Nicholas of Cusa's
On Learned Ignorance

KARSTEN HARRIES

Nicholas of Cusa's
On Learned Ignorance

A Commentary on *De docta ignorantia*

THE CATHOLIC UNIVERSITY OF AMERICA PRESS
WASHINGTON, D.C.

Copyright © 2024
The Catholic University of America Press
All rights reserved
The paper used in this publication meets the minimum
requirements of American National Standards for
Information Science—Permanence of Paper for Printed
Library Materials, ANSI z39.48-1992.
∞

Cataloging-in-Publication Data is available from the Library
of Congress

ISBN: 978-0-8132-3832-6
eISBN: 978-0-8132-3833-3

In Memoriam

Jasper Hopkins

November 8, 1936–January 23, 2023

No one has done more to make the
works of Nicholas of Cusa available to
the English-speaking world.

CONTENTS

BOOK TWO 227

BOOK THREE 329

ABBREVIATIONS

AP   Nicholas of Cusa, *Apologia Doctae Ignorantiae"*

CA   *Cribratio Alkorani*

DB   *De Beryllo*

DC   *De coniecturis*

DI   *De docta ignorantia.* Latin text in Nikolaus von Kues, *Philosophisch-theologische Werke*, I

DLG   *De Ludo Globi*

DLN   *De li non aliud*

DP   *Trialogus de Possest.*

DPL   *De dato patris luminum*

DSE   *Idiota de Staticis Experimentis*

DVD   *De Visione Dei*

GA   Martin Heidegger, *Gesamtausgabe*

IDM   Nicholas of Cusa, *Idiota de Mente*

IDS   *Idiota de Sapientia*

IL   John Wenck, *De Ignota Litteratura*

KSA   Nietzsche, *Sämtliche Werke, Kritische Studienausgabe*

OLI   Nicholas of Cusa, *On Learned Ignorance. A translation and appraisal by Jasper Hopkins*

PG   Patrologia Graeca

PL   Patrologia Latina

PTW   Nikolaus von Kues, *Philosophisch-theologische Werke.*

S   *Nicholas of Cusa's Early Sermons*

ST   Thomas Aquinas, *Summa Theologica*

TC   Nicholas of Cusa, *De theologicis complementis*

WWR   Schopenhauer, *World as Will and Representation*

Nicholas of Cusa's
On Learned Ignorance

Introduction

"The First Modern Philosopher?"

Many philosophers have become uneasy about what philosophy has become and where it has led us: Nietzsche and Heidegger, Derrida and Rorty are just a few names. Their uneasiness betrays widespread concern about the shape of our modern culture, the sustainability of our way of life. As more and more begin to suspect that the road on which we have been traveling may end in disaster, attempts are made to retrace steps taken; a search begins for missed turns and for those who may have misled us.

Among these, Descartes has long occupied a special place as a thinker whose understanding of proper method helped found not just modern philosophy, but modern science, and indeed the shape of our technological world. It is thus to be expected that attempts to question modernity, to confront it in order perhaps to take a step beyond it, should so often have taken the form of attempts to call into question Cartesian rationality. Think of Heidegger—although I think it far more difficult to meet the challenge of, while doing justice to, our Cartesian inheritance. What I attempt with this commentary is part of a related effort.

I am convinced that an attempt to take a step back from the *mathesis universalis* of Descartes to the *docta ignorantia* of Nicholas of Cusa still has much to teach us. To be sure, *On Learned Ignorance* is very much the product of an age that in many ways lies irrecoverably behind us. Faith in God is a presupposition of everything Nicholas of Cusa, or Nicolaus Cusanus, wrote, especially of this book. Not that he fails to recognize the claims of reason. Like no thinker before him, Cusanus recognized the godlike creativity and power of the human spirit. This led Cassirer to call Cusanus the first modern philosopher.

But to do justice to *On Learned Ignorance*, we may not forget that its author was a man of faith, a cardinal, and an outspoken and untiring defender of the Catholic Church. As Clyde Lee Miller puts it, "Cusanus was out to do nothing less than 'think God.'"[1] This attempt to think or name God is also an attempt to make sense of his faith—indeed, of faith itself. Bound up with it is the need to examine the limits of our reason. *On Learned Ignorance* lets us place the claims of reason in a more encompassing perspective. The need to do so remains.

In the last two hundred years the significance of Nicolaus Cusanus has been increasingly recognized. After centuries of comparative neglect,[2] what has been called a Cusanus Renaissance occurred at the then newly established Catholic Faculty of Theology of the University of Tübingen in the 1820s under the influence of Johann Adam Möhler

---

1. Clyde Lee Miller, *Reading Cusanus: Metaphor and Dialectic in a Conjectural Universe* (Washington, DC: The Catholic University of America Press, 2003), 1.

2. Morimichi Watanabe, "The Origins of Modern Cusanus Research in Germany and the Establishment of the Heidelberg *Opera Omnia*," in *Nicholas of Cusa: In Search of God and Wisdom*, ed. Gerald Christianson and Thomas M. Izbicki (Leiden: Brill, 1991), 19. Serious interest in Cusanus, however, predates these "origins." Cusanus's influence on Leonardo da Vinci (1452–1519) and especially Giordano Bruno (1548–1600) has received a great deal of attention, but his ideas had a much broader impact: see Günter Gawlick, "Zur Nachwirkung cusanischer Ideen im siebzehnten und achtzehnten Jahrhundert," in *Nicolo' Cusano: Agli Inizi del Mondo Moderno, Atti del Congresso internazionale in occasione del V centenario della morte di Nicolò Cusano*, Bressanone, 6–10 settembre 1964 (Sansoni: Firenze, 1964), 225–39, and Stephan Meier-Oeser, *Die Präsenz des Vergessenen: Zur Rezeption des Nicolaus Cusanus vom 15. bis 18. Jahrhundert*, Buchreihe der Cusanus-Gesellschaft 10 (Münster: Aschendorff, 1989). Especially Cusanus's claim that the earth is not the immovable center of the world generated a lively discussion, including Caelius Calcagnini (1479–1541), Giordano Bruno, Tomasso Campanella (1568–1639), Johannes Kepler (1571–1630), and Pierre Gassendi (1592–1655), as did his claim of a plurality of worlds, which spawned a whole literature fantasizing about life on other stars, especially the moon, but also met with expected opposition from those who, like Athanasius Kircher (1602–80), insisted that the fact that Christ was born here on earth was sufficient to establish its central position. The doctrine of learned ignorance led some thinkers such as Jean Bodin (c. 1530–96) to take him as a total skeptic; Richard H. Popkin, *From Erasmus to Descartes* (New York: Harper and Row, 1964), 84. The Aristotelian Martinus Schockius, too, considered him a modern skeptic; Popkin, *From Erasmus to Descartes*, 202. In a different vein, Cusanus's *De concordantia catholica* and especially *De pace fidei* caused him to be called, already at the time of the Reformation, "Lutheran before Luther"; Gawlick, "Zur Nachwirkung cusanischer Ideen," 226. In the eighteenth century, Enlightenment interest in religious tolerance generated renewed interest in *De pace fidei*. In 1779 Gotthold Ephraim Lessing asked Konrad Arnold Schmid to translate *De pace fide* into German; see Walter A. Euler, "Religionsfriede und Ringparabel: Die religionstheologischen Ideen von Cusanus und Lessing," *Cusanus Jahrbuch* 4 (2012): 3–24. Four years before the rationalist theologian Johann Salomo Semler (1725–91) had praised the "free and unusual" character of *De docta ignorantia* and called attention to the importance of *De pace fidei*, which he then published, accompanied by his own critical comments, in 1787: Semler, *Des Kardinals von Cusa Dialogus von der Übereinstimmung oder Einheit des Glaubens* (Leipzig, 1787); see Gawlick, "Zur Nachwirkung cusanischer Ideen," 239, and Morimichi Watanabe, "Cusanus, Islam, and Religious Tolerance," in *Nicholas of Cusa and Islam: Polemic and Dialogue in the Late Middle Ages*, ed. Ian Christopher Levy, Rita George-Tvrtković, and Donald Duclow, Studies in Medieval and Reformation Traditions 183

(1796–1838). In 1829 that faculty sponsored an essay contest on "A Description of the Life and the Ecclesiastical and the Literary Work of Cardinal and Bishop of Brixen, Nicholas of Cusa." The winner was a Möhler student, Franz Anton Scharpff. With the publication of his *Der Cardinal und Bischof Nicolaus von Cusa* (1843), "serious modern research in Cusanus can be said to have begun in Germany."[3] Scharpff also translated a number of Cusanus's most significant works, including *On Learned Ignorance*.[4] A great many studies followed in quick succession, including such important works as Johannes Uebinger's Würzburg dissertation *Die Philosophie des Nicolaus Cusanus* (1880), which he followed up with *Die Gotteslehre des Nikolaus Cusanus* (1888) and Richard Falckenberg's *Grundzüge der Philosophier des Nicolaus Cusanus mit besonderer Berücksichtigng der Lehre vom Erkennen* (1880), written in Jena. Still, as Morimichi Watanabe remarks, "Modern Cusanus research in nineteenth-century Germany was chiefly advanced by members of the Catholic School of Tübingen under the influence of Johann Adam Möhler."[5]

The current interest in Cusanus, however, is in large measure a result of the interest several members of the neo-Kantian school, such as Paul Natorp and Hermann Cohen in Marburg and Heinrich Rickert in Heidelberg, took in Cusanus, in whose works they saw provocative anticipations of Kant and of their conviction that a mathematical approach to reality is demanded by the nature of human reason. It was especially Cohen's most gifted student, Ernst Cassirer, who gave wide currency to the neo-Kantian understanding of Cusanus, calling him the first modern philosopher because of the way he based his thinking on an examination of the limits of our reason.[6]

Jasper Hopkins has discussed in illuminating detail many aspects of Cusanus's thought that might be cited by those who, following Cassirer, would like to consider Cusanus the first modern philosopher,[7]

(Leiden: Brill, 2014), https://doi.org/10.1163/9789004274761. In a letter to his brother of July 27, 1807, Friedrich Schlegel wrote, "I also read and leafed through in Nicolaus Cusanus,… a philosopher compared with whom Leibniz and his ilk seem flat and shallow"; cited in Stephan Meier-Oeser, *Die Präsenz des Vergessenen*, 62.

3. Watanabe, "Origins of Modern Cusanus Research in Germany," 22.

4. Franz Anton Scharpff: *Des Cardinals und Bischofs Nicolaus von Cusa wichtigste Schriften in deutscher Übersetzung* (Freiburg im Breisgau: Herder, 1862; repr. Frankfurt am Main: Minerva, 1966).

5. Watanabe, "Origins of Modern Cusanus Research in Germany," 25.

6. Ernst Cassirer, *Individuum und Kosmos in der Philosophie der Renaissance* (Leipzig: Teubner, 1927), 10. See also Cassirer, *Das Erkenntnisproblem in der Philosophie und Wissenschaft der neueren Zeit*, vol. 1, 2nd ed. (Berlin: Verlag Bruno Cassirer, 1911).

7. Jasper Hopkins, "Nicholas of Cusa (1401–1464): First Modern Philosopher?," *Midwest Studies in Philosophy* 26 (2002): 13–29. Earlier Hopkins had, however, himself called Cusans the "first modern philosopher": "Nicholas is rightly called the first modern

but, as the question mark in the title of his article, "Nicholas of Cusa (1401–1464): First Modern Philosopher?" suggests, he rejects an understanding of Cusanus as the or even one founding figure of modern philosophy.[8] The conclusion of Hopkins's essay, based on a thorough survey of the relevant literature, deserves to be quoted at length:

> In truth, Nicholas is *not* the first Modern thinker. For his "Modern themes" are not sufficiently developed for him to warrant this title. Moreover, certain of those themes are not really Nicholas's but are ascribed to him out of misunderstanding. In retrospect, Nicholas must be regarded as a transitional figure, some of whose ideas (1) were *suggestive* of new ways of thinking but (2) were not such as to conduct him far enough away from the medieval outlook for him truly to be called a Modern thinker. Spinoza, Kant, and Hegel never mention him, although Kepler, Descartes, and Leibniz do. His ideas were given a boost by the printing of his collected works (Paris, 1514) by Jacques Lefèvre d'Étaples. They were given a further boost when Giordano Bruno appropriated some of them. Nevertheless, Emerich Coreth's judgment remains cogent: "Cusa's direct influence on Modern thought is small; an immediate common-bond is scarcely confirmable."[9] Nicholas's intellectual influence on his own generation and on subsequent generations remained meager. Nevertheless, as Cassirer discerns, Nicholas commands our respect—though for reasons less pronounced than Cassirer himself gives. Looking back on Cusa, we find in his corpus of writings certain ideas that were developed by his Modern successors without his having directly influenced most of those successors through his own writings, of which they had scarcely any firsthand knowledge. The proper metaphor for assessing Cusa's historical role is that of *das Türöffnen:*[10] Nicholas

---

philosopher and the first German philosopher; but because of his continuity with the past and his lack of historical influence he cannot properly be given the title the Father of modern philosophy—an honor still rightfully Descartes's"; Hopkins, "Introduction," in *Nicholas of Cusa's Metaphysic of Contraction* (Minneapolis: Arthur J. Banning, 1983), 15–16; cf. 108–9. Hans Blumenberg, too, would have us consider Cusanus a medieval rather than a modern thinker; see Blumenberg, *Die Legitimität der Neuzeit* (Frankfurt am Main: Suhrkamp, 1966), 435–43. The 1976 edition was translated by Robert M. Wallace as *The Legitimacy of the Modern Age* (Cambridge, MA: MIT Press, 1983). A convincing critique of Blumenberg's understanding of Cusanus and the epochal threshold was provided by Elizabeth Brient: *The Immanence of the Infinite: Hans Blumenberg and the Threshold to Modernity* (Washington, DC: The Catholic University of America Press, 2002). See also Matthias Vollet, "Einleitung," in *Die Modernitäten des Nikolaus von Kues: Debatten und Rezeptionen*, ed. Tom Müller and Matthias Vollet (Bielefeld: transcript Verlag, 2014), 11–21.

8. See also David Albertson, "Mystical Philosophy in the Fifteenth Century: New Directions in Research on Nicholas of Cusa," *Religion Compass* 4, no. 8 (2010): 471–85.

9. Emerich Coreth, "Nikolaus von Kues, ein Denker an der Zeitwende," in *Cusanus Gedächtnisschrift*, ed. Nikolaus Grass (Innsbruck: Universitätsverlag Wagner, 1970), 15.

10. In the same spirit Rudolf Haubst had called Cusanus the "Pförtner der neuen Zeit,"

opens the door to Modernity—without himself ever crossing over the threshold that distinguishes the Middle Ages from Modernity. Thus, he does not help "legitimate" the Modern Age, to borrow Hans Blumenberg's title.[11] Instead, the reverse is true: the Modern Age helped "legitimate" certain of his ideas (with or without knowing them to be his)—for example, his notion of learned ignorance, his notion of the infinite disproportion between the finite and the infinite, his notion of the coincidence of opposites in God, his notion of the mobility of the earth, and his notion of the earth's being privatively infinite (that is, its being finite but unbounded). By themselves these five notions—being more in resonance with the Modern Age than with the medieval world—evidence for us that Nicholas's thought is, indeed, an unmistakable major boundary-marker on the pathway to Modernity. That is why these five themes in particular have been so intently explored by today's philosophers.

There is little in this thoughtful assessment I would quarrel with, although it fails to do justice to what Cusanus still must contribute to an understanding of our place in the world; nor does it speak to the novelty of Cusanus's thinking, of which he himself was so proud and repeatedly reminds the reader.[12] And the neo-Kantian reading of Cusanus should not be dismissed: Cassirer remains an invaluable guide to one side of Cusanus's thinking, even as those more thoroughly familiar with medieval thought have been right to remind us of how deeply rooted his thought remained in that of his predecessors. As Maurice de Gandillac observes, "It would seem to be the fate of all rich intellects, especially when they stand in a period of transition, that they give room to, if not contradictory, yet very different interpretations, because these rest on heterogeneous historical registers."[13]

What matters to me is what Cusanus still has to teach a modern reader. Concluding his still indispensable *Nikolaus von Kues*, Gandillac wrote, "The present world knows forces that tear it apart, not unlike

---

the doorkeeper of the modern age; Haubst, "Nikolaus von Kues: Pförtner der neuen Zeit," in *Kleine Schriften der Cusanus-Gesellschaft*, Heft 12 (Trier: Paulinus, 1988), 6.

11. Blumenberg, *Die Legitimität der Neuzeit*. Blumenberg, however, did not take Cusanus to have legitimated the modern age: the modern age was not in need of legitimation. According to Blumenberg there is nothing illegitimate about the self-assertion in response to nominalism and its absconded God in which he seeks the origin of modernity. Cusanus's thought remains theocentric and thus premodern, given Blumenberg's understanding of modernity.

12. Isabella Mandrella, "Begriff und Funktion der Neuheit in der Philossophie des Nicolaus Cusanus," in Müller and Vollet, *Die Modernitäten des Nikolaus von Kues*, 23–42.

13. Maurice de Gandillac, *Nikolaus von Kues: Studien zu seiner Philosophie und philosophischen Weltanschauung*, trans. Karl Fleischmann, vom Verfasser grundlegend überarbeitete Ausgabe (Düsseldorf: Schwan, 1953), 143.

those of the 15th century. It could be that the spirit in which the
shipper's son from Cues responded to the crisis of his days today may
once again, in healing fashion, give life to the indispensable effort
of people of good will."[14] I have written this commentary on *De docta
ignorantia, On Learned Ignorance* in the spirit of this remark. My interest is not primarily historical, although we need to place Cusanus's
writings in their historical context if we are to understand them. But
I am not concerned with defending claims that he either should or
should not be considered the first modern philosopher. Little is at
stake. A great deal depends here on how modernity is understood.
As Hans Blumenberg observed, "The supposed founding acts of the
modern age proved to be more and more mere crossing points of
strands reaching far back into the past and the founding figures suc-
cumbed to the erosion of historical diligence, which finally reduces
supposed revolutions to mere evolutions."[15] Every supposed beginning of modernity can be questioned. But there are "crossing points"
that have a special significance: something new emerges. If, despite
Blumenberg's justified caveat, we nevertheless want to posit a beginning of the modern world, I think that a good case can be made that
it should be located, if anywhere, in the Florence of Cosimo de Medi-
ci (1389–1464). Cusanus (1401–64) was not untouched by the many
new ideas that were then emerging in that city.

But what makes his thought important to me is not the way it anticipates a number of notions we have come to associate with the modern world. Nor is it the way he might be invoked to legitimate that
world, but rather the way he, notwithstanding his incipient modernity, invites us to call that legitimacy into question, the way his thought
continues to challenge often taken-for-granted presuppositions of
our worldview: most importantly, a distinctly modern self-assertion
or self-elevation that has made our human reason the measure of reality. There are indeed many passages in his works that can be cited in
support of just such a self-elevation: Cusanus thus cites with approval
the Protagorean "man is the measure of all things"[16] and calls man "a
second God" (*DB* 7). But he never loses sight of Genesis 1:27: that

14. Gandillac, *Nikolaus von Kues*, 497.
15. Blumenberg, *Die Legitimität der Neuzeit*, 437.
16. Nicholas of Cusa, *De beryllo, Opera Omnia*, ed. Hans G. Sänger and Karl Bormann
(Hamburg: Meiner, 1988), XI:6, abbreviated *DB*; trans. Jasper Hopkins, *On [Intellectual]
Eyeglasses* in *Nicholas of Cusa: Metaphysical Speculations* (Minneapolis: Banning, 1997). Page
references in the text are to the Meiner edition, given also in the margin of the translation.

God created man in his image. The ultimate measure of man is the incomprehensible infinite God.

Much of what Cusanus has to tell us in *On Learned Ignorance* may seem dated, steeped as it is in a Christian worldview that means very little to most of us today. The way that work is rooted in a tradition that includes Pythagoras, Plato, Plotinus, Proclus, Augustine, Boethius, Pseudo-Dionysius, Eriugena, Thierry of Chartres, and Meister Eckhart makes it difficult for a modern reader to find proper access to what it has to say. Nevertheless, as this commentary seeks to show, *De docta ignorantia* provides us with a continuing challenge. Inseparable from Cusanus's understanding of the doctrine of learned ignorance is an insight into the radical transcendence of reality, so different from the ontology implied by Descartes's insistence on the primacy of clear and distinct ideas, from what Nietzsche called "the unshakable faith that thought, using the thread of causality, can penetrate the deepest abysses of being, and that thought is capable not only of knowing being, but even of correcting it,"[17] a faith that in large measure still supports our science and technology and our modern world.

When someone uses the term "transcendence," we should ask just what is being transcended. With Cusanus it is first of all the reach of our human reason. Reality and our reason are thought to be finally incommensurable, as are the infinite and the finite.[18] This thought is inseparably bound up with Cusanus's understanding of the infinite transcendence of God, which must elude all our attempts to fully comprehend God and the creation. And yet, he insists, only this incomprehensible God provides our thinking and our actions with their proper measure. But how can the incomprehensible infinite provide us finite knowers with a measure? The way Cusanus addresses this question deserves and rewards a careful reading of *On Learned Ignorance.*

A Troubled Life

Before proceeding, a few facts about Cusanus's life: Given the many burdens placed on him by the church, which he served with such distinction, one can only wonder how he found the time and admire his ability to write as much as he did. As Karl Jaspers points out, "Cusanus was the only one of the great philosophers to have led a busy life in

17. Friedrich Nietzsche, *"The Birth of Tragedy" and "The Case of Wagner,"* trans. Walter Kaufmann (New York: Vintage, 1967), 95.
18. See Karsten Harries, *The Antinomy of Being* (Berlin: DeGruyter, 2019).

the world from an early age to the day of his death."[19] There is tension between his writings and the demands his busy life placed on him and the way he responded to them.

Cusanus is one of those thinkers who invite those concerned with their thought to visit the places with which they were associated. Niklas Cryfftz, or Krebs (Latin Nicolaus Cancer) was born as the first of four children to Johann Cryfftz and Katherina Roemer in 1401 in Kues, in Latin Cusa, a village on the Moselle, not too far from Trier, in a region long known for its superb wines. His father was a well-to-do merchant,[20] making his living off the river, especially with shipping. The connection with the river is suggested by the family name, Cryfftz, meaning crayfish, shown in the cardinal's coat of arms, which we can still see in a number of churches with which he was associated as prebendary and in the copper plate that in 1488 was placed over his heart, which, following his wishes, was buried in front of the altar of the chapel of the hospice, the Cusanus Stift, that with the help of his family he had founded in his hometown.

About the childhood of Cusanus we know next to nothing. It has been suggested repeatedly that he studied with the Brethren of the Common Life at the famous Latin school in Deventer, as Erasmus of Rotterdam was to do sixty years later.[21] This cannot be documented, but be this as it may, the spirit of the *devotio moderna*, inspired by Rhenish mysticism, which presided over that school, would seem to have affected Cusanus at an early age.

That he received an excellent education, providing him with a good command of Latin, is evident. Cusanus was only fifteen when, in 1416, he enrolled as a cleric from the diocese of Trier in the recently founded University of Heidelberg, then a center of nominalism,[22] to study the seven liberal arts, the *trivium* (grammar, logic, and rhetoric) and the *quadrivium* (arithmetic, geometry, astronomy, and music). After perhaps a year,[23] he left Heidelberg for Padua,[24] which had be-

---

19. Karl Jaspers, *Anselm and Nicholas of Cusa*, ed. Hannah Arendt, trans. Ralph Manheim (New York: Harcourt Brace Jovanovich, 1974), 26.

20. Cf. Erich Meuthen, ed., *Acta Cusana: Quellen zur Lebensgeschichte des Nikolaus von Kues*, Bd. I, 1 (Hamburg: Meiner, 1976), nos. 2–10, 13.

21. Cf. Gerd Heinz-Mohr, "Bemerkungen zur Spiritualität der Brüder vom gemeinsamen Leben," in *Nicolo' Cusano: Agli Inizi del Mondo Moderno*, 471.

22. The University of Heidelberg was founded in 1386 by Rupert I, Count Palatine of the Rhine. Its first rector was Marsilius of Inghen.

23. Cf. Meuthen, *Acta Cusana*, no. 11, 3–4.

24. For an account of what Padua had to offer Cusanus, see Erich Meuthen, *Nicholas of Cusa: A Sketch for a Biography* (Washington, DC: The Catholic University of America Press, 2010), 17–21.

come, following the Condemnation of 1277 that had weakened the University of Paris, perhaps the leading university in Europe, a center especially for legal studies, but also for the study of nature—a hundred years later Copernicus was to complete his studies there.

Cusanus stayed in Padua for six years, receiving his *doctor decretorum*, his doctor of canon law, in 1423. Some of the notes he took in a lecture course by the famous jurist Prosdocimus de Comitibus, in whose house he was a boarder, have survived in the library of the Cusanus Stift in Kues.[25] Although the illustrious canonist Francesco Zabarella (1360–1417) had left the university six years before Cusanus's arrival in Padua, his students kept his teaching alive: that a presupposition of legitimate government is the consent of the governed; that this holds for the church as much as for secular governments. A leading contributor to the Council of Constance (1414–18), Zabarella argued for the supremacy of such a general council over the pope, a position the young Cusanus would seem to have made his own.

Besides canon law, Cusanus also studied mathematics and astronomy. Especially important to Cusanus would seem to have been the lectures of Prosdocimo de' Beldomandi, renowned for his mastery of the mathematical arts that made up the medieval *quadrivium*. Padua had much to offer the young Cusanus. Especially significant were the friends he made there, most importantly the mathematician and doctor Paolo Toscanelli (1397–1482), to whom he was to remain close for the rest of his life and who was at his bedside when he died in Todi in 1464. With him he could share his interests in mathematics, astronomy, and geography. Important, too, was one of his teachers, the slightly older Julian Cesarini (1398–1444), then not yet a cardinal. To him, friend and patron, he was to dedicate the first three of his major works, *De concordantia catholica* (1433/34), *De docta ignorantia* (1440), and *De conjecturis* (1440–44).

A brief stay in Rome (1424) followed the years spent in Padua, but soon Cusanus was back in the Rhineland, where the award of a stipend of forty Gulden and the benefice of the parish church at Altrich on January 31, 1425, testify to the high esteem in which the young cleric was being held by the archbishop of Trier, Otto von Ziegenhain.[26] Thus supported, he was able to both teach and continue

---

25. Alois Krchnák, "Die kanonisschen Aufzeichnungen des Nikolaus von Kues in Cod. Cus. 220 als Mitschrift einer Vorlesung seines Lehrers Prosdocimus de Comitibus," in *Mitteilungen und Forschungsbeiträge der Cusanus-Gesellschaft* (Mainz: Matthias-Grünewald-Verlag, 1962), 67–84.

26. See Erich Meuthen, "Die Pfründen des Cusanus," in *Mitteilungen und Forschungsbeiträge der Cusanus-Gesellschaft* (Mainz: Matthias-Grünewald-Verlag, 1962), 2:16.

his studies in theology and philosophy at the university of Cologne, where he matriculated on March 26, 1425. The only slightly older Heymeric de Campo (1395–1460), an admirer of the neo-Platonists Ramon Llull, Albert the Great, and Pseudo-Dionysius, became his mentor and lifelong friend.[27] Cologne helped provide Cusanus with the philosophical tools that later allowed him to write *De docta ignorantia*.[28] Of special importance would seem to have been his study of Albert the Great's commentary on Dionysius's *Mystical Theology* and of Proclus's commentary on Plato's *Parmenides*.[29] While at Cologne, Cusanus would seem to have made a name for himself as a teacher of canon law; otherwise, it is difficult to understand the offer of a professorship at the recently founded university of Louvain that he received and rejected in 1428,[30] presumably because his archbishop had other plans for him and by then had called the young canon lawyer back to Trier as his secretary (*procurator*).

His stay in Cologne was all too brief. In 1426 Cusanus joined Cardinal Giordano Orsini as his secretary on a difficult mission to counter the Hussite heresy. In 1427 he was back in Rome, now as his archbishop's representative. His good relations with the humanist circle at the Roman Curia, presided over by Cardinal Orsini, led to the award of further benefices, most importantly his appointment as Dean of St. Florin in Koblenz, which in the following twelve years required his prolonged but often interrupted presence in that town. In 1428 he was able to travel to Paris, joined by Heymeric, looking for manuscripts, especially by Ramon Llull. On December 29, 1429, he was back in Rome.

In the following years Cusanus was to become ever more active in church politics. The death of his patron, Archbishop Otto, in 1430 had led to a contested episcopal election in Trier, which pitted the candidate elected by the majority of the chapter, Jakob von Sierck, against Ulrich von Manderscheid, who initially had received only two votes, but could count on the support of the local nobility: a local repetition of the Great Schism (1378–1417) threatened. The Schism had not long ago divided the church for forty years between popes in Rome and Avignon. Matters became more complicated when a third

---

27. See Andrea Fiamma, "Nicola Cusano ed Eimerico da Campo: Gli anni coloniensi," *Medioevo: Rivista di storia della filosofia medievale* XLI (2016): 217–57.

28. Fiamma, "Nicola Cusano ed Eimerico da Campo," 219.

29. M. L. Führer, "The Theory of the Intellect in Albert the Great and Its Influence on Nicholas of Cusa," in Christianson and Izbicki, *Nicholas of Cusa: In Search of God and Wisdom*, 46–56.

30. The invitation was repeated in 1435 and once again rejected.

pope was added: the Council of Pisa (1409) ineffectually sought to depose the two rivals, Gregory VII (Rome) and Benedict XIII (Avignon) and elected its own candidate, Alexander V, who was succeeded by Anti-pope John XXIII.[31] The Schism was ended definitively only in 1417 by the Council of Constance (1414–18), which, asserting the superiority of such a general council over all individuals, including even the pope, forced the abdication or deposition of all three popes and the election of Martin V. It was this pope who now attempted to end the schism in Trier—both candidates had traveled to Rome seeking papal confirmation—by appointing his own candidate, Raban von Helmstatt, bishop of Speyer, archbishop of Trier, even though the cathedral chapter by then had united behind Ulrich von Manderscheid. Ulrich refused to accept the decision, even using force to get his way. Without papal approval he reigned as archbishop from 1430 to 1436.[32] The pope responded by excommunicating him and his supporters, including Cusanus.[33] But by then excommunication was no longer the effective tool it had once been.

Ulrich had chosen the young canon lawyer, whom he had made his secretary and chancellor, to argue his rather shaky case before the Council convened by Pope Martin V in Basel in 1431 to complete the work begun in Constance. Cusanus had already made a name for himself as a legal scholar. He was made a member of the Council on February 29, 1432, and was assigned to the Commission on Matters of Faith.[34] Cusanus failed, however, after many presentations and delays, in his mission to persuade those assembled of the merits of his patron's case. On May 15, 1434, the Council decided against Ulrich. Cusanus accepted the verdict, although he continued to advise Ulrich, who appealed it, refusing to step down as archbishop. By then Cusanus had emerged as one of the most articulate and influential church politicians at Basel. His interest in Latin manuscripts had born fruit in his rediscovery in a Cologne monastery in 1428 of twelve comedies by Plautus , which he sent to Poggio Bracciolini, a scholar ever on the lookout for lost Latin manuscripts; this discovery had already secured him a certain reputation among Italian humanists.

The Council was in turmoil when Cusanus first arrived in Basel.

---

31. Cf. Paul E. Sigmund, *Nicholas of Cusa and Medieval Political Thought* (Cambridge, MA: Harvard University Press, 1963), 11–38.

32. Franz Xaver Kraus, "Ulrich von Manderscheid," in *Allgeméine Deutsche Biographie*, 39 (Leipzig: Duncker and Humblot, 1895): 39:234–35, https://www.deutsche-biographie.de/pnd13830551X.html#adbcontent.

33. Meuthen, *Nicholas of Cusa*, 34–38.

34. Meuthen, *Nicholas of Cusa*, 38.

On December 18, 1431, before it had really begun, Pope Martin's successor, Eugene IV, had issued a bull dissolving the Council, announcing a new one to meet in Bologna in eighteen months. By thus dissolving the Council, the pope placed himself above it in violation of what had been achieved in Constance. Most of those assembled in Basel were outraged. Among them was one of Cusanus's old friends from Padua, now Cardinal Julius Cesarini, who in 1431 had been appointed by Pope Martin V to preside over the Council as his legate, but now resigned that appointment in protest. The Council responded to the papal bull by reiterating the pope's subordination to a general council that had been proclaimed at Constance.[35] Supported by the emperor, the Council decided to suspend the pope, who eventually gave in to what the Council demanded and revoked his earlier bull.

Not surprisingly, given what he had learned in Padua and the cause that brought him to Basel, Cusanus, like his former teacher Cesarini, on his arrival actively supported the Council in its struggle with the pope—and as such a supporter he presents himself to us in his first major work, *De concordantia catholica* (1433/34), which supported the work of the Council by arguing for a moderate conciliarism. Given that all human beings were created by God equal and free, the authority of the ruler, be he pope or emperor, had to be based on the consent of the governed—mediated, however, by the hierarchically organized church or empire. In matters of faith a general council should be the final court of appeal.[36]

And yet, Cusanus knew all too well that in their present fallen state most human beings were not really free. The unruly crowd that constituted the Council of Basel was only a very inadequate representation of the mystical church, the body of Christ, marked by harmony and unity. Ideas that point forward to the modern liberal conception of the state were thus in tension with his elevated understanding of the church and his generally low opinion of the masses, confirmed by the often-raucous behavior of those assembled in Basel. In a very concrete way Cusanus confronted the problem of the one and the

35. For a detailed account of the conflict, see Joachim W. Stieber, *Pope Eugenius IV, The Council of Basel and the Secular and Ecclesiastical Authorities in the Empire: The Conflict over Supreme Authority and Power in the Church* (Leiden: Brill, 1978). See also Gandillac, *Nikolaus von Kues*, 11–44.

36. For an excellent discussion of *The Catholic Concordance* and Cusanus's subsequent refusal to claim the work as a significant achievement, see Morimichi Watanabe, "Political and Legal Ideas," in *Introducing Nicholas of Cusa: A Guide to a Renaissance Man*, ed. Christopher M Bellitto, Thomas M. Izbicki, and Gerald Christianson (New York: Paulist Press, 2004), 141–65.

many with which he later was to wrestle in his many writings, where he never left any doubt about the priority of the one. The unity of the church, and indeed of humanity, was a lifelong concern. That may help to explain why in May 1436 Cusanus turned away from the cause of the Council, which had found in his *De concordantia catholica* its most convincing literary expression. In the fractured and fractious Council of Basel he could not recognize an adequate representation of the church.

Be this as it may, famously or infamously, Cusanus switched sides and came to support the pope. It was hardly a sudden decision. For some time Cusanus had had increasing doubts concerning the authority of the Council. Already on May 11, 1435, he wrote Pope Eugene IV expressing such doubts while asking him to confirm the important benefice of the monastery of Münstereifel that he had just obtained.[37] Cusanus never lost sight of his finances and throughout his life looked out for his and his relatives' interests. In the fall of that year he befriended the pope's personal envoy to the Council, Ambrogio Traversari (1386–1439), prior general of the Camaldolese Order, an ardent advocate of papal primacy and then the leading authority on Pseudo-Dionysius. Given Cusanus's deep interest in Dionysius, we must look no further to explain their friendship. But no doubt Cusanus was also mindful of his own career.[38]

Was it then that opportunism with which his opponents charged him that turned him against the Council? Or the loss of his suit? Or had he learned from interminable discussions that seemed to accomplish very little to distrust the democratic process and to put greater faith in autocratic rule?[39] Given his lifelong striving for unity, he must have been troubled by the divisions that rent the Council, by its radicalization, its increasingly strident opposition to the pope, which went so far as to set the Council up as the church's supreme governing body and to insist that papal tax collectors send their money henceforth to Basel, not to Rome, claiming for itself the right to grant indulgences and canonizations.[40] One issue that divided the Council was a democratization that gave a simple parish priest or master

37. Meuthen, *Nicholas of Cusa*, 30.

38. Joachim W. Stieber, "The Hercules of the Eugenians's at the Crossroads: Nicholas of Cusa's Decision for the Pope and Against the Council in 1436/37—Theological, Political, and Social Aspects," in Christianson and Izbicki, *Nicholas of Cusa: In Search of God and Wisdom*, 233.

39. For a detailed account of the often-raucous proceedings in Basel, see Mandell Creighton, *The History of the Papacy during the Period of Reformation*, vol. 2, *The Council of Basel—The Papal Restoration, 1418–1464* (London: Longmans, Green, 1882).

40. Creighton, *Council of Basel*, 221, 227.

of arts the same vote as a bishop or cardinal, a development that caused many of the higher clergy to reconsider their challenge to the pope. What authority could such a divided council claim? Had Cusanus himself not argued that the mark of a valid council was "that it was concluded in harmony, by which he seems to have meant by unanimous agreement"?[41] How could negotiations that Aeneas Sylvius Piccolomini, one of the chroniclers of the Council, "compared unfavorably to drunkards in a tavern,"[42] claim superiority over the pope? "The council rent by divisions seemed to Cusanus to be not the church of God, but the synagogue of Satan."[43]

In a world where centrifugal forces threatened to tear church and Europe apart, Cusanus labored for unity. In 1436 the Byzantine Empire appealed to the Council for help against the threatening Ottoman Turks, opening up the possibility of reuniting the Eastern and the Western church, thus healing the Great Schism of 1054 that had split Christianity into Roman Catholic and Eastern Orthodox. Cusanus eagerly pursued this dream of unity. And so it seems fitting that his final break with the fractured and fractious Council should have come after a tumultuous meeting in the cathedral on May 7, 1437, a meeting at which the majority, fearing with good reason a reassertion of papal power, refused to honor the wishes of the Greek representatives, who for obvious reasons wanted the final negotiations to take place not in Basel, but in a place easier for them to reach, preferably an Italian seaport.[44] Appointed by the dissenting minority party, Cusanus left with two bishops and the Greek representatives for Bologna to get papal approval before traveling on to Constantinople to prepare for a council of reunification. When the pope later that year transferred the Council to Italy, the majority, remaining in Basel, once more attempted to reassert that Council's authority, ineffectually suspending the pope and stripping his supporters, including Cusanus, of their ecclesiastical offices.[45] On May 16, 1439, they pronounced the Council's superiority over the pope a dogma.[46] In Germany the Council retained strong support, especially in the universities.

41. Creighton, *Council of Basel*, 233.

42. Creighton, *Council of Basel*, 224. Cf. Will-Erich Peuckert, *Die Große Wende: Das apokalyptische Saeculum und Martin Luther* (Darmstadt: Wissenschaftliche Buchgesellschaft, 1948), 2:501–5.

43. Sigmund, *Nicholas of Cusa and Medieval Political Thought*, 229.

44. Sigmund, *Nicholas of Cusa and Medieval Political Thought*, 228.

45. Sigmund, *Nicholas of Cusa and Medieval Political Thought*, 225.

46. Wilhelm Baum, "Introduction," in *Nikolaus von Kues: Briefe und Dokumente zum Brixner Streit* (Vienna: Turia and Kant, 1998), 12.

No doubt considerations advanced by his friend Cesarini, who also made his definitive break with the Council when it refused to accommodate the Greeks, reinforced Cusanus's decision to desert the Council's cause. And we should not forget his friendship with Traversari. Was Cusanus also moved by that opportunism with which his enemies charged him? Was he bribed? Be this as it may, Basel changed Cusanus into an untiring defender of papal supremacy, a reversal that was to earn him the bitter and lifelong enmity of conciliarists, such as the zealous Gregor von Heimburg, who had first met Cusanus at the University of Padua, where he, too, earned the degree of Doctor of Canon Law shortly after Cusanus.[47] Heimburg had joined the Council representing the archbishop of Mainz. After Cusanus's break with the Council, Heimburg was to turn into his most strident and dangerous adversary. Heimburg saw clearly that the particularism of the princes and the flourishing cities in which a new sense of freedom was emerging had eroded the authority of both pope and emperor, these symbols of Christian unity. More decisively than Cusanus, he had already stepped across the epochal threshold that both joins and separates modernity and the Middle Ages.

In the contempt he felt for what he took to be Cusanus's betrayal of the Council's cause, Heimburg was by no means alone. A then widely circulating rhyme, *Cusanus et Lysura, pervertunt omnia iura*, "Cusanus and Lysura pervert all laws,"[48] speaks to the many enemies his conversion to the papal cause had made Cusanus.[49] His tireless efforts in support of the pope earned him the epithet "The Hercules of the Eugenians" from the humanist Aeneas Sylvius Piccolomini (1405–64), who later was to become Pope Pius II, but was then still an eloquent, but unprincipled man of the world. Aeneas Sylvius had come to the Council as secretary to Domenico Capranica, bishop of Fermo, who in 1432 had gone to Basel to protest Pope Eugene IV's refusal to confirm the cardinal's hat, which he had been granted by Martin V. In Basel Aeneas Sylvius and Cusanus began what was to evolve into a lifelong friendship. Not surprisingly, given the cause that brought him to Basel, like

---

47. On Cusanus and Heimburg, see Georg Pick, *Nikolaus von Kues: Vom Moseljungen zum Kardinal und Philosophen*, 3rd ed. (Frankfurt am Main: R. G. Fischer, 1996), 100–116.

48. Johannes Lysura (?–1459), named after his birthplace, Lieser, near Kues. He represented the archbishop of Mainz, Dietrich von Erbach, at the Council of Basel; Hartmut Boockmann, "Johannes Lysura," *Neue Deutsche Biographie* 10 (1974): 560–61, https://www .deutsche-biographie.de/pnd136317022.html#ndbcontent.

49. Tobias Daniels, *Diplomatie, politische Rede und juristische Praxis im 15. Jahrhundert: Der gelehrte Rat Johannes Hofmann von Lieser* (Göttingen: V. and R. Unipress GmbH, 2013).

Cusanus and Gregor von Heimburg, Aeneas Sylvius, too, initially supported the Council's supreme authority.[50] But ever alert to the way the political winds were blowing, in 1442, now serving Emperor Frederick III as poet laureate and secretary, Aeneas Sylvius, following the emperor, shifted support to the papal side. In 1445 he went to Rome to make peace between emperor and pope. In 1446, now in the service of the pope, this up to then worldly opportunist decided to take holy orders. "He resolved to live more cleanly, 'to abandon,' as he said, 'Venus for Bacchus.' He was ordained, and 'loved nothing so much as the priesthood.'"[51] His labors on behalf of both pope and emperor were rewarded when both nominated him bishop of Trieste. And Aeneas Sylvius did prove an untiring supporter of the papal cause, which for many years he had opposed. But now he was finally in full agreement with his old friend Cusanus.

Meanwhile Cusanus's tireless work for pope and church had also not gone unrewarded: sometime in the thirties he was ordained a priest, and on December 16, 1446, just before the pope's death, Eugene IV named Cusanus a cardinal *in pectore*, an appointment reconfirmed and made public by his successor Nicholas V (1447–55), who named Cusanus cardinal-priest on December 20, 1448, and on January 3 assigned to him the church San Pietro in Vincoli. The appointment was confirmed by Calixtus III (1455–58) and Pius II (his old friend Aeneas Sylvius, who in 1458 had become pope with the cardinal's support).

Throughout his career we see Cusanus involved in various attempts to reform the church, to restore unity to Christendom, to unite all humanity in one faith. When still a member of the Council, he thus negotiated with the Bohemian Hussites, and the compromise he had proposed in 1433, granting the Hussites the right to administer the holy sacrament in both kinds, bread and wine, although initially rejected, became the basis of the agreement that was reached in 1436: Compared to the need to preserve the unity of the church the difference in rites mattered little.[52] I have already mentioned his mission to Constantinople for discussions with the Eastern church, which, threatened by Ottoman expansion, was looking west for support. At the Council of Ferrara (1438), transferred to Florence in 1439, union was in fact achieved. The decree *Laetentur caeli*, issued on July 6, 1439, proclaimed the end of the schism that had for so long

---

50. Peuckert, *Die Große Wende*, 42.
51. Creighton, *Council of Basel*, 279–80.
52. Cf. Gandillac, *Nikolaus von Kues*, 22.

divided the Roman and Greek churches.[53] But the joy was short-lived: the different Eastern churches, including the Byzantine, refused to accept the agreement. And the hoped-for military support, while offered, proved sadly deficient in the end. On behalf of Pope Eugene IV, Cardinal Cesarini, having presided over the council of reunification, now helped organize a crusade that began in 1443. After some initial successes it ended with the total defeat of the crusader army by the Ottomans in the Battle of Varna (1444). Cusanus's mentor and friend Cesarini and Władysław, king of Poland and Hungary, both lost their lives in the battle. Constantinople could not be saved. Only a few years later, on May 29, 1453, it fell to Sultan Mehmed II. Its fall and the bloodbath that followed were to traumatize Christian Europe for centuries, reinforcing the negative view of Muslims that had prevailed in Europe for centuries. "In the immediate aftermath of the loss of Constantinople, nothing was more certain than the equation of the Muslim armies with the legions of the Antichrist."[54] Cusanus, too, was horrified. But familiar with the writings of Ramon Llull, who sought to engage Muslims in a dialogue in the hope of converting them, having studied the Koran, and, when he was in Constantinople, having helped thirteen Muslims who wanted to travel to Rome to be instructed in the Christian faith, Cusanus was to respond to this disaster in a very different way, writing a work that has not lost its relevance: *De pace fidei* (The Peace of Faith) (1453), which attempts to show that what divides the many different religions is only superficial.[55] Different practices and rites should not obscure the underlying faith in the same unfathomable God. *Religio una in rituum varietate.* To be sure, Cusanus left no doubt concerning the primacy of the Church of Rome.[56] And the irenic tone of the dialogue contrasts with his support for another crusade, called for especially by his old friend Aeneas Sylvius, by then bishop of Siena, at the Diet of Regensburg (1454).

Meanwhile, whatever had been achieved in Florence was shadowed not only by the Ottoman threat that culminated in the fall of Constantinople, but also by the continuing and increasing hostility

---

53. Watanabe, "Political and Legal Ideas," 146.

54. James E. Biechler, "Interreligious Dialogue," in Bellitto, Izbicki, and Christianson, *Introducing Nicholas of Cusa*, 271.

55. See Biechler's excellent discussion "Interreligious Dialogue," 270–96.

56. See Thomas McTighe, "Nicholas of Cusa's Unity Metaphysics and the Formula *Religio una in rituum varietate*," in Christianson and Izbicki, *Nicholas of Cusa: In Search of God and Wisdom*, 161–72; Hanna-Barbara Gerl-Falkovitz, "Nicolaus Cusanus, *De pace fidei* (1454)," in *Westliche Moderne, Christentum und Islam: Gewalt als Anfrage an monotheistische Religionen*, Edition Weltordnung, ed. Wolfgang Palaver, Roman A. Siebenrock, and Dietmar Regensburger (Innsbruck: Innsbruck University Press, 2008), 107–26.

of the Council of Basel, which had refused to accept the pope's decision to transfer the council to an Italian city, a stance that enjoyed a great deal of support, especially in Germany. The emperor refused to take sides. The turmoil prevented Cusanus from being present at the celebration of the union in Florence that he had worked so hard to achieve. The pope needed him to be in Germany to help sway wavering princes to the papal side. Convinced of its supreme authority, the Council of Basel answered the pope's decree that proclaimed the reunification of the church by deposing him and electing in 1439, with the eloquent support of the then still conciliarist Aeneas Sylvius, the Duke of Savoy, Amadeus VIII, as its own anti-pope Felix V. In 1440 that antipope made Cusanus's old enemy Gregor von Heimburg his secretary. The schism that once divided the church between Rome and Avignon seemed to have returned, keeping Cusanus busy. Ever more decisively he asserted the pope's supreme authority, challenging the authority of the Council at Basel at different meetings, especially at the diets of Nürnberg (1438), Mainz (1439 and 1441) Frankfurt (1442), and again Nürnberg (1444). Cusanus may deserve some credit for the fact that Felix V was to be the last antipope.

Busy as he was serving his pope, he did succeed in carving out a few months of free time that allowed him to write *De docta ignorantia* in the priory of Münstereifel, finishing it in his hometown Kues (December 1439 to February 12, 1440).

Heimburg, Cusanus, and Aeneas Silvius were to meet once more in 1446 at the Diet of Frankfurt, Heimburg still arguing against papal supremacy and Cusanus defending it as part of the papal legation, while Aeneas Sylvius represented Emperor Fredrick III. The compromise that was reached prepared for the Concordat of Vienna (1448), which regulated the relationship of pope and emperor until the end of the Holy Roman Empire in 1806. It was followed by the resignation of the antipope Felix V and the final signing in 1449 of what had been agreed upon. Papal authority was reaffirmed. Gregor von Heimburg's hopes for a more democratic church were shattered.

In the Jubilee year 1450,[57] Pope Nicholas V named Cusanus prince-

---

57. See Leviticus 25:8–12: "Count off seven sabbath years—seven times seven years—so that the seven sabbath years amount to a period of forty-nine years. 9. Then have the trumpet sounded everywhere on the tenth day of the seventh month; on the Day of Atonement sound the trumpet throughout your land. 10. Consecrate the fiftieth year and proclaim liberty throughout the land to all its inhabitants. It shall be a jubilee for you; each of you is to return to your family property and to your own clan. 11. The fiftieth year shall be a jubilee for you; do not sow and do not reap what grows of itself or harvest the untended vines. 12. For it is a jubilee and is to be holy for you; eat only what is taken directly from the fields." In

bishop of the Tyrolean Brixen (Bressanone), south of the Brenner. This last appointment was to prove a cursed reward. From the very beginning the papal appointee was considered an unwelcome intruder by the Tyroleans, who had already chosen Duke Sigismund's chancellor Leonhard Wiesmayer for their bishop but were forced by the emperor to accept the pope's decision.

Before being able to assume his post in Brixen, Cusanus was appointed by the pope legate to Germany and the Low Countries with the mission to preach the indulgence of the Jubilee year to those unable to travel to Rome and, more importantly, to strengthen support for the pope, to reform the secular clergy and monasteries, both very much in need of reform,[58] and to mediate conflicts.[59] The cause of conciliarism was still smoldering, supported by territorial interests that threatened church and empire with disintegration, and there were countless abuses that needed addressing. The Reformation that soon was to shatter Christian unity shows that Cusanus was, despite some successes, in the end less than successful: centrifugal proved stronger than centripetal powers. The center no longer would hold—a problem with which Cusanus struggled in different ways throughout his life, always concerned to preserve the unity of the Catholic Church.

In March 1451 Emperor Friedrich III finally invested Cusanus with the bishopric and made the shipper's son from Kues a prince of the empire. But only in April 1452 was Cusanus able to settle in Brixen—although "settle" is hardly the right word: although the Tyroleans and their popular Duke Sigismund had to accept the decision of pope and emperor to appoint Cusanus, they did so grudgingly. And while Cusanus proved a successful financial manager of his bishopric, his attempts to transform it into a model diocese proved less successful. His stiff-necked self-righteousness, his unwillingness to make concessions to all-too-human desires, separated the would-be good shepherd from his flock.[60] The cathedral chapter resented that their autocratic bishop should be a commoner and a foreigner. The unbending prince-bishop's attempts to use threats, church bans, and military force to bring about the reforms he thought necessary in his

---

the Catholic Church the tradition of holy or jubilee years dates back to Pope Boniface VIII, who in 1300 invoked such a year.

   58. Reform of the monasteries had also been a major concern of the Council of Basel.

   59. See Brian A. Pavlac, "Reform," in Bellitto, Izbicki, and Christianson, *Introducing Nicholas of Cusa*, 71–83.

   60. Hermann J. Hallauer, *Nikolaus von Kues als Bischof und Landesfürst in Brixen*, Trierer Cusanus Lecture (Trier: Paulinus, 2000); Pavlac, "Reform," 6:91–93.

diocese and his efforts to reassert long forgotten rights in an attempt to expand his secular domain at the expense of Duke Sigismund all led to counter-force, even a feigned or real threat to his life that in June 1457 led the frightened cardinal to seek refuge in the fortress Andraz and in 1458 caused him to leave for Rome, where his old friend Aeneas Sylvius, now Pope Pius II, was happy to have him. Having learned to respect the judgment of Cusanus, he appointed him vicar-general for the Papal States, [61] which Cusanus governed effectively, leaving the pope free to prepare for the congress of Mantua (1459), where he hoped to persuade the princes of Europe to follow his call for yet another crusade to meet the Ottoman threat. The attendance was disappointing. Cusanus did his best to mediate between the pope and the reluctant princes, while the pope attempted to mediate between Cusanus and Duke Sigismund—in both cases with little success, in part as a result of the eloquent opposition of Gregor von Heimburg, who had become the duke's adviser, still pursuing his opposition to papal authority. The pope responded on the 18th of January 1460 with the bull *Execrabilis*, which condemned conciliarism. It proved an impotent display of papal power. Four days before, a crusade had indeed been proclaimed, but the lukewarm support of the princes made it a hollow proclamation.

Early in 1460 Cusanus did return to his diocese. Still in fear of his life, he once again sought refuge in his castle Andraz. His fears were justified. In the Easter week of 1460 Duke Sigismund's mercenaries seized him in Bruneck, where Cusanus had come for a synod and to give some sermons. The duke's resolve to resist the pope and his appointee, despite the expected ecclesiastic penalties, was strengthened by Cusanus's old enemy Gregor von Heimburg.[62] The limited effectiveness of papal bans and interdict heralded the Reformation to come.

Released only after making concessions that he later revoked as coerced, Cusanus left the Tyrol on April 27, 1460, first for Cortina,

---

61. Erich Meuthen, *Die letzten Jahre des Nikolaus Cusanus* (Cologne and Opladen: Westdeutscher Verlag, 1958), 28.

62. See Albert Jäger's riveting, admirably detailed, but prejudiced *Der Streit des Cardinals Nicolaus von Cusa mit dem Herzoge Sigmund von Österreich als Grafen von Tirol*, 2 vols. (Innsbruck: Wagner, 1861). A necessary correction is provided by Herman Hallauer, "Die 'Schlacht' im Enneberg 1458: Neue Quellen zur Biographie des Nikolaus von Kues," in *Nicolo' Cusano: Agli Inizi del Mondo Moderno*, 447–69. See also Anselm Sparber's unreliable "Aus der Wirksamkeit des Kardinals Nikolaus von Kues als Fürstbischof von Brixen (1450–1464)," in *Nicolo' Cusano: Agli Inizi del Mondo Moderno*, 523–35, and Brian A. Pavlac, "Nicolaus Cusanus as Prince-Bishop of Brixen (1450–64): Historians and a Conflict of Church and State," *Historical Reflections/Reflexions Historiques* 21, no. 1, (1995): 131–53.

then for Rome. There Pope Pius kept him busy, although Cusanus's attempts at reform, which did not stop at the Roman Curia, made even the pope uneasy. Already in 1459 Cusanus had drafted his *Reformatio generalis*, which called for a general reform of the Roman Curia and would have subjected the pope to the judgment of outside visitors.

> Since the eye, which sees the blind spots (*maculas*) of the others, does not see its own blind spot, it cannot visit itself. For this reason it must submit itself to another visitor, who visits, corrects, and cleanses it in order to make sure that it is suitable to visit the members of the body.[63]

As they had in the Tyrol, in Rome, too, as later again in Orvieto, Cusanus's attempts at reform met with opposition and proved ineffective. The pope did not feel he needed to be corrected and cleansed; he resented being criticized for his monarchic attitude, while Cusanus, disheartened, threatened to withdraw from public life.[64]

Meanwhile, the situation in Brixen remained unresolved and even in his absence continued to take much of Cusanus's time. It took several years and the efforts of pope and emperor to finally work out a compromise with the Tyrolean duke that would have allowed Cusanus to return. But two weeks before that compromise was reached Cusanus died in Todi, on August 11, 1464, while on a mission for his pope to reenergize what remained of an army that had gathered in Ancona in preparation for Pius II's long-planned crusade against the Ottomans[65] (a crusade that, because of lukewarm support and poor organization, never materialized). Cusanus was also there to help adjudicate a dispute that had developed between the Catholic city of Breslau and the Bohemian Hussite king Podiebrad. His old friend Paolo Toscanelli traveled all the way from Florence to be at Cusanus's bedside. Cusanus was buried in San Pietro in Vincoli, the titular church he had been awarded when Pope Nicholas V had named him cardinal. Following his wishes, his heart was buried in the chapel of the hospice that he and his family had endowed in Kues.

His friend Pope Pius II died three days later in Ancona, to which

---

63. Johannes Hoff, trans., *The Analogical Turn: Rethinking Modernity with Nicholas of Cusa* (Grand Rapids, MI: Eerdmans, 2013), 226.

64. Hoff, *Analogical Turn*, 227.

65. The crusade, called for already by his predecessors Nicholas and Caixtus III, had been an obsession of Pope Pius II, who, as mentioned, had called on the princes of Europe to assemble in Mantua in June 1459 to support this project, but the response was disappointing. Continuing Ottoman expansion kept the project alive, but it never really gathered the necessary support. See Norman Housley, *Crusading and the Ottoman Threat, 1453–1505* (Oxford: Oxford University Press, 2012).

he had traveled, although already grievously ill, only to see the dissolute troops that had assembled there in response to his impassioned preaching for a crusade melt away.[66]

Given such a busy, turbulent life, one must wonder how Cusanus found the time and the concentration to write as much as he did—well over thirty significant treatises. And we should not forget the over two hundred sermons, often theological-philosophical treatises, that reward careful study.[67] That we have autographs even of the very first sermons he preached suggests how much Cusanus valued them.

That Cusanus represents a position between two ages appears to have been felt already by his contemporaries. Significantly, it is in a eulogy, included in Giovanni Andrea de Bussi's dedicatory epistle to Pope Paul II that accompanied his Apuleius edition (1469) and written shortly after the cardinal's death, that we see for the first time the expression "Middle Ages" (*media tempestas*) being used—for six years Bussi had been the cardinal's secretary, and with the cardinal's encouragement he established the first Italian printing shop in the Benedictine monastery of Subiaco (1465). In that epistle he praises Cusanus, this best of all men (*vir eo melior nunquam sit natus*) for, among other things, keeping in his memory not just the works of the ancient authors, but also those of both the earlier and the later Middle Ages, right down to our own time.[68] An epochal threshold had been crossed.[69] Bussi's characterization of the preceding centuries as *media tempestas* suggests, on the one hand, that one no longer felt part of it, that a new third age had commenced; on the other hand, his praise recognizes a desire on the part of Cusanus to preserve a certain continuity with the past.

That Cusanus felt himself to be occupying an epochal threshold is shown by a sermon he delivered less than a year after the completion of *On Learned Ignorance* in Augsburg of January 1, 1441: *Domine, in lumine vultus tui ambulant* (O Lord, in the light of Your countenance they walk) [Ps 88 (H89), 16].[70] The life of the church is there said to

66. Creighton, Council of Basel, *History of the Papacy*, 2:473–75; Meuthen, *Nicholas of Cusa*, 122–25; Housley, *Crusading and the Ottoman Threat*, 11.

67. See Lawrence F. Hundersmarck, "Preaching," in Bellitto, Izbicki, and Christianson, *Introducing Nicholas of Cusa*, 232–69.

68. "Vir ipse, quod rarum est in Germania, supra opinionem eloquens et Latinus, historias idem omnes non priscas modo, sed mediae tempestatis tum veteres, tum recentiores usque ad nostra tempora memoria retinebat."; cited in Nikolaus von Kues, *Vom Nichtanderen*, trans. Paul Wilpert (Hamburg: Meiner, 1952), 101n1. See also Paul Lehmann, "Vom Mittelalter und der lateinischen Philologie des Mittelalters," *Quellen und Untersuchungen zur lateinischen Philologie des Mittelalters* V, no. 1 (1914).

69. See Peuckert, *Die Große Wende*, 2:333–44.

70. Cusanus, Sermon XXIII: *Domine, in Lumine Vultus Tui*, 377–96.

imitate the life of Christ, where one year in the life of Christ is said to equal fifty years in the life of the church.

The childhood, until the visit in the temple, equals the years of the Church until 600 *usque ad tempus sancti Gregorii* [until the time of Saint Gregory]. The seventeen years of concealment follow—until the jubilee year 1450; *et nunc incipiet apparere ut potestatem habens proximo ex isto, et per 150 annos durabit apparitio eius* (but now begin the 3, i.e., 150 years of his *apparitio*, when Christ appears possessing power), years that begin in 1451 and last until 1600; they are followed by a final persecution of the Church and its victory, the ascension of the mystical body to eternal life: *deinde sequetur ultima persecutio crucifixionis, deinde resurrectio et ascensio corporis mystici ad vitam aeternam.*[71]

Thoughts of the beginning of a new year led Cusanus to thoughts of a new age, soon to begin. Cusanus thus thought of his own life as straddling the threshold separating an age of concealment from an age when Christ, the incarnated Logos, would manifest himself to all nations. Cusanus, to be sure, was well aware that what he has to say here is not to be taken too seriously: "These are the likely [sequences]; but they are not certain to us."[72]

71. Peuckert, *Die Große Wende*, 340.

72. *Nicholas of Cusa's Early Sermons*, trans. and intro. Jasper Hopkins (Loveland, Colo.: Arthur J. Banning, 2003), 381. See also Cusanus's *Coniectura de Ultimis Diebus* [A Surmise about the Last Days]: *Nicolai de Cusa Opera Omnia*, vol. IV, in *Opuscula* I, ed. Paul Wilpert (Hamburg: Meiner Verlag. 1959), 91–100, written five years later. For the translation by Jasper Hopkins, 2008, see *Coniectura de* Ultimis, https://jasperhopkins.info/Coniectura DeUltimisDiebus.pdf.

In this later conjecture, too, Cusanus suggests, drawing on his understanding of the church as the body of Christ, that fifty years in the life of the church correspond to one year of the life of Christ. "The foregoing parallelism, having to do with length-of-life, is inferred by Nicholas from a second exegetical norm: namely, that one ordinary year in the life of Jesus is to be interpreted as one jubilee year in the life of the Church"; Hopkins, "Introduction," 4. In this essay, too, drawing on the book of Daniel, Cusanus conjectures that the world may well end in the years 1700–1750. Once again, we are admonished not to make too much of such conjectures.

ON LEARNED IGNORANCE

BOOK ONE

Prologue

De docta ignorantia, On Learned Ignorance, the first and most significant of Cusanus's philosophical works, was begun in December 1439
in a monastery in the Eifel and finished in his hometown of Kues
(Cusa) on February 12, 1440.[1] It was thus written in just a bit over two
months. Not surprisingly, therefore, the argumentation often seems
a bit hurried. To be sure, the ideas developed in the book must have
occupied Cusanus for many years. A work like *De docta ignorantia* does
not suddenly burst into being. Some central ideas developed in the
text can indeed be traced back to his very first sermons:[2] the indefinability of the infinite thus occupies him in sermons 1, 4, 8, 11, 12,
and 17; in sermon 4 he plays already with the possibility of infinite
worlds;[3] and the very first sermon, *In principio erat verbum*, delivered in
1430, announces a theme that provides a key to Cusanus's thought:
that all being, the being of God, of the universe, and of man has a
triadic structure.[4] The thought of the coincidence of opposites looks
back to his study of Dionysius, Albert the Great, and Ramon Llull
with Heymeric de Campo in Cologne.[5] But such anticipations should
not lead us to discount the significance of the inspiration that, he
tells us, came to him while at sea, returning from Constantinople,
and provided him with the *regula doctae ignorantiae*, the principle of
learned ignorance, that allowed him to gather his speculations into a

1. Jasper Hopkins, "Preface," in *Nicholas of Cusa: On Learned Ignorance*, trans. Jasper
Hopkins (Minneapolis: Arthur J. Banning, 1981), vii.

2. See Pavel Floss, *The Philosophy of Nicholas of Cusa: An Introduction into His Thinking*
(Basel: Schwabe Verlag, 2020).

3. "Deus est infinitus in tantum quod, si mundi essent infiniti, ipse eos repleret, quia
non habet finem nec finibilis, sed finiens omnia"; cited in Floss, *Philosophy of Nicholas of
Cusa*, 37.

4. Floss, *Philosophy of Nicholas of Cusa*, 20–22.

5. Rudolf Haubst, "Das Leitwort der 'coincidentia oppositorum,'" in *Streifzüge in die
Cusanische Theologie* (Munich: Aschendorff, 1991), 117–40.

coherent whole. That, given the many demands placed on him by the church, he found the time to write this book following his mission to Constantinople and participation in the Council of Florence, which was to finally conclude only in 1445, testifies to a remarkable ability not to let his busy life prevent him from attending to what most profoundly mattered.

Both the Prologue and the concluding letter are addressed to Cardinal Julian Cesarini, his former teacher in Padua and the leader of the minority party at Basel that sided with the pope and that had authorized Cusanus to travel, with the approval of Pope Eugene IV, to Constantinople to prepare for the council of union with the Eastern church that was to take place in Ferrara. The spirit of Cesarini, so to speak, frames the work. Four years later, as mentioned, Cesarini was to lose his life in the Battle of Varna, the disastrous end of a crusade against the Ottoman Turks that he had helped organize.

As the concluding letter to Cesarini informs us, the fundamental thought came to Cusanus while at sea, returning from Greece.[6] He had left for Greece from Venice in the beginning of August 1437, arriving in Constantinople a month later. He began his return journey on November 27, 1437, in the company of, among many others, the Byzantine emperor John XIII Palaeologus, the patriarch Joseph II, and twenty-eight archbishops, including, and most importantly perhaps, given Cusanus's interests, the learned Metropolitan Bessarion, who combined a deep knowledge of neo-Platonism with the study of mathematics, physics, and cosmology. Given that the sea journey took over two months—the ship arrived in Venice on February 8, 1438—it is inconceivable that Cusanus would not have had many occasions to engage these learned Greeks in lengthy conversations. Having settled in Italy, Bessarion was made a cardinal in 1439. He was to remain a lifelong friend.[7]

Cusanus must have been exhilarated by what he thought had been achieved and by his conversations with Bessarion and other Greek theologians and was likely eager to study the many books he had acquired in Constantinople. No doubt he was still burdened by the chaos of Basel—the conciliar faction remained powerful and continued to demand his engagement—but was hopeful that his work for the reunification of the Roman and the Greek churches, which

6. See *De docta ignorantia*, Book III, ed. Hans Gerhard Senger (Meiner: Hamburg, 2002), note 263, 1f.

7. Morimichi Watanabe, *Nicholas of Cusa—A Companion to His Life and His Times* (London: Ashgate, 2013).

had been divided ever since the Great Schism of 1054, would be re-warded—that his dream of a truly united Catholic Church might yet become reality, as it seemed to when, as mentioned, a fragile and as it turned out all-too-fleeting union was at least formally achieved at the Council of Florence on July 6, 1439.

The letter to Cardinal Cesarini that concludes the book communicates something of the excitement that must have overcome Cusanus when the central thought of *De docta ignorantia* suddenly came to him—the thought that God, whom for so long he had struggled to understand, could be grasped only when, understanding the limits of our understanding, we are cast beyond them. Learned ignorance demanded a negative theology.[8] The reader, to be sure, may well wonder what here is a report of a sublime revelatory experience and what is rhetorical embellishment.[9] It is almost as if Cusanus wanted to exemplify something Augustine had written: "There is therefore in us a certain learned ignorance (*docta ignorantia*), so to speak—an ignorance which we learn from that Spirit of God who helps our infirmities."[10] Still, whatever texts or conversations helped ready Cusanus for the insight that came to him on his sea journey—in the later *Apologia doctae ignorantiae* (1449) he claims that at the time he "had not examined Dionysius or any of the true theologians" (*AP* 12)[11]—we should not dismiss his presentation of what then came to him as a divine gift: the conviction that only by transcending the rules that govern our reason is our intellect able to comprehend incomprehensibly the infinite God—and thinking God can be said to have been Cusanus's life-long fundamental project.[12]

8. See H. Lawrence Bond, "Redefining *Via Negationis*," in Bellitto, Izbicki, and Christianson, *Introducing Nicholas of Cusa*, 206–7.

9. See Marjorie O'Rourke Boyle, "Cusanus at Sea: The Topicality of Illuminative Discourse," *Journal of Religion* 71, no. 2 (April 1991): 180–201. Cusanus is said to have composed the letter as "epeidictic rhetoric," a genre that "had always been proper for the dedication of compositions to patrons and friends" (181). "As epeidictic in genre, it is not a brute fact that Cusanus experiencded the illumination 'at sea returning from Greece' with reference to an actual voyage on the Mediterrenean or the Adriatic. Considering the topic of the place in history of illuminative discourse, it is plausible that the reference, even if fundamentally literal, is more significantly symbolic" (182).

10. Augustine, *Epistolae* CXXX, no. XV (28): 1, https://orthodoxchurchfathers.com/fathers/npnf101/npnf1032.htm#P5022_2287573. See F. Edward Cranz, "The Transmutation of Platonism in the Development of Nicolaus Cusanus and Martin Luther," in *Nicolo' Cusano: Agli Inizi del Mondo Moderno*, 471, 81.

11. References in the text are to Jasper Hopkins, *Nicholas of Cusa's Debate with John Wenck: A Translation and Appraisal of "De Ignota Litteratura"* [*IL*] *and "Apologia Doctae Ignorantiae"* [*AP*]. Page references to *IL* are to the Latin text published by Hopkins in this volume, to *AP* to vol. II of *Opera Omnia*, Heidelberg Academy Edition, given in the margins of Hopkins's translations.

12. Cf. Miller, *Reading Cusanus*, 1.

> Receive now, Reverend Father, the things which I have long desired
> to attain by various doctrinal-approaches but could not—until, while
> I was at sea en route back from Greece, I was led (by, as I believe,
> a heavenly gift from the Father of lights, from whom comes every
> excellent gift) to embrace—in learned ignorance and through a
> transcending of the incorruptible truths which are humanly know-
> able—incomprehensible things incomprehensibly. Thanks to Him
> who is Truth, I have now expounded this [learned ignorance] in
> these books, which, [since they proceed] from [one and] the same
> principle, can be condensed or expanded. (*DI* III.263)[13]

The invocation of "the Father of lights, from whom comes every excellent gift," quoting James 1:17, may well strike us as a pious rhetorical flourish that need not detain us. But the fact that a few years later
Cusanus was to devote a brief treatise, *De dato patris luminum* [On the
Gift of the Father of Lights] (1445/1446)[14] to an explanation of the
phrase suggests that his invocation of the Father of lights is more
than that. With it Cusanus sought to assure the reader and perhaps
himself that the words that follow are not, as some of his critics were
to charge, the words of a false prophet, a self-inflated intellect, pre-
senting his own wild speculations as divinely inspired. As he explains
in the later treatise: with his words,

> the Apostle wanted to exclude the errors both of those who affirmed
> that God is the cause of evil and of those who elevated themselves by
> their own presumptiveness—as if a man, of himself and apart from
> the Father's gift of grace and His drawing, could attain to appre-
> hending wisdom. [The following] were sins of this kind: that most
> presumptuous sin (1) of the rational immaterial spirit Lucifer, who
> attempted to ascend by his own power to the likeness of the Most
> High, and (2) of the rational embodied spirit of [our first] ancestors,
> who were hoping that by means of the nourishment from the per-
> ceptible food of a tree they would attain unto a divine perfection of
> knowledge. From these examples we are taught that the actualizing
> [which is necessary] in order that we may apprehend wisdom (which
> is both a living light and the glorious quieting of our spirit's desire)
> cannot come either from ourselves or from lower, perceptible forms

---

13. References in the text are to the Latin text in Nikolaus von Kues, *Philosophisch-
theologische Werke*, Lateinisch-deutsch, vol, 1, *De docta* ignorantia, abbreviated *DI*. The numbers following are to paragraphs of the Latin text, found in the margins of Hopkins translation: Hopkins, *Nicholas of Cusa on Learned Ignorance*.

14. *De dato patris luminum* (1445/1446), in Paul Wilpert, ed., *Nicolai de Cusa Opera
Omnia*, Vol. IV (Opuscula I) (Hamburg: Felix Meiner Verlag, 1959), trans. Jasper Hopkins,
"On the Gift of the Father of Lights," in Nicholas of Cusa's Metaphysic of Contraction
(Minneapolis: J. Banning, 1983), 372–86. Abbreviated *DPL*.

of life, but can come [only] from the Father and Giver of forms, who alone has the prerogative of perfecting. (*DPL* 95)

True wisdom is a divine gift, not a human achievement.

In the concluding letter to Cardinal Cesarini, Cusanus speaks of a transcending of the incorruptible truths that are "humanly knowable." There are of course many such truths. According to Aristotle, the law of non-contradiction is the most fundamental of these, since our reason is bound by it.[15] But, according to Cusanus, the infinite God transcends these truths. They must therefore also be transcended by us if we are to open ourselves to and embrace the incomprehensible mystery of the Trinity in the only way open to us human knowers: incomprehensibly. This presupposes that we possess a faculty higher than our reason, an intellect that allows us to recognize and rise above the limits of reason—that is, to become learned about our essential ignorance. Only learned ignorance opens us to the mystery that is God. That is the insight that the Father of lights granted Cusanus.

But is this not to leave reason behind altogether and with it responsible thinking? This charge was leveled by Johannes Wenck, four years younger than Cusanus, a respected theologian who had studied at Paris and taught with distinction at the University of Heidelberg, but also someone who, as an ardent defender of the cause of the Council, bore a personal grudge against Cusanus ever since their Basel days, as displayed in his *De ignota litteratura*, written in 1442/43.[16] As Cusanus remarks, Wenck is speaking "from emotion" (*AP* 5). According to Wenck,

> This man of learned ignorance glories, telling the Cardinal that at sea, on his return from Greece, and being guided by supernal light, he found what he formerly had striven after by way of various doctrinal paths. And further specifying that which he found, he says: ... in order that I might embrace—in learned ignorance and through a transcending of the incorruptible truths which are humanly knowable—incomprehensible things incomprehensibly. He says that thanks to Him who is Truth he has expounded this [learned ignorance] in three books. Yet, that disciple whom Jesus loved exhorts us, in his first letter, chapter 4, not to believe every spirit but to test the spirits [in order to determine] whether they are from God. And he adds the reason why this is necessary: "because many false prophets

15. Aristotle, *Metaphysics* IV.3.1005.19–24.

16. For a searching discussion of Cusanus's debate with Wenck, see Blumenberg, *Legitimität*, 457–66. See also Donald Duclow, "Mystical Theology and Intellect in Nicholas of Cusa," *American Catholic Philosophical Quarterly* 64, no. 1 (Winter 1990): 115–29.

> have gone out into the world." Of which prophets the apostle in II Corinthians 1 says, speaking more specifically: "[They are] false apostles, deceitful workmen, who transform themselves into apostles of Christ." Among whose number is, perhaps, this man of learned ignorance, who under the guise of religion cunningly deceives those not yet having trained senses. For the teachings of the Waldensians, Eckhartians, and Wycliffians have long shown from what spirit this learned ignorance proceeds. (*IL* 22)

Wenck associates Cusanus's teaching of learned ignorance with views that the church had condemned as heretical.[17] A conservative defender of orthodoxy, he had good reason to be suspicious of such self-proclaimed inspirations. Cusanus in fact did not conceal his admiration for Meister Eckhart,[18] insisting on his orthodoxy even as he admitted that some of his utterances might well mislead careless readers (*AP* 25). As we shall see, Cusanus's proximity to Meister Eckhart does raise questions concerning his orthodoxy.

As Nietzsche knew so well, distance from what we take to be *terra firma* lets us wonder about just where we are and where we should be going. Thus he lets his Zarathustra address his doctrine of the eternal recurrence first to sailors, to those who, finding themselves at sea,[19] have left behind the familiar and the readily taken for granted. Cusanus must have experienced such a dislocation while at sea, wondering while out of sight of land whether our earth, like the ship on which he found himself, while providing those on board with the sense of a firm ground, might not actually be moving. Such wonder called into question the then taken-for-granted understanding of the earth as the firm center of the cosmos. But in his musings Cusanus must have gone much further: could it be that our reason, too, does not furnish us with a cognitive *terra firma*? That it remains bound to and limited by our finite human perspective? And is it not precisely an understanding of this essential limitation of our reason that opens a door to the most adequate grasp of the trinitarian God granted to us mortals?

---

17. See Donald Duclow, "Nicholas of Cusa in the Margins of Meister Eckhart: Codex Cusanus 21," in Christianson and Izbicki, *Nicholas of Cusa: In Search of God and Wisdom*, 57–69.

18. As Louis Dupré remarks, "Eckhart's influence on Cusa can hardly be exaggerated. One needs only to look at the extensive notes he wrote in the margins of the Eckhart codex in Kues to realize how seriously Cusa studied Eckhart's work"; Dupré, "The Question of Pantheism from Eckhart to Cusanus," in *Cusanus: The Legacy of Learned Ignorance*, ed. Peter J. Casarella (Washington, DC: The Catholic University of America Press, 2006), 75.

19. See Karsten Harries, "The Philosopher at Sea," in *Nietzsche's New Seas: Explorations in Philosophy, Aesthetics, and Politics*, ed. Michael Allen Gillespie and Tracy B. Strong (Chicago: University of Chicago Press, 1988), 21–44.

I accept Hans Blumenberg's suggestion that there is a significant similarity between Cusanus's teaching of the coincidence of opposites, the central thought of *On Learned Ignorance*, and Nietzsche's thought of the eternal recurrence.[20] Both are presented as inspirations.[21] Both are incomprehensible, monstrous thoughts (*monstra*), as Cusanus himself calls his own in his dedication of the book to Cardinal Julian Cesarini. The choice of *monstra* not only suggests his willingness to break with what had come to be established and accepted, but also a proud awareness of the novelty of what he has to say in this book. Cusanus speaks of the "boldness (*audacia*) by which [he] was led to deal with learned ignorance" (*DI* 1). But does the monstrous have a place in responsible discourse?

Given the way his sea journey may have made him wonder about the earth's place in the cosmos and the limits of our reason, it seems fitting that Cusanus should have chosen to organize the Prologue to *De docta ignorantia* around the theme of wonder (*admiratio, admirari*). Choosing this theme, Cusanus refers the reader back to Aristotle. Addressing his old teacher and friend Cesarini as his ideal reader, he suggests that this learned cardinal, "extremely busy with important public affairs," might well wonder what would lead his younger friend to publish his "foreigner's foolishness" (*barbaras ineptias*) and to select just him as judge. Cesarini was indeed "extremely busy" at the time: as already mentioned, even more than Cusanus, he played a leading part in the negotiations with the Greeks in Ferrara and then in Florence. But Cusanus also expresses the hope that the novelty of the title, *On Learned Ignorance*, would incite the cardinal's curiosity: "This wondering shall, I hope, induce your knowledge-hungry mind to take a look" (*DI*, Prologue, 1). By calling attention to the novelty of the seemingly paradoxical title, to the unusual, even monstrous things (*monstra*) found in this book, Cusanus himself thus invites the charge raised by Johannes Wenck:

20. Blumenberg has called Cusanus's thought of a circle whose radius becomes infinite, a thought offered to the reader as a representation of the *coincidentia oppositorum*, a *Sprengmetapher*, a metaphor meant to stretch what, first of all and most of the time, binds our understanding beyond the breaking point, seeking to explode these bonds, even as it reminds us of their inescapability. Georg Simmel, Blumenberg continues, invites us, in one of the fragments of his diary, to understand Nietzsche's thought of the eternal recurrence as another such *Sprengmetapher*; see Hans Blumenberg, *Schiffbruch mit Zuschauer: Paradigma einer Daseinsmetapher* (Frankfurt am Main: Suhrkamp, 1979), 84.

21. Friedrich Nietzsche, *Ecce Homo, Sämtliche Werke, Kritische Studienausgabe*, ed. Giorgio Colli and Mazzino Montinari (Munich, Berlin, and New York: Deutscher Taschenbuch Verlag and de Gruyter, 1980), 6:339, abbreviated as *KSA*, followed by volume and page number; translated by Walter Kaufmann and R. J. Hollingdale, *On the Genealogy of Morals and Ecce Homo* (New York: Vintage, 1989), 300.

> From an innate desire for health, the minds of my readers will be
> vigilant with regard even to this Unknown Learning. With spiritu-
> al weapons, however, I am going to rebut certain statements from
> Learned Ignorance—[rebut them] as being incompatible with our
> faith, offensive to devout minds, and vainly leading away from obe-
> dience to God. At the head of what must be said comes the [com-
> mand] in Psalms 45 ("Be still and see that I am God") as being
> the legitimate enlistment of all our mental activity. For if I behold
> the mind of the prophet: after the elimination of malevolent wars,
> which are repugnant to our God, and, moreover, after the weapons
> of treachery have been broken and knowledge is to be had of Christ,
> our peacemaker and defender, then comes the command "Be still
> and see that I am God." For He envisioned certain who were free to
> spend time in the Lord's vineyard and who are accused in Matthew
> 20: "Why do you stand here all day idle?" Very many see—not unto
> salvation, the end of our faith, but with regard to curiosity and vanity.
> (*IL* 19–20)

Novel, monstrous things are indeed likely to move us. But will they
move us as we should be moved? Wenck saw in Nicolaus Cusanus
someone likely to mislead uncritical readers. It is easy to understand
his concern. Had St. Augustine not warned against idle curiosity?

> To this is added another form of temptation more manifoldly dan-
> gerous. For besides the concupiscence of the flesh which consisteth
> of the delight of all the senses and pleasures, wherein its slaves, who
> go far from Thee, waste and perish, the soul hath, through the same
> senses of the body a certain vain and curious desire, veiled under the
> title of knowledge and learning, not of delighting in the flesh, but
> of making experiments through the flesh. The seat whereof being
> in the appetite of knowledge, and sight being the sense chiefly used
> for attaining knowledge, it is in Divine language called the lust of
> the eyes.[22]

Was Cusanus, by suggesting that just the novelty of his monstrous
thoughts might induce the busy cardinal to take a look at the book,
not appealing to just that curiosity condemned by St. Augustine?
Wenck certainly seems to have thought so. Jasper Hopkins echoes
that charge (*OLI* 30). But it was not an idle desire for novelty that
led Cusanus to his monstrous thoughts. No doubt he took pleasure
in and was proud of his own originality. His writings demonstrate
that.[23] But that originality Cusanus understood to be an expression

22. St. Augustine, *Confessions*, trans. Edward B. Pusey (New York: Modern Library,
1949), X, 231–32.
23. See Mandrella, "Begriff und Funktion," 23–42.

of that freedom that raises us human beings above the other animals and allows us to be creative and produce something genuinely new. Cusanus understood such creativity as the image of God's creativity, human freedom as an image of God's infinite freedom.[24] The pleasure Cusanus takes in his creativity, in his production of what may at first seem monstrous, is inseparable from his understanding of the human being and thus of himself as *imago Dei,* created in the image of God.[25] The doctrine of learned ignorance is born of a freedom willing to leave behind the security of the established and accepted. Such willingness recalls the courage of the sailor willing to leave *terra firma* behind.

24. See such dialogues as *Idiota de Mente, De Beryllo,* and *De Ludo Globi.* See also Mandrella, "'Amor liber est': Liebe und Freiheit bei Nicolaus Cusanus," In *Trierer Cusanus Lecture,* Heft 20 (Trier: Paulinus Verlag, 2016), and Jasper Hopkins, "Orienting Study, Part One: Expository Purview," in *Nicholas of Cusa: Metaphysical Speculations* (Minneapolis: Arthur J. Banning Press, 2000), 1:20–22.

25. See Isabelle Mandrella, *Viva imago: Die praktische Philosophie des Nicolaus Cusanus,* Buchreihe der Cusanus-Gesellschaft (Münster: Aschendorff, 2011); Wilhelm Dupré, "The Image of the Living God: Some Remarks on the Meaning of Perfection and World Formation," in *Cusanus: The Legacy of Learned Ignorance,* ed. Peter J. Casarella, 89–104.

I. LEARNED IGNORANCE

I. LEARNED IGNORANCE

How It Is That Knowing
Is Not-Knowing?

The title of this first chapter is paradoxical. How can knowing (*scire*) be not-knowing or ignorance (*ignorare*)? The chapter title promises to shed light on the book's similarly paradoxical title, *De docta igno-rantia, On Learned Ignorance*. The doctrine of learned ignorance is at the center not just of this book, but of Nicholas's system in its entirety. But what exactly is this doctrine? Only as we work our way through *De docta ignorantia* will we begin to do justice to all Cusanus has in mind. First, however, a preliminary question: How is the title of the book to be understood? Is the ignorance Cusanus has in mind to be understood as the end product of a learning process that teaches us that we know nothing, as Socrates claimed for himself? Or is *docta ignorantia* to be understood as the highest knowledge granted to us humans?

The way different German translators struggled with the title is instructive.[1] The first German translation by Franz Anton Scharpff (1862) has *Die Wissenschaft des Nichtwissens, The Science of Not-Knowing*.[2] This rather free translation loses the way the title presents us with a characterization of the ignorance under discussion: it is learned.

---

1. See Hopkins, *OLI*, "Introduction," 2–3.
2. Scharpff, *Des Cardinals und Bischofs*, 3–109.

I. LEARNED IGNORANCE

Half a century later Alexander Schmid translated the title as *Vom Wissen des Nichtwissens,*[3] *On the Knowledge of Not-Knowing.* The German is ambiguous: the genitive can be understood either objectively or subjectively—that is, not-knowing can be understood as the object of knowing or it can be understood as itself a knowing. Paul Wilpert, in the opening note to his German translation of Book One, suggests that the title is more correctly translated as *Die belehrte Unwissenheit,* ignorance that has been instructed about its ignorance, shifting the emphasis from knowledge to ignorance. The human being has been brought to recognize that what we call knowledge can never grasp the truth of things—is really ignorance.[4] As we shall see, much in the text can be cited to support that translation. But there are many other passages, including the concluding letter and the title of this first chapter, "How It Is That Knowing Is Not-Knowing?," that support Erich Meuthen's translation of the title as *Das gelehrte Nicht-Wissen.*[5] *Gelehrt,* however, is misleading in that it suggests not so much wisdom as academic learning, and this is not at all what Cusanus had in mind. As Hopkins points out, "This kind of wisdom Nicholas would not call erudition (and in this respect Wilpert is also right); for it is available to the common man as well as to the highly schooled. Thus, Nicholas will later write his *Idiotae,* in which he exalts the Wisdom of the layman. But such a layman, with such a wisdom as Socrates's, might appropriately be called *gelehrt* (and in this respect Wilpert's statements are misleading)."[6] But Cusanus's *Idiota* is not erudite; he is no *Gelehrter.*[7] For this reason I prefer Günther Gawlick's translation of the title as "Von der wissenden Unwissenheit,"[8] which suggests an ignorance that is wise. But Wilpert is right to point out that the state of ignorance Cusanus has in mind presupposes that we have been led to recognize—that is, have been *belehrt*—that our reason is incapable of fully grasping the truth. The meaning of *docta* in *docta ignorantia*

<hr>

3. Alexander Schmid, trans., *Cusanus, Nikolaus, vom Wissen des Nichtwissens,* trans. Alexander (Hellerau: Jakob Hegner, 1919).

4. Nikolaus von Kues, *Philosophisch-theologische Werke,* Lateinisch-deutsch (Hamburg: Felix Meiner Verlag/Wissenschaftliche Buchgesellschaft), 1:114n1, abbreviated *PTW.*

5. Erich Meuthen, *Nikolaus von Kues 1401–1464: Skizze einer Biographie,* 4th ed. (Münster: Aschendorff, 1979), 53.

6. *OLI,* "Introduction," 3.

7. On Cusanus's understanding of the *idiota,* see Gandillac, *Nikolaus von Cues,* 45–60. Gandillac, however, makes much of the impact on the young Cusanus of his supposed, but highly questionable, studies with the Brothers of the Common Life. In Deventer he would have met living examples of his *idiota.*

8. Nikolaus von Cues, "Von der wissenden Unwissenheit, ausgewählt und neu übertragen von Günther Gawlick," in *Nikolaus von Cues: Die Kunst der Vermutung; Auswahl aus den Schriften,* ed. Hans Blumenberg (Bremen: Carl Schünemann Verlag, 1957), 72–185.

oscillates between the distinction between *belehrt* and *gelehrt* and blurs it. So does the English "learned." As Hopkins remarks,

> The best English translation will therefore be the traditional one: viz., "On Learned Ignorance," where "learned" is understood in the double sense distinguished orally by the different pronunciations lurnd and lurnid—i.e., understood as both *belehrt* and *gelehrt.* For it is an ignorance which both distinguishes its possessor from the unlearned, or uninstructed, and elevates him to the place of the learned, or wise.[9]

My only reservation concerns the already mentioned academic flavor of *gelehrt* and *Gelehrter. Docta ignorantia* does not require erudition. For that reason I prefer, of all the translations of the title here considered, that of Alexander Schmid: *Vom Wissen des Nichtwissens,* where the objective and subjective readings of the genitive preserve the ambiguity of the title without making of knowledge or *Wissen* something properly at home only in the academic world.[10] From that world Cusanus sought to keep his distance.

Learned ignorance, as Cusanus understands it, has indeed come to recognize the limits of our reason, our essential ignorance: in this sense it has been *belehrt.* But it also confers a higher knowledge. It allows us to at least glimpse the truth that we all search for, precisely by leading us to recognize the inability of all our concepts to seize it. Never shall we know things as they really are. To become learned about our ignorance is to recognize that the truth of things, what they really are, inescapably transcends our comprehension.[11] Learned ignorance lets us recognize the limits of our reason in order to raise in us an awareness of what lies beyond these limits. So understood, the title gestures toward Cusanus's embrace of the coincidence of opposites and the higher insight into God that it opens up.

Following these preliminary remarks, let us consider the chapter in some detail. The beginning seems uncontroversial:

> We see that by the gift of God there is present in all things a natural desire to exist in the best manner in which the condition of each

9. Von Cues, "Von der wissenden Unwissenheit," 72–185.

10. Cf. Hans Blumenberg, "Von der wissenden Unwissenheit: Einführung," in Blumenberg, *Nikolaus von Cues: Die Kunst der Vermutung,* 71: "The attempt to translate *docta ignorantia* with *Wissen des Nichtwissens* allows, because of the ambiguity of the genitive, both for a Socratic and a Cusan interpretation: the objectve genitive yields the Socratic, the subjective genitive the Cusan formulation. Properly understood, this is justified by the fact that the Socratic meaning is not canceled by the Cusan, but preseved in it."

11. Cf. Karl-Heinz Volkmann-Schluck, *Nicolaus Cusanus: Die Philosophie im Übergang vom Mittelalter zur Neuzeit* (Frankfurt am Main: Klostermann, 1957), 1–11.

thing's nature permits this. And [we see that all things] act toward this end and have instruments adapted thereto. They have an innate sense of judgment which serves the purpose of knowing. [They have this] in order that their desire not be in vain but be able to attain rest in that [respective] object which is desired by the propensity of each thing's own nature. But if perchance affairs turn out otherwise, this [outcome] must happen by accident—as when sickness misleads taste or an opinion misleads reason. (*DI* I.1:2)

In agreement with what Aristotle had taught, all beings are said to be governed by the desire to attain the best possible state their nature allows. But we human beings, unlike the other animals, possess an intellect. And there is no intellect, properly speaking, where there is no freedom. What then is the best way in which a free intelligent being can exist? Cusanus suggests, agreeing with Thomas Aquinas, by freely embracing what it knows to be true.

Wherefore, we say that a sound, free intellect (*intellectus*) knows to be true that which is apprehended by its affectionate embrace. (The intellect insatiably desires to attain unto the true through scrutinizing all things by means of its innate faculty of inference.) Now, that from which no sound mind can withhold assent is, we have no doubt, most true. (*DI* I.1:2)

I would underscore the words "sound" (*sanus*) and "free" (*liber*). Both are needed. The mark of truth is here said to be the inability of a sound mind to withhold its assent from what is recognized to be true. Important is the reference to a "sound mind." The human mind may turn away from the love of truth. That possibility is inseparable from freedom.

"Most true" suggests degrees of truth. Cusanus is very much aware that what we hold to be true is often limited by various perspectives. But loving the truth, a free intellect will strive to rise above such limitations as best it can and, by transcending what it recognizes to be perspectival limitations, arrive at the truth that will bind it. To be truly free is to be bound by that truth. The love of truth here finds fulfillment.

But is truth, so understood, not denied to us human knowers? Are we not always limited in our pursuit of truth by our finite nature, by some perspective or other? Is there not always some distance between what we take to be "most true" and the truth? How do we pursue knowledge?

However, all those who make an investigation judge the uncertain proportionally, by means of a comparison with what is taken to be certain. (*DI* I.1:2)

Comparativa igitur est omnis inquisitio medio proportionis utens. All who investigate judge the uncertain proportionally (*proportionaliter*), relating what is being investigated to what is taken to be certain, where we may well wonder how secure a foundation is provided by what we take to be certain. When we attempt to understand something, we place it, as best we can, in the space of what is familiar and taken for granted.

The word *proportio*,[12] which plays such a central part in medieval discussions of analogy, invites further discussion. Hopkins translates it as "definite relation." An example would be the ratio 2:4. But such a relation need not be thought of in mathematical terms. A standard medieval example is provided by urine, which is said to be "healthy" by an analogy of proportion:—that is, urine is not literally healthy, but is called healthy because it is a sign of health. To understand the meaning of the analogy or metaphor, we have to understand the relevant relation (*proportio*)—that is, we must know what "healthy" here signifies.

Different is an analogy of proportionality, such as 2:4=x:y. It does tell us something about the relationship of x and y. Similarly, to speak of intellectual vision tells us something in that it asserts that the eye is related to the seen as the intellect is related to the understood. What the analogy leaves unaddressed is in what relationship 2 and x or eye and intellect stand. That requires us to put the two into some sort of definite relation.

In the late dialogue *De li non aliud*,[13] Cusanus speaks instead of *proportio*, of *definitio*. Consider: What is this? This is a cow. The matter in question is made definite by being brought into a definite relation (*proportio*) to the known. This is how inquiry proceeds.

Now, when, the things investigated are able to be compared by means of a close proportional tracing back to what is taken to be [certain], our judgment apprehends easily; but when we need many intermediate steps, difficulty arises and hard work is required. These points are recognized in mathematics, where the earlier propositions are quite easily traced back to the first and most evident principles but

12. A good introduction to medieval analogy is Tommaso de Vio Cajetan, *The Analogy of Names*, trans. Edward Bushinski and Henry Koren (1953; repr. Eugene, OR: Wipf and Stock, 2009).

13. Nicholas of Cusa, *On God as Not-Other: A Translation and an Appraisal of "De li non aliud,"* by Jasper Hopkins (Minneapolis: Banning, 1987).

> where later propositions [are traced back] with more difficulty be-
> cause [they are traced back] only through the mediation of the ear-
> lier ones. (*DI* I.1:2)

The following sentence provides a key to the doctrine of learned
ignorance:

> Therefore, every inquiry proceeds by means of a comparative rela-
> tion, whether an easy or a difficult one. Hence, the infinite, *qua* in-
> finite, is unknown; for it escapes all comparative relation. (*DI* I.1:3)

Our knowing is essentially finite. We have no difficulty understanding mathematical truths such as $2+3=5$ or $8^2=64$. But the infinite
must remain unknown. It cannot be reached by such inevitably finite
steps. Think of counting and of the impossible thought of the largest
number. To any number 1 can be added. The numerical maximum
transcends the reach of our finite reason: it is infinite. But while we
cannot comprehend the largest number, we can nevertheless think it,
are indeed inevitably led to this thought by our ability to count.

The maximum number serves Cusanus as a symbol of God. The
infinite God, too, cannot be comprehended. But to say even that, we
must have some insight into the infinite. Reflection on the finitude of
our reason presupposes that there is something in us that allows us to
transcend this limitation: that allows us to embrace the unknowable
unknowingly, so that our ignorance becomes learned.

We meet with the insight that reflection on the infinite and the
limits of our reason that it forces us to recognize presupposes a faculty higher than reason also in Descartes. Quite in the spirit of Cusanus,
Descartes states that God is to man as an infinite number is to a finite
number:

> For I readily and freely confess that the idea we have of the divine
> intellect, for example, does not differ from that we have of our own
> intellect, except insofar as the idea of an infinite number differs from
> that of a number raised to the second or fourth power. And the same
> applies to the individual attributes of God of which we recognize
> some trace in ourselves.[14]

Counting, we will never reach the largest—that is, infinite—number.
The very thought of such a number conflicts with our understanding
of what a number is, to which some other number can always be added. Descartes concludes from the fact that "I cannot reach a largest

---

14. René Descartes, *The Philosophical Writings of Descartes*, trans. John Cottingham, Robert
Stoothoff, and Dugald Murdoch (Cambridge: Cambridge University Press, 1985), 2:98.

number" that "in the process of counting" there is something that "exceeds my power." This is said to lead to the notion of "a being which is more perfect than I am." All finite numbers fall short of the maximum number in that to them you can always add one. The thought of a maximum number rules this out. The idea of such a maximum number exceeds thus the reach of my reason. The conclusion to be drawn, Descartes insists, is "not that an infinite number exists, nor indeed that it is a contradictory notion … , but that I have the power of conceiving that there is a thinkable number which is larger than any number that I can ever arrive at and hence that this power is something which I have received not from myself but from some other being which is more perfect than I."[15]

Although Cusanus is not mentioned here, we know that Descartes had read *De docta ignorantia*, although I know of only one direct reference to Cusanus: in a letter to Chanut of June 16, 1647.

To say that a number is thinkable, which, however, cannot be grasped by me, must make one wonder just how we are to understand "thinking" here. Our thought must be capable of transcending the limits of what our reason can comprehend—is indeed, by its very nature, led to this limit where the principle of non-contradiction is called into question, and in thinking this limit is cast beyond it. But this presupposes that our intellect transcends the reach of our reason.

"Number" is understood by Cusanus to be the presupposition of all comparative relations and thus of all understanding.

> But since *comparative relation* indicates an agreement in some one respect and, at the same time, indicates an otherness, it cannot be understood independently of number. Accordingly, number encompasses all things related comparatively. Therefore, number, which is a necessary condition of comparative relation, is present not only in quantity but also in all things which in any manner whatsoever can agree or differ either substantially or accidentally. Perhaps for this reason Pythagoras deemed all things to be constituted and understood through the power of numbers. (*DI* I.1:3)

Cusanus would seem to have Aristotle's *Metaphysics* in mind:

> *Meta* A.5.985b26ff: "Contemporaneously with these philosophers and before them (Leucippus and Democritus), the Pythagoreans, as they are called, devoted themselves to mathematics; they were the first to advance this study, and having been brought up in it they thought its principles were the principles of all things. Since of these

---

15. Descartes, *Philosophical Writings*, 2:100.

principles numbers are by nature the first.... they supposed the elements of number to be the elements of all things."

David Albertson suggests that this opening chapter of *De docta ignorantia* "could serve as an accurate digest of Boethius *De arithmetica*,"[16] placing *De docta ignorantia* in the tradition of a Christian neo-Pythagoreanism. Not that the conjunction of Christian thought and Pythagoras is unproblematic: There would seem to be tension between the infinity of God and the Pythagorean belief that the principles of our mathematics were the principles of all things. According to Cusanus the ability to count is a presupposition of our ability to understand anything whatsoever. But does this justify the Pythagorean claim of "the elements of number to be the elements of all things"? Or just of all things to the extent that we finite human knowers can understand them? Is Cusanus a Pythagorean?[17]

In the later dialogue *Idiota de mente*, Cusanus clarifies his relationship to Pythagoras:

Philosopher: You very much seem to be a Pythagorean, for [Pythagoras] asserted that all things are from number.

Layman: I don't know whether I am a Pythagorean or something else. But I do know that no one's authority guides me, even if it attempts to influence me. However, I deem the Pythagoreans—who, as you state, philosophize about all things by means of number—to be serious and keen [philosophers]. It is not the case that I think they meant to be speaking of number qua mathematical number and qua number proceeding from our mind. (For it is self-evident that that [sort of number] is not the beginning of anything.) Rather, they were speaking symbolically and plausibly about the number that proceeds from the Divine Mind—of which number a mathematical number is an image. For just as our mind is to the Infinite, Eternal Mind, so number [that proceeds] from our mind is to number [that proceeds from the Divine Mind]. And we give our name "number" to number from the Divine Mind, even as to the Divine Mind itself we give the name for our mind. And we take very great pleasure in occupying ourselves with numbers, as being an instance of our occupying ourselves with our own work.[18]

---

16. David Albertson, "'Boethius noster': Thierry of Chartres's *Arithmetica* Commentary as a Missing Source of Nicholas of Cusa's *De docta ignorantia*," *Recherches de Théologie et Philosophie Médiévales* 83, no. 1 (2016): 155.

17. See David Albertson, *Mathematical Theologies: Nicholas of Cusa and the Legacy of Thierry of Chartres* (Oxford: Oxford University Press, 2014).

18. *Idiota de Mente (The Layman on Mind)*, in Jasper Hopkins, *Nicholas of Cusa on Wisdom and Knowledge* (Minneapolis: Banning, 1996), 88; hereafter *IDM*. The numbers following refer to paragraphs to the Latin text in *PTW*, vol. 2.

Assuming the mask of the *idiota,* an untutored layman, Cusanus restates his often repeated conviction that numbers are a creation of the human mind. As such they cannot be "the beginning of anything." With this he distances himself from Pythagoras and Proclus. Pythagoras is said to have spoken only symbolically—that is to say, inadequately—about the number that proceeds from the divine mind. The depth of that inadequacy is indicated by the abyss that separates God's infinite and eternal mind from our finite mind. That abyss must be kept in mind if we are not to misunderstand Cusanus's characterization of mathematical number as an image of divine number. "Image" here is a metaphor for a relationship that eludes comprehension.

The need to distinguish human from divine mathematics may also have presented itself to Cusanus by his geometrical studies, which had made him well aware of the incommensurability of the diagonal and side of a square and of the incommensurability of the diameter and the circumference of a circle. "The old Pythagorean doctrine that the (natural) number is the measure of all things can no longer convince, in view of the incommensurable. To make man in the *sophistic* sense the measure of all things is out of the question. The Christian salvation account shows clearly that the divine is the measure of things, i.e. the infinite, and in the realm of the countable, the greatest possible number."[19] In the incommensurability he encountered in his geometrical studies Cusanus found a symbol of the incommensurability of God's creation and our concepts of divine and human mathematics.

Chapter 1 concludes with a reference to those earlier thinkers who have recognized the elusiveness of truth. Socrates deserves first place among these with his insistence in the *Apology* (23b) that the only thing he knew was that he knew nothing. Quite expectedly Solomon, who lamented that "the eye is not satisfied with seeing, nor the ear content with hearing" (Eccl 1:8) and Job, who said of wisdom that it is "hidden from the eyes of every living thing" (Jb 28:21) are invoked to show that the doctrine of learned ignorance had its biblical precursors. Of special interest is the reference to the beginning of the second book of Aristotle's *Metaphysics,* given the then still widespread understanding of Aristotle as *the* philosopher:

> The investigation of the truth is in one way hard, in another easy. An
> indication of this is found in the fact that no one is able to attain the

19. Joseph Ehrenfried Hofmann, "Sinn und Bedeutung der wichtigsten mathematischen Schriften des Nikolaus von Kues," in *Nicolo' Cusano: Agli Inizi del Mondo Moderno,* 386.

I. LEARNED IGNORANCE

truth adequately, while, on the other hand, no one fails it entirely, but everyone says something true about the nature of things, and while individually they contribute little or nothing to the truth, by the union of all a considerable amount is amassed. Therefore, since the truth seems to be like the proverbial door, which no one can fail to hit, in this way it is easy, but the fact that we can have a whole truth and not the particular part at which we aim shows the difficulty of it. (Take, for example, knowing that you are ill, but not what ails you.)

Perhaps, as difficulties are of two kinds, the cause of the present difficulty is not in the facts but in us. For as the eyes of the bats are to the blaze of day, so is the reason in our souls to the things that are by nature most evident of all.[20]

What is by nature most evident of all is not at all readily grasped by our reason. A gap separates the way things are from what our reason grasps—the order of being from the order of knowing.

With Cusanus this gap becomes an abyss: Our finite reason inevitably falls short of grasping the infinite God and his creation. Book One will thus conclude with the assertion that learned ignorance, an understanding of the limits of our finite reason, an understanding, however, that embraces an awareness of what lies beyond, is the goal of our knowledge. That is the truth that alone can satisfy our restless intellect, the maximum that our intellect can attain.

20. Aristotle, *Metaphysics* 1.993b.9ff.

CHAPTER 2

Preliminary Clarification
of What Will Follow

Providing an overview of the entire work, chapter 2 is necessarily sketchy, and the reader may well feel frustrated by such sketchiness. Too much is left unsaid, the argument underdeveloped.

The focus is provided by the idea of the Maximum. We are told that in *De docta ignorantia* the Maximum will be discussed in three ways: the first book will investigate Absolute Maximality—that is, the infinite God; the second book the Maximum contracted in plurality—that is, the boundless universe; the third book the Maximum as the most perfect of entities—that is, Jesus.

The way Cusanus introduces his central idea already let this reader stumble:

> Since I am going to discuss the maximum learning of ignorance (*maxima ignorantiae doctrina*), I must deal with the nature of Maximality. (*DI* I.2:5)

In just what sense does Cusanus understand the learning or doctrine of ignorance to be maximal? Does he take the meaning of this phrase to be so unproblematic that it can be taken for granted? Implicit is the claim that the doctrine of learned ignorance represents the apex to which human learning can ascend. Something of the sort is claimed in the later *Apologia doctae ignorantiae,* which sought to refute charges raised by Johannes Wenck: "Nevertheless, I affirm that learned ignorance alone excels incomparably every mode of contemplating God, even as all the saints also teach" (*AP* 57). Here he makes clear that at issue is knowledge of God, to whom all our conjectures are altogether inadequate. Negative theology is thus placed above positive theology.

But we should not make too much of this introductory sentence. The phrase *maxima ignorantiae doctrina* provides little more than a rhetorical entry to the discussion of the Maximum.[1]

> Now, I give the name "Maximum" to that than which there cannot be anything greater. But fullness befits what is one. Thus, oneness—which is also being—coincides with Maximality. But if such oneness is altogether free from all relation and contraction, obviously nothing is opposed to it, since it is Absolute Maximality. Thus, the Maximum is the Absolute One which is all things. And all things are in the Maximum (for it is the Maximum); and since nothing is opposed to it, the Minimum likewise coincides with it, and hence the Maximum is also in all things. And because it is absolute, it is, actually, every possible being; it contracts nothing from things, all of which [derive] from it. (*DI* I.2:5)

These few rather opaque sentences unfold in preliminary fashion the being of the Absolute Maximum. Very condensed, they are unpacked by the first book as a whole. Still, let us attempt to make some sense of what Cusanus here has to say: In what sense is the Absolute Maximum the Absolute One? In what sense is the Absolute One Being? Why does fullness befit the One? How are we to understand the coincidence of the Minimum with the Maximum? And how are we to understand: the Absolute One is all things and all things are in it? Is Cusanus a pantheist? Given the preliminary character of this chapter, the following remarks are also necessarily preliminary.

The fundamental thought seems easy enough to make some sense of if we are willing to follow Cusanus in his speculations about the Absolute Maximum—speculations that, as he insists, must necessarily leave our reason behind. This presupposes that our intellect should not be identified with our reason. The reach of human reason Cusanus takes to be circumscribed by its finitude. Reason is bound by the principle of non-contradiction. But our ability to think responsibly Cusanus

---

1. Paul Wilpert translates *maxima ignorantiae doctrina* as *die großartige Lehre des Nichtwissen.* Less literal than Hopkins, Wilpert thereby makes the first sentence less problematic, but he obscures its connection to what follows; *PTW* I, *DI* I, 2:5.

does not take to be limited to what our finite reason can comprehend. Cusanus thus places intellectual vision (*intellectus videns*) above reason (*ratio*). *De docta ignorantia* challenges the reader to make sense of that distinction, challenges him or her to follow Cusanus in investigations that require us, as he puts it, to think "incomprehensibly—above human reason" (*DI* I.2:5). The book demonstrates that we human beings are indeed capable of such thoughts, which, however, leaves the question of their truth value: can such incomprehensible thinking give us insight into God, as Cusanus claims? I shall return to this question at the end of this commentary.

We use the word "maximum" ordinarily with reference to something else—for instance, when we speak of the maximum amount of water some vessel can hold or the maximum number of people some room can hold. "Maximum" here is used in a way that is relative to a certain situation. It is a *maximum contractum*. The thought of the Absolute Maximum, which would have us think the maximum apart from any such relation is as elusive as the closely related thought of the maximum number. There is of course no such number: we can go on counting *ad infinitum*. And yet, to claim that there can be no such number presupposes that I have something in mind when I speak of the maximum number: even if self-contradictory, the expression is not without sense; the maximum number would be the end of the infinite number series. The thought of the maximum number would thus have us think the number sequence as both a whole and as infinite. This thought would seem to exceed our finite reason. But does it? It certainly is not altogether empty. Think of an infinite set, a whole with infinite members. Cusanus's thought of the maximum number is akin to the thought of the set of all cardinal numbers.

Similarly, even if we cannot comprehend Cusanus's Absolute Maximum, we nevertheless can think it in some fashion, he might say, incomprehensibly. The thought of the Absolute Maximum is the thought of an infinite whole that could not be greater: we might think of it as the set of all possible things. Given that thought, it makes sense to say that nothing can be added to the Absolute Maximum, for if something were added to it their sum would be greater. That is to say also that the Absolute Maximum cannot be thought of as lacking in any way: fullness befits it. Nothing other can be opposed to it. This lets Cusanus call it the Absolute One—absolute because it does not permit anything besides it, one because it is a whole from which nothing can be subtracted. The Absolute Maximum cannot be other than it is.[2] It falls outside the order that permits a greater and a less, a this and a that—that is to say, it exceeds all we can imagine or what our reason can grasp.

The same, it would seem, must be said of the Absolute Minimum: when we attempt to think it, it, too, is seen to fall outside the order that allows us to speak of a greater or a less. This lets Cusanus say of the Absolute Maximum that the Absolute Minimum coincides with it. Is this to say also that the Minimum coincides with the Maximum? Consider once more: "The Maximum is the Absolute One which is all things. And all things are in the Maximum (for it is the Maximum); and since nothing is opposed to it, the Minimum likewise coincides with it, and hence the Maximum is also in all things" (*DI* I.2:5). The passage invites us to think the relationship of the Minimum to God as being like the relationship of *all* things to God. It invites the question: is Cusanus a pantheist? But the very question betrays a misunderstanding of the text: the explanation Cusanus offers rejects the identity of God and creatures. "And because it [the Absolute One] is absolute, it is, actually, every possible being; it contracts nothing from things, all of which [derive] from it" (*DI* I.2.5). One is tempted to ask: if the Absolute One "is, actually, every possible being," is not every possible being God? But the question fails to do justice to the asserted asymmetry: all things are said to derive from the Absolute, which, however, is said to contract nothing from them. That suggests that Cusanus understands God as the transcendent ground of all possible things. Without him they would not be. But this is not to say that he would not be without them. God, we are tempted to say, here names the being of things. But if so, that being must be thought to transcend beings. God, so understood, is not another being. To say that all things derive from the Absolute is to suggest that the Absolute is in some sense constitutive of things: it is the mystery of their being. But how is such a constitution to be thought?

The passage similarly suggests that we should not assume that the coincidence of the Minimum with the Maximum means also the coincidence of the Maximum with the Minimum. Cusanus does not consider "Absolute Minimum" an appropriate name for God. As Gerda von Bredow remarks, we need to recognize "the fundamental irreversibility of the *coincidentia* of Maximum and Minimum."[3] The sig-

---

2. In *De li non aliud*, Cusanus considers the definition of God as the not-other the most adequate he has arrived at so far; see Nicholas of Cusa, *On God as Not-Other*, abbreviated *DLN*.

3. Gerda von Bredow, "Die Bedeutung des Minimim in der Coincidentia oppositorum," in *Nicolo' Cusano: Agli Inizi del Mondo Moderno*, 360.

nificance of Cusanus's insistence on the coincidence of the Minimum with the Maximum and on the irreversibility of that coincidence will become clearer in chapter 4.

As stated previously, the maximum number furnishes Cusanus with a symbol of the Absolute Maximum. The maximum number, however, has no being. There can be no such number. It is the product of a thinking that refuses to be bound by the limits of reason. Should we say the same of Cusanus's Absolute Maximum? Is it more than a thought construction that mirrors the thought of the maximum number? What allows Cusanus to say "oneness—which is also being—coincides with Maximality"? How are "oneness" and "being" to be understood?

Cusanus began this introductory chapter by stating the need to address the nature of Maximality. To think Maximality we must begin with thinking things that are large and ever larger until we arrive at the limiting thought of the Absolute Maximum, which transcends and bounds all possible beings; it is thus also a thought of the infinite. Elusive as this thought must be, it nevertheless haunts our understanding of anything as the ground of its being, present to us in the experience of the mystery that that thing is, just as the thought of the maximum number haunts our thought of any number, present to us in the awareness that to that number a greater number can always be opposed.

Cusanus states that the Maximum "is all things." He also states that the Maximum is "in all things." It is in all things as the principle of their being. But when our reason attempts to lay hold of this principle, it fails us. We cannot make sense of the Absolute Maximum or being as some sort of thing, as some super-entity. For it there is no place in logical space, in the space of our reason. The thought of the Absolute Maximum is, as Cusanus recognizes, inevitably a monstrous thought. But is it not therefore without sense?

As stated, chapter 2 is meant to provide little more than a promissory note: more discussion is needed, and this the First Book provides:

> In the first book I shall strive to investigate incomprehensibly—above human reason—this Maximum, which the faith of all nations indubitably believes to be God. [I shall investigate] with the guidance of Him "who alone dwells in inaccessible light." (*DI* I.2:5)

But must Cusanus's attempt to "investigate incomprehensibly—above human reason"—not be rejected by every responsible thinker? Jasper Hopkins calls the reasoning in this chapter specious (*OLI* 5). I wonder whether "specious" does it justice. We call "specious" an argument that seems to be correct or logical but is not so. But what Cusanus has to say here, in keeping with his demand that we "investigate incomprehensibly," so obviously transcends what our reason can grasp that it seems impossible to call such thinking correct or for that matter false—meaningless, perhaps, given a certain understanding of what makes our discourse meaningful, but not therefore without sense. What Cusanus says of Meister Eckhart, that he wrote in a way that invites misunderstanding (*AP* 25), must also be said of his own *On Learned Ignorance*. But how is it to be read and understood? Consider once more: God is all things, and all things are in God. The first book will unpack this.

I will just briefly consider the characterizations of the second and third books.

> Secondly, just as Absolute Maximality is Absolute Being, through which all things are that which they are, so from Absolute Being there exists a universal oneness of being which is spoken of as "a maximum deriving from the Absolute [Maximum]"—existing from it contractedly and as a universe. This maximum's oneness is contracted in plurality, and it cannot exist without plurality. Indeed, in its universal oneness this maximum encompasses all things, so that all the things that derive from the Absolute [Maximum] are in this maximum and this maximum is in all [these] things. Nevertheless, it does not exist independently of the plurality in which it is present, for it does not exist without contraction, from which it cannot be freed. In the second book I will add a few points about this maximum, viz., the universe. (*DI* I.2:6)

God is the being of all things. Their being gathers them into one universe. The universe, the totality of all things, is another maximum, but unlike God, the Absolute Maximum, it exists only as a boundless plurality of things.

Just as numbers can be ordered, so can the entities that make up the universe. Some are more perfect than others. Human beings are more perfect than animals; some human beings are more perfect than others. And just as judging one number to be greater than another leads to the thought of the greatest, the maximum number, to call one being more perfect than another leads to the thought of the most perfect being, which provides us with the measure of perfection.

> Thirdly, a maximum of a third sort will thereafter be exhibited. For since the universe exists-in-plurality only contractedly, we shall seek among the many things the one maximum in which the universe

actually exists most greatly and most perfectly as in its goal. Now, such [a maximum] is united with the Absolute [Maximum], which is the universal end; [it is united] because it is a most perfect goal, which surpasses our every capability. Hence, I shall add some points about this maximum, which is both contracted and absolute and which we name *Jesus*, blessed forever. [I shall add these points] according as Jesus Himself will provide inspiration. (*DI* I.2:7)

The chapter concludes with a paragraph explaining how this book is to be read.

However, someone who desires to grasp the meaning must elevate his intellect above the import of the words rather than insisting upon the proper significations of words which cannot be properly adapted to such great intellectual mysteries. Moreover, it is necessary to use guiding illustrations in a transcendent way and to leave behind perceptible things, so that the reader may readily ascend unto simple intellectuality. I have endeavored, for the purpose of investigating this pathway, to explain [matters] to those of ordinary intelligence as clearly as I could. Avoiding all roughness of style, I show at the outset that learned ignorance has its basis in the fact that the precise truth is inapprehensible. (*DI* I.2:10)

A reader focused on the literal meaning of the words will miss what *On Learned Ignorance* has to tell us. By their very nature, the mysteries to be discussed resist being put into words. Similarly, the examples provided are only pointers, steps in a ladder that must finally be cast away. But despite such caveats, Cusanus claims to have expressed himself as clearly as he was able, avoiding an unduly ornamental style, so that even an ordinary reader might be led to the root of the doctrine of learned ignorance and glimpse the incomprehensible precision of truth, which is the topic of the following chapter. The root of the doctrine of learned ignorance is an understanding of God as the incomprehensible Truth, presupposed by all our attempts to understand.

The Precise Truth Is Incomprehensible

The first two chapters have been introductory. Only with the third chapter does the discussion really get underway. At issue in this chapter is the essence of truth. By claiming that the precise truth is incomprehensible, the chapter's title also suggests that we should distinguish what we ordinarily mean by "truth" from this precise truth, raising the question of their relation. Cusanus is no skeptic.

The chapter begins with the reassertion of the gap that separates the infinite and the finite:

> *Quoniam ex se manifestum est infiniti ad finitum proportionem non esse,...*
>
> It is self-evident that there is no comparative relation of the infinite to the finite. (*DI* I.3:7)

Cusanus is hardly the first thinker to have made this, as he puts it, self-evident point. Nor does Cusanus use the phrase for the first time in *De docta ignorantia*. We meet with it already in a number of his sermons from the early 1430s.[1] Cusanus must have puzzled over the incomprehensibility of the infinite God long before he began work on *De docta ignorantia*. Jasper Hopkins suggests that Cusanus found the phrase in the once widely used *Compendium theologicae veritatis*, now

---

1. See *Nicholas of Cusa's Early Sermons: 1430–1441*, trans and intro. Jasper Hopkins (Loveland, Colo.: Arthur J. Banning, 2003). See https://jasper-hopkins; Nicholas of Cusa, sermons III (1431), IV (1431), VII (1431), XVI (1432).

thought to have been authored by Hugo of Strassburg (ca. 1205–68).[2] There he could read, *Creator a creatura cognisci non potest ad plenum in via vel etiam in patria, quia finiti nulla est proportio ad infinitum.* "Here below and also in Heaven the Creator cannot be fully known by reference to creatures because there is no comparative relation of the finite to the Infinite."[3] We should note that "cannot be fully known" suggests that the Creator can be known, if inadequately, from creatures. The *analogia entis* would thus appear to be preserved. But what sense can we make of this incomplete knowledge?

A compendium does not claim originality. Already in Aristotle's *De Caelo* we find the statement, "But there is no proportion between the infinite and the finite."[4] There it is introduced to support the thesis that "bodies of infinite weight and infinite lightness are equally impossible."[5] There can be no maximum or minimum weight. The statement invites being extended to all things: the maximum cannot exist.

Christian thinkers had to resist this conclusion: is God not the absolute maximum? In Thomas Aquinas's *De veritate* we meet with the formulation *infiniti autem ad finitum nulla est proportio*—there, however, to underscore the transcendence of God, not to deny his existence. But, as Aquinas recognizes, the phrase *infiniti ad finitum nulla est proportio* threatens to raise God so decisively above creation that he becomes irrelevant: "The medium through which a thing is known ought to be proportionate to that which is known through it. But the divine essence is not proportionate to a creature since it infinitely surpasses it, and there is no proportion between the infinite and the finite. Therefore, by knowing His own essence, God cannot know a creature." This conclusion Aquinas rejects: "Anaxagoras affirmed the existence of an intellect that was unmixed so that it could know all things; and for this he is praised by the Philosopher. But the divine intellect is unmixed and pure in the highest possible degree. Therefore, God knows all things in the highest possible degree, not only Himself but things other than Himself."[6] But what sort of knowledge can this be? Does God require a medium through which to know things? We must beware of reading our understanding of human knowledge into God. Human knowers do require a medium to know God. But if there is no proportion between the infinite and the finite,

2. Hugo Ripelin of Strassburg, *Compendium theologicae veritatis*, trans. and intro. Jasper Hopkins (August 2012); available on https://jasper-hopkins.info.

3. Hugo Ripelin of Strassburg, *Compendium*, 26.

4. Aristotle, *De Caelo* A.6.274a7.

5. Aristotle, *De Caelo* A.6.274a18.

6. Thomas Aquinas, *Questiones disputatae de veritate*, q. 2, a. 3 and 4, ad. 4.

it would seem that it is impossible for us to know anything about God. This conclusion, too, Aquinas rejects. But in the absence of a proper medium, what sense can we make of the *analogia entis,* the claim that an analogy joins Creator and creation that allows us to know God, even if such knowledge cannot claim to do him justice?

That God is infinite and transcends our finite understanding the Middle Ages took for granted. But it also took for granted that in our admittedly profoundly inadequate ways we can know a great deal about God. And is this not something every Christian must grant, despite the fact that there were theologians who would seem to have challenged this? Consider these words of Pope Benedict XVI:

> In all honesty, one must observe that in the late Middle Ages we find trends in theology which would sunder this synthesis between the Greek spirit and the Christian spirit. In contrast with the so-called intellectualism of Augustine and Thomas, there arose with Duns Scotus a voluntarism which, in its later developments, led to the claim that we can only know God's *voluntas ordinata.* Beyond this is the realm of God's freedom, in virtue of which he could have done the opposite of everything he has actually done. This gives rise to positions which clearly approach those of Ibn Hazm and might even lead to the image of a capricious God, who is not even bound to truth and goodness. God's transcendence and otherness are so exalted that our reason, our sense of the true and good, are no longer an authentic mirror of God, whose deepest possibilities remain eternally unattainable and hidden behind his actual decisions. As opposed to this, the faith of the Church has always insisted that between God and us, between his eternal Creator Spirit and our created reason there exists a real analogy, in which—as the Fourth Lateran Council in 1215 stated—unlikeness remains infinitely greater than likeness, yet not to the point of abolishing analogy and its language. God does not become more divine when we push him away from us in a sheer, impenetrable voluntarism; rather, the truly divine God is the God who has revealed himself as logos and, as logos, has acted and continues to act lovingly on our behalf. Certainly, love, as Saint Paul says, "transcends" knowledge and is thereby capable of perceiving more than thought alone (cf. Eph 3:19); nonetheless it continues to be love of the God who is Logos. Consequently, Christian worship is, again to quote Paul— "λογικὴ λατρεία," worship in harmony with the eternal Word and with our reason (cf. Rom 12:1). [10][7]

Should we count Cusanus among those who reject the *analgia entis,* the analogy of being? As we shall see, Cusanus does unfold the

---

7. Pope Benedict XVI, Regensburg address, September 12, 2006.

implications of *infiniti ad finitum nulla est proportio* in a way that must raise questions concerning the *analogia entis* and had to shatter the medieval worldview. But we also must recognize that throughout his writings Cusanus relies on what amounts to the *analogia entis* to speak of God, raising the question: what warrants such talk? Reason? Faith? Both together? Such talk can only be symbolic or metaphorical. The literal meaning must be left behind. Words can provide no more than uncertain pointers.

By its very nature the Absolute Maximum is infinite. With finite things you can always imagine something greater or less. But there can be no proportion—recall the preceding discussion—that allows us to bridge the divide that separates the finite and the infinite. But, to repeat the question: if that divide cannot be bridged, how can we say anything positive about God? Cusanus struggles with this question already in an early sermon: Is it only through Christ that we have access to God? Sermon Three, *Hoc facite*, seems to suggest this: "Your humanity is a ladder by means of which creatures ascend unto God. Of the finite to the infinite there is no proportion; nonetheless, there is a symbolic concordance between creatures and Your humanity."[8] But how do we ascend from Christ's humanity to his divinity? That requires faith. Only faith allows us to assert: Christ is God. But just what are we asserting? Must we not be able to give some content to the word "God" to make sense of the assertion? If we can think God only as the Infinite to which all we can say is altogether inadequate, does God not become simply irrelevant?

With his understanding of the finite/infinite divide, Cusanus would seem to call the doctrine of analogy, of such importance to medieval theology, into question. Such eminent scholars as Paul Wilpert, Josef Koch, and Wolfhart Pannenberg have thus suggested that Cusanus rejects the *analogia entis*.[9] And yet, as mentioned, throughout his works Cusanus draws on images drawn from this world to approach the being of God. Rudolf Haubst had good reason to insist that Cusanus relies centrally on the *analogia entis*.[10] And must we not agree with Johannes Hoff when he writes, "His gothic mind remained attached to the analogical rationality of the Dominican tradition throughout his whole life. For Cusa the pre-reflexive primacy of

8. Nicholas of Cusa, Sermo III, 11.

9. See Dennis Stammer, "Nikolaus von Kues und die analogia entis? Eine zum Panentheismusbegriff leitende Streitfrage der systematischen Theologie in begriffshistorischem Kontext," Draft-Version zum privaten Gebrauch, https://www.academia.edu/43231365

10. Rudolf Haubst, "Nikolaus von Kues und die analogia entis," in *Streifzüge in die cusanische Theologie* (Münster: Aschendorff, 1991), 232–42.

I. LEARNED IGNORANCE

being coincides with the primacy of the beautiful, the true, and the good that reveals itself through the 'science of praise'—*the scientia Dei et beatorum* of Thomas Aquinas"?[11] Does the doctrine that *nulla proportio inter infinitum et finitum est* really preclude the *analogia entis?* It does if we think that the latter precludes a reliance on symbols that transcend the reach of reason. But, as Cusanus recognizes, symbols are indispensable if there is to be any discourse about God. They have their ground in our pre-reflective experience of the world.

God as he is in himself is indeed unknowable. We must content ourselves with metaphors.[12] Even the description of God as the Absolute Maximum presupposes some intuition of what we call God that links it to our understanding of what is great and greater and extends it to what is infinitely great, exceeding the reach of our reason. We may want to speak of an analogy of inequality.

The chapter title asserts that the precise truth is incomprehensible, not just when dealing with God, but also when dealing with God's creation.

> Therefore, it is most clear that where we find comparative degrees of greatness, we do not arrive at the unqualifiedly Maximum; for things which are comparatively greater and lesser are finite; but, necessarily, such a Maximum is infinite. Therefore, if anything is posited which is not the unqualifiedly Maximum, it is evident that something greater can be posited. And since we find degrees of equality (so that one thing is more equal to a second thing than to a third, in accordance with generic, specific, spatial, causal, and temporal agreement and difference among similar things), obviously we cannot find two or more things which are so similar and equal that they could not be progressively more similar ad infinitum. Hence, the measure and the measured—however equal they are—will always remain different. (*DI* I.3:9)

Important is the insistence on the essential difference between "measure" and "measured." No matter how similar, two things could

---

11. Hoff, *Analogical Turn*, 131.

12. I disagree with Jasper Hopkins when he agrees with Josef Koch that in both *De docta ignorantia* and *De conjecturis* Cusanus excludes the *analogia entis.* But I take this disagreement to be superficial. At stake is just how the *analogia entis* is to be understood. That in *DI* Cusanus avoids the term *analogia* must be granted; see Hopkins, "Orienting Study, Part One: Analysis of Specialized Topics," 30. More importantly, I *agree with* Hopkins when he challenges Josef Koch's claim that there is a fundamental shift from *De docta ignorantia* to *De conjecturis*, from a metaphysics of being (*Seinsmetaphysik*) to a neo-Platonic metaphysics of unity (*Einheitsmetphysik*). Despite the evident evolution of Cusanus's thought, *DI* retains its authority to the very end; see Hopkins, "Orienting Study, Part One," *Nicholas of Cusa: Metaphysical Speculations*, 29–42, and Josef Koch, *Die Ars coniecturalis des Nikolaus von Kues* (Cologne: Westdeutscher Verlag, 1956).

always be more similar. No matter how adequate our description of some matter or thing, it could always be more adequate. Receiving its being from God, every created thing partakes of his infinity, is a contracted infinite, is like God, one and infinite. As such it is singular, unique. Whatever we can say about it will fail to capture its singularity.[13] The thing itself, the thing as it is in truth, transcends our comprehension, even though many things can be said about things that we with good reason take to be true, where we can distinguish between better and worse descriptions. But the truth of things escapes us human knowers. That was to remain Cusanus's life-long conviction, as he was to put in the last year of his life in the *Compendium* (1464):

> If you desire to make progress, then—first of all—assure yourself of the truth which the sound mind of every man acknowledges[14]: viz., that the singular is not plural and that the one is not many; and so, in many things the one cannot be present singularly and as it is in itself but [can be present only] in a way that is communicable to many. Moreover, we cannot deny that by nature a thing exists before it is knowable. Therefore, neither the senses, the imagination, nor the intellect attain unto the mode-of-being, since the latter precedes all these. Now, all the things that are arrived at by whatever manner of knowing signify only that antecedent mode-of-being. And, hence, they are not this reality itself but are likenesses, forms {*species*}, or signs of it. Therefore, there is no knowledge of the mode-of-being, although there is most certainly seen to be such a mode. (*Compendium* I.1)[15]

As already noted, we must distinguish our ordinary understanding of truth from the "precise truth," as Cusanus understood it, in keeping with the tradition, where there would be no gap between the thought of the thing and that thing. For our human purposes, what we have to say about something is often adequate, in this sense, but it will never be precise—that is, do full justice to the thing in question. To do so it would have to become identical with the thing. Such an identity requires God's creative intellect. The precise truth is denied to us. Yet

---

13. Christian Kny, "Einzelnes erkennt Einzelnes: Die Leistungsfähigkeit menschlicher Erkenntnis unter dem Gesichtspunkt der singularitas," in *Singularität und Universalität im Denken des Cusanus*, Beiträge der 5. Jungcusanertagung 11–13 Oktober 2012, ed. C. Ströbele (Regensburg: S. Roderer Verlag, 2015), 37–52.

14. Cf. *DI* I.2.

15. See also Hugo Ripelin of Strassburg, *Compendium* V.11: "However, since the perfection of signs admits of degrees, it will never be the case that any sign is so perfect and specific that it cannot be more perfect. Therefore, there is no givable sign of singularity, which does not admit of degrees. And so, what is singular is not knowable *per se* but only *per accidens*. For example, Plato, who does not admit of degrees [of being Plato], is seen only *per accidens*, by means of the visible signs that happen to characterize him."

some understanding of the gap between infinite and finite is constitutive of our understanding of the thisness, of the Scotist *haecceitas*, or of what Cusanus calls the "quiddity of things." The Kantian distinction between appearance and thing in itself comes to mind. When Kant called the thing in itself a noumenon, he, too, invoked its relationship to a divine nous. The medieval understanding of the truth of things here finds a distant echo.

The epistemological consequences of the incommensurability of infinite and finite are unpacked in the second paragraph:

> Therefore, it is not the case that by means of likenesses a finite intellect can precisely attain the truth about things. For truth is not something more or something less but is something indivisible. Whatever is not truth cannot measure truth precisely. (By comparison, a non-circle [cannot measure] a circle, whose being is something indivisible.) Hence, the intellect, which is not truth, never comprehends truth so precisely that truth cannot be comprehended infinitely more precisely. For the intellect is to truth as [an inscribed] polygon is to [the inscribing] circle. The more angles the inscribed polygon has the more similar it is to the circle. However, even if the number of its angles is increased ad infinitum, the polygon never becomes equal [to the circle] unless it is resolved into an identity with the circle. Hence, regarding truth, it is evident that we do not know anything other than the following: viz., that we know truth not to be precisely comprehensible as it is. For truth may be likened unto the most absolute necessity (which cannot be either something more or something less than it is), and our intellect may be likened unto possibility. Therefore, the quiddity of things, which is the truth of beings, is unattainable in its purity; though it is sought by all philosophers, it is found by no one as it is. And the more deeply we are instructed in this ignorance, the closer we approach to truth. (*DI* I.3:10)

Earlier Cusanus had written, "That from which no sound mind can withhold assent is, we have no doubt, most true." Now he asserts that "the quiddity of things, which is the truth of beings, is unattainable in its purity." That is to say: what we finite knowers take to be most true should not be confused with the truth of things. But to claim that "the quiddity of things, which is the truth of beings, is unattainable in its purity" is to suggest also that in our impure way we do have some sort of access to the truth of things. As the appeal to the polygons inscribed in a circle shows, Cusanus is no skeptic. But if the very idea of "the truth of things" requires us to think of God's creative intellect, does the scientific exploration of nature, which furnishes us with ever better approximations to the truth of things, not provide us with another ladder "by means of which creatures ascend unto God," unto God as creator of the world? Johannes Kepler thus considered astronomers "priests of Almighty God with respect to the Book of Nature."[16]

We are not used to speaking of the truth of things. Are not thoughts or propositions the sort of thing that can be true or false? Consider Thomas Aquinas's definition of truth as "the adequation of the thing and the intellect": *Veritas est adaequatio rei et intellectus.*[17] Does truth then depend on the existence of human beings who attempt to understand things? Aquinas, to be sure, would have rejected such a claim: the truth of our judgments or propositions has its measure in in the way things really are—that is, in the truth of things, and that truth is understood by Aquinas as the adequacy of the thing to the divine intellect. Aquinas, and Cusanus would have agreed, has a theocentric understanding of truth that gives human discourse its measure in God's creative Word, in the divine logos. The thing as it is in truth, what Cusanus, in keeping with tradition, calls the truth of beings, is understood as nothing other than the thing as present to the creative divine intellect. *Omne ens est verum.* "Every being is true." And, as Cusanus recognizes, given such an understanding of "the truth of beings," truth is indeed denied to us finite knowers.

We should note that the definition *veritas est adaequatio rei et intellectus,* "Truth is the adequation of the thing and the understanding," invites two readings: *veritas est adaequatio intellectus ad rem,* "Truth is the adequation of the understanding to the thing," and *veritas est adaequatio rei ad intellectum,* "Truth is the adequation of the thing to the understanding." And is the second not presupposed by the first? Is there not a sense in which the truth of our assertions presupposes the truth of things or what we can call ontological truth? If we are to measure the truth of an assertion about something, must that thing not disclose itself to us as it really is, as it is in truth? But what does "truth" now mean? How are we to understand "the truth of things"? Could it mean the adequation of the thing to our finite, perspective-bound understanding? Would that not substitute appearances for the things themselves? Or should we take it to mean the adequation of the thing to an ideal observer?

16. Job Kozhamthadam, SJ, *The Discovery of Kepler's Laws* (Notre Dame, IN: Notre Dame Press, 1994), 41, quoting letter to Herwart of March 25, 1598.

17. Thomas Aquinas, *Questiones disputatae de veritate,* q. 1, art. 1. See Martin Heidegger, *Einführung in die phänomenologische Forschung* (Wintersemester 1923/24); *Gesamtausgabe* (hereafter *GA*), vol. 17 (Frankfurt am Main: Klostermann, 1994), 162–94.

I. LEARNED IGNORANCE

Theology once had a ready answer: every created thing necessarily corresponds to the idea preconceived in the mind of God, and in this sense it cannot but be true. Here there is no gap separating thing and intellect. The truth of things, understood as *adaequatio rei (creandae) ad intellectum (divinum)*, "the adequacy of the (to be created) thing to the (divine) intellect," secures truth understood as *adaequatio intellectus (humani) ad rem (creatam)*, "the adequacy of the (human) intellect to the (created) thing."[18] Such talk of the truth of things does accord with the way we sometimes use the words "truth" and "true." For example, when we call something we have drawn "a true circle," we declare it to be in accord with our preconceived idea of what a circle is. What we have put down on paper accords with an idea in our intellect. Here the truth of things is understood as "the adequacy of the thing to the (human) intellect." Similarly, we may call someone a true friend. He meets our expectations concerning friendship. But in neither case is there an identity. The material object transcends whatever of our ideas it may satisfy. But in God's creative knowledge, idea and thing coincide.

What right do we have to think that our human intellect can bridge the abyss that separates God's infinite creative knowledge from our finite understanding? Or, to rephrase the question for a godless age: what right do we have to think that we can bridge the abyss that separates things in themselves from what we can perceive and understand? Or should we reject the very idea of things in themselves as unintelligible?[19]

Following tradition, Cusanus insists that there is an unbridgeable abyss that separates the human and the divine intellect. The truth could not possibly be other than it is. Whatever we finite knowers know about things can claim no such finality. And yet, as Cusanus suggests when he claims that we human knowers can grasp the truth only impurely or compares truth to a circle and our human attempts to grasp the truth to attempts to represent the circle by inscribing polygons in it, there are better or worse approximations. But this presupposes that even if our reason fails to comprehend the truth of things,

18. See Martin Heidegger, "Vom Wesen der Wahrheit," in *GA* 9 (1976), 178–82.

For a somewhat fuller discussion, see Karsten Harries, "The Antinomy of Being and the End of Philosophy," in *Division III of Being and Time: Heidegger's Unanswered Question of Being*, ed. Lee Braver (Cambridge, MA: MIT Press, 2015), 133–48.

19. Cf. Friedrich Nietzsche, "The 'thing in itself' (which is precisely what the pure truth, apart from any of its consequences, would be) is likewise something quite incomprehensible to the creator of language and some thing not in the least worth striving for"; Daniel Breazeale, *Philosophy and Truth: Selections from Nietzsche's Notebooks of the Early 1970s* (Atlantic Highlands, NJ: Humanities Press, 1979), 82.

that truth yet provides our descriptions with a measure, which presupposes some faculty in us that, even while it does not comprehend,
is yet, when perceiving things, in some sort of touch with the truth
of things and in a way that provides our assertions with a measure, as
the idea of the circle in the earlier quotation provides the inscribed
polygons with a measure. Not that the senses alone can provide that
measure. They present us with sensible schemata (*species*) or signs of
material things. But as Plato knew, what presents itself to our senses is
too bound to our body and its point of view to disclose the thing as it
is in truth. Reason is needed to interpret the material it is furnished
by the senses. Only our intellect, informed by the senses, perfecting
the sensible material, can get us ever closer to the truth of things.

To sum up: The Maximum is by its very nature infinite. That
means not only that an adequate understanding of the Absolute Maximum that is God is denied to us, but so is a fully adequate understanding of God's creation, of the truth of things. And yet, our propositions or thoughts, Cusanus points out, can be more or less adequate
to the truth of things. The idea of the truth of things provides our
pursuit of knowledge with a measure, leaving us with the question:
What access do we finite knowers have to this measure? This chapter
provides no more than a pointer.

II. THE COINCIDENCE OF OPPOSITES

The Absolute Maximum with Which the Minimum Coincides Is Understood Incomprehensibly

The chapter title repeats the claim that there can be understanding where there is no comprehension. That is to say: our intellect transcends the reach of our reason. Though incomprehensible, the infinite is present in our minds. Our ability to count bears witness to this, as docs our ability to understand in some fashion what lets Cusanus speak of the coincidence of the Absolute Minimum with the Absolute Maximum. But in what sense are we able to think it? We may well wonder whether this thought makes sense, whether thinking here does not lose touch with reality. Cusanus, to be sure, would insist on the opposite. The shipwreck of our reason lets us glimpse the infinite and put us in touch with reality.

The chapter begins with a reiteration of the incomprehensibility of the Absolute Maximum:

> Since the unqualifiedly and absolutely Maximum (than which there cannot be a greater is greater than we can comprehend [because it is Infinite Truth]), we attain unto it in no other way than incomprehensibly. For since it is not of the nature of those things which

II. THE COINCIDENCE OF OPPOSITES

> can be comparatively greater and lesser, it is beyond all that we can conceive. (*DI* I.4:11)

Anselm sought to prove the existence of God from the concept of a being than which nothing greater can be conceived. Cusanus rejects that formulation, for the Maximum, while it is indeed presupposed by all that is, cannot be conceived. We must attain to it incomprehensibly.[1]

God is incomparable. In the preceding chapter Cusanus had called it "most clear that where we find comparative degrees of greatness, we do not arrive at the unqualifiedly Maximum; for things which are comparatively greater and lesser are finite; but, necessarily, such a Maximum is infinite" (*DI* I.3:9). There can be no greatest similarity between any two existing things. Such similarity would be equality. But in this world maximum equality between two things, like absolute maximality, is not to be found. This does not mean that it cannot be conceived: we have no difficulty thinking of the equality of, say, 2 + 3 and 5 or of geometric figures—think of the Pythagorean theorem. Nor do we have difficulty understanding a claim such as: the number of people in this room equals the number of days in a week. Cusanus would not deny this. And how could he? But such conceptions are products of our own intellect; they are not things that actually exist— that is, things that are parts of God's creation. The number 7 is not to be found among these things. Nor is equality. When we judge existing things equal, in a certain respect we impose on them our human measures. These never exhaust their elusive being.

According to Cusanus every finite thing is unique, different from every other thing. As it presents itself to our reason, it could be other than it happens to be or possibly not be at all. But this is not true of the Absolute Maximum. We cannot think of it as possibly other than it is, nor as possibly not being, since it is presupposed by all entities. It is altogether actual. Or, should we rather say that in it possibility and actuality coincide, in that it is all that it could possibly be?[2]

> For whatsoever things are apprehended by the senses, by reason, or by intellect differ both within themselves and in relation to one

---

1. Cf. Jasper Hopkins, "Nicholas of Cusa's Intellectual Relationship to Anselm of Canterbury," in Casarella, *Cusanus: The Legacy of Learned Ignorance*, 54–73. Hopkins claims that "the primary tenet that Nicholas appropriates for himself is Anselm's twofold description of God, according to which God is both something than which a greater cannot be thought and something greater than can be thought" (57). But unlike Cusanus, Anselm thought that God's "existence can to some extent be both conceived and named by us analogically and non-symbolically—even if through a glass darkly" (59).

2. Cf. *DI* 1.2:5, and *Trialogus de possest* [hereafter *DP*], trans. Jasper Hopkins, in *A Concise Introduction to the Philosophy of Nicholas of Cusa*, vol. 3, *Actualized-Possibility* (Minneapolis: Banning, 1980).

> another—[differ] in such way that there is no precise equality among
> them. Therefore, Maximum Equality, which is neither other than nor
> different from anything, surpasses all understanding (*intellectum*).
> Hence, since the Absolutely Maximum is all that which can be, it is
> *altogether* actual. (*DI* 1.4:11)

To say that there is no precise equality among things is to claim that
things can be judged to be more or less equal. Such judgments presuppose some understanding of Maximum Equality, which provides
them with a measure.

The Maximum is said to fall outside the realm of the greater or
less. It follows that insofar as the Minimum, too, being maximally
small, is a maximum, it will coincide with the Maximum. The Minimum, too, is incomprehensible. There can be no such thing. Seeing
that Minimum and Maximum coincide presupposes an intellectual
vision (*visio intellectualis*) that is able to abstract the thought of the
maximum from our understanding of greater or less. What does such
an intellectual vision see? Not anything! It is a not-seeing seeing. Reason here suffers shipwreck. But in the shipwreck of reason our intellect glimpses the being of things, which is not anything we can see.
Being is not a thing.

> And just as there cannot be a greater, so for the same reason there
> cannot be a lesser, since it is all that which can be. But the Minimum
> is that than which there cannot be a lesser. And since the Maximum
> is also such, it is evident that the Minimum coincides with the Max-
> imum. (*DI* 1.4:11)

God is said to be all that can be, the greatest as well as the smallest. In
him Minimum and Maximum coincide. With this we have arrived at
the coincidence of opposites, where we should note that at first these
opposites appear separated by an infinite distance, but stretched to
the infinite, our reason loses its grasp of distance and infinite distance
collapses into coincidence.

But should we not rather say that the distinction of Maximum
and Minimum has to vanish as these terms lose their meaning and
with it also talk of the coincidence of opposites? Our reason cannot
make sense of this coincidence. Cusanus not only grants but emphasizes this: we comprehend the coincidence of opposites only incomprehensibly, in the foundering of reason. But we should note that
our reason is not altogether left behind. We must preserve a sense
of more and less to make any sense of the opposition of Maximum
and Minimum and thus of their coincidence. Reason is stretched to

II. THE COINCIDENCE OF OPPOSITES

a point where it snaps, but it is not jettisoned altogether. It provides a ladder that is then cast away. We therefore must be on guard when we say that God is the coincidence of maximum and minimum. In our attempt to think God as the Absolute Maximum, our reason is led to the thought of that coincidence, but thinking that thought, our reason suffers shipwreck. An abyss still separates that thought from God.

To reject such "incomprehensibly comprehending" as nonsensical is also to dismiss the trinitarian God as nonsensical. I shall have much more to say about the Trinity in chapters 7 to 10. I mention it here to suggest one reason Cusanus puts so much weight on comprehending incomprehensibly the coincidence of opposites. He recognizes that the space of reason has no place for the Christian God. To approach him we must be able to "look" in some sense beyond that space. The coincidence of opposites is the boundary that separates the space of reason from the beyond in which alone God, who cannot be seen, can yet be "seen," a seeing that presupposes that our mind is able to rise above our reason.

In *De visione Dei, The Vision of God,* Cusanus will call this boundary the *murus paradisi,* the wall of paradise.[3]

> The gate of this wall is guarded by a most lofty rational spirit; unless this spirit is vanquished the entrance will not be accessible. Therefore, on the other side of the coincidence of contradictories You can be seen—but not at all on this side. (*DVD* 9.39)

To vanquish this most lofty rational spirit we have to deprive him of his most powerful weapon: the law of non-contradiction. But to do so, must we not leave all reason behind? Or is it precisely reason that leads us to recognize the necessity of such a leave-taking?

> Hence, I experience the necessity for me to enter into obscuring mist and to admit the coincidence of opposites, beyond all capacity of reason, and to seek truth where impossibility appears. And when—beyond that [rational capacity] and beyond every most lofty intellectual ascent, as well—I come to that which is unknown to every intellect and which every intellect judges to be very far removed from the truth, there You are present, my God, You who are Absolute Necessity. And the darker and more impossible that obscuring haze of impossibility is known to be, the more truly the Necessity shines forth and the less veiledly it draws near and is present. (*DVD* 9.38)

---

3. For a searching discussion of the *murus paradisi,* see Bernard McGinn, "Seeing and Not Seeing: Nicholas of Cusa's *De visione Dei* in the History of Western Mysticism," in Casarella, *Cusanus: The Legacy of Learned Ignorance,* 44–47.

In chapter 2 Cusanus had written, "And all things are in the Maximum (for it is the Maximum); and since nothing is opposed to it, the Minimum likewise coincides with it, and hence the Maximum is also in all things" (*DI* I.2:5). Applied to the relationship of God to the creation, the coincidence of opposites would seem to imply the identity of God and all things. God is not other than these things. Is Cusanus then a pantheist? As mentioned, his assertion that the Absolute Maximum "contracts nothing from things" leaves no doubt about his answer. Coincidence cannot be understood as identity. "The Minimum coincides with the Maximum" does not imply "The Maximum coincides with the Minimum." But how then are we to understand the coincidence of opposites?

To help us approach what is incomprehensible Cusanus turns to quantity, only to leave it behind.

> The foregoing [point] will become clearer to you if you contract maximum and minimum to quantity. For maximum quantity is maximally large; and minimum quantity is maximally small. Therefore, if you free maximum and minimum from quantity—by mentally removing large and small—you will see clearly that maximum and minimum coincide. For maximum is a superlative just as minimum is a superlative. Therefore, it is not the case that absolute quantity is maximum quantity rather than minimum quantity; for in it the minimum is the maximum coincidingly. (*DI* 4:11)

Cusanus first asks the reader to contract maximum and minimum to quantity. Thus contracted, maximum and minimum are obviously opposed. We are then asked to "free maximum and minimum from quantity." But, as pointed out, when we attempt to do so we are unable to hold on to the opposition of maximum and minimum. Talk of the coincidence of maximum and minimum presupposes that we have not left the contraction to quantity and, that is to say, reason altogether behind. As the likening of the coincidence of opposites to the wall of paradise suggests, in the attempt to think it we confront the threshold that both joins and separates the space of reason from what lies beyond.

The Absolute is said to be beyond the opposition of great and small, as it is beyond all oppositions. God is thus also beyond the coincidence of opposites. But our reason cannot help but think in oppositions. Consider the limiting concept of the maximum number. The maximum number is infinitely distant from every number. In that sense it is equidistant from every number, although the thought of the maximum number presupposes that we can distinguish the

II. THE COINCIDENCE OF OPPOSITES

greater from the lesser. But that ability in turn presupposes a notion of the maximum number. In the thought of the maximum number finite and infinite thus intertwine. Reason is stretched to its limit. On the reef of the infinite our reason founders where the shipwreck of reason, when it attempts to comprehend the maximum number, can function as a symbol of the shipwreck of reason when it attempts to comprehend the Absolute Maximum. That shipwreck is a presupposition of comprehending God incomprehensibly.

At this point all discourse about the Maximum— that is, about God—threatens to dissolve in an "obscuring haze." God, so understood, would seem to be beyond all affirmation and all negation. Neither positive nor negative theologies can do justice to his being.

> Therefore, opposing features belong only to those things which can be comparatively greater and lesser; they befit these things in different ways; [but they do] not at all [befit] the absolutely Maximum, since it is beyond all opposition. Therefore, because the absolutely Maximum is absolutely and actually all things that can be (and is so free of all opposition that the Minimum coincides with it), it is beyond both all affirmation and all negation. And it is not, as well as is, all that which is conceived to be; and it is, as well as is not, all that which is conceived not to be. But it is a given thing in such a way that it is all things; and it is all things in such a way that it is no thing; and it is maximally a given thing in such a way that it is it minimally. (*DI* I.4:12)

Cusanus thinks God here in relation to all things—that is, a Creator. As Gerda von Bredow remarks, "In all saying of God the relationship of God to the world is contained. That must be kept in mind especially when interpreting the *coincidentia* of *Maximum* and *Minimum absolutum*. Here we are not concerned to think God as He is in Himself—absolute in the strictest sense, but to see God in terms of His relation to the world. What matters also is the continuation of the theological tradition, a synthesis of affirmative and negative theology that is more than just dialectically placing affirmative and negative statements next to each other, as the Areopagite does in the famous passage *Div. Nom.* VI.3."[4]

But how are we to think of this synthesis? As Jasper Hopkins remarks, according to the previous statements, "Since God is beyond all affirmation and negation, we may not, acceptably, affirm anything of Him or deny anything of Him. And yet, paradoxically, we may also,

---

4. Von Bredow, "Die Bedeutung des Minimum," 359.

acceptably, affirm of Him or deny of Him anything that is not unfitting."[5] I wonder what sense we can still make here of what is fitting or unfitting: all conceptions of God seem to be swallowed by the infinite. An answer, it would seem, can only be provided by Revelation, by Scripture and the incarnate Word. But to accept that answer requires faith. To reason God is an abyss.

> For example, to say "God, who is Absolute Maximality, is light" is [to say] no other than "God is maximally light in such way that He is minimally light." For Absolute Maximality could not be actually all possible things unless it were infinite and were the boundary of all things and were unable to be bounded by any of these things—as, by the graciousness of God, I will explain in subsequent sections. (*DI*.4:12)

The infinite distance that separates God as the unbounded boundary of all things and the things is stated clearly enough. To repeat: Cusanus is no pantheist. But what makes "God is maximally light in such way that He is minimally light" more fitting than "God is minimally light in such way that He is maximally light"? The latter Cusanus does not say. The asymmetry is significant.

As we have seen, Cusanus is well aware that the discourse of reason (*discursus rationis*) will not be able to make sense of the coincidence of opposites. That incomprehensible "seeing" that recognizes the Maximum to be infinite surpasses reason.

> However, the [absolutely Maximum] transcends all our understanding (*intellectus*). For our intellect cannot, by means of reasoning (*ratio*), combine contradictories in their Beginning, since we proceed by means of what nature makes evident to us. Our reason falls far short of this infinite power and is unable to connect contradictories, which are infinitely distant. Therefore, we see (*videmus*) incomprehensibly, beyond all rational inference (*rationis discursus*), that Absolute Maximality (to which nothing is opposed and with which the Minimum coincides) is infinite. But "maximum" and "minimum," as used in this [first] book, are transcendent terms of absolute signification, so that in their absolute simplicity they encompass—beyond all contraction to quantity of mass or quantity of power—all things. (*DI* I.4:12)

That we can "see" incomprehensibly presupposes that reason does not limit our "sight." Aristotelian logic may rule our reason, but it does not rule our mental capacity in its entirety: we are able to "see," incomprehensibly, what transcends our comprehension. To become

<hr>

5. Jasper Hopkins, "Orienting Study," Part One, "Expository Purview," 59.

II. THE COINCIDENCE OF OPPOSITES

learned about one's ignorance is to become aware not just of the limits of reason, but also of what transcends its reach. Only on the other side of the coincidence of opposites can God be glimpsed.

Both the coincidence of opposites and the implied coincidence of the Creator and creation invite question. Johannes Wenck seizes on both in his invective *De ignota litteratura*. He dismisses Cusanus's teaching of the coincidence of opposites as a stratagem designed to make all reasonable criticism impossible:

> Moreover, such teaching as this author's destroys the fundamental principle of all knowledge: viz., the principle that it is impossible both to be and not to be the same thing, [as we read] in *Metaphysics IV*. But this man cares little for the sayings of Aristotle. For he says that he always sets out from [one and] the same foundation and that he has elicited, beyond the usual approach of the philosophers, [teachings which will seem] unusual to many. (*IL* 21–22)

Wenck does agree with what Cusanus has to say about reason, but he cannot make sense of the claim that "only in the most learned ignorance (*doctissima ignorantia*) do we see most simple Being itself which is the Essence of all things" (*IL* 23). And Wenck is especially concerned to reject the suggested identity of God and creatures. Gathering snippets from *De docta ignorantia* into his First Thesis, he has Cusanus claim the following:

> All things coincide with God. This is evident because He is the Absolute Maximum, which cannot be comparatively greater and lesser. Therefore, nothing is opposed to Him. Consequently, God— on account of an absence of division—is the totality of things, as Hermes Trismegistus says. Hence, too, no name can properly befit Him, because of the absence of a distinct bestowal; for the bestowal of a name is based upon the determinate quality of that upon which the name is bestowed. (*IL* 24)

As Cusanus will point out in his *Apologia doctae ignorantiae*, the sentence "All things coincide with God" is not to be found in *De docta ignorantia*. Wenck may well have thought it to be implied by such statements as "the absolutely Maximum is absolutely and actually all things which can be (and is so free of all opposition that the Minimum coincides with it)" (*DI* 1.4:12). And he had reason to suspect a connection between what he found in Cusanus and the condemned views of Meister Eckhart. The proximity of aspects of the doctrine of learned ignorance to certain passages in Meister Eckhart is indeed troubling. That Wenck should have suspected Cusanus of heresy deserves serious consideration.

> This thesis is alluded to by Meister Eckhart in the vernacular book which he wrote for the queen of Hungary, sister of the dukes of Austria—[a book] which begins: "*Benedictus Deus et pater Domini nostri Ihesu Christi.*" [Here Eckhart] says: "A man ought to be very attentive to (1) despoiling and divesting himself of his own image and [of the image] of each creature, and to (2) knowing no father except God alone. [For] then there will be nothing which can sadden or disturb him—not God, not a creature, not any created thing or any uncreated thing. [For] his whole being, living, apprehending, knowing, and loving will be *from God, in God,* and *God.*"

> And in his sermons he [says]: "In the soul there is a certain citadel which sometimes I have called the guardian of the soul, sometimes the spark [of the soul]. It is very simple—as God is one and simple. It is so simple and so beyond every measure that God cannot view [it] according to measure and personal properties. And if it were to behold God, then this would be evident: viz., that He [is beyond] all His divine names and personal properties, because He is without measure and property. Now, insofar as God is one and simple and without measure and property, insofar as He is neither Father nor Son nor Holy Spirit, He can enter into this one thing which I am calling the citadel." (*IL* 25)

Wenck has to reject the view that in the mystical experience the individual "will be *from God, in God,* and *God,*" especially the last. But is this not implied by Cusanus's assertion "The absolutely Maximum is absolutely and actually all things which can be (and is so free of all opposition that the Minimum coincides with it)" (*DI* 1.4:12)?

To not just think, but experience or "see" God as Cusanus's Absolute Maximum we would indeed have to be able to ascend in thought to what Eckhart calls the citadel of the soul. This would require a movement of introversion, which would be at the same time a movement of self-transcendence, a flight of thought that rises above image, measure, and property, above all that can be more or less, that leaves beneath itself all that reason can grasp, everything finite. It would leave behind also the Trinity. Left would be only infinite simple oneness, an abyss, however, that we, as free-thinking beings, bear within ourselves. This ascent would let all content disappear. Eckhart calls what would remain "very simple—as God is one and simple."[6] Thoughts of that citadel within the soul and God inevitably blur. Man

6. Cf. Duclow, "Nicholas of Cusa in the Margins of Meister Eckhart," 64–65.

II. THE COINCIDENCE OF OPPOSITES

may feel himself to be one with God, but that experience has no content. Creation has here been left far behind or beneath and with it all thoughts of God as creator.

Cusanus, however, does not lose sight of God as creator. The very expression "Absolute Maximum" relates it to the created world in which things can always be greater. To repeat von Bredow's remark, "In all saying of God as the *Absolute* the relation of the world to God is already contained."[7] Cusanus understands the Absolute Maximum as the ground of creatures. He recognizes that the kind of experience envisioned by Eckhart, which would elide the distinction between creature and creator, is denied to us human knowers, that we must preserve the distance between the human being and God.

> For suppose someone sees—beyond all knowledge of mathematics (which posits limits and measures for things) and beyond all plurality and number and harmonious proportion—all things apart from measure, number, and weight. Then, assuredly, he sees all things in terms of a most simple oneness. And to see God in this manner is to see all things as God and God as all things. But through learned ignorance we know that God cannot in this manner be seen by us. (*AP* 9)

But do statements such as "God is all things" not invite claims to the kind of sight that, Cusanus here insists, learned ignorance teaches us to be impossible? Among the followers of Eckhart, some of them close to the brotherhood of the frees spirit, we do indeed find individuals who claimed just that. Wenck had reason to associate Cusanus's teachings with their heretical views.

> See what great evils swarm and abound in such very simple learned ignorance and such very abstract understanding. Wherefore, John, bishop of Strassburg, on the sabbath before the Feast of the Assumption of the Blessed Virgin Mary, in the year of our Lord 1317, conducted a trial against the Beghards and the sisters in his own city, who were claiming (1) that God is, formally, whatever is and (2) that they were God—not being distinct [from Him] in nature. (*IL* 25)

Cusanus recognizes that the statement "God is all things" invites misunderstanding, as he takes Wenck's invective to illustrate.

> And if there were Beghards who made such statements as our adversary alleges (viz., that, in nature, they were God), then they were rightfully condemned—just as Almericus too was condemned by Innocent III at a general council (about which [you may read] in the chapter "*Damnamus de Summa Trinitate*"). Almericus did not rightly

---

7. Von Bredow, "Die Bedeutung des Minimum," 359.

understand that God is all things by way of enfolding; some of his errors are cited by John Andrea in *Novella*. Men of little understanding chance to fall into error when they search out higher [truths] without learned ignorance. (*AP* 28–29)

The "is" in "God is all things" needs to be understood as all things are enfolded in God. In what follows I shall have more to say about Cusanus's understanding of creation as an unfolding of God, enfolded in him. We must, however, keep in mind that all talk of unfolding and enfolding, as it struggles to comprehend the incomprehensible mystery that is God, remains altogether inadequate. As Cusanus was to put it in *De Conjecturis*:

> And because by means of that ray of divinity intelligence sees that its conception is inadequate, it affirms (1) that Oneness-which-is-Trinity is to be understood as above all enfolding and unfolding and (2) that God cannot be conceived as He is. (*DC* 35)

Cusanus's response to his long-standing adversary Wenck is dismissive. He felt misunderstood. That Wenck should have mistakenly attributed to him the thesis "All things coincide with God" is taken to be just one particularly striking example of Wenck's failure to understand the meaning of *On Learned Ignorance*. To really understand such a text, we need to not just hear what the words have to tell us but see with our mental eye what the author saw. Cusanus compares himself to Socrates, who knew about his ignorance precisely because he was in possession of a higher knowledge:

> It was as the knowledge of the sun's brightness on the part of one who sees is to the knowledge of the sun's brightness on the part of one who is blind. For a blind man may have heard many [reports] about the sun's brightness—even that its brightness is so intense that it cannot be comprehended. [And he may] believe that on the basis of what he has thus heard he knows something about the sun's brightness; however, he remains ignorant of this brightness. By contrast, if one who has sight is asked regarding the sun's brightness "How bright is it?" he answers that he does not know. Moreover, he knows that he does not know; for since light is perceived by sight only, he knows by experience that the sun's brightness excels [the power of his] sight. (*AP* 2)

The theologians of his day, including Wenck, are said to be mostly unaware of their ignorance. They have failed to consider the limits of reason. When they have learned to speak like their teachers, they feel they have earned the right to call themselves theologians (*AP* 3).

II. THE COINCIDENCE OF OPPOSITES

They have not seen that "inaccessible Light in whom there is no darkness" (1 Jn 1:5). But thinking themselves learned, they may well judge those who have actually glimpsed that light blind because of their, to them, unintelligible speech.

> For mystical theology leads to a rest and a silence where a vision of the invisible God is granted to us. But the knowledge which is exercised for disputing is knowledge which looks for a victory of words and which is puffed up. It is far removed from the knowledge which approaches God, who is our peace. Hence, since [our adversary] proposes to hold a dispute—[a dispute] arising out of his knowledge—he could not conceal what kind of knowledge this was. For that which puffs up and arouses to conflict manifests itself—[showing] that it is not (as is learned ignorance) knowledge which, by means of rest, tends toward mental seeing. (*AP* 7–8)

Cusanus is unwilling to engage Wenck on his terms. Instead, he is concerned to exhibit the gap that separates mystical theology, and it is to that tradition, among others, that *De docta ignorantia* is indebted, and the tradition represented by Wenck for which Aristotle remains *the* philosopher. These remarks help us to understand how *De docta ignorantia* should be read: We should not tear snippets out of the whole, look for seeming contradictions, but recognize that to understand it, we must grasp the underlying meaning. That demands that we read the work at least twice, once to glimpse that meaning and then, having gained a first understanding of it, to test it by returning to the beginning to read it once more. And, as there are other works by the author, to consider these, too.

> For whoever examines the mind of someone writing on some point ought to read carefully all his writings and ought to resolve [his statements on this point] into one consistent meaning. For from truncated writings it is easy to find something which by itself seems inconsistent but which when compared with the whole corpus is [seen to be] consistent. (*AP* 17)

The point that gathers *De docta ignorantia* and Cusanus's works in their entirety into a whole is the thought of the vision of God granted to us human knowers. To describe that vision Cusanus uses the metaphor of looking at the sun, which is too bright to be looked at by us for more than a fleeting moment. Our eye is blinded by its brightness. Similarly, our mental eye is blinded by the intellectual brightness of God. We catch it, too, only in fleeting glimpses (*AP* 12).

CHAPTER 5

The Maximum Is One

As the Absolute Maximum cannot rationally be grasped, but is glimpsed only incomprehensibly, so it cannot be named, except unnameably. But what kind of a discourse is this unnameable naming?

Responsible discourse about things presupposes a world of objects that could be greater or less.

> Anything than which a greater or a lesser cannot be posited cannot be named. (*DI* I. 5:13)

That is to say, it will not find a place in our linguistic or logical space. But to be for us, must it not find its place in such a space? Are language and logic not constitutive of the way things can be for us? As the poet Stefan George, whom Heidegger liked to quote, put it, *Kein ding sei wo das wort gebricht*, "where the word is lacking, no thing may be."[1] God, understood as the Absolute Maximum, certainly is not a thing. God, so understood, cannot be in that sense, Cusanus insists. This raises a question about the meaning of "being." What do we mean when we say, "God is?"

> For by the movement of our reason names are assigned to things which, in terms of comparative relation, can be comparatively greater or lesser. And since all things exist in the best way they are able to

---

1. Harries, *Antinomy of Being*.

> exist, there cannot be a plurality of beings independently of number. For if number is removed, the distinctness, order, comparative relation, and harmony of things cease; and the very plurality of beings ceases. (*DI* I.5:13)

From naming, Cusanus thus turns to numbering, which he takes to be constitutive of naming. Number is thought to be constitutive of the space of things as they are for us. This recalls Pythagoras, but Cusanus here is thinking of beings *as they are for us,* not of things as they are in themselves. Number rules the world disclosed to us, a world in which there are countless things.

> But if number itself were infinite—in which case it would be actually maximal and the minimum would coincide with it—all of these would likewise cease, since to be infinite number and to be minimally number [that is, not at all to be number] amount to the same thing. (*DI* I.5:13)

If we were unable to count, we could not experience the many things of this world.

Once again Cusanus insists on the asymmetry of minimum and maximum: if number were infinite, the minimum would indeed coincide with the maximum, but then we would not be able to count. The numerical minimum is thus not identical with the numerical maximum. Cusanus is thinking of natural or counting numbers. Counting, I can go on ad infinitum. But the same does not hold when I descend on the number scale:

> Therefore, if in ascending the scale of numbers we actually arrive at a maximum number, since number is finite, still we do not come to a maximum number than which there can be no greater number; for such a number would be infinite. Therefore, it is evident that the ascending number-scale is actually finite, and that the [arrived at maximum number] would be in potentiality relative to another [greater] number. But if on the descending scale a similar thing held true of number, so that for any actually posited small number a smaller number were always positable by subtraction just as on the ascending scale a larger number [is always positable] by addition, [then the outcome] would still be the same [as in the case where number were infinite]. For there would be no distinction of things; nor would any order or any plurality or any degrees of comparatively greater and lesser be found among numbers; indeed there would not be number. Therefore, in numbering, it is necessary to come to a minimum than which there cannot be a lesser, viz., oneness (*unitas*). And since there cannot be anything lesser than oneness, oneness will be an

unqualifiedly minimum, which, by virtue of the considerations just presented, coincides with the maximum. (*DI* I.5:13)

The minimum and *principium* of number is oneness. Number is understood as generated from oneness, *unitas*, as its *explicatio*, its unfolding.[2] Oneness is said to be the beginning of number and its end (*principium* and *finis*). We can think of oneness so understood as the form of all natural numbers. Every number is a unity of one or more members. "The indivisible is present in the innermost depth of the divisible: one cannot separate it from it, without eliminating it; it is the inner law of counting, the mystery of its unlimited progress."[3]

The difference between the number one, other numbers, and the *principium unitas* invites question. We have no difficulty dividing or subtracting a number from one. And the number one can be divided ad infinitum: $\frac{1}{2}$ is obviously less than 1; and the infinite series of positive numbers is mirrored by an equally infinite series of negative numbers. So understood, the number one could not be considered to be a minimum. Cusanus, however, has a very different understanding of number as counting number—that is, as essentially related to things to be counted. According to the medieval theory of transcendentals, every being (*ens*) is one (*unum*). It is thus constituted by unity. Cusanus, too, follows the then generally accepted Pythagorean understanding of "oneness as not yet a number, but the source and origin of all natural numbers, which can be generated by a successive positing of unities."[4] As mentioned, Cusanus is concerned only with natural or counting numbers. Fractions are relations between such numbers. If there were not a minimum number, he can thus argue, if both ascending and descending the number scale could go on ad infinitum, there would be no bottom, and therefore there could not be a greater and a less. Nor could there be order or plurality.

We may want to distinguish between the transcendental one or oneness, which characterizes all that exists, the largest and the smallest, and every number, including "one" as number, the smallest

---

2. That one is not just another number Cusanus could read in Meister Eckhart, *Expos: Libri Sapientiae*, n. 149, Lateinische Werke II (Stuttgart: Kohlhammer, 1992), 486f. Thierry of Chartres had already taught that unity makes number—*unitas autem numerum facit*; Thierry of Chartres, *Commentum super Boethium De Trinitate (Librum hunc)*, ed. N. M. Haring, Archives de'Histoire Doctrinale et Littéraires de Moyen Age 35 (Paris: Librairie Philosophique J. Vrin, 1960), II.59.108, and *Lectiones in Boethii librum de Trinitate*, ed. N. M. Haring, Archives de'Histoire Doctrinale et Littéraires de Moyen Age 33 (Paris: Librairie Philosophique J. Vrin , 1958), VII.7.232, cited in *PTW* I, DI I:116n14.

3. Gandillac, *Nikolaus von Kues*, 253.

4. Hofmann, "Sinn und Bedeutung der wichtigsten mathematischen Schriften des Nikolaus von Kues," 386.

number, but a number among other numbers. But for Cusanus there is no number apart from counting, and we count by means of one. It is the *principium*, not only of all numbers, but of all things; in that sense it is unlike any other number—not really a number at all. With this understanding of number, Joseph Ehrenfried Hofmann points out, "Cusanus joins the old Pythagorean doctrine, with which Boethius had acquainted him. He did not follow Beldomandi, who as one of the first recognized one as a number."[5]

Do we have in the relationship of the transcendental "one" (*unitas*) to the number "one" a symbol of the relationship of Father and Son, who are two, yet one? We shall return to this question in our discussion of the Trinity.

Thinking about both, the coincidence of opposites and number, Cusanus hopes to have cast some light on the infinite oneness of God.

> See that by means of number we have been led to understanding (1) that "Absolute Oneness" quite closely befits the unnamable God and (2) that God is so one that He is, actually, everything which is possible. Accordingly, Absolute Oneness cannot be comparatively greater or lesser; nor can it be multiple. Thus, Deity is Infinite Oneness. Therefore, he who said "Hear, O Israel, your God is one" (Dt 6:4) and "Your Father and Teacher in Heaven is one" (Mt 23:8) could not have spoken more truly. (*DI* I.5:14)

Cusanus here offers us for God's creative power, which is said to be "everything which is possible," the symbol of our ability to count, where he understands counting as the unfolding of one: every possible number can be said to be an unfolding of one.

> And whoever would say that there are many gods would deny, most falsely, the existence not only of God but also of all the things of the universe—as will be shown in what follows. For the pluralities of things, which descend from Infinite Oneness, are related to Infinite Oneness [in such a way] that they cannot exist independently of it (just as number, which is an entity-of-reason produced by our [power of] relational discrimination, necessarily presupposes oneness as such a beginning of number that without this beginning there could not possibly be number). (*DI* I.5:14)

Cusanus understands both God's creative understanding and our re-creative understanding, which depends on numbering, as an

---

5. Joseph Ehrenfried Hofmann, "Einführung," Nikolaus von Cues, *Die mathematischen Schriften*, trans. Josepha Hofmann, intro. and notes Joseph Ehrenfried Hofmann (Hamburg: Meiner, 1952), xvii.

unfolding of oneness.[6] Our ability to count provides the key. Number is constitutive of the world known to us. Similarly, number can be said to be constitutive of God's creation, understood as the unfolded divine One. But we may not forget that such speaking is only symbolic or conjectural. God is understood by Cusanus in the image of the human being, said in the Bible to have been created in the image of God. Understanding ourselves, we human beings discover ourselves to be the image of God. As Cusanus put it in his sermon *Ubi Venit Plenitudo Temporis* (1454):

> For inasmuch as an image that is alive with an intellectual life knows itself to be an image, it knows that within it is the Truth and Exemplar and Form that gives being to it, with the result that it is an image. And this [Form] is the image's true life, which is present in the image as truth is present in its image. Next, an intellect that understands itself to be a living image has from God the power to liken itself more greatly to its exemplar and, thus, has the power to approach closer and closer to greater union with its own object, viz., with truth, so that it may be more pleasantly at rest.[7]

The thought that the human being is *imago Dei* is at the center of Cusanus's oeuvre in its entirety.[8] And inseparable from this thought is an awareness of the godlike creativity of man.

> For we are creators who make likenesses. Just as God the Creator creates and forms real things by understanding them, so we produce from our intellect the likenesses of things; and by means of the arts [and crafts] we show that we are makers of likenesses. And just as God actually enfolds within His own being all the things that exist or that can be made, so [our] intellect enfolds within its power all the likenesses of all things, and it unfolds by making likenesses, and this [making of likenesses] is the act of understanding.[9]

6. Clyde Lee Miller points out that in *De docta ignorantia* the language of "Unfolding and enfolding" "was restricted to God's creation, as the terms had been restricted in Boethius and Thierry of Chartres." Only in *De Conjecturis* does Cusanus use this language to describe "the procession of knowledge contents from the human mind"; Miller, "Nicholas of Cusa's *On Conjectures* (*De coniecturis*)," in Christianson and Izbicki, *Nicholas of Cusa: In Search of God and Wisdom*, 123. But this transference of the language of *explicatio/complicatio* from God to man is certainly suggested by what Cusanus has to say about number as an unfolding of the one in *De docta ignorantia*. See *DI* I.5:13 and 14; *DI* I.8:23; *DI* I.22:68.

7. Cusanus, *Sermo* CLXIX, 4.

8. Volkmann-Schluck, *Nicolaus Cusanus*, xv: "The entire metaphysics of Nicolaus of Cues has its foundation in a symbolic interpretation of the human being as *imago Dei*." See also Wilhelm Dupré, "The Image of the Living God: Some Remarks on the Meaning of Perfection and World Formation," in Casarella, *Cusanus: The Legacy of Learned Ignorance*, 89–104; Mandrella, *Viva imago*.

9. Cusanus, *Sermo* CLXIX, 6.

II. THE COINCIDENCE OF OPPOSITES

As Gadamer observes, "Here we really stand at the beginning of the entire modern essence. One only needs to think of one-point perspective, the great discovery of the age, which shaped western painting up to the threshold of our century. It is more than a discovery of the fine arts. It bears witness to a manner of thinking. The thought of the point of view, finite, changing, exchangeable, places an altogether new meaning into the thought of the singular individual."[10]

10. Hans-Georg Gadamer, "Nikolaus von Kues im modernen Denken," in *Nicolo' Cusano: Agli Inizi del Mondo Moderno*, 45.

The Maximum Is Absolute Necessity

Jasper Hopkins considers this a curious chapter, "perhaps the nadir of the entire treatise of three books," calling Cusanus's reasoning here "thoroughly implausible and unrigorous" (*OLI* 8). There is indeed much here that may seem to support such a negative judgment. But the reader should ask him- or herself whether the kind of rigor demanded by Hopkins has not been called into question by Cusanus's understanding of learned ignorance, which would have us embrace paradox.[1] Despite considerations that may at first appear lacking in rigor, the chapter deserves careful examination.

In expected fashion the chapter begins by contrasting what is limited and bounded with the Maximum, reiterating Cusanus's version of the ontological difference, the difference between the infinite and the finite.

In the preceding I indicated that everything except the one unqualifiedly Maximum is—in contrast to it—limited and bounded. Now,

---

1. See Eugen Russo, "Philosophy of Paradox in the Fifteenth Century: Nicolaus Cusanus's *De docta ignorantia* and Masaccio's *Trinity*" (master's thesis, Central European University, Budapest September 2014), 33. Challenging Hopkins's dismissive judgment, Russo argues that Cusanus's concerns here are dictated by the nature of his method, which embraces paradox, a method "to which the arguments he presents are entirely appropriate."

what is finite and bounded has a beginning point and an end point. (*DI* I.6:15)

The following sentence is puzzling:

> And we cannot make the following claim: viz., that "one given finite thing is greater than another given finite thing, [the series of finite things] always proceeding in this way unto infinity." (For there cannot actually be an infinite progression of things which are comparatively greater and lesser, since in that case the Maximum would be of the nature of finite things). (*DI* I.6:15)

As translated, the first sentence makes little sense. But I have trouble with Hopkins's translation. The Latin reads:

> *Et quia non potest dici quod illud sit maius dato finito et finitum ita semper in infinitum progrediendo, quoniam in excedentibus et excessis in infinitum actu fieri non potest, alias maximum esset de natura finitorum, igitur necessario est maximum actu omnium finitorum principium et finis.*

The question is: what does *illud* refer to here? I take it to refer to the Maximum that is the beginning and end of every finite thing. That cannot be said to be finite. It cannot be reached by a progression of ever greater finite things ad infinitum. Read in this way, this amounts to an affirmation of the abyss separating finite and infinite. But if, as Cusanus claims to have shown, the One coincides with the Maximum, then, as oneness is the beginning and end of all number, so the actually Maximum is the beginning and end of all that is finite.

Something that looks rather like a claim that the existence of God has thus been proven follows:

> Accordingly, it follows that the actually Maximum is the Beginning and the End of all finite things. (*DI* I.6:15)

Think once more of the series of natural numbers increasing ad infinitum. To every natural number we can add one. Although we can count ad infinitum, we will never arrive at the maximum number. To think of the maximum number we must leave natural numbers behind, must think the essence of number without reference to more and less. As pointed out, according to Cusanus every number is a whole or, if you wish, a set with one or more members. In that sense oneness can be said to be constitutive of number. A maximum number, too, can only be thought as one. But so understood, oneness is the beginning, the *principium* of cardinality.

Repeating the conclusion of chapter 5, Cusanus suggests that, as the maximum number is the beginning and end of all numbers, God is the beginning and end of all things.

> Moreover, nothing could exist if the unqualifiedly Maximum did not exist. For since everything nonmaximal is finite, it is also originated. But, necessarily, it will exist from another. Otherwise—i.e., if it existed from itself—it would have existed when it did not exist. Now, as is obviously the rule, it is not possible to proceed to infinity in beginnings and causes. So it will be the case that the unqualifiedly Maximum exists, without which nothing can exist. (*DI* I.6:15)

God is said to be *principium et causa*, the beginning and cause of creation. But how are we to understand "cause" when we call God the cause of the world? Descartes was asked this question by Arnauld and answered that our traditional understanding of cause will not do.

> To give a proper reply to this, I think it is necessary to show that, in between "efficient cause" in the strict sense and "no cause at all," there is a third possibility—namely, "the positive essence of a thing," to which the concept of an efficient cause can be extended. In the same way in geometry the concept of an arc of an indefinitely large circle is customarily extended to the concept of a straight line; or the concept of a rectilinear polygon with an indefinite number of sides is extended to that of a circle.[2]

When he says God is the cause of creation, Descartes claims to use the term in a way that stands in the same relation to efficient causation as the circle to the inscribed polygon. Cusanus, as we have seen, uses the relationship of circle to the inscribed polygon as a symbol of the relationship of the infinite to the finite, a relationship that exceeds the reach of our reason,

Just as, according to Cusanus, the maximum number is the *principium* of every number, so God is the *principium* or cause in this extended sense of everything. So understood, God can be said to exist necessarily.

> Furthermore, let us contract maximum to being, and let us say: it is not the case that anything is opposed to maximum being; hence, neither not-being nor minimally being [are opposed to it]. How, then, since minimally being is maximally being—could we rightly think that the Maximum is able not to exist? Moreover, we cannot rightly think that something exists in the absence of being. But Absolute Being cannot be other than the absolutely Maximum. Hence,

---

2. Descartes, *Philosophical Writings of Descartes*, 2:167.

II. THE COINCIDENCE OF OPPOSITES

we cannot rightly think that something exists in the absence of the [absolutely] Maximum. (*DI* I.6:16)

Open to the mystery of the being of things, we are open to the mystery of Divine being.

A puzzling paragraph follows. What is Cusanus trying to say here? It does indeed invite Hopkins's harsh judgment:

> Moreover, the greatest truth is the absolutely Maximum. Therefore, (1) it is most greatly true either that the unqualifiedly Maximum exists or that it does not exist, or (2) [it is most greatly true that it] both exists and does not exist, or (3) [it is most greatly true that it] neither exists nor does not exist. Now, no more [alternatives] can be either asserted or thought. No matter which one of them you say to be most greatly true, my point is made. For I have the greatest truth, which is the unqualifiedly Maximum. (*DI* I.6:16)

The first sentence makes some sense: if truth, as Thomas Aquinas, for instance, holds, is to be understood as the adequacy of intellect and thing, then the greatest truth would be the coincidence of the two. But God is that coincidence.

The following three propositions raise a question about the meaning of being.

1. The first proposition assumes that existence can be applied univocally to God and creatures: either something exists or it does not exist; that holds for God as much as it holds for a unicorn or a cow. God is understood here as a being, unique in that no greater being than the unqualifiedly Maximum can be conceived.

2. The second proposition embraces the paradox that God both exists and does not exist. It thus calls such a univocal use of "being" into question: can God be said to exist as a lion or a rose exists? How is the word "exists" to be understood when applied to God? By an analogy of proportion? But remember: when some medicine is said to be healthy because it is the cause of health, it is understood that it is not literally healthy. Is this to say then that in the sense in which the lion or the rose exists God does not exist? And conversely, that in the sense in which God exists the lion and the rose do not exist? In Meister Eckhart we find some such view. He sometimes denies being to God and sometimes to creatures. His declaration that creatures are nothing was among the propositions by Eckhart declared heretical in the papal bull *In agro dominico.*

> The twenty-sixth article. All creatures are one pure nothing.
> I do not say that they are a little something or anything,
> but that they are pure nothing.[3]

In Eckhart you will also find passages where God is said to be nothing. At issue is the question: what does it mean for God and things to be? Both cannot be said "to be" in the same sense. The word, it would seem, has to be understood analogically. But Eckhart's formulations open up an infinite abyss between God and creatures that threatens to rob analogy of its meaning. If creatures can be said to be, God is not; if God can be said to be, creatures are not.

But why then attribute being at all to both God and things? Thomas Aquinas might have said, because in him we discover the Creator, the ground of things, the *principium* of their being, the ground also of our being. God is said "to be" by us by an analogy of proportion or by what Cajetan will call an analogy of attribution. But what sort of analogy is that? As mentioned, a standard example in medieval texts is urine, which is said to be healthy by some doctor. Literally, of course, urine is not the sort of thing that can be sick or healthy. It is said to be healthy because it is a sign of health. That is to say, to really understand such an analogy we have to understand the relation involved. But in the case of the relation of finite creatures to God there is no definite relation that we can specify or comprehend. What do we mean when we call God the *principium* or ground of the being of all things, experienced in the mystery of their being? A nihilist might experience that mystery, but he would not want to personify or reify it and call it God. Eckhart in some places seems quite close to such a nihilism. Cusanus's proximity to Eckhart, whose teachings had been condemned by the church, had to make him suspect to more traditional theologians such as Johannes Wenck.

3. In keeping with some passages in Meister Eckhart, the third proposition denies the appropriateness of applying *esse* to God altogether. The preceding considerations may well lead us to this conclusion.

Cusanus now points out that whatever of these three options you claim to be the greatest truth, you have assumed that there is the greatest truth. But, as stated, the greatest truth is the Absolute Maximum— that is, God, the coincidence of intellect and thing. Therefore you

---

3. Meister Eckhart, *The Essential Sermons, Commentaries, Treatises, and Defense,* trans. and intro. Edmund Colledge, OSA, and Bernard McGinn (Mahwah, NJ: Paulist Press, 1981, 80.

have assumed that God exists. For Cusanus, to claim truth is to pre-suppose God's existence.

That Cusanus understood this to be a convincing argument for the existence of God is suggested by the fact that he presented it again, if in simplified form, in the sermon *Dies sanctificatus* on December 25, 1440, the first Christmas day following the completion of *De docta ignornatia*.

> Now, this First Beginning we call God, who cannot be understood not to exist. For God is Truth, which cannot be understood not to be; for truth is the object of the intellect. For whether God is understood to exist or understood not to exist: since either alternative is affirmed as true, God [who is Truth] is affirmed to exist. Consequently, God—who by means of either of the contradictory alternatives is seen, necessarily, to exist—is beyond all opposition and contradictoriness. (*S* XXII.9)[4]

Even those who deny the existence of God are said to presuppose it, because by denying it they assume that there is a truth of the matter. But God is Truth.[5] A modern reader may well respond with the Pilate question, "What is truth?" (Jn 18:38). Cusanus might have repeated, "Truth is the object of the intellect." Whenever we want to know something, we want to know what the matter in question really is, what is "is" in truth. Recall Thomas Aquinas's definition of truth as "the adequation of the thing and the intellect." That there is truth, so understood, is a presupposition of the intelligibility of the universe. For Cusanus the ground of that intelligibility is the coincidence of thing and intellect, where he would have us understand the trinity: thing, intellect, coincidence as signifying the Trinity of Father, Son, and Holy Spirit.

What the restatement of the argument in *Dies sanctificatus* has left out is the way the three propositions of *De docta ignorantia* raise the question of just what do we mean when we ascribe being to God.

> Wherefore, although it is evident through the aforesaid that the name "being" (*nomen esse*) (or any other name) is not a precise name for the Maximum (which is beyond every name) (Phil 2:9), nevertheless it is necessary that being befit it maximally (but in a way not

---

4. Cf. Gandillac, *Nikolaus von Kues*, 262: "The rational act that negates, like the act that affirms, meet not only in the common assertion that the truth is substantially different from error, but, one can say, that in its full significance and applied to the infinite being, the two formulations completely coincide. One must in fact affirm God just as one has to deny him. He stands above the contradiction, as the infinite circle transcends the opposed categories of curve and straight line."

5. Cf. Blumenberg, *Die Legitimität der Neuzeit*, 451–52.

nameable by the name "maximum") and above all nameable being. (*DI* I.6:17)

The struggle with the limits of language is evident. While the name "being" is said to befit (*convenire*) the Maximum, it cannot be said to name it. As Gandillac puts it, "When one speaks of *ens, esse,* or *essentia* one necessarily remains with a 'contracted' or foreshortened consideration on the level of reason, which, though admissible, is strictly speaking inadequate."[6] What Cusanus means by "being" calls for further discussion.[7]

Cusanus concludes the chapter by asserting that it is most true that the Maximum exists necessarily and exists as one.

> By such considerations, as well as by an infinity of similar ones, learned ignorance sees most clearly from the aforesaid that the unqualifiedly Maximum exists necessarily, so that it is Absolute Necessity. But I indicated that the unqualifiedly Maximum cannot exist except as one. [*Est autem ostensum non posse nisi unum esse maximum simpliciter.*] Therefore, it is most true that the Maximum exists as one. (*DI* I.6:17)

Cusanus has already shown to his satisfaction that the Maximum can exist only as one. There cannot be two or three maxima. This raises the question: what sense can Cusanus make of the Trinity? The following chapters address that question.

6. Gandillac, *Nikolaus von Kues*, 290.

7. See Jasper Hopkins, *A Concise Introduction to the Philosophy of Nicholas of Cusa,* 2nd ed. (Minneapolis: University of Minnesota Press, 1980), 9, where Hopkins takes issue with Armand Maurer's reading of the passage. I find the disagreement insubstantial. See Armand Maurer, "Nicholas of Cusa," *Encyclopedia of Philosophy* (New York: Macmillan. and Free Press), 5:497.

III. THE TRINITY

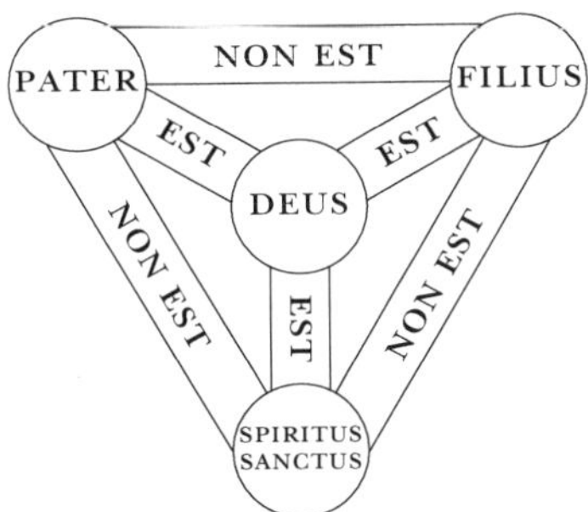

CHAPTERS 7 TO 10 DEVELOP THE CLAIM that the Maximum must be thought of as necessarily triune. That as a cardinal and ardent defender of *una, sancta, catholica, et apostolica ecclesia* Cusanus would have wanted to defend the Trinity is to be expected. Evident in these chapters is the cardinal's attempt to reconcile his philosophical understanding of the Maximum with the church's understanding of the Trinity; evident, too, however, is his conviction that any serious investigation into the Maximum will lead us, and not just believing Christians, to the triune God.

But should we really say that in these chapters Cusanus is trying to reconcile his understanding of the Maximum with the church's understanding of the Trinity? Should we not perhaps rather say that Cusanus's understanding of the Trinity shaped his understanding of the Maximum from the very beginning and that it would mean also his understanding of the coincidence of opposites and the doctrine of learned ignorance? As mentioned, Cusanus explored the Trinity already in his first sermon, *In principio erat verbum*, of 1430. Already in this sermon Cusanus shows great interest in a triadic model to explain created reality.[1] Imitating the Trinity, the universe, and man, too, are said to have a triadic structure. But to embrace the Trinity we must accept that the reach of our reason is limited and that the law of non-contradiction does not circumscribe reality. These core ideas of *De docta ignorantia* are thus present, *in nuce*, already in his very first sermon.

This does not diminish the significance of the often noted dependence of chapters 7 to 10 on the twelfth-century philosopher Thierry of Chartres and more generally the School of Chartres.[2] This dependence will become even more pronounced in the corresponding chapters 7 to 10 of Book Two, which discuss the Trinity of the universe.[3] In these chapters a Christian neo-Pythagoreanism focusing on the Trinity, indebted to Boethius's *De Trinitate*, finds striking expression.[4] The same can be said of *De docta ignorantia* as a whole.[5] The proximity of central ideas of that book to the work of Thierry of Chartres is indeed such that it led Pierre Duhem, as early as 1909, to charge Cusanus with plagiarism.[6] That overblown charge was dismissed by Edmond Vansteenberghe in 1920.[7] But Duhem's charge, if exaggerated, is of interest in that, coming right after Ernst Cassirer's celebration of Cusanus as the first modern philosopher,[8] it demonstrated that the cardinal's thinking owed a profound debt to the Middle Ages, more especially to a thinker of the twelfth century, inviting the reader to question the originality of Cusanus and, more importantly, the relationship of modernity to the Middle Ages: could it be that modernity evolved with some necessity from medieval thought?

As David Albertson has shown convincingly, about Cusanus's profound indebtedness to Thierry of Chartres and his circle there can be no doubt.[9] And, as he points out, Duhem's charge was given a

---

1. Floss, *Philosophy of Nicholas of Cusa*, 23.

2. *PTW* I:117–18n22.

3. *PTW* I:132–24n67.

4. See Thierry of Chartres, *Commentarius super Boethium de Trinitate (Librum hunc)*, ed. N. M. Haring, Archives de'Histoire Doctrinale et Littéraires de Moyen Age 35 (Paris: Librairie Philosophique J. Vrin, 1960), 80–134; Boethius, *De trinitate*, ed. C. Moreschini (Munich and Leipzig: Teubner, 2005).

5. See Albertson, *Mathematical Theologies*.

6. Pierre Duhem, "Thierry de Chartres et Nicolas de Cues," *Revues de Sciences Philos. et Théol.* 30 (1909): 325–31. For a thoughtful assessment of Cusanus's undeniable dependence on Thierry de Chartres and thinkers in his orbit, see David Albertson, "A Learned Thief? Nicholas of Cusa and the Anonymous *Fundamentum Naturae*: Reassessing the Vorlage Theory," *Recherches de Théologie et Philosophie médiévales* 77, no. 2 (2010): 351–90.

7. See E. Vansteenberghe, *Le Cardinal Nicolas de Cues (1401–1464): L'Action—La Pensée* (Paris: Édouard Champion, 1920), 411n7.

8. See also Cassirer, *Das Erkenntnisproblem*.

9. Albertson, *Mathematical Theologies*.

different twist and new weight by the discovery in 1995 of a short text, *Fundamentum naturae quod videtur physicos ignorasse* ("The Foundation of Nature, Which the Natural Scientists Apparently Do Not Know"), that had been in the possession of Georg Schwarz, a Dominican at Eichstätt, by Maarten J. F. M. Hoenen, who showed that "this brief text, written by someone with a deep understanding of the thought of Thierry of Chartres, parallels nearly verbatim the central sections of Book II of *De docta ignorantia*."[10] According to Hoenen, in it we find "the three leading concepts (*Grundbegriffe*) of *De docta ignorantia*, the 'rule' of learned ignorance, the concept of 'coincidence of opposites,' and 'Trinity.'"[11] Was Cusanus a "learned thief" after all?[12] I shall return to *Fundamentum* in my discussion of chapters 7 to 10 of Book Two. What matters here is the way this text underscores how indebted Cusanus is to Thierry of Chartres and to thinkers in his orbit.[13] How this fact should affect our reading of *De docta ignorantia* remains in question.

What Hoenen takes to be Cusanus's extensive borrowing from *Fundamentum* led him to contend "that the anonymous treatise contains *in nuce* many of the essential doctrines of *De docta ignorantia*."[14] "Cusanus must have seen the idea of *De docta ignorantia* clearly formulated for the first time in this text. The conjecture thus suggests itself that the philosophical thought to which Cusanus had already dedicated himself for some time, and for which he still searched for an adequate and comprehensive expression,... took form after studying the treatise and was able to develop into the overall teaching of *De docta ignorantia*."[15] Hoenen would seem to give to Cusanus's encounter with

10. Albertson, "Learned Thief," 354.

11. Albertson, "Learned Thief," 356.

12. Irene Caiazzo's discovery of a commentary on Boethius's *De arithmetica* that she convincingly attributes to Thierry of Chartres adds another chapter to the story of Cusanus's appropriation of Chartrian sources. David Albertson has shown that "there is considerable textual evidence that Nicholas used Thierry's *Arithmetica* commentary in the construction of *De docta ignorantia*"; David Albertson, "'Boethius noster,' Thierry of Chartres's *Arithmetica* Commentary as a Missing Source of Nicholas of Cusa's *De docta ignorantia*," *Recherches de Théologie et Philosophie Médiévales* 83, no. 1 (2016): 143–99. See also Thierry of Chartres, *The Commentary on the "De arithmetica of Boethius,"* ed. Irene Caiazzo (Toronto: University of Toronto Press, 2015).

13. Rudolf Haubst, *Das Bild des Einen und Dreieinen Gottes in der Welt nach Nikolaus von Kues* (Trier: Paulinus Verlag, 1952), 99–144.

14. Haubst, *Das Bild des Einen und Dreieinen Gottes*.

15. Maarten J. F. M. Hoenen, "'Ista prius inaudita': Eine neuentdeckte Vorlage der *De docta ignorantia* und ihre Bedeutung für die frühe Philosophie des Nikolaus von Kues," in *Medioevo: Rivista di Storia della filosofia medievale* 21 (1995): 435–36; cited in Albertson, "Learned Thief," 354. The relationship of *Fundamentum* to *De docta ignorantia* remains controversial. Jasper Hopkins's detailed critique of Hoenen's claim that *Fundamentum* is the *Vorlage* or model of *De docta ignorantia*—his proposal that the author of *Fundamentum* may

III. THE TRINITY

Fundamentum somewhat the same importance that Cusanus himself ascribed to that visionary experience he claims to have had while at sea returning from Constantinople. Cusanus's core ideas, Hoenen suggests, are already to be found in *Fundamentum*. They are indeed found already in his very first sermon, raising the question: when and where did Cusanus first discover the Chartrian texts, more especially *Fundamentum*, that were to become so important to him? Was it on his visit to Paris in 1428? Given their presumed importance to Cusanus, it is strange that none of these texts appear to have been part of the books that he, in his testament, bequeathed to the hospital he had founded in Kues.[16]

Albertson, while accepting Hoenen's claim that Cusanus made extensive use of this brief text, helps us to put it in its proper context. Cusanus, he remarks, "is no more a thief of that author's [the author of *Fundamentum*] ideas than he is of Thierry of Chartres's ideas.... To concede that Cusanus used *Fundamentum* in *De docta ignorantia* does not negate the originality of the 1440 work—precisely as Klibansky replied to Duhem—but it does compel us to reopen the unsolved case regarding Thierry of Chartres's broad impact on the German Cardinal. It also ought to shift the emphasis of research from Cusanus's philosophical or epistemological achievements toward his theological ones, especially the distinctive mystical Christology of Book III."[17]

To this reader it poses the question: does Cusanus's understanding of the Trinity present us with the very core of *De docta ignorantia*? And the more general question: suppose one accepts the orthodox understanding of the Trinity, does one not also have to accept the coincidence of opposites and some version of the doctrine of learned ignorance?

But what reason is there to assert the Trinity? Will a modern reader find much of philosophical significance in these four chapters? The very attempt to distinguish what is philosophically significant from what is theologically significant does violence to the thought of Cusanus, who insists that only learned ignorance and the associated understanding of the coincidence of opposites —and that means of

---

have relied on *De docta ignorantia*—is not easily dismissed. I find Albertson's critique of Hopkins not altogether convincing; see Hopkins, "Orienting Study," Part One, "Expository Purview," 4–11; Albertson, "Learned Thief," 363–68. See also Hans Georg Senger's note on the controversy in *PTW* I, *DI* II:123–24n67.

16. Giovanni Mantese, "Ein notartielles Inventar von Büchner und Wertgegenständen aus dem Nachlass des Nikolaus von Kues," in *Mitteilungen und Forschungsbeiträge der Cusanus-Gesellschaft* 2 (Mainz: Matthias-Grünewald-Verlag, 1962), 2:85–116.

17. Mantese, "Ein notartielles Inventar," 389–90.

the limits of the logic that presides over our reason—allow for a proper, if not at all adequate, understanding of the unity of Father, Son, and Holy Spirit, who, while different persons, are yet one God. As the example of Johannes Wenck shows, their commitment to reason may well make philosophers unwilling to follow Cusanus's path to learned ignorance. Would an understanding that in his sense had become learned about its ignorance not have us leave our reason behind? But is it perhaps that very reason that, recognizing its limits, forces us to transcend these limits in a way that opens a door to an appreciation of the philosophical significance of the Trinity? Recall that in chapter 2 Cusanus had pointed to God, understood as the Truth, as the root of the doctrine of learned ignorance. And does truth not have a trinitarian structure? Consider Thomas Aquinas's definition of truth as "the adequation of the thing and the intellect": *Veritas est adaequatio rei et intellectus.*[18] In perfect truth adequacy becomes equality. Precise truth is the equality of being and intellect. To a medieval thinker the unity of Father, Son (the Word), and the Holy Spirit had to suggest itself. In Alan of Lille's *Theologicae regulae* Cusanus could read, "*In Patre unitas, in Filio aequalitas, in Spiritu sancto unitatis aequalitatis connexio,*"[19] "In the Father unity, in the Son equality, in the Holy Spirt the connection of unity and equality."

18. Thomas Aquinas, *Questiones disputatae de veritate*, q. 1, art. 1.

19. Alanus ab Insulis, *Theologicae regulae* IV, PL 210:625. Alan of Lille appears to have been a student of Thierry of Chartres.

CHAPTER 7

The Trine and One Eternity

Cusanus begins this chapter with the rather difficult to accept claim that there never was a nation that did not worship God and believed him to be the Absolute Maximum and One. But it would seem to have been his conviction that, if perhaps only obscurely and in distorted fashion, every human being believed in the same triune God that he believed in. To support his claim he invokes, not very convincingly, the authority of Marcus Varro, who is said to have reported that the "Sissenii worshipped Oneness as the Maximum" (*DI* I.7:18)[1] and proceeds to point to Pythagoras, "a very famous man of undeniable authority as a thinker in his own time," who is said to have recognized that "this Oneness is trine" (*DI* I.7:18). In concluding the chapter Cusanus will return to Pythagoras's supposedly trinitarian conception of oneness. Rather surprisingly, the pagan Pythagoras frames this chapter on the Trinity.

As Paul Wilpert points out,[2] Cusanus may have drawn the questionable reference to Pythagoras, hardly sufficient to support his claim, from *De septem septenis,* a Chartrian text long attributed to John of

---

1. Wilpert *points* out that the *Antiquitates* of Varro have here been confused with those of Josephus, who, however, mentions the Essenes. The source on which Cusanus relied is unknown; see Paul Wilpert's note in *PTW* I, DI I:117n18.

2. *PTW* I, DI I:117n18.

Salisbury (c. 1120–80).[3] We are left with a question: What lets Cusanus invoke the "undeniable authority" of the pagan Pythagoras to support this assertion that "Oneness is trine"? The suggestion that Cusanus may have found the reference to Pythagoras in *De septem septenis* gives us a first answer: Cusanus would seem to owe his understanding of a trinitarian Pythagoras to the School of Chartres.

A more philosophical answer is suggested by the sentences that follow:

> As we investigate the truth about this [matter] and elevate our intellects more highly, let us assert (in accordance with the aforesaid): No one doubts that that which precedes all otherness is eternal. For otherness is identical with mutability. Now, everything which naturally precedes mutability is immutable and, hence, eternal. But otherness consists of one thing and another. Hence, otherness is subsequent to oneness, just as is number. Therefore, oneness is by nature prior to otherness; and since oneness naturally precedes otherness, it is eternal. (*DI* I.7:18)

The supposed insight of the pagan Pythagoras that number is subsequent to oneness is to be raised to a higher level. Cusanus invites us to think the relation of creation, marked by mutability, and this is to say otherness, to the eternal God, as being like the relation of number to oneness. Wilpert and Senger point out that "with his speculation on the concept of otherness Nikolaus follows to a large extent the doctrine of the School of Chartres, especially Thierry."[4] There he found confirmation of his conviction that number provides us finite knowers with a key to approaching the essence of God. In Thierry of Chartres Cusanus would seem to have found his Christian Pythagoras. Not that he knew him to be the author of some texts he became acquainted with and presumably acquired—perhaps while visiting Paris in 1428, looking for manuscripts. As Albertson suggests, Cusanus "may well have viewed Thierry's commentaries and the *Fundamentum* treatise as essentially the work of a single author," whom he associated especially with a commentary on Boethius's *De Trinitate.* This unnamed commentator Cusanus was to call in his *Apologia doctae ignorantia* "easily the most intelligent man of all those whom I have read" (*AP* 24)— high praise indeed for, as we now know, Thierry of Chartres.[5]

Drawing on Thierry, Cusanus offers us in chapter 7 what seems to

---

3. John of Salisbury, *De septem septenis,* sect. VII (PL 199, 961C). On the misattribution to John of Salisbury, see Albertson, "Boethius Noster," 149n6.

4. *PTW* I, DI I:117n18.

5. Albertson, "Learned Thief," 389.

be intended as some sort of proof of his triune God. Not surprisingly, given Cusanus's understanding of the limits of reason, the "proof" invites question. But let us consider the steps of the "argument."

1. Oneness (*unitas*) precedes otherness and is eternal. (*DI* I.7:18)
2. Equality (*aequalitas*) precedes inequality and is eternal. (*DI* I.7:19)
3. Union (*conexio*) is prior to separation and is eternal. (*DI* I.7:20)
4. There cannot be more than one eternal thing. (*DI* I.7:21)
5. Therefore oneness, equality, and union are one.

The association of oneness with the Father, equality with the Son, union with the Holy Spirit, common to Thierry and his school, makes the claim that the three are eternal hardly surprising. It is indeed inseparable from Cusanus's understanding of God as the Truth. Still, the association of what would seem to be first of all abstract concepts with the three persons of the Trinity invites question.

We may well be willing to grant the substance of the first three theses, to which I shall return: whatever concepts such as oneness, equality, and union name certainly does not seem subject to time. But what sort of being does it possess? Are oneness, equality, and union realities of some sort? By claiming that there can be only one eternal thing, Cusanus would seem to rule this out. But why can there be no plurality of eternal things? Plato's forms come to mind. And are numbers not also things in this sense? And if oneness can be said to be eternal, should we not say the same of otherness? That Cusanus would have us reject a plurality of eternal forms is evident. Should we then say that they are abstractions, dependent on human knowers? As such they would have only a derivative, at bottom temporal being. But that, too, Cusanus would have us reject. What he has in mind are not just abstract concepts: Oneness, equality, and union have an ontological significance. But if they do indeed have such a significance, must they not be considered separate "things" in some sense? What then justifies the claim that there can be no more than one such eternal "thing"? How are we to understand the claim that oneness, equality, and union are three and yet one? Cusanus might answer, only in learned ignorance, only by accepting the *coincidentia oppositorum*.

1. Let us take a closer look at the first thesis: When Cusanus speaks here of otherness, he is thinking not of an abstract concept, but of the countless things that make up God's creation, each one different from the other. All otherness, Cusanus had asserted earlier, presupposes number. But number, as we have seen, according to his neo-Platonic

III. THE TRINITY

mathematical thinking, has its *principium* in the One or Oneness, which is also the Maximum. Since the Maximum stands in no relation to an other, it could not be other; therefore it is not mutable, hence is eternal.

Is Cusanus justified to claim that the Maximum stands in *no* relation whatsoever to another? The very word "Maximum" would seem to presuppose thoughts of a series of things that can be greater or less, just as the maximum number that Cusanus is so fond of invoking makes reference to the number sequence and is said to be the *principium* or ground of every number. Similarly, the One—that is, God— must be thought of as the *principium* or ground of the world of things. For Cusanus God is not well understood by us as a self-sufficient plenitude. He must be thought of as Creator, as unfolding himself in the creation. But to think God both as the Absolute Maximum, which stands in no relation to an other, and as Creator, we have to embrace the *coincidentia oppositorum.*

We may well want to question Cusanus's identification of otherness with mutability. Mutability does imply otherness, and if the One precludes otherness, it makes sense to call it eternal. But does otherness imply mutability? For Cusanus all the things God created could be other than they happen to be. Given that understanding of God, Cusanus's identification of otherness and mutability seems justified. As mentioned, it implies a rejection of Platonism, which posits eternal realities other than God.

Cusanus's discussion of the Maximum as "oneness preceding otherness" invites comparison with his later discussion of the "Not-Other," which in *De li non aliud* he calls the most adequate name for God he has been able to come up with:

> I certainly do not mean that "Not other" is the name of that whose name is above every name. Rather through "Not-other" I disclose to you the name of my concept of the First. There does not occur to me any more precise name, which expresses my concept of the Unnameable, which, indeed, is not *other* than anything. (*DLN* 99)

Cusanus insists that he is naming not the unnameable Deity, but his "concept of the First"—that is, a human construct. All theology moves within the circle of such thought constructions. A fully adequate understanding of what we call God is denied to us, even as the unnameable God haunts us.

Everything finite could be other than it happens to be, could be greater or less. That is to say, whatever entity presents itself to us presents itself in a logical space in which everything could be other than it happens to be or not be at all, we can say: in the mode of otherness, of the *aliud*. *Non aliud* points in the same direction as the expression "in-finite." What it names is not an entity. It transcends the space of reason.

Cusanus's discussion of the Absolute Maximum brings to mind Kant's discussion of the sublime in the *Critique of Judgment*:

> That is sublime in comparison with which everything else is small. We can easily see here that nothing in nature can be given, however large we may judge it, that could not, when considered in a different relation, be degraded all the way to the infinitely small, nor conversely anything so small that it could not, when compared with still smaller standards, be expanded for our imagination all the way to the magnitude of a world; telescopes have provided us with a wealth of material in support of the first point, microscopes in support of the second. Hence, considered on this basis, nothing that can be an object of the senses is to be called sublime. [What happens is that] our imagination strives to progress towards infinity, while our reason demands absolute totality as a real idea, and so [the imagination,] our power of estimating the magnitude of things in the world of sense, is inadequate to that idea. Yet this inadequacy itself is the arousal in us of the feeling that we have within us a supersensible power; and what is absolutely large is not an object of sense, but is the use that judgment makes naturally of certain objects so as to [arouse] this (feeling), and in contrast with that use any other use is small. Hence what is to be called sublime is not the object, but the attunement that the intellect [gets] through a certain presentation that occupies reflective judgment.
>
> Hence we may supplement the formulas already given by another one: *Sublime is what even to be able to think proves that the mind has a power surpassing any standard of sense.*[6]

What Kant says of the absolutely large can also be said of Cusanus's *Maximum* and his *non aliud*. Both are ideas of reason that surpass every standard of sense and yet, since they can be thought, prove that we human beings possess a faculty that touches the infinite. Cusanus's *Maximum* is, in Kant's sense, an idea born of the collusion of the imagination that "strives to progress towards infinity" and reason, which "demands absolute totality": an idea of the infinite one.

To comprehend things we have to mentally bound them. It is when we experience things as exceeding our ability to comprehend

6. Immanuel Kant, *Critique of Judgment*, trans. Werner S. Pluhar (Indianapolis: Hackett, 1987), 105–6.

them that a feeling is aroused in us that "we have within us a super-sensible power"; within itself our mind discovers the infinite and becomes learned about its ignorance. Such a visionary sublime experience Cusanus would seem to have had on that ship that brought him back from Greece to Venice.

Let me return to the question: Why can there not be a multiplicity of eternal objects? I mentioned Plato's forms. Or think of numbers. But Cusanus does not take Plato's forms or numbers to be existing realities. They are thought by him to be products of the unfolding of our human mind in its effort to take the measure of God's creation, which Cusanus understands as the unfolding of the divine One, where he is aware that such understanding provides us only with symbols. Like the nominalists he encountered already in Heidelberg, like Aristotle, Cusanus cannot accept the view that Plato's forms are abstract eternal things. God is the only eternal reality Cusanus recognizes. Plato's forms are said to be products of our human mind. But they are produced in response to the essential differences we perceive in things. In this respect Cusanus would seem to be closer to Aristotle or to Thomas Aquinas than to Plato.

2. "Equality precedes inequality and is eternal." Given the association of equality with the Word, the thesis is hardly surprising.

> Moreover, every inequality is composed of an equal and a greater. Therefore, inequality is by nature subsequent to equality—something which can be proven very cogently by means of analysis. For every inequality is analyzable into an equality. For the equal is in between the greater and the lesser. So if you remove that [portion] which is greater, there will be an equal. But if there is a lesser, remove from the other that [portion] which is greater, and an equal will result. And you can continue to do this until, in the process of removing, you come to things simple. Clearly, then, every inequality is, by removing, analyzable into an equality. Therefore, equality naturally precedes inequality. (*DI* I.7:19)

Albertson suggests that the source of this argument may well be Thierry's recently discovered commentary on Boethius's *De arithmetica*.[7] But we do not need to know Cusanus's source to follow his discussion; the very word "inequality" already suggests the priority of "equality." Preceding inequality, equality also precedes otherness, for whenever there is inequality there is also otherness. The claim that equality is eternal raises once more the questions concerning the being of

7. Albertson, "Noster Boethius," 162.

what concepts like "equality" refer to, a question raised already by the first thesis.

3. Cusanus supports the third proposition, that union is prior to separation and is eternal, with similar considerations, once again following Thierry of Chartres.[8]

> Moreover, if there are two causes one of which is by nature prior to the other, the effect of the prior [cause] will be by nature prior to [the effect] of the subsequent [cause]. Now, oneness (*unitas*) is both union and a cause of union; for the reason things are said to be in union is that they are united (*unita*) together. Likewise, the number two is both separation and a cause of separation; for two is the first separation. Therefore, if oneness is a cause of union and if the number two is [a cause] of separation, then just as oneness is by nature prior to two, so union is by nature prior to separation. But separation and otherness are by nature concomitant. Hence, union is eternal (just as is oneness), since it is prior to otherness. (*DI* I.7:20)

We should note how Cusanus relies in his speculations on mathematics, even as he warns against an uncritical reliance on numbers. The mathematics he relies on is the mathematics of neo-Platonism, which lets him understand God as the unfolding One. This invites questions: what justifies it? Should we look for its ground to an intuition of the—according to Cusanus—incomprehensible nature of God? Or should we look rather to the nature of the human mind, which he also understands as an unfolding one, where counting is the first expression of that unfolding? Is God here understood in the image of man? Cusanus will address these questions explicitly in chapter 11 of *De docta ignorantia*.

Having "proved" that oneness, equality, and union are eternal, Cusanus concludes that they are one, since according to him, once more in agreement with Thierry of Chartres, there can be no more than one eternal thing, since he takes otherness to imply mutability. The three are one, although their being one remains incomprehensible, since equality and union would both seem to presuppose otherness. We are cast back to the incomprehensible Trinity: oneness, equality, and union differ and are yet one.

Returning to the beginning of the chapter, Cusanus concludes:

> And this is that trine Oneness which Pythagoras, the first philosopher of all and the glory of Italy and of Greece, affirmed to be worthy of worship. (*DI* I.7, I.21)

8. Albertson, "Noster Boethius," 162.

CHAPTER 8

Eternal Generation

Quite in the spirit of Thierry of Chartres, this very brief chapter continues the discussion of the Trinity, clarifying the need to go beyond a conception of God as simply One: It seeks to show that God must be thought as generative, as Creator. But to think God as the ground of both the existence and the essence of every thing, we have to think him as both Father, the ground of each thing's existence, and as Son, the Word, the Logos that was in the beginning, the ground of each thing's essence. A presupposition of the being of things, as Cusanus thinks it, is thus the generation of the Son.

> Let me now show very briefly that equality of oneness is begotten from oneness but that union proceeds from oneness and from equality of oneness. "*Unitas*" or "ὄντας," so to speak (from the Greek word "ὤν," which is rendered in Latin as "*ens*"), and *unitas* [oneness] is *entitas* [being], as it were.[1] For indeed, God is the being of things, for he is the Form of being and, hence, is also being. Now, equality of oneness is equality of being, as it were (*quasi*)—that is, equality of existing (*essendi sive exsistendi*). But equality of existing [that is, of being (*essendi*)] is the fact that in a thing there is neither too much nor too little—nothing beyond [measure], nothing below [measure]. For if in a thing there were present too much, [that thing] would be

1. Cf. *PTW* I:117–18n22, citing Thierry of Chartres, *Commentum* II.22.97.

monstrous; and if there were present too little, [that thing] would not even exist. (*DI* I.8:22)

Following Thierry of Chartres, in a way that may make us think of Heidegger, Cusanus draws on a questionable etymology to support his claim that *unitas* is *entitas*. Every *ens* is *unum*; its being cannot be separated from its oneness; its existence cannot be separated from its essence. As Oneness, God the Father is the *principium* of the existence of every being. As Equality of Oneness, as the Son, God is the *principium* of the essence of every being. God is thus "the being of things." And in every thing being is present in a manner proper to it.

Once more Cusanus approaches the key thought with a mathematical analogy, calling our attention to the difference between 1 and 1 understood as the product of 1 x 1, where the product of this multiplication, while different, is yet the same as the original 1. Similarly, Christ, the Son of the Father, and the Father, while different, are yet one God.

> When we pay attention to what generation is, we view clearly the generation of equality from oneness. For generation is the repetition of oneness or the multiplication of the same nature as it proceeds from a father to a son. This latter generation is found only in transient things. However, the generation of oneness from oneness is one repetition of oneness—that is, is oneness once [that is, oneness times one]. But if I multiply oneness two times or three times and so on, oneness will beget from itself another—for instance, the number two or the number three or some other number. But oneness once repeated [that is, oneness times one] begets only equality of oneness; this [repeating] can only be understood as oneness begetting oneness. And this generation is eternal. (*DI* I.8.23)

Here, too, Cusanus is following his Christian Pythagoras Thierry of Chartres. Even as he warns against an uncritical reliance on numbers—applied to God, they can yield only inadequate symbolic conjectures—he relies in his speculations on a metaphorical mathematics, drawn from the mathematics of neo-Platonism, which lets him understand God as the unfolding—that is, the generative One. The first unfolding of God is the Logos—that is, the Son. The Logos cannot be divorced from the being of beings: everything that exists has an essence.

The chapter's first sentence had promised a discussion of all three persons of the Trinity. But only in the following chapter does Cusanus turn explicitly to the Holy Spirit. Given Christian doctrine, this turn is to be expected. But a secular reader may well wonder whether there is a philosophical need for that turn. Is it not sufficient to point to our world, which can be said to presuppose the descent of some timeless logos into the material and temporal, of the divine Word into beings? In the *Symposium* Plato names the power that presides over this descent eros. Cusanus might have understood Plato's eros as a pagan's obscure understanding of the Holy Spirit, which has often been said to be love.

The Eternal Procession of Union

With this chapter Cusanus turns explicitly to the third person of the Trinity. Having "proved" to his satisfaction that oneness, equality, and union are eternal, Cusanus concludes that they are one, since, as discussed earlier, according to him there can be no more than one truly eternal thing. Given the preceding, such neo-Platonic reasoning intended to shed some light on the incomprehensible Trinity is not unexpected.

> Just as generation of oneness from oneness is one repetition of oneness, so the procession from both is oneness of the repetition of this oneness—or (if you prefer the expression) is oneness of oneness and of the equality of this oneness. However, "procession" signifies an "extension," as it were, from one thing to another—just as in the case where two things are equal, a certain equality (which conjoins and unites them in a certain way) is extended, as it were, from the one to the other. Therefore, union is rightly said to proceed from oneness and from equality of oneness. For union is not merely of one [of these]; rather it proceeds from oneness to equality of oneness and from equality of oneness to oneness. Therefore [union] is rightly said to proceed from both, since it is extended, as it were, from the one to the other. (*DI* I.9:24)[1]

1. Once again, Cusanus would appear to be following Thierry of Chartres and Clarenbald of Arras; *PTW* I, DI I:118n24.

III. THE TRINITY

Of interest is the following explanation:

> But we do not say that union is begotten from oneness or from
> equality of oneness, since union is not from oneness either through
> repetition or through multiplication. And although equality of one-
> ness is begotten from oneness and although union proceeds from
> both [of these], nevertheless oneness, equality of oneness, and the
> union proceeding from both are one and the same thing—as if we
> were to speak of [one and] the same thing as this, it, the same (*hoc,
> id, idem*). The fact of our saying "it" is related to a first thing; but
> our saying "the same" unites and conjoins the related thing to the
> first thing. Assume, then, that from the pronoun "it" there were
> formed the word "itness," so that we could speak of oneness, itness,
> and sameness: itness would bear a relation to oneness, but sameness
> would designate the union of itness and oneness. [In this case, the
> names "Oneness" (*unitas*), "Itness" (*iditas*), and "Sameness" (*identi-
> tas*)] would nearly enough befit the Trinity. (*DI* I.9:25)

Cusanus could find the simile of *hoc, id, idem*, "this, it, the same," for
Father, Son, and Holy Spirit in Boethius's *De trinitate*; *unitas, iditas*,
and *identitas* appear to be Cusanus's own formulations.[2] They invite
closer consideration. Saying, with reference to some thing, "this"
suggests that we are pointing to it in some sense. Saying "this is it"
presupposes some understanding of what sort of thing this "this" is;
it attributes to what is an essence. The copula joins the two. In the
structure of a simple sentence, say, "This is a rose," Cusanus thus finds
a symbol of the Trinity. "It" unfolds "this," as the One unfolds itself in
the creative word, in the *Logos*. But what joins the two, what lets the
One become creative? An overflowing love. In every thing Cusanus
would appear to have experienced the image of the Trinity.

The chapter concludes by addressing the relationship of this discussion of oneness, equality, and union to what the church has taught
about Father, Son, and Holy Spirit. The church fathers are said to
have used these names "because of a certain likeness to these tran-
sient things. Just as the Deity is present as much in the Son as in the
Father, so humanity is present in the son as much as it is in the father,
from whom it passed to the son. This is why the father loves the son
more than any other human being" (*DI* I.9:26). Love is the bond that
joins the two, just as the Holy Spirit joins Father and Son.

We are told not to forget that talk of Father and Son is "only in relation to creatures" (*DI* I.9.26). Cusanus finds oneness, equality, and

2. *PTW* I, DI I:118–19n25.

union more adequate terms to describe the incomprehensible triune Deity. But is such talk, too, not only in relation to our human understanding? Once more Cusanus reminds us of the way he has drawn on texts that belong to a tradition that he traces back to Pythagoras:

> And in my judgment, this is a very clear investigation (in accord with the Pythagorean investigation) of the ever adorable Trinity in oneness and Oneness in trinity. (*DI* I.9:88)

An Understanding of Trinity in Oneness Transcends All Things

Chapter 10 concludes Cusanus's discussion of the Trinity in Book One. It takes for its point of departure a statement by Martian, which Cusanus once again found in John of Salisbury, who substitutes for Martian's "philology" "philosophy."[1]

> Let us now inquire about what Martian is getting at when he says that Philosophy, desiring to ascend unto a knowledge of this Trinity, left behind circles and spheres. (*DI* I.10:27)

Hopkins's translation is rather tame. *Evomuisse* is translated as "left behind," but *emovere* means "to spit out, to vomit forth." Cusanus points out that the most perfect corporeal figure, the sphere, the most perfect surface figure, the circle, and the most perfect rectilinear figure, the triangle, as well as simple straightness, must be "spit out" if we are to raise ourselves to an understanding of the Maximum. Mathematics provides us with a ladder, but in the end this ladder must be cast away. How are we to understand that? And what are left with?

Cusanus insists that we have not rightly left the sphere, the circle, and the like behind, unless we understand that maximal oneness is

---

1. *PTWI*, DI I:119n27.

necessarily trine. Why should this be so? Why not simply one? That to do justice to the *unicum, simplicissimum maximum,* the "unique, most simple maximum" (*DI* I.10:27), we must leave behind sphere, circle, triangle, and straight line is easy enough to understand, given the preceding. There can be no maximum sphere, circle, triangle, or straight line. The attempt to imagine these as maxima must suffer shipwreck. All plurality would also seem to have to be spit out. But would that not include trinity? Cusanus, to be sure, insists that perfect oneness is triune, fully aware that this surpasses the reach of our reason and requires faith illuminated by learned ignorance.

> Consequently, we must leave behind the things which, together with their material associations, are attained through the senses, through the imagination, or through reason—[leave them behind] so that we may arrive at the most simple and most abstract understanding, where all things are one, where a line is a triangle, a circle, and a sphere, where oneness is threeness, (and conversely), where accident is substance, where body is mind (*spiritus*), where motion is rest, and other such things. (*DI* I.10:27)

Once more we may wonder whether the Maximum, so understood, leaving behind plurality, does not also have to leave behind the Trinity. Having left behind plurality, what sense can we make of "oneness is threeness (and conversely)"? That faith would have us assert this is clear enough. But does this assertion not require us to hold on to some sense of plurality to make the paradoxical claim that oneness is threeness? Maximal oneness, Cusanus insists, is necessarily trine. What considerations other than faith can Cusanus adduce to support that claim?

As mentioned, to think oneness as maximal is to think it in relation to a realm where we find the greater and less—that is, plurality. Cusanus thinks the Maximum in relation to creation as its *principium.* But to understand maximal oneness as the *principium* of creation is to think it as generative, as procreative.

Cusanus seeks to clarify this by means of what he calls an *exemplum:*[2]

> To use examples suitable to the foregoing [point]: We see that oneness of understanding is not anything other than that which understands, that which is understandable, and the act of understanding. (*DI* I.28)

---

2. Wilpert points to Ramon Llull as the source of this example, citing Eusebio Colomer, SJ, *Nikolaus von Kues und Raimund Llull: Quellen und Studien zur Geschichte der Philosophie* (Berlin: De Gruyter, 1961), 2:9ff.

When we really understand something, say, an equilateral triangle, there is no distance between subject and object. In the act of understanding they appear united.

Cusanus transfers this reflection on human understanding to God's. And is such a transference not justified if we accept that God created man in his image?

> So suppose you want to transfer your reflection from that which understands to the Maximum and to say that the Maximum is, most greatly, that which understands; but suppose you do not add that the Maximum is also, most greatly, that which is understandable together with being the greatest actual understanding. In that case, you do not rightly conceive of the greatest and most perfect Oneness. For if Oneness is the greatest and most perfect understanding (which without these three mutual relations cannot be either understanding or the most perfect understanding), then whoever does not attain to the trinity of this Oneness does not rightly conceive of oneness. (*DI* I.10:28)

Key here is the identification of Oneness with the most perfect understanding. Recall the earlier discussion of the truth of things, which provides our investigations of nature with a measure. The truth of things is nothing other than "the greatest and most perfect understanding." Here God who understands and the understood are thought to be one in God's creative understanding. We may well wonder about the claim "Oneness is the greatest and most perfect understanding." Is this not to read he human knower into God? But does the thought of the infinite we bear within ourselves not build a bridge to the Godhead?

> For oneness is only threeness, since oneness indicates indivision, distinctness, and union. Indeed, indivision is from oneness—as are also distinctness and union (*unio sive conexio*). Hence, the greatest Oneness is not other than indivision, distinctness, and union. Since it is indivision, it is eternity and without beginning. (The eternal is not divided by anything.) Since it is distinctness, it is from immutable eternity. And since it is union (*conexio sive unio*), it proceeds from both [indivision and distinctness]. (*DI* I.10:28)

Next we are invited to reflect on "Oneness is maximal."

> Moreover, when I say "Oneness is maximal," I indicate threeness. For when I say "oneness," I indicate a beginning without a beginning; when I say "maximal," I indicate a beginning from a beginning; when I conjoin and unite these two through the word "is," I indicate a procession from both. (*DI* I.10:29)

To say "Oneness is maximal" is to think Oneness as the Trinity. Oneness is as the Word that is said to have been in the beginning: "And the Word was with God, and the Word was God." (Jn 1:1)

As pointed out, the asserted need for theology to spit out circles and spheres calls for a consideration of the function mathematics and mathematical examples have in Cusanus's discourse. Chapters eleven to eighteen will show us in just what sense Cusanus would have us both make use of and leap beyond (*transilire*) sphere, circle, triangle, and straight line.

IV. THE POWER OF MATHEMATICS

FOR CUSANUS MATHEMATICS had been a lifelong companion. It opened a door to the infinite he bore within himself and in which he experienced the presence of the infinite God. The door to that experience was the coincidence of opposites.

We don't know much about Cusanus's early years. Thus, we do not know when he first became interested in mathematics. But we can assume that already in Heidelberg, as a student in the faculty of the arts, he became acquainted with the *Institutiones arithmeticae* of Boethius and its number mysticism, as well as with Bradwardine's *Arithmetica speculativa* and, more importantly, his *Geometria speculativa,* a popular textbook that acquainted students with the simpler parts of Euclid's *Elements.*[1] Given his lifelong fascination with numbers and figures, it seems more than likely that later, while at Padua, Cusanus studied not only law, but also mathematics and astronomy with Prosdocimo de' Beldomandi, perhaps joined by his friend Toscanelli, who studied medicine with Beldomandi, but, like Cusanus, had interests that covered the whole *quadrivium.* Beldomandi, who had been appointed professor of music and astrology in 1422, had established himself as a master of the four mathematical arts of the *quadrivium,* arithmetic, geometry, astronomy, and music theory, where it is the last for which he is perhaps best known today. Judging by his later work, the young Cusanus may well have been struck by the way Beldomandi taught that the astronomer could not claim certainty for his mathematical models. Even the question of whether the apparent motion of the fixed stars was sufficient to establish that the stars really moved was

1. Hofmann, "Einführung," in Nikolaus von Cues, *Die mathematischen Schriften,* x. See also Joseph Ehrenfried Hofmann, "Sinn und Bedeutung der wichtigsten mathematischen Schriften des Nikolaus von Kues," in *Nicolo' Cusano: Agli Inizi del Mondo Moderno,* 385–98.

IV. THE POWER OF MATHEMATICS

open for discussion, even though Beldomandi did not find persuasive the thesis that it was not the firmament, but the earth, that moved.[2]

As those of Cusanus's later writings that concern the extension and squaring of the circle show, he did have an interest in a problem that today we are tempted to call purely mathematical. That interest earned him a place in the history of mathematics.[3] To be sure, as the focus on this problem shows, for Cusanus, as already for Boethius, mathematical and theological problems could not be divorced. Dante, in the last canto of the *Divine Comedy*, considers the impossibility of squaring the circle a symbol of our inability to comprehend paradise. For Cusanus, work on that problem was no doubt part of his effort to symbolically approach the being of God. I will return to the significance the problem held for Cusanus later.

Cusanus's interest in neo-Platonic mathematics must have been reinforced when he was in Cologne teaching law and studying philosophy with the slightly older Heymeric de Campo, who followed Albert the Great and Proclus. It was Heymeric who had encouraged Cusanus to travel to Paris to look for works by Ramon Llull. The success of that trip is suggested by the fact that there are more works by Llull in Cusanus's library than by any other thinker. Of interest is that "in the year 1428 he himself copied Llull's *Treatise on the Squaring and Triangulation of the Circle* and significantly only the first mathematical part, but not its symbolic-theological continuation."[4] That trip also may have led him to discover works by Thierry of Chartres and his followers. The School of Chartres, as mentioned, had a decisive impact on Cusanus's Christian neo-Pythagorean understanding of the significance of mathematical symbols. It is curious, however, that none of these works can be found in his library.

A modern reader not particularly interested in the historical context may still wonder about the truth content of what Cusanus has to say, regardless of how original or how derivative. As the cardinal himself recognized, his evident fondness for mathematical symbols in his attempts to find ever more adequate symbols to explain the

2. Mieczyslaw Markowski, "Die kosmologischen Anschauungen des Prosdocimo de' Beldomandi," in *Studi sul XIV secolo in memoria di Anneliese Maier*, ed. Alfonso Maierù and Agostino Paravicini (Rome: Ed. di Storia e Letteratura, 1981), 268–69.

3. Moritz Cantor, *Vorlesungen über Geschichte der Mathematik* (New York: B. G. Teubner Verlagsgesellschaft, 1965); Hofmann, "Einführung," ix–lii; Jean-Marie Nicolle, "Innovation in Mathematics and Proclusean Tradition in Cusanus's Thought," in *Nicholas of Cusa: A Medieval Thinker for the Modern Age*, ed. Kazuhiko Yamaki (London and New York: Routledge, 2011), 85–88.

4. Nikolaus von Cues, *Die Mathematischen Schriften*, xii –xiii.

incomprehensible being of God calls for discussion. What justifies it? His love of mathematics is not a good enough answer. Nor is reference to the evident impact Chartrian texts had on his thinking.[5] How are we to understand the power of such symbols? Chapter 11 of *On Learned Ignorance* addresses that question quite directly.

5. See Albertson, *Mathematical Theologies.*

CHAPTER 11

Mathematics Assists Us Very Greatly in Apprehending Various Divine [Truths]

Cunsanus begins this chapter by invoking Romans 1:20: "Ever since the creation of the world his invisible nature, namely his eternal power and deity, has been clearly perceived in the things that have been made," and Corinthians 13:12: "For now we see in a mirror dimly, but then face to face."

There is some tension between these two biblical passages. The first states that in the things God created his eternal power and deity can be clearly perceived, while the second asserts that in our present condition we see it in a mirror dimly. Cusanus's opening statement joins the two:

> All our wisest and most divine teachers agree that visible things are truly images of invisible things and that from created things the Creator can be knowably seen as in a mirror and a symbolism. (*DI* I.11:30)

Cusanus drops the "clearly," but keeps "in a mirror" and adds "symbolism": *in speculo et in aenigmate.* What kind of mirror and what sort of symbolism does he have in mind? How does he understand the image character of visible things? In what way are they truly "images of invisible things"?

> But the fact that spiritual matters (which are unattainable by us in themselves) are investigated *symbolically* has its basis in what was said earlier. For all things have a certain comparative relation to one another ([a relation that is], nonetheless, hidden from us and incomprehensible to us), so that from out of all things there arises one universe and in [this] one maximum all things are this one. And although every image (*imago*) seems to be like its exemplar, nevertheless except for the Maximal Image (which is, in oneness of nature, the very thing which its Exemplar is) no image is so similar or equal to its exemplar that it cannot be infinitely more similar and equal. (These [doctrines] have already been made known from the preceding [remarks]). (*DI* I.9:30)

All things are images of the Maximum, all speak of God in their ever different ways. But once more the question: how does Cusanus understand this image character? When we think of an image or picture, we think of an object that resembles the original in some specific way, while different. To understand the nature of that resemblance we must understand the relevant form of representation. Think of a map. Something visible represents something visible. Such a representation will never do complete justice to the original. As Cusanus writes, "No image is so similar or equal to its exemplar that it cannot be infinitely more similar and equal." All our images or descriptions of things could no doubt be better. Some are more adequate than others and often, if not precise, adequate enough for our purposes. In that sense we can claim truth for some of our representations, even if these lack absolute precision. In all these cases the exemplar provides the image with its measure. But what access do we have to this exemplar? Do our senses give us adequate access? As Plato knew, the inevitably perspectival character of perception rules this out. Cusanus, too, denies that the exemplar is ever perceived by us as it is: what we see is also only an image of what remains invisible.

"Image" (*imago*) here thus does not have its usual meaning: Cusanus understands *imago* not as "a picture of some original, but a presentation that makes visible something invisible."[1] But to make the invisible visible, the *imago* must be such that it lets us recognize that it is only *imago* and thus casts us beyond itself—we might say toward its exemplar, toward the thing as it is in truth. The truth of the thing

---

1. Volkmann-Schluck, *Nicolaus Cusanus*, 25.

IV. THE POWER OF MATHEMATICS

is the measure of all our images—that is, the coincidence of image and exemplar. But that coincidence, the absolute truth, is God. As the truth, God is the ultimate measure of every image. There is thus a sense in which we can call whatever we see—say, a rose, an image of God. Not that the rose resembles the Maximum. But in that rose we can experience the presence of the Creator when open to the mystery of its being. So experienced, the rose is a theophany. The same can be said of all creatures. The Maximum is to us the incomprehensible bond that gathers all things into a universe, a boundless plurality of things, yet one. So understood, God is experienced as the theme of the world.

I use the word "theme" here, thinking of a much later philosopher, Alexander Gottlieb Baumgarten (1714–62), the founder of aesthetics. Here is his definition:

> By theme we mean that whose representation contains the sufficient reason of other representations supplied in the discourse, but which does not have its own sufficient reason in them.[2]

In creating a unity out of a manifold the poet is thought by Baumgarten to be like another god, the work he creates like another world, having its own perfection and closure. The simile leads Baumgarten to make the following provocative claim:

> We observed a little while ago that the poet is like a maker or creator. So the poem ought to be like a world. Hence by analogy whatever is evident to the philosophers concerning the real world, the same ought to be thought of a poem.[3]

This is to say that whatever the philosophers have said about the world is by analogy true of the poem. When Baumgarten speaks here of the philosophers, he has in mind first of all Gottfried Wilhelm Leibniz (1646–1716) and his follower Christian Wolff (1679–1754). Consider Leibniz's *Monadology*, which represents the world as a perfectly ordered whole. The philosopher's discourse, to be sure, as demanded by rationalist metaphysics, aims to be clear and distinct. Challenging such cognitive confidence, Cusanus would say that our understanding of the way God gathers the world into a whole, into one universe, will never be clear and distinct, will always remain "hidden from us and incomprehensible to us." In this sense our understanding of the

---

2. Alexander Gottlieb Baumgarten, *Reflections on Poetry* [Meditationes philosophicae de nonnullis ad poema pertinentibus], par. 66, trans. Karl Aschenbrenner and William B. Holther (Berkeley and Los Angeles: University of California Press, 1954), 62.

3. Baumgarten, *Reflections on Poetry*, par. 68, p. 63.

Creator's presence in creation would seem to be more like Baumgarten's poetic understanding. A poem cannot be translated into a clear and distinct discourse. Nor, according to Cusanus, can the way the world speaks to us of God. Whatever we can say about it remains a more or less inadequate conjecture.

Note what Baumgarten's simile suggests: the creation resembles a poem that has God for its theme. Cusanus might agree, but he would add that this "poem" is interpreted best when the interpreter relies on the language of mathematics.

> Now, when we conduct an inquiry on the basis of an image, it is necessary that there be no doubt regarding the image, by means of whose symbolical comparative relation we are investigating what is unknown. For the pathway to the uncertain can be only through what is presupposed and certain. But all perceptible things are in a state of continual instability because of the material possibility abounding in them. In our considering of objects, we see that those which are more abstract than perceptible things, viz., mathematicals (not that they are altogether free of material associations, without which they cannot be imagined, and not that they are at all subject to the possibility of changing) are very fixed and are very certain to us. Therefore, in mathematicals the wise wisely sought illustrations of things that were to be searched out by the intellect. (*DI* I.11:31)

What kind of symbolism should be chosen? There should be "no doubt concerning the image." Before we can ask whether a model we are offered in explanation of some state of affairs is a good model, we have to be clear about that model. Just as we cannot decide the truth or falsity of a proposition unless we first understand its meaning, so we should be clear about the symbolism we are employing. That, according to Cusanus, explains the superiority of mathematical symbols: they "are very fixed and are very certain to us." Think of $2 + 2 = 4$ or a circle!

In his high estimation of mathematics Cusanus was of course by no means alone. He knew himself to be part of a tradition, inaugurated by Pythagoras and Plato. He could also have invoked the authority of St. Thomas, who insists that unlike physics or theology, mathematics can claim to provide us with firm knowledge.[4]

---

4. Isabelle Mandrella, "Der wissenschaftstheoretische Primat im Denken des Cusanus: Mathematik oder Metaphysik?," in *Das Mathematikverständnis des Nikolaus von Kues: Mathematische, naturwissenschaftliche und philosophisch-theologische Dimensionen*, ed. Friedrich Pukelsheim and Harald Schwaetzer, Mitteilungen und Forschungsbeiträge der Cusanus-Gesellschaft 29 (Trier: Paulinus, 2005), 183–200.

IV. THE POWER OF MATHEMATICS

The two other kinds of theoretical science one could call opinion rather than scientific conception; theology because its object does not appear and is incomprehensible, physics because its matter is unstable and not clear. Mathematics alone will provide those who pursue it with a firm and secure faith in their investigation, as the proof follows indubitable ways.[5]

The greater reliability of mathematics does not mean that it should be ranked above theology, which investigates divine matters, matters that transcend what we can comprehend. And we must not forget that the reliability of mathematics is bought at the price of leaving reality behind: what grants mathematics its power, according to Aquinas, is the *abstractio formalis*, which abstracts from the qualitative properties of the material object to arrive at an object that is now thought in purely quantitative terms. "Line or circle are accordingly in their being, i.e. in reality always material, but they can be thought without recourse to the materiality our senses can perceive (*materia sensibilis*). The materiality which belongs to them according to the understanding Thomas calls *materia intelligibilis*, pure extension, which should be attributed to an object before definite qualities."[6]

Cusanus's understanding of the power of mathematics is not so very different. He, too, takes the mathematician to be concerned with a *materia intelligibilis* gained by leaving the sensible behind. But there is one crucial difference: Cusanus does not think that St. Thomas's understanding of *abstractio formalis* provides us with an adequate account of the genesis of mathematicals. "The human being does not find mathematical objects as given, which he then makes his own by means of a formal abstraction, but he first constructs them."[7] With his senses man does experience a world ordered in measure, number, and weight (Ws 11:21). That order informs his *anima sensitiva*, the sensible soul, which provides our reason with material by providing it with species—that is, with already ordered sensible information. That information provides the occasion for the construction of mathematical objects.[8]

Consider once more a circle! The mental image we form of a circle does presuppose the faculty of sight. But the circle we think by

---

5. Thomas Aquinas, *Expositio super De trinitate*, q. 6, a. 1, q. 2, ed. Bruno Decker (Leiden: E. J. Brill, 1965) 209, 21–26), cited in Mandrella, "Der wissenschaftstheoretische Primat," 188.

6. Mandrella, "Der wissenschaftstheoretische Primat," 187.

7. Mandrella, "Der wissenschaftstheoretische Primat," 197.

8. See Cusanus, *Compendium*, trans. Jasper Hopkins, in *Nicholas of Cusa on Wisdom and Knowledge* (Minneapolis: Banning, 1996), chapter 11, 35–36.

means of that image is not subject to change. It has no definite extension. Mathematicals are thus said by Cusanus to transcend the changeable material realm, and yet, dependent as they are on the imagination, they are said to be not altogether "free of material associations." Thus they provide us with something like a bridge joining the material and temporal to the invisible and eternal. Any material circle, no matter how well drawn, will fall short of the perfect circle in our mind (*IDM* 103), and yet we "see" the latter in the former. As Cusanus was to state this point some ten years later, in *De theologicis complementis* (1453), here using the example of a triangle:

> When a mathematician forms a polygon, he looks unto its infinite exemplar. For example, when he draws a trigonal quantity, he does not look unto a trigonal quantity but unto what is unqualifiedly trigonal and is free of all quantity and quality, of all magnitude and multitude. Hence, the fact that he draws something quantitative does not result from the exemplar; nor does he himself intend to make something quantitative. But because he cannot draw it [except in such a way] that the triangle which he mentally conceives becomes perceptible, there happens to it quantity, without which it cannot become perceptible. Therefore, the triangle unto which he looks is neither large nor small nor delimited in magnitude or multitude. Therefore, it is infinite.[9] (*TC* 755)

The right triangle Pythagoras had in mind when he proved his theorem was not some material object in time and space. It has no definite size. In that sense it can be said to be infinite. There is thus a sense in which the mathematician is in touch with what is infinite and timeless. To be sure, to make his triangle perceptible, Pythagoras had to draw it. But whatever triangle he may have drawn is not the "infinite exemplar" that allowed him to prove his theorem.

But how then do we arrive at the idea of the "infinite exemplars" of a timeless triangle or a timeless circle? By abstracting it from changeable experience? But how can what is temporal generate something infinite and timeless? In subsequent works Cusanus returns to this question.

In the trialogue *Idiota de Mente, The Layman on Mind* (1450), Cusanus invokes quite explicitly the mind's immutability to account for the generation of such timeless exemplars:

9. Nicholas de Cusa, *Complementary Theological Considerations* [*De Theologicis Complementis*], trans. Jasper Hopkins, in *Nicholas of Cusa: Metaphysical Speculations; Six Latin Texts*, trans. Jasper Hopkins (Minneapolis: Banning, 1998); hereafter *TC*.

IV. THE POWER OF MATHEMATICS

> Hereafter, when our mind (not insofar as it is operative in a body that it enlivens but insofar as it is mind per se, yet unitable to a body) looks unto its own immutability, it makes assimilations of forms not as they are embedded in matter but as they are in and of themselves. And it conceives the immutable quiddities of things, using itself as its own instrument, apart from any instrumental [corporeal] spirit—as, for example, when it conceives a circle to be a figure from whose center all lines that are extended to the circumference are equal. (*IDM* 103)

The circle in the mind is such an assimilation. In the world there can be no two things that are precisely equal. In it we will never find a perfect circle—that is, one with radii that are all precisely equal. But things are different when we turn to mathematicals. Looking at a circle in some patterned pavement or imagining a circle, we have no difficulty thinking of a perfect circle, a circle that cannot be found in what is material and changing. That immutable circle exists only in our mind. Looking at some material circle, we create it. Such creation shows that our mind transcends its temporal condition.

Numbers are similar creations. We never will encounter, say, a "7" in the world, but we have no difficulty counting the days of the week or the eggs in some basket. Number as we know it is also a creation of the human mind, an unfolding of the one. But man was created in the image of God. Number, too, therefore has its divine counterpart:

> Hence, number, which is derived from mind, must be judged to be something different insofar as it is from the oneness of the Uncreated Mind and insofar as it is from a created mind. For the oneness of the former number is analogous to natural form, whereas the oneness of the latter number is analogous to an artificial form. (*TC* 10)

Something analogous can be said of the concepts we form of things. We create these artificial forms not ex nihilo, as God created the world, but in response to God's creation as it presents itself to our senses in which we glimpse, if only *in speculo et aenigmate*, the natural form created by God. To speak here of abstraction is misleading if meant to suggest that the concept "tree," named by the word, existed in some fashion already in nature. To be sure, there are trees. Looking at them our intellect is furnished with ordered sensible material. But "circle," "7," and "tree" are first of all creations of the human mind, responding to what we experience as an ordered nature. What we comprehend as the "immutable quiddities of things" are our creations but, to repeat, creations made in response to what we experience. Their immutability, however, has its foundation not in nature, but in the immutability of our human mind, which, transcending time and space, unfolds itself in assimilating itself to nature.[10]

There is, to be sure, a decisive difference between the concept of a circle and the concept of a tree. The concept of a tree is formed in response to our experience of a family resemblance between certain things. That experience provides the concept with something like a measure in nature, where for Cusanus that measure has its foundation in the divine Word that created the universe as an order of countless individual things, ordered in a way that invites us to speak of genera and species. The concepts of a circle, or of the number 7, on the other hand, provide us with the rule for their construction. There is no need here to appeal to nature. They are products of an unfolding of the human mind, which, to be sure, is awakened by its experience of nature, but with its mathematical constructions transcends nature and leaves it behind.

The mathematical sciences are understood by Cusanus as the products of this unfolding:

> Because mind as it is in itself, i.e., as free from matter, makes these assimilations [of immutable quiddities], it assimilates itself to abstract forms. In accordance with this power [of assimilation] it produces the mathematical branches of knowledge, which [deal in] certainty. (*IDM* 104)

What then grants mathematical signs their certainty? Cusanus points to the fact that here the mind is concerned with its own creations. We understand what we can create. The definition of a circle provides us with a rule for its construction; to understand the meaning of "7" requires only the ability to count, which Cusanus takes to be a presupposition of all thinking. Only hinted at in *De docta ignorantia*, this doctrine is unpacked in his later writings, especially in *Idiota de Mente*, *De Beryllo*, and *De Possest*:

> For regarding mathematical [entities], which proceed from our reason and which we experience to be in us as in their source [*principium*]: they are known by us as our entities and as rational entities; [and they are known] precisely, by our reason's precision, from which they proceed. (In a similar way, real things [*realia*] are known precisely, by the divine [intellect's] precision, from which they proceed into being.)

---

10. Cf. Führer, "Theory of the Intellect in Albert the Great," 48: "Nicholas is clearly carrying forward the Albertist idea that the assimilative intellect operates as a microcosm in this mirror-like operation of assimilation."

IV. THE POWER OF MATHEMATICS

> These mathematical [entities] are neither an essence (quid) nor a
> quality (*quale*); rather, they are notional entities elicited from our
> reason. (*DP* 43)

The human mind creates the measures it brings to things and, for
Cusanus more importantly, to God. Numbers provide the form of
these measures. Number can thus be considered the principle of our
reason. But we must not forget that Cusanus takes our creative mind
to be an image of the Creator.

I would like to underscore "to us" in the statement that mathematical symbols "are very fixed and are very certain to us" (*DI* I.11:31).
Cusanus takes the certainty of mathematics to be relative to us human knowers. He is not thinking here of a divine mathematics, which
must be thought to be beyond the *coincidentia oppositorum* and thus
as beyond our comprehension. God could no doubt square the circle. But to this divine mathematics our reason has no access. But as
we human beings were created in the image of God, so the human
mind—which, with the help of mathematics, unfolds itself in the progressive comprehension of nature—is an image of God, who unfolds
himself in the creation.

Just how the analogy of human to divine mathematics is to be
thought transcends our comprehension, even as it is a condition of
the comprehensibility of nature.

Let me return to the claim that, by their relative freedom from
material associations and their fixed character, mathematical symbols
are to be preferred. That every material circle, say one drawn on a
piece of paper, no matter how perfect, can never be more than an
approximation to the thought circle requires no further discussion.
Yet there are of course better and worse approximations. Cusanus
delights in the incommensurability of the mental measure and the
material thing measured. To him it is a sign that our mind transcends
what is material and perishable.

It is not only what he takes to be the "incorruptible certainty"
of mathematical signs that lets them open up "the pathway for approaching divine matters" (*DI* I.11:32), but, as the following chapters
show, the way they, by their very nature, lead us to the limit of what
our reason can comprehend and thus let us become learned about
our ignorance. Cusanus is thus fascinated by the incommensurability
between geometrical figures such as circle and square or of curved
and straight lines and the way such incommensurability vanishes
when we expand such figures ad infinitum. Aristotle had declared

that there can be no figure that is both circular and rectilinear.[11] Cusanus would grant this as far as our reason is concerned; but when we attempt to comprehend the infinite or the infinitesimal, our reason is forced to recognize its limits. I mentioned Dante, who found in the impossibility of squaring the circle a symbol of our inability to comprehend paradise. Cusanus found in it an expression of the inability of the *ratio* to comprehend the mathematically infinite, symbolizing the infinite God. But the very fact that human beings have attempted to square the circle presupposes some understanding of what success would involve and thus of the infinite. And does this not show that our mind is able to transcend the limits of reason in some sense, that there is in us a faculty, the intellect (*intellectus*), that allows us to rise above them?

Like Aristotle, Cusanus was convinced of the incommensurability of curved and straight lines and thus of the incommensurability of circle and square. As he puts it in *De Conjecturis*:

> The diameter of a circle is disproportional to the circumference, because reason does not attain the coincidence of such different things.
>
> To state many points very briefly: nothing in mathematics can be known by means of any other root [than the root-belief that a coincidence of opposites is unattainable]. Whatever [in mathematics] is demonstrated to be true is [shown to be] true from a consideration of the fact that unless it were true, a coincidence of opposites would be implied, and this result would constitute a going beyond reason. (*DC* 76–77)

But the reach of our intellect exceeds that of our reason. The incommensurability of diameter and circumference invites thoughts of a higher geometry where what our geometry finds incommensurable would be resolved. For Cusanus, too, the attempt to square the circle—that is, to construct a square with straightedge and compass, possessing an area exactly equal to a given circle—is a symbol of the, in the end, impossible attempt to comprehend the infinite essence of God. That helps to explain his fascination with the problem.

Cusanus knew that to solve that problem would be equivalent to providing the exact value of π. Albert of Saxony and with him "almost the entire Middle Ages"[12] had taken the value of π to be $3\frac{1}{7}$. Cusanus

11. Aristotle, *Metaphysics* H.10422b.

12. Cantor, *Vorlesungen über Geschichte der Mathematik*, 192. I would like to thank Katherine O'Brien, whose senior essay, "Cardinality and the Cardinal: Reflecting on Historical Constructions of the Infinite and God" (2007) taught me a great deal about the significance

would have encountered that value in Bradwardine's *Geometria speculativa*, which invokes the authority of Archimedes, although without familiarity with his work. Cusanus knew better: Archimedes had just been translated into Latin, and a copy of the translation had been given to Cusanus, who, as he tells us, read it with great interest.[13] Archimedes had established that the value of π had to be between $3\frac{1}{7}$ and $3\frac{10}{71}$.

In his conviction that it is impossible to square the circle, Cusanus was correct,[14] although it was only in 1768 that Johann Heinrich Lambert was able to prove the irrationality of π. And, as Ferdinand von Lindemann proved in 1882, the relation of diameter to circle can also not be expressed with the help of such algebraic operations as addition, squaring, and drawing the square root, π also cannot be constructed geometrically. We thus call π not only, like the square root of 2, an irrational, but a transcendental number. Cusanus, to be sure, would have resisted calling such numbers "numbers." "Number" to him meant a natural or counting number. This led him to insist that the area of a square can never be comprehended by us as equal to that of a circle. To us that seems counterintuitive, despite the fact that we know that the circle cannot be squared. But we are willing to consider π a number, albeit an irrational and transcendental number, and we may well want to agree with Leibniz that his "unification of geometry and arithmetic through algebraicization provides us with a perfect solution of this conundrum."[15] Cusanus's much more restricted understanding of number led him to reject what mathematicians have come to call the "intermediate value theorem."[16] Consider

---

of Cusanus's mathematical speculations. The essay includes a translation of the Cusanus chapter of Moritz Cantor's *Vorlesungen*, although the essay is primarily concerned with the way Cusanus anticipates some of Georg Cantor's key ideas.

13. As Cusanus tells us in *De mathematicis complementis*, the geometrical writings of Archimedes had been translated into Latin on behalf of Pope Nicholas V by Jacopus Cremonensis in 1450. The pope sent the translation to Cusanus, who responded by dedicating *De mathematicis complementis* to him; see Cusanus, *Von den mathematischen Ergänzungen* (*De Mathematicis complementis*), in Nikolaus von Cues, *Die mathematischen Schriften*, 68–69; see also 215n3; cf. Hofmann, "Einführung," xxi.

14. Hopkins denies this: "And his several mathematical writings evidence the attentiveness that he gave to geometry and to attempts to 'square the circle'—attempts that he did not know to be futile"; Hopkins, *Orienting Study*, I.14. But Cusanus did know them to be futile, as did Aristotle. To succeed we would have to comprehend the coincidence of curved and straight line, which our *visio intellectualis* allows us to think, but our reason cannot achieve, although with its contructions it can in principle appoach the sought solution ad infinitum so that, as far as our senses are concened, a difference can no longer be detected. Only in this sense can the circle be squared; see Hofmann, "Einführung," xix.

15. Johannes Hoff, *Analogical Turn*, 66.

16. Hofmann, "Einführung," xxi.

the following passage from chapter 1 of Book Three of *On Learned Ignorance*:

> Similarly, a square inscribed in a circle passes—with respect to the size of the circumscribing circle—from being a square which is smaller than the circle to being a square larger than the circle, without ever arriving at being equal to the circle. And an angle of incidence increases from being lesser than a right [angle] to being greater [than a right angle] without the medium of equality. (*DI* III.1:188)

The first sentence denies that the circle can be squared. But the intermediate value theorem holds that there can be no gap in the series of continuously expanding squares that Cusanus invites us to imagine, their area at first smaller, then larger than the area of some given circle.[17] It seems only reasonable to suppose that there has to be a square with an area exactly equal to the area of the given circle, even if to establish this we have to invoke the transcendental number π: $A = \pi r^2$. But Cusanus cannot make sense of such numbers. He is convinced that our reason is incapable of comprehending a square with an area precisely equal to a given circle, and that means that with its mathematical constructions our reason will never arrive at such a square. But he also recognizes what such a squaring of the circle would involve: a step that leaves reason, as he understands it, behind. Just as our intellect allows us to think of a circle with an infinite radius, where circumference and tangent, curved and straight line would coincide, so our intellect allows us to think of a polygon with infinite infinitesimal sides that would coincide with the circle. The intellect glimpses the infinitesimal for which the *ratio* has no room. And, as his wrestling with this problem in his mathematical treatises demonstrates, Cusanus is also convinced that in principle it is possible to get ever closer to the solution of the problem, so close in fact that the difference between what our reason can achieve and the precise value would no longer be perceptible. Cusanus, as Johannes Hoff remarks, would have been delighted at how well modern calculus works, even

---

17. Tamara Albertini claims that "On learned Ignorance does not allow for a merging of circle and polygon in the finite realm. Cusanus, however relaxed his stance in *On Squaring the Circle* (*De circuli quadratura*), where he introduced a new principle stating that 'where more and less can be given, equal can be given as well' (*ubi est dabile magis et minus, est et dabile equale*)"; Albertini, "Mathematics and Astronomy," in Bellitto, Izbicki, and Christianson, *Introducing Nicholas of Cusa*, 376. But in *De circuli quadratura* Cusanus disagrees with those scholars who rely on this principle. He grants, however, that if we mean by equality not absolute equality, but an approximation so great that our reason can no longer determine the difference—that is, that this difference becomes infinitesimal, then the circle can for all practical purposes be squared; see *Von der Quadratur des Kreises* (*De circuli quadratura*), in Nicolaus von Cues, *Die mathemaischen Schriften*, 37 and 41.

IV. THE POWER OF MATHEMATICS

if our mathematics, as Cusanus understands it, is such that it denies us the sought solution.[18] In the material world, he thought, the circle could be squared for our human purposes, and he did his best to provide a better approximation of π than his predecessors. As already mentioned, his efforts, which in places seem to leave all theology behind, have earned him a place in the history of mathematics, even if the great mathematician Regiomontanus (1436–76), a generation younger, was quite contemptuous of Cusanus's ability as a geometer, demonstrating that the efforts to which he had access failed to fall within the limits established by Archimedes. Regiomontanus was unaware of the *Transmutationes geometricae* (1445), where Cusanus did come up with an approximation that falls within the Archimedean limits, if in an intuitive way, lacking mathematical rigor.[19] Regiomontanus no doubt would not have been satisfied.

Notwithstanding his many efforts to square the circle, Cusanus was convinced "that the *coincidence of opposites* cannot be achieved on the level of rational comparisons (*coincidentiam vitandam*),[20] and that, consequently, mathematical comparisons can only provide us with *conjectures* and not *precise descriptions* of our analogical world."[21] As Hoff puts it, "We are not inhabiting a digital universe."[22]

The second sentence of the passage cited previously makes essentially the same point. The example of the angle of incidence, by which Cusanus means what Bradwardine called *angulus semicirculi*, the angle formed by the diameter of a circle and the semicircle, an angle larger than any acute angle, but smaller than a right angle, is clear enough: there would seem to be no such angle. Once again, the intermediate value theorem seems not to hold. And yet we have no difficulty seeing how the semicircle swings away from the perpendicular.[23] Both examples show that the infinite, both as minimum and as maximum, lurks in our geometrical constructions, lurks also in our mind, which is provoked by its elusive presence to think of the infinite God.

Even though in some of his writings Cusanus would appear to have

18. Hofmann, "Einführung," xxi. See also Hofmann, "Sinn und Bedeutung," 394–95.

19. Tony Phillips, "How Not to Square the Circle," in *Monthly Essays on Mathematical Topics*, Posted May 2011, American Mathematical Society, www.ams.org/feature-column/fcarc-cusa.

20. Nicholas de Cusa, *De Coniecturis*, ed. Josef Koch, Karl Bormann, and Hans G. Senger (Hamburg: Meiner Verlag, 1972) (hereafter *DCI*); Translation *De coniecturis: On Surmises*, by Nicholas of Cusa, in *Nicholas of Cusa: Metaphysical Speculations*, trans. Jasper Hopkins (Minneapolis: Banning, 2000), I.n77.

21. Hoff, *Analogical Turn*, 67.

22. Hoff, *Analogical Turn*, 68. My emphasis.

23. Hoff, *Analogical Turn*, 68. See also *PTW* I.105–6n188, 106–8.

come to think as a pure mathematician, "grappling with mathematical subjects as a true scientist, who, in an objective proof, will admit only facts and logical conclusions based on fact,"[24] his interest in mathematics remained subordinate to his desire to exhibit the power of mathematical symbols to lead us to a better understanding of the incomprehensible deity. He cites Boethius, "the most learned of the Romans," as a thinker who insisted that some understanding of mathematics was a presupposition of gaining some understanding of divine matters (*DI* I.31).[25] Presupposed is Cusanus's conviction that there is an analogy between divine and human mathematics, an analogy that, while incomprehensible, is yet supported by his understanding of the human being as *imago Dei*. In this conviction he feels himself confirmed by the Pythagorean-Platonic tradition:

> Did not Pythagoras, the first philosopher both in name and in fact, consider all investigation of truth to be by means of numbers? The Platonists and also our leading [thinkers] followed him to such an extent that our Augustine,[26] and after him Boethius,[27] affirmed that, assuredly, in the mind of the Creator number was the principal exemplar of the things to be created. (*DI* I.11:33)

Even Aristotle is said to have relied on mathematical symbols to explain the difference of species[28] or how one form can be in another.[29]

> Proceeding on this pathway of the ancients, I concur with them and say that since the pathway for approaching divine matters is opened to us only through symbols, we can make quite suitable use of mathematical signs because of their incorruptible certainty. (*DI* I.11:32)

But it is not just the incorruptible certainty of mathematical symbols that lets Cusanus embrace them in his attempts to approach the timeless deity but, as already suggested and as the following chapters demonstrate, the way the mathematical imagination is inescapably drawn to the infinite. Having been created in the image of the infinite God, the human mind bears the infinite within itself. It is to God's "infinite fecundity" that the mathematician looks with his creations. (*TC* 6)

---

24. Joseph Ehrenfried Hofmann, *The History of Mathematics*, trans. Frank Gaynor and Henrietta O. Midonick (New York: Philosophical Library, 1957), 78.

25. Boethius, *De Institutione Arithmetica*, I.1, ed. G. Friedlein (1867; repr. Frankfurt: Minerva, 1966), 9–11.

26. Augustine, *Ad Orosium contra Pricillianistas et Origenistas* 8, PL 42:674.

27. Boethius, *De Institutione Arithmetica* I.2.12.

28. Aristotle, *Metaphysics* VIII.3.1044a.10–11.

29. Aristotle, *De Anima* II.414b29.1–32.

The Way in Which Mathematical Signs Ought to Be Used in Our Undertaking

Chapter 12 is once more introductory: it is to help the reader to better understand Cusanus's use of mathematical symbols, his symbolic investigation of the Absolute (*symbolice investigare*) in the following six chapters. How are mathematical symbols, which according to Cusanus are necessarily finite, to help us think the infinite being of God? Gregor von Heimburg, Cusanus's implacable enemy ever since the latter's embrace of the papal cause at the Council of Basel, ridiculed Cusanus's "attempts to explain the mysteries of the true religion with mathematical superstition."[1] But these attempts are not dismissed quite so easily.

> Since from the preceding [points] it is evident that the unqualifiedly Maximum cannot be any of the things which we either know or conceive: when we set out to investigate the Maximum symbolically, we must leap beyond simple likeness. For since all mathematicals are finite and otherwise could not even be imagined if we want to use finite things as a way for ascending to the unqualifiedly Maximum, we must first consider finite mathematical figures together with their characteristics and relations. (*DI* I.12:33)

1. Jäger, *Der Streit des Cardinals Nicolaus von Cusa*, 2:236.

Consider the relationships that hold between finite mathematical figures, such as a circle and an inscribed polygon! Try to determine the angle formed by the circle and the side of the inscribed polygon. Here, as in the attempt to square the circle, although concerned with finite figures that are easily constructed, we find ourselves already involved with relations that our reason cannot quite fathom. The infinite lurks in the finite. Such incommensurability showed itself to the Pythagoreans when they tried to determine the relationship of the side of a square to the diagonal: the square root of 2 proved to be irrational. But "in all realms of mathematics we meet with the irrational incommensurability that so upset the Pythagoreans. The infinite is productive not only because it makes possible an ever-improving approximation, but also because it forces us to suppose as a real limit the precise existence of the irrational proportion."[2] It also forces us to recognize that our reason is incapable of comprehending that proportion. It transcends the reach of our reason and its logic. Such irrationality is an expression of the lack of proportion between the infinite and the finite, even as it shows the presence of irrationality in the finite.

> Next, [we must] apply these relations, in a transformed way, to corresponding infinite mathematical figures. (*DI* I.12:33)

Consider once more the relation of tangent to circle. As we increase in our imagination the radius of the circle to infinity, straight and curved line will come to coincide, an example of the coincidence of opposites.

Cusanus would then have us rid ourselves of all reference to figures:

> Thirdly, [we must] thereafter in a still more highly transformed way, apply the relations of these infinite figures to the simple Infinite, which is altogether independent even of all figure. At this point our ignorance will be taught incomprehensibly how we are to think more correctly and truly about the Most High as we grope by means of a symbolism. (*DI* I.12:33)

Think of an infinite triangle as a symbol of the Trinity: the three persons will be seen to coincide in the Infinite One.

Cusanus's *ex imagine inquisitio,* his image-based inquiry into the Absolute (*DI* I.12:31), proceeds thus in three steps:

<hr>

2. Gandillac, *Nikolaus von Kues,* 168.

IV. THE POWER OF MATHEMATICS

1. First comes a consideration of the unchanging forms of geometry and their relationships—for instance, the relationship of circle and inscribed polygon.

2. These geometrical figures are then expanded in our imagination to infinity. Circle and polygon now come to coincide.

3. These infinite figures and the coincidence of opposites that they show are then transformed by pushing our intellect to jettison all figures into a symbol of the incomprehensible Absolute.[3]

The following chapters exemplify both the power and the limits of this *inquisitio ex imagine*.

The chapter concludes with examples that by now are not unexpected:

> Operating in this way, then, and beginning under the guidance of the maximum Truth, I affirm what the holy men and the most exalted intellects who applied themselves to figures have stated in various ways. The most devout Anselm compared the maximum Truth to infinite rectitude. (Let me, following him, have recourse to the figure of rectitude, which I picture as a straight line.) Others who are very talented compared to the Super-blessed Trinity a triangle consisting of three equal right angles. Since, necessarily, such a triangle has infinite sides, as will be shown, it can be called an infinite triangle. (These men I will also follow.) Others who have attempted to befigure infinite oneness have spoken of God as an infinite circle. But those who considered the most actual existence of God affirmed that He is an infinite sphere, as it were. I will show that all of these [men] have rightly conceived of the Maximum and that the opinion of them all is a single opinion. (*DI* I.12:34)

In *De veritate* Anselm symbolized the highest truth (*summa veritas*) by the straight line.[4] The infinite triangle and circle Cusanus could find in Heymeric de Campo's *Tractatus de sigillo aeternitatis*, which he owned[5] The infinite sphere, a key metaphor for Cusanus, he found in Meister Eckhart, who in turn found it in the *Book of the XXIV Philosophers*.[6] In Alan of Lille's *Regulae Theologicae* we meet with the closely

---

3. See Johannes Hoff, "Die sich selbst zurücknehmende Inszenierung von Reden und Schweigen: Zur mystagogischen Rhetorik des Nikolaus von Kues," in *Religion und Rhetorik: Entwicklungen und Paradoxien ihrer unvermeidlichen Allianz, Religionswissenschaft heute*, ed. Holt Meyer and Dirk Uffelmann (Stuttgart: Kohlhammer, 2007), 224.

4. Anselm of Canterbury, *De veritate* I and X, trans. J. Hopkins and H. Richardson (New York: Mellen 1976), 2:77 and 91–92; cf. Jasper Hopkins, "Nicholas of Cusa's Intellectual Relationship to Anselm of Canterbury," in Casarella, *Cusanus: The Legacy of Learned Ignorance*, 60.

5. See *PTW* I:120n345.

6. See Dietrich Mahnke, *Unendliche Sphäre und Allmittelpunkt* (Halle: Niemeyer, 1937),

related description of God as an intelligible sphere.[7] Cusanus would seem to have made use of this text as well.[8] His preference for *infinitus* rather than *intelligibilis* invites question. So does his characterization of the infinite sphere as a particularly apt symbol for "the most actual existence of God," *actualissimam dei existentiam?* I shall return to the symbol of the infinite sphere in my discussion of chapter 23 and again in my discussion of Book Two.

---

and Herbert Wackerzapp, "Der Einfluss Meister Eckharts auf die ersten philosophischen Schriften des Nikolaus von Kues," *Beiträge zur Geschichte der Philosophie in der Theologie des Mittelalters* 39, no. 3 (1962): 140ff.

7. Alanus ab Insulis, *Regulae Theologicae, Regula* XIIII, PL 210:627. See also ab Insulis, *Sermo de sphaera intelligibili: Textes inédits,* ed. M. Th. d'Alverny, Études de Philosophie Médiévales 52 (Paris: Vrin, 1965), 297–306.

8. Edward J. Butterworth, "Form and Significance of the Sphere in Nicholas of Cusa's *De Ludo Globi,*" in Christianson and Izbicki, *Nicholas of Cusa: In Search of God and Wisdom,* 89–100.

The Characteristics of a Maximum Infinite Line

In the preceding chapter Cusanus had outlined an image-based inquiry into the Absolute: The forms of geometry and their relationships are expanded in our imagination to infinity so that what were opposites are now seen to coincide. That coincidence of opposites is taken to symbolize the incomprehensible infinite Absolute.[1] Chapter 13 provides us with examples of this three-step inquiry. The point of departure is a straight line. Two diagrams are to help us "see" "that if there were an infinite line, it would be a straight line, a triangle, a circle, and sphere" (*DI* I.13:35). The subjunctive is important: as pointed out, there can of course be no such line. When we attempt to imagine an infinite line, we are unable to fully comprehend what we trying to imagine; and that goes also for the distinction between line, triangle, circle, and sphere: we can imagine them only as finite. The turn to the infinite lets the distinction between them evaporate. But does this justify the claim that triangle, circle, and sphere coincide with the infinite line? That thought would seem to require us to hold on to the distinction even as we are forced to let go of it. Cusanus's claim certainly calls for some explanation.

1. See Hoff, "Die sich selbst zurücknehmende Inszenierung von Reden und Schweigen," 224.

To support this claim Cusanus offers us two diagrams. The first invites us to think of the relationship of ever-expanding circles to their tangent.[2]

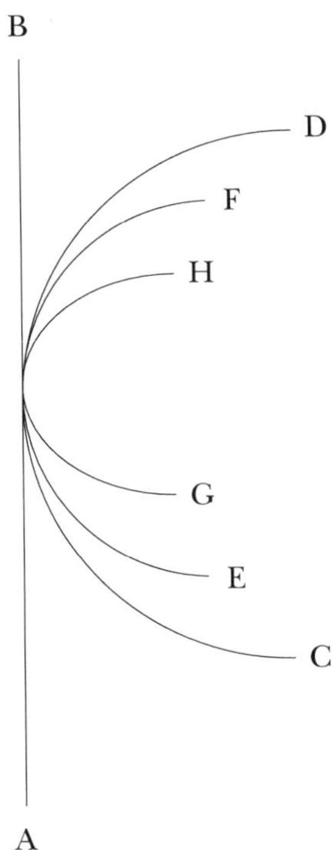

That the circumference of the maximum circle appears to be minimally curved and maximally straight is easily granted. We can, as Cusanus puts it, "visually recognize that it is necessary for the maximum line to be maximally straight and minimally curved" (*DI* I.13:35). Whether we begin with a straight line or a circle does not matter. Given a circle with an infinite radius, straight and curved line could no longer be distinguished. "In the maximum line curvature is straightness" (*DI* I.13:35).

The "proof" offered for the claim that the infinite line is a maximum triangle, circle, and square invites question. To say that the thought of an infinite line lets the distinction between line, circle, and sphere evaporate is one thing; to say that in the infinite line,

2. The source would seem to be Bradwardinus, *Geometrria speculativa,* tract. II, cap. 4., concl. 6. See *PTW* I:121n35, and Hofmann, "Einführung," xi.

IV. THE POWER OF MATHEMATICS

line, circle, and sphere are one quite another. The reader is asked to embrace the paradox that in the infinite line these three are one.

> Secondly, I said that an infinite line is a maximum triangle, a maximum circle, and a [maximum] sphere. In order to demonstrate this, we must in the case of finite lines see what is present in the potency of a finite line. And that which we are examining will become clearer to us on the basis of the fact that an infinite line is, actually, whatever is present in the potency of a finite line. (*DI* I.13:36)

Once again a diagram is to help us accept this difficult to accept claim.

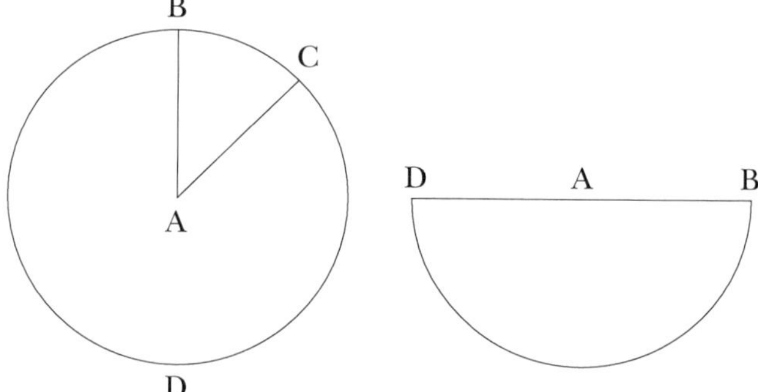

Hopkins calls our attention to the shift from the subjunctive of the beginning, "if there were an infinite line," which denies that there is an actual infinite line to the indicative: the infinite line is said to be "actually" all the finite line can be (*OLI* 10). Cusanus, however, does not claim that there exists an actual infinite line. But given some finite straight line, the possibility of extending it to infinity suggests itself. And then we can inquire into what properties such a line "actually" must possess.

Cusanus's appeal to "the potency of a finite line" raises questions. In our imagination a straight line can be extended or expanded ad infinitum. And so can any other line. In that sense we can say that an infinite line is present in the potency of a finite line. But that potency resides not so much in the potency of the finite line as in our intellect, which can play with that line in countless ways. So understood, the potency of the line is not exhausted by its extendability, as shown by the second diagram. Consider some such line AB. It can be rotated around A first in two, then in three dimensions so that triangle, circle, and finally sphere are generated.

> And the sphere is the termination of the potency of the line. The sphere exists in complete actuality since it is not in potency with respect to any further derivable figure. Therefore, if these figures are present in the potency of a finite line and if an infinite line is actually all the things with respect to which a finite line is in potency, then it follows that an infinite line is a triangle, a circle, and a sphere. Q.E.D. (*DI* I.13:36)

Despite the triumphant Q.E.D., Cusanus has not provided us with a convincing proof. Any line can in our imagination be expanded ad infinitum. Such a line can also be rotated as suggested, generating triangle and circle and sphere. Since the space of our imagination is three-dimensional, the sphere can be said not to be in potency with respect to any further derivable figure, unlike line and circle, which can be rotated to generate circle and sphere. Cusanus does not consider the possibility of a fourth dimension. But when we attempt to extend the straight line AB in our imagination to infinity and then try to repeat the rotation, we find it difficult to do so. Does the infinite line have a beginning point, an A? We need such an A to construct a triangle, a circle, a sphere. The move to the infinite lets the distinction between these figures evaporate. As Cusanus puts it, in the infinite line triangle, circle, and sphere coincide. But this formulation supposes that even as the distinction between these figures evaporates as we extend them to the infinite, there is yet some sense in which we can hold on to it. This allows him to say, "If these figures are present in the potency of a finite line and if an infinite line is actually all the things with respect to which a finite line is in potency, then it follows that an infinite line is a triangle, a circle, and a sphere." Cusanus's interest in leading us to a better understanding of the Trinity is a presupposition of his "proof." That much here remains less than clear he recognizes:

> And because, presumably, you would like to see more clearly how it is that the infinite is actually those things that are present in the potency of the finite, I will now make you very certain thereof. (*DI* I.13:36)

An Infinite Line Is a Triangle

An infinite triangle cannot be imagined; but, Cusanus insists, it can be thought. That this thought leads into paradox he not only recognizes but welcomes: as long as we remain committed to the law of non-contradiction, the mystery of the Trinity will have no meaning for us. The problematic ascent from what can be imagined to what can only be thought is demanded by Cusanus's image-based inquiry into the Absolute. To clarify the nature of this ascent Cusanus begins chapter 14 by calling our attention to the distinction between imagination and intellect.

> Since in the case of quantitative things a line and a triangle differ incomparably, the imagination, which does not transcend the genus of perceptible things, does not apprehend that the former can be the latter. However, this [apprehending] will be easy for the intellect. It is already evident that there can be only one maximum and infinite thing. Moreover, since any two sides of any triangle cannot, if conjoined, be shorter than the third, it is evident that in the case of a triangle whose one side is infinite, the other two sides are not shorter [that is, are together infinite]. And because each part of what is infinite is infinite, for any triangle whose one side is infinite, the other sides must also be infinite. And since there cannot be more than one infinite thing, you understand transcendently that an infinite triangle cannot be composed of a plurality of lines, even though it is the greatest and truest triangle, incomposite and most simple. (*DI* I. 14:37)

The claim that we can think an infinite triangle, that the infinite triangle is "the greatest and truest triangle, incomposite and most simple," invites question. That Cusanus speaks of the infinite triangle as he does shows that there is a sense in which we are able to think such a triangle. But to take that thought seriously we must embrace a paradox. That of course is Cusanus's very point. Every attempt to raise something finite to infinity will end with a paradox. Here, it is the attempt to think an infinite triangle. Since the sum of any two sides of a triangle cannot be smaller than the third, in the case of a triangle with an infinite side, the sum of the other two sides must also be infinite, and since Cusanus thinks he has shown that there can be only one infinite (*DI* I.14:37), the three sides become one in the infinite line, a symbol of the Trinity.[1]

To help us ascend from a finite triangle to one that is infinite and transcends the reach of our reason and to find in this "non-quantitative triangle" a symbol of the incomprehensible Trinity, Cusanus offers us a second example: increase one angle of the triangle until it equals two right angles. At this point the triangle collapses and becomes a line.

> Furthermore, you can be helped to understand the foregoing if you ascend from a quantitative triangle to a non-quantitative triangle. Clearly, every quantitative triangle has three angles equal to two right angles. And so, the larger the one angle is, the smaller are the other two. Now, any one angle can be increased almost but (in accordance with our first premise) not completely up to the size of two right angles. Nevertheless, let us hypothesize that it is increased completely up to the size of two right angles while the triangle remains [nonetheless a triangle]. In that case, it will be obvious that the triangle has one angle which is three angles and that the three angles are one. (*DI* I.14:38)

We may want to question the hypothesis that "the triangle remains" when one angle is increased to 180 degrees. Cusanus would grant that our imagination and reason would have us reject this hypothesis. But think of a series of ever flatter triangles, which terminates in a triangle that coincides with the base line. Just as the maximum number is said by Cusanus to remain a number, so the triangle flattened to coincide with the line is said to remain a triangle.

We may want to object: but now we no longer have a triangle. Cusanus grants this: as long as we think of quantitative triangles, the

---

1. Georg Cantor would disagree. Cusanus might reply that Cantor's infinite is not yet the negative infinite that he has in mind.

resulting line can no longer be called a triangle. But our ability to think, he claims, is not limited in that way:

> Hence, by means of this hypothesis, which cannot hold true for quantitative things, you can be helped in ascending to non-quantitative things; that which is impossible for quantitative things, you see to be altogether necessary for non-quantitative things. Hereby it is evident that an infinite line is a maximum triangle. Q.E.D. (*DI* I.14:39)

To be sure, the hypothesis that the triangle collapsed into a line still remains a triangle is difficult to accept. The difficulty is analogous to the difficulty we have considering the maximum number a number. And yet Cusanus's reasoning is not difficult to follow. If we are willing to accept his hypothesis of a non-quantitative triangle, we can also accept his conclusion: that an infinite line is a maximum triangle. But a non-quantitative triangle is a wooden iron, analogous to that of the maximum number. Cusanus offers us his examples to help us ascend to what he knows is paradoxical. But the coincidence of opposites is the gate in the wall of reason that allows us to glimpse paradise.

CHAPTER 15

The Maximum Triangle Is a Circle and a Sphere

Given the preceding, the claim that the infinite triangle should coincide with the infinite circle cannot surprise. But to accept it we must be able to make sense of Cusanus's non-quantitative figures. To follow his examples, we must hold on to essentially finite figures, even as we expand them and let them become infinite. That this translation into the infinite lets the difference between triangle and circle disappear we can grant. But to still speak here of the coincidence of triangle and circle we must also be able to hold on in a non-quantitative way to both triangle and circle.

To support his claim, Cusanus once again invites the reader to consider a diagram. As suggested, we can follow the argument that the maximum triangle is a circle if we are prepared to grant Cusanus that it makes sense to speak of a maximum, and that means infinite and thus non quantitative, triangle and circle:

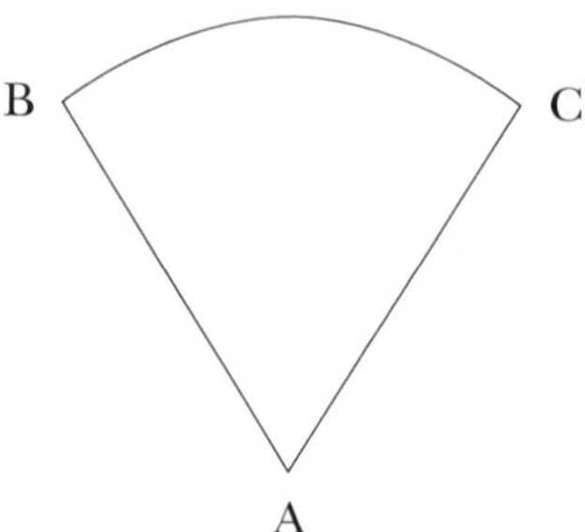

Next, we shall see more clearly that a triangle is a circle. Let us postulate the triangle ABC, formed by rotating the line AB—A remaining stationary—until B comes to C. There is no doubt that if line AB were infinite and B were rotated until it came all the way back to the starting point, a maximum circle would be formed, of which BC would be a portion. Now, because BC is a portion of an infinite arc, BC is a straight line. And since every part of what is infinite is infinite, BC is not shorter than the whole arc of infinite circumference. Hence, BC will be not only a portion but the most complete circumference. Therefore, it is necessary that the triangle ABC be a maximum circle. And because the circumference BC is a straight line, it is not greater than the infinite line AB; for there is nothing greater than what is infinite. Nor are there two lines, because there cannot be two infinite things. Therefore, the infinite line, which is a triangle, is also a circle. And [this is] what was proposed [for proof]. (*DI* I.15:40)

To accept this argument, we must grant Cusanus that in thinking about geometric figures our intellect is not bound by the imagination. And must we not grant it? We have no difficulty thinking about a fourth dimension, although the imagination is left behind. This, to be sure, is a thought foreign to Cusanus. But his claim that the human intellect is not bound by the imagination must be accepted. This raises, however, the question: what is the being of that infinite line that is also an infinite triangle, an infinite circle, and an infinite sphere? Is it more than a paradoxical mental construct that can have no relation to reality? What justifies Cusanus's understanding of it as a symbol of the triune God?

The argument of the quoted paragraph depends on the claim that there cannot be different infinites, one greater than the other. Is that obvious? Georg Cantor, for one, would have denied that. But given Cusanus's understanding of the infinite as the maximum, it would seem that the claim can be accepted: if there were two infinites, we could add the two and a greater infinite would result, but this would be incompatible with the presupposed understanding of the infinite as the maximum. God is the Maximum. But surely Cusanus does not want to say that the maximum line, which is a triangle, a circle, and a sphere, is God: it is a symbol of God. But do we then not have to distinguish between infinites after all? The geometric maximum is a human construct, which has no being except in our mind. What makes the generation of that construct possible is an idea of the infinite that is inseparably bound up with our freedom. God, the Absolute Maximum, however, is thought to exist, and not only in our mind. That the geometric maximum can symbolize the Absolute Maximum has its foundation in Cusanus's understanding of the human being as *imago Dei*. Unfolding itself in whatever it can comprehend and think, it resembles God, the infinite One, who unfolds himself in whatever is and can be. The human infinite we can think in some fashion. But what about the divine infinite?

Despite Cusanus's assertion that it is most clear, *manifestissimum* (*DI* I.14:41), the "proof" of the second claim, that the maximum triangle is a sphere, seems hardly perspicuous. How are we to understand the turn from the second to the third dimension? Does the distinction among the three dimensions even make sense once we have left behind quantitative figures?

> Moreover, that an infinite line is a sphere becomes very obvious in the following way: The line AB is the circumference of the maximum circle—indeed, it is the [maximum] circle, as was just proved. And, in the triangle ABC, AB was brought from B to C, as was previously stated. But BC is an infinite line, as was also just proved. Hence, AB [which is the maximum circle] reached C by a complete coming around upon itself. And since this is the case, it follows of necessity that from such a coming around of a circle upon itself a sphere is originated. And given that we previously proved that ABC is a circle, a triangle, and a line, we have now proved that it is also a sphere. And these are [the results] we set out to find. (*DI* I.15:44)

What makes the "proof" less than perspicuous is once more that, with the demanded infinitization of finite figures such as that in the illustration, we lose hold of the distinction between them and thus of his image of a circle rotating around its axis to generate a sphere. To follow Cusanus's mathematical examples we must retain one foot in the finite even as our intellect reaches for the infinite. Must the same then not also be said of all our attempts to understand God? Take away that foot in the finite and God vanishes.

CHAPTER 16

In a Symbolic Way the Maximum Is to All Things as a Maximum Line Is to [All] Lines

In this chapter Cusanus begins to unpack the symbolic significance of his mathematical play with the infinite. That we human beings can play with thoughts of the infinite as he does demands consideration. Despite whatever questions we may have, we can follow Cusanus in some fashion and think the coincidence of the infinite triangle and the infinite circle. This does show that our intellect is not bound to the finite—that we are free to transcend the finite in our thoughts, free even to embrace what is paradoxical.

That our freedom knows no boundaries was later emphasized by Descartes in Meditation IV: "It is only the will, or freedom of choice, which I experience within me to be so great that the idea of any greater faculty is beyond my grasp; so much so that it is above all in virtue of the will that I understand myself to bear in some way the image and likeness of God."[1] Cusanus would have agreed. An awareness of the infinite is inseparable from our freedom. It allows us to imagine what is possible and oppose it to the actual; and it allows us to transcend the imagination altogether. Our intellect is not limited by what we can

---

1. Descartes, *Philosophical Writings of Descartes*, 2:40.

imagine or by what our reason can comprehend. It is the boundless freedom of thought that Cusanus, too, takes to show that we have been created in the image of God. And it is the freedom of thought that allows us to follow Cusanus's *ludi mathematici*, his mathematical games.

> Now that we have seen how it is that an infinite line is actually and infinitely all that which is in the possibility of a finite line, we likewise have a symbolism for seeing how it is that, in the case of the simple Maximum, this Maximum is actually and maximally all that which is in the possibility of Absolute Simplicity. For whatever is possible, this the Maximum is actually and maximally. [I do] not [mean] that it is from what is possible but rather that it is [what-is-possible] maximally. By comparison, a triangle is educed from a line; but an infinite line, [though a triangle], is not a triangle as [a triangle] is educed from a finite [line]; rather, [the infinite line] is actually an infinite triangle, which is identical with the [infinite] line. Moreover, absolute possibility is, in the Maximum, not other than actually the Maximum—just as an infinite line is actually a sphere. The situation is otherwise in the case of what is non-maximum. For in that case the possibility is not the actuality—even as a finite line is not a triangle. (*DI* I.16:42)

Just as the infinite line is understood by Cusanus to be the maximum of every possible finite figure or line, so God is said to be the Maximum of all that is and can possibly be. We should note the coincidence of possibility and actuality in the Maximum. From our human, inevitably finite, perspective God is all that is and can be. But the distinction between actual and possible, while it holds in the realm of the finite, cannot be applied to God.[2]

We may want to ask: what account can Cusanus then give of the creation of this actual world? What distinguishes it from the infinitely many other possible worlds we can think up? But to view things in this way *sub specie possibilitatis* is to remain subject to our human perspective. The creation of this world is not to be understood as a matter of God considering countless different possibilities, choosing to realize the best of all possible worlds.

> Hence, we notice here an important speculative consideration which, from the foregoing, can be inferred about the Maximum: viz., that the Maximum is such that in it the Minimum is the Maximum, and thus the Maximum infinitely and in every respect transcends all opposition. From this principle there can be elicited about the

---

2. See Cusanus, *Trialogus de possest.*

IV. THE POWER OF MATHEMATICS

> Maximum as many negative truths as can be written or read; indeed,
> all humanly apprehensible theology is elicited from this very great
> principle. (*DI* I.16:43)

We may well wonder whether such a negative theology is at all sufficient: so understood, God threatens to become an unfathomable
abyss, irrelevant to our human concerns. Must not a positive theology
supplement negative theology if God is to matter to us? To repeat:
must our thinking about God not retain one foot in the finite?

Cusanus claims to be following Dionysius the Areopagite, believed
by him, despite some doubts, to have been the Athenian convert of
St. Paul mentioned in Acts 17:34. As such the author of the *Corpus
Areopagiticum* identified himself, lending his work a false aura. Only
a few years after the composition of *De docta ignorantia* Lorenzo Valla
was to show in his commentaries on the New Testament (1457) that
the author's self-identification as the convert mentioned in Acts had
to be rejected. His dependence on the neo-Platonic tradition, especially on Proclus, is evident. So the author of the *Corpus Areopagiticum*
is now referred to as Pseudo-Dionysius and is dated to the late fifth
or early sixth century. To the reader of *De docta ignorantia* this matters
little. Cusanus's profound and problematic debt to the neo-Platonic
tradition, and especially to Pseudo-Dionysius, dating back at least to
his Cologne days with Heymeric de Campo, is evident and emphasized by Cusanus over and over.[3]

> Accordingly, the greatest seeker of God, Dionysius the Areopagite,
> declares in his *Mystical Theology*[4] that most blessed Bartholomew mar-
> velously understood theology, having called it the greatest and the
> least. For whoever understands this [point] understands all things;
> he transcends all created understanding. For God, who is this Maxi-
> mum, "is not this thing and is not any *other* thing; He is not *here* and
> is not *there*," as the same Dionysius says regarding the divine names[5];
> for just as He is all things, so He is not any of all the things. For, as
> Dionysius concludes at the end of *The Mystical Theology*: "above all
> affirmation God is the perfect and unique Cause of all things; and
> the excellence of Him who is unqualifiedly free from all things and
> is beyond all things is above the negation of all things."[6] Hence, he

3. See especially *De li non aliud,* which includes a florilegium of Dionysian texts.

4. Pseudo-Dionysius, *De mystica theologia* I.3, PG 3:1000.B; *Dionysiaca* I.572. Cusanus is
using the 1436 translation by Ambrosius Traversari; *PTW* I:121n453.

5. Pseudo-Dionysius, *De divinis nominibus* V.8, in PG 3.824AB; *Dionysiaca* I:355–56; *PTW*
I:121n43.

6. Pseudo-Dionysius, *De mystica theologia* I.3, PG 3:1048B; *Dionysiaca* I:601–2; *PTW*
I:121n43.

concludes in his *Letter to Gaius*[7] that God is known above every mind and all intelligence. (*DI* I.16: 43)

In Dionysius Cusanus could thus find his doctrine of the coincidence of opposites,[8] which, as mentioned, in *De Visione Dei*, he will liken to the wall of paradise. Only beyond that wall is God to be found.

The following reference to Moses Maimonides, called by Cusanus here Rabbi Solomon, is not based on a reading of the *Guide for the Perplexed*, but on quotations he had found in Meister Eckhart's *Exodus* commentary.[9] That Cusanus does not hesitate to join the Rabbi to Pseudo-Dionysius is of some interest, showing his interest in and openness to other religions.[10]

> And in harmony with this [verdict] Rabbi Solomon states that all the wise agreed that the sciences do not apprehend the Creator. Only He Himself apprehends what He is; our apprehension of Him is a defective approximation of His apprehension [*est defectus appropin-quandi apprensioni eius*—our apprehension is not just defective, it is that very failure to apprehend him]. Accordingly, Rabbi Solomon elsewhere says by way of conclusion, "Praised be the Creator! When His existence (*essentia*) is apprehended, the inquiry of the sciences is cut short, wisdom is reckoned as ignorance, and elegance of words as fatuity." And this is that learned ignorance which we are investigating. Dionysius [himself] endeavored to show in many ways that God can be found only through learned ignorance—[found] by no other principle, it seems to me, than the aforesaid. (*DI* I.16:44)

We are left with the question: what does such an understanding of God "through learned ignorance" have to offer us human beings?

---

7. Pseudo-Dionysius, *Epistula I ad Gaium* V.8, in PG 3:1065A; *PTW* I:121n43; *Dionysiaca* I:607.

8. Miller, *Reading Cusanus*, 20–24.

9. Wackerzapp, *Der Einfluss Meister Eckharts*, 8.

10. See Cusanus, *De Pace Fidei*.

Very Deep Doctrines from the Same [Symbolism of an Infinite Line]

Chapter 17 leads to the very core of Cusanus's thinking.

> Still more on the same topic: A finite line is divisible, and an infinite line is indivisible; for the infinite, in which the maximum coincides with the minimum, has no parts. However, a finite line is not divisible to the point that it is no longer a line, because in the case of magnitude we do not arrive at a minimum than which there cannot be a lesser—as was indicated earlier. Hence, a finite line is indivisible in its essence [*ratio*]; a line of one foot is not less a line than is a line of one cubit. It follows, then, that an infinite line is the essence of a finite line. Similarly, the unqualifiedly Maximum is the Essence of all things. But the essence (*ratio*) is the measure (*mensura*). Hence, Aristotle rightly says in the *Metaphysics* that the First is the measure [*metrum et mensura*] of all things because it is the Essence of all things. (68.17.47)

Cusanus calls the infinite line the essence of the finite line. What he has in mind is clear enough: every line is infinitely divisible. But dividing it we will only arrive at shorter lines, never at the point, although every line can be considered an unfolding of the point. In that sense all lines have the same essence. Similarly, by extending a line we will only arrive at ever longer lines, never at the maximum line, although every line can be considered a contraction of the infinite line. But infinite line and point cannot really be opposed if we accept the coincidence of maximum and minimum, of the infinite line and the point. Every line is divisible ad infinitum, but the essence of all lines, be it point or infinite line, is indivisible.

The thought invites being transferred to time. Every stretch of time would seem to be infinitely divisible and infinitely extendable. In that sense they all have the same essence: infinite time. How is infinite time to be thought? As the maximum, eternity, that coincides with the minimum, the moment?[1] Cusanus might remind us that the infinite line coincides with a circle. Nietzsche's doctrine of the eternal recurrence comes to mind. Should the essence of time then be said to be eternity? In this connection, consider Nietzsche's suggestion that the thought of the eternal recurrence represents the greatest "Annäherung des Werdens an das Sein,"[2] the greatest approximation of becoming to being. The measure of that approximation would be the coincidence of becoming and being. Cusanus would invoke God.

Questions are raised by Cusanus's claim that the Maximum of all things is both the essence and the measure of all things. That Cusanus should call the infinite line the essence of all finite lines is no surprise. But, being out of proportion with all finite lines, how can the infinite line provide finite lines with a measure? Not that Cusanus asserts this in the cited passage. Taking the infinite line to be a fitting symbol for God, he claims analogously that the essence of all things, their thingliness, is the infinite God. But what justifies the claim that "the essence is the measure"? Do finite things not require a finite measure? How can the Maximum, said to transcend and to be out of proportion with all things, also be the measure of all things? Cusanus's rather questionable invocation of the authority of Aristotle does not really help. Here the relevant passage:

> *Metaphysics* X.1.1052b.14–21: The name "element" means that it has this attribute, that there is something which is made of it as a primary constituent. And so with "cause" and "one" and all such terms. For this reason to be one is to be indivisible (being essentially a "this"

---

1. Cf. Cesare Catà, "Die paradoxale Frage der drei Weisen," 16, citing Cusanus sermon CCXVI: "Et attende, quod locus temporis est aeternitas sive nunc seu praesentia, et locus motus est quies, et locus numeri est unitas, etc. Nam quid videtur esse in tempore, nisi praesentia? Fluit enim tempus, et non est fluxus eius nisi de esse in esse." Cf *DI* II.2.

2. See Miriam Ommeln, "Die Aufnahme von Nietzsches Philosophie in die surrealistischen Ideen oder: Die Verkörperung von Nietzsches Ästhetik ist der Surrealismus," in *Die Auflösung des abendländischen Subjekts und das Schicksal Europas (Mit Nietzsche Denken)*, ed. Beatrix Vogel and Harald Seubert (Munich: Allitera Verlag, 2005), 173.

IV. THE POWER OF MATHEMATICS

and capable of existing apart either in place or in form or thought) or perhaps to be whole and indivisible; but it is especially to be the first measure of a kind, and above all of quantity; for it is from this that it has been extended to the other categories.

One is indeed the measure of number. But is it not the number one, rather than oneness, that is the measure of number? Oneness is constitutive of all numbers, but not their measure. It would seem therefore that if the Maximum is to provide finite things with a measure it must descend into the finite, as Cusanus's numerical Maximum can be said to do when the numerical minimum, one, is said to coincide with the maximum. But what among things can be said to furnish them with a measure, as one furnishes numbers with a measure? An answer will be provided in Book Three.

The symbol of the infinite line suggests to Cusanus the eternity and immutability of God.

> Furthermore: Just as an infinite line, which is the essence of a finite line, is indivisible and hence immutable and eternal, so also the Essence of all things, viz., Blessed God, is eternal and immutable. And herein is disclosed an understanding of the great Dionysius,[3] who says that the Essence [*essentia*] of things is incorruptible, and of others who have said that the Essence [*ratio*] of things is eternal. (*DI* I.17:48)

Given the preceding, this passage is clear enough. We should note, however, once more that, given the symbol of the infinite line, the essence of things can mean little more here than their being, their thingliness.

Of interest in this connection is the following passage, where Cusanus gives us his own understanding of Plato's theory of forms, based on a third-hand understanding of Plato.[4]

> For example, [let me mention] the divine Plato, who, as Chalcidius reports, stated in the *Phaedo* that, as it exists in itself, there is one Form or Idea of all things but [that] with respect to things, which are plural, there seems to be a plurality of forms. For example, when I consider a two-foot line, a three-foot line, and so on, two things appear: (1) the line's essence, which is one and equal in each and every line and (2) the difference which there is between a line of

---

3. Pseudo-Dionysius, *De mystica theologia* IV.23, in PG 3:724D; *PTW*, 122n48.

4. Wilpert points out that the erroneous reference to the *Phaedo*, instead of to the *Timaeus*, suggests that Cusanus was not relying on Chalcidius, *Commentarius in Platonis Timaeum*, but on some source citing Chalcidius without sufficient care; *PTW* I:122n48. Cf. Plato, *Timaeus* 31A.

> two feet and a line of three feet. And so, the essence of a two-foot line and the essence of a three-foot line seem to be different. However, it is obvious that in an infinite line a line of two feet and a line of three feet do not differ. Now, an infinite line is the essence of a finite line. Hence, there is one essence of both lines; and the difference between the things, or the lines, does not result from a difference of the essence, which is one, but results accidentally, because the lines do not participate equally in the essence. Hence, there is only one essence of all lines, and it is participated in different ways. (*DI* I.17:48)

This suggests that there is really only one form: God. The seeming multiplicity of forms is said to happen "accidentally," a product of the unequal participation of things in the divine essence, comparable to the unequal participation of numbers in the numerical Maximum. But how are we to understand this "accidentally"? Does God's omnipotence not rule out an appeal to accident to account for the multiplicity of forms and things? And what sense can we make of an unequal participation in the infinite God?

As mentioned, in the case of numbers their unequal participation depends on the number one, the numerical Minimum, said to coincide with the Maximum. It provides all numbers with a measure. But the infinitesimal point cannot provide lines with the needed measure, since point and line are incommensurable. We do, of course, speak of shorter and longer lines, but is the most fundamental measure not provided here by our own body? Think of a foot. Should something similar be said about things?

Cusanus attempts to shed light on the unequal participation of things in the divine essence by appealing to the fact that no thing can be exactly like another:

> But as for there being differences of participation: this occurs because (as we proved earlier), there cannot be two things which are exactly similar and which, consequently, participate precisely and equally in one essence. For only the Maximum, which is Infinite Essence, can participate with supreme equality in essence. Just as there is only one Maximum Oneness, so there can be only one Equality of Oneness. Because it is Maximum Equality, it is the Essence of all things. (*DI* I.17:49)

The Equality of Oneness is, of course, another name for the divine Word. Cusanus, too, identifies Plato's forms with the Divine Logos. But this does not tell us how we are to understand the unequal

IV. THE POWER OF MATHEMATICS

participation of things in the Divine Logos. Once again Cusanus offers us a mathematical analogy:

> Moreover, in a line of two feet an infinite line is neither longer nor
> shorter than the two-foot line, as was stated earlier. And similarly
> regarding lines of three feet and more. Now, since an infinite line is
> indivisible and one, it is present as a whole in each finite line. But it
> is not present as a whole in each finite line according to participa-
> tion and limitation; otherwise, when it was present as a whole in a
> line of two feet, it could not be present in a line of three feet, since
> a line of two feet is not a line of three feet. Therefore, it is present
> as a whole in each line in such way that it is not present in any line
> insofar as one line is distinct from the others through limitation.
> Therefore, the infinite line is present as a whole in each line in such
> [a] way that each line is present in it. Now, this [point] must be
> considered in both its aspects; for then we will see clearly how it is
> that the Maximum is in each thing and in no thing. This [symbolism
> of a line] symbolizes none other than the Maximum, since by sim-
> ilar reasoning the Maximum is [seen to be] in each thing, even as
> each thing [is seen to be] in it; moreover, [this symbolism] displays
> the reason that the Maximum exists in itself. Accordingly, the fact
> that the Maximum is the measure [*metrum et mensura*] of all things
> is not other than the fact that the unqualifiedly Maximum exists in
> itself—i.e., that the Maximum is the Maximum. Therefore, no thing
> exists in itself except the Maximum; and everything exists in itself
> insofar as it exists in its Essence [*ratio*], because its Essence (*ratio*) is
> the Maximum. (*DI* I.17:50)

Just as the infinite line is fully present in every finite line as its essence, no matter what its length, so God is fully present in every finite
thing as its essence. But as soon as a thing is experienced as distinct
from other things, it is infinitely distant from God. The mystery of
being is the mystery of God.

Cusanus's use of mathematical symbols can be read as an anticipation of Georg Cantor's set theory. Cusanus's discussion of infinite lines can be considered "a looser and more geometrical form
of [Cantor's] proof that the aggregate which holds all natural numbers is the same in size (or cardinality) as that which holds only even
ones." Cusanus "discovered that the common arithmetic of the finite
leaves the infinite unaffected."[5] Cantor, to be sure, proved that in
this mathematical sense there exists not just one infinite: cardinality

---

5. Katherine O'Brien, "Cardinality and the Cardinal: Reflecting on Historical Constructions of the Infinite and God," 26. Paper written for my seminar *Nicholas of Cusa and
Alberti*, Fall 2005.

does not exhaust the being of number; according to Cantor there exist transfinite numbers, "built from infinite sets in the same manner that finite numbers were built from finite ones."[6] The set of natural numbers, while infinite, is thus of a lower magnitude than the set of real numbers. Cusanus would have questioned Cantor's Platonic faith in the objective reality of numbers, including his transfinite numbers. He would have had to consider them, like all numbers, human constructions, constructions, however, that, like his own mathematical symbols, show that the human mind, having been created in the image of God, is open to the infinite—and that is to say, also to God. Cantor himself insisted on the relevance of his speculations to theology. "His discussion of the set of all sets,... he suggested, proved the existence of an Absolute God because it could not be well-defined by mathematics. In his writings, Cantor refers to these collections in explicitly theological terms. He explained that 'the true infinite or Absolute, which is in God, permits no determination' and embraced even Russell's paradoxes under this interpretation."[7] Although unable to accept Cantor's mathematical realism, Cusanus could have embraced the conclusion: the true infinite—that is, the Maximum— permits no determination. It presents itself to our understanding as no thing, in this sense as nothing.

Cusanus had no doubt that the symbolism of the infinite line can help us approach God in learned ignorance:

> From these [considerations] the intellect can be helped; and by the illustration of an infinite line, the intellect can in sacred ignorance very greatly advance beyond all understanding and toward the unqualifiedly Maximum. For here we have now seen clearly how we can arrive at God through removing the participation of beings. For all beings participate in Being. Therefore, if from all beings participation is removed, there remains most simple Being itself, which is the Essence (*essentia*) of all things. And we see such Being only in most learned ignorance; for when I remove from my mind all the things which participate in Being, it seems that nothing remains. Hence, the great Dionysius says that our understanding of God draws near to nothing rather than to something. But sacred ignorance teaches me that that which seems to the intellect to be nothing is the incomprehensible Maximum. (*DI* I.17:51)

What remains of God when we try to comprehend him by removing "the participation of beings"? To the intellect God, the incomprehensible

6. O'Brien, "Cardinality and the Cardinal," 6.
7. O'Brien, "Cardinality and the Cardinal," 6.

IV. THE POWER OF MATHEMATICS

Maximum, seems to be nothing. It would seem that so understood, God cannot be called the creator of a world comprised of indefinitely many things, each thing different from every other thing, participating—if we follow Cusanus—unequally in the Maximum. How are we to understand such participation? The following chapter attempts to provide an answer.

CHAPTER 18

From the Same [Symbolism] We Are Led to an Understanding of Participation in Being

In keeping with his faith, things are said by Cusanus to receive their being from God. To help us understand the unequal way things participate in God's being, he once again makes use of mathematical symbols. The way the being of finite things is said to derive from God's being is symbolized by the way the being of a curve is said to derive from straightness.

> Furthermore, our insatiable intellect, stimulated by the aforesaid, carefully and with very great delight inquires into how it can behold more clearly this participation in the one Maximum. And being once again aided by the illustration of an infinite straight line, it remarks: A curve, which admits of more or less, cannot be a maximum or a minimum. Nor is a curve, qua curve, anything—since it is a deficiency of what is straight. Therefore, the being which is in a curve derives from participation in straightness, since a curve, considered maximally and minimally, is only something straight. Therefore, the less a curve is a curve (e.g., the circumference of a quite large circle), the more it participates in straightness. [I do] not [mean] that it takes a part of it, because infinite straightness is not partible. Now,

IV. THE POWER OF MATHEMATICS

the longer a straight finite line is, the more it seems to participate in the infinity of an infinite, maximum line. (*DI* I.18:52)

There are thus degrees of participation in the Maximum: just as a straight line participates more fully in the infinite line than a curved line, substance participates more fully in the Maximum than accidents. This allows Cusanus to fit Aristotle's substance-accident ontology into his scheme: straight is to curved line as substance is to accident.

> Moreover, through this [illustration] we see how it is that there can be only beings which participate in the being of the First either through themselves or through other than themselves—just as there are only lines, either straight or curved. Wherefore, Aristotle was right in dividing all the things in the world into substance and accident. (*DI* I.15:53)

Neither "substance" nor "accident" applies to God. Substances, however, are said to participate more fully in the being of the First than accidents. For this reason, Dionysius is said to have been right when he called God super-substantial rather than super-accidental. But, as he reminds us, Cusanus is not interested in developing the ontology of substance and accident further (*DI* I.18:54). He is content to express some agreement with Aristotle, of whom he is so often very critical.

Given his first figure, Cusanus's attempt to shed some light on the participation of things in the Maximum with the analogy of more or less curved lines that have their measure in the straight tangent makes intuitive sense. But this impression depends on an image that lets us compare segments of smaller and larger circles. To the intellect, which looks beyond the visual presentation, all circles are equally curved. Doubling the diameter does not make a circle less curved.

Cusanus's claim that "the longer a straight finite line is, the more it seems to participate in the infinity of an infinite, maximum line" also invites questions. To be sure, just as a larger number seems to be closer to the numerical maximum than a smaller number, so a longer straight line seems to participate more fully in the infinite straight line than a shorter straight line, and a less curved line seems to participate more fully in straightness than a more strongly curved line.

> Just as an infinite line [is the measure] of a straight line and of a curved line, so the Maximum [is the measure] of all things which participate [in it], no matter how differently. (*DI* I.18:52)

But when we call one straight line longer than another, does the infinite line really provide the measure? Comparing the two lines is sufficient. As Cusanus recognizes, neither line can be considered a larger or smaller part of the infinite line. From that line both can be said to be infinitely distant. And following his analogy between lines and things, should we not say the same about things? Can the Maximum, so understood, function as their measure and in a way that allows us to say that they participate unequally in God?

We do, of course, distinguish between larger and smaller things. The most fundamental measure would be seen to be provided by the human body: a foot, an ell. Presupposed is also the human ability to count. That, as we have seen, can progress ad infinitum, but counting, we shall never arrive at a maximum. A finite measure is needed to measure things that are finite, just as the number "one" is needed to measure numbers. But where are we to find that measure? The God of Dionysius cannot provide Cusanus with what is needed.

V. EXCURSUS

Mathematics and the Study of Nature

CUSANUS'S ADVOCACY of mathematical symbols to describe the being of God makes it easy to overlook that the superiority of such symbols applies, according to him, not just to the pursuit of divine knowledge, but also to the study of God's creation, of nature. Just as Cusanus's interest in mathematics merited him a chapter in Moritz Cantor's monumental *Vorlesungen über Geschichte der Mathematik*,[1] his conviction that mathematical symbols will lead us to a deeper understanding of nature similarly deserves the attention of the historian of science. In this connection the little dialogue *Idiota de staticis experimentis, On Experiments Done with Weight-Scales*,[2] is of special interest.

Slight as it is, *De staticis experimentis* forces us to question Alexandre Koyré's claim that, "in deep opposition to the fundamental inspiration of the founders of modern science and the modern world-view, who, rightly or wrongly, tried to assert the panarchy of mathematics, [Cusanus] denies the very possibility of the mathematical treatment of nature."[3] As *De staticis experimentis* shows, there is a sense in which Cusanus did not at all deny that possibility. Quite the opposite! Long before Galileo and Kepler, Cusanus advocated a mathematical treatment of nature. Ernst Cassirer had good reason to see in Cusanus the beginning of the modern age.

And yet there is a profound incompatibility between the approach

---

1. Cantor, *Vorlesungen über Geschichte der Mathematik*.

2. Nicolaus Cusanus, *Idiota de staticis experimentis*, trans. Jasper Hopkins, in *On Experiments Done with Weight-Scales*, in Hopkins, *Nicholas of Cusa on Wisdom and Knowledge*, hereafter *DSE*.

3. Alexandre Koyré, *From the Closed World to the Infinite Universe* (New York: Harper Torchbook, 1958), 19.

to nature advocated by Cusanus and the thinking of a Copernicus, a Galileo, or a Kepler, and Koyré is right to point to the way the "founders of modern science and the modern world-view … tried to assert the panarchy of mathematics." Cusanus challenged such an assertion, at least as far as our human, as opposed to divine mathematics is concerned, and this challenge, I want to suggest, remains important. But, to repeat, Cusanus not only does not deny the possibility of a mathematical treatment of nature but calls for just such a treatment.

Idiota de staticis experimentis is the fourth and last of the *Idiota* dialogues. The first two bear the title *Idiota de sapientia*, "The Layman on Wisdom," the third the title *Idiota de mente*, "The Layman on Mind." In all four dialogues Cusanus opposes a modest, untutored layman, a craftsman interested in making things, to an orator, proud of his book learning. In this concluding dialogue Cusanus's interest in mathematics takes a decidedly worldly, empirical turn that leaves the theological neo-Platonic concerns that usually occupy him in his writings, especially when they turn to his mathematical symbolism, pretty much behind. What concerns him here are such matters as medicine, weather forecasting, the merits of (or rather the false claims made by) alchemy and astrology. He throws out numerous, at times bizarre, suggestions as to how his insight into the power of mathematical measures might be put to use. Not that the busy cardinal is likely to have taken the time to test any of the hypotheses he advances and to engage in actual experimentation. But what is important is the intuition underlying this little dialogue: that all of nature, notwithstanding its infinite variety, can yet be counted, measured, and weighed and is in this sense commensurable. As Hans Blumenberg observes," The universal quantifiability of all natural appearances and processes is one of the most important presuppositions of modern science."[4]

Consider the very beginning of the dialogue. To the Orator's praise of the metaphor of the scales of justice, a metaphor that suggests that just decisions are made by a careful weighing of the evidence, the Layman replies by taking a closer look at the vehicle of the metaphor, taking it literally and applying it to all of nature.

> Layman: Although in this world nothing can attain unto preciseness, nevertheless we know from experience that the verdicts of weight-scales are quite accurate and that, therefore, they are generally accepted. But since with regard to objects that have different origins it

---

4. Hans Blumenberg, ed., *Nikolaus von Cues: Die Kunst der Vermutung; Auswahl aus den Schriften* (Bremen: Carl Schünemann Verlag, 1957); "Einführung," in *Die Experimente mit der Waage*, 298.

is not possible for equal weights to be present in identically sized objects, please tell me whether or not anyone has [ever] written down the different experimental results pertaining to weights. (*DSE* 161)

The Layman begins thus by reiterating the central thesis of *On Learned Ignorance*: the unvarnished truth will always elude us finite knowers. But what interests this wise craftsman is something else: the way a determination of the specific gravity of different substances promises deeper insight into nature. As McTighe notes, "Cusa's treatment of specific gravity comes nowhere near the sophistication of a thirteenth-century treatise on the problem."[5] Busy as he was, Cusanus was content to make a promising suggestion, and so he has his Layman ask the Orator whether he knows of any attempt to record the specific gravity of different substances. After the Orator replies that he has not heard of any such attempt, the Layman continues:

> It seems to me that by reference to differences of weight we can more truly attain unto the hidden aspects of things and can know many things by means of more plausible surmises (*coniectura*). (*DSE* 162)

The Orator agrees with the Layman's intuition that careful weighing of different substances might reveal to us more about their usually hidden nature, where that intuition presupposes a conviction that, while "the verdict of weight-scales" will not in principle be altogether accurate and that it could always be infinitely more precise, it nevertheless can be "quite accurate," accurate enough for our human purposes. And though Cusanus insists that the size of any two objects can never be perfectly identical, here he has his craftsman speak of identically sized objects. What he has in mind is not perfect identity, but identity that is good enough for our practical purposes. The craftsman's conviction that the determination of the specific gravity of things will lead us to a deeper understanding of nature presupposes his conviction that there is a certain attunement of the judgments of the weight scales to the way things really are, which means to the way God made them.

The Orator supports such conviction, appealing, however, not to experience, as the Layman had done, but to the authority of the Bible.

---

5. Thomas McTighe, "Nicholas of Cusa's Theory of Science and Its Metaphysical Background," in *Nicolo' Cusano: Agli Inizi del Mondo Moderno*, 318–19. McTighe cites Marshall Clagett, *The Science of Mechanics in the Middle Ages* (Madison: University of Wisconsin Press, 1959), 97.

V. EXCURSUS

> Your point is well taken. For a certain prophet said that weight and
> weight-scales are the judgment of the Lord, who created all things
> in number, weight, and measure and who balanced the fountains of
> waters and weighed the foundations of the earth, as [Solomon] the
> wise writes. (Wis 11:21; see also Prv 16:11).[6] (*DSE* 162)

The Orator here offers scriptural support to a thought that was to
become important to Galileo, Kepler, and Descartes, who were convinced that God has written the book of nature in the language of
mathematics. Cusanus may well have been thinking here also of Augustine, who in *The City of God*, the *Confessions*, and *On the Trinity* offers theological interpretations of the passage from Wisdom to which
Cusanus's Orator refers us, inviting thoughts of the theological source
not just of Cusanus's emphasis on the weight-scale, but of the just
emerging scientific spirit.[7] And does the evident success of a mathematical approach to nature not presuppose that nature is amenable
to such an approach—that is to say, given the historical context, that
God created the world in such a way that it invites such an approach?

We should note how Cusanus's *Idiota* refuses to be interrupted by
the Orator's pious observation, as indeed in this entire dialogue this
wise layman, unlike Cusanus himself, appears quite uninterested in
theological issues. And so he just continues:

> So if the amount of water from one source is not of the same weight
> as is a similar amount [of water] from another source, then a judg-
> ment about the difference-of-nature between the one source and the
> other source is better arrived at by means of a weight-scale than by
> means of some other instrument. (*DSE* 162)

The Orator once again agrees and finds this intuition supported, this
time by the authority of the pagan Vitruvius.[8] Once more the Layman
refuses to be deflected from his train of thought. Convinced as he is
that there is much to be learned from a comparison of the different
weights of things, he thus calls for tables of the specific gravity of different substances, something he thinks might prove particularly useful in medicine. He thus calls on doctors to rely not just on secondary

---

6. Ws 11:21: "… but thou hast ordered all things in measure, and number, and weight";
Prv 16:11: "A just weight and balance are the LORD's: all the weights of the bag are his work."

7. See Andrea Fiamma, "'Iudicium Staterae verius experimur': Augustinus von Hippo
als Quelle der *De staticis experimentis* bei Nikolaus von Kues," *Freiburger Zeitschrift für Philosophie und Theologie* 63, no. 1 (2016): 175–95.

8. In 1450 Cusanus and Leon Battista Alberti studied Vitruvius's *De architectura* together
and mentioned it in their texts; Fiamma, "'Iudicium,'" 179, citing Kurt Flasch, "Cusano e
gli intellettuali italiani del Quattrocento," in *Le filosofie del Rinascimento*, ed. Cesare Vasoli
(Milan: Bruno Mondadori, 2002), 179.

qualities, such as the color or the smell of urine, to diagnose a certain illness, but to weigh and record the specific gravity of the urine or blood of sick and healthy individuals.

> Orator: Do you think that in all cases the situation is as you indicated it to be in the case of water?
>
> Layman: Yes, I do. For identical sizes, of whatsoever different things, are not at all of the same weight. Accordingly, since the weight of blood or the weight of urine is different for a healthy man and for a sick man, for a youthful man or for an elderly man or for a German and an African, wouldn't it be especially useful to a physician to have all these differences recorded? (*DSE* 163)

It is especially medicine that, Cusanus thinks, would gain from a more quantitative approach, and so he has his *Idiota* continue: "I think that a physician can make a truer judgment from the weight of the urine together with its color than from just its color, which is misleading." Turning to a more quantitative approach, he suggests, doctors might gain a clearer understanding of just how much of a certain medicine to prescribe. And he goes on to suggest that the weighing of water might lead to more accurate time-keeping devices.

What matters here is the privileging of what can be measured and weighed over what can be seen, of primary over secondary qualities, which looks ahead to Galileo and Descartes. The proposal strikes at the very heart of Aristotle's science of nature. Consider the way Aristotle constructs his table of elements. Crucial are two pairs of secondary qualities, hot and cold and dry and moist. They yield the four elements fire, air, water, earth.

	dry	moist
hot	fire	air
cold	earth	water

By privileging primary over secondary qualities we rob the Aristotelian understanding of the four sublunar elements and thus his physics of their foundation. Not that Cusanus no longer thinks in terms of the Aristotelian four elements: "He adheres, of course, to the traditional theory of four elements. But these are not ultimate indivisibles. Insofar they are regarded as pure indivisibles they are conjectural entities."[9]

We should note the recurrent suggestion in the dialogue that it would be very helpful to have reliable information on the specific

____

9. McTighe, "Nicholas of Cusa's Theory of Science," 336.

v. EXCURSUS

gravity of different substances under different circumstances. As the Orator puts it in concluding the dialogue:

> You have now explained sufficiently the reasons why you wish for the weights of things to be measured by means of a weight-scale and to be recorded both serially and multiply. For indeed, we see that that book would be very useful. And we see that the undertaking of it by great men ought to be urged, so that in different provinces [experimental weights] would be registered and would be collected into one [book], so that we would more readily be brought to many things that are [now] hidden from us. And I will not cease everywhere to promote its being done. (*DSE* 195)

It would indeed have been useful. Consider the following observation by the Layman:

> Elements are, in part, transformed one into another. For example, in the case of a plate-of-glass placed in the snow, we experience that air on the glass is condensed into water, which we find as a fluid on the glass. Similarly, we experience that a certain [kind of] water is turned into stones (just as water is turned into ice) and that a hardening, petrifying power is present in certain springs [of water] which harden into stone objects placed into them. Likewise, there is said to be found a certain kind of water from Hungary that turns iron into copper because of the power-of-glazing that is in that water. From a consideration of such powers it is evident that [the various] waters are not purely elemental things but are things composed of elements. And it would be very delightful to know the weights of the various powers of all such waters, so that from the differences of weight in air and in oil we might make closer surmises about the powers. (*DSE* 177)

Such a careful measuring of the specific gravity of different substances would indeed lead to a better understanding of the elements of which they are composed, would lead eventually to a questioning of the then still prevailing Aristotelian theory of the four elements.

Such measuring, Cusanus's *Idiota* suggests, might also yield a better understanding of what makes one soil fertile, another barren. And it would tell us whether coins were indeed of pure gold. The technique "would also avail very much for knowing how greatly the adulterated products of alchemy veered from the real thing." (*DSE* 171)

And just as careful use of the balance scale will show just how much or rather how little the alchemists are able to accomplish—a thought quite in the spirit of Archimedes—so an insistence on grounding the pronouncements of science in what can be observed and measured lets Cusanus's layman be suspicious of astrology. Not that all its predictions can simply be dismissed. He himself claims to have had some success foretelling the future. But where astrology appears successful, he suggests, such success rests on no science and has in all probability little to do with the stars.

> However, when I have paid attention to [someone's] countenance, his clothes, his eye-movements, to the form of his words and their weightiness, to the state of things I requested him to make known to me, at repeated moments, then I have suspected that surmises can be made by one to whom something quite true comes to mind unreflectingly—someone in whom a certain presaging spirit seems to speak. However, I think that with regard to this [predictive activity] no [structured] art is possible and that one who has [this] sense-of-judgment cannot pass it on and that a wise man ought not to busy himself with these predictive activities. (*DSE* 190)

The supposed science of astrology—Cusanus uses the term *ars*—here masks an intuitive psychological understanding. Not all our understanding, Cusanus is prepared to grant, is well grounded. But a wise man ought to base his predictions on results achieved by following a proper method.

The Orator once again agrees and cites yet another authority in support, this time St. Augustine, who speaks of a drunkard who could read other people's minds and "exposed thieves and brought to light, in an amazing way, other hidden matters—although he was very flighty and not at all wise" (*DSE* 191).[10] The *Idiota* once again is unimpressed by the Orator's appeal to this eminent authority and claims a similar power for himself, only to dismiss it:

> I know that I have often foretold many things, according as my spirit brought [them] to mind; and yet, I did not at all know the basis for [my prediction]. In the end it seemed to me not to be permitted to a serious man to speak without a basis, and I thenceforth kept silent. (*DSE* 191)

While Cusanus is unwilling to deny the occasional success of such an intuitive understanding and might thus have been willing to grant doctors and astrologers who relied on Renaissance magic a measure of success, he also is profoundly suspicious of it. And what lets him be suspicious is that it does not rest on anything that deserves to be called science. A presupposition of science, as he understands it, is that it is in possession of a sound method. And such a method should

---

10. Augustine, *Contra Academicos* I.6.17 (PL 32:915).

privilege primary qualities, qualities that can be quantified, and it should privilege mathematics.

Cusanus here presents himself to us as more modern than Ficino, a generation younger, or Pico, or—150 years later—Bruno or Campanella, who all remained tied to a premodern, magical worldview. And yet there would still seem to be an abyss that separates the cardinal's amateurish thought experiments from the science inaugurated by Copernicus, Galileo, Kepler, and Descartes. And the difference is not adequately explained by pointing out that Cusanus is indeed just an amateur who does not have or take the time to seriously pursue what he is here calling for—content to throw out conjectures, as he calls them, that he does not bother to test. But what matters here is his advocacy of a mathematical approach to nature. How are we to understand such advocacy? How does it differ from that embraced by the founders of the new science? Cusanus's down to earth *Idiota* appeals to experience to support the mathematical approach he advocates, but as the preceding three dialogues make clear, his advocacy of a mathematical approach to nature has a different foundation.

As we have seen, whatever separates Cusanus from the new science is not, as Koyré claims, that he denies the possibility of the mathematical treatment of nature. Quite the opposite: he calls for it. And yet Koyré is right to insist that Cusanus does not belong with the "founders of modern science and the modern world-view." Despite the pious words that Cusanus puts into the mouth of his Orator, that God "created all things in number, weight, and measure," there is a sense in which Cusanus refuses to assert what Koyré calls the "panarchy of mathematics." One way of putting this is to say that Cusanus refused to endorse what Cassirer called the Christian Platonism that he took to be a presupposition of the new science.[11]

If Aristotle's philosophy of nature had been an obstacle standing in the way of the emerging new science, Plato, with his emphasis on mathematics (think of the *Timaeus*), offered a more congenial

---

11. Ernst Cassirer, *The Individual and the Cosmos in the Renaissance*, trans., intro. Mario Domandi (New York and Evanston, Ill.: Harper and Row, 1964), 168–69. See also Cassirer, *Das Erkenntnisproblem in der Philosophie und Wissenschaft der neueren Zeit* (1911; repr. Darmstadt: Wissenschaftliche Buchgesellschaft, 1994), 1:389–90. What separates Galileo from Plato is similarly stressed by Edmund Husserl: "For Platonism the real had a more or less perfect methexis in the ideal. This afforded ancient geometry possibilities of a primitive application to reality. [But] through Galileo's mathematization of nature, nature is idealized under the guidance of the new mathematics; nature itself becomes—to express it in a modern way—a mathematical manifold"; Husserl, *The Crisis of European Sciences and Transcendental Phenomenology: An Introduction to Phenomenological Philosophy*, trans. and intro. David Carr (Evanston, IL: Northwestern University Press, 1970), 23.

philosophy. Recall the famous passage from Galileo's *Assayer*, where he claims that "philosophy is written in this grand book, the universe." To write this book God is said to have used the language of mathematics. And this language, Galileo insisted, is a language that we human beings are able to understand. Plato, to be sure, would have had difficulty with the claim that God used the language of mathematics to write the book of nature. A Pythagorean might have thought so, but, as Cassirer points out, Plato did not think that philosophy was written in the book of nature. Within itself the mind finds access to the invisible cosmos of the ideas. The material world is of course informed by the forms—as shown by the creation account in the *Timaeus*—but matter also always offers resistance to such formation. In the material world the forms are never completely victorious. Plato thus thinks in terms of the opposition of matter and form, an opposition that easily leads to a certain demonization of the material and the sensuous, which is seen as a force that alienates us from our spiritual home and drags us and the logos down into time.

Just on this point there is a decisive difference between the Christian and the Platonic understanding of nature. If God is omnipotent, the all-powerful creator of all that is, then there can be nothing outside and resisting his creative power. If then this God, like Plato's demiurge, is also a geometer, must not matter, too, be geometrical in its very essence? And so Kepler could insist *Ubi materia, ibi geometria*, "Where there is matter, there is geometry."[12]

Cassirer not only speaks of Galileo's Platonism, but he also suggests that Cusanus's call for a mathematical approach to nature may be understood as just another corollary of his Platonism. And if Galileo's Platonism is a Christian Platonism, at odds with what Plato thought, the same can be said of the Platonism of Cusanus. But, and this is crucial, Cusanus, emphasizing the infinity of God, insists on the unbridgeable gap that separates the divine from the human mind, divine from human mathematics. Number as we humans know it is, as we have seen, understood by Cusanus to be a human creation. "Number exists only from mind; indeed, whoever lacks a mind cannot number. Therefore, mind is the efficient cause of [mathematical] form. Hence, every [mathematical] form is a likeness of a mental conceiving on the part of Infinite Power" (*TC* 760). God created man in his image. But the nature of that likeness remains hidden from us. "Hence, number, which is derived from mind, must be judged to be

12. Johannes Kepler, Thesis XX, *De fundamentis astrologiae certioribus*, in *Opera Omnia*, 1:423 (Frankfurt am Main and Erlangen: Heyden and Zimmer, 1858).

something different insofar as it is from the oneness of the Uncreated Mind and insofar as it is from a created mind. For the oneness of the former number is analogous to natural form, whereas the oneness of the latter number is analogous to an artificial form" (*TC* 10). When we create our concepts we respond to the natural form of things, but we grasp that form not as it is, but as refracted by our senses and our reason. God's infinite reason transcends what human finite reason can grasp, even as it provides the latter with a measure, but it does so in a way we cannot comprehend. The same holds for divine and human mathematics. The former does indeed provide the latter with a measure, as shown by the fact that mathematics allows us to "make closer surmises about the powers" of nature, but these remain conjectures. If God can be said to have written the book of nature in the language of mathematics, this is a metaphor that speaks to the success of a mathematical approach. Cusanus could endorse Plato's claim that it is not in nature, but in the mind that we human knowers find the key to mathematical knowledge, but, unlike Plato, he would have refused to give to mathematicals an independent being. They are creations of our own reason, which, however, has its divine measure but, to repeat, in a way that eludes us.

A great many and usually very favorable references to Plato are scattered throughout Cusanus's writings. But once this has been said, it is necessary to add that the cardinal does not hesitate to criticize Plato when he thinks it necessary. This critique brings out the profound distance that separates the two thinkers, as it casts light on what would have made it impossible for Cusanus to endorse the very different Platonism of a Kepler or a Galileo.

That Cusanus is very much aware of what separates him from Plato is shown by this quotation from his dialogue *De beryllo*:

> Know, too, that I have found, as it seems to me, a certain additional failing on the part of [those] seekers of truth. For Plato said (1) that a circle can be considered insofar as it is named or defined—insofar as it is mentally depicted or mentally conceived—and (2) that from these [considerations] the nature of the circle is not known, but (3) that the circle's quiddity (which is simple and incorruptible and free of all contraries) is seen by the intellect alone. Indeed, Plato made similar statements regarding all [such things]. For if Plato had considered that [claim], assuredly he would have found that our mind, which constructs mathematical entities, has these mathematical entities, which are in its power, more truly present with itself than as they exist outside the mind." (*DB* 55)

Cusanus here is challenging the Platonic claim that we have an intellectual vision of mathematicals as independent realities existing outside the mind. They are said to be constructions of the human mind. And the same is said to hold for Plato's understanding of the forms. Cusanus proceeds to explain what he has in mind:

> For example, man knows the mechanical art, and he has the forms of this art more truly in his mental concept than as they are formable outside his mind—just as a house, which is made by means of an art, has a truer form in the mind than in the pieces of wood. For the form that comes to characterize the wood is the mental form, idea, or exemplar. (*DB* 55)

Of interest is the way Cusanus invites us to think what it is for us human knowers to understand something in the image of a craftsman's know-how, a simile Descartes will later rely on in the *Discourse on Method.* Unlike Plato, Cusanus sees no reason to reify the idea of the house and to give it an independent reality. All such things, he insists, have their origin not in nature, but in the creative human spirit responding to the world in which we find ourselves (*DB* 55). To be sure, here Cusanus is speaking of artifacts, not of natural objects. They would seem to require a different account. But Cusanus extends what he has said about the forms that govern the creation of artifacts to numbers and to the forms we discover in nature.

Numbers, as we have seen, are understood by Cusanus as an unfolding of the human mind, which, created in the image of the divine mind, bears oneness within itself as the most fundamental measure. For him already, as later for Descartes, there is a sense in which we fully comprehend things only to the extent that we can produce or reproduce them. And just this explains why mathematical representations deserve to be ranked above others. When dealing with mathematicals, the mind is dealing with its own creations. The language of mathematics is therefore transparent as no other language can be. When I have understood the definition of a circle, I possess what Descartes would have called a "clear and distinct understanding" of it, because the definition gives the rule for its construction. Here the mind is concerned with what it has created. It is this greater adequacy of mathematical descriptions to our mind's mode of operation, more than the presupposed understanding of nature as a book God wrote using the language of mathematics, that lets Cusanus call for the mathematization of the science of nature. To the extent that I can represent nature mathematically I can recreate it in my mind.

V. EXCURSUS

What matters here are not the details, but the general direction in which Cusanus would have us proceed: number gives us the key to how to represent and learn more about the workings of nature. Like ruler and clock, the weight-scale is an instrument that helps us to re-describe nature in a way that makes it more commensurable with our mind's mode of operation. Implicit in such a mathematization of the science of nature is a shift away from the heterogeneity of the immediately experienced world to the homogeneity of a world subjected to the measure of number.

But, to repeat, with Cusanus this privileging of mathematics does not have its foundation, first of all, in the nature of things but is relative to the nature of human understanding. We can imagine a being who knows what is by means of genetic definitions, somewhat in the way that the definition of a circle gives us a rule for its construction. God may perhaps be understood as such a being. But we human beings do not construct the world we experience. In this respect a tree is very different from a circle. What we construct in such cases is never more than a similitude, an image, or a picture. By their form such pictures should conform to the nature of the human spirit. They should be as comprehensible as possible. But they should not be confused with the things pictured. These we shall never adequately comprehend, although, in a way that we cannot fully comprehend, they provide our conjectures with a measure. But this measure does not present itself to us. Our best access to it is by measuring and representing nature relying on our mathematics. This understanding of the task of science invites comparison with Alberti's understanding of the art of painting.[13]

In this connection the fact that both Cusanus and the slightly younger Alberti should have defended the then much-maligned Protagoras deserves special attention.[14] Let me cite first Alberti: "Perhaps Protagoras, by saying that man is the mode and measure of all things, meant that all the accidents of things are known through comparison

---

13. Cf. Karsten Harries, "On the Power and Poverty of Perspective: Cusanus and Alberti," in Casarella, *Cusanus: The Legacy of Learned Ignorance*, 105–26; Charles H. Carman, *Leon Battista Alberti and Nicholas Cusanus: Towards an Epistemology of Vision for Italian Renaissance Art and Culture* (Farnham Surrey: Ashgate, 2014); and my review of Carman in *Renaissance Quarterly* 68, no. 3 (Fall 2015): 989–90. According to Carman, Alberti's intention was not to create "artful pictorial illusion," but to visualize the divine infinite. I have difficulty detecting such an intent in *On Painting*.

14. On Alberti's use of Protagoras, see Charles Trinkaus, "Protagoras in the Renaissance: An Exploration," in *Philosophy and Humanism: Essays in Honor of Paul Oskar Kristeller*, ed. Edmund Mahoney (New York: Columbia University Press, 1976), 195–98.

to the accidents of man."[15] We meet with a similar reference in his *Libri della famiglia* (1433/34). In this rehabilitation of the sophist, which challenges both Plato and Aristotle, humanistic self-assertion finds striking expression.

We find the same rehabilitation of Protagoras in Cusanus, who explicitly defends the sophist against the critique of Aristotle in *De beryllo*, which appeared in 1458.[16] Did Cusanus here borrow from Alberti? It is worth noting that both authors in places wrote "Pythagoras" where they should have written "Protagoras"; Cusanus may have been misled by a copy of Bessarion's translation of Aristotle's *Metaphysics* that he owned, although in a marginal note he himself points out the confusion. But should we consider this a mere confusion? Cusanus's understanding of mathematics invites a blurring of the distinction between Pythagoras and Protagoras. His neo-Pythagoreanism is a Protagorean neo-Pythagoreanism.

There can be no doubt that Cusanus had read *On Painting* or at least was familiar with the substance of the book when he began work on *On Learned Ignorance*. An earlier version of Alberti's treatise with the title *Elementa picturae* is still to be found in the library of the Cusanus Stift in Kues.[17] But what matters here is not Cusanus's possible indebtedness to the slightly younger painter. His meditations on infinity had to lead to a denial of any available absolute center or measure in the realm of creatures. God, to be sure, is said to be the center and measure of creatures, but he is so in a way that transcends our comprehension. This elusiveness of the divine generates the demand for a more readily available center and measure. Cusanus finds that center in the human being, who, as the Bible teaches, was created in the image of God. Cusanus understood this to mean that the free human being, too, is a creator. Alberti's representation of the painter offered him a vivid example of the creative power of the human being.[18]

The decentering that is a consequence of thoughts of the infinity of God invites a humanist recentering. The thought of Cusanus invites us to understand the anthropocentrism of the Renaissance as a response to the decentering power of reflection on the infinity of

15. Leon Battista Alberti, *On Painting*, trans., introduction John R. Spencer, rev. ed. (New Haven: Yale University Press, 1966), 55.

16. See Trinkaus, "Protagoras," 199–204.

17. The entire codex is illustrated in Elena Filippi, *Umanesimoe misura viva: Durer tra Cusano e Alberti* (San Giovanni Lupatoto: Arsenale, 2011).

18. Elena Filippi, "The Heritage of Cusanus's New Anthropology and Its Impact on Visual Culture in Fifteenth-Century Germany and Flanders," *American Cusanus Society Newsletter* 31 (2014): 34–43.

God. The rehabilitation of Protagoras belongs in this context. Not that such rehabilitation can have been based on much more than what was suggested by the much-quoted line that man is the measure of all things, with which Protagoras's lost book, *Truth*, is said to have begun. Neither Plato's *Protagoras* nor his *Theaetetus* were then available. What was readily available was Aristotle's widely repeated dismissal of Protagoras in his *Metaphysics*:

> Knowledge, also, and perception, we call the measure of things, for the same reason, because we come to know something by them— while as a matter of fact they are measured rather than measure other things. But it is with us as if someone else measured us and we came to know how big we are by seeing that he applied the cubit-measure a certain number of times to us. But Protagoras says man is the measure of all things, meaning really the man who knows or the man who perceives, and these because they have respectively knowledge and perception, which we say are the measures of objects. They are saying nothing, then, while they appear to be saying something remarkable.[19]

Aristotle insists that more fundamentally our knowledge of things has its measure in these things. They are, as it were, the natural measures of knowledge. Protagoras, on the other hand, is said by Aristotle to have held that what presents itself to us in knowledge or perception is therefore true. But what presents itself to one person may be incompatible with what presents itself to another; what presents itself to us at one time may be incompatible with what presents itself to another. Aristotle thus thought that the Protagorean saying "man is the measure of all things" violated the law of non-contradiction: "If all opinions and appearances are true, all statements must be at the same time true and false. For many men hold beliefs in which they conflict with one another, and all think those mistaken who have not the same opinions as themselves."[20] Medieval commentators on Aristotle's *Metaphysics*, such as Siger of Brabant and Thomas Aquinas, followed Aristotle. It is not man who is the measure of all things, but the wise man, and the wise man knows that he is measured by things.[21] But this appeal to the wise man invites question. Where is he to be found?

I am aware of only one medieval thinker who defended Protagoras against the Aristotelian critique long before Alberti and Cusanus:

19. Aristotle, *Metaphysics* X.1.1053a31–1053b4.
20. Aristotle, *Metaphysics* IV.5.1009a6–1009a10.
21. Dallas G. Denery II, "Protagoras and the Fourteenth-Century Invention of Epistemological Relativism," *Visual Resources* 25, no. 1 (March 2009): 34–38.

Nicholas of Autrecourt, who in 1347 was condemned for his heretical views.[22] He questioned this appeal to the wise man: in what sense are things the way the wise man judges them to be? This is the question Autrecourt (ca. 1299–ca. 1369), a theology student at the University of Paris, would ask in the 1330s. "We must next consider the question," Nicholas writes in the *Exigit ordo*, "whether everything that appears is true and whether everything that appears to be true is true." He then immediately suggests that the Protagorean thesis is a "generally accepted rule" and "should not be modified or restricted unless necessary."[23] At first glance, it is an absurd assertion, one that willfully ignores the unanimous tradition of anti-Protagorean commentary that had grown up around Aristotle's *Metaphysics*.[24]

As Cusanus was to do, Nicholas of Autrecourt already would have us question the authority of Aristotle. We would do better to consider what we experience without Aristotelian blinders. Not that what we experience will allow us to comprehend the underlying reality. Cusanus might have said we have to settle for more or less adequate conjectures. Nicholas of Autrecourt invokes "metaphysical probability."[25]

Since we cannot evaluate competing theories in terms of the appearances themselves, Nicholas argues, we must evaluate them from our own perspective in terms of what we hope to accomplish with them. Our perspective operates like a regulative ideal or framework for guiding, organizing, and assessing competing theories about the world. Nicholas is quite explicit about this when he introduces and defends Protagoras's thesis. If we hope to explain how certitude might be possible, what the world and our relation to it must be like if we hope to construct a cognitive theory that secures for us some means of making justified statements about the world, then the Protagorean thesis is more probable than its Aristotelian-Scholastic rejection.[26]

But how are we to understand that perspective is said to operate like a regulative ideal or framework? Is it the perspective of the individual located in a particular place and time? The inadequacy of that perspective is recognized by the appeal to the wise man. Cusanus, too, insists that the perspective of the individual must be transcended.

22. Hans Seed Thijssen, "Nicholas of Autrecourt," in *Stanford Encyclopedia of Philosophy*, ed. Edward N. Zalta (Spring 2016 ed.), https://plato.stanford.edu/archives/spr2016/entries/autrecourt/.

23. Edition of the *Exigit Ordo* and the theological question "*Utrum visio alicuius rei naturalis possit naturali intendi*," in J. R. O'Donnell, "Nicholas of Autrecourt," *Mediaeval Studies* 1 (1939): 179–28; see especially 228, lli. 5–12.

24. Denery, "Protagoras," 39.

25. Denery, "Protagoras," 43.

26. Denery, "Protagoras," 43–44.

V. EXCURSUS

The truth of things is denied to us. Our experience gives us access to things, but that access is inevitably limited by our point of view and the make-up of our senses. To gain a more adequate understanding of things we must subject what we observe to a measure furnished by our reason. But this is not an individual, but a human measure. Cusanus, too, thus feels compelled to defend Protagoras against his Aristotelian critics.

As mentioned, Cusanus found the line "man is the measure of all things" in Aristotle's *Metaphysics*. That one line was all he needed. And the same can be said of Alberti. There are striking similarities between the way Alberti and Cusanus appeal to Protagoras. Here is Cusanus in *De beryllo*:

> Thirdly, note the saying of Protagoras that man is the measure of things. With the sense man measures perceptible things, with the intellect he measures intelligible things, and he attains unto supra-intelligible things transcendently. Man does this measuring in accordance with the aforementioned [cognitive modes]. For then he knows that the cognizing soul is the goal of things knowable, he knows on the basis of the perceptive power that perceptible things are supposed to be such as can be perceived. And likewise [he knows] regarding intelligible things that [they are supposed to be such] as can be understood, and [he knows] that transcendent things [are to be such] as can transcend. Hence, man finds in himself, as in a measuring scale, all created things.[27]

All created things have their place in a mental space of our own construction.

As mentioned, Cusanus had actually written "Pythagoras" instead of "Protagoras."[28] This seemingly obvious "mistake" was corrected in the critical edition by Ludwig Baur with the interesting comment: "Nicolaus scripsit Pytagorae. Hunc errorem inde repetendum esse puto, quod in codice Cusano 184 fol. 71 r in translatione Metaphysicae a Bessarione redacta legitur: 'Pytagoras omnium rerum hominem mensuram aiebat'; sed in codice additur; 'Credo dici debere

---

27. Nicholas of Cusa, *De Beryllo*, in *Opera Omnia*, ed. Hans G. Sänger and Karl Bormann (Hamburg: Meiner, 1988), XI:6; trans. Jasper Hopkins, *On [Intellectual] Eyeglasses*, in *Nicholas of Cusa: Metaphysical Speculations*, 37.

28. Cf. Trinkaus, "Protagoras," 195: "Protagoras was frequently confused with Pythagoras, an easy orthographical error, though some modern scholars do indeed relate his thinkimg to the Pythagorean school, and there remains the mystery of Protagoras's choice of the word *metron*—'measure'—whatever its and his authentic meaning, which could also serve to associate him with Pythagoras." Alberti, too, confused the two thinkers; Trinkaus, "Protagoras," 199.

Protagoras.'" Cusanus, Baur suggests, was thoughtlessly following Bessarion's mistaken translation. But Cusanus himself later corrected the mistake in his copy of Bessarion's translation of the *Metaphysics*, reason enough to correct the mistake in the critical edition. But I find the confusion of Protagoras with Pythagoras to be more than just a simple mistake. I find it revealing. As suggested, Cusanus can be said to represent a Protagorean Pythagoreanism. About his indebtedness to the Christian Pythagorean tradition as represented by Boethius, Augustine, and Thierry of Chartres there can be no doubt.[29] But Cusanus reads Protagoras into Pythagoras, and just this opens his thought to the future.

What does the cited passage tell us about what Cusanus found so significant in the saying of Protagoras? To the extent that we can know things at all, they must be capable of entering our consciousness, either as objects of sense, or as objects of thought, or as mysteries that transcend the power of reason. Just as the painter's representation of the world has its center in the perceiving eye, the world as we know it has its center in the knowing subject. And if this suggestion that the human being is the center of things known ascribes a quasi-divine creativity to man, this should not seem too surprising, given that God was thought to have created man in his own image. Cusanus understands this image character first in terms of man's ability to create a second world, the world of concepts, which allows us to take the measure of what we experience. The key to that creation is provided by mathematics. Rather like Alberti's perspective construction, this second world provides the linguistic or logical space in which what we perceive must take its place if it is to be understood at all. Cusanus therefore continues:

> Fourthly, note that Hermes Trismegistus states that man is a second god. For just as God is the creator of all real beings and of natural forms, so man is the creator of conceptual beings and of artificial forms that are only likenesses in his intellect, even as God's creatures are likenesses of the Divine intellect. (*DB* 7)

Like Alberti, Cusanus insists here on the godlike character of man. As God's creative reason unfolds itself in creation, so the human intellect unfolds itself in whatever it knows. The known world resembles the world created by Alberti's painter. That world, to be sure, has its measure in what presents itself to our eyes.

29. See Albertson, *Mathematical Theologies*.

V. EXCURSUS

Later in *De beryllo* Cusanus returns to Protagoras:

> There still remains one thing: viz., to see how it is that man is the measure of all things. Aristotle says that by means of this [expression] Protagoras stated nothing profound. Nevertheless, Protagoras seems to me to have expressed [herein] especially important [truths]. I consider Aristotle rightly to have stated, at the outset of his *Metaphysics,* that all men by nature desire to know. He makes this statement with regard to the sense of sight, which a man possesses not simply for the sake of working; rather, we love sight because sight manifests to us many differences. If, then, man has senses and reason not only in order to know, then perceptible objects have to nourish man for two purposes: viz., in order that he may live and in order that he may know. But knowing is more excellent and more noble, because it has the higher and more incorruptible goal. Earlier on, we presupposed that the Divine Intellect created all things in order to manifest itself; likewise the Apostle Paul, writing to the Romans, says that the invisible God is known in and through the visible things of the world. (*DB* 65)

This, to be sure, hardly sounds like a critique of Aristotle. Quite the opposite: Cusanus sounds like a humanist Aristotelian when he, here and elsewhere, embraces the visible things of the world in all their variety as an epiphany of the Divine. Jasper Hopkins has thus argued that Cusanus is misappropriating Protagoras.[30] But is he? Trinkaus links this passage to Alberti's invocation *of la più grassa Minerva* to suggest a new emphasis on visible form.[31] But what impresses Cusanus here is not just the beauty and wealth of the visible, but the way all we see is dependent on the fact that we possess eyes: Aristotle is said to have seen "this very point: viz., that if perceptual cognition is removed, perceptible objects are removed. For he says in the *Metaphysics*: 'If there were not things that are enlivened, there would not be either senses or perceptible objects'" (*DB* 69).[32] Cusanus extends this thought and claims that the same holds for the objects of our knowledge. Is Protagoras then not right when he "stated that man is the

30. *DB* 273n18.

31. Charles Trinkaus, "Protagoras in the Renaissance: An Exploration," in *Philosophy and Humanism: Essays in Honor of Paul Oskar Kristeller,* ed. Edmund Mahoney (New York: Columbia University Press, 1976), 203. On the phrase *la più grassa Minerva,* see John R. Spencer's introduction to his translation of Alberti's *On Painting,* 18–19.

32. The reference is to *Metaphysics* IV.5 (1010b.30–1011a.2), which Ross translates as follows: "And, in general, if only the sensible exists, there would be nothing if animate things were not; for there would be no faculty of sense. The view that neither the objects of the sensations nor the sensations would exist is doubtless true (for they are affections of the perceiver), but that the substrata which cause the sensation should not exist even apart from sensation is impossible."

measure of things"? "Because man knows—by reference to the nature of his perceptual [cognition]—that perceptual objects exist for the sake of that cognition, he measures perceptible objects in order to apprehend, perceptually, the glory of the Divine Intellect" (*DB* 69). The being of whatever presents itself is a being relative to the human perceiver and knower.[33] Cusanus charges Aristotle with having failed to pay sufficient attention to such relativity and, as a consequence, to have failed to do justice to Protagoras.

Consider once more Aristotle's critique of Protagoras, where that very critique may have encouraged humanists who had come to associate the Stagirite with the scholasticism they rejected to give the maligned sophist a kinder reception.[34] Aristotle insists that our knowledge of things has its measure in these things. They are, as it were, the natural measures of knowledge. It is as if we were handed a yardstick and decided by that how tall we were.

For Cusanus, too, our knowledge begins with perception. There would be no knowledge if our senses did not provide us with aspects of things.[35] But perception does not give us an unmediated access to God's creation. What we perceive is always limited by the make-up of our senses and our point of view. Even the yardstick example invites more questions than may at first appear. Does our understanding of the length of a "yard" not presuppose an understanding of its relationship to our body? That relationship becomes explicit when we say. "A yard is three feet." Perception already imposes a human measure on whatever presents itself to our senses. And this dependence on the subject is compounded by the way perception is entangled in understanding. To be sure, when I call this an oak tree, the proposition's truth or falsity is decided by whether this tree is indeed an oak tree. But when I see this object as an oak tree, is such seeing not itself dependent on the humanly created concept "oak tree," as it is dependent on the make-up of our eyes. From the very beginning we have subjected appearance to our human measures.

One could, to be sure, challenge Protagoras by invoking Cusanus's own doctrine of learned ignorance or the beryl of the dialogue. There is, indeed, as Aristotle recognized, a sense in which knowledge and perception must be said to measure things. Do we not lose the distinction between appearance and reality when we make man the

---

33. This invites comparison with Heidegger's understanding of Being in *Being and Time*.
34. Cf. Trinkaus, "Protagoras," 193.
35. Clyde Lee Miller, "Perception, Conjecture, and Dialectic in Nicholas of Cusa," *American Catholic Philosophical Quarterly* 54, no. 1 (Winter 1990): 35–43.

measure of all things? Was Cusanus's teaching of learned ignorance and in *De beryllo* not meant to block precisely such an undue self-elevation of the human knower by reminding us that the final measure of all human knowing is God? Remember the context of these references to Protagoras. And consider Plato's remark on Protagoras in the *Theaetetus*, a remark Cusanus is unlikely to have known, since Ficino finished his translation of that dialogue only some years later: "He says, you will remember, that 'man is the measure of all things—alike of the being of things that are and of the not-being of things that are not.'... He puts it in this sort of way, doesn't he, that any given thing 'is to me such as it appears to me, and is to you as it appears to you,' you and I being men?"[36] Plato already accuses Protagoras of confusing appearance and reality or of confusing perceiving and knowing. But for Cusanus the seeming obviousness of this distinction is rendered questionable by a higher-order reflection: does the knower, too, not impose on what he claims to know his human measures? It is precisely because of this that Cusanus, like Alberti, calls man a second God, a creator of conceptual forms in which he mirrors or unfolds himself and by means of which he reconstructs or recreates in his own image the manifold presented to his senses.

Let me conclude this excursus by returning to a statement I made in the very beginning of this commentary: Cusanus, I said, is a thinker who continues to challenge me. What I find especially challenging, as no doubt did Cassirer, is the way he calls for a mathematical approach to nature even as he insists that such an approach never will allow us to comprehend things as they are in themselves. All that it can provide are approximations, conjectures. This way of putting the matter suggests Kant, and there is indeed a way in which Cusanus, like Kant, insists on the insuperable gulf that separates phenomena from noumena, a gulf that is obscured when science claims to be in possession of the language in which the book of nature is written.

Why is it important to insist on this gulf? As Kant recognized, and this is why he had to write a second and a third *Critique*, there is a sense in which nature or reality is elided by the very pursuit of objective truth. Such an elision is inscribed into the conception of reality or the metaphysics of nature that is presupposed by science, as inaugurated by Copernicus, Galileo, Kepler, and Descartes. That conception, we may not forget, is a human construction. Science aims at a

---

36. Plato, *Theaetetus* 152a. Translated by F. M. Cornford. In *The Collected Dialogues Including the Letters*, edited by Edith Hamilton and Huntington Cairns. Bollingen Series. (Princeton: Princeton University Press, 1962).

perspicuous—and that means also objective—representation of the world that ideally would include everything that deserves to be called real. But so understood, science tends to elide reality, tends to mistake reality for what it can represent. That such objectification must transform that reality we experience first of all and most of the time, is evident: our first access to reality is always bound to particular perspectives, mediated by our bodies, colored by our concerns and interests. But as soon as we understand a perspective as such, in thought at least we are already beyond the limits it would impose. Such reflection on perspective and point of view leads inevitably to the idea of a subject that, free of all perspectives, would understand things as they really are. And it leads with equal necessity to the thought that the reality that gives itself to our eyes, and more generally to our senses, is the mere appearance of an objective reality that no eye can see, no sense can sense, that only a rational thinking can attempt to reconstruct.

The pursuit of truth, so understood, demands objectivity. And objectivity demands that we not allow our understanding to be clouded by our inevitably personal desires and interests. It wants just the facts. With good reason Wittgenstein could therefore say in the *Tractatus*, "In the world everything is as it is and happens as it does happen. In it there is no value—and if there were, it would be of no value" (6.41). It would be just another fact that, like all facts, could be other than it happens to be. If there is something that deserves to be called a value, it will not have a place in the world of science. To find it we must step outside that world. And the same goes for freedom. That means that persons as persons are not part of the scientific world picture. They are ruled out by the mathematical form of representation that governs it.

But is this not to say that whatever makes life meaningful must be sought outside the reality known to science? To identify reality with what science so understood can grasp is to leave no room for what Kant called "things in themselves." But every time we experience a person as a person, we experience such a thing in itself. There is no experience of persons without at least a trace of respect. In this sense we can agree with Kierkegaard that subjective truth is higher than objective truth, where we must resist the temptation to translate such subjective truth into some version of objective truth, as phenomenology too often has attempted to do. To the extent that the modern world reduces reality to the reality science can know, it becomes a prison that denies us access to the reality of persons and things. To experience the aura of the real that gives to persons and things their proper weight, we must escape from that prison, must open a door or at least a window in the world known to science, a window to what we can call the truth of things, but now "truth" may no longer be understood as objective truth. Copernicus had put the pursuit of objective truth on the right track. But just because he did, it remains important to consider both the legitimacy and the limits of that pursuit. Here the thought of Cusanus's teaching of learned ignorance can be of help. In this connection, book three of *De docta ignorantia* deserves our special attention.

VI. NAMING GOD

Throughout his life Cusanus was preoccupied and struggled with the problem of how to name and think about the infinite, incomprehensible triune God. Already the first part of his very first sermon, *In Principio Erat Verbum*, delivered on Christmas Day, 1430, perhaps in Koblenz, addresses the issue at some length. Where are we to find a fitting name for God? Creatures we can point to and name, as Adam named the animals. But God is not to be found among the things we encounter. And so Cusanus states in this first sermon that "this so immense God remains unnameable, inexpressible, and fully unknowable by any creature" (*Sermo* I.3). And yet to worship the mystery that is God, human beings must somehow name the unnameable: "Hence, He is assigned names with different human words, in different languages of different nations, although His own name is unique, supreme, infinite, ineffable, and unknown" (*Sermo* I.3).

All the names human beings have given to God are of course inadequate, but they cannot be totally so. This would make such naming idle verbal play. So while God is said by the young Cusanus to be unnameable and "fully unknowable," in that sermon he has quite a bit to say about God, in keeping with the Christian tradition that had shaped him and his audience. And Cusanus does not hesitate to judge certain names more adequate than others. That presupposes an understanding of God that he could expect his audience to share: God is the most perfect being. Cusanus thus claims it to be evident "that supreme being, supreme duration (that is, eternity), supreme power, supreme majesty, supreme glory, supreme justice, supreme truth are one simple God, outside of whom there is nothing supreme and nothing infinite" (*Sermo* I.2). That understanding allowed the Hebrews to call him by names that recognized his perfection:

> When the created intellect ascends in order to apprehend the power
> of such a Supreme Good, (1) it finds Him alone to be the most just
> Provider: hence, among the Jews the created intellect gave Him the
> name "El." (2) It finds Him to be the Governor of the universe who
> foresees all things: [hence,] it called [Him] "Adonai." (3) It finds
> [Him to be] most powerful: [hence,] it called [Him] "Jah." (4) It
> finds [Him to be] most kindly: [hence,] it called [Him] "Sabaoth,"
> "Schaddai," etc. And according to the tradition of the Hebrews there
> are eight such names. However, the one most holy [name], whose
> meaning the human intellect cannot apprehend, is given by God. It
> is "Tetragrammaton," i.e., "of four letters." It is ineffable; i.e., it is in-
> conceivable by the intellect. And it is voiced by the Jews only once a
> year after a preceding fast. This name is "Jehova." And wherever this
> name occurs in the Hebrew Bible we have [in our Bible the name]
> "Dominus" ["Lord"]. (*Sermo* I.3)

All the names, except the last, look to this world to name God. Some
quality, considered praiseworthy, is raised to a maximum. But the tie
to this world is preserved in tension with the initial claim that God is
"infinite, ineffable, and unknown." Only the last name, the Tetragrammaton YHWH, is exempt from the defect of all other names, because
God thus named himself: "I am who I am." The reference is to Exodus
3:14–15, where Moses asks God what to tell the people of Israel when
challenged about his promise to lead them out of Egypt: "Say this to
the people of Israel: 'The Lord, the God of your fathers, the God of
Abraham, the God of Isaac, and the God of Jacob, has sent me to you.'
This is my name forever, and thus I am to be remembered throughout
all generations." But what this name names, even though preceded by
the explanation, "I am who I am," remains a mystery. "It is ineffable;
that is, it is inconceivable by the intellect," as Cusanus puts it.

While Cusanus embraces what the Old Testament had to say about
God, nothing said so far addresses what already, here and throughout
his writings, is a central concern: to establish that the ineffable God
should be thought as triune. The way he supports this view in this first
sermon deserves our attention, for it casts light on what will remain a
key presupposition of his thinking:

> And since it is the case that no idleness can possibly be found in
> the Supreme Being, it follows that He is of supreme activity. But
> in every action there are found, necessarily, three perfect correla-
> tions. For nothing acts on itself but on an object of the action that
> is distinct from the agent. And from the agent of the action and the
> object of the action there arises a third thing: viz., the doing. In the
> Divine Being these correlations will be the three Persons by reason

of which we call God trine. For God whom we call Father deifies, begets, justifies, loves (along with infinite other perfect activities). And God is deifiable, begettable, justifiable, lovable, etc.; and we call Him the Son, who proceeds from the Father. And, thirdly, there is the Deifying on the part of the One who deifies and on the part of the One who is deifiable, i.e., the Deifying on the part of the Father and on the part of the Son (and, similarly, there is the Justifying, the Begetting, and the Loving on the part of the One who loves and on the part of the One who is lovable); and we call this the Holy Spirit, who proceeds from both [the Father and the Son]. (*Sermo* I.6)

Quite in keeping with the biblical tradition, Cusanus thinks God in the image of a human actor. In every action we can distinguish the actor, the object of the action, and the action. Similarly, we can distinguish in God the Father as the perfect actor, the Son as the perfect object of his action, and the Holy Spirit as the perfect action that joins both. Cusanus's understanding of God in the image of man invites the charge of an undue anthropomorphism. But God, Cusanus can counter, created man in his image. As his image, our being too has a triadic structure. And we bear the image of his infinity within ourselves, manifest in our freedom. Only this allows our intellect to ascend to an understanding of the infinite God that, while altogether inadequate, is yet sufficient for us human beings to fulfill our vocation.

In this sermon Cusanus appears quite confident in his ability to convince us that God must be thought as a Trinity: "I, too, when once disputing, discerned that wise Jews can be influenced to believe in the Trinity" (*Sermo* I.7). In *De docta ignorantia*, as we have seen and shall see, he develops these considerations at great length. But if Cusanus is confident that he can make a strong case for the Trinity, to convince a non-Christian believer in God of the Incarnation is quite a different matter. "But as for the fact that, in God, the Son became incarnated: this is [a teaching] against which they have become hardened and want to hearken neither to arguments nor to the Prophets" (*Sermo* I.7).[1] This response cannot surprise us: Are there any persuasive arguments Cusanus can present in support of the Incarnation? Book Three of *De docta ignornatia* will provide an answer to that question.

The question of how to name God to which the first part of *Sermo* I is devoted was to remain a central concern throughout Cusanus's life. It pervades *De docta ignorantia*. Chapters 19 to 25, to which I shall now turn, address it directly.

---

1. See also Cusanus's letter of December 29, 1454, to archbishop Johannes of Segovia, in Baum, *Nikolaus von Kues: Briefe und Dokumente*, 272–73.

CHAPTER 19

The Likening of an Infinite Triangle to Maximum Trinity

After the excursus and a brief look at *Sermo* I, let us return to *De docta ignorantia*. Chapter 6 discussed the use of mathematical symbols: they are to help us come to a better understanding of God. But how much help are they? Cusanus calls them paradigms (*paradigmata*), which Hopkins translates as symbols, Paul Wilpert as *Beispiele,* examples. What is a Cusan paradigm? Kant's understanding of symbolic hypotyposis in the *Critique of Judgment* is of help here. Kant there compares a despotic state to a handmill: they do not resemble each other, but there is an analogy in the way we think about both. That would seem to fit Cusanus's use of his *paradigmata*: an analogy links the way we think about the geometrical infinite and the way we think about God.

An example of a Cusan paradigm is the infinite triangle. Such a triangle, discussed at length in chapters 13 and 14, exists no more than a square circle; it is an idea of reason that stretches reason to a point where it founders on the reef of the infinite. Is this how we should think about God?

> Regarding what was stated and shown, viz., that a maximum line is a maximum triangle: let us now become instructed in ignorance. We have seen that a maximum line is an [infinite] triangle; and because

[this] line is most simple, it will be something most simple and three. Every angle of the triangle will be the line, since the triangle as a whole is the line. Hence, the infinite line is three. But there cannot be more than one infinite thing. Therefore, this trinity is oneness. (*DI* I.19:55)

We can agree: given this kind of reasoning, trinity is indeed oneness, but can the same then not be said about any other figure—for example, a square or a pentagon? Do they furnish equally perspicuous paradigms? To be sure, in keeping with his faith, Cusanus privileges the triangle, but he recognizes that the preceding does not adequately establish this privilege.

Furthermore, a maximum line is just as much a triangle, a circle, and a sphere as it is a line; it is truly and incompositely all these, as was shown. (*DI* I.19:56)

And would the argument not work for any figure? Why should these three, triangle, circle, and sphere, and especially the triangle, be privileged? The next chapter will attempt to tackle this question. But a first answer is obvious enough: Cusanus is concerned here to show us, with his paradigm of the identity of infinite triangle and infinite line, how, grappling with thoughts of the infinite, we can make sense of the mystery of the Trinity, where one is three and three are one, though to make sense of this we must embrace the coincidence of opposites:

For example, in God we must not conceive of distinction and indistinction as two contradictories but [must conceive of] them as antecedently present in their own most simple Beginning, where distinction is not anything other than indistinction; and then we will conceive more clearly that the trinity and the oneness are the same thing. For where distinction is indistinction, trinity is oneness; and, conversely, where indistinction is distinction, oneness is trinity. And similarly, about the plurality of persons and the oneness of essence: for where plurality is oneness, trinity of persons is the same as oneness of essence; and, conversely, where oneness is plurality, oneness of essence is trinity of persons. (*DI* I.19:57)

Augustine is cited in support of the proposition that "when you begin to number the Trinity, you depart from the Truth" (*DI* I.19:57). Cusanus, to be sure, in agreement with both Aristotle and Aquinas, takes counting to be the paradigm of what we ordinarily consider knowing. In that sense God cannot be known. Nor does the coincidence of the infinite line and the infinite triangle make sense to our reason. Only by rising above reason can our intellect make sense of both.

CHAPTER 20

Still More regarding the Trinity

There Cannot Be Fourness, [Fiveness,] Etc., in God

In chapters 7 through 9 Cusanus had already discussed the Trinity at
length. He now reiterates what matters:

> Furthermore, the truth of the Trinity—a Trinity which is Triunity—
> requires that the trine be one, because [the trine] is spoken of as
> tri-une. But the triune comes under a concept only in the manner in
> which a mutual relationship unites distinct things and an order distin-
> guishes them. Now, when we construct a finite triangle there is first
> one angle, then another, and then a third from the first two; and these
> angles bear a mutual relationship to one another, so that from them
> there is one triangle. By comparison, then, [this mutual relationship
> obtains] infinitely in the infinite. Nevertheless, we must view this [mu-
> tual relationship] in the following way: viz., that priority is conceived
> to be in the eternity in such way that posteriority does not contradict
> it. For priority and posteriority could not belong in any other way to
> the infinite and eternal. Hence, it is not the case that the Father is pri-
> or to the Son and that the Son is posterior [to the Father]; rather, the
> Father is prior in such way that the Son is not posterior. The Father is
> the first person in such [a] way that the Son is not subsequently the
> second person; rather, just as the Father is the first person without
> priority, so the Son is the second person without posteriority; and, in a
> similar way, the Holy Spirit is the third person. (*DI* I.20:60)

VI. NAMING GOD

If faith in a triune God explains Cusanus's choice of the infinite triangle for his paradigm, the reader may still wonder about the "logic" of this choice. Why not choose some other figure, a square, for example? As pointed out in the preceding chapter, the argument that "a maximum line is just as much a triangle, a circle, and a sphere as it is a line" (*DI* I.19:56) can be extended to all figures. Cusanus anticipates the challenge:

> However, you might like to note, regarding this ever-blessed Trinity, that the Maximum is three and not four or five or more. This point is surely noteworthy. For [fourness or fiveness, etc.] would be inconsistent with the simplicity and the perfection of the Maximum. (*DI* I.20:60)

What needs to be shown is that being four or five would indeed "be inconsistent with the simplicity and the perfection of the Maximum." Cusanus invokes the idea of a simplest element:

> For example, every polygonal figure has a triangular figure as its simplest element; moreover, a triangular figure is the minimal polygonal figure—than which there cannot be a smaller figure. Now, we proved that the unqualifiedly minimum coincides with the maximum. Therefore, just as one is to numbers, so a triangle is to polygonal figures. Therefore, just as every number is reducible to oneness, so [all] polygons are [reducible] to a triangle.... For [a quadrangle] could not be a congruent measure of triangular figures, because it would always exceed them. Hence, how could that which would not be the measure of all things be the maximum? Indeed, how could that which would derive from another and would be composite, and hence finite, be the maximum? (*DI*.20:60)

Just as the number one is privileged among numbers, the triangle is privileged among polygons. As all numbers are an unfolding of the one, all polygonal figures are said to be an unfolding of the triangle.[1] Recall the way the number one has been discussed as the *principium* of all numbers. Every number is an aggregate of ones. In similar fashion, the triangle is now said to be the *principium* of all polygonal figures. Every such figure can be analyzed into an aggregate of triangles. We may well wonder about the exclusion of less regular figures—say, an ellipse. Given finite figures, such figures cannot be resolved into an aggregate of triangles. Transferred to the infinite, they all can be said to coincide with the infinite line. But this does not explain why

---

1. The thought that the triangle is the *principium* of all figures Cusanus found in Boethius, *De institutione arithmetica* II.6, ed. G. Friedlein (Leipzig, 1867), 92, 6f.; *PTW* I:123n61: *Adeo haec figura princeps est latitudinis ut ceterae omnes superficies in hanc resolvantur.*

we should single out the triangle as the measure of all figures. We may recall here Cusanus's claim that straight line is to curved line as substance is to accident (*DI* I.18:53). That may help to explain why here he is concerned with polygons.

Important are the ideas of measure and potency.

> It is now evident that from the potency of a simple line there first arises a simple triangle (as regards polygons), then a simple circle, and then a simple sphere; and we do not arrive at other than these elemental figures which are disproportional to one another in finite things and which enfold within themselves all figures. Hence, if we wanted to conceive of the measures of all measurable quantities, first we would have to have, for length, a maximum, infinite line, with which the minimum would coincide; then, similarly, for rectilinear size [we would have to have] a maximum triangle; and for circular size, a maximum circle; and for depth, a maximum sphere; and with other than these four we could not attain to all measurable things. (*DI* I.20:61)

Cusanus has in mind the preceding discussion, which generated triangle, circle, and sphere out of the line. Important to him is the need to recognize the generative power of the Maximum. God must be thought of as creator, and that means in relation to creation. He must be thought of as the Word that unfolds all that is. Cusanus is concerned to show how God provides us human beings, indeed all creatures, with a measure. To do so he must manifest himself in the creation. Once again Cusanus relies on mathematical analogies: Just as we can arrive at the idea of the maximum number with which the numerical minimum, the number one, the element and measure of all numbers coincides, or at the idea of a maximum triangle with which the finite triangle, the element and measure of all rectilinear figures coincides, so we can arrive at the idea of the infinite Maximum with which the element and measure of all creatures coincides. Christ will be the subject of Book Three.

It is difficult to take such analogies too seriously. Once again Gregor von Heimburg's dismissal of Cusanus's speculations as "mathematical superstition" comes to mind. But in his playful way Cusanus is grappling with the elusive essence of God. Only as the Trinity does God become relevant to our human existence:

> By comparison, then, since the unqualifiedly Maximum is the measure of everything, we predicate of it those attributes without which we do not consider it to be able to be the measure of everything. Hence, although the Maximum is infinitely above all trinity, we call it

> trine; for otherwise we would not be considering it to be the simple
> Cause and Measure of the things whose oneness of being is a trini-
> ty—even as, with regard to figures, triangular oneness consists of a
> trinity of angles. Yet, in truth: if this consideration is eliminated, then
> neither the name "trinity" nor our concept of trinity at all befit the
> Maximum; rather, [the name and the concept] fall infinitely short of
> this maximal and incomprehensible Truth. (*DI* I.20:61)

The statement that the "Maximum is infinitely above all trinity" has
to raise questions in the minds of the orthodox. Do we consider God
a Trinity only given our human perspective, which lets us ask for the
"Cause and Measure of the things whose oneness of being is a trinity—
even as, with regard to figures, triangular oneness consists of a trinity
of angles"? To us finite human knowers, Cusanus seems to be saying,
God presents himself as a trinity. But in truth the name "Trinity" does
not befit the Maximum at all. As suggested already in *Sermo* I, we human beings tend to look at things, including God, in our own image as
actors: capable of action. We have some end in mind and act to realize
that end. To counter the objection that this is to unduly anthropomor-
phize God, we can point to Genesis 1:27: "God created mankind in his
own image." Still, the statement that the "Maximum is infinitely above
all trinity" is troubling.

Cusanus discovers this trinitarian structure in activities, thoughts,
volitions, and likenesses.

> And so, we regard the maximum triangle as the simplest measure
> of all trinely existing things—even as activities are actions existing
> trinely (1) in potency, (2) in regard to an object, and (3) in actu-
> ality. The case is similar regarding perceptions, thoughts, volitions,
> likenesses, unlikenesses, adornments, comparative relations, mutual
> relations, natural appetites, and all other things whose oneness of
> being consists of plurality—e.g., especially a nature's being and activ-
> ity, which consist of a mutual relationship between what acts, what is
> acted upon, and what derives commonly from these two. (*DI* I.20:62)

We should note that the distinction between potency and actuality does
not apply to Cusanus's Maximum. Human actors choose among different possibilities. To our finite understanding, this world offers itself as
an island in the ocean of what could be. We are thus tempted to ask
why God chose to create this world with its countless imperfections. We
demand a reason explaining why it is as it is. But in God possibility and
actuality are one. To repeat: God did not first consider countless possible worlds and then choose to realize the one he deemed best. This is
the world God created: the unfolding of his infinite essence.

CHAPTER 21

The Likening of the Infinite Circle to Oneness

If an equilateral triangle offers itself as an obvious symbol of the Trinity, a circle offers itself as "a perfect figure of oneness and simplicity"—that is, as a symbol of the Oneness of God (*DI* I.21:63). To be sure, to do justice to God's infinity, we must think this circle as one and three. And yet, the difference between triangle and circle is not preserved in the infinite circle: "For the identity in an infinite circle is so great that it precedes all oppositions—even relative oppositions. For in an infinite circle *other* and *different* are not opposed to identity" (*DI* I.21:63). We must wonder whether an understanding of God drawing on the paradigm of the infinite circle is compatible with a robust understanding of God as the Trinity.

We should not forget that Cusanus's infinite circle is only a human thought construction, a symbol designed to cast some light on the ineffable being of God. But the emphasis on simplicity and oneness is such that the paradigm of the circle threatens to obscure the lessons of the paradigm of the triangle.

> Therefore, [by comparison]: since the Maximum is of infinite oneness, all the things which befit it are it, without difference and otherness. Thus, its goodness is not different from its wisdom but is the same thing; for in the Maximum all difference is identity. Hence,

> since the Maximum's power is most one, its power is also most power-
> ful and most infinite. The Maximum's most one duration is so great
> that in its duration the past is not other than the future, and the
> future is not other than the present; rather, they are the most one du-
> ration, or eternity, without beginning and end. For in the Maximum
> the beginning is so great that even the end is—in the Maximum—the
> beginning. (*DI* I.21:3)

The phrase "all the things which befit it" raises questions. In what
sense can anything be said to befit a Maximum said to be without difference and otherness? Must we not say that all things befit it equally
or not at all? Why do goodness and wisdom befit it better than cruelty
and ignorance?

The unity of the Maximum entails that God is beyond time, for
if the Maximum leaves no room for difference, it certainly leaves no
room for the difference between past, present, and future. In the
Maximum all distinctions collapse. So understood, eternity is the essence of time. I note once more how close Cusanus here comes to
Nietzsche's doctrine of the eternal recurrence. In God the end is said
to be the beginning. Thought in relation to God the timeline is an
infinite circle. Just as actuality and possibility coincide in God, so do
past, present, and future in the thought of "one duration, or eternity,
without beginning and end."

> All these [points] are exhibited by the infinite circle, which is eter-
> nal, without beginning and end, indivisibly the most one and the
> most encompassing. Because this circle is maximum, its diameter is
> also maximum. And since there cannot be more than one maximum,
> this circle is most one to such an extent that the diameter is the cir-
> cumference. Now, an infinite diameter has an infinite middle. But
> the middle is the center. Therefore, it is evident that the center, the
> diameter, and the circumference are the same thing. (*DI* I.21:64)

Cusanus offers these mathematical *paradigmata* to illuminate the relationship of God to creation:

> Accordingly, our ignorance is taught that the Maximum, to which the
> Minimum is not opposed, is incomprehensible. But in the Maximum
> the center is the circumference. You see that because the center is
> infinite, the whole of the Maximum is present most perfectly within
> everything as the Simple and the Indivisible; moreover, it is outside
> of every being—surrounding all things, because the circumference
> is infinite, and penetrating all things, because the diameter is in-
> finite. It is the Beginning of all things, because it is the center; it is
> the End of all things, because it is the circumference; it is the Middle

> of all things, because it is the diameter. It is the efficient Cause, since
> it is the center; it is the formal Cause, since it is the diameter; it is
> the final Cause, since it is the circumference. It bestows being, for
> it is the center; it regulates being, for it is the diameter; it conserves
> being, for it is the circumference. And many similar such things.
> (*DI* I.21:64)

That in the maximum circle center, diameter, circumference are said
to coincide repeats what has been said. This is, of course, not so with
finite figures. Taking the relationship of finite figures to the infinite
as a symbol of the relationship of creatures to God, Cusanus can say
that from our creaturely perspective God appears as trine: as the efficient cause of all created things—that is, as the ground of the existence of creatures; as their formal cause—that is, as the ground of
their essence; as their final cause—that is, as the ground of their end.
As in the infinite circle center, diameter, and circumference are one
and the same, so Father, Son, and Holy Spirit are one and the same
in God. Is the Trinity then to be understood as the way God manifests
himself to us human knowers? It would seem that any orthodox Christian has to reject this. Johannes Wenck thus charges that Cusanus
speaks expressly against the Athanasian creed when he writes:

> In the oneness of the Trinity the identity is so great that it precedes
> even all relative oppositions. This is evident because in the Trinity,
> other and different are not opposed to identity. For since the Maxi-
> mum is of infinite oneness, all the things which befit it are it without
> difference and otherness. Hence, it is not Father, not Son, and not
> Holy Spirit. For it is only infinity—not [an infinity] which begets or
> is begotten or proceeds. (*IL* 34–35)

Although not quite quoting *De docta ignorantia,* Wenck is not distorting what Cusanus had written. To be sure, there are, as we have seen,
many passages in *On Learned Ignorance* where Cusanus explicitly affirms
the orthodox position that God is three and one. And so, answering
Wenck's criticism, Cusanus writes in his *Apologia Doctae Ignorantiae.*

> Nevertheless, [the doctrine of] the Super-blessed Trinity is com-
> patible with this [doctrine of the divine simplicity]. For the infinite
> simplicity allows that God is one in such way that He is three, and is
> three in such way that He is one—even as this [point] is explained
> more clearly in the books of *Learned Ignorance.* (In like manner, we
> read that Pope Celestine, in professing his faith, spoke as follows:
> "We confess our belief that the indivisible holy Trinity—Father, Son,
> and Holy Spirit—is one in such way that it is three, and is three in
> such way that it is one.") (*AP* 23)

VI. NAMING GOD

But there is a strand in *De docta ignorantia* that puts such emphasis on the transcendence of the infinite Maximum that, as all difference, otherness, and number are left behind, so is the Trinity. Much here recalls Meister Eckhart, to whom Cusanus is so obviously indebted. Wenck, as we have seen, is very much aware of that proximity, as he is of Eckhart's proximity to condemned heretics such as the Beghards and Lollards of Strassburg (*IL* 30). In his *Apology* Cusanus accepts his proximity to Eckhart, praises his "genius and ardor," but adds that "he wished that his books be removed from public places, for the people are not suited for the statements Eckhart often intersperses contrary to the custom of the other teachers; nevertheless, intelligent men find in them many subtle and useful [points]" (*AP* 25). When one reads Eckhart's articles that were condemned in the bull "*In agro dominico*" issued by Pope John XXII in 1329, one is struck by the way some of them anticipate the teachings of Cusanus. Consider article 23, which focuses on God's unity.

> God is one in all ways and according to every respect so that he cannot find any multiplicity in himself either in intellect or in reality. Anyone who beholds the number two or who beholds distinction does not behold God, for God is one, outside and beyond number, and is not counted with anything. There follows: No distinction can exist or be understood in God himself.[1]

The Oneness of God is emphasized in this passage taken from Eckhart's *Exodus* commentary in a way that appears to deny the Trinity. It is of course only an excerpt, but everything asserted in the condemned article can be found in *De docta ignorantia*. Bernard McGinn, in his "Theological Summary" of Eckhart's thinking, is concerned to defend Eckhart's orthodoxy, notwithstanding such texts. Since his defense is easily transferred to Cusanus, it deserves being quoted here:

> Such texts provided the grounds for the suspicions of Eckhart's judges and many later interpreters concerning the validity of his doctrine of God from the standpoint of Christian trinitarianism. In order to be fair to Eckhart, though, we must also avert to another series of texts. In the Meister's writings there is no lack of passages that stress the absolute identity of the three Persons with the divine essence; there are also texts that seem to hint at, if not to develop fully, a dialectical relationship between the indistinct divine ground and the relational distinction of the Persons of the Father Son, and Holy Spirit.

---

1. Eckhart, *Essential Sermons, Commentaries, Treatises, and Defense,* 79. The bull is citing Eckhart's *Commentary on Exodus.* The first sentence of the condemned article quotes Moses Maimonides, *Guide for the Perplexed.*

Thus in *Sermon* 10: "Distinctions come from the Absolute Unity, that is the distinction in the Trinity. Absolute Unity is the distinction and distinction is the Unity. The greater the distinction, the greater the Unity, for that is the distinction without distinction."[2] Eckhart seems to be asserting that the God beyond God, the hidden ground of the Trinity, is the more indistinct insofar as he is distinct, the more one insofar as he is three.[3]

Again and again Eckhart distinguishes between the Godhead and God—between "God, the hidden ground of the Trinity" and God as he is with us human knowers. Insofar as we are finite creatures, bound to a particular place in space and time, our understanding, too, is finite and bound to particular perspectives. But we are more than finite creatures. We possess a spirit that is capable of reaching up to the infinite. Within himself the human being discovers thus the infinite, where thoughts of this infinity within merge with thoughts of the infinity of God—not, to be sure, God as creatures conceive him, but God as he is in himself. The Trinity, it would seem, for Eckhart belongs with the former. It does not describe the Godhead. It cannot be described.

In many places Cusanus is close to Eckhart.[4] Eckhart answers to an important strand in his own thinking, but one that leaves him dissatisfied, as demonstrated by chapters 7 to 10 of Book One, chapters 7 to 10 of Book Two, and especially by Book Three. Cusanus is too aware of our essential ignorance to think that we can grasp God as he is in himself. We cannot escape our human perspective.

But let us return to the conclusion of chapter 21. Cusanus here comments on the circular character of all theology in a way that threatens to render theology mute precisely by allowing it to make an infinite number of supposedly obvious points.

I call attention only to the following: that all theology is circular and is based upon a circle. [This is true] to such an extent that the names for the [divine] attributes are predicated truly of one another in a circular manner. For example, supreme justice is supreme truth, and supreme truth is supreme justice; and similarly for all the others. Accordingly, if you want to prolong the inquiry, an infinite number of theological [points] which are now hidden from you can be made very obvious to you. (*DI* I.21:66)

2. *DW* I:178.
3. Eckhart, *Essential Sermons, Commentaries, Treatises, and Defense,* 36–37.
4. See Wackerzapp, "Der Einfluss."

VI. NAMING GOD

The circularity of all theology, a thought Cusanus appears to have found in Ramon Llull,[5] is here tossed off as if it raised no serious questions. Cusanus speaks of positive attributes such as justice and truth. Just as in the infinite the triangle has been said to coincide with the circle, so in God supreme justice is said to coincide with supreme truth. That is demanded by God's infinite unity. Given such an understanding of God, that can be said of every divine attribute: in God they all coincide. But how do we human knowers determine what is a properly divine attribute? What of negative attributes such as injustice and deception? What is it about God that makes the latter inappropriate? In such an infinite God all attributes would seem to coincide. The circularity that Cusanus here attributes to theology threatens to render it meaningless.

5. Colomer, *Nikolaus von Kues und Raimund Llull*, 88ff.

CHAPTER 22

How God's Foresight Unites Contradictories

With this chapter we return to the problem of time and, intertwined with it, to the problem of freedom.

> But so that we may also come to see how through the previous points we are led to a deep understanding, let us direct our inquiry to [the topic of] God's foresight. Since it is evident from the foregoing that God is the enfolding of all things, even of contradictories, [it is also evident that] nothing can escape His foresight. For whether we do some thing or its opposite or nothing, the whole of it was enfolded in God's foresight. Therefore, nothing will occur except in accordance with God's foreseeing. (*DI* I.22:67)[1]

Striking is the claim that God enfolds not only all that is possible, but even contradictories, a claim made already by Eriugena.[2] This is to say also that whatever we will choose to do or will fail to do cannot escape God's foresight. God will have foreseen whatever will happen. Consider Aristotle's famous statement about the sea fight that either will or will not take place tomorrow. "A sea-fight must either take

---

1. For a discussion of Cusanus's appropriation and transformation of Thierry of Chartres's concept of folding, see Albertson, *Mathematical Theologies*, 184ff.

2. Dermot Moran, "Pantheism from John Scottus Eriugena to Nicholas of Cusa," *American Catholic Philosophical Quarterly* 64, no. 1 (Winter 1990): 144.

place tomorrow or not, but it is not necessary that it should take place tomorrow, neither is it necessary that it should not take place, yet it is necessary that it either should or should not take place tomorrow."[3] The future, Aristotle insists, is open. The principle of bivalence, that every meaningful proposition is either true or false, does not seem to hold in such cases: if I hold that to be meaningful a statement must be either true or false, statements about future contingencies, such as "the sea-fight will take place tomorrow" are not really meaningful. But if God foresees all that will happen, must we not say that the proposition that the sea-fight will take place tomorrow is now either true or false? To be sure, we may not know what will happen, but God knows. Determinism would seem to follow. But Cusanus would not claim that we have a knowledge of divine foreknowledge that allows us to claim this. Whatever will happen is indeed, he claims, enfolded in God's foresight. But in God possibility and actuality coincide, and this coincidence surpasses our understanding. By claiming that God's foresight unites contradictories, Cusanus can reconcile God's foresight with human freedom.

The following discussion is puzzling:

> Hence, although God could have foreseen many things which He did not foresee and will not foresee and although He foresaw many things which He was able not to foresee, nevertheless nothing can be added to or subtracted from divine foresight. By way of comparison: Human nature is simple and one; if a human being were born who was never even expected to be born, nothing would be added to human nature. Similarly, nothing would be subtracted from human nature if [the human being] were not born—just as nothing [is subtracted] when those who have been born die. This [holds true] because human nature enfolds not only those who exist but also those who do not exist and will not exist, although they could have existed. In like manner, even if what will never occur were to occur, nothing would be added to divine foresight, since it enfolds not only what does occur but also what does not occur but can occur. Therefore, just as in matter many things which will never occur are present as possibilities so, by contrast, whatever things will not occur but can occur: although they are present in God's foresight, they are present not possibly but actually. Nor does it follow here from that these things exist actually. (*DI* I.22:68)

The comparison of God's relationship to what has been, is, and will be the case to humanity's relationship to whatever human beings

---

3. Aristotle, *De Interpretatione* 9.19a.30.f.

were, are, or will be invites an understanding of God as the essence or Being of whatever was, is, or can be. Such a God may not be thought of as a being. Something like Heidegger's *ontologische Differenz* seems to open up here. *Gottheit* (Godhead), the essence of God or gods, would thus be a better term than *Gott*. Eckhart liked the former term to speak of the God beyond God. The difference between *Gottheit* and *Gott* invites an understanding of *Gottheit* that, as I just suggested, would approach Heidegger's understanding of Being, where Heidegger was well aware of his proximity to Meister Eckhart. So was Cusanus. But such an understanding fails to capture what orthodoxy would have to insist on: that God be understood as the creator of the world, as the author of the law, as the savior who took away the sting of death. *Gottheit* so understood would seem to be closer to logical space that has room not only for all that was, is, and will be, but also for all that could possibly be. But would we want to attribute foresight to logical space?

I have already suggested the relevance of Cusanus's understanding of God to the problem of reconciling freedom and divine providence. The coincidence of opposites provides Cusanus's answer to this problem.

> Hence, divine foresight is inescapable and immutable. Nothing can transcend it. Hence, all things related to it are said to have necessity—and rightly so, since in God all things are God, who is Absolute Necessity. And so, it is evident that the things which will never occur are present in God's foresight in the aforesaid manner, even if they are not foreseen to occur. It is necessary that God foresaw what He foresaw, because His foresight is necessary and immutable, even though He was able to foresee even the opposite of that which He did foresee. For if enfolding is posited (*posita complicatione*), it is not the case that the thing which was enfolded (*res complicata*) is posited; but if unfolding is posited (*posita explicatione*), enfolding (*complicatio*) is [also] posited. For example, although I am able to read or not to read tomorrow: no matter which of these I shall do, I will not escape [God's] foresight, which embraces [that is, enfolds] (*complectitur*) contraries. Hence, whatever I shall do will occur in accordance with God's foresight. (*DI* I.22:69)

God enfolds contraries. All that is actual and all that is possible is folded together or enfolded in God, but God unfolds himself only in what is actual. Just as humanity is constitutive of every possible human being, it is realized only in those that were, are, or will actually exist. But to think of God in human fashion as first foreseeing these different possibilities and then willing some of these to exist, perhaps because they would make this the best of all possible worlds, would be to violate the unity of God.

In this connection Kant's Third Antinomy is of some interest. The thesis claims that the causality that science presupposes is insufficient to explain everything that happens in the world. Everything is not so determined. We also need to have recourse to explanations that recognize freedom, that recognize that it makes sense to speak of a genuine origin, be it the origin of the cosmos, be it a free decision. The antithesis insists that everything that happens is indeed ruled by the laws that govern nature, that there is no freedom. The thesis counters that such causal explanations lead to an infinite regress, that there must be something such as absolute spontaneity—that is, so to say, another sort of groundless causality. The antithesis replies that such a causality is unthinkable, and once again it does not matter whether we are thinking of human or divine freedom.

Returning to Cusanus's example, we could say that the thesis has its counterpart in the view that I am free to decide whether I shall read or not read tomorrow. The antithesis will insist that whatever I shall be doing is determined by God's foresight and is thus determined. The solution lies in recognizing that God is beyond the principle of non-contradiction. Kant would say that the solution lies in recognizing that what our understanding can comprehend is transcended by the thing-in-itself.

CHAPTER 23

The Likening of the Infinite Sphere to the Actual Existence of God

Given Cusanus's earlier remarks about the infinite sphere, what he has to say about the likening of the infinite sphere to the actual existence (*ad actualem existentiam*) of God is to be expected.[1] I pointed out earlier that Cusanus found the metaphor in Meister Eckhart, who in turn found it in the *Book of the XXIV Philosophers*.[2] As mentioned, in Alan of Lille he is likely have encountered the closely related formulation *Deus est spaera* [*sic*] *intelligibilis, cuius centrum ubique, circumferentia nusquam*.[3] So understood, *sphaera intelligibilis* and *sphaera infinita* would seem to say the same.

The sphere is a familiar symbol of perfection. To say that it has its center everywhere is to say that we are not dealing with any sphere that we can encounter or imagine. But we can make some sense of

1. Cusanus had already mentioned the infinite sphere as a name for "the most actual existence of God" in chapter 12, but without further discussion.

2. Clemens Baeumker, "Das pseudo-hermetische 'Buch der 24 Meister' (Liber XXIV philosophorum): Ein Beitrag zur Geschichte des Neupythagoreismus und Neuplatonismus im Mittelalter," Beiträge zur Geschichte der Philosophie und Theologie des Mittelalters 25 (1928). See Mahnke, *Unendliche Sphäre und Allmittelpunkt*, and Wackerzapp, "Der Einfluss," 140ff.

3. On the relation of Alan of Lille's and Cusanus's use of the symbol of the sphere, see Butterworth, "Form and Significance of the Sphere in Nicholas of Cusa's *De Ludo Globi*," in Christianson and Izbicki, *Nicholas of Cusa*, 89–100.

it. To say that the intelligible sphere has its center everywhere is to suggest that God is fully present in even the smallest part of creation. Any sphere we can imagine is to the intelligible sphere as the creation is to God. God cannot be imagined. But *intelligibilis* still suggests intelligibility. *Infinitus*, on the other hand, better preserves God's radical transcendence, a central Cusan concern.

Of interest is that Cusanus considers the infinite sphere an especially appropriate *paradigma* for the actual existence of God. "Actual," *Actualis*, suggests activity. The symbol invites us to think of God as infinitely creative. As we shall see, in Book Two the figure of the infinite sphere will play a central and explosive part in the cosmology of Cusanus.

The discussion of the infinite sphere in this chapter holds no surprises.

> It is fitting to reflect upon still a few more points regarding an infinite sphere. In an infinite sphere we find that three maximum lines—of length, width, and depth—meet in a center. But the center of a maximum sphere is equal to the diameter and to the circumference. Therefore, in an infinite sphere the center is equal to these three lines; indeed, the center is all three: viz., the length, the width, and the depth. It will therefore be the Maximum[4]—infinitely and most simply—all length, width, and depth; in the Maximum these are the one most simple, indivisible Maximum. As a center, the Maximum precedes all width, length, and depth; it is the End and the Middle of all these; for in an infinite sphere the center, the diameter, and the circumference are the same thing. And just as an infinite sphere is most simple and exists in complete actuality, so the Maximum exists most simply in complete actuality. And just as a sphere is the actuality of a line, a triangle, and a circle, so the Maximum is the actuality of all things. Therefore, all actual existence has from the Maximum whatever actuality it possesses; and all existence exists actually insofar as it exists actually in the Infinite. Hence, the Maximum is the Form of forms and the Form of being, or maximum actual Being. (*DI* I.23:70)

The reader is invited to reflect further on the properties of an infinite sphere. Such a sphere cannot really exist: it is a thought construction. When we increase the radius of a sphere to infinity the properties that Cusanus ascribes to his sphere can indeed be granted, although we may also want to say that when a sphere is so stretched to

---

4. Translation changed. Hopkins translates *Erit itaque maximum* as "And so, [by comparison] the Maximum will be,..." The inserted [by comparison] certainly makes the text less jarring.

infinity, we lose our grasp on what it is to be a sphere. Given that the infinite sphere is a paradigm that is to help us understand the actual existence of God, what sense does it make to say that "an infinite sphere is most simple and exists in complete actuality"? What kind of being does the infinite sphere possess? Given the preceding, we can understand what lets Cusanus call the infinite sphere "the actuality of a line, a triangle, and a circle." But this cannot mean that it exists as Cusanus takes God to exist. Cusanus presents it as a paradigm that helps to shed some light on the way God is the actuality or the being of all things: "the Form of forms and the Form of being, or maximum actual Being."

The importance this paradigm will have in Book Two is hinted at by the following:

> Since the Maximum is like a maximum sphere, we now see clearly that it is the one most simple and most congruent measure of the whole universe and of all existing things in the universe; for in it the whole is not greater than the part, just as an infinite sphere is not greater than an infinite line. Therefore, God is the one most simple Essence (ratio) of the whole world, or universe. (*DI* I.23:72)

To say that the infinite sphere is "the one most simple and most congruent measure of the whole universe" is to suggest that the shape of the universe cannot be comprehended. The finite spherical cosmos of Aristotle and Ptolemy is an inappropriate description. That point will be developed at length in Book Two.

To say that the infinite sphere is "the one most simple and most congruent measure of … all existing things in the universe" is to say that the things that make up the universe are similarly infinite, and how they are in truth will be similarly incomprehensible. Consider once more the second proposition of the *Book of the 24 Philosophers*, which is the ultimate source of Cusanus's paradigm, who found it cited, as already mentioned, in Meister Eckhart: *Deus est sphaera infinita cuius centrum est ubique, circumferentia nusquam*, "God is an infinite sphere whose center is everywhere and his circumference nowhere."[5] To say that the center is everywhere is to say that God is fully present in everything. Consider this passage from one of Meister Eckhart's sermons:

> The least one knows of God, for example, to see a flower get its Being from him, is more perfect knowledge than any other. To know

---

5. Kurt Flasch, *Was Ist Gott? Das Buch der 24 Philosophen*, Lateinisch-Deutsch (Munich: Beck, 2011).

VI. NAMING GOD

the least of creatures as one of God's Beings, is better than knowing an angel.[6]

A dung heap can become an epiphany of the divine.

The question the metaphor of the infinite sphere raises is: if God is fully present in everything, how are we to rank one thing, place, or action above another? The paradigm of the infinite sphere thus threatens all attempts to assert hierarchies among beings. It threatens also what Kierkegaard called a "teleological suspension of the ethical."

6. Meister Eckhart, *Meister Eckhart: A Modern Translation,* trans. Raymond B. Blakney (New York: Harper Torchbooks, 1969), 171.

CHAPTER 24

The Name of God; Affirmative Theology

Cusanus begins his discussion of affirmative theology by reiterating that no name can properly befit the Maximum. In that sense it is unnameable.

> Since the Maximum is the unqualifiedly Maximum, to which nothing is opposed, it is evident that no name can properly befit it. For all names are bestowed on the basis of a oneness of conception [*ratio*] through which one thing is distinguished from another. But where all things are one, there can be no proper name. (*DI* I.24:74)

So understood, naming is essentially heterothesis: something is understood to be this and not that. Whatever is posited by naming it is necessarily opposed to what is other. Heterothesis is thus constitutive of understanding (*ratio*). But as Cusanus thinks God, he cannot be opposed to an other. That is to say, God has no place in logical or conceptual space. If proper naming is inseparable from conceiving, there can be no proper name for God.

> Hence, Hermes Trismegistus rightly says, "Since God is the totality of things, no name is proper to Him; for either He would have to be called by every name or else all things would have to be called by

His name";[1] for in His simplicity He enfolds the totality of things. (*DI* I.24:75)

The reference to Hermes Trismegistus invites the charge of pantheism. The distance between creation and creator appears to have been eliminated: either we name God when naming anything at all or "God" is a name for anything. Meister Eckhart comes to mind, as does the metaphor of the infinite sphere: the center is everywhere; God is fully present in everything, no matter how insignificant.

> Hence, as regards His own name, which we say to be ineffable and which is "tetragrammaton" (i.e., "of four letters") and which is proper because it befits God according to His own essence, not according to any relation to created things: He ought to be called "One-and-all," or better, "All-in-one." And in like manner we previously discovered [the name] "Maximum Oneness," which is the same thing as "All-in-one"; indeed, the name "Oneness" seems still closer and still more suitable than the name "All-in-one." Wherefore the prophet says: "On that day there will be one God, and His name will be one."[2] (*DI* I.24:75)

As mentioned, the tetragrammaton יהוה is the biblical name for "Yahweh." What matters to Cusanus is that this ineffable name refuses to relate God to anything other than himself: God is God. But what can we call him, if we are not content with this empty tautology? Hermes Trismegistus's "no name is proper to him; for either he would have to be called by every name or else all things would have to be called by his 'name'" provides a pointer. And so Cusanus goes on to suggest that "One-and-all" and "All-in-one" would be good names for God; but even more suitable would be "Oneness."

> However, it is not the case that "Oneness" is the name of God in the way in which we either name or understand oneness; for just as God transcends all understanding, so, a fortiori, [He transcends] every name. Indeed, through a movement of reason, which is much lower than the intellect, names are bestowed for distinguishing between things. But since reason cannot leap beyond contradictories: as regards the movement of reason, there is not a name to which another [name] is not opposed. Therefore, as regards the movement of reason: plurality or multiplicity is opposed to oneness. Hence, not "oneness" but "Oneness to which neither otherness nor plurality

---

1. Hermes Trismegistus, *Asclepius* 20, in *Corpus Hermeticum*, 2nd ed., ed. A. D. Nock (Paris: Société d'Edition "Les Belles Lettres," 1945), 2:321, lines 8–9. See *PTW* I:125n75.

2. Zachariah 14:9. Once again Cusanus is drawing on Meister Eckhart's *Exodus* commentary. See *PTW* I:125n75.

nor multiplicity is opposed" befits God. This is the maximum name, which enfolds all things in its simplicity of oneness; this is the name which is ineffable and above all understanding. (*DI* I.24:76)

With this we are very close to the "name" *non aliud*, "not-other," which in the later trialogue *De li non aliud* Cusanus will call the most precise name to express his concept of the Unnameable, which is indeed not other than anything, that has occurred to him.[3] Still, there is no adequate name, although, and this is important to consider, some names are certainly thought to be more adequate than others. This presupposes that, while we lack an adequate concept of God, our intellect nonetheless provides us with an intuition of God that allows us to judge one name more adequate than another.

> Although "Oneness" seems to be a quite close name for the Maximum, nevertheless it is still infinitely distant from the true Name of the Maximum—[a Name] which is the Maximum. (*DI* I.24:77)

A fully adequate name would have to be nothing other than the thing named. That holds for all names. All are inadequate. But they are especially inadequate when we attempt to speak of God. Affirmative names befit God only "infinitesimally."

> And so, from these considerations it is evident that the affirmative names we ascribe to God befit Him [only] infinitesimally [*per infinitum diminute*]. For such [names] are ascribed to Him in accordance with something found in created things. Therefore, since any such particular or discrete thing, or thing having an opposite, can befit God only very minutely [*diminutissime*] affirmations are scarcely fitting, as Dionysius says.[4] For example, if you call God "Truth," falsity is the contradistinction; if you call Him "Virtue," vice is the contradistinction; if you call Him "Substance," accident is the contradistinction; and so on. But since God is not a substance which is not all things and to which something is opposed, and is not a truth which is not all things without opposition, these particular names cannot befit Him except very infinitesimally. (*DI* I.24:78)

This raises the question: what allows any names to befit him at all? All names are bestowed on God in relation to our understanding of created things. But if between the finite and the infinite there is no proportion, as we are told by Cusanus, what sense can we make even of his "except very infinitesimally"?

3. Nicholas of Cusa, *De li non aliud*, trans. Jasper Hopkins, in *Nicholas of Cusa, On God as Not-Other: A translation and an Appraisal* (Minneapolis: Banning, 1987), 6.

4. Pseudo-Dionysius, *De coelesti hierarchia*, *Dionysiaca* II:750. Cusanus is relying on the translation by Johannes Scottus Eriugena; *PTW* I:125n35.

VI. NAMING GOD

But does it even make sense to speak of God, except in relation to creation? Cusanus would seem to grant that there must be such a relation when he claims that the affirmative names we ascribe to God befit him only *per infinitum diminute* or *diminutissime*. His mathematical paradigm comes to mind—the way the curvature of a circle is diminished as its radius is increased to infinity, until in the infinite circle, circle and straight line come to coincide. In this case we can speak of more or less curved lines—that is, of more or less inadequate approximations of the infinite line, although every finite circle, no matter how large, will be unable to bridge the gap that separates the finite and the infinite.

> The aforesaid is so true of all affirmations that even the names of the Trinity and of the persons—viz., "Father," "Son," and "Holy Spirit"—are bestowed on God in relation to created things. For because God is Oneness, He is Begetter and Father; because He is Equality of Oneness, He is Begotten, or Son; because He is Union of both [Oneness and Equality-of-Oneness], He is Holy Spirit. Accordingly, it is clear that the Son is called Son because He is Equality of Oneness, or of Being, or of existing. Hence, from the fact that God was eternally able to create things—even had He not created them—it is evident [that] He is called Son in relation to these things. For He is Son because He is Equality of being [these] things; things could not exist beyond or short of Equality. Thus, He is Son because He is Equality of being of the things which God was able to make, even had He not been going to make them. Were God not able to make these things, He would not be Father, Son, or Holy Spirit; indeed, He would not be God. Therefore, if you reflect quite carefully, [you will see that] for the Father to beget the Son was [for Him] to create all things in the Word. Wherefore, Augustine maintains that the Word is both the Art and the Idea in relation to created things. Hence, God is Father because He begets Equality of Oneness; but He is Holy Spirit because He is the Love common to both [Oneness and Equality of Oneness]; and He is all these in relation to created things. (*DI* I.24:80–81)

To think God as the Trinity is to think him in relation to creation. But this is the only way we human beings can think him. Any attempt to think God as he is in himself leads to silence.

CHAPTER 25

The Pagans Named God in Various Ways in Relation to Created Things

Of interest is what Cusanus has to say about the way the pagans named God. In countless different ways they all sought to capture something essential about God, even though they are said to have been too focused on the things of the world to do justice to God's transcendent unity. Thus they fell into idolatry, mistaking things that were unfoldings of God for the divine reality. But this presupposes that the pagans did have some understanding of the essence of God.

It is of course not just the pagans who are in danger of replacing God with something that is just an unfolding of God. All affirmative theology names God in relation to created things and thus inadequately. Even Father, Son, or Holy Spirit are said by Cusanus to be but inadequate names that veil the divine essence. Our task is to remain aware of the essential inadequacy of all our names. But we also need to distinguish more or less adequate ways of naming God, where the elusive measure has to be provided by our intellect, which in its glimpse of the Maximum is able to transcend the finite.

VI. NAMING GOD

> The pagans likewise named God from His various relationships to
> created things. [They named Him] Jupiter because of marvelous
> kindness (for Julius Firmicus[1] says that Jupiter is a star so auspicious
> that had he reigned alone in the heavens, men would be immor-
> tal); similarly, [they named Him] Saturn because of a profundity
> of thoughts and inventions regarding the necessities of life; Mars
> because of military victories; Mercury because of good judgment in
> counseling; Venus because of love which conserves nature; Sun be-
> cause of the force of natural movements; Moon because of conser-
> vation of the fluids upon which life depends; Cupid because of the
> unity of the two sexes (for which reason they also called Him Nature,
> since through the two sexes He conserves the species of things).
> (*DI* I.25:83)

Cusanus presupposes here that positive attributes such as kindness,
immortality, thoughtfulness, strength, good judgment, and love befit
God better than negative attributes, such as hate or deceit. Presupposed once again is an intuition of God that makes the positive attributes more appropriate.

Of interest is the way Cusanus dwells on the last God he mentions
in the cited paragraph, on Cupid:

> Hermes[2] said that not only all [species of] animals but also all [spe-
> cies of] non-animals have two sexes; wherefore, he maintained that
> the Cause of all things, viz., God, enfolds within Himself both the
> masculine and the feminine sex, of which he believed Cupid and
> Venus to be the unfolding. Valerius,[3] too, the Roman, making the
> same affirmation, professed that Jupiter is the omnipotent Divine
> Father and Mother. Hence, in accordance with one thing's desiring
> (*cupit*) another, they gave to the daughter of Venus, i.e., of natural
> beauty, the name "Cupid." But they said that Venus is the daughter
> of omnipotent Jupiter, from whom Nature and all its accompani-
> ments derive. (*DI* I.25:83)

We should note the shifting characterizations of Cupid, which all
seem groping anticipations of Cusanus's triune God. "Cupid" thus
first appears as a name for the cause of all things—we might say as

---

1. Firmicus Maternus, *Mathesis*, ed. W. Kroll, F. Skutsch, and K. Ziegler (1897; repr.
Leipzig: B. G. Teubner, 1913), 1:56, 30–37.

2. Hermes Trismegistus, *Asclepius* 21, in *Corpus Hermeticum* II:321, lli. 18–21.

3. Cusanus found the reference to Valerius Soranus in Augustine, *De Civitate Dei* VII.9.
The two lines quoted by Augustine, citing Varro, are all that that has survived of Soranus's
poetry: *Iuppiter omnipotens regum rerumque deumque/progenitor genetrixque deum, deus unus et
omnes* ("Almighty Jove, progenitor of kings, and things, and gods, / And eke the mother of
the gods, and one and all"); St. Augustine, *The City of God*, trans. Marcus Dods, DD (New
York: Random House, 1950), 217.

natura naturans, which through the two sexes and the bond that unites them "conserves the species of things." The cause of all things is thus understood to unfold itself in a trinity. In similar fashion Hermes Trismegistus is said to have understood Cupid and Venus as the result of the unfolding of God in whom the difference between masculine and feminine is enfolded. Here Cupid appears, so to speak, as the Son of an androgynous deity and Venus as his bride. The Romans are *said to have* given us yet a third understanding: Cupid is now said to be the daughter of Venus, who in turn is said to be the daughter of Jupiter. Venus is here identified with natural beauty, and beauty gives rise to desire, which embracing beauty seeks to give birth. Plato's *Symposium* and its account of eros comes to mind. Jupiter gives birth to beauty, and beauty awakens desire or love. Taken together, these three accounts present Cupid first as Father, then as Son, and finally as love or desire, the offspring of Venus. Cupid appears thus as both one and three, echoing the Trinity.

How should we understand "All these names are unfoldings of the enfolding of the one ineffable name" (*DI* I.25:84)? The plenitude enfolded in God's ineffable name is unfolded in the potentially countless names that we human beings have given him. The pagans attempted to unfold the essence of God in their gods, where, as we should expect, Cusanus discovers in them anticipations of the Trinity.

To the pagans, who worshipped many gods, Cusanus contrasts the Jews, who worship one infinite God and for that very reason were derided by them. And yet, fundamentally, the pagans are said to have worshipped that same God, even if all too often they fell into idolatry. Cicero is cited in support: "The wise, however, continued rightly to believe in the oneness of God, as will be known to anyone who carefully examines Cicero's *On the Nature of the Gods,* as well as the ancient philosophers" (*DI* I.84). Further support is said to be offered by works of architecture:

> The Temple of Peace, the Temple of Eternity, the Temple of Harmony, and the Pantheon (in which there was in the middle, under the open air, the altar of the Infinite Limit, of which there is no limit)— and other such [edifices] inform us that the pagans named God in various ways in accordance with His relationship to created things. All these names are unfoldings of the enfolding of the one ineffable name [the tetragrammaton] (*DI* I.84)

The necessity of naming God in accordance with his relationship to created things brings with it the danger that the mundane vehicle will obscure the divine tenor. Idolatry is worshipping God in created things. In an extended sense one could say that idolatry is holding up some finite thing as the absolute. Think of the golden calf. This brings to mind Hermann Broch's understanding of radical evil, or Kitsch.[4] Without learned ignorance it would seem that Christianity, too, easily falls into something very much like idolatry. Dogmatism and idolatry are related. Dogmatism is incompatible with learned ignorance.

4. See Karsten Harries, "Decoration, Death, and Devil," in *Hermann Broch: Literature, Philosophy, Politics; The Yale Broch Symposium 1986* (Columbia, S.C.: Camden House, 1988), 279–97.

CHAPTER 26

Negative Theology

The concluding chapter of Book One begins with a reaffirmation of the indispensability of affirmative theology. We cannot worship an empty infinite transcendence. To worship God we must be able to think of him in ways that make him supremely praiseworthy.

> The worshipping (*cultura*) of God, who is to be worshiped in spirit and in truth [John 4:23–24], must be based upon affirmations about Him. Accordingly, every religion, in its worshipping, must mount upward by means of affirmative theology. [Through affirmative theology] it worships God as one and three, as most wise and most gracious, as Inaccessible Light [1 Tm 6:16], as Life, Truth, and so on. And it always directs its worship by faith which it attains more truly through learned ignorance. It believes that He whom it worships as one is All-in-one, and that He whom it worships as Inaccessible Light is not light as is corporeal light, to which darkness is opposed, but is infinite and most simple Light, in which darkness is Infinite Light; and [it believes] that Infinite Light always shines within the darkness of our ignorance but [that] the darkness cannot comprehend it [Jn 1:5]. (*DI* I.26:86)

As the beginning of the Gospel of John, which Cusanus is here invoking, suggests, when the evangelist speaks of Light he is thinking of the Word through which all things were made—that is to say, he is thinking God in relation to creation, as every religion must do. Religion cannot dispense with metaphors drawn from the created world. But for that very reason it must guard against doing violence to God by making him into a being like other creatures; it must preserve his transcendence. Learned ignorance helps to guard worship (*cultura*) from idolatry, preventing words from drowning faith (*fides*).

> And so, the theology of negation is so necessary for the theology of affirmation that without it God would not be worshiped as the Infinite God but, rather, as a creature. And such worship is idolatry; it ascribes to the image that which befits only the reality itself. Hence, it will be useful to set down a few more things about negative theology. (*DI* I.26:86)

Negative theology is necessary to save affirmative theology from idolatry! Without it, Cusanus suggests, God would be worshipped as another being, the highest being perhaps, but a being among beings, nonetheless. Just as straight line, triangle, circle, and sphere must be translated into the infinite to become fitting symbols of God, so names such as Father, Son, and Holy Spirit must be translated into the infinite to become fitting names for God. Such translation presupposes some understanding of the ineffable infinite one. The task of negative theology is to help us guard such understanding. But divorced from affirmative theology it leaves us only with an abyss: the infinity of God, which bears no relation to creation. So understood, God threatens to dissolve into an empty transcendence. The Dionysian tradition to which Cusanus is so indebted is shadowed by that threat:

> Sacred ignorance has taught us that God is ineffable. He is so because He is infinitely greater than all nameable things. And by virtue of the fact that [this] is most true, we speak of God more truly through removal and negation—as [teaches] the greatest Dionysius, who did not believe that God is either Truth or Understanding or Light or any-thing which can be spoken of.[1] (Rabbi Solomon[2] and all the wise follow Dionysius.) Hence, in accordance with this negative theology, according to which [God] is only infinite, He is neither Father nor Son nor Holy Spirit. Now, the Infinite qua Infinite is neither Begetting, Begotten, nor Proceeding. (*DI* I.26:87)

Negative theology thus leaves no room for the Trinity. The Trinity, however, is central to Cusanus's understanding of God, as has been

---

1. Pseudo-Dionysius, *De mystica theologia* V, in *Dionysiaca* I:597–600.

2. The reference to Moses Maimonides, called here Rabbi Solomon, is based on a reference Cusanus had found in Meister Eckhart's *Exodus* commentary; *PTW* I:n87. Cusanus no doubt thinks of Eckhart as one of the wise who follow Dionysius.

shown again and again in the preceding chapters. But there is tension in his thinking between a neo-Platonic strand that includes Proclus, Pseudo-Dionysius, John Scotus Eriugena, and Meister Eckhart and a trinitarian strand that includes St. Augustine, Boethius, and Thierry of Chartres. As Cusanus points out, as soon as the persons of the Trinity are distinguished, we have left negative theology behind. But we must leave negative theology behind if God is to matter to us, if he is to have any relevance to our existence here on earth, if we are to understand God as creator, as giver of the law, and as savior.

Concluding Book One and in an effort to mediate between these two strands, Cusanus invokes Hilary of Poitiers (c. 310–c. 367).

> Therefore, when Hilary of Poitiers distinguished the persons, he most astutely used the expressions "Infinity in the Eternal," "Beauty in the Image," and "Value in the Gift" [*In aeterno, inquit, infinitas, species in imagine, usus in munere*]. He means that although in eternity we can see only infinity, nevertheless since the infinity which *is* eternity is negative infinity, it cannot be understood as Begetter but [can] rightly [be understood] as eternity, since "eternity" is affirmative of oneness, or maximum presence. Hence, [Infinity-in-the-Eternal is] the Beginning without beginning, "Beauty in the Image" indicates the Beginning from the Beginning, "Value in the Gift" indicates the Procession of the two." (*DI* I.26:87)

Even with Cusanus's explanation, the cited passage is not easy to understand. It helps to read it in its original context, in Hilary of Poitiers, *De Trinitate* II.I:

> He bade them baptize in the Name of the Father, and of the Son, and of the Holy Ghost, that is with confession of the Creator and of the Only-begotten, and of the Gift. For God the Father is One, from Whom are all things; and our Lord Jesus Christ the Only-begotten, through Whom are all things, is One; and the Spirit, God's Gift to us, Who pervades all things, is also One. Thus all are ranged according to powers possessed and benefits conferred—the One Power from Whom all, the One Offspring through Whom all, the One Gift Who gives us perfect hope. Nothing can be found lacking in that supreme Union which embraces, in Father, Son and Holy Spirit, infinity in the Eternal, His Likeness in His express Image, our enjoyment of Him in the Gift.[3]

---

3. Hilary of Poitiers, *De Trinitate* II.I (PL 10:51A); E. W. Watson and L. Pullan, trans., *From Nicene and Post-Nicene Fathers*, second series, vol. 9, ed. Philip Schaff and Henry Wace (Buffalo, NY: Christian Literature, 1899), revised and edited for New Advent by Kevin Knight, http://www.newadvent.org/fathers/3302.htm.

VI. NAMING GOD

Recall what Cusanus had said earlier about the Romans who, inadequately glimpsing the Trinity, posited the procession of Cupid from Venus, of Venus from Jupiter: Jupiter, cause of all things, gives birth to beauty and beauty awakens love. Hilary of Poitiers presents us with a similar procession. As Cusanus points out, an understanding of God as "only infinity" cannot capture what finds inadequate expression in an understanding of God as Father or Begetter. But by writing *infinitas in aeterno*, Hilary takes a first step away from such negativity: "eternity," Cusanus suggests, affirms oneness, maximum presence. *Infinitas in aeterno* names thus the "Beginning without beginning." *Species in imagine* suggests the splendor or beauty of the Son, of both the Word through which all things are said to be and more especially the splendor of Christ, the paradigm of beauty here on earth. *Usus in munere* suggests the enjoyment of the gift the Holy Spirit bestows on the faithful.

To be sure, all such affirmations are highly inadequate. But the corresponding negations, while true, are altogether insufficient, and so Cusanus concludes:

> From these [observations] it is clear (1) that in theological matters negations are true and affirmations are inadequate, and (2) that, nonetheless, the negations which remove the more imperfect things from the most Perfect are truer than the others. For example, it is truer that God is not stone than that He is not life or intelligence; and [it is truer that He] is not drunkenness than that He is not virtue. The contrary [holds] for affirmations; for the affirmation which states that God is intelligence and life is truer than [the affirmation that He is] earth or stone or body. All these [points] are very clear from the foregoing. (*DI* I.26:89)

Presupposed is an intuition of perfection. We can distinguish the less from the more perfect. The presupposed measure of perfection we human beings do not find in the world, but bear within ourselves as images of God—not that we shall ever grasp God's perfection. But the shadow of that perfection lies on every thing we judge to be more or less perfect.

> Therefrom we conclude that the precise truth shines incomprehensibly within the darkness of our ignorance. This is the learned ignorance we have been seeking and through which alone, as I explained, [we] can approach the maximum, triune God of infinite goodness—[approach Him] according to the degree of our instruction in ignorance, so that with all our might we may ever praise Him,

who is forever blessed above all things, for manifesting to us His incomprehensible self. (*DI* I.26:89)

Recall Cusanus's earlier attempt to show how the infinite, despite its incommensurability with the finite, can yet provide us with a measure that allows us to call one thing or description more or less adequate to God's infinite being: God is fully present in every thing, just as the infinite line is: present in every line, no matter how short. And yet, to us a longer straight line seems to participate more fully in the infinite straight line than a shorter line. To us human knowers there appear to be degrees of participation in the Maximum, just as there are more or less adequate names or descriptions of God, even though none are able to bridge the abyss that separates the infinite from the finite. God is incomprehensible. The precise truth eludes us. But this does not mean that we wander, cognitively, in total darkness. The precise truth "shines incomprehensibly" into that darkness, providing our attempts to understand him and his creation with an elusive measure. Incomprehensible as it must remain, the splendor of the triune God is nonetheless manifest to us.

BOOK TWO

I. THE UNIVERSE

M ORE THAN THE OTHER TWO BOOKS, it is Book Two of *On Learned Ignorance* that with its projection of a boundless universe presents the reader with, as Cusanus puts it, "previously unheard of [doctrines]," which, he claims, learned ignorance shows us to be true (*DI* II.11:156). Shattering the medieval cosmos, these doctrines were indeed likely to amaze the reader. Challenging what was then well-established common sense, many readers, like Johannes Wenck, no doubt, felt they had to reject what Cusanus had to say as nonsense. How could one reconcile this denial of the central position of the earth, the claim that there are countless stars inhabited by intelligent beings, with Aristotle's understanding of the cosmos, with the biblical account of the creation, and, more importantly, with the Christian salvation account? How could a cardinal claim truth for such radical views? One hundred and fifty years later Giordano Bruno embraced the cardinal's conception of a boundless universe with an evangelical fervor. On February 17, 1600, Bruno was burned on the Piazza Campo de' Fiori in Rome for his views. How the church had changed! But geocentrism could not be saved.

Already as a student in Padua Cusanus demonstrated his deep interest in the mathematical arts, especially astronomy. While a member of the Council of Basel he was able to put what he had learned in the lectures of Prosdocimo de' Beldomandi to good use when composing his *De correctione kalendarii* (1436). The issue was of considerable interest. "The most fundamental difficulty is that there is a slight difference between the actual year and the Julian calendar year of 365.25 days. The actual solar year is a fraction of a day shorter. Over more than a millennium and a half, the date of the actual Vernal Equinox had slipped back nearly ten days earlier than the assumed date of March 21. This caused a discrepancy in the date of Easter, which was the point of ecclesiastical interest."[1] I mention this early learned treatise here because it shows that Cusanus's knowledge of astronomical matters far exceeded that of all but a few of his contemporaries.[2]

The second book begins with a brief Prologue, once again addressed to Cardinal Julian Cesarini. Cusanus reminds the reader of what has been discussed in Book One concerning the Absolute Maximum from which every created thing derives. That book had concluded with the seemingly paradoxical and for that very reason thought-provoking statement that while the precise truth is denied to us, it yet "shines incomprehensibly within the darkness of our ignorance" (*DI* I.26:89). The Prologue of Book Two picks up this thought:

> Through certain symbolic signs we have in the foregoing way discussed instruction in ignorance as it regards the nature of the Absolute Maximum. Through [the assistance of] this Nature, which shines forth a bit to us in a shadow, let us by the same method inquire a bit more about those things which are all-that-which-they-are from the Absolute Maximum. (*DI* II.P:90)

Instead of "shines incomprehensibly within the darkness of our ignorance," we now read "shines forth a bit to us in a shadow," recalling 1 Corinthians 13:12: "For now we see in a mirror, dimly, but then face to face. Now I know in part; then I shall understand fully, even as I have been fully understood." In our present mortal condition we are denied an adequate understanding of God. And yet, the mirror of our own understanding presents us with symbols such as infinite line, triangle, circle, and sphere that give us at least some insight into the nature of the incomprehensible Deity.

From the Creator Cusanus turns to the creation.

> Since what is caused derives altogether from its cause and not at all from itself and since it conforms as closely [*propinquius et similius*] as it can to the Fount and Form [*ratio*] from which it is that which it is: clearly, the nature of contraction is difficult to attain if the Absolute Exemplar remains unknown. Therefore, it is fitting that we be learned-in-ignorance beyond our understanding [*apprehensio*], so that (though not grasping the truth precisely as it is) we may at least be led to seeing that there is a precise truth which we cannot now comprehend. This is the goal of my work in this part. May Your Clemency judge this work and find it acceptable. (*DI* II.90)

---

1. Hunter, "What Did Nicholas of Cusa Contribute to Science," 103.

2. Cusanus's efforts did not lead to the needed reform of the Julian calendar. That had to wait for the reform instituted by Pope Gregory XIII in 1582.

In keeping with his age, Cusanus, too, understands every thing as an *ens creatum*. Both that it is and what it is it owes to God, who is therefore both its Fount (*origo*) and Form (*ratio*), both Father and Son—that is, the Word. That Cusanus is speaking here not of God as he is in himself, but he reveals himself to us in his creation should be kept in mind. He speaks of God as he appears in the mirror provided by our understanding.

Cusanus claims that since the Maximum remains unknown, there can also be no precise truth concerning the things of this world, for all things created by God partake of his infinity, a thought presented already in the very first chapter of *De docta ignorantia*. And yet, Cusanus insists, attempting to grasp the truth about things, attempts that will inevitably fall short of their goal, we may nevertheless be led "to seeing that there is a precise truth which we cannot now comprehend." That the precise truth is incomprehensible was shown in some detail in chapter 3 of Book One. There we saw also how this incomprehensible truth provides our search for the truth with a measure. It functions as a regulative ideal.

That there can be no precise truth does not mean that there cannot be better or worse descriptions of God's creation. And, as Book Two will show, Cusanus is convinced that he has good reasons to reject the then prevailing, fundamentally still Aristotelian worldview, which places the earth at the center of a finite spherical cosmos. That view can appeal to the way we experience the world around us first of all and most of the time: sunrise and sunset, the revolution of the heavens, seem to support a geocentric worldview, which assigns us our place near the center of the cosmos. But such support is shaken by reflection on the way the position and make-up of both our body and our mind shape the way things present themselves to us. Different points of view inevitably limit our access to the truth. To become aware of the power of perspective to distort our understanding of reality is to become learned about our essential ignorance.

CHAPTER 1

Corollaries Preliminary to Inferring One Infinite Universe

The chapter title already raises a question: if whatever is not the Absolute Maximum is finite, that Maximum alone would seem to deserve to be called infinite. How then can Cusanus now apply the term to the universe? What is its being? In what sense can it be said to be infinite? In what sense finite?

Cusanus begins by reminding the reader of the principle he had established in the beginning of *De docta ignorantia*:

> It will be very advantageous to set forth, from out of our beginning [*ex principio nostro*], the preliminary corollaries of our instruction in ignorance. For they will furnish a certain facility regarding an endless number of similar points which in like manner can be inferred; and they will make clearer the points to be discussed. (*DI* II.1:91)

By *principium nostrum* Cusanus refers to the *regula doctae ignorantiae*, the rule of learned ignorance, that outside the Absolute Maximum— that is, in this world where there is always a more and a less—there can be no true equality and therefore no precise truth. Consider once more his articulation of that principle in chapter 3 of Book One:

> If anything is posited which is not the unqualifiedly Maximum, it is evident that something greater can be posited. And since we find

> degrees of equality (so that one thing is more equal to a second thing
> than to a third, in accordance with generic, specific, spatial, causal,
> and temporal agreement and difference among similar things), ob-
> viously we cannot find two or more things which are so similar and
> equal that they could not be progressively more similar ad infinitum.
> (*DI* I.3:9)

Creation is the realm of the more and the less, where each thing
possesses an identity uniquely its own and no two things will ever be
exactly the same. "Hence, the measure and the measured—however
equal they are—will always remain different" (*DI* I.9).

Cusanus now restates this principle and applies it to the way we
measure motion:

> I maintained, at the outset of my remarks, that with regard to things
> which are comparatively greater and lesser we do not come to a max-
> imum in being and in possibility. Hence, in my earlier [remarks]
> I indicated that precise equality befits only God. Wherefore, it follows
> that, except for God, all positable things differ. Therefore, one mo-
> tion cannot be equal to another; nor can one motion be the measure
> of another, since, necessarily, the measure and the thing measured
> differ. (*DI* II.1:91)

Taken in the ordinary sense of "measure," this cannot be right. We
do of course measure one motion by another all the time. Think of
clocks. As the dialogue *De staticis experimentis* shows, Cusanus was very
much aware of the power and the importance of human measuring
and measuring devices, such as rulers, scales, and time-keeping devices. But Cusanus is thinking here of absolutely precise measurements
that cannot be improved on. Such measurements, he insists, are denied to us human knowers.

To show the fruitfulness of his principle, Cusanus proceeds to apply it to the medieval quadrivium, to the mathematical arts of arithmetic, geometry, astronomy, and music. As David Albertson remarks,
"The Boethian quadrivium is an exemplary illustration, if not a practical proof, of *docta ignorantia*."[1] Cusanus turns first to astronomy.

> Although these points will be of use to you regarding an infinite
> number of things, nevertheless if you transfer them to astronomy,
> you will recognize that the art of calculating lacks precision, since
> it presupposes that the motion of all the other planets can be mea-
> sured by reference to the motion of the sun. Even the ordering of
> the heavens—with respect to whatever kind of place or with respect

---

1. Albertson, *Mathematical Theologies*, 184.

to the risings and settings of the constellations or to the elevation of
a pole and to things having to do with these—is not precisely knowable. And since no two places agree precisely in time and setting, it
is evident that judgments about the stars are, in their specificity, far
from precise. (*DI* II.1:91)

What Cusanus has to say here about the judgments of astronomers
being "far from precise" did not challenge the then prevailing view:
had not Aristotle admitted that the astronomer had to settle for less
than absolute truth, suggesting that the number of spheres necessary
to explain the observed phenomena could reasonably be assumed to
be forty-nine or perhaps fifty-five? "The assertion of necessity must
be left to more powerful thinkers."[2] And Ptolemy had been forced to
grant that the order of the spheres of sun, moon, and the five planets
could not be definitively established and that his all too often ad hoc
constructions of the motions of the planets could be reasonably challenged by other hypotheses.[3] In the same spirit Thomas Aquinas had
pointed out that constructions using eccentrics and epicycles were
not sufficient to establish truth, since other explanations are also able
to save the phenomena.[4] Supported by such authorities, the Middle
Ages were pretty much convinced that astronomers, who were concerned with the to us inaccessible superlunar world, had to settle for
less than the truth—that is, had to be content with human constructions or conjectures able to save the phenomena, a phrase that goes
back to Plato[5]—had to be content to construct explanatory models
to explain what they observed as best they could. So what Cusanus
here has to say did not go against the consensus of the learned. But
Cusanus supports his claim that our accounts of stellar movements
are inevitably far from precise with reasoning that applies equally to
the sublunar world: in all our attempts to understand this world, precision is not to be found. With this the Aristotelian scientists of his
day would have disagreed. Not that Cusanus is a skeptic: we can distinguish between better and worse conjectures. But we cannot claim
to understand nature as it really is. In this respect his thought is more
compatible with the practice of modern science than that of Copernicus, Kepler, or Galileo.

Cusanus turns next to geometry, pointing out that while it is

2. Aristotle, *Metaphysics* XII.8.1074a10–17, trans. W. D. Ross.

3. *Ptolemy's Almagest*, trans., annotated G. J. Tomer (Princeton: Princeton University
Press, 1998), XI.1 and 2, 419–23.

4. Thomas Aquinas, *Summa Theologica* II, q. 32, art. 1, ad 2; *Commentaria in libr. Arist. de
caelo et mundo* XII.17.

5. Plato, *Timaeus* 29b–d.

possible in geometry to prove one area equal to another, actually, for instance, when the two are put on paper, precise equality is impossible. There will always be some small, perhaps imperceptible, difference. This qualifies the claim that equality is found only in God. That claim is true when we confine ourselves to what exists actually, but when we are concerned with constructions of our own mind we do meet with equality.

> If you subsequently adapt this rule to mathematics, you will see that equality is actually impossible with regard to geometrical figures and that no thing can precisely agree with another either in shape or in size. And although there are true rules for describing the equal of a given figure as it exists in its definition, nonetheless equality between different things is actually impossible. (*DI* II.1:92)

Crucial is the distinction between "actually" and "in its definition." That we human beings are capable of thinking equality, as is presupposed when we judge things unequal, testifies to the way human reason transcends the material world. The same can be said of our ability to prove, say, the Pythagorean theorem. When dealing with what exists in our definitions—that is, in constructions produced by human reason, and this for Cusanus most definitely includes mathematics—we are able to claim truth that is more than an approximation. The same is true of judgments such as "There are two persons in this room." Not that there exists some "two" in the room. "Two" is a product of our reason, as is the concept "person." But that I can call the judgment "there are two persons in this room" true does not conflict with Cusanus's claim that there can be no equality between actually existing things. Our reason does possess the godlike ability to create a conceptual space in which things must find their place to be comprehended by us. And when we entertain the incomprehensible thought of the numerical maximum, we recognize that the human intellect transcends the reach of reason and reaches up to the infinite.

Turning to music, Cusanus similarly claims that here on earth "precise comparative relation is seen only formally; and we cannot experience in perceptible objects a most agreeable, undefective harmony, because it is not present there" (*DI* II.1:93). The never quite perfect harmonies we do hear on earth have their measure in perfect harmonies that we can conceive but never quite realize in the music we make. But having its measure in perfect harmony, the harmonies that delight us in this life point to the pleasure that awaits the faithful in the life beyond.

> A certain immensely pleasant contemplation could here be engaged in—not only regarding the immortality of our intellectual, rational spirit (which harbors in its nature incorruptible reason, through which the mind attains, of itself, to the concordant and the discordant likeness in musical things), but also regarding the eternal joy into which the blessed are conducted, once they are freed from the things of this world. But [I will deal] with this [topic] elsewhere. (*DI* II.1:93)

The closing promissory remark is to *De conjecturis*, which will have a bit more to say about music and about the joy someone experiences when he glimpses in earthly harmonies the perfect harmony that is inseparable from God (*DC* II.2:83; II.6:105).

In actuality there can be no perfect harmony, just as there can be no absolutely equal areas. And yet our intellect bears within itself the idea of such a harmony, just as it bears within the idea of equality. And this provides us with the regulative ideal presupposed when we judge harmonies.

To conclude the discussion of the applicability of his principle to the quadrivium, Cusanus turns to arithmetic:

> Furthermore: If we apply our rule to arithmetic, we see that no two things can agree in number. And since with respect to a difference of number there is also a difference of composition, complexity, comparative relation, harmony, motion, and so on ad infinitum, we hereby recognize that we are ignorant. (*DI* II.1:94)

We may want to challenge this: are there not countless ways that two things can agree in number, say, in the number of legs and arms two human beings can be said to possess? In this respect at least, can they not be said to agree in number? But, as already suggested, Cusanus might reply that we are dealing here with abstractions, with things as they exist in our thoughts. In our conceptual space there can indeed be equality, but not when we are dealing with what is real.

> No one [human being] is as another in any respect—neither in sensibility, nor imagination, nor intellect, nor in an activity (whether writing or painting or an art). Even if for a thousand years one [individual] strove to imitate another in any given respect, he would never attain precision (though perceptible difference sometimes remains unperceived). Even art imitates nature as best it can; but it can never arrive at reproducing it precisely. Therefore, medicine as well as alchemy, magic, and other transmutational arts lacks true precision, although one art is truer in comparison with another (e.g., medicine is truer than the transmutational arts, as is self-evident). (*DI* II.1:94)

I. THE UNIVERSE

Here we should raise the question: in just what respect is medicine truer than the transmutational arts—that is, alchemy? What makes one imitation of nature superior to the other? Cusanus appears to look to art for a model. The slightly younger Alberti had shown how with the help of the mathematical art of perspective a painter could create representations of the observed that under the right circumstances could fool the eye. The measure of our representations is provided here by what we perceive. As Cusanus recognizes, differences between the imitation and the imitated can become so small as to be imperceptible. But there will always be a difference.

Understanding has often been understood in the image of seeing. But as Plato knew and as Descartes attempted to show with his example of a piece of wax, it is not the eye that lets us understand what the thing is in truth. Nor is it our reason, Cusanus would have challenged Descartes. As the painter replaces seen reality with his paintings, so our reason replaces the things of this world with thought constructions. But our intellect teaches us that in both cases these constructions should not be confused with things as they are in truth. The truth of things is denied to us.

The material world is the realm of the more or less. But from the finite there is no transition to the infinite: no matter how I refine and expand my descriptions, never will they exhaust the being of the thing before me and arrive at the perfect description, just as, no matter how long I count, I will never get to the maximum number. No matter how large a number, I can always add 1. In this sense the number sequence is endless and in this sense infinite. And just as I will never arrive at a largest number by adding number to number, so I will never be able to comprehend the universe as a bounded whole. I will never come to some wall or boundary where the universe ends. That would be like coming to a number to which one could not be added. The universe has no boundaries. In that sense it is infinite.

This leads Cusanus to a distinction between the negatively and the privatively infinite.[6] The universe is infinite in the latter sense: it

6. While Jasper Hopkins is right to insist that according to Cusanus the universe falls "infinitely and disproportionally short of Absolute Infinity," I find it misleading to say that "he still regards the universe as finite," suggesting that he did not break with Aristotelian science in any fundamental way; Hopkins, *Nicholas of Cusa: Metaphysical Speculations* (Minneapolis, Minn.: Arthur J. Banning Press, 2000), "Orienting Study, Part Two: Analysis of Specialized Topics," 2:88. Hopkins's footnote refers us to *DI* II.4:113, 8–13; *DI* II.11:156, 27–28; and *DI* II.8:139, 1–5. But these passages all affirm the infinity of the universe, even as they insist that there is no proportion between God's absolute infinity and the privative infinity of the boundless universe. It would be less misleading to say with Cusanus that it is "in this respect ... neither finite nor infinite." Hopkins would seem to agree: see "Orienting

lacks boundaries; I cannot conceive of a beyond. But God is infinite
in a different sense:

> Therefore, only the absolutely Maximum is negatively infinite.
> Hence, it alone is whatever there can at all possibly be. But since the
> universe encompasses all the things which are not God, it cannot
> be negatively infinite, although it is unbounded and thus privatively
> infinite. And in this respect it is neither finite nor infinite. For it
> cannot be greater than it is. (*DI* II.1:97)

The universe, thought as the totality of "the things which are not
God," cannot be thought greater than it is, because then we would
have to think of a possible beyond, but this we cannot do. We are
unable to count all the finite things that God created; in this sense we
cannot comprehend the world's finitude. We cannot understand the
universe as a finite whole.

> This results from a defect. For its possibility, or matter, does not ex-
> tend itself farther. For to say, "The universe can always be actually
> greater" is not other than saying, "Possible being passes over into
> actually infinite being." But this latter [statement] cannot hold true,
> since infinite actuality—which is absolute eternity, which is actually
> all possibility of being—cannot arise from possibility. Therefore, al-
> though with respect to God's infinite power, which is unlimitable, the
> universe could have been greater: nevertheless, since the possibility-
> of-being, or matter, which is not actually extendible unto infinity,
> opposes, the universe cannot be greater. And so, [the universe is]
> unbounded; for it is not the case that anything actually greater than
> it, in relation to which it would be bounded is positable. (*DI* II.1:97)

The claim that God's infinite power could have created a greater universe, while in agreement with the church's position, as it had found
binding expression in the Condemnation of 1277, lacks content,
however, given Cusanus's understanding of the incomprehensibility
of the Absolute Maximum. We cannot posit anything greater than the
universe, understood as the totality of all that is, just as we cannot posit anything greater than the totality of all numbers. Both "the totality
of all that is" and "the totality of all numbers" are limiting concepts
that surpass the reach of our reason. There is thus a sense in which
the universe, too, is *infinitum* and *maximum*. But since it is finite all the

---

Study, Part One: Expository Purview," 16–17, in *Nicholas of Cusa's Metaphysic of Contraction*,
88–89: "Though in this sense the universe is 'not limited'—i.e., is 'unlimited,' or 'infinite'—
it is nonetheless actually finite, in the sense that it has a determinate measure (known to
God alone). In other words, the universe is finite but unbounded; and as such, it can be
called a finite infinity."

same, the universe must be an infinite maximum in a diminished, or as Cusanus puts it, in a contracted manner: it is the *maximum contractum*. But what is the meaning of this *contractio*?

Contractio makes something definite, into a "this." Thus it is related to definition, to the word, where we should also think of the divine Word. But any specific "this" stands in a relation to others. The universe is a contracted maximum in that it is a boundless plurality of different things. It stands in somewhat the same relationship to God as the idea of all finite numbers stands to the maximum number.

Created Being Derives from the Being of the First in a Way That Is Not Understandable

This point, reiterated in the *Apologia doctae ignorantiae*, speaks of the essential impossibility of arriving at a clear understanding of the relationship of Creator and creation. The following discussion could be cited as an illustration of this point: It is anything but clear.

Not surprisingly, Cusanus suggests that no privation can be a result of the Maximum, and that has to raise the question: how could God create a world that in so many ways seems less than perfect?

> Sacred ignorance has already taught us that nothing exists from itself except the unqualifiedly Maximum (in which from itself, in itself, through itself, and with respect to itself are the same thing: viz., Absolute Being) and that, necessarily, every existing thing is that which it is, insofar as it is, from Absolute Being. For how could that which is not from itself exist in any other way than from Eternal Being? But since the Maximum is far distant from any envy, it cannot impart diminished being as such. Therefore, a created thing, which is a derivative being, does not have everything which it is (e.g., [not] its corruptibility, divisibility, imperfection, difference, plurality, and the like) from the eternal, indivisible, most perfect, undifferentiated, and one Maximum—nor from any positive cause. (*DI* II.2:98)

I. THE UNIVERSE

But if not from God, what is the cause of the diminished being of creatures (*ab-esse*)? Must it not also derive from the Maximum in some way? Cusanus denies this. But how is the creation then to be understood? Cusanus attempts to provide an explanation relying on his by now familiar mathematical symbolism.

> An infinite line is infinite straightness, which is the cause of all linear being. Now, with respect to being a line, a curved line is from the infinite line; but with respect to being curved, it is not from the infinite line. Rather, the curvature follows upon finitude, since a line is curved because it is not the maximum line. For if it were the maximum line, it would not be curved, as was shown previously. Similarly with things: since they cannot be the Maximum, it happens that they are diminished, other, differentiated, and the like—none of which [characteristics] have a cause. Therefore, a created thing has from God the fact that it is one, distinct (*discreta*), and united to the universe; and the more it is one, the more like unto God it is. However, it does not have from God (nor from any positive cause but [only] contingently) the fact that its oneness exists in plurality, its distinctness in confusion, and its union in discord. (*DI* I.2:99)

The diminished being (*ab-esse*) of creatures, Cusanus insists, follows from their finitude. But is their finitude not inseparable from their being creatures? If we are to think of God as Creator, must we not think the unfolding of God in creation as inseparable from his essence? The cited passage seems to invite us to think created being as a result of a conjoining of absolute necessity and contingency. Should we understand the creation of the world then as an incomprehensible accident? But that is hardly compatible with the faith that the creation declares the glory of God, a faith that Cusanus explicitly shares. And how can Cusanus oppose absolute necessity and contingency, given his insistence that the Maximum cannot be opposed to some other? What is Cusanus's understanding of "contingency"?[1] How can we oppose God to the world he created? The creation remains a mystery.

---

1. Jasper Hopkins suggests that "the introduction of the word 'contingency' signals that Nicholas has no intelligible explanation to offer. He is thus reduced further and further into unintelligibility"; *OLI* 19. Challenging that suggestion, Thomas McTighe claims that "far from being a sign of failure, what we have here is "a necessary consequence of Cusa's *Einheitsmetaphysik*—not a doctrinal collapse but a genuinely creative effort to bypass inconsistent features of his Platonic and Neoplatonc sources"; McTighe, Contingentia and *Alteritas* in Cusa's Metaphysics," *American Catholic Philosophical Quarterly* 64, no. 1 (Winter 1990): 56. "Here we have the heart of Cusa's theory of differentiation from which the later works do not depart in any essential way. It can be summarized in a kind of equation: A is not B because A is not God" (59). But why is there an A and a B? McTighe's answer: "Both formal and material diversity are a function of contingency" (66n47). But that answer is

> Who, then, can understand created being by conjoining, in created being, the absolute necessity from which it derives and the contingency without which it does not exist? For it seems that the creation, which is neither God nor nothing, is, as it were, after God and before nothing and in between God and nothing—as one of the sages[2] says: "God is the opposition to nothing by the mediation of being." Nevertheless, [the creation] cannot be composed of being and not-being. Therefore, it seems neither to be (since it descends from being) nor not to be (since it is before nothing) nor to be a composite of being and nothing. (*DI* II.2:100)

As Hopkins points out, Cusanus's explanation is "altogether unsatisfactory" (*OLI* 19). Creation, and thus the being of created things, remains unintelligible. But how could there be an intelligible explanation? To offer such an explanation, our reason, Cusanus points out, would have to be capable of leaping beyond contradictories.

> Now, our intellect, which cannot leap beyond contradictories, does not attain to the being of the creation either by means of division or of composition, although it knows that created being derives only from the being of the Maximum. Therefore, derived being (*ab-esse*) is not understandable, because the Being from which [it derives] is not understandable—just as the adventitious being (*adesse*) of an accident is not understandable if the substance to which it is adventitious is not understood. And, therefore, the creation as creation cannot be called one, because it descends from Oneness, nor [can it be called] many, since its being derives from the One; nor [can it be called] both one and many conjunctively. But its oneness exists contingently and with a certain plurality. Something similar, it seems, must be said about simplicity and composition and other opposites. (*DI* II.2:100)

The following paragraph had to trouble a conservative reader such as Johannes Wenck, raising questions, as it does, about God, the creation, and the eternity of the world. Creation is said to be nothing other than God's being all things.

> But since the creation was created through the being of the Maximum and since—in the Maximum—being, making, and creating are the same thing: creating seems to be not other than God's being all things. Therefore, if God is all things and if His being all things

---

unsatisfactory. That Adam is different from Eve is not just a matter of contingency; the creation remains a mystery. Cusa's supposed *Einheitsmetaphysik* here deconstructs itself.

2. Pseudo-Hermes Trismegistus, *Liber XXIV philosophorum*, propos. 14. Cusanus's source, according to Herbert Wackerzapp, is Meister Eckhart: *PTW* I:118n20.

> is creating: how can we deem the creation not to be eternal, since God's being is eternal—indeed, is eternity itself? Indeed, insofar as the creation is God's being no one doubts that it is eternity. Therefore, insofar as it is subject to time, it is not from God, who is eternal. Who, then, understands the creation's existing both eternally and temporally? For in Being itself the creation was not able not to exist eternally; nor was it able to exist before time, since "before" time there was no *before*. And so, the creation always existed, from the time it was able to exist. (*DI* I.2:101)

How does Cusanus understand the creation of the universe? His claim that "insofar as the creation is God's being no one doubts that it is eternity" is difficult to accept: how are we to reconcile it with the biblical creation account? Johannes Wenck thus objects: "This thesis destroys [the status of] the creation, for a condition of the creation is that it has not always existed (*IL* 35:35). But can we make sense of an origin of this universe? Kant's first antinomy remains with us. Its thesis, in agreement with the medieval worldview, claims that "the world has a beginning in time, and is also limited as regards space," the antithesis that "the world has no beginning, and no limits in space; it is infinite as regards both time and space." The argument for the thesis rests on the claim that to really comprehend something we must think it as a whole—that is to say, as enclosed within limits. Cusanus could agree that the comprehensibility of the world demands its constructability, and that means its finitude. To think the world as such a constructed whole is to think it as bounded. But the thought of a limit of the world in time or space is the thought of a barrier that thought in its freedom inevitably leaps across. That also holds for the big bang with which our universe is supposed to have begun. Such a leap of thought would be no leap at all were there no thought of the other side of that barrier. Neither a finite or an infinite world is intelligible, and that, for Kant, too, meant that our universe is at bottom incomprehensible. Cusanus would have agreed.

In his gloss on "For in Being itself the creation was not able not to exist eternally," Jasper Hopkins writes, "The word 'in' is here crucial. The universe as enfolded in God is ontologically prior to its unfolded, temporal existence in God, says Nicholas. Insofar as it is unfolded and temporal, however, it is neither God nor from God (that is, from God in the sense of God's having caused its temporality and plurality); rather, its temporality and plurality derive from contingency" (*OLI* 193n21). The same point, it would seem, could be made with respect to every created thing: As enfolded in God it is God. But temporality would seem to be constitutive of our embodied being. Is it not from God? Is not time, too, "a gift of the Father, who created us all," as the Marschallin sings in Richard Strauss's *Rosenkavalier*? To say that temporality and plurality derive from contingency is to empty the creation account of all meaning. Time and its relation to God and with it the creation of the world remain a mystery.

Cusanus, of course, insists on the incomprehensibility of creation, especially in this chapter:

> Who, in fact, can understand that God is the Form of being and nevertheless is not mingled with the creation? For from an infinite line and a finite curved line there cannot arise a composite, which cannot exist without comparative relation; but no one doubts that there can be no comparative relation between the infinite and the finite. How, then, can the intellect grasp the following?: that the being of a curved line is from an infinite straight line, though the infinite straight line does not inform the curved line as a form but rather as a cause and an essence. The curved line cannot participate in this essence either by taking a part of it (since the essence is infinite and indivisible) or as matter participates in form (e.g., as Socrates and Plato [participate] in humanity), or as a whole is participated in by its parts (e.g., as the universe [is participated in] by its parts), or as several mirrors [partake of] the same face in different ways (for it is not the case that as a mirror is a mirror before it receives the image of a face, so created being exists prior to derivative, [participating] being; for created being *is* derivative being). Who is he, then, who can understand how it is that the one, infinite Form is participated in different ways by different created things? (*DI* II.2:102)

Cusanus rejects here various ways in which we might think the relation of the creation to the Creator: that relation is not like that of essence and particular existent or form and matter; it is not like that of a whole and its parts; it is not like that of a face to its images in some mirror, for the mirror has an independent existence. And yet, Cusanus is unwilling to jettison the mirror metaphor.

> Who is he, then, who can understand how it is that the one, infinite Form is participated in in different ways by different created things? For created being cannot be anything other than reflection—not a reflection received positively in some other thing but a reflection which is contingently different. Perhaps [a comparison with an artifact is fitting]: if the artifact depended entirely upon the craftsman's idea and did not have any other being than dependent being, the artifact would exist from the craftsman and would be conserved as a result of his influence—analogously to the image of a face in a

> mirror (with the proviso that before and after [the appearance of the image] the mirror be nothing in and of itself). (*DI* II.2:102)

Symbolically speaking, the creation can be said to be the mirror image of the Creator, but the mirror in question comes into being only with the mirrored image. Ursula Renz suggests that this is the first time that Cusanus presents us with an explicit commentary on this potent image.[3]

Not content with this suggestive, but nevertheless inadequate image, Cusanus continues his discussion of the elusive Deity:

> Nor can we understand how it is that God can be made manifest to us through visible creatures. For [God is] not [manifest] analogously to our intellect, which is known only to God and to ourselves and which, when it commences to think, receives from certain images in the memory a form of a color, a sound, or something else. Prior [to this reception] the intellect was without form, and subsequently thereto it assumes another form—whether of signs, utterances, or letters—and manifests itself to others [besides itself and God]. (*DI* II.2:103)

The analogy, or rather the rejection of the analogy between God and the intellect, is of interest. Our intellect, too, is not manifest as such. In itself, it is formless. To become manifest to others and to itself, it must express itself—in bodily gestures, for example, or in language. This presupposes that there is something to be expressed—that is, thoughts that in turn presuppose experience, which forms these thoughts. But God is not in need of anything other than himself in order to create. He does not need to be informed, but is the origin of all forms, the form of forms.

All things are said by Cusanus to be in the image of the Maximum. They differ from it only contingently, where such contingency remains incomprehensible.

> Who could understand the following?: how all things are the image of that one, infinite Form and are different contingently [*ex contingenti*]—as if a created thing were a god manqué [*occasionatus*], just as an accident is a substance manqué, and a woman is a man manqué. For the Infinite Form is received only finitely, so that every created thing is, as it were, a finite infinity or a created god, so that it exists in the way in which this can best occur. (*DI* II.2:104)

3. Ursula Renz, "Lebendiger Spiegel oder Spiegel des Lebendigen? Subjektivität und Performanz in Cusanus' Spiegelsymbolik," in Paul Michel, ed., *Präsenz ohne Substanz: Zur Symybolik des Spiegels*, Schriften zur Symbolforschung 14 (Zürich and Freiburg i. Br.: Pano, 2003), 95–108.

The word "manqué" (*occasionatus*) and the reference to woman deserves some comment. *Occasionatus*, not found in classical Latin, suggests that something that came into being did so in an accidental fashion. Cusanus's choice of *occasionatus* looks back to Thomas Aquinas, who follows Aristotle's account of generation, but supplements it in an interesting way.[4] In his *Summa Theologiae* (I, q. 92, a. 1) Aquinas writes the following:

> With respect to the particular nature the female is something defective and *occasionatum*, for the active force in the male semen intends to produce a perfect likeness of itself in the male sex; but if a female should be generated, this is because of a weakness of the active force, or because of some indisposition of the material, or even because of a transmutation [brought about] by an outside influence.... But with respect to universal nature the female is not something *occasionatum*, but is by nature's intention ordained for the work of generation. Now the intention of universal nature depends on God, who is the universal author of nature. Therefore, in instituting nature, God produced not only the male but also the female.

That casts an interesting light on Cusanus's understanding of the relationship of the Creator to the creation. God is said to be to the creation as man is to woman, but as woman is said to be "with respect to the particular nature," something defective and *occasionatum*," yet necessary to nature's "work of generation" and thus to nature, so creation would seem to be something defective, compared to God's perfection, but in fact necessary to the being of the Creator.

Still, the creation and its perfection remain unintelligible. The appeal to contingency offers little help in that it invites us to oppose it to God as something other. But such an understanding of contingency is ruled out by Cusanus's insistence that we cannot oppose an other to the Maximum. That also holds for contingency and temporality.

A more obvious objection to what Cusanus has to say about the eternity of the world is that it seems to challenge the creation account found in the Bible. I doubt that Jasper Hopkins's explanation that the universe as enfolded in God is God, but "insofar as it is unfolded and temporal,... is neither God nor from God (i.e., from God in the sense of God's having caused its temporality and plurality); rather, its temporality and plurality derive from contingency" would have satisfied a Johannes Wenck, who found the way Cusanus refused to be

---

4. See Michael Nolan, "What Aquinas Never Said about Women,"
November 1998, http://www.firstthings.com/article/1998/11/003-what-aquinas-never
-said-about-women.

bound by the rules of Aristotelian logic unacceptable. Here Wenck's statement of Cusanus's Seventh Thesis, which joins propositions from the second and the third chapter of Book Two:

> The creation always existed, from the time it was able to exist; for the creation is God's being. Who, indeed, can understand that God is the Form of being and nevertheless is not mingled with the creation but is one enfolding of all things? For God is the enfolding of all things in that all things are in Him; and He is the unfolding of all things in that He is in all things—just as, by way of illustration, number is the unfolding of oneness, and just as a point is the perfection of magnitudes, identity, the enfolding of difference, equality [the enfolding] of inequality, and simplicity, [the enfolding] of divisions. (*IL* 35)

Earlier I cited Wenck's claim that "this thesis destroys [the status of] the creation; for a condition of the creation is that the creation has not always existed" (*IL* 35–36). He continues, "Moreover, since God Himself always exists, how can the creation be God's being?"

The reply given by Cusanus in *Apologia doctae ignorantiae* emphasizes that all that chapters 2 and 3 really claim is that the way in which the being of creation derives from Absolute Being can neither be expressed nor understood.

> The Teacher picked up a copy of *Learned Ignorance* and read the second and the third chapters of Book Two. And he showed clearly that the seventh thesis, together with its corollaries, was excerpted perversely. For in those chapters nothing is expressly dealt with other than [the view] that the being of creation derives from Absolute Being in a manner which can neither be expressed nor understood; there is no other assertion, although different modes of discourse are touched upon. (*AP* 33)

With this we have to agree. Yet much is suggested by Cusanus in these chapters, if obliquely, that invites reflection. And how could a discourse concerning the mystery of creation be anything but hermetic?

CHAPTER 3

In a Way That Cannot Be Understood the Maximum Enfolds and Unfolds All Things

In this chapter Cusanus addresses the question "in what sense may things be said to be in God and God in things?" The question is of special importance, given the recurring charge that Cusanus is a pantheist.[1] Crucial here is the pair *complicatio* (enfolding) and *explicatio* (unfolding): all things are said to be enfolded in God, as every number is enfolded in oneness; the universe is the unfolding of God, as quantity is the unfolding of oneness.

The chapter begins with, given the difficulty of the topic, a remarkably self-confident and succinct statement of what Cusanus thinks has been established in Book One:

> Nothing not enfolded in the first part [i.e., Book One] can be stated or thought about the ascertainable truth. For, necessarily, everything that agrees with what was there stated about the First Truth is true; the rest, which disagrees, is false. Now, in Book One we find it indicated that there can be only one Maximum of all maxima. But the Maximum is that to which nothing can be opposed and in which

1. See Moran, "Pantheism from John Scotus Eriugena to Nicholas of Cusa," 131–52.

I. THE UNIVERSE

even the Minimum is the Maximum. Therefore, Infinite Oneness is the enfolding of all things. Oneness, which unites all things, bespeaks this [enfolding of all things]. Oneness is maximal not simply because it is the enfolding of number[2] but because [it is the enfolding] of all things. And just as in number, which is the unfolding of oneness, we find only oneness, so in all existing things we find only (*non nisi*) the Maximum. (*DI* II.3:105)

The "only" in the concluding sentence invites question. Consider two different numbers, say four and seven; do we find in them *only* oneness? Or consider two different things, say a rose and a lily; do we find in them *only* the Maximum? Does this not elide what makes them different, what makes them what they are? In chapter 5 of Book One Cusanus had opposed oneness to number, which can be greater or less, as the beginning or principle (*principium*) and end (*finis*) of all number (*DI* I.5:14). Analogously, he had opposed "Absolute Maximality" to the countless things that make up this world, all of them different, as their principle. The "only" makes sense only if we are looking for the *principium* of four and seven, rose and lily. Then we will find only oneness in the case of numbers, which are an unfolding of our mind (cf. *DI* I-14), and only God in the things of this world.

Cusanus uses the relationship of the point to line, surface, or material object as a symbol of the relationship of God to all things, which are enfolded in God and God's unfolding.

With respect to quantity, which is the unfolding of oneness, oneness is said to be a point. For in quantity only a point is present. Just as everywhere in a line—no matter where you divide it—there is a point, so [the same thing holds true] for a surface and a material object. And yet, there is not more than one point. This one point is not anything other than infinite oneness; for infinite oneness is a point which is the end, the perfection, and the totality of line and quantity, which it enfolds. The first unfolding of the point is the line, in which only the point is present. (*DI* II.3:105)

Just as the point is understood by Cusanus as the *principium* of space, so the present is understood by him as the *principium* of time. Rest is enfolded motion, motion, unfolded rest. The present enfolds time, time is the unfolded present. The present is the truth of time.

In like manner, if you consider [the matter] carefully: rest is oneness which enfolds motion, and motion is rest ordered serially. Hence, motion is the unfolding of rest. In like manner, the present, or the

---

2. Cf. Boethius, *De Institutione Arithmetica* I.3, ed Friedlein, 13; *PTW* I:119n36.

now, enfolds time. The past was the present, and the future will become the present. Therefore, nothing except an ordered present is found in time. Hence, the past and the future are the unfolding of the present. The present is the enfolding of all present times; and the present times are the unfolding, serially, of the present; and in the present times only the present is found. Therefore, the present is one enfolding of all times. (*DI* II.3:106)

The passage brings to mind a passage from Schopenhauer's *World as Will and Representation*:

> Above all, we must clearly recognize that the form of the phenomenon of the will, and hence the form of life or of reality, is really only the *present*, not the future or the past. Future and past are only in the concept, exist only in the connexion and continuity of knowledge insofar as this follows the principle of sufficient reason. No man has lived in the past, and none will live in the future; the present alone is the form of all life, but it is also life's sure possession which can never be torn from it. The present always exists together with its content; both stand firm without wavering, like the rainbow on the waterfall. For life is sure and certain to the will, and the present is sure and certain to life. (*WWR* I.278)

To further explain the relation of Creator and creation Cusanus once again draws on the number analogy:

> To explain my meaning by numerical examples: Number is the unfolding of oneness. Now, number bespeaks reasoning. But reasoning is from a mind. Therefore, the brutes, which do not have a mind, are unable to number. Therefore, just as number arises from our mind by virtue of the fact that we understand what is commonly one as individually many: so the plurality of things [arises] from the Divine Mind (in which the many are present without plurality, because they are present in Enfolding Oneness). (*DI* II.3:108)

Cusanus can justify his fondness for mathematical symbols by pointing to Genesis 1:26: "Let us make man in our image, after our likeness." As I observed earlier, if God created us human beings in his image, are we not entitled to think God in our own image? Just as oneness unfolds itself in number, so our intellect is a oneness that unfolds itself in whatever things our reason can comprehend. And so Cusanus thinks God as Oneness unfolding itself in the countless things that make up this universe. To be sure, an infinite distance separates us finite creatures from the infinite God. But the fact that we human beings are capable of thinking, if not of comprehending, the infinite Maximum shows that there is a sense we bear within ourselves the image of the infinite God. The presupposed analogy between the human and the divine mind provides the key to what Gregor von Heimburg dismissed as Cusanus's "mathematical superstition."[3]

Cusanus takes counting to be the paradigm of all knowing, a thought familiar to both Aristotle and Aquinas.[4] Number he has shown to be the unfolding of oneness by reason. As he was to write in *De conjecturis*: *Nec est aliud numerus quam ratio explicata,* "Nor is number something other than reason unfolded" (*DC* II.7).[5] The comprehended cosmos is thus an unfolding of the human mind, enfolded in the human mind, where we must take care not to confuse the comprehended with the divinely created cosmos; to repeat once more: we shall never know things as they are in truth but have to settle for conjectures.

Drawing on the analogy between the human and the divine mind, but careful to guard against misunderstanding, Cusanus goes on to insist that divine enfolding and unfolding surpass our comprehension:

> However, the mode of enfolding and unfolding surpasses [the measure of] our mind. Who, I ask, could understand how it is that the plurality of things is from the Divine Mind? For God's understanding is His being; for God is Infinite Oneness. If you proceed with the numerical comparison by considering that number is the multiplication, by the mind, of the common one: it seems as if God, who is Oneness, were multiplied in things, since His understanding is His being. And, yet, you understand that this Oneness, which is infinite and maximal, cannot be multiplied. How, then, can you understand there to be a plurality whose being comes from the One without [there occurring] any multiplication of the One? That is, how can you understand there to be a multiplication of Oneness without there being a multiplication [of Oneness]? Surely, [you can] not [understand it] as [you understand the multiplication] of one species or of one genus in many species or many individuals; outside of these [individuals] a genus or a species does not exist except through an abstracting intellect. Therefore, no one understands how God (whose oneness of being does not exist through the understanding's abstracting from things and does not exist as united to, or merged with, things) is unfolded through the number of things.

<hr>

3. Jäger, *Der Streit des Cardinals Nicolaus von Cusa,* 2:236.

4. See Aristotle, *Metaphysics.* X.1.1053b4: "Evidently then, being one in the strictest sense, if we define it according to the meaning of the word, is a measure, and especially of quantity, and secondly of quality." See also Aquinas, *ST* I, q. 11, a. 2, in *The Basic Writings of St. Thomas Aquinas,* vol. 2, ed. Anton C. Pegis (New York: Random House, 1945): "For *one* implies the idea of a primary measure; and number is *multitude* measured by *one.*"

5. *PTW* II:11.

> If you consider things in their independence from God, they are nothing—even as number without oneness [is nothing]. If you consider God in His independence from things, He exists and the things are nothing. If you consider Him as He is in things, you consider things to be something in which He is. And in this regard you err, as was evident in the preceding chapter. For it is not the case that the being of a thing is another thing, as a different thing is [another thing]; rather, its being is derivative being. If you consider a thing as it is in God, it is God and Oneness. (*DI* II.3:109)

Of interest is Cusanus's rejection of the attempt to understand the unfolding of God in the things of this earth as being like the way in which a genus could be said to unfold itself in species and species in individuals. Genera and species, Cusanus holds, do not actually exist. The only being they have is in the abstracting intellect. The analogy tempts us to think of God as another human abstraction, supported by our understanding of all things as being. So understood God would be the most encompassing abstraction but possessing being only in our mind. That Cusanus must reject such an understanding of God, which would deny him an independent being, requires no comment.

But how are we to understand "In the beginning God created the heavens and the earth" (Gn 1:1)? Would it help us to say that the plurality of creation results from God's presence in nothing? How then are we to think the relationship of this nothing to God? How are we to think this "nothing"? As the nothing that separates Father and Son?

> There remains only to say that the plurality of things arises from the fact that God is present in nothing. Take away God from the creation and nothing remains (*DI* II.3:110).

Tolle Deum a creatura et remanet nihil. I have difficulty with the thought of nothing remaining. It threatens to make nothing into some sort of thing after all. Cusanus might have said: take away God from the creation and only God remains. Presumably that is what Cusanus means to say. But taken literally, the statement claims that nothing remains, neither the creation nor God. Take away God from the creation and nothing remains. Is this to say that without the creation God is nothing? This would suggest that God can be said to be only as creator. In expected fashion Wenck objects to this claim:

> This corollary deprives God of His own being—since, in nothing, being is nothing. (*DIL* 36)

I. THE UNIVERSE

Attempting to clarify this point, Cusanus draws on the relationship of substance to accident.

> Take away substance from a composite and no accident remains; and so, nothing remains. How can our intellect fathom this? For although an accident perishes when the substance is removed, an accident is not therefore nothing. However, the accident perishes because its being is adventitious being. And hence, a quantity, for example, exists only through the being of a substance; nevertheless, because quantity is present, the substance is quantitative by virtue of quantity. But [the relationship between God and the creation is] not similar. For the creation is not adventitious to God in a correspondingly similar manner; for it does not confer anything on God, as an accident [confers something] on a substance. Indeed, an accident confers [something] on a substance to such an extent that, as a result, the substance cannot exist without some accident, even though the accident derives its own being from the substance. But with God a similar thing cannot hold true. (*DI* II.3:110)

As he had rejected the comparison of God's unfolding himself in creation to the way genera and species might be said to unfold themselves in individuals, so he now rejects the comparison of God's relationship to creatures to that of substance to accident. For while accidents cannot be without substances, substances cannot be without some accidents. But God, Cusanus claims, cannot be said to depend for his Being in any way on creation.

But can his being be separated from creation? The creation is unfathomable. "It belongs to the unfathomable being of God himself."[6]

And yet we do seem to know something about God.

> You might reply: "God's omnipotent will is the cause; His will and omnipotence are His being; for the whole of theology is circular." If so, then you will have to admit that you are thoroughly ignorant of how enfolding and unfolding occur and that you know only that you do not know the manner, even if you know (1) that God is the enfolding and the unfolding of all things, (2) that insofar as He is the enfolding, in Him all things are Himself, and (3) that insofar as He is the unfolding, in all things He is that which they are, just as in an image the reality itself (*veritas*) is present. (*DI* II.3:111)

That leaves the nature of enfolding and unfolding unilluminated. Insofar as God is understood as the enfolding of all things, they are said to be nothing other than God. That is demanded by the Oneness

---

6. Hanna-Barbara Gerl-Falkovitz, "Nicolaus Cusanus, *De pace fidei* (1454)," 116.

of God. But with this the difference between things vanishes and with it their being. Insofar as God is understood as the unfolding of all things, he is said to be just what they are. So understood God vanishes and with it his being. Only creatures remain,

But we must read the sentence in its entirety: "He is that which they are, just as in an image the reality itself (*veritas*) is present." Does this not suggest that Cusanus agrees with Thomas Aquinas, who does think that creatures bear a likeness to God, but an image cannot be said to preserve the reality of the exemplar? But by writing that in the image "the reality itself (*veritas*) is present," Cusanus resists such a reading. As Dermot Moran glosses this passage: "Again the Platonic metaphysics of the image is here modified through the Cappadocian and Eriugenian tradition such that the image only has reality in so far as it has the reality of the exmplar."[7] Meister Eckhart comes to mind: in the sense creatures are said to be, God is nothing; in the sense in which God can be said to be, creatures are nothing.

What we must grant Cusanus is this: the creation is incomprehensible.

7. Moran, "Pantheism," 141.

The Universe, Which Is Only the Contracted Maximum, Is a Likeness of the Absolute [Maximum]

"Universe" names the totality of things. As shown in the preceding chapter, Cusanus takes the universe to be infinite in the sense that when we attempt to comprehend it as a whole we come to no end, just as we come to no end counting. But if the number series and the universe can both be said to be infinite, they can be said to be so only privatively, in that both lack closure and can thus be said to go on and on, The Absolute Maximum, on the other hand, is the infinite one.

Since it is understood to include all things, the universe, too, is a maximum. Were we to try to think of some thing beyond the universe, it would be, given the definition, part of the universe. To us human knowers the infinity of the universe manifests itself in boundless plurality, as is the case with the endless number series. Cusanus thus calls the universe a contracted maximum. The medium of contraction could be said to be plurality in time and space.

Although an infinite abyss separates the Absolute Maximum from the contracted maximum that is the universe, Cusanus asserts nevertheless an analogy in the way we think about these two maxima:

> Therefore, [regarding] those things which in Book One were made
> known to us about the Absolute Maximum: as they befit the maxi-
> mally Absolute absolutely, so I affirm that they befit in a contracted
> way what is contracted. (*DI* II.4:112)

Cusanus seeks to explain the analogy further in the following passage:

> God is Absolute Maximality and Oneness, who precedes and unites
> absolutely different and separate things—i.e., contradictories—be-
> tween which there is no middle ground. Absolute Maximality is,
> absolutely, that which all things are: in all things it is the Absolute
> Beginning of things, the [Absolute] End of things, and the [Abso-
> lute] Being of things; in it all things are—indistinctly, most simply,
> and without plurality—the Absolute Maximum, just as an infinite
> line is all figures. So likewise the world, or universe, is a contracted
> maximum and a contracted one. The world precedes contracted op-
> posites—i.e., contraries. And it is, contractedly, that which all things
> are: in all things it is the contracted beginning of things, the con-
> tracted end of things, and the contracted being of things; it is a con-
> tracted infinity and thus is contractedly infinite; in it all things are—
> with contracted simplicity and contracted indistinction and without
> plurality—the contracted maximum, just as a contracted maximum
> line is contractedly all figures. (*DI* II.4:113)

What Cusanus has to say here about God recapitulates what he had
said in Book One. Familiar, too, is the simile that invites us to think
the presence of God in all things as being like the presence of the
infinite maximum line in all figures, which Cusanus discussed as unfoldings of the infinite line. "An infinite line is all figures," but as
their *principium* or essence. This suggests that we do not do justice to
Cusanus's understanding of the universe when we understand it simply as the totality of all things in space and time. That fails to capture
the way Cusanus thinks of the universe as the *principium* of all things.
Consider the earlier discussion of the maximum number, which is
also one, as the *principium* of every number. Every number can be said
to be contraction or unfolding of the maximum number. Similarly,
Cusanus suggests, the universe is present in every thing as its *principium*. What is it to be a thing? To be a unique particular in boundless
space and time, related to countless other such particulars. That is its
essence, the same for every thing. This is not to say that every thing is
the universe absolutely: it is the universe in a contracted way, as this
unique particular thing. Key here is the concept of contraction.

> Hence, when one rightly considers contraction, the whole matter
> becomes clear. For contracted infinity, simplicity, or indistinction is,

> with regard to its contraction, infinitely lower than what is absolute, so that the infinite and eternal world falls disproportionally short of Absolute Infinity and Absolute Eternity, and [so that] the one [falls disproportionally short] of Oneness. Hence, Absolute Oneness is free of all plurality. But although contracted oneness (which is the one universe) is one maximum: since it is contracted, it is not free of plurality, even though it is only one contracted maximum. Therefore, although it is maximally one, its oneness is contracted through plurality, just as its infinity [is contracted] through finitude, its simplicity through composition, its eternity through succession, its necessity through possibility, and so on—as if Absolute Necessity communicated itself without any intermingling and yet necessity were contractedly restricted in something opposed to it. [For example, it is] in itself, absolute being apart from any abstracting on the part of our intellect, and as if what is white were contractedly white from whiteness; in this case whiteness would be restricted by non-whiteness in something actually white, so that that which would not be white without whiteness is white through whiteness. (*DI* II.4:114)

Words such as "infinity," "oneness," or "eternity" all have their contracted sense—for example, when we speak of one infinite and eternal universe. "Infinite," as pointed out earlier, is used here in a privative sense, which falls infinitely short of the Absolute Maximum in which Infinity, Oneness, Eternity, and Necessity cannot be separated. The infinity of the universe, however, is contracted through finitude—the universe is the totality of countless finite things: its oneness is contracted through plurality; similarly, its eternity is contracted through a succession of countless moments; necessity is contracted through countless possibilities. We can speak thus of infinite space, infinite time, infinite possibilities.

The example Cusanus offers us to illustrate his point is of interest in the way it both invites and resists a Platonic interpretation of contraction. Whiteness, according to Cusanus, is a universal—as such, a human abstraction. But such an abstraction presupposes a recognition of something that all white things share in their individual ways. The human abstraction responds to something that we experience in things, say a certain family resemblance. This may lead us to think of whiteness not as a mere humanly constructed universal, but as a Platonic form from which all white things derive their whiteness. Contraction could then be thought of as being like Platonic participation. Cusanus, however, rejects such a reification of what he takes to be human abstractions. But he also does not lose sight of the fact that these abstractions respond to something real. It has its basis in the way God ordered the world—that is, in the Word. The meaning of "whiteness" thus hovers between its human and its divine origin.

Cusanus invites us to think of the way the universe is contracted in things analogously. This invites the question: does Cusanus think of the universe as a similar abstraction, resembling a Platonic form from which all things derive their worldly being? But once again we should not reify the universe and make it into some sort of thing. It is the totality of all things, which as members of the universe share a certain family resemblance, just as all human beings share their humanity. That humanity is not another thing, but it is more than just a product of the human intellect. It has its basis in the way God ordered the world and gathered it into a whole.

The analogy between God and the universe Cusanus proposes raises then the further question: would he have us think God, too, as such an abstraction, based on a perception of a family resemblance between all created things, as the word "creator" may suggest? Cusanus would no doubt resist such a suggestion. As the image of God, the human being, which with its intellect and in its freedom reaches up to infinity, bears the idea of God more immediately within itself. That justifies talk of God as a person.

> From these [observations] an inquirer can infer many points. For example, just as God, since He is immense, is neither in the sun nor in the moon, although in them He is, absolutely, that which they are: so the universe is neither in the sun nor in the moon;[1] but in them it is, contractedly, that which they are. Now, the Absolute Quiddity of the sun is not other than the Absolute Quiddity of the moon (since [this] is God Himself, who is the Absolute Being and Absolute Quiddity[2] of all things); but the contracted quiddity of the sun *is* other than the contracted quiddity of the moon (for as the Absolute Quiddity of a thing is not the thing, so the contracted [quiddity of a thing] is none other than the thing). Therefore, [the following] is clear: that since the universe is contracted quiddity, which is contracted in one way in the sun and in another way in the moon, the identity of the universe exists in difference, just as its oneness exists in plurality. Hence, although the universe is neither the sun nor the moon, nevertheless in the sun it is the sun and in the moon it is the moon. However, it is not the case that God is in the sun the sun and

---

1. David Albertson suggests that Cusanus appears to have found the example of sun and moon in *Fundamentum*, "A Learned Thief? Nicholas of Cusa and the Anonymous *Fundamentum Naturae*: Reassessing the Vorlage Theory," *Recherches de Théologie et Philosophie médiévales* 77, no. 2 (2010): 366.

2. This idea, too, he appears to have found in *Fundamentum*; Albertson, "Learned Thief," 366.

> in the moon the moon; rather He is that which is sun and moon without difference, *Universe* bespeaks *universality*—i.e., a oneness of many things. Accordingly, just as humanity is neither Socrates nor Plato but in Socrates is Socrates and in Plato is Plato, so is the universe in relation to all things. (*DI* II.115)

God is said to be neither the sun nor the moon, but he is said to be in them what they are in an absolute manner. That is, "He is that which is sun and moon without difference." Jasper Hopkins points out that in the later dialogue *De li non aliud*, Cusanus "is willing to make such statements as 'In the sky God is the sky.'"[3] Did Cusanus change his mind, as Hopkins asserts? I wonder. The difference between "in the sun God is the sun in an absolute manner" expands on the sense in which God can be said to be the sun in the sun. To understand things "in an absolute manner" should be compared with an understanding of things in the mode of the *non aliud,* the not other. In the later dialogue Cusanus is struggling to give more adequate expression to what I take to be essentially the same thought. Like all things, both sun and moon owe both that they are and what they are to God. That is implied by the medieval understanding of every thing as *ens creatum* and *ens verum.* In this respect there is no difference between them. God is the absolute quiddity of both. In God they are God and in them God is what they are absolutely.

In contrast, the universe is said to be neither the sun nor the moon, but is said to be in them what they are, but now not absolutely, but in a contracted manner. As the contraction of God, the universe exists only in countless individuals. "The identity of the universe exists in difference." As already mentioned, to understand the universe as just the totality of all things does not quite capture what Cusanus has in mind. "*Universe* bespeaks *universality*—i.e., a oneness of many things" (*DI* II.153). To say that in the sun the universe is the sun is to say that the sun, by its very nature, is related to countless other things, is part of one universe. So understood, "universe" would seem to mean something like the essence of what it is to be a created thing— that is, "thingliness," just as the maximum number was thought by Cusanus to be the *principium* of number. And just as every number has its unique place in the boundless number series, so every thing has its place in one boundless whole. We should note the way in which with Cusanus terms like "oneness," "universe," "humanity" tend to straddle the ontic-ontological divide. The Universe names both, the totality of

---

3. *OLI* 194n50. Cf. Hopkins, *Nicholas of Cusa's Metaphysic of Contraction,* 111.

all things and the being of each thing, just as "humanity" means both "the totality of human beings: the human race: humankind" and "the quality or state of being human."

Wenck criticizes this view, calling the view that "the Absolute Quiddity of the sun is not other than the Absolute Quiddity of the moon," since "it is God Himself, who is the Absolute Being and Absolute Quiddity of all things" "abominable" and the view that in the sun the universe is the sun, in the moon the moon "incompatible with every philosophy" (*IL* 36). Cusanus's reply in the *Apologia* is brief and dismissive, repeating his position and insisting on the orthodoxy of the view (*AP* 33).

The chapter concludes with a concise statement of Cusanus's understanding of the creation of the universe.

> But since, as was said, the universe is only the contracted first,[4] and in this respect is a maximum, it is evident that the whole universe sprang into existence by a simple emanation[5] of the contracted maximum from the Absolute Maximum. But all the beings that are parts of the universe (and without which the universe, since it is contracted, could not be one and whole and perfect) sprang into existence together with the universe; [there was] not first an intelligence, then a noble soul, and then nature, as Avicenna and other philosophers maintained.[6] Nevertheless, just as in a craftsman's design the whole (for instance, a house) is prior to a part (for instance, a wall), so because all things sprang into existence from God's design, we say that first there appeared the universe and thereafter all things—without which there could not be either a universe or a perfect [universe]. Hence, just as the abstract is in the concrete, so we consider the Absolute Maximum to be antecedently in the contracted maximum, so that it is subsequently in all particulars because it is present absolutely in that which is contractedly all things [viz., in the universe]. For God is the Absolute Quiddity of the world, or universe. But the universe is contracted quiddity. *Contraction* means contraction to [that is, restriction by] something, so as to be this or that. Therefore, God, who is one, is in the one universe. But the universe is contractedly

4. Dermot Moran suggests that *primum contractum* is better translated as "the first contracted [thing]"; Moran, "Pantheism," 147n33. I find this suggestion unconvincing: is the universe a thing? As the *maximum contractum* the universe is not a thing, just as God as the *maximum absolutum* is not a thing; see Jasper Hopkins, "Review of Special issue on Nicolaus Cusanus edited by Louis Dupré," *American Catholic Philosophical Quarterly* 64, no. 1 (Winter 1990): 211–28.

5. Cusanus found the expression *emanatio simplex* in Meister Eckhart; see sermon XLIX, 2n511; *PTW* I:121n48.

6. Avicenna, *Metaphysica* IX.4, Opera Omnia (Venice, 1508; repr. Louvain: Ed. de la bibliothèque S.J., 1961), *PTW* I:121n49.

> in all things. And so, we can understand the following: (1) how it is
> that God, who is most simple Oneness and exists in the one universe,
> is in all things as if subsequently and through the mediation of the
> universe, and (2) [how it is that] through the mediation of the one
> universe the plurality of things is in God. (*DI* II.4:116)

Following Eckhart, Cusanus would have us understand the universe
as the simple emanation of God. But the universe exists only in the
plurality of things that make up the universe. Apart from these it has
no being. That God "is in all things *as if* subsequently and through
the mediation of the universe" (*est quasi ex consequnti mediante uni-
verso in omnibus*) should not lead us to understand the universe as
somehow existing apart from the things that make it up, as if it were
some third entity mediating between God and things. The *quasi* that
Cusanus will repeat in the following chapter argues against such a
reading. There are no such mediating entities between things and
God. To be sure, the Creator has often been thought in the image of
a craftsman. And a craftsman will have some idea or plan of what he
is to make. That idea could be said to mediate between the craftsman
and his work. The thought of the universe as a divine plan, mediating
between God and the creation, suggests itself. But it is only we who,
relying on the craftsman metaphor, say that first there appeared the
plan of the universe and thereafter all things. We say this, responding to the marvelous interconnectedness of all things that suggests a
divine plan. In the same way Cusanus speaks of the mediation of the
universe to stress that things are what they are only as unique parts of
the boundless, well-ordered cosmos.

CHAPTER 5

Each Thing in Each Thing

Jasper Hopkins calls this a bizarre thesis.[1] At first blush one has to agree: the thesis seems to make little sense. What did Cusanus have in mind when he embraced the Anaxagorean fragment, "Each thing is in each thing," *Quodlibet in quolibet*? Why did this thesis, which he may have found in commentaries on Artistotle's *Physics* by Albertus Magnus or Thomas Aquinas,[2] become important to him?

The argument Cusanus presents seems straightforward, if questionable. In each created thing the universe is said to be contracted as this created thing. But the universe is the totality of all created things—that is to say, in each created thing the totality of all created things is said to be contracted as this created thing, just as in each human being humanity is contacted as this human being.

But the analogy between the universe and humanity, which Cusanus invokes in this chapter, immediately raises questions. Like "universe

1. *OLI* 24.

2. J. S. Kirk and J. E. Raven, *The Presocratic Philosophers* (Cambridge: Cambridge University Press, 1957), 375–76. The fragment has been preserved by Simplicius in *In Aristotelis Physicorum libros quattuor priores et posteriores commentaria*, ed. H. Diels, *Commentaria in Aristotelem Graeca IX–X* (Berlin: Reimer, 1882, 1885). Simplicius's commentary had been translated into Latin in the thirteenth century. The formula *Quodlibet est in quolibet*, with the ascription to Anaxagoras, Cusanus could have found in Albertus Magnus's or Thomas Aqiuinas's commentaries on Aristotle's Physics; without the ascription to Anaxagoras, it appears repeatedly in the writings of Meister Eckhart; see *PTW* I:121n52. Gandillac points to Proclus and Raymundus Lullus as possible sources; Gandillac, *Nikoklaus von Cues*, 120.

I. THE UNIVERSE

(*universum*)," as used by Cusanus, "humanity (*humanitas*)" is, as mentioned in the preceding chapter, profoundly ambiguous: it can mean either the totality of human beings or the essence of what it is to be a human being, humanness. The two meanings are quite distinct. Humanity can be said to exist in contracted fashion in each human being, as the abstract has been said by Cusanus to exist in contracted fashion in the concrete. But that, it would seem, does not entitle us to say that each human being is in each human being, although all share a common humanity. Similarly, all things can be said to share a common essence insofar as they are things. To be a thing is to be just one of the countless things that make up the universe. But that does not seem to entitle us to say that each thing is in each thing. If all Cusanus means to assert is that all things, as parts of the universe, share a common essence, this hardly seems to deserve a separate chapter. But the title makes a stronger and far more questionable claim. And to make this stronger claim Cusanus must rely on an understanding of "universe" that blurs the difference between an understanding of the universe as the totality of all things and an understanding of the universe as the essence of each thing, which is to be understood as a unique contraction of the universe. How are we to understand Cusanus's willingness to blur what it would seem must be distinguished?

Let us consider his argument in greater detail.

> If you pay close attention to what has already been said, you will not have trouble seeing—perhaps more deeply than Anaxagoras—the basis of the Anaxagorean truth "each thing is in each thing." From Book One it is evident that God is in all things in such way that all things are in Him; and it is now evident [from II.4] that God is in all things through the mediation of the universe, as it were. Hence, it is evident that all is in all and each in each. For the universe, as being most perfect, preceded all things "in the order of nature," as it were [*quasi ordine naturae*], so that in each thing it could be each thing. For in each created thing the universe is this created thing; and each thing receives all things in such way that in a given thing all things are, contractedly, this thing. Since each thing is contracted, it is not the case that it can be actually all things; hence, it contracts all things, so that [in it] they are it. Therefore, if all things are in all things, all things seem to precede each given thing. Therefore, it is not the case that all things are many things, since it is not the case that plurality precedes each given thing. Hence, in the "order of nature," [as it were] all things preceded, without plurality, each thing. Therefore, it is not the case that many things are in each thing actually; rather, [in each thing] all things are, without plurality, this respective thing. (*DI* II.5:117)

Question provoking is the way Cusanus asserts that "it is not the case that all things are many things" (*non igitur omnia sunt plura*). How are we to understand "all things" (*omnia*)? The German *das All* comes to mind, which can be translated as the universe, but suggests not so much a plurality of things, but more strongly something all-embracing. The universe is the totality of all things. Only in these countless things does it have actual existence. How then are we to understand "Hence, in the 'order of nature,' [as it were] all things preceded, without plurality, each thing"? So understood, as a whole, embracing all things without plurality, the universe is said to mediate between God and things: "God is in all things through the mediation of the universe, as it were."

We should note the "as it were." Cusanus is not saying that the universe actually mediates between God and things as an existing third entity. Nor is he saying that the universe, understood as "all things without plurality," actually precedes each thing. The universe after all actually exists only in these countless things. But these things exist only as a universe—that is, gathered into one, each thing having its place in the cosmic order and as such related to every other thing. The universe can thus be said to be the *principium* of all things. In this way, as the universe, all things imitate the Oneness of God. This *principium* should not be thought of as an independently existing entity, mediating between God and things, just as Cusanus would not have us think whiteness as existing independently of white things— say, as a Platonic form, mediating between God and white things. As pointed out in the preceding chapter, they are first of all abstractions formed by us in response to what we perceive. We experience all created things as having their place in space and time. Just as whiteness can be said to be in all white things, which without whiteness would not be what they are, the universe can be said to be in all things, which without it would not be what they are, parts of an all-embracing whole. In this sense the universe can be given a certain priority: "For the universe, as being most perfect, preceded all things 'in the order of nature' [as it were], so that in each thing it could be each thing." But the precedence, "'in the order of nature,' [as it were]," is established by the way we human knowers understand the relationship of the things of the world order to God, a relationship that appears mediated by the universe.

That Cusanus is not claiming that the things that make up the universe are in their plurality in contracted fashion in each thing is made clear by the paragraph's concluding sentence: "Therefore, it is not the case that many things are in each thing actually; rather, [in each thing] all things are, without plurality, this respective thing" (*DI* II.5:117).

> But everything which exists actually, exists in God, since He is the actuality of all things. Now, actuality is the perfection and the end of possibility. Hence, since the universe is contracted in each actually existing thing, it is evident that God, who is in the universe, is in each thing and that each actually existing thing is immediately in God, as is also the universe. (*DI* II.5:118)

Every actually existing thing is said to contract all things not as particulars, but "without plurality." How are we to think all things without plurality? Cusanus might invite us to draw on the analogy with numbers: how are we to think of all numbers without plurality? Cusanus would seem to think the universe as having a being somewhat like that of the maximum number, which does not exist and yet provides all numbers with their *principium*. The idea of the maximum number is demanded by our reason, which would have us think what is privatively infinite—that is, the endless number series, as a whole, which is also the thought of the essence of number. Analogously, Cusanus would have us think the countless things that make up the universe as a whole, a whole that does not actually exist as things exist but is yet the *principium* of every thing.

> Therefore, to say that each thing is in each thing is not other than [to say] that through all things God is in all things and that through all things all things are in God. The following very deep [truths] are apprehended clearly by an acute intellect: that God is, without difference, in all things because each thing is in each thing and that all things are in God because all things are in all things. But since the universe is in each thing in such way that each thing is in it: in each thing the universe is, contractedly, that which this thing is contractedly; and in the universe each thing is the universe; nonetheless, the universe is in each thing in one way, and each thing is in the universe in another way. (*DI* II.5:119)

The quote is made difficult by Cusanus's use of "all things" (*omnia*). Recall his assertion: "It is not the case that all things are many things." "All things" can mean the countless things that exist; but it can also mean the universe as the all-embracing unity of all things. Cusanus would seem to shift from one meaning to the other. So understood, the passage can be taken to reassert the mediating function of the universe. As a contraction of the universe each thing is in God and God is in each thing as a contraction of the universe.

To clarify this puzzling passage, Cusanus draws once again on the by now familiar mathematical analogy of the infinite line from which every finite line is said to have its being:

> Therefore, in the finite line all that which the infinite line is—viz., line, triangle, and the others—is that which the finite line is. Therefore, in the finite line every figure is the finite line. In the finite line there is not actually either a triangle, a circle, or a sphere; for from what is actually many, there is not made what is actually one. For it is not the case that each thing is in each thing actually; rather, in the line the triangle is the line; and in the line the circle is the line; and so on. (*DI* II.5:119)

Analogously, every thing is not actually in every thing. "See, then, how it is that the oneness of things, or the universe, exists in plurality and, conversely, the plurality [of things] exists in oneness." (*DI* II.5:119)

The oneness of the universe is said to imitate the oneness of God. Cusanus finds an analogy in the oneness of an organism:

> For since the eye cannot actually be the hands, the feet, and all the other members, it is content with being the eye; and the foot [is content with being] the foot. And all members contribute [something] to one another, so that each is that which it is in the best way it can be. Neither the hand nor the foot is in the eye; but in the eye they are the eye insofar as the eye is immediately in the man. And in like manner, in the foot all the members [are the foot] insofar as the foot is immediately in the man. Thus, each member through each member is immediately in the man; and the man, or the whole, is in each member through each member, just as in the parts the whole is in each part through each part. (*DI* II.5:121)

The analogy lets Cusanus claim that the universe, too, is such a harmonious whole, where every part is content to be just what it is.

> Consider more closely and you will see that each actually existing thing is tranquil because of the fact that in it all things are it and that in God it is God. You see that there is a marvelous oneness of things, an admirable equality, and a most wonderful union, so that all things are in all things. (*DI* II.5:120)

Given the troubled times Cusanus lived in and his stormy life, which, as we saw, was anything but tranquil, one has to wonder how he squared the discord that so obviously mars human affairs with the rosy picture of the universe that he here presents. Is there a sense in which we human beings have lost our place in the universe, in which every part is said to be tranquil, because "not able to exist in any other way or any better way" (*DI* II.120–21)? What place does freedom have in Cusanus's picture of the universe? Here Cusanus does not seem concerned with such questions. What interests him is rather the way the universe, imitating God, exhibits "a marvelous oneness of things, an admirable equality, and a most wonderful union." Its trinitarian structure will be the topic of chapter 7.

To sum up what he had said in chapters 4 and 5, Cusanus offers us yet another questionable analogy. Once again Cusanus invokes the idea of humanity:

> Therefore, suppose you consider humanity as if (*quasi*) it were some-thing absolute, unmixable, and incontractible; and [suppose you] consider a man in whom absolute humanity exists absolutely and from which humanity there exists the contracted humanity which the man is. In that case, the absolute humanity is, as it were (*quasi*), God; and the contracted humanity is, as it were (*quasi*), the universe. The absolute humanity is in the man principally, or antecedently, and is in each member or each part subsequently; and the contracted humanity is in the eye eye, in the heart heart, etc., and so, in each member is contractedly each member. Thus, in accordance with this supposition, we have found (1) a likeness of God and the world, and (2) guidance with respect to all the points touched upon in these two chapters, together with (3) many other points which follow from this [comparison]. (*DI* II:122)

The repeatedly used *quasi* demands our attention. Cusanus is asking us to think something he knows our reason must reject as impossi-ble. Humanity is, first of all, an abstraction. Humanity has no being apart from human beings. The thought of humanity as something absolute—that is, in no relation to other things—is to think it in a way to which we can give no content. That humanity, so understood, is said to be, "as it were (*quasi*), God" is not surprising if we recall the chapter on negative theology. The thought of an absolute humanity thus figures the thought of the Absolute Maximum. Cusanus asks us next to think of a man "in whom absolute humanity exists absolutely and from which humanity there exists the contracted humanity which the man is." To think of such a man would be to think of something like the maximum number, which shares its being as a number with other numbers and yet as a maximum is not just another number, which is essentially one of many. That Cusanus should liken such a man to the universe is not surprising: contracted in time and space, the universe is like the countless things of this world. But it, too, is a maximum, contracted in each of these things.

The thought of the man "in whom absolute humanity exists absolutely" has to bring to mind Christ, the incarnated Word. Is there a sense in which the universe is a similar incarnation? Book Three will give us occasion to pursue this thought further.

And as each organ has been understood by Cusanus as a contraction of the whole human being, so each part of the universe is a contraction of the whole. There is, to be sure, this decisive difference: the whole human being is a thing, as are the organs that are said by Cusanus to be its contractions. The part-whole relation here is a relation among things. But no more than the maximum number can the universe be comprehended as such a whole.

As mentioned, Hopkins considers the thesis that "each thing is in each thing" bizarre, supported by "an altogether dubious notion of the relation of part and whole" (*OLI* 25). Questionable it is, but in the sense of the German *fragwürdig*: worthy of being questioned. How are we to think the being of the universe? The universe continues to resist comprehension. The parallelism among God, world, and man, God, macrocosm, and microcosm, which concerns Cusanus in this chapter, will continue to occupy us.

CHAPTER 6

The Enfolding, and the Degree of Contraction, of the Universe

In this chapter especially Cusanus's use of mathematics, here to support his endorsement of Aristotle's theory of ten categories, invites questioning. Inadequately supported, it seems almost playful:

> In the foregoing we found, beyond all understanding, that the world, or universe, is one. Its oneness is contracted by plurality, so that it is oneness in plurality. And because Absolute Oneness is first and the oneness of the universe is derived from it, the oneness of the universe will be a second oneness, consisting of a plurality. And since (as I will show in *Conjectures*) the second oneness is tenfold and unites the ten categories, the one universe will, by a tenfold contraction, be the unfolding of the first, absolute, and simple Oneness. Now all things are enfolded in the number ten since there is not a number above it. (*DI* II.6:123)

As it stands this would seem to be an absurd claim: are there not countless numbers above ten? Cusanus does not deny this. What then are we to make of his claim?

Cusanus refers us to his forthcoming *De Conjecturis*, a companion text to *De docta ignorantia*, also dedicated to cardinal Cesarini, a text on which he was then apparently already working. The beginning of that work states clearly how he understands the being of the comprehended cosmos: it is, as we have already seen, the product of an unfolding of the human mind in response to what we experience with our senses; and we must not confuse our conjectures about things with the things themselves, which are an unfolding of the divine mind. To be sure, our conjectures have their measure in the divinely created cosmos as presented to us by our senses. Its intelligibility presupposes some sort of resemblance between our human and divine numbers. But the nature of that resemblance remains hidden from us. We have no access to this cosmos that is not mediated by our mind and that, for Cusanus, means also mediated by number, the unfolding of our mind. Cusanus's appropriation of the Aristotelian categories is thus hardly in the spirit of Aristotle. As Ernst Cassirer recognized, it is closer to the spirit of Kant.

> It must be the case that surmises (*conjecturae*) originate from our minds,[1] even as the real world originates from Infinite Divine Reason. For when, as best it can, the human mind (which is a lofty likeness of God) partakes of the fruitfulness of the Creating Nature, it produces from itself, qua image of the Omnipotent Form, rational entities, [which are made] in the likeness of real entities. Consequently, the human mind is the form of a surmised (*conjecturalis*) [rational] world, just as the Divine Mind is the Form of the real world (*DC* 5).

The comprehended, rational world is an unfolding of the human mind as such a conjecture. Our conjectures, to be sure, are "in the likeness of real entities." "By *coniectura* we must understand genuine, if not altogether adequate, knowledge, ever confronted with experience, knowledge, however, that has its foundation first of all in the most 'divine' function of the human being: the mathematical."[2] Our conjectures are likenesses of the truth. The precise nature of that likeness remains hidden from us. The infinite thus shows us two sides: a negative side that renders all our conjectures inadequate and a positive side that renders them approximations of the truth. That our conjectures are indeed "in the likeness of real entities" shows itself in the way they allow us to cope with nature.

The origin of all our conjectures is number. Number therefore provides us with a key to the comprehended universe.[3]

---

1. I prefer "conjecture" to "surmise" as a translation of *conjectura.*
2. Gandillac, *Nikoklaus von Cues,* 160.
3. See chapter 6, "The Power of Mathematics," and chapter 7, "Excursus: Mathematics and the Study of Nature," in Book One.

> Number is a certain natural, originated beginning that is of reason's making; for those [creatures] that lack a mind, e.g., brute animals, do not number. Nor is number anything other than reason unfolded; for number is proved to be the beginning of those things that are attained by reason—proved to such an extent that if number is removed, then reason shows that none of those things [attained by reason] would remain. Moreover, reason's unfolding of number and its using number to make surmises is nothing other than reason's using itself and mentally fashioning all [surmised] things in a natural, supreme likeness of itself—just as in and through His Co-eternal Word, God (who is Infinite Mind) communicates being to things. (*DC* 7)

As we shall see, Cusanus's understanding of the way we count provides the key to his privileging of the number ten and to his embrace of Aristotle's ten categories. Hopkins points to chapter 6 as one place where Cusanus makes clear his desire to remain close to the Aristotelians,[4] although, as pointed out, his embrace of Aristotle here would seem to be hardly in the spirit of Aristotle.

> And in this way the Peripatetics speak the truth [when they say that] universals do not actually exist independently of things. For only what is particular exists actually. In the particular, universals are contractedly the particular. Nevertheless, in the order of nature universals have a certain universal being which is contractible by what is particular. [I do] not [mean] that before contraction they exist actually and in some way other than according to the natural order ([that is, other than] as a contractible universal which exists not in itself but in that which is actual, just as a point, a line, and a surface precede, in progressive order, the material object in which alone they exist actually). For because the universe exists actually only in a contracted way, so too do all universals. Although universals do not exist as actual apart from particulars, nevertheless they are not mere rational entities. (By comparison, although neither a line nor a surface exists apart from a material object, they are not on this account mere rational entities; for they exist in material objects, even as universals exist in particulars.) (*DI* II.6:125)

The comparison raises questions: if line and surface are not mere rational entities, what are they? Do they also have a divine supra-rational being? In his attempt to steer a middle course between Platonism and nominalism, Cusanus relies on his understanding of the human being as *imago Dei*. The unfolding of the human mind in the comprehended

4. *OLI* 25.

cosmos mirrors in a way that eludes our comprehension the unfolding of the divine mind in the cosmos, where "unfolding" and "mind," when applied to God, are altogether inadequate metaphors.

The general is said to exist only in particular things. Universals are first of all products of our thinking about things (*universalia post rem*). They are arrived at by a process of abstraction, which presupposes the intelligibility of things: we must recognize that the family resemblances we detect in things and that let us group them as we do are not imported by us into these things. This much we must grant the Platonists: they have their foundation in reality. In that sense we are justified in speaking of *universalia ante rem*. Cusanus is no nominalist. But what is the being of these *universalia ante rem*? They have being only in the divine mind, and there multiplicity is not to be found. There, Plato's many forms coincide in what we may call "one form" or "exemplar." We must therefore not take them to be independently existing entities of some sort. The order of the universe has its foundation in the divine Word, which takes the place of Plato's forms. Only with respect to the many things of this world can we speak of a multiplicity of forms.[5] It is this middle course that, if essentially incapable of being rendered clear and distinct, we nevertheless must steer.

> For example, dogs and the other animals of the same species are united by virtue of the common specific nature which is in them. This nature would be contracted in them even if Plato's intellect had not, from a comparison of likenesses, formed for itself a species. Therefore, with respect to its own operation, understanding follows being and living; for [merely] through its own operation, understanding can bestow neither being nor living nor understanding. Now, with respect to the things understood: the intellect's understanding follows, through a likeness, being and living and the intelligibility of nature. Therefore, universals, which it makes from comparison, are a likeness of the universals contracted in things. (*DI* II.6:126)

To repeat: the human mind unfolds itself in the comprehended cosmos, as God unfolds himself in the created cosmos. The way God unfolds himself in the cosmos surpasses our understanding, even as it provides it with a measure. But God's creation, and in just what relation it stands to the comprehended cosmos, remains a mystery.

Nothing that has been said so far helps us to understand the remarkable claim that there is no number above the number ten. What

<hr>

5. Johannes Hirschberger, "Das Platon-Bild bei Nikolous von Kues," in *Nicolo' Cusano: Agli Inizi del Mondo Moderno*, 119.

prompts this privileging of the number ten in which Cusanus finds a key to the organization of the universe?

> Therefore, the tenfold oneness of the universe enfolds the plurality of all contracted things. As ten is the square root of one hundred and the cube root of one thousand, so—because the oneness of the universe is in all things as the contracted beginning of all—the oneness of the universe is the root of all things. From this root there first arises the "square number," so to speak, as a third oneness; and the cubic number [arises thereafter] as a fourth and final oneness. The first unfolding of the oneness of the universe is the third oneness, viz., one hundred; and the last unfolding is the fourth oneness, viz., one thousand. (*DI* II.6:123)

The question returns: how are we to understand the privileging of the number ten, the mapping of the sequence 1—10—100—1,000 unto the sequence God—categories—genera—species? The point seems forced. In *De Conjecturis* Cusanus was to offer an explanation of sorts:

> It is expedient that you contemplate the nature of number more keenly the more deeply you are endeavoring to investigate other things by means of a likeness to number. Turn your attention, first of all, to number's progression, and you will ascertain that its progression is completed in the number four. For 1, 2, 3, and 4, added together, will make 10, which unfolds the numerical power of simple oneness. Indeed, from the number ten, which is a second oneness, the squared unfolding of the root [ten] is attained by means of a similar four-term progression: [for] 10, 20, 30, and 40, when added together, are 100, which is the square of the root ten. Similarly, by means of a like movement, centenary oneness [that is, the number 100], gives rise to 1,000: [for] 100, 200, 300, and 400, when added together, are 1,000. There is no continuing on in this way (as if there remained something further), although there is no denying that after 10 (viz., with 11, where, after 10, a return is made to oneness) the process repeats itself, just as it also does after 1,000. (*DC* 10)

The claim that the progression of number is completed in the number four follows the Pythagorean understanding of the Tetractys, a triangular figure consisting of ten points arranged in four rows: one, two, three, and four points in each row."

The Tetractys represented the organization of space:

1. the first row represented zero *dimensions* (a *point*)

2. the second row represented one dimension (a *line* of two points)

3. the third row represented *two dimensions* (a *plane* defined by a *triangle* of three points)

4. the fourth row represented *three dimensions* (a *tetrahedron* defined by four points).[6]

Representing the generation of space from a point, the Tetractys thus offered itself as a symbol of the creation of the universe and is thus venerated in this Pythagorean prayer:

> Bless us, divine number, thou who generated gods and men! O holy, holy Tetractys, thou that containest the root and source of the eternally flowing creation! For the divine number begins with the profound, pure unity until it comes to the holy four; then it begets the mother of all, the all-comprising, all-bounding, the first-born, the never-swerving, the never-tiring holy ten, the keyholder of all.[7]

It also offered itself to Cusanus as such a symbol. The decimal system underscores the potency of 10: 10 is the square root of 100 and the cubic root of 1,000, numbers whose special significance had indeed also been recognized by the Roman way of counting. But the Arabic numerals on which Cusanus relies in *De Coniecturis* underscore that significance. Although promulgated already by Leonardo Fibonacci in his *Liber Abaci* (1202), at the time, Arabic numerals were still a relatively novel way of marking numbers, which Cusanus had to explain to his readers. Most people then still used Roman numerals.[8]

Cusanus was hardly alone in thinking the decimal system to have its foundation in the natural way of counting, "independent of any arithmetic convention."[9] Its wide use is explained by our tendency to count with our ten fingers. The number ten is of course the base of the decimal system, which uses one of the first nine integers or 0 in each place and lets each place value of a number be a power of ten. This help us to understands Cusanus's claim that there is no number above the number ten—that is, that with eleven "a return is made to oneness." Cusanus's assertion that there is "no continuing on in this way" after we have reached 1,000—once we have squared and cubed

---

6. Tobias Dantzig, *The Language of Science: A Critical Survey Written for the Cultured Non-Mathematician* (New York: Macmillan, 1930).

7. Dantzig, *Language of Science*, 42.

8. *PTW* II:219n11, 1.

9. Gandillac, *Nikoklaus von Cues*, 319.

ten, that it makes no sense to speak of a higher power—is supported by his highly questionable understanding of the intimate connection between arithmetic and geometry. There are of course infinitely
many numbers larger than 1,000, but according to Cusanus we get to
these by an ever-repeated return to oneness.

Given his understanding of number as the unfolding of the human
spirit, providing the form of the comprehended cosmos, it is not surprising that we should find in his still in many ways Aristotelian understanding of nature analogies to the sequence 1—10—100—1,000—
namely, God—categories—genera—species.

> And so, we find three universal onenesses descending by degrees to
> what is particular, in which they are contracted, so that they are actu-
> ally the particular. The first and absolute Oneness enfolds all things
> absolutely; the first contracted [oneness enfolds] all things contract-
> edly. But order requires [the following]: that Absolute Oneness be
> seen to enfold, as it were, the first contracted [oneness], so that by
> means of it [it enfolds] all other things; that the first contracted
> [oneness] be seen to enfold the second contracted [oneness] and,
> by means of it, the third contracted [oneness]; and that the second
> contracted [oneness be seen to enfold] the third contracted one-
> ness, which is the last universal oneness, fourth from the first, so that
> by means of the third contracted oneness the second oneness arrives
> at what is particular. (*DI* II.6:124)

While Cusanus is thus concerned to show that his understanding of
the universe is in agreement with Aristotle's distinction between categories, genera, and species, what would seem to matter more to him
is the way mathematics provides comprehended nature with its form.
But we may not forget the distinction between human and divine
mathematics. Mathematics is understood here first of all as an unfolding of the human mind. To be sure, when we attempt to understand
nature we imitate, as best we can, God's creative understanding. But
learned ignorance has taught us that the abyss that separates the finite
and the infinite, human and divine mathematics, will not be bridged.
The Pythagorean One is only a very inadequate symbol of God.

II. THE TRINITY OF THE UNIVERSE

THE NEXT FOUR CHAPTERS are held together by the concept of the Trinity. Cusanus has claimed that all things imitate God as best as they can. They all thus have a trinitarian structure. That holds especially for man, said to have been created by God in his image. A nonbeliever might wonder whether the asserted similarity between the trinitarian God and man has its foundation rather in the fact that man created God in his image. The thought would seem to be not altogether alien to Cusanus: recall that in accordance with negative theology, God is said to be "only infinite, He is neither Father nor Son nor Holy Spirit. Now, the Infinite qua Infinite is neither Begetting, Begotten, nor Proceeding" (*DI* II:87). Affirmative theology can only furnish us with more or less adequate conjectures that inevitably will bear the mark of us human beings: made of the earth, possessing a form, and capable of motion. In this sense the human being, too, is thought by Cusanus to be a trinity. And this trinity Cusanus also finds in the universe, which, as we saw, he takes to be the first contracted oneness, following the oneness of God. Just as God, the Absolute Maximum, must be thought by us to be a trinity, so must the universe, the contracted maximum (discussed in chapter 7). The trinity that marks the universe is that of matter (discussed in chapter 8), of form, (discussed in chapter 9), and of motion (discussed in chapter 10), echoing the Trinity of Father, Son, and Holy Spirit.

That the universe has a trinitarian structure is a thought Cusanus shares with quite a number of medieval thinkers.[1] In these chapters Cusanus draws heavily on texts by Thierry of Chartres, his school, and thinkers influenced by him. such as Alan of Lille and including, it would seem, especially *Fundamentum*, which bears a startlingly close relationship to chapters 7–10, paralleling "nearly verbatim"

1. *PTW* I:123nn69, 70.

II. THE TRINITY OF THE UNIVERSE

what Maarten J. F. M. Hoenen considered the central sections" of Book II of *De docta ignorantia*."[2] As already mentioned, Hoenen saw in this short text the source or *Vorlage* of these chapters, pointing to the circle of students around Heymeric de Campo, an interesting suggestion that invites further consideration of the time Cusanus spent in Cologne and his friendship and collaboration with Heymeric. As I pointed out, the suggestion that Cusanus used this text as a *Vorlage* did not go unchallenged. But philosophically, not all that much is at stake in this controversy. Throughout *De docta ignorantia* Cusanus appropriated the ideas of others, but in a way that is unmistakably his own. The arguments must speak for themselves.

2. Albertson, "A Learned Thief?," 154.'

The Trinity of the Universe

Chapter 7 has an introductory character, preparing for the following three chapters. It begins by restating what in Book I had been said about God as the Trinity and continues by pointing out how the unity of Father, Son, and Holy Spirit in God differs from the trinitarian structure of the universe, which in its contracted way imitates the divine Trinity.

> In God it is not the case that Oneness exists contractedly in Trinity as a whole exists [contractedly] in its parts or as a universal exists [contractedly] in particulars; rather, the Oneness is the Trinity. Therefore, each of the persons [of the Trinity] is the Oneness; and since the Oneness is Trinity, one person is not another person. But in the case of the universe a similar thing cannot hold true. Therefore, [in the case of the universe] the three mutual relationships—which in God are called persons—have actual existence only collectively in oneness. (DI II, 7:127)

According to Cusanus a trinitarian structure is present in all God has created, especially in the universe as the *principium* of every created thing, which, however, has existence only in these things.

> For there cannot be contraction without (1) that which is contractible, (2) that which causes contracting [*contrahens*], and (3) the union which is effected through the common actuality [*actum*] of these two. (*DI* II.7:128)

II. THE TRINITY OF THE UNIVERSE

The model provided by human making once again suggests itself, which had already provided Aristotle with the key to his understanding of the being of things in terms of four causes. Think of a piece of wax on which a form is imposed by some actor and of the formed wax that results.

> But since that which causes contracting delimits the possibility of that which is contractible, it descends from Equality of Oneness. For Equality of Oneness is Equality of Being. For being and one are convertible. Hence, since that which causes contracting equalizes the possibility for being one thing or another contractedly, it is rightly said to descend from Equality-of-Being, which, in God, is the Word. (*DI* II:129)

God is thought here, quite in keeping with tradition, in the image of a craftsman: to make, say, a bed is to delimit the possibility provided by the wood. But the making of anything presupposes an idea of what is to be made. The making of the bed requires reason at work. To active human reason corresponds the divine Word (Equality of Oneness, which is Equality of Being), which bears a relationship to Plato's realm of the forms, although, as we have seen, Cusanus denies that there is actually a plurality of forms. Just as human reason is one, unfolding itself in countless ideas, so the Word is one, unfolding itself in what appears to us as the order of the universe, unfolded in categories, genera, and species.

> And since the Word, which is the Essence (*ratio*) and Idea and Absolute Necessity of things, necessitates and restricts the possibility through such a cause of contracting, some [thinkers] called that which causes contracting "form" or "the world-soul" (and they called possibility "matter"); others [spoke of it as] "fate substantified"; others, e.g., the Platonists, [spoke of it as] a "connecting necessity." For it descends from Absolute Necessity, so that it is a contracted necessity and contracted form, as it were, in which all forms truly exist. (*DI* II.7:129)

Just as only the realization of the idea in the mind of the carpenter in the successful transformation of the wood results in a bed, so only the union of the Word and possibility results in particular things. But the totality and principle of all things is the universe. To be a thing is to be part of the universe, along with countless other things.

> Therefore, the oneness of the universe is three, since it is from possibility, connecting necessity, and union—which can be called possibility [*potentia*], actuality [*actus*] and union [*nexus*]. (*DI* II.7:130)

I am not altogether satisfied by the translation of *actus* as actuality. Wilpert translates *actus* as *Wirklichkkeit*, in which we hear the word *wirken*, to bring something about. In medieval Latin *actus* translates the Greek *energeia*. The English "actuality" does not seem to me to preserve the sense of being active, of being at work, as opposed to the result of such work. As the *nexus* of *actus* and *potentia* the universe is one, just as the bed is one as the product of the working of the wood by the craftsman.

In analogy to the distinction between craftsman, his being at work, the work produced, and the material used, Cusanus thus, following closely Thierry of Chartres,[1] arrives at four modes of being, where we must keep in mind that, as Cusanus is well aware, the craftsman metaphor, taken from the human sphere, can provide us only with a highly inadequate account of God's creation. That inadequacy shadows what follows:

> And herefrom infer four universal modes of being. There is the mode of being which is called Absolute Necessity, according as God is Form of forms, Being of beings, and Essence (*ratio*) or Quiddity of things. With regard to this mode of being: in God all things are Absolute Necessity itself. Another mode [of being] is according as things exist in the connecting necessity; in this necessity, just as in a mind, the forms-of-things, true in themselves, exist with a distinction, and an order, of nature. We shall see later whether this is so. An other mode of being is according as, in determined possibility, things are actually this or that. And the lowest mode of being is according as things are possible to be, and it is absolute possibility (*possibilitas pura*). (*DI* II:130)[2]

The four modes of being are thus:

1. Absolute Necessity (*absoluta necessitas*): God as Form of forms, Being of beings, and the essence or quiddity of things.

2. Connecting Necessity (*necessitas comlexionis*), understood as the principle of the order of nature: to be things must have their distinct places in a space of forms, a logical space, a nexus.

3. Determined possibility: (*possibilitas determimata*). Things have to be actually this or that; they occupy distinct places in that space.

4. Absolute possibility (*possibilitas pura*).

---

1. For a discussion of Thierry's modal theory, see Albertson, *Mathematical Theologies*, 127–38; see especially Table 5-2 on 128.

2. The passage is almost identical with a passage in *Fundamentum*, cited in Albertson, *Mathematical Theologies*, 352n88.

Of interest is the way Cusanus separates the first mode of being from the following three. These three modes of being are said to have actual existence only in particular things as conditions of their being. The only existents Cusanus admits are God and particular beings, which owe their being to God. This must make us wonder what kind of being he can ascribe to the second and fourth mode.

Every particular being is necessarily (a) a specific determination of possibility, (b) a determination that presupposes absolute possibility as it presupposes (c) connecting necessity as the principle of the order in which particular things have their place. Taken together, these three modes of being provide the *principium* of the being of things. But earlier Cusanus had determined the universe to be that *principium*.[3] These three modes would thus seem to name different aspects of the universe.

In the following, Cusanus appropriates once again the wording of *Fundamentum*:[4]

> The last three modes of being exist in one universality which is a contracted maximum. From these there is one universal mode of being, since without them not anything can exist. I say modes of being. For the universal mode of being is not composed of the three things as parts in the way that a house [is composed] of a roof, a foundation, and a wall. Rather it is from modes of being. For a rose which in a rose garden is in potency in winter and in actuality in the summer has passed from a mode of possible being to something actually determined. Hence, we see that the mode of being of possibility, the mode of being of necessity, and the mode of being of actual determination are distinct. From them there is one universal mode of being, since without them there is nothing; nor does the one mode actually exist without the other. (*DI* II.7:131)

All four modes of being are difficult to comprehend, the first and fourth more so than the second and the third. The first and fourth can be thought only by following the *via negationis*. "They are not two juxtaposed or opposing 'existents,' but two 'limits' that become meaningful only on the level of a supra-rational analysis."[5] The second mode, too, raises the question: what kind of being it is supposed to possess? We should note Cusanus's careful wording: "In this necessity, just as in a mind, the forms-of-things, true in themselves, exist with a distinction, and an order, of nature. We shall

---

3. Albertson, *Mathematical Theologies*, 226 and 227.
4. Albertson, *Mathematical Theologies*, 352n89.
5. Gandillac, *Nikolaus von Kues*, 400.

see later whether this is so." The third mode is said to refer to the way "things are actually this or that." The two middle modes are thus "no longer ontologically opposed realities, but one represents the world as it thought by a unifying consciousness, the other as it is given objectively in the unlimited possibility of its relations."[6] About the incomprehensibility of God enough has been said. But how are we to understand absolute possibility? Cusanus's example of the rose that is said to be in potency in winter is of no help: here we have an example of possibility very much restricted by the being of the rose—that is, an example of contracted possibility. Does it even make sense to speak of absolute possibility?[7] How is it related to Absolute Necessity—that is, to God? The following chapter will shed some light on that question.

6. Gandillac, *Nikolaus von Kues*, 400–401.

7. The author of *Fundamentum* rejects Thierry's fourth mode as incoherent. He also rejects the second mode: "Because the world is contracted there can be no mediators between the world and God, since such mediations claim to enjoy an uncontracted status beyond the world but less than God"; Albertson, *Mathematical Theologies*, 159. Cusanus would seem to agree to with this critique of Thierry's four modes.

CHAPTER 8

The Possibility or Matter
of the Universe

The equation of possibility and matter lets us think of Aristotle's prime matter, and it is indeed with a discussion of prime matter that Cusanus begins this chapter.

> To expound here, at least briefly, upon the things which can make our ignorance learned, let me discuss for a moment the previously mentioned three modes of being—beginning with possibility. The ancients made many statements about possibility; the opinion of them all was that from nothing nothing is made. And so, they maintained that there is a certain absolute possibility of being all things and that it is eternal. They believed that in absolute possibility all things are enfolded as possibilities. (*DI* II.8:132)

The argument that there must be something like prime matter as the ground of the possibility of all things Cusanus could find in Aristotle (*Metaphysics* 12062b.24ff.; *Physics* 187a.27ff.). The thesis, *ex nihilo nihil fit,* "from nothing nothing is made," is, however, difficult to square with the Christian understanding of God, who is said to have created the world *ex nihilo,* out of nothing.

Despite that apparent incompatibility, Cusanus found the Aristotelian account suggestive:

> They conceived this [absolute] matter, or possibility, by reasoning in a reverse way, just as in the case of absolute necessity. For example, they conceived a body incorporeally by abstracting from it the form of corporeity. And so, they attained unto matter only ignorantly [*non nisi ignoranter*]. For how can a body be conceived incorporeally and without form? They said that by nature possibility precedes everything, so that the statement "God exists" is never true without the statement "Absolute possibility exists" also being true. Nevertheless, they did not maintain that absolute possibility is co-eternal with God, since it is from God. Absolute possibility is neither something nor nothing, neither one nor many, neither this nor that, neither quidditive nor qualitative; rather, it is the possibility for all things and is, actually, nothing of all things. (*DI* II.8:132)

What makes this passage difficult to interpret is that the view Cusanus here attributes to the ancients, where he relies on Thierry of Chartres,[1] would seem to be in many ways close to his own understanding of matter, certainly a conjecture worth taking seriously. The statement that they "attained unto matter only ignorantly [*non nisi ignoranter*]" should not be understood as a simple dismissal. Would a better translation perhaps be, "They did not attain unto matter, except ignorantly"—that is, in the mode of learned ignorance? The difficulty of thinking a body incorporeally is akin to the difficulty of thinking an infinite triangle. The statement "God exists" is never true without the statement "Absolute possibility exists" also being true, coupled with the statement "They did not maintain that absolute possibility is co-eternal with God, since it is from God" would seem to be an expression of the unlimited creativity of God. That creativity surpasses our comprehension. The final sentence of the quoted passage brings to mind negative theology.

Cusanus turns next to a similarly sympathetic consideration of the Platonists and what is said by him to be their trinitarian conception of possibility. Once again Cusanus seems eager to point to the way the Platonists seem to have anticipated his own convictions.

> The Platonists called absolute possibility "lack" [*carentia*], since it lacks all form. Because it lacks, it desires. And by virtue of the following fact it is aptitude [*aptitudo*]: viz., it obeys necessity, which commands it (i.e., draws it toward actually being), just as wax [obeys] the craftsman who wills to make something from it. But formlessness [*informitas*] proceeds from, and unites, lack and aptitude—so that absolute possibility is, as it were, incompositely trine. For lack, aptitude, and

---

1. Cf. *PTW, DC* II:12688, 89, referring the reader to Thierry, *Commentum* II:19 and 28.

II. THE TRINITY OF THE UNIVERSE

> formlessness cannot be its parts; for if they were, something would
> precede absolute possibility—which is impossible. Hence, [lack, apti-
> tude, and formlessness] are modes in whose absence absolute possi-
> bility would not be absolute. For lack exists contingently in possibility.
> For from the fact that possibility does not have the form it can have,
> it is said to be lacking. Hence, it is lack. (*DI* II.8:133)

But the comparison of the way a craftsman decides to shape wax into,
say, a statue and the way absolute possibility is informed by the forms,
as formless matter is brought to life when the world-soul mingles with
it, raises the question of how to understand the aptitude of absolute
possibility. The wax has properties that predispose it to be shaped in
certain ways, just as the wood has properties that allow a craftsman to
make it into a chest. Possibility is here contracted in ways determined
by the material in question. And must something analogous not also
be said about the universe? As Cusanus remarks:

> Furthermore, unless the possibility of things were contracted, there
> could not be a reason for things, but everything would happen by
> chance, as Epicurus falsely maintained.[2] That this world sprang
> forth rationally from possibility was necessarily due to the fact that
> the possibility had an aptitude only for being this world. Therefore,
> the possibility's aptitude was contracted and not absolute. The same
> holds true regarding the earth, the sun, and other things: unless
> they had been latently present in matter—[present] in terms of a
> certain contracted possibility—there would have been no more rea-
> son why they would have been brought forth into actuality than not.
> (*DI* II.8:138)

Here Cusanus appears to reject Thierry's fourth mode of being. Absolute possibility cannot be divorced from the being of God.

We meet here with a problem anyone faces who attempts to account for the being of things in terms of the imposition of form on
formless matter, where we may want to consider both the creation
account of the *Timaeus* and Kant's account of the formation of objects
as a result of the informing of the material of sensibility as paradigms,
one ontological, the other epistemological. What determines that
there are, say, cats and dogs? The material must already be disposed
to be informed in certain ways—that is, in the language of Cusanus,

---

2. The source of the Epicurus reference is John of Salisbury, to whom Cusanus also
would seem to owe much of his understanding of the *Timaeus*. We should keep in mind that
until Ficino's complete translation, the *Timaeus* was the only Platonic dialogue known to the
Middle Ages, and that only in an incomplete translation (to 53c) by Chalcidius (ca. 321),
who accompanied it with a widely read commentary. Cf. *PTW* I, *DI* II:128n102.

possibility cannot be absolute, but must already have been contracted in certain ways by the material in question.

> Hence, Hermes[3] said that hyle is the nourisher of bodies and that formlessness is the nourisher of souls. And someone among us[4] said that chaos naturally preceded the world and was the possibility of things—in which chaos that formless power resided, and in which power all souls exist as possibilities. Hence, the ancient Stoics said that all forms are actually in possibility but are hidden and appear as a result of a removal of the covering—just as when a spoon is made from wood only by the removal of portions [of the wood]. (*DI* II.8:134)

As Senger points out,[5] the early Christian church tended to either equate chaos with the nothing from which God is said to have created the world or, as Augustine, for instance, thought, to think it as God's first creation: *Primo ergo materia facta est confusa et informis ... quod credo a Graecis chaos apellari*, "first therefore matter was made confused and formless ... which, I believe, the Greeks called chaos."[6] But although formless, chaos has to be such as to be capable of being shaped by God into the world, just as the limewood had to possess certain properties to be fashioned by some sculptor into a statue of the Virgin. The Stoics—we do not know on what source Cusanus is relying—therefore had good reason to think that the forms, although still hidden, were already present in the material, to be revealed by, say, the sculptor: Dürer was to speak of the form sleeping in the matter that the artist had to liberate.

Cusanus, however, rejects the thesis that the form is already present in matter. He finds the Aristotelian position more acceptable.

> However, the Peripatetics said that forms are in matter only as possibilities and are educed by an efficient cause. Hence, it is quite true that forms exist not only from possibility but also through an efficient cause. (For example, he who removes portions of a piece of wood, in order that a statue be made from it, adds with respect to form.) This is obvious. (*DI* II.8:135)

But in order to make his statue, the material used by the sculptor has to possess certain properties, a certain aptitude. Possibility has been contracted in a specific way. The wood used by the sculptor is itself

---

3. Hermes Trismegistus, *Asclepius* 14.2:313.
4. Gandillac suggests Bernhardus Silvestris in *Nikolaus von Kues*, 401n48.
5. *PTW* I, DI II:127n95.
6. St. Augustine, *De genesi contra Manichaeos*, PL 34:I.5.

II. THE TRINITY OF THE UNIVERSE

already shaped matter and as such presupposes matter in a more fundamental and more formless way. This brings us back to prime matter as absolute possibility.

> Thus, [the Peripatetics] said that the totality of things is present, as possibility, in absolute possibility. Absolute possibility is boundless and infinite because of its lack of form and because of its aptitude for all forms—just as the possibility of shaping wax into the figure of a lion or a hare or whatever else, is boundless [*interminata*]. Now, this infinity contrasts with the infinity of God because it is due to a lack, whereas [the infinity] of God is due to an abundance, since in God all things are actually God. Thus, the infinity of matter is privative, [but the infinity] of God is negative. This is the position of those who have spoken about absolute possibility. (*DI* II.8:135)

We have to question the claim that the possibility of shaping wax into various figures is boundless. As pointed out, all material is contracted possibility. As Cusanus recognizes, absolute possibility is difficult to make sense of. As we strip away from matter all determination, all form, we end up with nothing, a privative infinite, which Cusanus is concerned to distinguish from the negative infinite that is God, negative because all our positive determinations fall infinitely short of capturing God's infinite perfection.

Having spent the greater part of this chapter reviewing the positions of "those who have spoken about absolute possibility," Cusanus presents his own view: he rejects the view that there is such a thing as absolute possibility. All possibility we comprehend is contracted possibility, contracted through actuality (*DI* II.8:137).

> Through learned ignorance we find that it would be impossible for absolute possibility to *exist*. For since among things possible nothing can be less than absolute possibility, which is nearest to not-being (even according to the position of [earlier] writers), we would arrive at a minimum and a maximum with respect to things admitting of greater and lesser degrees; and this is impossible. Therefore, in God absolute possibility is God, but it is not possible outside Him. For we cannot posit anything which exists with absolute potency since everything except for the First is, necessarily, contracted. (*DI* II.8:136)

Whatever we consider the matter of which the universe is made to be, it has to be thought of as contracted in such a way that it made it possible for this universe to be as it is.

> Hence, although God is infinite and therefore had the power to create the world as infinite, nevertheless because the possibility was, necessarily, contracted and was not at all absolute or infinite aptitude, the

world—in accordance with the possibility of being—was not able to be actually infinite or greater or to exist in any other way [than it does]. (*DI* II.8:139)

The passage is difficult to understand: God, being infinite, is said to have had the power to create an infinite world; and yet since there can be no absolute possibility other than God, when we consider the genesis of the universe we have to recognize that in this case, too, possibility was necessarily contracted and in such a way that its mode of existence had to be as it is. But in what sense could God have created an infinite world? That there can be only one Absolute Maximum is a central tenet of *De docta ignorantia*. The infinity of whatever world God might have created could only have been a contracted infinite. One would think that if God had the power to create an infinite world, he had the power to create countless other such worlds. But this Cusanus rejects: given the way God contracted possibility when creating the universe, the universe had to be as it is, not actually infinite, but also in such a way that it could not have been greater, for that would mean that the universe were bounded.

What Cusanus has to say here brings to mind the Condemnation of 1277,[7] an expression of the collision of an Aristotelian understanding of nature and Christian theology. The former had to reject a *creatio ex nihilo*. Consider the condemned propositions 188, "That it is not true that something comes from nothing or was made in a first creation," and 189, "That creation is not possible, even though the contrary must be held according to faith." As Cusanus was to do in *De docta ignorantia*, the Condemnation defends the doctrine of divine omnipotence, and must this not mean that natural science cannot claim to understand the way things have to be? But Cusanus could grant the Aristotelian that as far as our reason reaches, we cannot make sense of a *creatio ex nihilo*. Having become learned about our ignorance, we have come to recognize the limits of our reason. The contraction of possibility that is a presupposition of the genesis of the universe remains incomprehensible. Today we might think of the big bang.

Hence, from a knowledge of possibility we see how it is that contracted maximality comes from possibility which, of necessity, is contracted. This contraction [of possibility] does not result from contingency, because it occurs through actuality. And so, the universe has a rational and necessary cause of its contraction, so that

7. "Condemnation of 219 Propositions" (of 1277), in *Philosophy in the Middle Ages*, ed. Arthur Hyman and James J. Walsh (Indianapolis: Hackett, 1973), 542–49.

> the world, which is only contracted being, is not contingently from God, who is Absolute Maximality. This [point] must be considered more in detail. Accordingly, since Absolute Possibility is God: if we consider the world as it is in Absolute Possibility, it is as [it is] in God and is Eternity itself. If we consider [the world] as it is in contracted possibility, then possibility, by nature, precedes only the world; and this contracted possibility is neither eternity nor coeternal with God; rather, it falls short of eternity, as what is contracted [falls short] of what is absolute—the two being infinitely different. (*DI* II.8:139–40)

Two ways of looking at the world are here contrasted. One is the way of our reason. Following that way, we are led to something like prime matter, the most fundamental material underlying the universe. It may not be understood with Aristotle and Aquinas as an altogether passive receptacle for the forms. Cusanus rejects an understanding of prime matter as absolute possibility as incoherent: Prime matter must have an "aptitude" to receive specific forms; it must be such that it allows for the development of all things, culminating in humanity. It is a contracted possibility. Why it is contracted the way it is we cannot fathom. That the world is as it is to us appears contingent or accidental.

But there is another way of viewing the matter, opened up by learned ignorance: if we consider the world as it is in Absolute Possibility—that is, as [it is] in God, there is no room for contingency. In him Absolute Possibility and Absolute Necessity coincide. So understood, the world appears as having to be just as it is, but this necessity surpasses our understanding.

The chapter concludes with a tantalizing question:

> What is said about potency or possibility or matter needs to be qualified, in the foregoing manner, according to the rules of learned ignorance. How it is that possibility proceeds by steps to actuality, I leave to be dealt with in the book *Conjectures*. (*DI* II.8:140)

There, and in other of Cusanus's writings, we do find passages that flesh out what here is only hinted at, passages that suggested to Rudolf Haubst the possibility of claiming Cusanus as a representative of a "Christian evolutionism" that connected the biblical creation account with evolution, inviting comparison with Teilhard de Chardin's account of "the evolution of life from matter and the birth of consciousness from bios."[8] A passage like the following from *De conjecturis* is indeed suggestive:

---

8. Rudolf Haubst, "Der Evolutionsgedanke in der cusanischen Theologie," in *Nicolo' Cusano: Agli Inizi del Mondo Moderno*, 297–98; Haubst, "Nikolaus von Kues und der Evolutionsgedanke," *Scholastik* 39 (1964): 481–94.

Hence, a vegetative spirit conceals in its darkness an intellectual spirit; but certain signs of the intellectual spirit appear in the branches for supporting the fruit and in the leaves and coverings for protecting the fruit. However, we experience more numerous intellectual signs in animals, where the intellectual spirit is more visible. For we experience more clearly and more closely signs of intellectual activity [first] in animals' powers-of-sense, then to a greater degree in their power-of-imagination, and to a still greater degree in their power-of-reason. Moreover, among animals with reasoning powers there are more fully visible signs of foresight in the case of men than in the case of other animals. From these signs we infer that, in the case of men, there is brighter intelligence. (*DC* II.10:123)

I will not rehearse here Haubst's suggestive essay, but its guarded conclusion deserves more discussion:

As a philosophical-metaphysical thinker Nicolaus has so attuned especially his image of the unity of the universe to the possibility of a biological evolution from a primordial creation (*Urschöpfung*) that at first consisted only of elements that one may call this attunement—if not the thesis—but the latent hypothesis of a successive evolution one of his fertile guiding ideas.[9]

9. Haubst, "Der Evolutionsgedanke," 306–7.

CHAPTER 9

The Soul, or Form, of the Universe

The title of this chapter may seem a bit puzzling: soul (*anima*) and form (*forma*) would seem to have different connotations: soul suggests an active, animating principle, form something like a structure imposed on matter. But the conjunction makes sense, given that in these chapters Cusanus is attempting to exhibit the trinitarian structure of the universe: absolute possibility, discussed in chapter 8, provides the universe with the ground of its being, corresponding to the first person of the Trinity, while chapter 9 turns to the Word, which is said to have been in the beginning, providing the universe with both its soul and its form. Chapter 10 will deal with the Holy Spirit.

In the present chapter the discussion moves in a way from soul to form. Once again, the ancients provide the initial point of reference.

All the wise agree that possible being cannot come to be actual except through actual being; for nothing can bring itself into actual being, lest it be the cause of itself; for it would be before it was. Hence, they said that that which actualizes possibility does so intentionally, so that the possibility comes to be actual by rational ordination and not by chance. Some called this excellent [actualizing] nature "mind"; others called it "Intelligence," others "world-soul," others "fate substantified," others (e.g., the Platonists) "connecting necessity." The Platonists thought that possibility is necessarily determined through this necessity, so that possibility now actually is that which it was be-forehand able to be by nature. (*DI* II.9:141–42)

When Cusanus speaks here of "all the wise," he also has in mind Aristotle[1] and his many followers, including Albertus Magnus and Thomas Aquinas.[2] But in this chapter he is more interested in the Platonists, where he was thinking of Proclus, Augustine, and Boethius and his interpreters, especially Thierry of Chartres and his School.[3]

The concept of a world-soul can be traced back to the *Timaeus* (*Tim.* 34b), available to Cusanus in the incomplete translation by Chalcidius.[4] Here is the relevant passage:

> Such was the whole plan of the eternal God about the god that was to be; he made it smooth and even, having a surface in every di-rection equidistant from the center, a body entire and perfect, and formed out of perfect bodies. And in the center he put the soul, which he diffused throughout the body, making it also to be the ex-terior environment of it, and he made the universe a circle moving in a circle, one and solitary, yet by reason of its excellence able to converse with itself, and needing no other friendship or acquain-tance. Having these purposes in view he created the world a blessed god. (trans. Benjamin Jowett)

The world is here understood in the image of a self-sufficient animat-ed body: just as the soul gives life to the body, so the world-soul ani-mates the universe. That Christian Platonists such as Basil of Caesarea, Boethius, Augustine, and Abelard should have understood Plato's world-soul as an anticipation of the Holy Spirit cannot surprise us.[5] Cusanus is aware of this tradition, aware also of the fact that the Coun-cil of Sens (1140) had condemned Abelard's thesis that the Holy Spirit is the soul of the world. This did not dampen his interest in the *Timae-us* and in what it had to say about the world-soul, even if he could not have endorsed Abelard's appropriation of the dialogue.

But in this chapter he is concerned primarily with the form of the universe—that is, with the second person of the Trinity, with the Word. The Holy Spirit is discussed in the following chapter. At the center of the present chapter is Cusanus's appropriation and critique of the Platonic doctrine of forms. Like the Aristotelian author of

---

1. Aristotle, Metaphysics IX.1049b, 24–29.
2. *PTW* I, *DI* II:129n106.
3. *PTW* I, *DI* II:129n107.
4. *PTW* I, *DI* II:128–29n105.
5. Andrea Fiamma, "La réception du Timée par Nicolas de Cues (*De docta ignorantia* II, 9)," *Revue des sciences religieuses* 91, no 1 (2017): 40.

II. THE TRINITY OF THE UNIVERSE

Fundamentum, Cusanus is concerned to eliminate a third ontological realm between the creation and the Creator, such as the world-soul or a realm of forms, in which the forms of worldly things are said to actually exist, just as these forms are said to be enfolded in the mind of God. Such an understanding of the world soul as an unfolding of the divine mind, a *tertium,* mediating between God and the world, had to be rejected for failing to do justice to the unity of God.[6] Johannes Wenck misunderstands Cusanus on this point:

> The first corollary of the same eighth thesis: *The world-soul is the unfolding of the Divine Mind. This is evident because all things—which in God are one Exemplar—are, in the world-soul, many distinct [exemplars].* (*IL* 36)

Wenck objects that this introduces a complexity into the world-soul that the Christian must reject. Cusanus would have agreed. But he had attributed the view Wenck condemns to the Platonists, without fully endorsing it:

> However, [the following view] was acceptable to the Platonists: that such a distinct plurality of exemplars in the connecting necessity is—in a natural order—from one infinite Essence, in which all things are one. Nevertheless, they did not believe that the exemplars were created by this [one infinite Essence] but that they descended from it in such way that the statement "God exists" is never true without the statement "The world-soul exists" also being true. And they affirmed that the world-soul is the unfolding of the Divine Mind, so that all things—which in God are one Exemplar—are, in the world-soul, many distinct [exemplars]. (*DI* II.9:143)

According to Cusanus, as we have seen, nothing exists to mediate between God and creation. And he also rejected the claim that the plurality of exemplars followed with necessity from the one infinite Essence, as Plotinus taught.[7] That denied divine freedom. The disagreement with the Platonists, but also Cusanus's appreciation of their conjectures, is apparent. As he states his own position in concluding the chapter:

> God alone is absolute; all other things are contracted. Nor is there a medium between the Absolute and the contracted as those imagined who thought that the world-soul is mind existing subsequently to God but prior to the world's contraction. For only God is "world-soul" and "world-mind"—in a manner whereby "soul" is regarded as

6. Fiamma, "La réception du Timée par Nicolas de Cues," 43.
7. Plotinus, *Enneads* VI.7.

something absolute in which all the forms of things exist actually. (*DI* II.9:150)

Albertson calls our attention to the fact that this passage is taken almost verbatim from *Fundamentum,* as is much in *DI* II.8–10. But I cannot accept his claim that the position expressed here by the author of *Fundamentum* is not also that of Cusanus—that it is "not Cusan at all."[8] Cusanus's understanding of the relationship of God and the Tetractys leaves no room for Thierry's second mode. God exists and creatures exist. Cusanus recognizes no other existents. "Therefore, forms do not have actual existence except (1) in the Word as Word and (2) contractedly in things" (*DI* II.9:150). Thierry and his followers taught that the forms exist enfolded in the one God and unfolded in the many things that make up this world.[9] In *De docta ignorantia* Cusanus appropriates their understanding of the process of creation as an unfolding of God. But, like the author of *Fundamentum,* he rejects the elevation of the forms into a mode of being actually mediating between God and creatures.

But what are we to say then about universals? What the concept of, say, a dog refers to does seem to transcend particular dogs. Cusanus would grant this; but this, he insists, should not lead us to attribute to it an independent being. Concepts, as pointed out, are our creations and have being only in the human mind. Cusanus agrees with Aristotle: "They *are* the intellect, whose operation is to understand by means of an abstract likeness" (*DI* II.9:150).

How are we to think this process of abstraction? How are we to understand the presence of universals in things? If, agreeing with Aristotle and the nominalists, Cusanus rejects an existing realm of forms, he yet thinks, as this chapter shows, that the Platonists—where Cusanus is thinking first of all of the Chartrian texts available to him[10]— did greater justice to the intelligibility of the world.

> And so, the mode-of-being that is in the world-soul is [the mode] in accordance with which we say that the world is intelligible. The mode of actual being—which results from the actual determination of possibility by way of unfolding—is, as was said, the mode of being according to which the world is perceptible, in the opinion of the Platonists. They did not claim that forms as they exist in matter are

8. Albertson, *Mathematical Theologies,* 368nn115 and 116.

9. See David Albertson, "Gott als Mathematiker? *Mitteilungen und Forschungsbeiträge der Cusanus Gesellschaft* 33 (2012): 110–11; Fiamma, "La réception du Timée par Nicolas de Cues," 45.

10. *PTWI, DI* II:129n117.

II. THE TRINITY OF THE UNIVERSE

> other than forms which exist in the world-soul but [claimed] only
> that forms exist according to different modes of being: in the world-
> soul [they exist] truly and in themselves; in matter [they exist] not
> in their purity but in concealment—as likenesses. [The Platonists]
> added that the truth of forms is attained only through the intellect;
> through reason, imagination, and sense, nothing but images [are at-
> tained], according as the forms are mixed with possibility. And [they
> maintained] that therefore they did not attain to anything truly but
> [only] as a matter of opinion. (*DI* II.9:144)

With much of this Cusanus could agree. Things present themselves
to us exhibiting significant resemblances. That renders them intelligible. With the creation of concepts our reason responds to this. The
Platonists are right to insist that the intelligibility of the world resides
in it, not in us. But they went astray in reifying what makes things intelligible and in positing forms as a mode of being mediating between
God and the things of this world. In an important sense there is only
one form, and that is the divine Word.

To support his critique of the Platonists, Cusanus appeals to his
earlier discussion of the Maximum, which can only be one.

> Therefore, there cannot be many distinct exemplars, for each ex-
> emplar would be maximum and most true with respect to the things
> which are its exemplifications. But it is not possible that there be
> many maximal and most true things. For only one infinite Exemplar
> is sufficient and necessary; in it all things exist, as the ordered exists
> in the order. (*DI* II.9:148)

We should note, however, how close Cusanus, despite this difference,
remains all the same to the Platonists.

> The Platonists thought that all motion derives from this world-soul,
> which they said to be present as a whole in the whole world and as
> a whole in each part of the world. Nevertheless, it does not exer-
> cise the same powers in all parts [of the world]—just as in man the
> rational soul does not operate in the same way in the hair and in
> the heart, although it is present as a whole in the whole [man] and
> in each part. Hence, the Platonists claimed that in the world-soul
> all souls—whether in bodies or outside [of bodies]—are enfolded.
> For they asserted that the world-soul is spread throughout the en-
> tire universe—[spread] not through parts (because it is simple and
> indivisible) but as a whole in the earth, where it holds the earth
> together, as a whole in stone, where it effects the steadfastness of the
> stone's parts, as a whole in water, as a whole in trees, and so on for
> each thing. The world-soul is the first circular unfolding (the Divine
> Mind being the center point, as it were, and the world-soul being the

circle which unfolds the center) and is the natural enfolding of the whole temporal order of things. Therefore, because of the world-soul's distinctness and order, the Platonists called it "self-moving number" and asserted that it is from sameness and difference. They also thought that the world-soul differs from the human soul only in number, so that just as the human soul is to man so the world-soul is to the universe. [Moreover,] they believed that all souls are from the world-soul and that ultimately they are resolved into it, provided their moral failures do not prevent this. (*DI* II.9:145)

The thought that the soul is present in the whole body was widely accepted in the Middles Ages. The transference of this thought to the world-soul Cusanus could find in the Chartrian writings he had access to.[11] Following the *Timaeus* and its interpreters, including Proclus,[12] Cusanus once again draws on geometrical metaphors. The world-soul is likened to a circle that has God for its center. It is the unfolding of God. In it all things are enfolded. We should keep in mind that in the infinite circle, center and circumference coincide. The same must be said of world-soul and God. The infinitization of the circle hints at what separates Cusanus from the Platonists.

Christian thinkers, Cusanus points out, found this an attractive account, making of Plato's forms timeless concepts residing in God's creative mind.

> [These Christians] support their view by the authority of divine Scripture: "God said 'Let there be light,' and light was made." If the truth of light had not been naturally antecedent, what sense would it have made for Him to say, "Let there be light"? And if the truth of light had not been antecedent, then after the light was temporally unfolded, why would it have been called light rather than something else? Such [Christians] adduce many similar considerations to support this view. (*DI* II.9:146)

According to Cusanus, these Christians recognized something that the Aristotelians missed:

> The Peripatetics, although admitting that the work of nature is the work of intelligence, do not admit that there are exemplars. I think that they are surely wrong—unless by "intelligence" they mean God. (*DI* II.9:147)

But Aristotle does not know an intelligent creator God. This lets Cusanus side with the Platonists, if with reservations:

---

11. *PTW* I, *DI* II:129–30n118.
12. *PTW* I, *DI* II:130n119.

II. THE TRINITY OF THE UNIVERSE

> The Platonists spoke quite keenly and sensibly, being reproached, unreasonably, perhaps, by Aristotle, who endeavored to refute them more concerned with the verbal surface than with the intellectual core (*qui potius in cortice verborum quam medullari intelligenti eos redarguere nisus est*).[13] But through learned ignorance I shall ascertain what the truer [view] is. I have [already] indicated that we do not attain to the unqualifiedly Maximum and that, likewise, absolute possibility or absolute form (i.e., [absolute] actuality) which is not God cannot exist. And I indicated that no being except God is uncontracted and that there is only one Form of forms and Truth of truths and that the maximum truth of the circle is not other than that of the quadrangle. Hence, the forms of things are not distinct except as they exist contractedly; as they exist absolutely they are one, indistinct [Form], which is the Word in God. (*DI* II.9:148)

What the Platonists attempted to express with their conception of the world-soul is thus understood by Cusanus as an inadequate conjecture concerning what is understood more adequately, with the help of learned ignorance, as the second person of the Trinity, the divine Word, the form of all forms.

13. Translation changed.

CHAPTER 10

The Spirit of All Things

With this chapter Cusanus turns to the third person of the Trinity, to the Holy Spirit. Once again traditional thinkers furnish the point of departure.

> Certain [thinkers] believed that motion, through which there is the union of form and matter, is a spirit—a medium, as it were, between form and matter. They considered it as pervading the firmament, the planets, and things terrestrial. The first [motion] they called "Atropos"—"without turning," so to speak; for they believed that by a simple motion the firmament is moved from east to west. The second [motion] they called "Clotho," i.e., turning; for the planets are moved counter to the firmament through a turning from west to east. The third [motion they called] "Lachesis," i.e., fate, because chance governs terrestrial things. (*DI* II.10:151)

Once again Chalcidius's commentary on the *Timaeus* would seem to be the ultimate source, mediated however by writers associated with the school of Chartres, such as John of Salisbury.[1] The general picture is Platonic-Aristotelian.

> The motion of the planets is as an unrolling of the first motion; and the motion of temporal and terrestrial things is the unrolling of the motion of the planets. Certain causes of coming events are latent in

---

1. *PTW* I, *DI* II:132n133.

II. THE TRINITY OF THE UNIVERSE

> terrestrial things, as the produce [is latent] in the seed. Hence, [these thinkers] said that the things enfolded in the world-soul as in a ball are unfolded and extended through such motion. For the wise thought as if [along the following line]: a craftsman [who] wants to chisel a statue in stone and [who] has in himself the form of the statue, as an idea, produces—through certain instruments which he moves—the form of the statue in imitation of the idea; analogously, they thought, the world-mind or world-soul harbors in itself exemplars-of-things, which, through motion, it unfolds in matter. (*DI* II.10:151)

Aristotle thought that terrestrial motion presupposed the motion of the planets and this in turn the motion of the firmament. Once again, the metaphor of the craftsman who has in his mind an idea of what he wants to create and then proceeds to realize it provides the fundamental schema. Analogously the world-soul is said to bear the forms (*exemplaria*) of all things within itself in order to realize them in matter. Such realization presupposes the power to mediate and unite form and matter.

> They said that this uniting spirit proceeds from both possibility and the world soul. For matter has—from its aptitude for receiving form—a certain appetite, just as what is base desires what is good and privation desires possession; furthermore, form desires to exist actually but cannot exist absolutely, since it is not its own being and is not God. Therefore, form descends, so that it exists contractedly in possibility; that is, while possibility ascends toward actual existence, form descends, so that it limits, and perfects, and terminates possibility. And so, from the ascent and the descent motion arises and conjoins the two. This motion is the medium-of-union of possibility and actuality, since from movable possibility and a formal mover, moving arises as a medium. (*DI* II.10:152)

This uniting spirit that pervades the universe is called nature, an identification Cusanus could find in John of Salisbury, who in turn invokes the authority of Hermes Trismegistus.[2] To elucidate the way this uniting spirit operates, Cusanus offers an analogue that we find in Chalcidius's *Timaeus* commentary.[3] Consider a sentence such as *Deus est* (*DI* II:153): hearing the sentence, made up by joining letters, syllables, and words into a whole, we immediately understand the meaning the speaker wanted to communicate. The spirit of the speaker communicates itself in the discourse, a spirit that in turn is said to descend from the Holy Spirit.

2. *PTWI*, *DI* II:132n139.
3. *PTWI*, *D* II:133n140.

> Hence, just as in an act of speaking there is a certain spirit [or breath] which proceeds from him who speaks—[a spirit] which is contracted into a sentence, as I mentioned—so God, who is Spirit, is the one from whom all motion descends. For Truth says: "It is not you who speak but the Spirit of your Father who speaks in you" (Mt 10:20). A similar thing holds true for all other motions and operations. (*DI* II.10:153)

Cusanus is still reporting here the views of others, but in the preceding passage he makes no attempt to distance his own views from those of the Platonists, whose views he summarizes. But the preceding discussion should have led us to expect that, as we shall see in some detail in the following chapters, Cusanus's understanding of learned ignorance must call the hierarchically ordered cosmos of Plato, Aristotle, and the medievals into question. It does not allow for the existence of a firmament. And thus he concludes the chapter with a statement of his own position:

> Therefore, it is not the case that any motion is unqualifiedly maximum motion, for this latter coincides with rest. Therefore, no motion is absolute, since absolute motion is rest and is God. And absolute motion enfolds all motions. Therefore, just as all possibility exists in Absolute Possibility, which is the Eternal God, and all form and actuality exist in Absolute Form, which is the Father's divine Word and Son, so all uniting motion and all uniting proportion and harmony exist in the Divine Spirit's Absolute Union, so that God is the one Beginning of all things. In Him and through Him all things exist in a certain oneness of trinity. They are contracted in a like manner in greater and lesser degree (within [the range between] the unqualifiedly Maximum and the unqualifiedly Minimum) according to their own gradations, so that in intelligent things, where to understand is to move, the gradation of possibility, actuality, and their uniting motion is one gradation, and in corporeal things, where to exist is to move, [the gradation] of matter, form, and their union is another gradation. I will touch upon these points elsewhere. Let the preceding [remarks] about the trinity of the universe suffice for the present. (*DI* II.10:155)

The denial of absolute rest and motion will prove of special importance in the concluding chapters of Book Two.

III. THE CONDITION OF THE EARTH

MORE THAN ANYTHING ELSE, it is his rejection of geocentrism that lets Cusanus be remembered today. In his Introduction to *De docta igmoratia*, Jasper Hopkins invites us to understand this rejection as an expression of his age:

> What can be discerned most of all in his speculative cosmology is what can also be discerned principally in his metaphysics: viz., a burning desire for nouveautés. This is the desire that drives him to view every created thing as a finite infinity and to view the universe as "neither finite nor infinite." He lived in an age in which the old ways of looking at things were beginning to be experienced as confining. A world whose celestial motions were supposed to be precisely measurable and whose sole living inhabitants were to be found exclusively at its center no longer seemed sufficiently adventurous. *DI*'s own venturesome picture of the world testifies to the fact that as early as 1440 the dawn of the Renaissance had commenced for German intellectuality. (*OLI* 30)

Hopkins claims that it is its spirit of adventure that distinguishes the Renaissance from the Middle Ages and that in Cusanus this spirit finds particularly striking expression. But this fails to do justice to the way the traditional understanding of God as infinite had to invite thoughts that called into question the very foundation of the medieval worldview. The "dawn of the Renaissance" should not be understood as somehow casting a light into the darkness of the Middle Ages, but as emerging from the very center of medieval thought: from a wrestling with the infinity of God.[1] To suggest that what we discern in the speculative cosmology of Cusanus is a burning desire for *nouveautés* is to fail to do justice to the way it, too, is the product of a wrestling with the idea of infinity, an idea that cannot be separated from our self-awareness as free human beings. Today we are still wrestling with that idea.

1. Karsten Harries, *Infinity and Perspective* (Cambridge, MA: MIT Press, 2001).

Corollaries Regarding Motion

Perhaps supporting Jasper Hopkins's remark that in Cusanus's speculative cosmology we can discern "a burning desire for *nouveautés*," chapter 11 begins in a way that shows that Cusanus is quite aware of and takes pride in the novelty of his ideas.

"Perhaps those who will read the following previously unheard of [doctrines] will be amazed, since learned ignorance shows these [doctrines] to be true" (*DI* II.11:156).[1]

Key here is once more the by-now-familiar thought that in the realm of the finite we will not find something that could not be larger or smaller. In any genus it is impossible to arrive at an unqualifiedly maximum or minimum. Applied to the universe, this means that there is neither a fixed center nor a circumference. Applying the coincidence of opposites, Cusanus claims that "therefore the center of the world coincides with the circumference" (*DI* II.11:156). That center is God.

Cusanus appeals to the preceding chapters to justify his trinitarian understanding of the creation and creatures:

> We already know from the aforesaid (a) that the universe is trine,
> (b) that of all things there is none which is not one from possibility,

---

1. Hoenen took this passage to refer to the preceding chapters 7–10; "'Ista prius inaudita,'" 435. For a convincing rejection of this reading, see Hopkins, "Orienting Study, Part One: Expository Purview," 9–10.

III. THE CONDITION OF THE EARTH

> actuality, and uniting motion, and (c) that none of these [three]
> can at all exist without the other [two], so that of necessity these
> [three] are present in all things according to very different degrees.
> [They are present] so differently that no two things in the universe
> can be altogether equal with respect to them, i.e., with respect to
> any one of them. However, it is not the case that in any genus—even
> [the genus] of motion—we come to an unqualifiedly maximum
> and minimum. Hence, if we consider the various movements of the
> spheres, [we will see that] it is not possible for the world-machine to
> have, as a fixed and immovable center, either our perceptible earth
> or air or fire or any other thing. For, with regard to motion, we do
> not come to an unqualifiedly minimum—i.e., to a fixed center. For
> the [unqualifiedly] minimum must coincide with the [unqualifiedly]
> maximum; therefore, the center of the world coincides with the cir-
> cumference. (*DI* II.11:156)

Cusanus invites the reader to consider the then generally accepted
picture of the cosmos, which has different spheres revolving around
a fixed center, associated with our earth. But if there were such a
center, it would be an absolute minimum. That such a minimum
would have to coincide with the absolute maximum Cusanus claims
to have shown in Book One. There, already, he had discussed the
coincidence of center and circumference as a metaphor for God. Key
here is the incomprehensibility of space. We cannot make sense of a
boundary of space. But that means we cannot make sense of a center
of space. And that means we cannot make sense of absolute motion
or absolute rest. Our understanding of motion, center, and boundary is inescapably relative to some assumed framework. But no such
framework can claim truth. The very idea of an existent absolute center makes no sense to Cusanus:

> Hence, the world does not have a [fixed] circumference. For if it
> had a [fixed] center, it would also have a [fixed] circumference; and
> hence it would have its own beginning and end within itself, and it
> would be bounded in relation to something else, and beyond the
> world there would be both something else and space (*locus*). But all
> these [consequences] are false. Therefore, since it is not possible
> for the world to be enclosed between a physical center and [a phys-
> ical] circumference, the world—of which God is the center and the
> circumference—is not understood. And although the world is not
> infinite, it cannot be conceived as finite, because it lacks boundaries
> within which it is enclosed. (*DC* II.11:156)

The fact that there can be no minimum motion leads Cusanus to a
denial of the claim that the earth is at rest at the center of the cosmos.

Not that there is a better candidate to occupy the center—say, the sun. Given a boundless cosmos, the very concepts of absolute rest and an absolute center of the cosmos cannot be made sense of. Not only Aristotle and Ptolemy, but Copernicus and Kepler, who placed the sun at the cosmic center, are left behind by such speculations. The very idea of such a central position is claimed to be no more than an illusion, based on the mistaken absolutization of some framework.

But is a radical rejection of a geocentric cosmos really the position of Cusanus? In this chapter we sense his struggle to free himself from the then generally taken-for-granted geocentric cosmos. It is not always altogether clear just what he is asserting. Does it really entail a radical break with the Aristotelian-Ptolemaic understanding of the cosmos, or does it just introduce into it something like an uncertainty principle?

> Therefore, the earth, which cannot be the center, cannot be devoid of all motion. Indeed, it is even necessary that the earth be moved in such a way that it could be moved infinitely less. Therefore, just as the earth is not the center of the world, so the sphere of fixed stars is not its circumference—although when we compare the earth with the sky, the former seems [*videatur*] to be nearer to the center, and the latter nearer to the circumference. (*DI* II.11: 157)[2]

That the earth cannot be the center of the universe follows from Cusanus's claim that there can be no absolute minimum motion. Still, someone who wants to argue that Cusanus has not really abandoned geocentrism can point out that Cusanus, while he claims that the earth moves, as Albert of Saxony (1316–98) had indeed done before him in his *Quaestiones in libros de caelo et mundo*,[3] there nevertheless is a strand in his discussion that ascribes to the earth a lesser motion than to all the other planets and stars, which would make his a modified geocentric position. Consider the following:

> From these [foregoing considerations] it is evident that the earth is moved. Now, from the motion of a comet, we learn that the elements of air and of fire are moved; furthermore, [we observe] that the moon [is moved] less from east to west than Mercury or Venus or the sun, and so on progressively. Therefore, the earth is moved even less than all [these] others; but, nevertheless, being a star, it does

not describe a minimum circle around a center or a pole. Nor does
the eighth sphere describe a maximum [circle], as was just proved.
(*DI* II.11:159)

Cusanus here assumes a framework much like that provided by
Ptolemy. Given that framework, it does indeed seem to be the case
that the earth is moved less than all other stars. This may suggest that
the earth is indeed close to the center. Experience would seem to
support geocentrism. The earth does appear to be at the center of
the observed cosmos.

But, as pointed out, this is an appearance only. The boundlessness
of the universe forces us to recognize that all our judgments of motion are relative to some reference point posited by us. Our perception of our earth's central position cannot mean that the earth is at
or near the center of the world. The boundless universe prevents us
from making sense of a cosmic center.

> Therefore, just as the earth is not the center of the world, so the
> sphere of fixed stars is not its circumference—although when we com-
> pare the earth with the sky, the former seems [*videatur*] to be nearer
> to the center, and the latter nearer to the circumference. Therefore,
> the earth is not the center either of the eighth sphere or of any other
> sphere. (*DI* II.11:157)

Cusanus grants that the appearances support geocentrism. The earth
is said to be "moved even less" than all the other stars. But the boundless universe causes every attempt to locate its center to suffer shipwreck. In reality there are no fixed poles, although we have to presuppose such fixed reference points whenever we measure motion.

How radical Cusanus's thinking is is shown by the following:

> And since we can discern motion only in relation to something
> fixed, viz., either poles or centers, and since we presuppose these
> [poles or centers] when we measure motions, we find that as we go
> about conjecturing, we err with regard to all [measurements]. And
> we are surprised when we do not find that the stars are in the right
> position according to the rules of measurement of the ancients, for
> we suppose that the ancients rightly conceived of centers and poles
> and measures. (*DI* II.11:159)

That we recognize motion only in relation to something assumed to
be fixed is a thought familiar already to the ancients—for instance, to
Virgil. Cusanus may have encountered it in the writings of William of
Conches (c. 1090—after 1154),[4] an eminent member of the School

____

4. *PTW* I, *DI* II:135n159.

of Chartres, to whom Cusanus's speculations about the universe are indebted. The radicality of Cusanus's cosmology becomes apparent in the chapter's concluding paragraph:

> Therefore, if with regard to what has now been said you want truly to understand something about the motion of the universe, you must merge the center and the poles, aiding yourself as best you can by your imagination. For example, if someone were on the earth but beneath the north pole [of the heavens] and someone else were at the north pole [of the heavens], then just as to the one on the earth it would appear that the pole is at the zenith, so to the one at the pole it would appear that the center is at the zenith. And just as antipodes have the sky above, as do we, so to those [persons] who are at either pole [of the heavens] the earth would appear to be at the zenith. And at whichever [of these] anyone would be, he would believe himself to be at the center. Therefore, merge these different imaginative pictures so that the center is the zenith and vice versa. Thereupon you will see—through the intellect, to which only learned ignorance is of help—that the world and its motion and shape cannot be apprehended. For [the world] will appear as a wheel in a wheel and a sphere in a sphere—having its center and circumference nowhere, as was stated. (*DI* II.11:161)

Given a boundless universe, which has neither center nor circumference, it makes no sense to ascribe to it motion and shape.[5]

---

5. I disagree with Jasper Hopkins when he suggests that Cusanus here "regards it as having a motion and a shape which are unknowable to finite minds"; *OLI* 198n129. "Motion" and "shape" have no meaning ex*cept for finite* minds.

CHAPTER 12

The Conditions of the Earth

This has come to be perhaps the most often cited chapter of *De docta ignorantia.*[1] Wenck well recognized its novelty: much of what Cusanus has to say about the earth and its place in the universe had indeed never been heard before (*IL* 37). As Giordano Bruno was to remark 150 years later, the "divine Cusanus," as he called him, had shattered the closed world of the medievals. Bruno felt as if released from a prison. A new age, an age of freedom, was about to begin. Small wonder that he called Cusanus alone, among his many precursors, divine.[2] But that was hardly the reception with which the chapter was received by Cusanus's contemporaries. Too much here was at odds with the still prevailing worldview. The first response to the chapter must have been mostly incomprehension.

The chapter begins with a thought experiment that no doubt reflects an experience that Cusanus had when he returned from Greece, as the concluding letter to Cardinal Cesarini suggests, an experience that furnished him with the one great thought that according to Heidegger is at the center of every great philosopher's thought.

1. See Gawlick, "Zur Nachwirkung cusanischer Ideen im siebzehnten und achtzenten Jahrhundert," 225–39, especially 228ff.
2. Giordano Bruno, *The Ash Wednesday Supper,* ed., trans. Edward A. Gosselin and Lawrence S. Lerner (Hamden: Archon, 1977), 139.

What struck him while he was aboard the ship must have been the relativity of our perception of motion and rest. Cusanus was not the first to have noted it. As already mentioned, he could have found this thought in William of Conches's *Philosophia*. But Cusanus pushes this thought much further: can we even make sense of an absolute center of space? Related is the question: is not a boundary of space unthinkable? Will our mind not fly beyond any such supposed boundary and venture into the space beyond? And if we cannot make sense of a center of the universe, if whatever such center we propose turns out to be something we finite knowers have posited, what about other supposedly firmly established centers? Are not all such supposed centers posited by us human knowers, dependent on the make-up of our body and mind and the place we happen to occupy? An understanding of perspective provides the key to the doctrine of learned ignorance.

The experience Cusanus appeals to is familiar. Cusanus's Paduan teacher Prosdocimo de Beldomandi had used it in his commentary on Sacrobosco's *Sphaera* (1418) to make more plausible the view attributed by him to some ancient astronomers that the sphere of the fixed stars was actually at rest while the earth rotated on its axis.[3] Copernicus was to invoke it two centuries later to prepare the reader for the reception of his *De Revolutionibus*:

> And why are we not willing to acknowledge that the appearance of a daily revolution belongs to the heavens, its actuality to the earth? The relation is similar to that of which Virgil's Aeneas says: "We sail out of the harbor, and the countries and cities recede." For when a ship is sailing along quietly, everything which is outside of it will appear to those on board to have a motion corresponding to the motion of the ship, and the voyagers are of the erroneous opinion that they with all that they have with them are at rest. This can without doubt also apply to the motion of the earth, and it may appear as if the whole universe were revolving.[4]

The experience on the ship carrying him back to Italy must have made Cusanus meditate not just on the way our perception of motion is relative to what is assumed to be stable, even though it may in fact be moving, but also to the supposedly unshakable convictions that divided the church, on the way so much that we hold to be true is in

---

3. Markowski, "Die kosmologischen Anschauungen," 268–69.

4. Nicholas Copernicus, *De revolutionibus Orbium Celestium* I.8; English trans. in *The Portable Renaissance Reader*, ed. James Bruce Ross and Mary Martin McLaughlin (New York: Viking, 1953), 591.

III. THE CONDITION OF THE EARTH

fact but a perspectival appearance shaped by what happens to be our point of view.

> The ancients did not attain unto the points already made, for they lacked learned ignorance. It has already become evident to us that the earth is indeed moved, even though we do not perceive this to be the case. For we apprehend motion only through a certain comparison with something fixed. For example, if someone did not know that a body of water was flowing and did not see the shore while he was on a ship in the middle of the water, how would he recognize that the ship was being moved? And because of the fact that it would always seem to each person (whether he were on the earth, the sun, or another star) that he was at the "immovable" center, so to speak, and that all other things were moved: assuredly, it would always be the case that if he were on the sun, he would fix a set of poles in relation to himself; if on the earth, another set; on the moon, another; on Mars, another; and so on. Hence, the world-machine will have its center everywhere and its circumference nowhere, so to speak; for God, who is everywhere and nowhere, is its circumference and center. (*DI* II.12:162)

The example of the moving ship is to alert us to the power of perspective and perspectival illusion. The reader is invited to apply it to the earth: is our earth not like such a ship? The ancients are said to have paid insufficient attention to the way what we experience is ruled by our point of view.

We meet with this application of the insight into the relativity of our perception of motion, furnished by the example of the moving ship, to cosmology already in Nicole Oresme's French translation and commentary on Aristotle's *On the Heavens* (1370s). Oresme already asks, How would the earth look to someone placed somewhere in the sky? "Thus, it is apparent," he concludes, "that one cannot demonstrate by any experience whatever that the heavens move with diurnal motion; whatever the fact may be, assuming that the heavens move and the earth does not or that the earth moves and the heavens do not, to an eye in the heavens which could see the earth clearly, it would appear to move; if the eye were on the earth, the heavens would appear to move."[5] Experience and human reason provide no sure answers.[6]

5. Nicole Oresme, *Le Livre du ciel et du monde*, ed. Albert D. Menut and Alexander J. Denomy, trans. Albert D. Menut (Madison: University of Wisconsin, 1968), 536 (lines 344–49).

6. Dallas G. Denery II, "Protagoras and the Fourteenth-Century Invention of Epistemological Relativism," *Visual Resources* 25, no. 1 (March 2009): 31.

Oresme's intent is not to shake the foundations of the geocentric cosmos. He never doubts that the earth rests immobile at the center of the cosmos: common sense, tradition, and faith make that clear and guarantee the truth of that judgment. He is simply pointing out that unaided natural reason, limited as it is by our senses and our existence as particular individuals, occupying a concrete here and now, cannot always definitively reach those same conclusions.[7]

Does Oresme then not anticipate Cusanus's doctrine of learned ignorance? But there is a decisive difference. Cusanus is willing to assert the boundlessness of the cosmos and to deny the earth its central position. This presupposes a different understanding of the power of reason. Even if our reason is never fully adequate to the truth of things, the thought of the coincidence of intellect and thing nevertheless provides our reason with a measure. The more our finite understanding rises above the limitations of perspective, the more adequate our understanding, especially of the universe.

Reflection on the gap that separates intellect and thing also leads Cusanus to wonder about the sphericity of the earth. That it cannot be a perfect sphere follows from the preceding: created things can only approximate the perfection of geometric figures such as the circle or the triangle. To be sure, Cusanus accepts the traditional privileging circle and sphere,[8] but only as a regulative ideal, never quite realized. He even gives an argument in support of this privilege:

> Moreover, the earth is not spherical, as some have said; yet, it tends toward sphericity, for the shape of the world is contracted in the world's parts, just as is [the world's] motion. Now, when an infinite line is considered as contracted in such way that, as contracted, it cannot be more perfect and more capable, it is [seen to be] circular; for in a circle the beginning coincides with the end. Therefore, the most nearly perfect motion is circular; and the most nearly perfect corporeal shape is therefore spherical. Hence, for the sake of the perfection, the entire motion of the part is oriented toward the whole. For example, heavy things [are moved] toward the earth and light things upwards; earth [is moved] toward earth, water toward water, air toward air, fire toward fire. And the motion of the whole tends toward circular motion as best it can, and all shape [tends toward] spherical shape—as we experience with regard to the parts of animals, to trees, and to the sky. Hence, one motion is more circular and more perfect than another. Similarly, shapes, too, are different. (*DI* II.12:164)

7. Denery, "Protagoras," 33.
8. See Aristotle, *On the Heavens*, Book II.3 and 4.

III. THE CONDITION OF THE EARTH

While the Platonic axiom of the perfection of circular motion and spherical shape remains as a regulative ideal, for Cusanus there can be no perfectly circular motion. On this point he would have questioned Copernicus, for whom the circularity of the orbits of the planets was to remain an axiom of nature. One can only imagine how difficult it must have been for Kepler to break with this axiom, where we should keep in mind that an ellipse is an obliquely seen circle. Both Copernicus and Kepler remained convinced that heavenly bodies moved in perfect geometric figures, be they circles or ellipses, just as they remained convinced of the finitude of the universe, which allowed the astronomer to make sense of absolute motion. Cusanus challenges both. The astronomer's explanations of the movement of the planets, like all scientific theories, can never be more than conjectures.

Important is Cusanus's rejection of cosmic heterogeneity—that is, of the radical distinction between the sublunar world in which there is change, death, and decay and the superlunar world with its untiring circular motions. This rejection robs both Aristotle's then generally accepted cosmology and his physics of their foundation. Aristotle's understanding of sublunar motion is relativized and extended to the universe. The thesis of cosmic homogeneity, now a presupposition of our science,[9] can be understood as a corollary of an understanding of God, who in his infinity is equally close to or equally distant from every created thing. There is no absolute up and down. The world above the moon is essentially no different from our earth. The stars are essentially no different from our earth, made up of the same four elements—earth, water, air, and fire—as our earth. In every star we meet with an up and a down: heavy things fall, light things rise. In the heavens, too, there is change. In place of the Greek and medieval opposition of a sublunar realm that knew change, decay, and death and a changeless superlunar realm, we now have a presumption that things are pretty much the same throughout the cosmos.

This leads Cusanus to place the earth on the same level as the other stars. He is concerned to make sun and earth appear as much alike as possible:

> Therefore, the shape of the earth is noble and spherical, and the motion of the earth is circular; but there could be a more perfect [shape or motion]. And because in the world there is no maximum

---

9. Blumenberg speaks of "the true, abiding triumph of Cusan cosmology...; here the Cusan really goes beyond Copernicus"; *Legitimität*, 472.

or minimum with regard to perfections, motions, and shapes (as is evident from what was just said), it is not true that the earth is the lowliest and the lowest. (*DI* II.12:164)

The position challenged by Cusanus was generally accepted at the time. Thomas Aquinas was just one thinker to follow Aristotle, who argued against the Pythagoreans, who would put fire as the most precious thing at the center of the cosmos, that the center of the cosmos should not be so privileged: "But to the mere position we should give the last place rather than the first. For the middle is what is defined, and what defines it is the limit, and that which contains or limits is more precious than that which is limited, seeing that the latter is the matter and the former the essence of the system."[10] Did Dante not place the devil near the center of the earth and thus of the cosmos, a place devoid of light and warmth and furthest removed from the Empyrean Heavens, the dwelling place of God? Cusanus dismisses all such considerations. "For although [the earth] seems more central with respect to the world, it is also for this same reason nearer to the pole, as was said" (*DI* II.12:164). That the earth seems more central is readily granted, but how are we to understand that "it is also for this same reason nearer to the pole"? Cusanus refers the reader to what had been said in the preceding chapter: given the boundlessness of the universe, whatever we take to be center or pole is only relative to our perspective. Absolutely speaking, they coincide, as minimum and maximum coincide. But such coincidence surpasses our understanding.

> Moreover, the earth is not a proportional part, or an aliquot part, of the world. For since the world does not have either a maximum or a minimum, it also does not have a middle point or aliquot parts [expressible in a mathematical ratio], just as a man or an animal does not either. For example, a hand is not an aliquot part of a man, although its weight does seem to bear a comparative relation to the body—and likewise regarding its size and shape. (*DI* II.12:164)

Since there can be no proportion between the finite and the infinite, it is impossible to express the proportion of the earth's volume to that of the universe as a mathematical ratio. Thought-provoking is the analogy to man or an animal. As Cusanus points out, the weight of, say, a hand can be compared with the weight of the body, even if such comparison may never be such that it could not be made more

10. Aristotle, *On The Heavens* II.13.293b:12–15.

precise. But to weigh the body is not to comprehend the organism. The human being has no center that could be located in space.

The following observations, farfetched as they may seem to us, are of interest in that they show not only the extent of Cusanus's commitment to the axiom of cosmic homogeneity and, that is to say, to his break with the still-prevailing Aristotelian world picture, but also the difficulty he has to jettison that picture altogether. They provide thus a striking example of the difficulty of effecting a paradigm shift. His commitment to cosmic homogeneity leads Cusanus to apply what Aristotle had said about the physics of the sublunar realm to the sun, the moon, and to all the other stars. The Aristotelian world-picture posits an absolute up and down. Every element seeks its proper place. The earth in heavy things causes them to fall. Cusanus relativizes this account: the element of earth that provides the center of every star causes heavy things to fall there, too. Cusanus might be said to take a small step here toward what was to become the modern theory of gravity. But the hold of Aristotle's physics remains strong: the collision of the commitment to cosmic homogeneity and the Aristotelian theory of the four elements and their proper places leads Cusanus to conjectures that, while they may seem bizarre to us, make sense, given his position on the threshold of modernity.

> Moreover, [the earth's] blackness is not evidence of its lowliness. For, if someone were on the sun, the brightness which is visible to us would not be visible [to him]. For when the body of the sun is considered, [it is seen to] have a certain more central "earth," as it were, and a certain "fiery and circumferential" brightness, as it were, and in its middle a "watery cloud and brighter air," so to speak—just as our earth [has] its own elements. Hence, if someone were outside the region of fire, then through the medium of the fire our earth, which is on the circumference of [this] region, would appear to be a bright star—just as to us, who are on the circumference of the region of the sun, the sun appears to be very bright. Now, the moon does not appear to be so bright, perhaps because we are within its circumference and are facing the more central parts—i.e., are in the moon's "watery region," so to speak. Hence, its light is not visible [to us], although the moon does have its own light, which is visible to those who are at the most outward points of its circumference; but only the light of the reflection of the sun is visible to us. On this account, too, the moon's heat—which it no doubt produces as a result of its motion and in greater degree on the circumference, where the motion is greater, is not communicated to us, unlike what happens with regard to the sun. Hence, our earth seems to be situated between the region of the sun and the region of the moon;

and through the medium of the sun and the moon it partakes of
the influence of other stars which—because of the fact that we are
outside their regions—we do not see. For we see only the regions of
those stars which gleam. (*DI* II.12:164–65)

That Cusanus's fantastic constructions fail to do justice to the many
differences that in fact exist between heavenly bodies requires no
comment. But that does not diminish the significance of his conviction, based on his understanding of God's relation to creation, that
one physics must hold throughout the universe. That he should have
looked to Aristotle for an outline of this physics is hardly surprising.

> Therefore, the earth is a noble star which has a light and a heat and
> an influence that are distinct and different from [that of] all other
> stars, just as each star differs from each other star with respect to its
> light, its nature, and its influence. And each star communicates its
> light and influence to the others, though it does not aim to do so,
> since all stars gleam and are moved only in order to exist in the best
> way [they can]; as a consequence thereof a sharing arises (just as
> light shines of its own nature and not in order that I may see; yet, as
> a consequence, a sharing occurs when I use light for the purpose of
> seeing). (*DI* II.12:166)

The earth has become a star among stars, in its way just as valuable
as the sun. Its smaller size is no argument against this. Curious and
altogether unconvincing, but of interest as it illustrates his attempt
to apply Aristotelian sublunar physics to other stars, is Cusanus's suggestion that every star has something like an earth surrounded by a
watery, an airy, and finally a fiery region. When we look at the sun, we
look at its fiery region, not at its earthly core. And here on earth we
do not see this earth's fiery region.

Although concerned only to exist in the best way it can, each star
has an influence on other stars. The most obvious example for us
here on earth is the sun. It shines only to shine, but without its light
and warmth there would be no life here on earth. Cusanus finds here
a sign of God's providence:

> Blessed God created all things in such way that when each thing de-
> sires to conserve its own existence as a divine work, it conserves it in
> communion with others. Accordingly, just as by virtue of the fact that
> the foot exists merely for walking, it serves not only itself but also the
> eye, the hands, the body, and the entire human being (and similarly
> for the eye and the other members), so a similar thing holds true
> regarding the parts of the world. For Plato referred to the world
> as an animal. If you take God to be its soul, without intermingling,

III. THE CONDITION OF THE EARTH

> then many of the points I have been making will be clear to you.
> (*DI* II.12:166)

The reference is once more to the *Timaeus*.[11] Plato's demiurge created the world as a body with a soul possessing reason, a single living intelligent creature, containing within itself all living things. Cusanus, having rejected the idea of an independently existing world soul, invites us to take God to be that soul. He created the world in such a way that each part, while striving to be the best it can be, yet contributes to the whole. As the work of God, each part possesses its own distinctive dignity. That is also true of the earth.

> Moreover, we ought not to say that because the earth is smaller than the sun and is influenced by the sun, it is more lowly [than the sun]. For the entire region-of-the-earth, which extends to the circumference of fire, is large. And although the earth is smaller than the sun—as we know from the earth's shadow and from eclipses—we do not know to what extent the *region* of the sun is larger or smaller than the region of the earth. (*DI* II.12:167)

The axiom of cosmic homogeneity leads Cusanus to insist that intelligent life must exist on countless heavenly bodies, a claim that was later enthusiastically embraced by Giordano Bruno. It proved especially provocative and influential: our astronomers are still led by it to look for intelligent life on other stars.

Cusanus was by no means the first to suggest this: the thought of possible inhabitants of the moon and the planets he could find in Plato's *Timaeus* (42d), as translated by Chalcidius, who in his commentary already provided the explanation, appropriated by Cusanus, that no place in the universe be left deserted.[12]

> For example, [we cannot rightly claim to know] that our portion of the world is the habitation of men and animals and vegetables which are proportionally less noble [than] the inhabitants in the region of the sun and of the other stars. For although God is the center and circumference of all stellar regions and although natures of different nobility proceed from Him and inhabit each region (lest so many places in the heavens and on the stars be empty and lest only the earth—presumably among the lesser things—be inhabited), nevertheless with regard to the intellectual natures a nobler and more perfect nature cannot, it seems, be given (even if there are inhabitants of another kind on other stars) than the intellectual

11. Plato, *Timaeus* 30b, 38e.
12. *PTW* I, *DI* II:136n172.

nature which dwells both here on earth and in its own region. For man does not desire a different nature but only to be perfected in his own nature. (*DI* II.12:169)

There is tension in this passage between the thesis of cosmic homogeneity, which demands intelligent life on countless other stars, and the perfection ascribed to our intellectual nature, which does seem to claim a certain uniqueness for the earth, a uniqueness impossible to reconcile with the thesis of cosmic homogeneity. As a cardinal and good Christian, Cusanus must have been aware of the incompatibility of cosmic homogeneity with the Christian salvation account: does this not demand that the earth as the place of the birth and death of our savior have a unique significance? And the same, it seems, would have to hold for us human beings, since in Christ God became man.

Cusanus avoids here addressing this tension. We shall have occasion to return to it in Book Three. Here Cusanus seems to dismiss the problem by pointing out how little we can know of these distant stars and their inhabitants. Our conjectures lack the experiential support needed to take them very seriously. Of the inhabitants of other stars, we have no experience whatsoever, even if the asserted homogeneity of the cosmos gives us reason to assert their existence. But our lack of knowledge renders them quite irrelevant to our life here on earth. For all practical purposes we are alone.

> Therefore, the inhabitants of other stars—of whatever sort these inhabitants might be—bear no comparative relationship to the inhabitants of the earth (*istius mundi*). (*DI* I.12:169–70)

> Hence, since that entire region is unknown to us, those inhabitants remain altogether unknown. By comparison, here on earth it happens that animals of one species—[animals] which constitute one specific region, so to speak—are united together; and because of the common specific region, they mutually share those things which belong to their region; they neither concern themselves about other [regions] nor apprehend truly anything regarding them. For example, an animal of one species cannot grasp the thought which [an animal] of another [species] expresses through vocal signs—except for a superficial grasping in the case of a very few signs, and even then [only] after long experience and only conjecturally. But we are able to know disproportionally less about the inhabitants of another region. We surmise that in the solar region there are inhabitants which are more solar, brilliant, illustrious, and intellectual—being even more spirit-like than [those] on the moon, where [the inhabitants] are more moonlike, and than [those] on the earth, [where they are] more material and more solidified. (*DI* II.12:171)

III. THE CONDITION OF THE EARTH

The remark about how little animals of one species understand the thoughts of another species is of interest in that it suggests that each animal species lives in a particular region, a world that is pretty much its own. That region limits its awareness of the larger world of which it is a part. But we human beings are also animals, if rational animals. What do we know of the inner life of other animals? Only after long experience do we gain a superficial understanding of what we think a cat or a dog might think. But of extraterrestrials we have no experience whatsoever. Our surmises are therefore idle.

According to the medieval worldview, death and decay are limited to the sublunar world. The axiom of cosmic homogeneity denies this.

> Moreover, the earthly destruction-of-things which we experience is not strong evidence of [the earth's] lowliness. For since there is one universal world and since there are causal relations between all the individual stars, it cannot be evident to us that anything is altogether corruptible; rather, [a thing is corruptible only] according to one or another mode of being, for the causal influences—being contracted, as it were, in one individual—are separated, so that the mode of being such and such perishes. Thus, death does not occupy any space, as Virgil says. For death seems to be nothing except a composite thing's being resolved into its components. And who can know whether such dissolution occurs only in regard to terrestrial inhabitants? (*DI* II.12:172)

The chapter concludes with a brief summary of different views that have been held concerning what happens after death, where the Platonists think of a return to the world-soul, others to a return to the star to which they belong. But these are idle speculations that have little weight.

> Of himself a man cannot know these matters; [he can know them] only if he has [this knowledge] from God in a quite special way. Although no one doubts that the Perfect God created all things for Himself and that He does not will the destruction of any of the things He created, and although everyone knows that God is a very generous rewarder of all who worship Him, nevertheless only God Himself, who is His own Activity, knows the manner of Divine Activity's present and future remuneration. Nevertheless, I will say a few things about this later, according to the divinely inspired truth. At the moment, it suffices that I have, in ignorance, touched upon these matters in the foregoing way. (*DI* II.12:174)

As already mentioned, the obvious tension between the Christian salvation account, which would seem to imply the uniqueness of the earth, and the thesis of cosmic homogeneity, receives no discussion here.

CHAPTER 13

The Admirable Divine Art
in the Creation of the World
and of the Elements

The title of this last chapter of Part Two raises questions. That it should praise the way the visible world declares the glory of God is expected and in keeping with tradition. But the special mention of the elements deserves comment. Did Cusanus feel that his extension of the Aristotelian-medieval theory of elements from the sublunar world to the universe remained problematic and deserved further discussion? But if this extension of a theory restricted to the sublunar world to the universe does indeed raise questions, they remain unaddressed. For one, this extension demands an altogether new theory of motion. In this chapter there is no mention of the revolutionary consequences of Cusanus's destruction of the prevailing cosmology.

Perhaps Cusanus was thinking more of Plato's *Timaeus* than of the works of Aristotle and their medieval reception. The rather sketchy account of the world in the *Timaeus* describes it as a single whole, made up of all four elements.[1] That is in keeping with Cusanus's understanding of the universe. Cusanus would have rejected, of course,

1. Plato, *Timaeus* 32c–33a,

III. THE CONDITION OF THE EARTH

the spherical shape Plato ascribes to the world. But repeatedly the discussion of this chapter brings to mind the *Timaeus* and its medieval interpreters.

Still, the discussion of the elements in this chapter does not challenge the then accepted, fundamentally Aristotelian cosmology—indeed, appropriates its language in a way that must obscure the originality of Cusanus's vision of an infinite cosmos. In concluding Part Two, did Cusanus want to leave the reader with the impression that his views were not all that radical after all?

The beginning of the chapter invokes the consensus of the tradition.

> Since it is the unanimous opinion of the wise that visible things—in particular, the size, beauty, and order of things—lead us to an admiration for the divine art and the divine excellence, and since I have dealt with some of the products of God's admirable knowledge, let me (with regard to the creation of the universe and by way of admiration) very briefly add a few points about the place and the order of the elements. (*DI* II.13:175)

In familiar fashion God is likened to an artist, where that metaphor should not lead us to forget that *infiniti ad finitum nulla est proportio*, that all affirmative statements about God are inadequate. Here Cusanus speaks about God in a way that invites us to forget that inadequacy and thus the very core of his teaching of learned ignorance.

In the creation of the world, God is said to have used arithmetic, geometry, music, and astronomy—that is, the same arts that Cusanus's learned contemporaries were expected to use when investigating things. Key to the organization of the quadrivium is number, which, according to Cusanus, also provides the key to our study of nature. Arithmetic studies number as such, geometry number in space, music number in time, and astronomy number in space and time. The suggestion that in the creation of the world God used the same arts that we use to understand his creation suggests that in our admittedly limited way we can understand the ways of God and gain access to the truth of things. But just this Cusanus had denied in the preceding chapters. Galileo's claim that to write the book of nature God used the language of mathematics does seem to agree with Cusanus's claim here that God created the world relying on the arts of the quadrivium. But Cusanus denied that the language God used to create the world is a language that we are able to understand: the gap between human science and divine creation cannot be bridged.

Thus, even though Cusanus asserts that God arranged everything in an admirable order, we are unable to really understand that order.

To be sure, that there must be some sort of correspondence between divine mathematics and ours is suggested by the way our mathematically based scientific conjectures concerning God's creation do give us real insight into the workings of nature, even if they could always be better. The truth of things provides our conjectures with a measure. Although we cannot comprehend that truth, we can approach it by using mathematics to make sense of what we experience.

In this concluding chapter Cusanus is especially concerned with the theory of the elements, fully aware that what he has to say is only a conjecture indebted to Plato, Aristotle, and their many followers.

> For through arithmetic God united things. Through geometry He shaped them, in order that they would thereby attain firmness, stability, and mobility in accordance with their conditions. Through music He proportioned things in such way that there is not more earth in earth than water in water, air in air, and fire in fire, so that no one element is altogether reducible to another. As a result, it happens that the world-machine cannot perish. Although part of one [element] can be reduced to another, it is not the case that all the air which is mixed with water can ever be transformed into water; for the surrounding air would prevent this; thus, there is ever a mingling of the elements. Hence, God brought it about that parts of the elements would be resolved into one another. And since this occurs with a delay, a thing is generated from the harmony of elements in relation to the generable thing itself; and this thing exists as long as the harmony of elements continues; when the harmony is destroyed and dissolved, what was generated is destroyed and dissolved. (*DS* II:175)[2]

Cusanus here is concerned only with the first three members of the quadrivium: astronomy is not mentioned! Did Cusanus think that astronomy had been treated sufficiently in the preceding chapters? Its absence, at any rate, leaves the proposed account quite incomplete.

What Cusanus has to say here presupposes the medieval understanding of the sublunar world: the spherical earth encircled by the sphere of water, it in turn by the sphere of air, and it by the sphere of fire. But this understanding of the sublunar world cannot be divorced from an understanding of the whole cosmos. Think of the sun and its effect in the seasons; or of the *primum mobile*, according to Ptolemy the tenth outermost concentric sphere, which, revolving around the

---

2. See Albertson, *Mathematical Theologies*, 183.

III. THE CONDITION OF THE EARTH

earth, causes all celestial bodies to revolve with it and is ultimately the cause of all motion. That account of motion is not available to Cusanus. The thesis of cosmic homogeneity, which reads the make-up of the sublunar realm into the whole universe, demands an alto-gether new theory of motion. His discussion of the elements in this chapter barely touches on this demand.

Cusanus points out that each sphere cannot contain only its ele-ment. For how could we then account for differences in things—for instance, in the specific gravity of things? All things should be thought to be composites of the four elements in different proportions. In some there is thus more earth than in others: they are heavier. That wood floats suggests that earth here mingles with both air and water. These composites can disintegrate and come into being, but the elements will remain. Death, as pointed out in the preceding chapter, should thus be understood not as annihilation, but as a dissolution of a particular harmonious configuration of elements.

The persistence of the spheres is said to presuppose that while the four elements are present in ever different proportions in all things, the dominant element is present in its sphere in greater abundance. Elements of water will thus be present in the earth, but not to such an extent that the integrity of the sphere of water would be threatened by the absorption of the water into the earth.

> And so, God, who created all things in number, weight, and measure, arranged the elements in an admirable order. [Wis 11:12] (Number pertains to arithmetic, weight to music, measure to geometry.) (*DI* II:176)

The biblical citation gives some rhetorical support to the problematic absence of the fourth member of the quadrivium, astronomy, from the discussion.

> For example, heaviness is dependent upon lightness, which restricts it (for example, earth, which is heavy, is dependent upon fire in its "center," so to speak); and lightness depends upon heaviness (e.g., fire depends upon earth). And when Eternal Wisdom ordained the elements, He used an inexpressible proportion, so that He fore-knew to what extent each element should precede the other and so that He weighted the elements in such way that proportionally to water's being lighter than earth, air is lighter than water, and fire lighter than air—with the result that weight corresponds to size and, likewise, a container occupies more space than what is contained [by it]. Moreover, He combined the elements with one another in

> such a relationship that, necessarily, the one element is present in the other. With regard to this combination, the earth is an animal, so to speak. according to Plato. It has stones in place of bones, rivers in place of veins, trees in place of hair; and there are animals which are fostered within its hair, just as worms [*vermiculi*, little worms, grubs, vermin] are fostered in the hair of animals. (*DI* II.13:176)

The four spheres, Cusanus suggests, depend on each other. The earth has its place in the center of the most encompassing sphere, fire. As we move outward from the earth, the elements get progressively lighter and the corresponding spheres larger. But in all things, all the elements are present, in ever different proportions.

In the *Timaeus* Plato likened the cosmos to an animal,[3] as Cusanus had done in the preceding chapter, referring the reader to this passage. Here he applies it to the earth. Cusanus may have been thinking of another passage in the *Timaeus* where Plato likens the planets to animals.[4] Since Cusanus thought there was no essential difference between the earth and the planets, the invocation of the authority of Plato seems justified. Thinking of the first *Timaeus* passage, Senger suggests that Cusanus was distorting Plato's text by substituting the earth for the cosmos.[5] Perhaps, but if so, the substitution might well have seemed justified to him, given the similarity he saw between both: God fashioned the universe in such a way that all its different parts, each striving to maintain its own particular being, yet had an influence on the other parts, contributing to the functioning of the whole. Thus he called God the soul of the universe. Something similar can be said of the earth, although in the case of the earth the power that animates and organizes the whole is the element of fire, which is, so to speak, the god of the earth.

> And, so to speak: earth is to fire as the world is to God. For fire, in its relation to earth, has many resemblances to God. [For example,] there is no limit to fire's power; and fire acts upon, penetrates, illumines, distinguishes, and forms all earthly things through the medium of air and of water, so that, as it were, in all the things which are begotten from earth there is nothing except fire's distinct activities. Hence, the forms of things are different as a result of a difference in fire's brightness. But fire is intermingled with things; it does not exist without them; and terrestrial things do not exist [without it]. (*DI* II.13:177)

---

3. Plato, *Timaeus* 30b.
4. Plato, *Timaeus* 30e. See *Laws*, 898.
5. *PTW* I, *DI* II:141n179.

III. THE CONDITION OF THE EARTH

Present in all things, fire is said to be the element that by means of air and water transforms earth in such a way that all the different earthly things emerge. Without the element of fire there would not be the many things we encounter, nor would there be life. The creative power of fire, however, should not lead us to confuse it with God.

> God, however, is only absolute. Hence, God, who is light and in whom there is no darkness [1 Jn 1:5], is spoken of by the ancients as absolute consuming fire [Dt 4:24; Hb 12:29] and as absolute brightness. All existing things endeavor, as best they can, to participate in His "brightness and blazing splendor," so to speak (*quasi*)—as we notice with regard to all the stars, in which participated brightness is found materially contracted. Indeed, this distinguishing and penetrating participated brightness is contracted "immaterially," so to speak (*quasi*), in the life of things which are alive with an intellective life. (*DI* II.13:177)

As the repeated *quasi* suggests, Cusanus is very much aware that his understanding of the element fire as a contraction of the divine fire is only a metaphor, as is his understanding of the intellect as an "immaterial" contraction of the same. In the *Timaeus* already the element of fire is said to be a condition of the visibility of things.[6] Analogously, Cusanus suggests, the intelligibility of things presupposes an intellectual fire, present in things that possess an intellect, a *lumen naturale*.

Nothing in this discussion of the elements could have provoked the medieval reader. The concluding paragraphs of the chapter return to the expected praise of God.

> Who would not admire this Artisan, who with regard to the spheres, the stars, and the regions of the stars used such skill that there is—though without complete precision—both a harmony of all things and a diversity of all things? [This Artisan] considered in advance the sizes, the placing, and the motion of the stars in the one world; and He ordained the distances of the stars in such way that unless each region were as it is, it could neither exist nor exist in such a place and with such an order—nor could the universe exist. (*DI* II.13:178)[7]

We may wonder whether this rhetoric of praise is really supported by the universe as we experience it. No doubt, the many biblical references Cusanus makes in concluding this discussion of the universe offer what at the time may have seemed authoritative support. But how justified is it to understand God in the image of an artist? That

6. Plato, *Timaeus* 31b.
7. Albertson, *Mathematical Theologies*, 183.

the metaphor readily suggests itself when we attempt to think the relationship of the universe to a God assumed to be wise, good, and all-powerful is readily granted. But does Cusanus really think that we understand the universe so well that we can confidently speak of it as harmoniously ordered whole in which every part has to be just as it is? The boundless universe he has projected suggests sublimity rather than beauty. We do not comprehend the harmony the conclusion praises.

The phrase "without complete precision" raises questions. Why did this all-mighty artisan create the world without precision? That we human knowers cannot comprehend the universe with precision is a claim Cusanus has made over and over; that our human conjectures present us with pictures of the world that inevitably lack precision is a key consequence of the doctrine of learned ignorance. But can we say that God created the world without precision? Such a statement would seem to substitute an all-too-human conjecture for the truth of things. Learned ignorance would have us be more modest in our claims.

> With regard to these objects, which are so worthy of admiration, so varied, and so different, we recognize—through learned ignorance and in accordance with the preceding points—that we cannot know the rationale for any of God's works but can only marvel; for the Lord is great, whose greatness is without end. (*DI* II.13:179)

We cannot understand the ways of the creator. When judging a work of art, we presuppose that it is the product of an intentional doing. The artist had an end in mind. In the case of God, we do not know of such an end. We do not comprehend God in a way that justifies the artist metaphor. Cusanus thus insists on the muteness of things.

> But all things reply to him who in learned ignorance asks them what they are or in what manner they exist or for what purpose they exist: "Of ourselves [we are] nothing, and of our own ability we cannot tell you anything other than nothing. For we do not even know ourselves; rather, God alone—through whose understanding we are that which He wills, commands, and knows to be in us—[has knowledge of us]. Indeed, all of us are mute things. He is the one who speaks in [us] all. He has made us; He alone knows what we are, in what manner we exist, and for what purpose. If you wish to know something about us, seek it in our Cause and Reason, not in us. *There* you will find all things, while seeking one thing. And only in Him will you be able to discover yourself. (*DI* II.13:180)

III. THE CONDITION OF THE EARTH

No longer does nature offer itself to us as a book in which we can read. No longer can we say with Alan of Lille:

> Omnis mundi creatura
> Quasi liber et pictura
> Nobis est et speculum
>
> Nostrae vitae, nostrae mortis,
> Nostrae status, nostrae sortis
> Fidele signaculum.

"All the world's creatures are like a book, a picture, or a mirror to us, the truthful sign of our life, death, condition, and destiny." Having become learned about our ignorance, we should not search out the final cause of things. We really understand things only to the extent that we ourselves can make them. A new reality principle announces itself; and corresponding to this reality principle a new insistence on the godlike creativity of the human knower: *homo faber.*

To justify the artist metaphor we have to discover ourselves in God, and that means also God within ourselves, in a way that transcends reason. Part Two thus concludes with a paragraph that once more restates the limits of human reason, but also expresses the confidence that to those who truly seek God, God will disclose himself. Only faith responding to grace can endow talk of God as the supreme artist with meaning. Only faith can render our life meaningful.

> See to it, says our learned ignorance, that you discover yourself in Him. Since in Him all things are Him, it will not be possible that you lack anything. Yet, our approaching Him who is inaccessible is not our prerogative; rather, it is the prerogative of Him who gave us both a face which is turned toward Him and a consuming desire to seek [Him]. When we do [seek Him], He is most gracious and will not abandon us. Instead, having disclosed Himself to us, He will satisfy us eternally "when His glory shall appear." (Ps 16:15 (17:15)
>
> May He be blessed forever. (*DI* II.13:180)

BOOK THREE

Like the prologues to books one and two, the prologue to Book Three is addressed to cardinal Cesarini. The "concept of Jesus," which Cusanus proposes to develop in this book, is easy enough to grasp if impossible to fully understand, for Jesus is said to be both Absolute Maximum and contracted maximum. The concept of Jesus is that of the maximal—that is, unsurpassable finite creature, which as such coincides with the Absolute Maximum. But given Cusanus's understanding of creation, what sense does this concept make? Has he not argued that in the realm of the finite there can be no absolute maximum, that something greater or less can always be imagined? And what room does the principle of cosmic homogeneity, which in chapters 11 and 12 of Book Two Cusanus opposes to the Aristotelian principle of cosmic heterogeneity, leave for the "concept of Jesus"? As the metaphor of the infinite sphere suggests, is God not equally, indeed infinitely close to every creature? Cusanus's new cosmology, so enthusiastically embraced by Giordano Bruno, makes it difficult to make sense not just of the Christian creation account, but of the Christian salvation account, of the unique significance of both the earth and of Christ. How can we reconcile the religious understanding of the fall, of Christmas, Good Friday, Easter, and Pentecost with conjectures about intelligent life on countless other heavenly bodies? The new cosmology and central dogmas of the church seem impossible to reconcile. How did Cusanus reconcile them?

Could Book Three be deleted without a serious loss of philosophical substance? That Hans Blumenberg, in his edition of a selection of the works of Cusanus, including most of *De docta ignorantia*, chose to include only the first four chapters of Book Three, which do not presuppose faith in Christ, is easy to understand.[1] What does Cusanus's speculative Christology have to teach us moderns? That most philosophers interested in Cusanus have tended to have little to say about Book Three is not surpising.

But such neglect of Book Three invites questioning. Consider Jasper Hopkins's very different evaluation of Book Three:

> The innovativeness of Nicholas's theory of redemption strikingly surpasses, in significance, the novelty of his cosmological speculation. For this theory is more centrally linked to the originality and distinctiveness of his entire program of learned ignorance than are the "corollaries of motion" and the "conditions of the earth" found in Book Two, chapters 11 and 12. Indeed, without some such theory, the labors of Books One and Two could not have come to fruition. And the unity-of-thought which was being sought would have remained hauntingly unattained. (*OLI* 30)

By emphasizing the significance of Cusanus's theory of redemption while downplaying his cosmogical speculations as the product of his "burning desire for nouveautés" (*OLI* 29), Hopkins places the theologian above the philosopher. Hopkins's belittling of Cusanus's cosmogical speculations invites challenge: even if in obvious tension with his Christology, the significance of Cusanus's cosmology is not so easily dismissed. It has its foundation in his understanding of the Absolute Maximum.

But this much we must grant: No reading of *De docta ignorantia* that forgets the cardinal can convince. *De docta ignorantia* can indeed be read as a commentary on the *Credo*. The first two books unfold the *Credo*'s beginning: *Credo in unum Deum, Patrem omnipotentem/factorem coeli et terroe, visibilium omnium et invisibilium*, "I believe in one God, the Father Almighty, / maker of heaven and earth, of all things visible and invisible." Book Three follows closely the order of the *Credo*'s remaining lines. Cusanus's concern to use his docrine of learned ignorance to shed new light on traditional dogmas is evident throughout the chapters of Book Three. They leave no doubt concerning his originality and orthodoxy.

But what is their philosophical significance? Did Hans Blumenberg not have good reason to exclude most of Book Three from his abridged version of *De docta ignorantia*? What modern reader can be expected to find much of significance in Cusanus's Christology?

---

1. Hans Blumenberg, *Nikolaus von Cues.*

What, if any, philosophical reason is there for introducing the concept of Jesus? But we fail to do justice to *De docta ignorantia* when we oppose the philosopher to the theologian. Hopkins's remark that Book Three was needed to bring "the labors of Books One and Two … to fruition" must be accepted.

The first two books must leave the reader dissatisfied: The Absolue Maximum has been shown by Cusanus to be separated by an abyss from our world that reason alone cannot bridge: *infiniti ad finitum nulla est proportio.* So understood, God threatens to become irrelevant to life here on earth. To be relevant God must bridge the abyss that separates the infinite and the finite. A first way in which God does so is as the creator "of all things visible and invisible." Not that we can comprehend his action. The questions "why did God create the world?," "why did he create this in so many ways imperfect world?" have no good answers.

But, as the central chapters of Books One and Two demonstrate, Cuasanus's arguments that to think God as creator we must think him as triune are not easily dismissed. Cusanus is confident that his arguments for the Trinity are strong enough to convince non-Christian believers in God, such as Jews and Moslems.[2]

The Incarnation of the Word, to be sure, is an altogether different matter. No reason will convince those who do not believe in Christ. Faith is thus neccessary to accept most of what Cusanus has to say in Book Three as plausible conjectures. Why then did Cusanus think Book Three was necessary to bring *De docta ignorantia* to a proper conclusion? We are given a pointer by Cusanus's understanding of the universe as the contracted maximum, infinite, comprised of countless stars, many of them likely to be home to intelligent life. Are we mortals not lost in infinite space, our existence here on earth a brief firework that soon vanishes? The privative infinity of the universe threatens to render our life here on earth insignificant. Where are we to find the center and measure needed to make life truly meaningful?

Jesus Christ, this second way in which God bridges the abyss that separates the infinite and the finite, provides Cusanus with the answer. In him God and creature are one. Book Three is needed to join Book One, concerned with God, the Absolute Maximum, and Book Two, concerned with the universe, the contracted maximum. Without this synthesis of the infinite and the finite in Jesus Christ, the lack of proportion between the infinite and the finite would leave us mortals incurably dissatisfied: as Sartre was to put it, a vain passion.

2. Cf. Cusanus, *Sermo* I.7.

I. THE NEED FOR CHRIST

I N BOOK THREE Cusanus is struggling with how, given his understanding of the abyss that separates God, understood as the Absolute Maximum, from the boundless universe, understood as the contraction of the Absolute into a plurality of countless things, we human knowers, caught up as we are in our perspectives, can justify our value judgments. Is God, as the ground of Being, not equally close to every creature? What measure allows us to judge one thing higher than another? And given the principle of cosmic homogeneity, what sense can we make of the unique significance of places such as Bethlehem or Jerusalem, of this earth, of the unique significance of Christ? Can the infinite God of Cusanus, the Absolute Maximum, ground our human values? How can Cusanus reconcile the radical consequences of his insight into the infinite with the views of the cardinal of the Catholic Church? Will Book Three provide us with a convincing answer?

A Maximum Which Is Contracted to This or That and Than Which There Cannot Be a Greater Cannot Exist Apart from the Absolute [Maximum]

Cusanus's discussion in support of this claim is curiously indirect. Most of the chapter unpacks the first part of the title: "A maximum which is contracted to this or that and than which there cannot be a greater cannot exist." That, it turns out, has significant implications for his understanding of the organization of nature in terms of genera and species. Discussion of the title's conclusion, that such a maximum entity "cannot exist apart from the Absolute [Maximum]," is pretty much left to the following chapter.

Chapter 1 begins by recalling the discussion of the preceding two books:

> Book One shows that the one absolutely Maximum—which is incommunicable, unfathomable, incontractible to this or that—exists in itself as eternally, equally, and unchangeably the same. Book Two thereafter exhibits the contraction of the universe, for the universe exists only as contractedly this and that. Thus, the Oneness of the Maximum exists absolutely in itself; the oneness of the universe exists contractedly in plurality. (*DI* III.I:182)

I. THE NEED FOR CHRIST

Expected is Cusanus's insistence that in the universe there can be no entity that could not be more or less. But if so, what sense does it make to speak of "a maximum which is contracted to this or that and than which there cannot be a greater"? Christ of course is understood by Cusanus to be just such an entity. The following discussion underscores the difficulty we have making sense of Christ's existence.

> With regard to contracted things, there cannot be an ascent or a descent to an absolutely maximum or an absolutely minimum. Hence, just as the Divine Nature, which is absolutely maximal, cannot be diminished so that it becomes finite and contracted, so neither can the contracted nature become diminished in contraction to the point that it becomes altogether absolute [that is, altogether free of contraction]. (*DI* III.1:183)

But if the Divine Nature "cannot be diminished so that it becomes finite and contracted," and if in no creature contraction can become so minimal that it "becomes altogether absolute," how are we to understand the Incarnation? Reason must consider it a wooden iron, an idea of something that like a square circle cannot exist. Only a thinking that having become learned about its ignorance embraces the coincidence of opposites can accept it,

Cusanus has shown to his satisfaction that among created things there can be no equality. Every created thing is different from every other, "either (1) in genus, species, and number or (2) in species and number or (3) in number—so that every thing exists in its own number, weight, and measure" (*DI* III.1:182). Every thing possesses an identity that is uniquely its own. And every thing is a contraction of the Maximum, but not to the same degree as any other such thing. Some things are less remote from God than others. "Any given thing is comparatively greater or lesser than any other given thing" (*DI* III.1:183). We should note that with this understanding of creation as contraction we have left the metaphor of the infinite sphere behind. So understood, the act of creation establishes a hierarchy: the different degrees of contraction establish a natural rank order among created things. But do we human knowers have access to this rank order? If we cannot comprehend the Maximum, what sense can we make of degrees of contraction? We do of course rank the entities that make up the universe: plants rank above stones, animals above plants, human beings above the other animals. But the measure by which we judge to be higher and lower would seem to be provided by our own being. But what justifies our anthropocentrism? Is not the true measure of perfection God? How are these two measures, the human and the divine, related? Who can claim to have an adequate grasp of degrees of contraction? Is our human being not the only measure available to us? A humanist anthropocentrism answers to the elusiveness of God.

There can be no creature that could not be more or less. "Therefore, it is not the case that any contracted thing attains to the limit either of the universe or of genus or of species; for there can exist a less greatly contracted thing or a more greatly contracted thing [than it]" (*DI* III:184). Like the universe, plant or animal genera or species can have no sharp boundaries. Is there a sharp boundary separating birds and dinosaurs? Or think of the species *homo sapiens* and of other now extinct members of the genus *homo*. Where does one species begin or end? In his claim that there can be no sharp boundary that separates genus from genus, species from species, Cusanus thinks himself supported by the Aristotelian natural philosophy of his day, pointing to "oysters, sea mussels, and other things" (*DI* III.1:186).[1]

Cusanus does not hesitate to extend this point to human beings:

Therefore, no species descends to the point that it is the minimum species of some genus, for before it reaches the minimum it is changed into another species; and a similar thing holds true of the [would-be] maximum species, which is changed into another species before it becomes a maximum species. When in the genus animal the human species endeavors to reach a higher gradation among perceptible things, it is caught up into a mingling with the intellectual nature; nevertheless, the lower part, in accordance with which man is called an animal, prevails. Now, presumably there are other spirits.[2] ([I will discuss] these in *Conjectures*.) And because of a certain nature which is capable of perception they are said, in an extended sense, to be of the genus animal. But since the intellectual nature in them prevails over the other nature, they are called spirits rather than animals, although the Platonists believe that they are intellectual animals. Accordingly, it is evident that species are like a number series which progresses sequentially and which, necessarily, is finite, so that there is order, harmony, and proportion in diversity, as I indicated in Book One. (*DI* III.1:187)

1. See *PTW* I, *DI* III, 103, n. 186.13.
2. *Fortassis*: "Perhaps" may be a better translation. Cusanus appears not very interested in and quite noncommittal about the existence of such spirits. The reader who hopes to find more about Cusanus's position on the existence of demons in *De coniecturis* will be disappointed.

I. THE NEED FOR CHRIST

Cusanus places the human species between the higher animals and more totally spiritual beings. Without naming them, he refers here to the Platonists, without committing himself to their views. He may have been thinking of Apuleius (c. 124–c. 170), who speaks in his *De deo Socratis*, which Cusanus owned and annotated, of demons as belonging to the genus animals, a remark often cited in the Middle Ages, so by Augustine and Aquinas. Chalcidius, too, includes demons among the animals in his commentary of the *Timaeus*. So do many other writers, such as William of Conches.[3] While Cusanus does not seem particularly interested in the question of whether demons exist, he does think that in the genus animal higher, more spiritual species than the human species are possible. Today we may want to think about the evolution of the genus homo. *Homo sapiens* may well evolve someday into some higher species. We are left with the question: How does Cusanus fit Jesus into this account? If he is both a human being and a maximum that cannot be greater, does it make sense to posit possible species higher than the human species?

What does Cusanus mean when he likens a species to a number series? He refers the reader back to Book One, where he had pointed out in chapter 5 that every number, no matter how large, is finite, an unfolding of oneness. Every number series is a finite set of numbers, rising from a minimum to a maximum. The distinction between higher and lower is inseparable from our human understanding of number. Cusanus suggests that we can speak of species and genera in analogous fashion. They are finite sets of members that can be ranked higher and lower.

> It is necessary that, without proceeding to infinity, we reach (1) the lowest species of the lowest genus, than which there is not actually a lesser, and (2) the highest [species] of the highest [genus], than which, likewise, there is not actually a greater and higher—even though a lesser than the former and a greater than the latter could be respectively posited. Thus, whether we number upward or downward we take our beginning from Absolute Oneness (which is God)—i.e., from the Beginning of all things. (*DI* III.1:188)

In the margin of his copy of Bessarion's translation of Aristotle's *Metaphysics* Cusanus wrote at *Metaphysics* I.6.987b.15ff.: *aristoteles interpretatur species numeros*.[4] In that particular passage, Aristotle was sketching the view of Plato, who is said to place numbers between the Forms

3. *PTW* I:104n187, 12.
4. *PTW* I:105n187, 13f.

and sensible things, and the Pythagoreans, who are said to have identified sensible things and numbers. Cusanus thinks of a genus as a
finite set of species, a species as a finite set of particulars, just as he
thinks of a number as a finite set of iterations of one. Just as numbers
can be ranked, so can genera and species. But, agreeing with Aristotle, Cusanus denies that genera, species, or numbers actually exist.
They have their origin in our mind as it strives to make sense of the
sensible world. In Aristotle's *Metaphysics* Cusanus could thus find his
understanding of the similarity of species and numbers confirmed.

As numbers can be ranked, we discover degrees of perfection in
the creation. There are higher and lower species and genera and,
within these, higher and lower individuals. This rank order of existing things is not infinite. It has a bottom and a top. But God is the
measure of perfection, and God has been shown to be beyond our
comprehension. That must render our rankings and our judgments
of perfection precarious.

> Hence, species are as numbers that come together from two oppo-
> site directions—[numbers] that proceed from a minimum which is
> a maximum and from a maximum to which a minimum is not op-
> posed. Hence, there is nothing in the universe which does not enjoy
> a certain singularity that cannot be found in any other thing, so that
> no thing excels all others in all respects or [excels] different things
> in equal measure. By comparison, there can never in any respect be
> something equal to another, even if at one time one thing is less than
> another and at another [time] is greater than this other, it makes
> this transition with a certain singularity, so that it never attains pre-
> cise equality [with the other]. (*DI* III:188)

This less than perspicuous formulation invites question. I discussed
his attempt to support the counterintuitive claim that something can
at first be smaller and then become greater than some other thing
without ever being precisely equal to it by appealing to the impossibility of squaring a circle and of determining the angle of incidence at
some length in chapter 11 of Book One. What matters here is Cusanus's insistence that in no respect can one entity be precisely equal
to another. As the contracted Maximum, every individual is unique.
We need to appreciate its godlike uniqueness as such, without comparing it to another, judging it superior or inferior. Any attempt to
establish a hierarchy among genera, species, and individuals is here
called into question. Cusanus recognizes that we constantly compare
entities, especially our fellow human beings, applying to them our
human perspective-bound measures.

I. THE NEED FOR CHRIST

> Individuating principles cannot come together in one individual in
> such harmonious comparative relation as in another [individual];
> thus, through itself each thing is one and is perfect in the way it can
> be. And in each species—e.g., the human species—we find that at
> a given time some individuals are more perfect and more excellent
> than others in certain respects. (For example, Solomon excelled oth-
> ers in wisdom, Absalom in beauty, Sampson in strength; and those
> who excelled others more with regard to the intellective part de-
> served to be honored above the others.) Nevertheless, a difference
> of opinions—in accordance with the difference of religions, sects,
> and regions—gives rise to different judgments of comparison (so
> that what is praiseworthy according to one [religion, sect, or region]
> is reprehensible according to another); and scattered throughout
> the world are people unknown to us. Hence, we do not know who
> is more excellent than the others in the world; for of all [individu-
> als] we cannot know even one perfectly. God produced this state of
> affairs in order that each individual, although admiring the others,
> would be content with himself, with his native land (so that his birth-
> place alone would seem most pleasant to him), with the customs of
> his domain, with his language, and so on, so that to the extent pos-
> sible there would be unity and peace, without envy. For there can be
> [peace] in every respect only for those who reign with God, who is
> our peace which surpasses all understanding. (*DI* III.1:189)

There is tension between "through itself each thing is one and is perfect in the way it can be" and "some individuals are more perfect and
more excellent than others in certain respects," where Cusanus adds
that "those who excelled others more with regard to the intellective
part deserved to be honored above the others." But are we in possession of a standard that allows us to make such judgments? And so he
follows this claim and concludes the chapter in a way that reminds of
the way our value judgments are bound by cultural perspectives. As
Nietzsche's Zarathustra was to put it, "Much that was good to one people was scorn and infamy to another: thus I found it. Much I found
called evil here, and decked out with purple honors there. Never did
one neighbor understand the other: ever was his soul amazed at the
neighbor's delusion and wickedness."[5]

To become learned about one's ignorance is to recognize that not
only our belief in geocentrism but our religious and value judgments
are bound by different perspectives. We human beings cannot claim
to be in possession of the absolute truth. No country, no religion

---

5. Friedrich Nietzsche, *Zarathustra*, in *The Portable Nietzsche*, ed. and trans. Walter
Kaufmann (Harmondsworth: Penguin, 1976), 170.

can claim to be the guardian of absolute values. But human beings need to be rooted in a particular region and culture to feel at home in the world. It is natural and good to love one's country, language, and customs, but such love should be attended by the recognition that there are other perspectives that deserve to be respected. Love of our home should lead us to be content with who we are and our situation without comparing ourselves enviously with those we think are better off and without feeling a need to impose our customs and convictions on others.

In 1436, a few years before writing *On Learned Ignorance*, Cusanus had drawn on his insight into the perspectival character of religious convictions in his attempt to settle the Hussite controversy. Later in the dialogue *De Pace Fidei, On the Peace of Faith*, written after the fall of Constantinople in May 29, 1453, to the Ottomans and the bloodbath that followed, he attempted to show that all that separated Christians, Muslims, and Jews were superficial differences, that they all believed in their different ways in the same finally unfathomable deity, that only idolatry, the mistaking of finite things for the Maximum, had led to unending religious strife. Cusanus left no doubt, however, that Christianity is the one true religion,[6] quite aware that reason alone could not support such conviction. A reasonable critic might well ask whether the identification of a human being with the Maximum is not an example of what Cusanus calls idolatry.

6. See Thomas McTighe, "Nicbolas of Cusa's Unity Metaphysics," 161–72.

The Maximum Contracted [to a Species] Is Also the Absolute [Maximum; It Is Both] Creator and Creature

Only with this chapter do we get to the central concern of Book Three, to the Christology of Cusanus. What sense can we make of a being supposed to be both creature and Creator, both man and God, where the "and" must be understood not additively, but in terms of the coincidence of opposites? As far as our reason reaches, there can be no such being. But, as Cusanus has shown, our intellect is able to transcend the reach of reason and to entertain what reason declares impossible.

Cusanus begins this chapter by reiterating that we are not able to conceive an actual maximum for any given species, genus, or even a maximum genus, where we must keep in mind that for Cusanus, genera and species, like all universals, have no actual existence, and yet the creation of their concepts by our intellect does respond to an order that we perceive in things. But except for God, only particular entities have actual being.

Cusanus now asks: what if there were, despite all that has been said, an actually contracted individual of some species that would also be its maximum? That individual would provide all the other members of the species with a measure. That can be granted. But the question that we may well feel tempted to raise is, why engage in such thought experiments with what our reason judges to be impossible? Think of some species, say of the species *rosa*—that is, rose. It is easy to see why we posit such a species: It is part of our making sense of the world. To comprehend it we need to ascertain a certain order in nature. We recognize family resemblances among certain particulars and form words or concepts in response to, say, different roses and roselike plants. Think now of particular roses: some strike us as more perfect than others. How are our judgments related to our concept "rose"? We do seem to be in possession of a somewhat ill-defined image of what a rose should look like; Kant would speak of the normal idea of a rose that allows us to make such judgments. But is there a rose so perfect that no more perfect rose could be imagined? Such an ideal would provide us with something like a concrete measure, which we could then apply to other roses to judge them more or less perfect. But is there such an ideal? Cusanus denies this. He would dismiss our supposedly ideal rose as a kind of golden calf that may well become an obstacle to being open to the always unique beauty of individual roses.

> It is thoroughly clear that the universe is only contractedly many things; these are actually such that no one of them attains to the unqualifiedly Maximum. (*DI* III.2:190).

But such a denial seems to leave no room for Jesus Christ, who is both man and God.

> I will add something more: if a maximum which is contracted to a species could be posited as actually existing, then, in accordance with the given species of contraction, this maximum would be actually all the things which are able to be in the possibility of that genus or species. And just as the [Absolute] Minimum coincides with the Absolute Maximum, so also the contractedly minimum coincides with the contracted maximum. A very clear illustration of this [truth] occurs with regard to a maximum line, which admits of no opposition, and which is both every figure and the equal measure of all figures, and with which a point coincides—as I showed in Book One. Hence, if any positable thing were the contracted maximum individual of some species, such an individual thing would have to be the fullness of that genus and species, so that in fullness of perfection it would be the means, form, essence, and truth [*via, forma, ratio, atque veritas*) of

I. THE NEED FOR CHRIST

> all the things which are possible in the species. This contracted max-
> imum individual would exist above the whole nature of that [given]
> contraction—[exist] as its final goal. (*DI* III.2:190–91)

The maximum line is, of course, not something that actually exists,
and one might admit that a contracted maximum, thought in analogy
to such a line, similarly can be thought in some fashion, but insist that
it is impossible for it to actually exist. That such a maximum, were it
to exist, would have to be both God and creature can be granted, giv-
en the preceding discussion. And although Cusanus is not yet men-
tioning Christ, that his counter-rational construct is pointing to him
is suggested by the claim that such a being would be *via, forma, ratio,
atque veritas*. The reference is to John 14:6, where Jesus says of himself
that he is "the way and the truth and the life," *Via et veritas et vita.*

> And herefrom it is evident—in conformity with the points I exhibited
> a bit earlier—that the contracted maximum [individual] cannot exist
> as purely contracted. For no such [purely contracted thing] could
> attain the fullness of perfection in the genus of its contraction. Nor
> would such a thing qua contracted be God, who is most absolute.
> But, necessarily, the contracted maximum [individual]—i.e., God
> and creature—would be both absolute and contracted, by virtue of a
> contraction which would be able to exist in itself. (*DI* III.2:192)

That such a union must surpass our understanding requires no comment:

> Who, then, could conceive of so admirable a union, which is not as
> [the union] of form to matter, since the Absolute God cannot be
> commingled with matter and does not inform [it]. Assuredly, this
> [union] would be greater than all intelligible unions; for what is
> contracted would (since it is maximum) exist there only in Absolute
> Maximality—neither adding anything to Maximality (since Maxi-
> mality is absolute) nor passing over into its nature (since it itself is
> contracted).... For such a [being] would have to be conceived by
> us as (1) in such way God that it is also a creature, (2) in such way a
> creature that it is also Creator, and (3) Creator and creature without
> confusion and without composition. Who, then, could be lifted to
> such a height that in oneness he would conceive diversity and in
> diversity oneness? Therefore, this union would transcend all under-
> standing. (*DI* III.2:194)

Having gone this far with his speculations, Cusanus will proceed to ask
in the following chapter: of what nature would such a twofold maximum be? His answer is to be expected: it would have to be a human
being.

Only in the Case of the Nature of Humanity Can There Be Such a Maximum [Individual]

In this chapter Cusanus attempts to show that if there were some truly perfect entity—that is, a being that was both creature and Maximum—it would have to be a human being. The chapter does not claim that such a being exists. It invites us only to consider what such a being would have to be like if it existed. Such a being would provide humanity with an ideal measure.

Cusanus's argument for this thesis invites comparison with Kant's argument that only human being permits us to speak of an ideal of beauty. What is it that allows Cusanus and Kant to privilege the human species in that way? With Kant it is the fact that human beings alone, possessing reason, can provide themselves with an ideal image that should guide their actions and that becomes visible in the ideal of beauty.

> An ideal of beautiful flowers, of beautiful furnishings, or of a beautiful view is unthinkable. But an ideal of beauty that is accessory to determinate purposes is also inconceivable, e.g., an ideal of a beautiful mansion, a beautiful tree, a beautiful garden, etc., presumably

> because the purposes are not sufficiently determined and fixed by
> their concept, so that the purposiveness is nearly as free as in the
> case of vague beauty. [This leaves] only that which has the purpose
> of its existence with itself—man. Man can himself determine his pur-
> poses by reason; or, where he must take them from outer perception,
> he can still compare them with essential and universal purposes and
> then judge the former purposes' harmony with the latter ones aes-
> thetically as well. It is man, alone among all objects in the world, who
> admits of an ideal of beauty, just as the humanity in his person [that
> is, in man considered as an intelligence], is the only [thing] in the
> world that admits of the ideal of perfection.[1]

Kant presupposes that moral self-determination can become visible in
a particular person in a way that allows it to be represented by an artist. But moral self-determination presupposes freedom, and freedom
is not to be found in nature. The gulf that separates the infinite and
the finite appears to be bridged here.

Important is Kant's distinction between the standard or normal
idea and the rational idea of a human being. Human beauty, or the
beauty of a horse, or that of a building presupposes some understanding of the kind of thing we are judging. But the ideal of beauty requires more:

> But this [ideal of beauty] has two components. The first is the aes-
> thetic standard idea, which is an individual intuition (of the imag-
> ination) [by] which [we] present the standard for judging man as
> a thing belonging to a particular animal species. The second is the
> rational idea, which makes the purposes of humanity, insofar as they
> cannot be presented in sensibility, the principle for judging his fig-
> ure, which reveals these purposes, as their effect in appearance.[2]

Difficult to understand is the claim that, while the purposes of humanity "cannot be presented in sensibility," we can yet recognize "their
effect in appearance." How are we to think such recognition? Kant can
point to our recognition of persons as free, responsible agents:

> Now it is true that this visible expression of moral ideas that govern
> man inwardly can be taken only from experience. Yet these moral
> ideas must be connected, in the highest purposiveness, with every-
> thing that our reason links with the morally good: goodness of soul,
> or purity, or fortitude, or serenity, etc.; and in order for this connec-
> tion to be made visible, as it were, in bodily expression (as an effect
> of what is inward), pure ideas of reason must be united with a very

1. Kant, *Critique of Judgment*, 80–81.
2. Kant, *Critique of Judgment*, par. 17, 81.

strong imagination in someone who seeks so much as to judge, let alone exhibit, it.[3]

That we experience certain phenomena as the visible expression of moral ideas Kant takes to be evident. But this is to say that there must be experiences that bridge the divide between phenomena and things in themselves. Art that succeeds in exhibiting the ideal establishes such a bridge.

Cusanus's understanding of Christ has a similar bridging function, where we should keep in mind that medieval thinkers thought of beauty in just these terms and of Christ as the ideal of beauty. Here is a passage by St. Augustine who here is commenting on Psalm 45:

> He then is beautiful in heaven, beautiful on earth; beautiful in the womb, beautiful in his parents' arms; beautiful in his miracles; beautiful under the scourge; beautiful when inviting to life … beautiful in laying down his life; beautiful in taking it up again; beautiful on the cross; beautiful in the sepulchre; beautiful in heaven.[4]

Cusanus is indebted to this tradition.

To establish that a human being alone is the proper vehicle for the coincidence of Creator and creature, Cusanus appeals to the distinction between higher and lower creatures. We may want to ask once more whether this distinction is not called into question by Cusanus's cosmology with its claim of cosmic homogeneity. Is God not equally close to every creature? Is this not suggested by the metaphor of the infinite sphere? But the argument of Book Three depends on a reassertion of that hierarchical conception of the cosmos that figured so importantly already in chapter 1. In a way that anticipates Pico della Mirandola's *Oration on the Dignity of Man* (1486), Cusanus asserts that the special dignity of the human being, which makes it the only proper vehicle for the coincidence of Creator and creature, is tied to the way human beings, possessing both body and spirit, occupy the middle position in the hierarchy of creatures.

> It is first of all evident that the order of things necessarily requires that some things be of a lower nature in comparison with others (as natures devoid of life and intelligence are), that some things be of a higher nature (viz., intelligences), and that some things be of an in-between [nature]. Therefore, if Absolute Maximality is in the most universal way the Being of all things, so that it is not more of

---

3. Kant, *Critique of Judgment*, par. 17, 83–84.

4. St. Augustine, *Enarrationes in Psalmos* 44.3, cited in Gerald O'Collins, "The Beauty of Christ," 2005, www.theway.org.uk/back/444OCollins.pdf.

one thing than of another: clearly, that being which is more common to the totality of beings is more unitable with the [Absolute] Maximum. (*DI* III.3:195)

Cusanus could justify his claim that it is evident that some things are of a lower and other of a higher nature not only by invoking experience, but by pointing to the way we count. As we have seen, following Aristotle and Aquinas, Cusanus takes counting to be the principle of all knowing. We human beings cannot help but rank things.

But why privilege the human being? Why not an angel? To support that privilege Cusanus first offers an argument as to why a line cannot serve this function. He had discussed the properties of the maximum line at length in chapters 13 to 17 of Book One.

> Now, if the nature of lower things is considered and if one of these lower beings were elevated unto [Absolute] Maximality, such a being would be both God and itself. An example is furnished with regard to a maximum line. Since the maximum line would be infinite through Absolute Infinity and maximal through [Absolute] Maximality (to which, necessarily, it is united if it is maximal): through [Absolute] Maximality it would be God and through contraction it would remain a line. And so, it would be, actually, everything which a line can become. But a line does not include [the possibility of] life or intellect. Therefore, if the line would not attain to the fullness of [all] natures, how could it be elevated to the maximum gradation? For it would be a maximum which could be greater and which would lack [some] perfections. (*DI* III.3:196)

A similar argument could show why a plant or an animal would not be a suitable candidate. But what about a creature more spiritual than we human beings—say, an angel? Cusanus replies that lacking a body, such a spirit, too, could not "attain to the fullness of [all] natures."

> Therefore, a middle nature, which is the means of the union of the lower [nature] and the higher [nature], is alone that [nature] which can be suitably elevated unto the Maximum by the power of the maximal, infinite God. For since this middle nature—as being what is highest of the lower [nature] and what is lowest of the higher [nature]—enfolds within itself all natures: if it ascends wholly to a union with Maximality, then—as is evident—all natures and the entire universe have, in this nature, wholly reached the supreme gradation. (*DI* III.3:197)

The only plausible candidate for the elevation of a creature to the Maximum is thus a human being. We can speak of Cusanus's anthropocentrism, where we should note that geocentrism and anthropocentrism do not here go together. Nor do they in Copernicus or in the new science. Only a human being can provide all beings, be they lower or higher, with their measure. For the cardinal the ideal human being is, of course, Christ. Cusanus has thus prepared the conceptual place for Christ in his system:

> Now, human nature is that [nature] which, though created a little lower than the angels, is elevated above all the [other] works of God; it enfolds intellectual and sensible nature and encloses all things within itself, so that the ancients were right in calling it a microcosm, or a small world. (*DI* III.3:198)

Cusanus is still speaking in the subjunctive: if there were such a being, it would be man and also God, would be God and also man (*DI* III.3:199); it would be the perfection, not just of man, but of every thing.

Being the perfection of man, such a being would also be the ideal knower—that is, the truth. In such a being all our efforts to know would find their measure. The question "how are we to understand the intelligibility of nature?" would receive an answer.

> But [it is] qua Equality-of-being-all-things [that] God is Creator of the universe, since the universe was created in accordance with Him. Therefore, supreme and maximum Equality-of-being-all-things-absolutely would be that to which the nature of humanity would be united, so that through the assumed humanity God Himself would, in the humanity, be all things contractedly, just as He is the Equality of being all things absolutely. Therefore, since that man would, through the union, exist in maximum Equality of Being, He would be the Son of God—just as [He would also be] the Word [of God], in whom all things were created. That is, [He would be] Equality-of-Being, which is called Son of God, according to what was previously indicated. Nevertheless, He would not cease being the son of man, just as He would not cease being a man—as will be explained later. (*DI* III.3:200)

Cusanus is still speaking in the subjunctive, although what he has to say follows closely the beginning of the Gospel of John: "(1) In the beginning was the Word, and the Word was with God, and the Word was God. (2) He was in the beginning with God. (3) All things were made through him, and without him was not any thing made that was made.... (14) And the Word became flesh and dwelt among us, and we have seen his glory, glory as of the only Son from the Father, full of grace and truth." The structure of *De docta ignorantia* echoes these lines: Book One discussed the being of God who is one with the

Word, the Second Book the universe created through the Word; Book Three is devoted to Christ, the word become flesh, in whom the abyss that separates God and the creation is closed. The previous passage covers the same points, *still in the subjunctive, as a kind of thought experiment.* As Equality-of-Being—that is, as the Word—God created and ordered the world. But if the Word were to become man, the logos that created and ordered nature would also reside in humanity. Both would be inseparably joined in him who is both son of God and son of man. His truth would provide all human beings with a measure.

> But if a human nature (*homo*) is elevated unto a oneness with this Power—so that the human nature is a creature existing not in itself but in oneness with Infinite Power—then, this Power is limited not with respect to the creature but with respect to itself. Now, this [work, viz., such an elevated nature] is the most perfect work of the maximum, infinite, and unlimitable power of God; in it there can be no deficiency; otherwise it would not be either Creator or creature. How would it be a creature [existing] contractedly from the Divine Absolute Being if contraction could not be united with it? Through it all things, qua existing, would be from Him who exists absolutely; and, qua contracted, they would be from Him to whom contraction is supremely united. Thus, God exists first of all as Creator. Secondly, [He exists as] God-and-man (a created humanity having been supremely assumed into oneness with God); the universal-contraction-of-all-things [that is, the humanity] is, so to speak, "personally" and "hypostatically" united with the Equality-of-being-all-things). Thus, in the third place, all things—through most absolute God and by the mediation of the universal contraction, viz. the humanity—go forth into contracted being so that they may be that-which-they-are in the best order and manner possible. (*DI* III.3:202)

Once again we meet with the triad God, the universe, Christ, that provided Cusanus with the structure of *De docta ignorantia.* But the order has now been changed: the universe now follows God and Christ. The things that make up the universe are now said to depend on the mediation of humanity—that is, Christ, the Word.

> But this order should not be considered temporally—as if God temporally preceded the Firstborn of creation. And [we ought not to believe] that the Firstborn—viz., God and man—preceded the world temporally but [should believe that He preceded it] in nature and in the order of perfection and above all time. Hence, by existing with God above time and prior to all things, He could appear to the world in the fullness of time (in *plentitudine temporis*), after many cycles had passed. (*DI* III.3:202)

We should not think that first there was God, then the Son, and then the universe. Cusanus is speaking of an essential priority, a priority "in the order of perfection." As an understanding of the Trinity demands, the Son existed "with God above time and prior to all things." That the Word became flesh must be understood as the coincidence of time and eternity.

Cusanus speaks of "the fullness of time"? How are we to understand this "fullness of time"? The reference is to Paul's Letters to the Galatians (4:4):

> But when the time had fully come, God sent forth his Son.

and to the Ephesians (1:9–10):

> For he has made known to us in all wisdom and insight the mystery of his will, according to which he set forth in Christ as a plan for the fullness of time, to unite all things in him, things in heaven and things on earth.

The following chapters will have much more to say about the fullness of time. Clear is that, with this notion, time is no longer to be understood as an endless sequence of nows. Time now acquires something like a center, as also does space.

Throughout chapter 3, Cusanus is speaking in the subjunctive: Christ is presented as an idea that surpasses the reach of our reason, comparable to that of the numerical maximum. To reason Christ is an impossibility, but an impossibility that like Kant's ideal of beauty provides our life with a measure.

CHAPTER 4

Blessed Jesus, Who Is God and Man, Is the [Contracted Maximum Individual]

In the beginning of this rather brief chapter, Cusanus reminds us that faith has guided his considerations. But even if that has obviously been the case, to understand and even to accept much of his thinking up to this point, one does not have to be a believing Christian. Giordano Bruno is a good example. And, as I tried to suggest by drawing a parallel between Kant's conception of the ideal of beauty and Cusanus's conception of the maximum created being, even the beginning of Book Three should interest a philosopher. The need for an ideal image of man that can provide us human beings with a measure can be defended without claiming that any human being measures up to that ideal, and more specifically, without identifying this ideal with the historical Jesus. But with chapter 4 of Book Three faith takes over. Only faith allows Cusanus to shift from the subjunctive he used in the preceding chapter to the indicative. Chapter 4 leaves no doubt that Cusanus did not question the veracity of the New Testament's account of the historical Jesus.

Cusanus makes quite clear that, while the speculations of chapter 3 were still the product of a thinking that, while elevated by the doctrine of learned ignorance, did not require faith, what follows presupposes it. That the cardinal would have thought his idea of the contracted maximum individual to have become reality in Jesus cannot surprise us.

> In sure faith and by such considerations as the foregoing, we have now been led to the place that without any hesitancy at all we firmly hold the aforesaid to be most true. Accordingly, I say by way of addition that the fullness of time (*temporis plentitudo*) has passed and that ever-blessed Jesus is the Firstborn of all creation. (*DI* III.4:203)

The last sentence cites Colossians 1:15, which calls Christ "the image of the invisible God, the firstborn of all creation." Cusanus is convinced that his speculations will help us to better understand such biblical statements.

That there is tension between Cusanus's vision of a boundless cosmos and his faith in Jesus requires no further comment. There is indeed an abyss that separates a worldview based on secular reason, be it pagan or modern, from a worldview based on revealed religion. To quote the Jewish scholar Franz Rosenzweig:

> The difference between pagan thought and any revealed religion [is] that for pagan thinking there are many worlds and possibilities, reasons and accidents, for [revealed religion] everything is given only in one exemplar. For revelation founds an up and a down, a Europe and an Asia, as it founds an earlier and a later, a past and a future. The infinite descends to earth and from the place of its descent it draws boundaries in the ocean of space and in the river of time.[1]

The fullness of time is precisely that moment when the infinite is thought to descend to earth, when the vertical of the eternal intersects linear time in a particular place, at a particular time, providing not just the earth and its history, but the universe with a center. The mystery of the Incarnation is the mystery of that intersection. Faith restores the earth to its central position.

> On the basis of what Jesus, who was a man, divinely and suprahumanly wrought and on the basis of other things which He, who is found to be true in all respects, affirmed about Himself—[things to which] those who lived with Him bore witness with their own blood

---

1. Franz Rosenzweig, *Briefe* (Berlin: Schocken Verlag, 1935), 211, quoted by Hans Blumenberg, in *Die Genesis der kopernikanischen Welt* (Frankfurt am Main: Suhrkamp, 1981), 439fn146.

and with an unalterable steadfastness that was formerly attested to by countless infallible considerations—we justifiably assert that Jesus is the one (1) whom the whole creation, from the beginning, expected to appear at the appointed time and (2) who through the prophets had foretold that He would appear in the world. For He came "in order to fill all things," because He willingly restored all [human beings] to health. Being powerful over all things, He disclosed all the secrets and mysteries of wisdom. As God, He forgave sins, raised the dead, transformed nature, commanded spirits, the sea, and the winds. He walked on water and established a law in fullness of supply for all laws. (*DI* III.4:203)

Cusanus accepts the New Testament account of Jesus's life as historical truth. That truth shows that Jesus was not just another human being. If, through the prophets Jesus foretold that he would appear at the appointed time, Jesus must have preceded himself as this historical person. This precedence should not be understood temporally. As the phrase "the Word became flesh" (Jn 1:14) asserts, in the order of being the Word preceded Jesus, as it preceded all of creation that would not be without it, "In the beginning was the Word, and the Word was with God, and the Word was God" (Jn 1:1).

The language of the previous quotation is very much informed by the Bible. Cusanus could expect his readers to pick up the biblical references. "In order to fill all things" refers to Ephesians 4:10: "He who descended is the very one who ascended higher than all the heavens, in order to fill the whole universe." "Restored all to health" lets the reader think of Matthew 12:9–13, which tells of a man whose shriveled hand Jesus restored all [to health]. The Acts of the Apostles tell of St. Stephen, who became the first Christian martyr, bearing witness to Christ with his own blood. His martyrdom was witnessed by St. Paul before his conversion.

Cusanus's indebtedness to St. Paul is made clear by the long quote from Colossians 1:14–20 that he chose to include in this chapter:

He is the Image of the Invisible God, the Firstborn of all creation because in Him all things were created, in heaven and on earth, visible and invisible, whether thrones or dominions or principalities or powers; all things were created through Him and in Him; and He is prior to all things, and in Him all things exist. And He is the head of the body, the church; He is the Beginning, the Firstborn from the dead, so that He holds the primacy in all respects. For it was pleasing that all fullness dwell in Him and that through Him all things be reconciled unto Him. (*DI* III.4:203)

In the words of the divinely inspired apostle, Cusanus finds further confirmation of what he took the Gospels to have established: that Jesus is indeed man and God.

> Such testimonies, together with more elsewhere, are exhibited by the saints regarding the fact that He is God and man. In Him the humanity was united to the Word of God, so that the humanity existed not in itself but in the Word; for the humanity could not have existed in the supreme degree and in complete fullness otherwise than in the divine person of the Son. (*DI* III.4:204)

The Word of God is the creative logos. Having its measure in Christ who is the maximum of the human species, all of nature is thus established as knowable by us human knowers, created in the image of God. As mentioned previously, the thought of Jesus is also the thought of the ideal knower, who provides our attempts to understand creation with a measure, even as this measure ultimately eludes our grasp. Cusanus's confidence in the power of mathematics to help us understand nature is thus supported by his Christian faith. Cusanus is well aware that, unaided by faith, our reason and intellect will not allow us to assert that Jesus is man and God. That requires us to conceive Jesus "above all our intellectual comprehension and in learned ignorance, as it were."

To give us some understanding of how Jesus is subsumed in the Divinity, Cusanus invites us to think it in analogy to the way our perceptual, embodied being is subsumed in our intellectual nature. We should note the focus on both the problem of knowledge and on the problem of incarnation.

> For since the intellect of Jesus is most perfect and exists in complete actuality, it can be personally subsumed only in the divine intellect, which alone is actually all things. For in all human beings the [respective] intellect is potentially all things; it gradually progresses from potentiality to actuality, so that the greater it [actually] is, the lesser it is in potentiality. But the maximum intellect, since it is the limit of the potentiality of every intellectual nature and exists in complete actuality, cannot at all exist without being intellect in such way that it is also God, who is all in all. (*DI* III.4:206)

The example of the polygon inscribed in the circle is used once again to clarify the point.

> By way of illustration: Assume that a polygon inscribed in a circle were the human nature and the circle were the divine nature. Then, if the polygon were to be a maximum polygon, than which there cannot be

> a greater polygon, it would exist not through itself with finite angles but in the circular shape. Thus, it would not have its own shape for existing—[that is, it would not have a shape that was] even conceivably separable from the circular and eternal shape. (*DI* III.4:206)

The example applies also to understanding anything whatsoever—say, a rose. A totally adequate understanding of the rose would be nothing other than the rose. Knowledge and being would here coincide.[2] But such a coincidence is a mark of God's creative knowledge.

A brief reflection on the body of Christ concludes the chapter.

> Now, the maximality of human nature's perfection is seen in what is substantial and essential [about it]—i.e., with respect to the intellect, which is served by human nature's corporeal features. Hence, the maximally perfect man is not supposed to be prominent with regard to accidental features but with regard to His intellect. For example, it is not required that He be a giant or a dwarf or [that He be] of this or that size, color, figure—and so on for other accidents. Rather, it is necessary only that His body so avoid the extremes that it be a most suitable instrument for His intellectual nature, to which it be obedient and submissive without recalcitrance, complaint, and fatigue. Our Jesus—in whom were hidden (even while He appeared in the world) all the treasures of knowledge and wisdom [Col 2:3], as if a light were hidden in darkness—is believed to have had, for the sake of His most excellent intellectual nature, a most suitable and most perfect body (as also is reported by the most holy witnesses of His life). (*DI* III.4:207)

As mentioned, Jesus provides us also with the ideal of beauty. To think that ideal, embodied in Jesus, we should not think it as tied to "this or that size, color, figure." From our human point of view these are accidental features. As is true of Kant's ideal, what matters is that the body of Jesus be thought of as "a most suitable instrument for His intellectual nature." There is no obvious scriptural support for such an idealization of the body. But there is an affinity with Renaissance humanism—think of Leonardo or Michelangelo. The ideal human body with its proportions provides the visual arts with its measure.

---

2. Cf. Cusanus, *De li non aliud.*

II. EXCURSUS

Is There a Measure on Earth?

FAITH IN CHRIST is needed to accept what Cusanus has to tell us in the remaining chapters of Book Three. This raises the question: is faith of some sort, not necessarily faith in Christ, needed to live a meaningful life? Is reason, unaided by faith, able to establish the measure needed to provide our lives with the necessary orientation? This excursus addresses that question.

The title is taken from a text by the poet Friedrich Hölderlin:

> May, if life is sheer toil, a man
> Lift his eyes and say: so
> I too wish to be? Yes. As long as kindness
> The Pure, still stays with his heart, man
> Not unhappily measures himself
> Against the godhead. Is God unknown?
> Is he manifest like the sky? I'd sooner
> Believe the latter. It's the measure of man.
> Full of merit, yet poetically, man
> Dwells on this earth. But no purer
> Is the shade of the starry night,
> If I might put it so, than
> Man, who's called an image of the godhead.
> Is there a measure on earth?
> There is None?[1]

1. Martin Heidegger, "... dichterisch wohnet der Mensch," in *Vorträge und Aufsätze,* Gesamtausgabe (Frankfurt am Main: Klostermann, 2000), 7:197–98); "Poetically Man Dwells," in *Poetry, Language, Thought,* trans. and intro. Albert Hofstadter (New York: Harper and Row, 1971), 219–20.

Interpreting this text, Martin Heidegger calls human dwelling poetic and understands poetry as a measuring.

> Man, as man, has always measured himself with and against something heavenly. Lucifer, too, is descended from heaven. Therefore, we read in the next lines (28 to 29): Man measures himself against the godhead." The godhead is the "measure" with which man measures out his dwelling, his stay on the earth beneath the sky. Only insofar as man takes the measure of his dwelling in this way is he able to be commensurately with his nature. Man's dwelling depends on an upward-looking measure-taking of the dimension, in which the sky belongs just as much as the earth.[2]

In light of the Catholic faith in which he was raised, Heidegger's reading of Hölderlin's text is hardly surprising. As Cusanus, too, emphasizes, God is said to have created man in his image—that is to say that human beings have their measure in God. But how is this measure given to us earth-dwellers? According to the poet, on earth no measure is to be found. But is the invisible God known to us mortals in such a way that he provides our human dwelling with a measure? Already in the first chapter I called attention to the connection between an insistence on the infinity of God, which prevents our reason from comprehending him, and a human self-assertion that turns to the human being as the only available measure. I pointed to the connection between Eckhartian mysticism and Renaissance humanism. In the preceding excursus I called attention to the remarkable fact that we find both Alberti and Cusanus concerned to defend the much-maligned Protagoras and his claim that man is the measure of all things. And yet, to measure all things, including our own actions and judgments, responsibly, Heidegger tells us, following Hölderlin, that we human beings must measure ourselves against the Godhead. Cusanus would agree. But what sense can we make of such a measuring?

A striking embodiment of Cusanus's understanding of the claim that man is the measure of all things would seem to be his Layman, the Socratic protagonist of the four Idiota dialogues, a simple craftsman who finds in his craft a key to wisdom.

In *Idiota de Mente* Cusanus has his Layman conjecture "that mind [*mens*] takes its name from measuring [*mensurare*]" (*IDM* 57). In a sermon from 1455 (CLXVII) Cusanus appeals to Albertus Magnus, who, relying on a false etymology, had tied the word *mens* (mind) to *metior* (to measure).[3] He could also have appealed to Thomas

---

2. Heidegger, "Poetically Man Dwells."
3. See Gandillac, *Nikolaus von Kues*, 152.

Aquinas.[4] What matters, however, is not the etymology, but the claim that the proper activity of the *mens* is *mensurare*. How are we to understand this measuring?

Cusanus would have us distinguish between the divine and the human mind. God requires no external measure. But where does human measuring find the proper measures?[5] Cusanus can answer that we human beings, having been created in the image of God, find the most fundamental measure within ourselves, where Cusanus is thinking first of all not of the body, which provides Alberti's perspective construction with a human measure, but of the mind itself, which he understands as an unfolding unity, ever in search of unity as it confronts God's creation, spread out in countless things. Plato already had understood thought as a process seeking unity.[6] Sight, and more generally the senses, furnish us only ever different aspects of things. What, then, are these things in truth? Demanded is an understanding of the thing in question that would allow us to gather these perceived aspects into a higher unity. Quite in the spirit of Plato, Cusanus, too, understands the human intellect as essentially in between a unity that draws it and the manifold of the world to which it is tied by the body and its senses and desires. This lived tension of the one and the many demands resolution. The human being demands unity and is yet prevented from seizing that unity by the manifold world in which contradiction is always present. The task is to bring this manifold under a unity.[7]

The beginning of the first of the *Idiota* dialogues, *Idiota de Sapientia*, exemplifies the nature of this process.[8] Having proclaimed, citing scripture, that wisdom cries out in the streets, the Layman points to the activities that take place in the marketplace. They see moneytellers, oil being measured, produce being weighed. In each case a unit measure is applied to what is to be measured. And can we not observe something of the sort wherever there is understanding? When we call this thing a rose, do I not apply to what is before me a human measure?

The activities observed on the marketplace invite the thought that just insofar as he is the being who measures, the human being

4. See Gandillac, *Nikolaus von Kues*, 152, who refers us to *De Veritate* X, art. 1, *In sent.* I.35.1: "*Mens dicitur a metior, metiris.*"

5. Cf. Christian Kny [pre-edited version], "Messen ohne Maß? Nicolaus Cusanus und das Kriterium menschlicher Erkenntnis," *Das Mittelalter* 23 (2018): 92–108.

6. Plato, *Republic* VII.524E–25A. Cusanus owned two copies of the *Republic* in the translation of Pier Candido Decembrio.

7. Cf. Ernst Cassirer, *Philosophie der symbolischen Formen* (Berlin: Cassirer, 1923), I:9.

8. Nicholas of Cusa, *Idiota de Sapientia*; trans. *The Layman on Wisdom*, in Jasper Hopkins, *Nicholas of Cusa on Wisdom and Knowledge* (Minneapolis: Banning, 1996).

transcends the beast. *Animal rationale* comes to be understood first of all as *animal mensurans*. How then do we measure? The layman points out that we always measure by means of some unit—that is to say, by means of the one. The principle of all knowing is thus counting, a thought familiar to both Aristotle and Aquinas.[9] But both, as we have seen, insist that man is more fundamentally measured than measure. And something like that must be true if we are not to confuse reality and fiction and is indeed presupposed by Cusanus when he suggests that we seek to see and understand in order to better appreciate the glory of the Divine Intellect. As a Christian thinker, he never loses sight of the importance of the distinction between God's creative knowledge and human re-creative knowledge. The human knower may indeed be likened to Alberti's painter, but we should not forget that this is a painter who paints creation in order to lead himself and others to a greater appreciation of the beauty of creation, which remains the ground of his re-creation.

All this implies that, as is indeed obvious, even if counting is constitutive of measuring, the latter nevertheless cannot be reduced to the former: counting is not yet measuring. Thus, if unity is indeed the primary measure, that measure must be incarnated in some concrete unit measure if there are to be activities such as weighing flour or measuring the length of a piece of cloth. And these concrete measures are not to be found in the human mind; they must be established by human beings in response to the world in which they live. The *braccio* that plays such an important part in Alberti's perspective construction provides a good example. That measure, an arm's length, is read off the human body. In that sense it has its foundation in an already ordered nature. Not that a different unit of length might not have been chosen instead, which reminds us that such measures are indeed humanly created, but not ex nihilo. That just this measure is chosen by the Florentine Alberti has to do with the way the arm offers itself naturally when we measure cloth. Other activities might have suggested the foot or the digit of a finger as the appropriate measure. The creation of the measure has its ground in a human practice. It is a human creation that does not imitate some

---

9. See Aristotle, *Metaphysics* X.1.1053b4: "Evidently then, being one in the strictest sense, if we define it according to the meaning of the word, is a measure, and especially of quantity, and secondly of quality." See also Thomas Aquinas, *Summa Theologica* I, q. 11, a. 2, in *The Basic Writings of St. Thomas Aquinas*, vol. 1, ed. Anton C. Pegis (New York: Random House, 1945): "One implies the idea of a primary measure; and number is multitude measured by one."

natural object. Godlike, the human being here provides himself with the needed measure.

An even more striking example of the godlike creativity that makes us human beings human is the spoon that Cusanus has his Layman carve in *Idiota de Mente*. It too, is a human creation grounded in a human practice that does not imitate some natural object. That lets the Layman claim that his art of spoon-carving is more godlike than the art of the painter in that it does not depend on an external model.[10] The example is striking in a number of ways: traditionally the representational art of the painter had been ranked far above mere craft. Cusanus's *Idiota* challenges this: making something without depending on some natural model is ranked above representation. *Homo faber* is given a new dignity.

> Having taken, a spoon in hand, the Layman said: "A spoon has no other exemplar, except our mind's idea [of the spoon]. For although a sculptor or a painter borrows exemplars from the things that he is attempting to depict, nevertheless I (who bring forth spoons from wood and bring forth dishes and jars from clay) do not [do so]. For in my [work] I do not imitate the visible form of any natural object, for such forms of spoons, dishes, and jars are perfected by human artistry alone. So my artistry involves the perfecting, rather than the imitating, of created visible forms, and in this respect it is more similar to the Infinite Art." (*IDM* 62)

When the Layman speaks of "the perfecting, rather than the imitating, of created visible forms," this may suggest that making a spoon is a sort of imitation after all, as suggested by Jasper Hopkins.[11] No doubt, it presupposes an experience of natural forms, but not one of these has provided him with a model. That the form-of-spoonness is a human creation requires no discussion. Different spoons are informed by this form.

> Layman: Suppose, then, that I wanted to explain my art and to make perceptible the form-of-spoonness, through which a spoon is constituted a spoon. With respect to its nature, the form of spoonness is not attainable by any of the senses; for it is not white or black or of any other color; nor is it characterized by any sound, odor, taste, or touch.

10. Cf. Andreas Wolfsteiner, "Die Natur löffelt nicht: Modellszenarien in den Laienschriften des Nicolaus Cusanus um 1450," in *Modell und Risiko: Historische Miniaturen zu dynamischen Epistemologien*, ed. Peter Löffelbein and Michael Lorber (Wiesbaden: Harrassowitz, 2019), 95–114. See also Nathan J. Taylor, "Beispiellose Exemplarität: Hans Blumenbergs Idiot," *Zeitschrift zum Beispiel*, no. 3., *Hagener Beiträge zur Literatur- und Medienwisssenschaft Themenheft, Handgreifiche Beispiele, Zweite Lieferung* (2019): 73–94.

11. Jasper Hopkins, "Introduction," in *Nicholas of Cusa on Wisdom and Knowledge*, 28.

Nevertheless, I will endeavor to make the form of spoon-ness perceptible in the way in which this can be done. Hence, I hew out, and hollow out, a material (viz., wood) by means of various movements of the tools that I use. [I continue] until in the wood there comes to be the requisite proportion, wherein the form of spoonness shines forth fittingly. In this way you see that in the befiguring proportion of the wood the simple and imperceptible form of spoonness shines forth, as in an image of itself. Hence, the true nature and the precision of spoonness, which is unmultipliable and incommunicable, cannot at all be made perfectly perceptible by any tools whatsoever or by any man at all. And in all spoons there shines forth variously only that most simple form, [shining forth] to a greater degree in one spoon and to a lesser degree in another, but not [appearing] in a precise way in any spoon. (*IDM* 63)

That recalls Plato. But the form the *Idiota* has in mind is a human creation. The example of the spoon invites thus a challenge to Plato's epistemology. That challenge is implied already in the way the Layman, when introduced to the learned Philosopher by the Orator, who is embarrassed to find him engaged in such menial tasks, introduces himself, and in the Philosopher's response:

Layman: I am gladly engaging in these tasks, which constantly nourish both mind and body. I am of the opinion that if this man whom you have brought is a philosopher, then he will not look down on me simply because I am applying myself to the craft of spoon-making.

Philosopher: Perfectly correct. For we read that even Plato painted now and then—something that he is thought to have done only because it did not interfere with his speculation. (*IDM* 54)

As the Orator adds, not only did painting not interfere with his speculations, but it offered Plato examples that allowed him to communicate "profound matters." The same is true, the Layman responds, of his craft: "I inquire symbolically into what I choose to, and I nourish my mind; I sell spoons and feed my body. In this way I acquire, in sufficient measure, all that I need" (*IDM* 55). Both Plato and the Layman use symbols drawn from art to communicate profound matters. But Plato is said to have drawn them from a representational art, while the Layman draws them from the art of spoon-making, which has no external model. Human creativity is given an altogether new significance.[12]

---

12. Cf. Taylor, "Beispiellose Exemplarität," 90–91. In this connection Cusanus's invention of his bowling game in *De ludo globi* also deserves consideration.

And does the example of spoon-making not also cast light on the genesis of our concepts or words? They too are products of our mind, tools of a sort that help us to cope with and establish our place in the world. To use one of Cusanus's favorite terms, they are conjectures, where Maurice Gandillac suggests that in the Latin *coniectura* Cusanus hears the German *Mut-massung* it translates, which suggests a measuring with the mind. We can call such conjectures human creations, provided we keep in mind that, like *braccio* and "foot," they are not created ex nihilo, but are rooted in a practice, created in response to certain experiences of an already ordered reality.

We have no way of understanding God's creation as he understands it. Things are not available to us in their truth. And yet that truth, the truth of things, measures our truths. In that sense we may want to agree with the poet Hölderlin: God is the measure of man. But that measure must in some way present itself to us here on earth. How is such a presentation to be thought? Can it be comprehended? As soon as there is experience there is also the interpreting activity of the human mind. Constitutive of whatever we experience is thus our way of understanding it, our human perspective, our human measure. This Cusanus takes to be the profound insight of Protagoras. But if there is a sense in which the human mind can be called a living unity that unfolds itself in number and measure, such an unfolding must respond to a world it has not created if it is not to substitute arbitrary invention for understanding. The unfolding of the living unity that we ourselves are must at the same time be a return to the divine unity that illuminates the countless particulars that make up our world.

This means that whatever presents itself in perception must present itself as already illuminated by logos.[13] If the mind is to gather some perceived manifold into a unity, that manifold must present itself as inviting just such a gathering. In his perspective construction, as we have seen, Alberti turns to the body to furnish him with a measure to mediate between the eye's point of view and what is to be represented. Cusanus similarly recognizes the need for measures to mediate between the mind, thought as an unfolding unity, and what is to be represented. Here, too, successful representation of the world in which we find ourselves requires that we furnish ourselves with measures that will allow us to take the measure of what is to be

---

13. *Timaeus* 69b–c. See Elizabeth Brient, "The Immanence of the Infinite: A Response to Blumenberg's Reading of Modernity" (Ph.D. diss., Yale University, 1995), 113–14.

represented. Such measures must be fitting. To be such, the mind that creates these measures must do so in response to what it would measure.

That human beings, when looking for a form of representation that would do justice to the workings of their own mind, should have turned to mathematics is only to be expected. As I showed in the first Excursus, that holds especially for our attempts to understand the workings of nature. But we should keep in mind that according to Cusanus the comparative transparency of such a mathematical representation of the world has its foundation in the chosen form of representation. This raises the question of whether the other side of such transparency, as in the case of Alberti's artificial perspective construction, is not the elision of the substance of reality that must escape such comprehension.

Cusanus would have us understand that the concepts embodied in our language are human creations. But he would also have us see that they may not be understood as creations ex nihilo. To give us insight into the world, our measures must respond to that very world in which and to which we apply them. But if so, experience may not be reduced to a mere perception of *sensibilia*, the mind to a tabula rasa. The fitting establishment of such measures requires an altogether different kind of perception, a perception that bears a certain resemblance to a perception of Platonic forms in things, even though Cusanus found what he took to be Plato's reification of the forms inadequate. But what sort of perception could that be, a perception that invites or calls for concepts and words that in turn are then applied to the perceived?

The philosopher, who is the layman's main interlocutor in this dialogue, invites the latter to clarify his position by relating it to the different views held by Plato and Aristotle:

> Aristotle claimed that no concept is concreated with our mind or soul, inasmuch as he likened the mind to a blank tablet. But Plato maintained that concepts are concreated with our mind or soul, but [he said] that because of the burden of the body the soul has forgotten [them]. What do you believe to be true in this regard? (*IDM* 77)

The Layman finds both positions lacking. He cannot agree with Plato's denigration of the body:

> Doubtlessly, our mind was put into this body by God for its own development. Therefore, it is necessary that the mind have from God all that without which mind cannot attain unto [this] development.

> Therefore, we ought not to believe that concreated with the soul
> there were concepts which the soul forgot in the bodily state; rather,
> we ought to believe that the soul has need of the body in order that
> its concreated power may proceed toward being actualized. (*IDM* 77)

God placed the mind in the body so that it could become what it
should be. Plato's theory of recollection is rejected. But Aristotle was
wrong to compare the mind to a blank tablet. That fails to do justice
to the mind's creative power, its originality, which makes it an image
of the divine mind. We should not think that our concepts are to
be found in nature, products of some simple process of abstraction.
Their creation requires the power of judgment.

> But since mind cannot learn if it lacks all power of judgment (even
> as a deaf man could not at all learn to become a lyre player, since
> he would possess no judgment regarding harmony—through which
> judgment he would be able to judge whether he were learning), our
> mind has—concreated with it—power-of-judgment (*concreatum iudi-*
> *cium*),[14] without which it could not learn. This power of judgment is,
> by nature, concreated with the mind. Through it the mind makes its
> own judgments about rational considerations—[judging] whether
> they are weak or strong or conclusive. If by "concreated concept"
> Plato meant this power, then he did not at all err [in this respect].
> (*IDM* 77)

What Plato attempted to explain with his forms the Layman,
speaking for Cusanus, attempts to explain by appealing to a power
of judgment said to be concreated with the mind. Cusanus places
this power of judgment above rational considerations as a kind of
judge. It decides whether they are "weak or strong or conclusive."
But what does this power of judgment look to when so judging? What
kind of compass does it rely on? The comparison of this *concreatum
iudicium* to the ability to judge harmony is suggestive: Is the power of
judgment Cusanus has in mind like an aesthetic judgment? In what is
presumably his last work, the *Compendium*, Cusanus invokes the *splendor aequalitatis*:

> The human mind naturally beholds in its own self—its own self as
> a living and intelligent manifestation of Equality—a singular mani-
> festation of Equality, a manifestation which we call a singular thing
> [constituted] in Equality's resplendent reflection. For the human

---

14. See Hans-Georg Gadamer, "Nikolaus von Kues im modernen Denken," in *Nicolo'
Cusano: Agli Inizi del Mondo Moderno*, 43; Christian Kny, "Messen ohne Maß?," 92–108. See
also Kny, "Einzelnes erkennt Einzelnes, 37–52.

mind—as being the first manifestation of the knowledge which the Prophet calls the light-of-God's countenance emblazoned upon us— is nothing but a sign of that [divine] Co-equality. Hence, man naturally knows the good, the equal, the just, and the right, because they are resplendent reflections of Equality. (*Com.* X.33–34.)

As a living manifestation of equality the human being by its very nature knows how to make sound judgments. The mind, itself a "thing [constituted] in Equality's resplendent reflection," recognizes in the things it encounters "resplendent reflections of Equality." Their splendor is a reflection of the Word's splendor.

Cusanus develops the mind's ability to make sound judgments in a way that recalls Plato:

Moreover, [man has] the innate [intellectual] forms (*cognatas species*) of the imperceptible virtues of justice and of equality, in order that he may know what is just, what is right, what is praiseworthy, what is beautiful, what is delightful and good (and may know the opposites of these), and may choose good things and become good, virtuous, prudent, chaste, courageous, and just. (*Com.* VI.17)

This may suggest that Cusanus has revised his rejection of Plato's forms and is now admitting that at least the highest forms are innate. But we should not be too quick to take *species* here to refer to a Platonic form. What is innate in us is the ability to recognize what makes something just, right, praiseworthy, beautiful, delightful, and good. As Jasper Hopkins points out, "Nicholas here means what Augustine meant in *De Trinitate* 8.3, where he spoke of the good as a *notio impressa.* This 'impressed concept'—for Augustine and also for Nicholas—is understood to be an innate capability-of-judgment, whereby that which is good is recognizable as such. A similar point holds for what is just, beautiful, equal, and right. None of these are explicit concepts that can be articulated and defined by every human agent early in life."[15] That capability is the presence of the divine measure in us. It provides our judgments with the needed compass.

Guided by the power of judgment, the mind is able to create fitting concepts for what it experiences:

From the foregoing [observation] we learn that mind is that power which, when stimulated, can assimilate itself to every form and can make concepts of all things, even though, [initially], it lacks all conceptual form. (*IDM* 78)

15. Hopkins, *Nicholas of Cusa on Wisdom and Knowledge,* 515–16n40.

But must the material furnished to the mind by the senses not already be experienced in a way that allows the power of judgment to assimilate itself to every form in appropriate ways? Cusanus, as we have seen, rejects both Aristotelian abstraction and Platonic recollection. Where then does the human creation of these concepts find its measure? In forms present in things. But how does their presence manifest to us? The appeal to the *iudicium cocreatum* seems insufficient. The ability to recognize what is true, good, or beautiful, equal, would idle if our experience of God's creation were not such as to stimulate the mind to create fitting concepts for all things.

Consider once more the example of Cusanus's Layman carving a spoon. It provides us with a pointer worth pursuing.[16] Hollowing out the wood, he shapes it until finally the form of spoonness shines forth fittingly, *convenienter resplendeat*, that same form that in varying degrees shines forth (*relucet*) in all spoons. When the art of the craftsman succeeds in shaping the wood in such a way that the form shines forth fittingly, we call his work beautiful. And does something similar not hold also of what is not an artifact, but an object of nature, having its origin in God? In the sermon *Tota pulchra es, amica mea* of 1456,[17] Cusanus, invoking the authority of Cicero as cited by Albertus Magnus, points out that we call the human body beautiful *ex resplendencia coloris super membra proportionata* (51, 5–6). *Proporcio* and *resplendencia* are taken to define the beautiful: *id quod materiale est in pulchritudine, puta proporcio, et formale puta resplendencia: Primum quia unitas, secundum quia lux* (56, 23–25). Proportion means unity, resplendence means

16. The last part of this excursus appeared in Harries, "On the Power and Poverty of Perspective," 105–26.

17. Giovanni Santinello, "Nicolai De Cusa: Tota pulchra es, amica mea (Sermo de pulchritudine): Introduzione ed ediz. critica," in *Atti e Memorie dell' Accademia Patavina* 71 (Padova, 1959), 21–58. Page and line references in the text are to this edition. A French translation, "Sermon: Tu es toute belle, ma bien-aimée," appeared in Francis Bertin, *Nicolas de Cues: Sermons Eckhartiens et Dionysiens, Introduction, traduction, notes et commentaires* (Paris: Les Éditions du Cerf, 1998), 317–85. Following Santinello, Bertin emphasizes how much of the sermon is made up of passages lifted from Ambrosius Traversari's translation of Dionysius's *De divinis nominibus* and from Albertus Magnus's commmentary on that text. Toscanelli had brought the former to Cusanus in 1443, on behalf of Pope Nicholas V. See Nicolaus von Cues, *Vom Nichtanderen*, intro. and notes by Paul Wilpert (Hamburg: Meiner, 1952), 14n6. See also Giovanni Santinello, "Nicoló Cusano e Leon Battista Alberti: Pensieri sul bello e sull'arte," in *Leon Battista Alberti: Una visione estetica del mondo e della vita* (Firenze: Sansoni, 1962). An English translation by Jasper Hopkins has also appeared: "Tota Pulcra Es, Amica Mea," Sermon CCXLIII, in *Nicholas of Cusa's Didactic Sermons: A Selection*, trans. and intro. Jasper Hopkins (Loveland, CO: Arthur J. Banning, 2008), 168–77. See also Hopkins, "'Non est quicquam expers pulchritudinis's The Theme of Beauty in Nicholas of Cusa's sermons," August 2009, https://jasper-hopkins.info/Cusanusonbeauty.pdf.

a spiritual light. A well-proportioned beautiful body is likened to a light, an observation that we find already in Xenophon's *Symposium*, where the beauty of the young Autolycus is likened to a light at night that draws all eyes to itself. To liken beauty to light is to suggest that beauty renders the beautiful more visible. Beauty opens our eyes; it lets us see.[18] But ever since Plato, understanding has been understood in the image of sight. If light lets us see, must there not also be a higher light that lets us understand? It is this simile that is presupposed by the example of the ruby Cusanus offers us in *De li non aliud* to help us to a better understanding of his thought of God as the not-other.

> You see this carbuncle stone, which the peasants call a ruby. Do you see that at this third hour of the night—at a very dark time and in a very dark place a candle is not needed because there is light in the stone? When this light wants to manifest itself, it does so by means of the stone. For in itself the light would be invisible to the sense [of sight]; for it would not be present to the sense and so would not at all be sensed, because the sense perceives only what is presented to it. Therefore the light which is in the stone conveys to the light which is in the eye what is visible regarding the stone. (*NA* 41)

The light in the stone answers to the light in the eye, which, without it, could not see. But the light in the ruby, no more than its glowing red, is said to be neither its essence nor its substance. That substance cannot be seen, does not present itself to our eyes. "The substance, which precedes accident, has nothing from the accidents. But the accidents have everything from the substance, since they are its accidents, i.e., the shadow, the image of the substantial light."[19] The light by which we see figures thus the substantial light that gathers this thing so that it is not other than just this thing, as it gathers all things. And while this light is invisible, Cusanus yet insists that it shows itself in the visible, and, as in the case of the spoon, more clearly in some than in others. Thus "the substantial light of the carbuncle shows itself more clearly—as in a closer likeness—in the glow of brighter splendor," in *clarioris fulgore splendentiae se clarius ostendit*. What is here called *fulgor splendentiae* is the ground of Plato's construction of the

---

18. Cf. Plato, *Pheadrus* 250d: "Now beauty, as we said, shone bright amidst these visions, and in this world below we apprehend it through the clearest of our senses, clear and resplendent. For sight is the keenest mode of perception vouchsafed us through the body; wisdom, indeed, we cannot see thereby—how passionate would had been our desire for her, if she had granted us so clear an image of herself to gaze upon—nor yet any other of those beloved objects, save only beauty; for beauty alone this has been ordained, to be most manifest to sense and most lovely of them all"; trans. R. Hackforth.

19. Hopkins, *On God as Not-Other*, 81.

forms. This *fulgor splendentiae* is *splendor formae*, is beauty. In the visible world experiences of the beautiful open windows to the transcendent ground of our knowing, let us glimpse the divine Word, which being also the ground of beauty can be called beautiful in a pre-eminent sense, as can each person of the Trinity. Jasper Hopkins calls our attention to Cusanus's Sermon CLXXXVII, where he identifies "the three Persons of the Divine Trinity by the names 'Begetting Beauty,' 'Begotten Beauty,' and 'Glorious Beauty' (or simply 'Glory'—a Glory that arises from Begetting Beauty and Begotten Beauty)."[20]

Following Albertus Magnus, Cusanus, too, defines the beautiful as *splendor forme, sive substancialis sive accidentalis, super partes materie proportionatas et terminatas.*[21] "The splendor of the form, either substantial or accidental, upon the proportioned and bounded parts of matter." That definition draws a distinction between two kinds of beauty, one where the *splendor formae* is substantial, the other where it is accidental. The beauty of the spoon is an example of the latter. As Cusanus says in *De Ludo Globi* of his globe: *Deus dator est substantiae, homo accidentis, seu similitudinis substantiae. Forma globi data ligno per hominem, addita est substantiae ligni.* "God is the Giver of substance; man is the giver of an accident, i.e., of a likeness-of-substance. A bowling-ball's shape, given to the wood by man, is joined to the wood's substance" (*DLG* 25). The beauty of the human body is an example of substantial beauty. As we read in *De ludo globi*:

> Now, a whole shines forth in all its parts, since a part is a part of the whole. Just as the whole man shines forth in the hand, which is proportioned to the whole, but, nevertheless, the whole perfection of man shines forth in a more perfect manner in the head: so the universe shines forth in each of its parts, for all things have their respective relation and proportion to the universe, but, nevertheless, the universe shines forth more greatly in that part which is called man than in any other part. (*DLG* 42)

Cusanus likens the human being to a kingdom gathered into one by its king. The body's beauty is the splendor of such a gathering. Just as "Trajan's power shines forth [*relucet*] in the preciousness" of his column, which his will defined and delimited, God's power shines forth in the well ordered universe (*NA* 34) and in every one of its parts, most perfectly, according to Cusanus, in the human being, the

20. Jasper Hopkins, "'Non est quicquam expers pulchritudinis': The Theme of Beauty in Nicholas of Cusa's Sermons," 7, japser-hopkns.info.gin.
21. Santinello, "Nicolai De Cusa: Tota pulchra es, amica mea," 51:3–4.

being that "enfolds intellectual and sensible nature and encloses all things within itself, so that the ancients were right in calling it a microcosm or a small world" (*DI* III.198). It is the only being that "can suitably be elevated to the Maximum by the power of the maximal, infinite God." Thus the sermon *Tota pulchra es, amica mea* concludes by calling Christ, the bridegroom of the Song of Songs, *pulchritudo absoluta*.[22] Such beauty calls the bride, the human soul, with the most beautiful word, *amica*, beloved. But our soul experiences an echo of this call, the call of the divine logos, in all that is beautiful. The beauty of creation opens windows in the house our reason has built.[23] Only by thus opening ourselves to what lies outside that house can our life and thought gain the measures that are a presupposition of all responsibility. Faith is Love of the Beauty that calls us. But for Cusanus that Beauty calls us most perfectly in Jesus, whose beauty is absolute.

22. Cusansus, "Tota pulchra es," 58, 11.

23. Only recently I realized that with this train of thought I have been unpacking something I had written in my dissertation (Harries, "In a Strange Land," 153–54) more than sixty years ago: "When I see an object in its ineffable particularity, I see it in the mode of the *non aliud*.... Rephrasing Kierkegaard's dictum we can say: purity of heart is to see one thing: the beautiful. Whenever I look at something and see it as some object among others, I see it not as it is in itself, not in the mode of the *non aliud*, and its beauty escapes me. It follows from this definition of beauty that anything can become beautiful if I look at it in the right way. A tree, a cloud, and old roof can appear to me as nothing other than what it is. Without the notion of another, I can no longer think of possibility. But 'where I touch on reality without its transformation into possibility, I touch on transcendence' [Karl Jaspers, *Philosophie* (Berlin: Springer, 1932), 3:9]."

III . CHRIST'S BIRTH, DEATH, AND RESURRECTION

As I mentioned, Giordano Bruno, who takes so much from chapters 11 and 12 of Book Two of *On Learned Ignorance*, found little of interest in Book Three. Key to Bruno's thought is his commitment to a freedom that knows no limits and refuses to be bound by either the church with its dogmas or by Aristotelian science. Bruno's pantheism left no room for the biblical God who is supposed to have created this world, to have given us his law, and to have so loved the world that he gave us his son, who died on the cross so that we might be redeemed. Bruno's cosmology implies the death of the biblical God, who, according to the church, revealed himself in nature, in scripture, and in Jesus Christ, the Word become flesh. Thus Bruno places us on the threshold of a Nietzschean nihilism.

Bruno, to be sure, was himself an evangelist of sorts, who found in the Copernican revolution a figure of a revolution that would bring with it a liberation of human beings from all sorts of despotic regimes and from the faith that once provided ethics and politics with a foundation. But freedom unbound denies that foundation. Once again, we are confronted with the question: in the absence of faith, what is to bind human freedom? To many of us moderns the still obvious answer to this question is reason. And is this not the answer we have to give? Is there an alternative? Kant's categorical imperative is difficult to get around. But is the egoist who cares only about his own happiness unreasonable? If the faith that once provided life with measure and meaning could not survive the Enlightenment's liberation of humanity, the faith in reason that the French revolution tried to establish when, having dethroned God, it placed its "Goddess of Reason" on the high altar of Notre Dame, also proved vulnerable to objections

III. CHRIST'S BIRTH, DEATH, AND RESURRECTION

raised by reason. As the poet Hermann Broch observed, "As things proceed rationally in the kingdom of reason, this 'Goddess of Reason' was soon forgotten."[1] Reason soon turned against itself and demonstrated its inability to furnish the kind of certainty and measure demanded. The history that followed has demonstrated the impotence of pure practical reason again and again. But what is to bind freedom? That was the question with which Nietzsche had to struggle. It is a question with which we are still struggling. And this question makes it difficult to dismiss the third book of *De docta ignorantia* quite as easily as so many philosophers, including Giordano Bruno and Hans Blumenberg, were able to do. The death of God has only given special weight to the question "what is to bind freedom?" Cusanus finds his answer in the faith in which he was raised, quite prepared to grant that such faith must accept what to reason must appear folly: the incarnation of the infinite God in a mortal human being that is the mystery of Christmas, said by him to have its foundation in God's love. But learned ignorance opens a door to faith: Human love must answer God's love if our life is to gain meaning and measure.

1. Hermann Broch, "Einige Bemerkungen zum Problem des Kitsches," in *Essays*, vol. 1, *Dichten und Erkennen* (Zurich: Rhein, 1955), 295–309. English translation, "Notes on the Problem of Kitsch," in Gillo Dorfles, *Kitsch: The World of Bad Taste* (New York: Universe Books, 1969), 59.

Christ, Conceived through the Holy Spirit, Was Born of the Virgin Mary

The title already tells us that what Cusanus has to say about Christ is in keeping with the position of the church that he served as a cardinal. Supported by the Gospels of Matthew (1:18–24) and Luke (1:26–35), which say that Mary was a virgin and that Jesus was conceived by the Holy Spirit, that doctrine was not really challenged by Christians before the Enlightenment.

Given the central place of the Virgin Birth in the Christian narrative, the way Cusanus fits that narrative into the metaphysical framework developed in the preceding chapters should not seem surprising.

Furthermore, we must consider that since the most perfect humanity, which is subsumed upwards, is the terminal contracted precision, it does not altogether exceed [the limits of] the species of human nature. Now, like is begotten from like; and, hence, the begotten proceeds from the begetter according to a natural comparative relation. But since what is terminal is free of termination, it is free of limitation and comparative relation. Hence, the maximum human being is not begettable by natural means; and yet, He cannot be altogether free of origin from that species whose terminal perfection

III. CHRIST'S BIRTH, DEATH, AND RESURRECTION

> He is. Therefore, because He is a human being, He proceeds partly according to human nature. And since He is the highest originated [being], most immediately united to the Beginning: the Beginning, from which He most immediately exists, is as a creating or begetting [Beginning], i.e., as a father; and the human beginning is as a passive [beginning] which affords a receiving material. Hence, [He comes] from a mother apart from a male seed. (*DI* III.5:208)

That Christ should actually have lived here on earth reason cannot make sense of. As far as reason is concerned there can be no "maximum human being," just as there can be no maximum number. But faith demands that we accept what the New Testament tells us as historical fact, even if our reason declares it to be impossible. Faith thus demands that we become learned about our ignorance and accept that coincidence of opposites where our reason suffers shipwreck.

As a mortal Jesus must be born by a mortal; as "maximum human being" he must be "most immediately united to the Beginning"—that is, to God. We speak of Jesus as the Son of God. In Book One Cusanus had insisted that 'Son' and 'Father' are metaphors, that all such talk is "only in relation to creatures." Such metaphors threaten to emphasize the difference between Father and Son in a way that obscures the incomprehensible unity of the triune God. But given the humanity of Jesus, we must speak of God "in relation to creatures," since in Jesus the Word became flesh—that is, God became a creature. Like every human being he must have a mother. Cusanus invokes the principle that like is generated from like. But as he is also God, he must be begotten by God.

We should note a certain analogy between the creation and the Incarnation. In both cases the Divine Word becomes visible in matter, once as the universe and again as a person. Given that God is said to have created man in his image, the visibility of the Word in the creation helps us understand the intelligibility of nature: our reason, unfolding itself in our progressive understanding of nature is an image of the creative Word.

"In the beginning was the Word, and the Word was with God, and the Word was God. He was with God in the beginning. Through him all things were made" (Jn 1:1–3). To understand that much, Cusanus thought, does not require faith, as demonstrated by Books One and Two. But faith is required to accept what follows: "And the Word became flesh and dwelt among us, and we have seen his glory, glory as of the only Son from the Father, full of grace and truth" (Jn 1:14). With the Incarnation, a standard of excellence is introduced into creation.

Christ, reason might say, represents the gift of the ideal. Kant thinks of the ideal as a product of the imagination, set into a work of art by the creative artist. Faith would have us understand it as God's gift to us mortals: In Christ the ideal has become actual, concrete, and visible. Creation is given measure and center.

In this connection we may want to think of recurrent iconoclastic controversies, which insisted on the inability of images to do justice to the divine essence. From its very beginning biblical religion has thus been shadowed by iconoclasm. Did the second commandment not say, "You shall not make for yourself any graven image, or any likeness of anything that is in heaven above, or that is in the earth beneath, or that is in the water under the earth" (Ex 20:4)? Israel's God is invisible. Think of Moses smashing the golden calf. "Do not make a picture of Christ," Asterius of Amasea (c. 350–c. 410 A.D.) warns us: "The humiliation of the Incarnation to which He submitted of His own free will and for our sake was sufficient for Him to endure—rather let us carry around in our soul the incorporeal world."[1]

But must we understand the Incarnation as a humiliation of Christ? Must we not rather understand the descent of the divine into the material as a mysterious necessity? Must the fact that God first created the world and then incarnated himself and thus closed the gap between spirit and body not be understood as inseparable from the triune essence of God? Should we not join those who appealed to the Incarnation to defend art, this human incarnation of spirit in matter as another manifestation of the fact that God created us in his image, where that image character is particularly conspicuous in the artist? But the modern world has difficulty accepting the Incarnation, which confronts us with the paradox that Mary, most definitely a human being, should be God's mother, daughter, and bride, just as it has difficulty granting more than an aesthetic significance to art. Many Christians today tend to relegate the Incarnation to a past that lies behind us. Christianity has become the religion of the no longer present, the dead God, the religion of a spiritual and increasingly empty transcendence.

But if, with Cusanus, we accept the Incarnation, accept also that God is three and one, must we not also accept that Mary in giving birth to Jesus gave birth not just to a human being, not just to a mask assumed by God for our sake, but to God in the full sense, as illustrated

---

1. Arnold Hauser, *The Social History of Art*, trans. Stanley Godman (New York: Vintage, 1951), 1:138.

III. CHRIST'S BIRTH, DEATH, AND RESURRECTION

by the shrine madonnas of the Middle Ages, which show the Trinity in Mary's womb? The Trinity here turns into a Quaternity, as Mary is made coequal. We are made to think of Isis. The best-known examples are today in in the Cluny Museum in Paris and the Germanisches Nationalmuseum in Nürnberg.[2] That the church rejected these expressions of Marian piety is to be expected.

The statues have been characterized as abhorrent and erroneous by such luminaries as the fifteenth-century chancellor of the University of Paris Jean Gerson (d. 1429) and the Flemish Catholic theologian and king's censor Johannes Molanus (d. 1585). In a 1402 sermon on the Nativity, Gerson expressed dismay at the sight of a trinitarian shrine madonna he encountered in a Parisian Carmelite monastery, which had "the Trinity within its womb, as if the entire Trinity took flesh in the Virgin Mary." Such a statue, he said, has "neither beauty, nor pious sentiment, and can be a cause of error and lack of devotion." The sentiment was repeated nearly verbatim by Molanus, and it is through his *De picturis et imaginibus sacris* that Pope Benedict XIV likely knew about Gerson's original injunction. In 1745, Benedict XIV outlawed trinitarian shrine madonnas, referencing Gerson in his papal bull.[3]

Cusanus would probably have agreed with Gerson. But the piety that finds expression in these shrine madonnas is a response to the mystery of Christmas that can claim to base itself on a literal reading of the Nicene Creed. The shrine madonnas invite further reflection. At least since Plato there has been a tendency to place spirit above matter in a way that has to devalue or even demonize matter, a devaluation extended to woman. The shrine madonnas challenge that devaluation, suggesting that the Trinity would not be without Mary, that spirit would not be without matter.

But let me return to chapter 5 of Book Three: I called the Incarnation a gift of the ideal. In analogous fashion God created the universe.

> But every operation proceeds from a spirit and a love which unites the active with the passive, as I earlier indicated in a certain passage. [The reference is to Book II, chapter 7 on the Trinity.] Hence, necessarily, the maximum operation (which is beyond all natural comparative relation and through which the Creator is united to

2. Elina Gertsman, *Worlds Within: Opening the Medieval Shrine Madonna* (College Station: Pennsylvania State University Press, 2015); Gudrun Radler, *Die Schreinmadonna/"Vierge Ouvrante"* (Frankfurt: Kunstgeschichtliches Inst. der Johann-Wolfgang-Goethe-Universität, 1990).

3. Elina Gertsman, "The Lives and Afterlives of Shrine Madonnas," *California Italian Studies* 6, no. 1 (2016): 4, https://escholarship.org/uc/item/6sboj1st.

the creation and which proceeds from a maximum uniting Love) is, without doubt, from the Holy Spirit, who is absolutely Love. Through the Holy Spirit alone and without the assistance of a contracted agent, the mother was able to conceive—within the scope of her species—the Son of God the Father. Thus, just as God the Father formed by His own Spirit all the things which by Him came forth from not-being into being, so by the same most holy Spirit He did this more excellently when He worked most perfectly [i.e., when He formed Jesus]. (*DI* III.5:209)

The ground of this gift, in which humanity finds its measure, is a love that surpasses all reason. Faith responds to God's love.

Reminding us of the inevitable inadequacy of such metaphors, Cusanus likens God to a teacher who in order to communicate his thoughts to his students has to incarnate them in words (*DI* III.210).

By means of this admittedly very remote likeness, we are momentarily elevated in our reflection—[elevated] beyond that which we can understand. For through the Holy Spirit (who is consubstantial with the Father) the Eternal Father of immense goodness (who willed to show us the richness of His glory and all the fullness of His knowledge and wisdom) indued with human nature the Eternal Word, His Son (who is this fullness and the fullness of all things). Making allowance for our weaknesses—since we were unable to perceive [the Word] in any other way than in visible form and in a form similar to ourselves—the Father manifested the Word in accordance with our capability. As a sound [is formed] from inbreathed air, so, as it were, this Spirit, through an outbreathing, formed from the fertile purity of the virginal blood the animal body. He added reason so that it would be a human nature. [To it] He so inwardly united the Word of God the Father that the Word would be human nature's center of existence. (*DI* III.5:211)

The universe, too, can be understood as an incarnation of God, but being boundless, in it no center is to be found. The Incarnation was necessary to provide nature and more especially us human beings with the center of our existence.

Cusanus defends the Virgin's Immaculate Conception, a controversial thesis in the medieval church that was taken up by the schismatic Council of Basel, which endorsed it on September 17, 1439, meeting however with opposition, especially from the Dominicans, who could point out that the Immaculate Conception had been denied by St. Thomas Aquinas and St. Bonaventure.[4] Long before it

---

4. See Rudolf Haubst, *Die Christologie des Nikolaus von Kues* (Freiburg: Herder, 1956), 241–46; *PTW* I:120 n; 212n19f.

III. CHRIST'S BIRTH, DEATH, AND RESURRECTION

became a dogma in 1854, when Pope Pius IX declared the Immaculate Conception ex cathedra in the bull *Ineffabilis Deus*, it had come to be generally accepted by the Catholic Church. Pope Pius IX invoked an argument presented by the Franciscan Duns Scotus: "This argument is that of 'preventive Redemption,' according to which the Immaculate Conception is the masterpiece of the Redemption brought about by Christ because the very power of his love and his mediation obtained that the Mother be preserved from original sin. Therefore Mary is totally redeemed by Christ, but already before her conception. Duns Scotus's confreres, the Franciscans, accepted and spread this doctrine enthusiastically and other theologians, often with a solemn oath, strove to defend and perfect it."[5] .

Cusanus would seem to have been in substantial agreement.

> No one should doubt that this mother, who was so full of virtue and who furnished the material, excelled all virgins in the perfection of every virtue and had a more excellent blessing than all other fertile women. For this [virgin-mother], who was in all respects foreordained to such a unique and most excellent virginal birth, ought rightfully to have been free of whatever could have hindered the purity or vigor, and likewise the uniqueness, of such a most excellent birth. For if the Virgin had not been pre-elected, how would she have been suited for a virginal birth without a male seed? If she had not been superblessed of the Lord and most holy, how could she have been made the Holy Spirit's sacristy, in which the Holy Spirit would fashion a body for the Son of God? If she had not remained a virgin after the birth, she would beforehand have imparted to the most excellent birth the center of maternal fertility not in her supreme perfection of brightness but dividedly and diminishedly—not as would have befit [this] unique, supreme, and so great son. Therefore, if the most holy Virgin offered her whole self to God, for whom she also wholly partook of the complete nature of fertility by the operation of the Holy Spirit, then in her the virginity remained—before the birth, during the birth, and after the birth—immaculate and uncorrupted, beyond all natural and ordinary begetting. (*DI* III.5:212)

Duns Scotus insists that the Incarnation should not be thought of as something that became necessary only because of the fall. "In the opinion of Duns Scotus the Incarnation of the Son of God, planned from all eternity by God the Father at the level of love is the fulfillment of creation and enables every creature, in Christ and through

---

5. Benedict XVI, General Audience, Wednesday, July 7, 2010 (Vatican City: Libreria Editrice Vaticana, 2010), w2.vatican.va/content/benedict-xvi/en/audiences/.../hf_ben -xvi_aud_20100707.html.

Christ, to be filled with grace and to praise and glorify God in eternity. Although Duns Scotus was aware that in fact, because of original sin, Christ redeemed us with his Passion, Death and Resurrection, he reaffirmed that the Incarnation is the greatest and most beautiful work of the entire history of salvation, that it is not conditioned by any contingent fact but is God's original idea of ultimately uniting with himself the whole of creation, in the Person and Flesh of the Son."[6] Inseparable from this "original idea" is the Virgin Mary.

We may well wonder why the Immaculate Conception became such an important issue in the church: Just what was at stake? We should consider how difficult it is to accept what is here being asserted: Mary is said to have been pre-elected to give birth to the Son of God. But the Trinity forces us to think the Son as God. Does Mary, too, then not, like her son, belong inseparably to the very essence of God? Her motherhood is here ennobled in a way that also implies an ennobling of the material world. In the Absolute, matter and spirit are so intimately joined that one cannot be placed above the other. We do violence to God, and to the human being created in His image, when we either sacrifice spirit to matter or matter to spirit.

But if Mary was pre-elected to give birth to the Son of God, that birth took place at a particular time and in a particular place. That raises the question of how to think the relationship of the eternal God to this temporal world: Must the infinite God not be thought to be equally close to every moment and every place? That is an implication of the metaphor of the infinite sphere that helped shape the cosmology of Cusanus. And yet the time of Christ's birth would seem to be privileged in an obvious. way, just as Christ, the concrete maximum, is privileged in the realm of creation. Cusanus recognizes this privilege: the Virgin birth is said to have required a fullness of perfection in time. But just as the Virgin's perfection, her fullness of fertility, eludes our understanding, so does the idea of the fullness of time.

> For from the virgin-mother [Jesus] was able to exist as a human being only temporally—and from God the Father only eternally; but the temporal birth required a fullness of perfection in time, just as [it required] in the mother a fullness of fertility. Therefore, when the fullness of time arrived: since [Jesus] could not be born as a human being apart from time, He was born at the time and place most fitting thereto and yet most concealed from all creatures. For the supreme bounties (*plenitudines*) are incomparable with our daily

6. Ibid.

III. CHRIST'S BIRTH, DEATH, AND RESURRECTION

> experiences. Hence, no reasoning was able to grasp them by any
> sign, even though by a certain very hidden prophetic inspiration
> certain obscure signs, darkened by human likenesses, transmitted
> them; and from these signs the wise could reasonably have foreseen
> that the Word was to be incarnated in the fullness of time. But the
> precise place, time, or manner was foreknown only to the Eternal
> Begetter, who ordained that when all things were in a state of mod-
> erate silence, the Son would in the course of the night descend from
> the Heavenly Citadel into the virginal womb and would at the or-
> dained and fitting time manifest Himself to the world in the form of
> a servant. (*DI* III.5:213–14)

Following the Nicene Creed, Cusanus here speaks of a twofold birth
of Christ, an eternal birth from God the Father and a temporal birth
from the Virgin. But Jesus is not just a terrestrial mask assumed by the
divine Word: He is the Word. The humanity of Christ is the humanity
of God. And that is to say that Mary is the mother of God. With this
the opposition of time and eternity, of Creator and creation, is called
into question. Confronted with the mystery of Christmas, our reason
fails us: The proper response is silence.

I single out the phrase, "When all things were in a state of moderate silence, [*dum medium silentium tenerent omnia*] the Son would in the
course of the night descend from the Heavenly Citadel." What are we
to make of this? In Revelations there is said to be silence in heaven for
about half an hour when the Lamb opens the Seventh Seal (Rv 8:1). A
number of biblical passages refer to the middle of the night.[7] Cusanus
would also appear to have been thinking of the time of the Incarnation
as the middle between the fall—that is, the beginning of history, and
the end of time. We meet with this thought already in his first sermon,
In Principio Erat Verbum:

> For the course of all time is a single hour; the first half of the hour is
> the time before the Incarnation; the other half is the time after the
> Incarnation. Wisdom 16 [says]: "While all things were in the midst
> of silence and night was in the midst of her course … ," etc. In other
> words, it is as half an hour from the time of man's sin to the time of
> Christ, in whom silence came about, in whom a pact was awaited be-
> tween Truth and Mercy, Peace and Justice, man and God. (*Sermo* I.22)

Just as faith in what has been revealed endows space with a spiritual center, an *axis mundi*, so it endows time with a center. That both
should have such a center surpasses reason.

7. See *PTW* I:121n214, 12f.

CHAPTER 6

The Mystery of the Death of Jesus Christ

With this chapter we turn from the mystery of Christmas to the mystery of Good Friday. Why did Christ have to suffer a painful death to save us? Once again Cusanus's intent is not just to reconcile his understanding of God with established doctrine, but to shed new light on the mystery of the Cross.

The chapter begins with a digression that provides us with a brief sketch of both the anthropology and the ethics of Cusanus. An understanding of the lack inseparable from our humanity is to prepare us for an understanding the necessity of Christ's shameful death on the cross.

Cusanus, too, understands the human being as the *animal rationale*, the animal possessed of a rational soul, but that definition does not do justice to the fact that God created us human beings in his image. Created in his image, we possess an intellect, and that means also a freedom that lets us be in touch with the infinite and eternal. Cusanus thus places reason between intellect and sense, between spirit and animal, between time and eternity.

> It accords with the expression of my intent that a short digression here be made—in order to attain more clearly unto the mystery of the Cross. There is no doubt that a human being consists of senses,

> intellect, and reason (which is in between and which connects the other two). Now, order subordinates the senses to reason and reason to intellect. The intellect is not temporal and mundane but is free of time and of the world. The senses are temporally subject to the motions of the world. With respect to the intellect, reason is on the horizon, so to speak; but with respect to the senses, it is at the zenith, as it were; thus, things that are within time and things that are beyond time coincide in reason. (*DI* III.6:215)

The understanding of human being that we are presented with here is broadly Platonic. A look at the *Phaedo* seems especially relevant: there is in us an intellect (*nous*) that is free of time and the world. We testify to that supratemporal intellect every time we lay claim to truth. When I claim truth for some proposition, I do not claim that it is true here and now. Every such claim is made *sub specie aeternitatis*. According to Cusanus, reason joins the sensible and temporal to the intellect, which allows us in reflection to transcend our time-bound being.

The animal in us is said by Cusanus, following Thomas Aquinas,[1] to be governed by two drives: concupiscence (*potentia concupiscibilis*), the drive "toward carnal desire," and anger (*potentia irascibilis*), the desire "to ward off what hinders it" (*DI* III.216). Reason allows us to rule over desire's passions so that we may satisfy our intellect's spiritual desire for the eternal.

> The senses, which belong to the animal [nature], are incapable [of attaining unto] supratemporal and spiritual things. Therefore, what is animal does not perceive the things which are of God, for God is spirit and more than spirit. Accordingly, perceptual knowledge occurs in the darkness of the ignorance of eternal things; and in accordance with the flesh it is moved, through the power of concupiscence, toward carnal desires and, through the power of anger, toward warding off what hinders it. (*DI* III.6:216)

The animal in us seeks out what is pleasurable and seeks to avoid pain. Utilitarianism answers to the animal we are. To quote Jeremy Bentham, "Nature has placed mankind under the governance of two sovereign masters, pain and pleasure. It is for them alone to point out what we ought to do, as well as to determine what we shall do."[2] Cusanus would object that nature so understood does not and should not govern us: our intellect bids us rise above our animal being, and

---

1. Aquinas, *ST* I, q. 81, a. 1.

2. Jeremy Bentham, *The Principles of Morals and Legislation* (Amherst, N.Y.: Prometheus, 1988), 1.

our reason allows us to check the rule of Bentham's two sovereign masters. Cusanus sums up his ethical position in a few lines:

> But supraexcellent reason contains—in its own nature and as a result of its capability of participating in the intellectual nature—certain laws through which, as ruler over desire's passions, it tempers and calms the passions, in order that a human being will not make a goal of perceptible things and be deprived of his intellect's spiritual desire. And the most important of [these] laws are that no one do to another what he would not want done to himself, that eternal things be preferred to temporal things, and clean and holy things to unclean and base things. The laws which are elicited from reason by the most holy lawgivers and are taught (according to the difference of place and time) as remedies for those who sin against reason work together to the foregoing end. (*DI* III.6:216)

Cusanus points out that the laws that should rule our actions have their foundation in what he calls supraexcellent reason, reason that, by its tie to the intellect, is raised above "the temporal and mundane" (*DI* III.6:215). Kant's pure practical reason comes to mind. These laws are universal, although, as Cusanus recognizes, they have been refracted by differences of time and place.

In the cited passage Cusanus names three of these laws—in first place, what Anglican theologians much later were to call the golden rule. Jesus reaffirmed it in the Sermon on the Mount: "So whatever you wish that men would do to you, do so to them; for this is the law and the prophets" (Mt 7:12).[3] Cusanus speaks of the law that "no one do to another what he would not want done to himself" and claims that it is founded in reason enlightened by the intellect. It does not depend on a special revelation. It is thus not confined to the Christian or the Western tradition, but, as Cusanus recognizes, found all over the world, if shaped by regional differences.

Jasper Hopkins calls our attention to the fact that Cusanus formulates the rule negatively: "He thereby tacitly implies that the New Testament formulation surpasses the natural law."[4] But the New Testament is hardly unique in formulating the rule positively. Both positive and negative formulations are found in many different religions. I do not see why Cusanus should have thought that the New Testament formulation surpasses the natural law. Does Jesus not present it as a reaffirmation of the law and the teachings of the prophets? In the

---

3. See also Luke 6:31: "And as you wish that men would do to you, do so to them."
4. Hopkins, *Nicholas of Cusa on Learned Ignorance*, 202n63.

III. CHRIST'S BIRTH, DEATH, AND RESURRECTION

Compendium Cusanus will indeed cite the positive formulation as an example of what we human beings recognize by nature (*naturaliter*) (*Com.* X.34).

In keeping with the doctrine of the fall, Cusanus takes human being to be marked by a profound lack. Our animal nature is said to deprive us from the enjoyment of the most excellent good, which is intellectual and eternal:

> Even if the senses were subject to reason in every respect and did not follow after the passions which are natural to them, the intellect— soaring higher [than reason]—sees that nonetheless man cannot of himself attain to the goal of his intellectual and eternal desires. (*DI* III.6:217)

Our intellect desires more. That is to say, a life ruled by reason alone— think of a Kantian ethic—finally leaves us dissatisfied.

But even the demand of the conditional, "if the senses were subject to reason in every respect," cannot be met by us mortals.

> For since from the seed of Adam man is begotten with carnal delight (in whom, in accordance with propagation, the animality prevails over the spirituality): his nature—which in its basis of origin is immersed in the carnal delights through which the man springs forth into existence by way of a father—remains altogether unable to transcend temporal things in order to embrace spiritual things. Accordingly, if the weight of carnal delights draws reason and intellect downward, so that they consent to these motions and do not resist them, it is clear that a man so drawn downward and so turned away from God is altogether deprived of the enjoyment of the most excellent good, which, in the manner of the intellectual, is upward and eternal. But if reason governs the senses, still it is necessary that the intellect govern reason in order that the intellect may adhere— by formed faith and above reason—to the Mediator, so that it can be drawn unto glory by God the Father. (*DI* III.217)

In keeping with tradition, Cusanus invokes the doctrine of the fall. But that doctrine is not needed to make sense of what he has to say here about the human condition. We cannot deny our animal desires, even as we may attempt to do our best to live a life of reason. We may pay lip service to the golden rule, but our actions will show that we lack the strength to live up to it. Kantian morality remains an ideal we daily betray in our behavior. And the same goes for the utilitarian commandment that we serve the greatest good of the greatest number, a commandment difficult to reconcile with Bentham's principle of utility cited earlier, which would have us place personal above public interest.

But even if we were able to live a life ruled by reason, reason by itself would still not be able to overcome that lack that is bound up with our mortal animal being. We know that someday all that we are and can accomplish will be past, gone like smoke. And as we must perish, so must humanity, so must this earth. Time denies us what we so deeply desire: to be in a way that will not be overtaken by time. This "ill will against time," as Nietzsche was to call it, is at the very center of the Platonic tradition and more specifically of its conception of eros that seeks a plenitude incompatible with our temporal condition. But what will banish the terror of time? What will take away the sting of death?

Christ alone, both man and God, is said by Cusanus to have been exempt from the lack constitutive of fallen humanity. In Christ human nature was able to return to God the Father of its own power. Our true homecoming is said to be possible only through faith in Christ, faith in what reason is unable to comprehend and must indeed judge impossible. But to have become learned about our ignorance is to have recognized that our reason, subject to the principle of non-contradiction, is unable to comprehend reality as it is in itself. That opens a door to faith. But it does no more than that: faith cannot be willed. It must come through that door from without. The cause of faith cannot be found within the individual. Cusanus is in agreement with Thomas Aquinas:

> The Pelagians held that this cause [of faith] was nothing else than man's free choice, and consequently they said that the beginning of faith is from ourselves, inasmuch as, namely, it is in our power to be ready to assent to the things which are of faith, but the consummation of faith is from God Who proposes to us the things we have to believe. But this is false, for since, by assenting to what belongs to faith, man is raised above his nature, this must need come to him from some supernatural principle moving him inwardly, and this is God. Therefore faith, as regards the ascent which is the chief act of faith, is from God moving man inwardly by grace.[5]

Cusanus speaks of "formed faith" (*fides formata*), faith formed and perfected by love," working through love to create good works.[6] Such faith requires a power over oneself that cannot be willed, that can only come to us through grace.

> Except for Christ Jesus, who descended from Heaven, there was never anyone who had [enough] power over himself and over his own

---

5. Thomas Aquinas, *ST* II-II, q. 4, a. 1, reply.
6. Gal 5:6. See also Thomas Aquinas, *ST* II-II, q. 4, a. 4.

III. CHRIST'S BIRTH, DEATH, AND RESURRECTION

> nature (which in its origin is so subject to the sins of carnal desire) to
> be able, of himself, to ascend beyond his own origin to eternal and
> heavenly things. Jesus is the one who ascended by His own power
> and in whom the human nature (begotten not from the will of the
> flesh but from God) was not hindered from mightily returning to
> God the Father. (DI III.6:218)

Unable to save ourselves, we mortals require a savior, as St. Anselm
explained in *Cur Deus Homo?*, in keeping with a long tradition.[7] This
is why God became man.[8] Cusanus appropriates that answer.

> But Christ the Lord willed to mortify completely—and in mortifying
> to purge—by means of His own human body all the sins of human
> nature which draw us toward earthly things. [He did this] not for
> His own sake (since He had committed no sin) but for our sakes, so
> that all men, of the same humanity with Him, would find in Him the
> complete purgation of their sins. The man Christ's voluntary and
> most innocent, most shameful, and most cruel death on the Cross
> was the deletion and purgation of, and the satisfaction for, all the
> carnal desires of human nature. (*DI* III.6:218)

Christ is that one human being whose self-control was such that carnal desires had no power over him. To speak of "satisfaction" here is
to suggest that just by our carnal desires we human beings are indebted to God. Anselm likens man to a most perfect pearl, God's most
precious possession, which we soiled with Adam's fall to which we
all remain subject and soil further with every sin. To render God the
satisfaction we owe him, we would have to cleanse ourselves, but we
lack the power to do so. Not so Christ: his voluntary death undoes the
consequences of Adam's fall.

> Whatever humanly can be done counter to the love for a neighbor
> is abundantly made up for in the fullness of Christ's love, by which
> He delivered Himself unto death even on behalf of His enemies.
> Therefore, the humanity in Christ Jesus made up for all the defects
> of all men. For since it is maximum [humanity], it encompasses the
> complete possibility of the species, so that it is such equality-of-being
> with each man that it is united to each man much more closely than
> is a brother or a very special friend. For the maximality of human
> nature brings it about that in the case of each man who cleaves to
> Christ through formed faith Christ is this very man by means of a

---

7. For a detailed discussion of Anselm's influence on Cusanus's theory of atonement, see Hopkins, "Nicholas of Cusa's Intellectual Relationship to Anselm of Canterbury," 61–67.

8. Cf. Anselm, *Cur deus homo? Complete Philosophical and Theological Treatises of Anselm of Canterbury*, trans. Jasper Hopkins and Herbert Richardson (Minneapolis: Arthur J. Banning, 2000), 295–389.

> most perfect union—each's numerical distinctness being preserved.
> (*DI* III.6:219)

How are we to understand that an individual "who cleaves to Christ through formed faith" becomes Christ, even while "each's numerical distinctness being preserved"? The humanity of Christ is said to be maximum humanity. He embodies the perfection of the human species. Cleaving to Christ we cleave to that perfection. But have we not substituted for the living Christ an abstract ideal?

The difficulty we have thinking the union of a person who cleaves to Christ with Christ while preserving numerical distinctness seems analogous to the difficulty we have understanding how the persons of the Trinity are yet one God. But is that analogy at all appropriate? Does it not elide the unbridgeable abyss that separates us finite human beings from God? That Johannes Wenck should have considered what Cusanus here has to say "poisonous" [*IL* 39] is not surprising. Wenck objects particularly to the way Cusanus moves from the individual Christ to his maximal humanity. Cusanus seems to suggest that the union of the believer with Christ is to be understood as being like the union of the individual with his species, with his humanity, in the case of the believer, with Christ's perfect or maximal humanity. But the union of the individual with his species does not imply personal immortality. And does what Cusanus has to say not destroy, Wenck objects, "the individuality of Christ's humanity," making Christ into "universal man" [*IL* 39]?

Cusanus dismisses this and similar challenges by Wenck to his understanding of Jesus. Wenck is said to belong with those who have not become learned about their ignorance. Cusanus admits that what he has written cannot do justice to the mystery of the Word become flesh but adds that this must be said of all writings about him, no matter how excellent, where Cusanus mentions in the first place John the Evangelist [*AP* 34]. The union of the faithful with Christ remains as incomprehensible as the Incarnation.

> Because of this union the following statement of Christ's is true: "Whatever you have done to one of the least of my [brethren], you have done to me." And, conversely, whatever Christ Jesus merited by His suffering, those who are one with Him also merited—different degrees of merit being preserved in accordance with the different degree of each [man's] union with Christ through faith formed by love. Hence, in Christ the faithful are circumcised; in Him they are baptized; in Him they die; in Him they are made alive again through resurrection; in Him they are united to God and are glorified. (*DI* III.6:219)

CHAPTER 7

The Mystery of the Resurrection

Having discussed the mysteries of Christmas and Good Friday in the preceding two chapters, in this chapter Cusanus is concerned with the mystery of Easter, with the necessity of Christ's death and resurrection. In the preceding chapter we saw Cusanus giving the traditional answer to the question, "Why did God become man?" But this does not yet answer the question, "Why did he have to suffer death, and not just death, but such a particularly painful and shameful death?" How can, or rather, why must this ultimate negativity be included in our understanding of Christ's perfect humanity? And since, like the Father, the Son, too, is God, how is this negativity to be reconciled with an understanding of God as perfect, good, and all powerful? It would seem that, if we accept Cusanus's understanding of the Trinity, such negativity cannot be separated from God's very essence any more than can Christ's humanity. But does this make sense?

In *Cur Deus Homo?* Anselm has his Boso give voice to objections that the infidels raise against the Christian salvation account, which they find unreasonable:

> What especially astounds unbelievers is that we call this liberation redemption. Indeed, they ask: "In what captivity, in which prison, or in whose power were you being held from which God could free you only by redeeming you through so much effort and, in the end, through His own blood?" We answer: He has redeemed us from sins

and from His own wrath and from Hell and from the power of the Devil, whom He came to vanquish on our behalf because we ourselves were unable to conquer him; moreover, He has bought back the Kingdom of Heaven for us. And because He has done all these things in this way, He has manifested how much He loves us.

But when [we make this reply] to them, they retort:

If you maintain that God, whom you say created all things by His command, was unable solely by His command, to do all the things [you have just mentioned], then you contradict yourselves, because you make Him powerless. On the other hand, if you say that He was able [to do these things solely by His command] but willed [to do them] only in the foregoing manner, then how can you show to be wise Him who you claim willed to suffer so many unbecoming things for no reason at all? For all the things which you set forth depend upon His will. For example, God's wrath is nothing other than His will-to-punish.[1]

Anselm's answer, "When God does some thing, then even though we do not see why He wills [to do it], His will ought to suffice us as a reason. For the will of God is never unreasonable,"[2] does not satisfy Boso. Nor does Anselm's statement, "And if the Son is correctly said not to have spared Himself but to have delivered Himself up willingly for us, who would deny it to be correctly said that the Father, from whom the Son possessed such a willingness, did not spare the Son but delivered Him up for us and willed His death?"[3] But why could God not have saved man in some other way? Why did he allow the snake to enter paradise and Adam to fall in the first place?

A nonbeliever may want to grant that the biblical account of fallen humanity well describes the human condition. Cusanus, as we have seen agrees with this. And he also agrees with Anselm that the happiness we mortals seek requires the remission of sin and that it cannot be attained, given our fallen condition. "Therefore, let us suppose the incarnation of God and the things we say about *that* man never occurred. And let us agree that (1) man was created for happiness, which cannot be possessed in this life, that (2) no one can attain happiness unless his sins have been forgiven, and that (3) no man passes through this present life without sin. And let us agree about the other things with respect to which faith is necessary for eternal salvation."[4] The happiness we mortals most deeply desire, Anselm and Cusanus

---

1. Anselm, *Cur Deus Homo*, book I, chapter 6, 305–6.
2. Anselm, *Cur Deus Homo*, book I, chapter 8, 309.
3. Anselm, *Cur Deus Homo*, book I, chapter 10, 315–16.
4. Anselm, *Cur Deus Homo*, book I, chapter 10, 318.

III. CHRIST'S BIRTH, DEATH, AND RESURRECTION

agree, we cannot gain by our own effort. It is denied to us by our temporal condition. To gain it requires an overcoming of that condition. But would such an overcoming not mean death? This is not to say that the rational nonbeliever might not agree with Anselm and Cusanus that the happiness we seek is denied to us by our temporal condition. But he might conclude with Sartre that what we most profoundly desire is denied to us.

A brief look at Kant's *Critique of Practical Reason* shows that the problem with which Cusanus here wrestles possesses a timeless significance. Kant, too, takes the desire for happiness (*Glückseligkeit*) to be constitutive of our human being.

> The realization of the highest good in the world is the necessary object of a will determinable by the moral law. But in this will the *perfect accordance* of the mind with the moral law is the supreme condition of the highest good. This then must be possible, as well as its object, since it is contained in the command to promote the latter. Now, the perfect accordance of the will with the moral law is *holiness*, a perfection of which no rational being of the sensible world is capable at any moment of his existence. Since, nevertheless, it is required as practically necessary, it can only be found in a *progress in infinitum* toward that perfect accordance, and on the principles of pure practical reason it is necessary to assume such a practical progress as the real object of our will.
>
> Now, this endless progress is only possible on the supposition of an *infinite* duration of the *existence* and personality of the same rational being (which is called the immortality of the soul). The highest good, then, practically is only possible on the supposition of the immortality of the soul; consequently, this immortality, being inseparably connected with the moral law, is a *postulate* of pure practical reason (by which I mean a *theoretical* proposition, not demonstrable as such, but that is an inseparable result of an unconditional a priori *practical* law).[5]

With much of this Cusanus could have agreed: He too takes the desire for happiness to be part of the human condition; he takes a moral life to be a necessary condition for the attainment of true happiness. He could have agreed with Kant that "the immortality of the soul is a postulate of pure practical reason."[6] He, too could say that

---

5. Immanuel Kant, *Kritik der praktischen Vernunft*, trans. Thomas Kingsmill Abbott, in *Kant's Critique of Practical Reason and Other Works on the Theory of Ethics*, 4th rev. ed. (London: Longman, Green, 1889), IV, "The Immortality of the Soul as a Postulate of Pure Practical Reason," A 219–20.

6. Kant, *Kritik der praktischen Vernunft*, A 219.

holiness, "the perfect accordance of the will with the moral law," is an ideal that we children of Adam cannot hope to realize, that it requires an ascent of our human being *in infinitum*. But Cusanus understands Christ to be the perfect human being, happy to grant Kant that such perfection can be thought by us only as demanding an infinite ascent. That is precisely how Cusanus understands maximal humanity. The realization of what Kant calls a postulate of practical reason Cusanus takes to have become reality with Christ: with him we mortals can rise to eternal lie. Our desire for a perfect happiness is not in vain; man is not a useless passion, as Sartre thought.

Cusanus turns to his understanding of the Incarnation to shed some light on the mystery of the Resurrection:

> The man Christ, being passible [able to suffer] and mortal, could attain unto the glory of the Father (who is Immortality itself, since He is Absolute Life) by no other way than [the following]: that what was mortal put on immortality. And this was not at all possible apart from death. For how could what is mortal have put on immortality otherwise than by being stripped of mortality? How would it be free of mortality except by having paid the debt of death? Therefore, Truth itself says that those who do not understand that Christ had to die and in this way enter into glory are foolish and of slow mind. But since I have already indicated that for our sakes Christ died a most cruel death, I must now say the following: since it was not fitting for human nature to be led to the triumph of immortality otherwise than through victory over death, [Christ] underwent death in order that human nature would rise again with him to eternal life and that the animal, mortal body would become spiritual and incorruptible. [Christ] was able to be a true man only if he was mortal; and he was able to lead mortal [human] nature to immortality only if through death human nature became stripped of mortality. (*DI* III.7:221)

Cusanus here stays close to scripture: in his First Letter to the Corinthians St. Paul had written:

> When the perishable puts on the imperishable, and the mortal puts on immortality, then shall come to pass the saying that is written:
>
> > "Death is swallowed up in victory?"
> > "O death, where is thy victory?
> > O death, where is thy sting?"
> >
> > (1 Cor 15:54–53)

III. CHRIST'S BIRTH, DEATH, AND RESURRECTION

The dead shall be raised, Paul preaches, as Christ has been raised from the dead. That Christ was indeed raised from the dead Paul accepts as a fact, supported by many witnesses, most of whom are said by him to have then been still alive. Cusanus, too, accepts this as historical reality. Had Christ himself not called those who did not believe that he had risen from the dead "foolish" and "slow of heart" (Luke 24, 25)? And is Christ, the divine Word, not the Truth, as Cusanus paraphrases Luke? But this truth our human reason cannot comprehend. In Christ the abyss that separates Creator and creature is mysteriously bridged, but the nature of this bridging exceeds the reach of our reason.

In speaking about Christ, there is an inevitable, but incomprehensible fusion of the very different ways we speak about his human and divine nature. Given the union of Christ's human and divine nature, the divine nature has also human characteristics just as the human nature has also divine characteristics, and this reflects itself in the ways we speak about both, speech in which we allow human and divine things to coincide, knowing that such speech transcends what reason can grasp. But the intellect finds in such speech pointers to the mystery of the resurrection.

> In what precedes I indicated that the maximum man, Jesus, was not able to have in Himself a person that existed separately from the divinity. For He is the maximum [human being]. And, accordingly, there is a sharing of the respective modes of speaking [about the human nature and the divine nature], so that the human things coincide with the divine things; for His humanity—which on account of the supreme union is inseparable from His divinity (as if it were put on and assumed by the divinity [*quasi per divinitatem induta et assumpta*]—cannot exist as separate in person. (*DI* III.7:223)

Following the Athanasian Creed, Cusanus insists on the hypostatic union of Christ's human and divine nature. That explains why in speaking of Christ our words will oscillate and blur the distinction between the human and the divine. The explanatory *quasi per divinitatem induta et assumpta* weakens, however, Cusanus's insistence that Christ's humanity and divinity cannot exist as separate in person in that it invites us to think of Christ's humanity as being somewhat like a garment put on by God or as something taken up by God, inviting thoughts of the mortal Jesus and the divine Word as distinct persons, a position declared heretical by the Council of Chalcedon (451 A.D.), which proclaimed that the selfsame Christ is both man and God[7]—

---

7. *PTW* I.III.126n2s25, 4–6.

that is, is one "person," as, following Tertullian, Boethius understood the term: "an individual substance of a rational nature."[8] Notwithstanding the aforementioned formulation, Cusanus accepts the orthodox understanding of the Incarnation, as explained at length by Thomas Aquinas.[9] The human Jesus is not just a mask assumed by the divine Word. Christ does have two separate natures, one human and the other divine, but in him the two coincide so that there remains one person, as in God the persons of the Trinity coincide, retaining, however, their separate natures. As a human being Jesus must die. As the Word he transcends time. With Johannes Hoff, who here draws on Rowan Williams's *Christ, the Heart of Creation* (2018), we can speak here of "two perspectives on the unique ('hypostatic') being of Jesus Christ. The first perspective focuses on the encounter with Jesus in the history of salvation, the second on Christs atemporal, intra-Trinitarian being."[10] But, as Hoff points out, it is difficult to make sense of this attempt "to secure the asymmetry between creator and creature, in accordance with the teaching of Christian orthodoxy: God is inherently distinct from his temporal, creaturely manifestations."[11] Consider the crucifixion. Christ's death cannot mean a separation of his divine and his corporeal being. They would violate the proclaimed union of Christ's human and divine nature in one person.

> But a man is a union of a body and a soul—the separation of which is death. Therefore, because the maximum humanity is subsumed in the divine person: at the time of [Jesus's] death neither the soul nor the body could have been separated (not even with respect to spatial separation) from the divine person, without which the man [Jesus] did not exist. (*DI* III.7:223)

This seems to assert that, since the mortal Jesus existed in essential unity with the divine person, he could not really die. But what sense are we to make then of his death on the cross?

> Therefore, Christ did not die as if His person had forsaken Him; rather He remained hypostatically united with the divinity—there not being even spatial separation with regard to the [personal] center, in which the humanity was subsumed. (But in accordance with the

---

8. Boethius, *De persona et duabus naturis*, chapter 3, Patrologia Latina, ed. J. Migne (Paris: Migne, 1878–90), 64:1345.

9. Thomas Aquinas, *ST* III, q. 32, a. 2.

10. Johannes Hoff, "Ontology after the God Delusion: The Performative Sources of Nicholas of Cusa's Trinitarian 'Definition of All Things,'" 6, https://www.academia.edu/40401311/Ontology_After_the_God_Delusion_The_Performative_Sources_of_Nicholas_of_Cusas_Trinitarian_Definition_of_All_Things_.

11. Hoff, "Ontology after the God Delusion."

III. CHRIST'S BIRTH, DEATH, AND RESURRECTION

> lower nature—which in conformity with the truth of its own nature was able to undergo a separation of the soul from the body—a separation was made temporally and spatially, so that at the hour of death the soul and the body were not together at the same place and at the same time.) Therefore, in His body and soul no corruptibility was possible, since they were united with eternity. (*DI* III.7:224)

Cusanus distinguishes here between Christ's lower nature, sharing with all human beings their subjection to time and their mortality, and his divinity. The mortal Jesus died on the Cross. But not the person: as the human maximum Jesus Christ transcended time. The human being is body and soul: we cannot separate the soul from the body and retain a robust sense of self. As the human maximum Christ is the perfection of our embodied being, "the truth of the humanity that is beyond time." In Christ so understood, body and soul, too, transcend time and remained united, even as Christ died on the cross, and, as far as his lower nature is concerned, soul and body were separated.

To take that thought at all seriously requires learned ignorance—that is, the acceptance of the coincidence of opposites, which, as the discussion of the Trinity showed, preserves both distinctness and unity. The acceptance of that thought's truth requires faith. Hoff thus suggests that "the 'singularity' of created entities has a theophanic character that transcends the horizon of rational representations." For the believer Jesus is the most striking example. Cusanus, he suggests, would have sympathized with Ludwig Wittgenstein's mantra, "Don't think, but look!"[12] Considering the historical Jesus the believer sees in him the unity of the human and the divine.

Cusanus takes Christ to be the timeless truth of humanity. If we are to make any sense of the saving power of Christ's resurrection, we must keep in mind the transfiguration of Christ's body.

> But the temporal birth was subject to death and temporal separation, so that when the circle of return (from temporal composition to dissolution) was completed and when, furthermore, the body was freed from these temporal motions, the truth of the humanity that is beyond time and that, as united to the divinity, remained undestroyed united (as its truth required) the truth of the body with the truth of the soul. Thus, when the shadowy image of the truth of the man who appeared in time departed, the true man arose, free from all temporal passion. Hence, the same Jesus most truly arose above

---

12. Hoff, "Ontology after the God Delusion," 10.

> all temporal motions (through a union of soul to body—[a union]
> beyond all temporal motion) and was never again going to die. With-
> out this union the truth of the incorruptible humanity would not
> have been unconfusedly and most truly united hypostatically with
> the nature of the divine person. (*DI* III.7:215)

Much here recalls Plato. Just as Plato might call some actually existing tree the shadow image of the true tree—that is, the Platonic form— the mortal Jesus is described here as the shadowy image of the true Jesus. The linear development of Christ's life from birth to death is interpreted as a circle that returns to its timeless divine origin. Are we then to understand our own lives, too, as just shadowy images of our true timeless selves?

To help us understand these difficult matters, Cusanus presents us with an interpretation of the parable of the kernel of wheat, which Jesus offered to point to the significance of his imminent death: "The hour has come for the Son of Man to be glorified. Very truly I tell you, unless a kernel of wheat falls to the ground and dies, it remains only a single seed. But if it dies, it produces many seeds" (Jn 12:23–24).

> Assist your smallness of intellect and your ignorance by Christ's ex-
> ample about the grain of wheat. In this example the numerical dis-
> tinctness of the grain is destroyed, while the specific essence remains
> intact; by this means nature raises up many grains. But if the grain
> were maximum and most perfect, then when it died in very good
> and very fertile soil, it could bring forth fruit not only one hundred-
> fold or one thousandfold but as manifold as the nature of the spe-
> cies encompassed in its possibility. This is what Truth means [when it
> says] that [the grain] would bring forth much fruit; for a multitude
> is a limitedness without number. (*DI* III.225)

Falling on fertile ground a grain of wheat, though dying, will gener-ate new grains. Were this a most perfect grain, it would yield a bound-less harvest. Question provoking, however, is the way Cusanus invokes "the nature of the species." The perfect dying grain stands here for Christ in whom all that is possible in the nature of the human species is enfolded. But here there is no suggestion of a personal resurrec-tion. What survives is the nature of the species unfolded in countless individuals that bear Christ's image.

The following explanation does not really put such concerns to rest:

> Therefore, discern keenly: with respect to the fact that the humanity
> of Jesus is considered as contracted to the man Christ, it is likewise

III. CHRIST'S BIRTH, DEATH, AND RESURRECTION

understood to be united also with his divinity. As united with the divinity, [the humanity] is fully absolute; [but] as it is considered to be that true man Christ, [the humanity] is contracted, so that Christ is a man through the humanity. And so, Jesus's humanity is as a medium between what is purely absolute and what is purely contracted. Accordingly, then, it was corruptible only in a given respect; but absolutely it was incorruptible. Therefore, it was corruptible according to temporality, to which it was contracted; but in accordance with the fact that it was free from time, beyond time, and united with the divinity, it was incorruptible. (*DI* III.7:225)

Johannes Wenck's objection cannot surprise:

This corollary is altogether noxious in itself because it destroys [the doctrine of] the true humanity of Christ. For if in accordance with His humanity the man Christ had a soul and human flesh (as the Athanasian Creed states), then how can the humanity of Christ be fully absolute? Nor does the supporting reason remain standing, because the humanity-of-Christ which was assumed by the Word was not free from time. For (by the testimony of the apostle) "when the fullness of time was come," Christ was sent. Therefore, His humanity was not free from time. Nor was it above time and incorruptible absolutely; for in that case Christ would not have been truly dead. Moreover, in such a supporting reason [this author] denies the truth of Christ's body and denies the resurrection of His body—[denies them] by universalizing Christ's humanity. (This universalization was fallaciously suggested to him by his own abstract understanding.) In this way he deprives us of the freely given benefits of Christ which are most graciously exhibited to us in Christ's temporal humanity. (*IL* 39–40).

Wenck accuses Cusanus of universalizing Christ's humanity. How does Cusanus understand the Resurrection? Is it Christ's concrete body that is resurrected? How are we to understand "the truth of the body"? Cusanus speaks of the body "freed from … temporal motions" (*DI* III.7:225). But what sense does this make, unless we speak of the essential body, but is that not a product of our abstract understanding?

In his *Defense of Learned Ignorance* Cusanus does not attempt to answer Wenck's objection. It is just one of many objections raised by Wenck against Book Three that Cusanus "does not care to comment on," scorning the ignorance of his adversary (*AP* 33). That is unfortunate. Wenck's charge that Cusanus universalizes Christ's humanity deserves serious consideration. We are left to wonder about Cusanus's understanding of human immortality. How does it relate to Plato's understanding of the immortality of Socrates? Is the living Socrates but an image of the timeless, essential Socrates? Is the mortal Jesus but an image of the essential Jesus?

> But truth, as temporally contracted, is a "sign" and an "image," so to speak, of supratemporal truth. Thus, the temporally contracted truth of the body is "shadow," so to speak, of the supratemporal truth of the body. So, too, the [temporally] contracted truth of the soul is, as it were, a "shadow" of the soul which is free from time. For when the soul is in time, where it does not apprehend without images, it seems to be the senses or reason rather than the intellect; and when it is elevated above time it is the intellect which is free from images. (*DI* III.7:226)

Cusanus can cite Paul's Letter to the Corinthians to support his talk of "the supratemporal truth of the body": "So is it with the resurrection of the dead. What is sown is perishable; what is raised is imperishable. It is sown in dishonor; it is raised in glory. It is sown in weakness; it is raised in power. It is sown a natural body; it is raised a spiritual body. If there is a natural body, there is also a spiritual body" (1 Cor 42–44). But how we are to think "the supratemporal truth" of the body remains a mystery? Are we to understand the body of the resurrected Christ, as he showed himself to the apostles, as still only a shadow of the supratemporal truth of the body? The very meaning of "body" seems tied to matter and time. A "timeless body" seems an oxymoron. But, as we have seen, unlike our reason, our intellect, according to Cusanus, is able to rise above all images and is not bound by the principle of non-contradiction.

The conclusion of this chapter brings out once more the paradoxical nature of Christ's resurrection:

> And since the humanity was inseparably rooted on high in the divine incorruptibility: when the temporal, corruptible motion was completed, the dissolution could occur only in the direction of the root of its incorruptibility. Therefore, after the end of temporal motion ([an end] which was death) and after the removal of all the things which temporally befell the truth of the human nature, the same Jesus arose—not with a body which was burdensome, corruptible, shadowy, passible (and so on for the other things which follow upon temporal composition) but with a true body which was glorious, impassible, unhindered, and immortal (as the truth which was free from temporal conditions required). Moreover, the truth of the hypostatic union of the human nature with the divine nature

III. CHRIST'S BIRTH, DEATH, AND RESURRECTION

necessarily required this union [of body and soul]. Hence, Blessed Jesus had to arise from the dead, as He Himself says when He states: "Christ had to suffer in this way and to arise from the dead on the third day" (Lk 24:46). (*DI* III.7:226)

By affirming his death, by sacrificing himself for our sake, Christ is said to have conquered death and stripped human nature of mortality. That self-sacrifice for the sake of humanity is the gate to true life is a theme that has a long history. Think of the *Symposium*, where Alcestis is rewarded with true life for her willingness to die for her husband! Or of the death of Socrates!

Christ, the Firstfruits of Those Who Sleep, Ascended to Heaven

Turning to Christ's Ascension, chapter 8 continues the discussion.

> Now that the foregoing points have been exhibited, it is easy to see that Christ is the Firstborn from the dead (Col 1:18). For before Him no one was able to arise [from the dead]—since human nature had not yet, in the course of time, reached a maximum and was not yet united with incorruptibility and immortality, as it was in Christ. For all human beings were powerless until the coming of Him who said: "I have the power to lay down my life and the power to take it up again" (Jn 10:18). Therefore, in Christ, who is the Firstfruits of those who sleep (1 Cor 15:20, 23), human nature put on immortality. But there is only one indivisible humanity and specific essence of all human beings. Through it all individual human beings are numerically distinct human beings, so that Christ and all human beings have the same humanity, though the numerical distinctness of the individuals remains unconfused. Hence, it is evident that the humanity of all the human beings who—whether temporally before or after Christ—either have existed or will exist has, in Christ, put on immortality. Therefore, it is evident that the following inference holds: the man Christ arose; hence, after [the cessation of] all motion of temporal corruptibility, all men will arise through Him, so that they will be eternally incorruptible. (*DI* III.227)

III. CHRIST'S BIRTH, DEATH, AND RESURRECTION

Once again Cusanus relies on scripture. Of special importance is the Gospel According to John:

> For this reason the Father loves me because I lay down my life, that I may take it again. No one takes it from me, but I lay it down of my own accord. I have power to lay it down, and I have power to take it again; this charge I have received from my Father. (Jn 10:17–18)

Christ here states clearly that his death is in his power. The crucifixion was something he chose to suffer for the sake of humanity, not something forced upon him by the Father. The latter would indeed be incompatible with the orthodox understanding of the Trinity. "I and the Father are one," Christ proclaims a bit later (Jn 10:30), provoking the Jews who hear him to want to stone him "for blasphemy: because you, being a man, make yourself God" (Jn 10:33).

As Cusanus understands him, Christ changed the very meaning of humanity. All human beings, Cusanus insists, share one indivisible humanity. But Christ is a human being. With Christ humanity comes to signify not mortality, but immortality.

> Therefore Christ is the one through whom according to the nature of his humanity, our human nature has contracted immortality and through whom, as well we (who were born altogether subject to motion) will (when motion ceases) rise beyond time and unto a likeness of Him. This will occur at the end of time. (*DI* III.228)

Cusanus is here referring to Paul's First Letter to the Corinthians:

> The first man was from the earth, so are those who are of the dust; and as is the man of heaven, so are those who are of heaven. I tell you this, brethren: flesh and blood cannot inherit the kingdom of God, nor does the perishable inherit the imperishable. (1 Cor 15:47–50)

Since our sense of who we are is so intimately tied to our body and thus to temporality, it is impossible to understand how the individual will be transfigured into a likeness of Christ at the end of time. For our time-bound self-understanding the promised immortality remains an unintelligible mystery. What sense can we make of human nature rising beyond time when all motion ceases? Cusanus has shown that there is a sense in which our intellect allows us to transcend time. But this self-transcendence does not furnish us with a sense of self that is not dependent on time. The resurrection remains a mystery. Cusanus would no doubt grant this, but remind us that once we have become learned about our ignorance we will have come to understand that what our reason finds intelligible does not circumscribe reality.

In Sermon XXII, *Dies Sanctificatus*, Cusanus finds the following words for the immortality of the soul: "Christ Jesus the human nature, qua exalted unto the Divinity, is the perfection of the universe and, especially, is the perfection of our human nature. For in that [Christ's human nature] reaches the highest gradation of human nature, than which there is no higher gradation, it enfolds every other [human] nature. And it unifies all the things that are subject to the nature, transforming them into Christ" (*Sermo* XXII.36). That suggests that all human beings are enfolded into Christ's humanity and indeed transformed into Christ. Cusanus bids his listeners "take note of the fact that Christ coincides with the nature of humanity, through which all men are men" (*Sermo* XXII.37).

Wenck objects that Cusanus understands the union of human beings with Christ, which is yet said to preserve the distinct individuality of each human being, in a way that is appropriate only when speaking of the union of Christ's humanity and his divinity: "Only to the Divine Nature is it befitting to be multiplied hypostatically, or personally, in identity of nature" (*IL* 40). The objection deserves a thoughtful answer. Cusanus, to be sure, does not bother to answer such objections made by someone who has not become learned about sacred ignorance: we should not attempt to comprehend what by its very nature must remain a mystery.

That the maximum and most perfect man Christ has to be identified with God, as Christ himself proclaims, follows from Cusanus's understanding of maximal humanity. Cusanus criticizes the Saracens for not recognizing this.

> If I am not mistaken, you see that [a religion] which does not embrace Christ is not a perfect religion, leading men to the final and most coveted goal of peace. Think of how discordant is the belief of the Saracens, who (1) affirm that Christ is the maximum and most perfect man, born of a virgin and translated alive into Heaven but (2) deny that He is God. Surely they have been blinded, because they assert what is impossible. But even from the points stated in the foregoing manner one who has understanding can see, clearer than day, that a man who is not also God cannot be maximum and in all respects most perfect, supernaturally born of a virgin. These [Saracens] are mindless persecutors of the Cross of Christ, being ignorant of His mysteries. They will not taste the divine fruit of His redemption, nor are they led to expect it by their law of Mohammed, which promises only to satisfy their cravings for pleasure. In the hope that these cravings are extinguished in us by the death of Christ, we yearn to apprehend an incorruptible glory. (*DI* III.229)

III. CHRIST'S BIRTH, DEATH, AND RESURRECTION

That Cusanus should have felt a need to contrast Christian belief with the belief of the Saracens is not surprising, given that Islam was then challenging Christianity not just spiritually, but militarily, the Ottomans threatening to seize Constantinople, the Eastern Rome, as indeed they were to do just a few years later. Ever concerned to strengthen the unity of humanity, Cusanus was eager to find commonalities between Christianity and Islam and reasons that might not only convince followers of Mohammed that they and Christians believed in the same God, but also would persuade them of the superiority of the Christian faith.

Cusanus's claim that the Koran affirmed that Christ is the maximum and most perfect man, born of a virgin and translated alive into Heaven, is based on his careful reading of the book, which he owned in the rather loose Latin translation by Robert of Ketton, *Lex Mahumet pseudoprophete* (1143), which he obtained while in Basel, as he tells us in the Prologue to his *Cribatio Alkorani*.[1] That already at the time of the Council of Basel he should have been concerned with Islam is not surprising, given that it was the threat posed by the Ottomans to the Byzantine Empire that had made the Eastern church receptive to the idea of reuniting the church. Islam was thus a topic of concern. In John of Segovia, who represented the University of Salamanca at the Council, Cusanus found someone able to discuss what separated the Koran from the Bible with some authority.[2] It was to him that he entrusted his treasured copy of the Koran when he left for Constantinople. In Constantinople that interest intensified. There he found discussion partners able to throw more light on the relationship of Islam to Christianity.

Not surprisingly, Cusanus was struck by the passages in the Koran that speak of the Virgin birth of Jesus and of his bodily ascent to Heaven. The Koran, too, thus affirms the uniqueness of Jesus.[3] Reason must declare both impossible. And yet, like the Bible, the Koran,

---

1. Jasper Hopkins, *Nicholas of Cusa's De Pace Fidei and Cribatio Alkorani*, translation and analysis, 2nd ed. (Minneapolis, Banning, 1994), *Cribatio Alkorani*, Prologue, 965.

2. John of Segovia (c. 1395–May 24, 1458) had come to the Council of Basel as a supporter of the pope, but soon was to become one of the most eloquent defenders of the conciliarist position, to which he remained faithful for the rest of his life. Their shared interest in Islam would seem to have brought Cusanus and John of Segovia together in Basel, and after their opposed positions on the authority of the council estranged them, "their common views on Islam kept their friendship from disintegrating"; James E. Biechler, "A New Face toward Islam: Nicholas of Cysa and John of Segovia," in Christianson and Izbicki, *Nicholas of Cusa: In Search of God and Wisdom*, 189.

3. The quotations following are from *The Holy Qur'an*, trans. Abdullah Yusuf Ali, online translation.

too, declared both to have really happened. For Cusanus the only way to make sense of this was to accept that Jesus was the maximum human being: both man and God.

Of special interest is the Koran's version of the Virgin birth. Since most readers of this commentary are unlikely to be familiar with the Koran, I quote the relevant passages at some length:

Surah 19 is dedicated to Mary:

> 16. Relate in the Book (the story of) Mary, when she withdrew from her family to a place in the East.
>
> 17. She placed a screen (to screen herself) from them; then We sent her our angel, and he appeared before her as a man in all respects.
>
> 18. She said: "I seek refuge from thee to (Allah) Most Gracious: (come not near) if thou dost fear Allah."
>
> 19. He said: "Nay, I am only a messenger from thy Lord, (to announce) to thee the gift of a holy son.
>
> 20. She said: "How shall I have a son, seeing that no man has touched me, and I am not unchaste?"
>
> 21. He said: "So (it will be): Thy Lord saith, 'that is easy for Me': and (We wish) to appoint him as a Sign unto men and a Mercy from Us: It is a matter (so) decreed."
>
> 22. So she conceived him, and she retired with him to a remote place.
>
> 27. At length she brought the (babe) to her people, carrying him (in her arms). They said: "O Mary! truly an amazing thing hast thou brought!
>
> 28. "O sister of Aaron! Thy father was not a man of evil, nor thy mother a woman unchaste!"
>
> 29. But she pointed to the babe. They said: "How can we talk to one who is a child in the cradle?"
>
> 30. He said: "I am indeed a servant of Allah. He hath given me revelation and made me a prophet;
>
> 31. "And He hath made me blessed wheresoever I be, and hath enjoined on me Prayer and Charity as long as I live;
>
> 32. "(He) hath made me kind to my mother, and not overbearing or miserable;
>
> 33. "So peace is on me the day I was born, the day that I die, and the day that I shall be raised up to life (again)!"
>
> 34. Such (was) Jesus the son of Mary: (it is) a statement of truth, about which they (vainly) dispute.
>
> 35. It is not befitting to (the majesty of) Allah that He should beget a son. Glory be to Him! when He determines a matter, He only says to it, "Be," and it is.

The Virginity of Mary is extolled also in Surah 21:

> 91. And (remember) her who guarded her chastity: We breathed into her of Our spirit, and We made her and her son a sign for all peoples.

and Surah 66:

> 12. And Mary the daughter of 'Imran, who guarded her chastity; and We breathed into (her body) of Our spirit; and she testified to the truth of the words of her Lord and of His Revelations, and was one of the devout (servants).

The differences between the accounts found in the Gospels and in the Koran are obvious enough. In the later *Cribratio Alkorani* (1460/61), Cusanus was going to discuss them in great detail. Particularly striking is the confused description of Mary's family found in the Koran, for Cusanus sufficient reason to dismiss the claim that it had God for its author:

> The Koran says that the Virgin Mary, the mother of Jesus, was the sister of Aaron and the daughter of Amram. Now, it is most certain that the one who reported these [details] to Muhammad erred and was ignorant of the Gospel's true narrative. For Mary the daughter of Amram and sister of Moses and Aaron was dead and buried in the desert more than a thousand years before [the time of] the Virgin Mary, the glorious mother-of-Jesus-Christ, who lived (as is read in this same Koran) at the time of Zacharias, the father of John the Baptist. (*CA* 981:32)

But even if distorted by faulty sources, the way the Koran stresses the virginity of Mary impressed Cusanus, even though the Koran refuses to call God the father of Jesus. And although the Koran denies that Jesus is the son of God, let alone God, it does assert that Jesus ascended bodily to Heaven.

> Surah 4:156. That they (the Jews) rejected Faith; that they uttered against Mary a grave false charge;
>
> 157. That they said (in boast), "We killed Christ Jesus the son of Mary, the Messenger of Allah;—but they killed him not, nor crucified him, but so it was made to appear to them, and those who differ therein are full of doubts, with no (certain) knowledge, but only conjecture to follow, for of a surety they killed him not:—
>
> 158. Nay, Allah raised him up unto Himself; and Allah is Exalted in Power, Wise;—

The crucifixion is here denied. Allah is said to have deluded the Jews into thinking that Christ Jesus died on the cross. But he did not die, but was bodily raised by Allah unto Himself.

Cusanus had to consider this an appropriation of the Gospel account that missed what was most essential: the redemptive power of Christ's death on the cross and resurrection, inseparable from his divinity; but even through the distorted account we can at least glimpse the truth: The virgin birth and Christ's being raised bodily by Allah unto himself are sufficient to show that Christ was not just another human being. Given the Koran's insistence on the uniqueness of Jesus, which Cusanus, reading his understanding of the human maximum into the Koran, takes to mean insistence on Jesus as the most perfect man, the followers of Mohammed should have recognized that such maximality required that he was God. Should it then not be possible to engage them in discussion so that their eyes would be opened to the truth?

I mentioned the death of Cusanus's teacher and friend Cesarini in the Battle of Varna (1444), which was followed by the fall of Constantinople to the Ottomans in 1453. It must have made the need to engage Islam seem still more pressing to Cusanus. Presumably still in that same year he wrote *De Pace Fidei, On the Peace of Faith*. He imagines a Heavenly symposium, where representatives of different religions, including especially Islam, end up agreeing that they share a single faith manifested in different rites. All religions have glimpsed the truth more or less adequately. The greater adequacy of Christianity is taken for granted, but no religion grasps the truth completely, and no religion misses the truth altogether.

A less irenic and more detailed confrontation with the Koran is found in *Cribatio Alkorani* (1461), dedicated to his friend Pope Pius II, who, as mentioned, was planning a crusade that fizzled in the end; but even here Cusanus takes the Koran to provide us with at least a partial glimpse of the truth.

Cusanus criticizes the Koran for its failure to recognize that the most perfect, maximum man, which, according to Cusanus, the Koran, too, takes Jesus to be, must also be God. Such recognition to be sure presupposes that the authors of the Koran were in a position to share Cusanus's understanding of the Maximum and of Jesus as the maximum man.

An analogous criticism is made of the Jews.

III. CHRIST'S BIRTH, DEATH, AND RESURRECTION

The Jews likewise confess with the Saracens that Messiah is the maximum, most perfect, and immortal man; but, held back by the same diabolical blindness, they deny that He is God. They also do not hope (as do we servants of Christ) to obtain the supreme happiness of enjoying God—even as they also shall not obtain it. And what I deem to be even more remarkable is that the Jews, as well as the Saracens, believe that there will be a general resurrection but do not admit its possibility through the man who is also God. For suppose [the following] be granted: that if the motion of generation and corruption ceases, the perfection of the universe cannot occur apart from resurrection, since human nature (which is an intermediate nature) is an essential part of the universe; and without human nature not only would the universe [not] be perfect but it would not even be a universe. And [suppose it also be granted] that therefore the following is necessary: that if motion ever ceases, either the entire universe will cease or men will rise to incorruptibility. (In these men the nature of all intermediate things is complete, so that the other animals will not have to arise, since man is their perfection.) Or [suppose] the resurrection be said to be going to occur in order that the whole man will receive, from a just God, retribution according to his merits. [Even if all of the foregoing be said], still, above all, Christ—through whom alone human nature can attain unto incorruptibility—must be believed to be God and man. (*DI* III.230)

The confrontation with Islam and Judaism leads Cusanus to reaffirm his conviction that faith in the general resurrection, which both Islam and Judaism suppose to take place at the end of the world, is vain unless such faith is also faith in Jesus Christ as both man and God. We mortal human beings are unable to save ourselves from the rule of time. We find it difficult to think of our own death and of the end of the world as anything but total annihilation. But Cusanus consoles us with the thought that a perfect God could not will the destruction of what he created. As he had written in chapter 12 of Book II:

Although no one doubts that the Perfect God created all things for Himself and that He does not will the destruction of any of the things He created, and although everyone knows that God is a very generous rewarder of all who worship Him, nevertheless only God Himself, who is His own Activity, knows the manner of Divine Activity's present and future remuneration. Nevertheless, I will say a few things about this later, according to the divinely inspired truth. At the moment, it suffices that I have, in ignorance, touched upon these matters in the foregoing way. (*DI* II.12:174)

What in Book Two had remained unsaid is developed in the present chapter, in which Cusanus relies on what he takes to be divinely inspired truth. Faith, he recognizes, is required to believe in a general resurrection, and Christian faith to accept the claim that such a resurrection presupposes the resurrection of Jesus who is God and man. To someone lacking faith, both resurrections make no sense.

To support his claim that a general resurrection is necessary, Cusanus invites us to think of the end of the universe when all motion ceases and time itself comes to an end. To the nonbeliever that would mean total annihilation. But God, being perfect, Cusanus insists, does not will the destruction of any of the things he created. The end of time therefore cannot mean the annihilation of the world; it must mean its transfiguration. But if, as Cusanus claims, without human nature, the universe would not even be a universe, the transfiguration of the universe must also be the transfiguration of humanity.

How are we to understand the claim that without human nature, the universe would not be a universe, let alone be transfigured? Cusanus was to repeat this claim in the sermon *Dies sanctificatus.*

> For unless God had assumed a human nature, then (since that human nature, as being something intermediate, enfolds in itself [all] other [human natures]) the entire universe would neither be perfect nor, indeed, would exist. (Here note that among created natures human nature (*homo*), by reason of its universality, enfolds all [other natures], both immaterial and material.) And hence, too, human nature was created as the goal of all beings, so that all things are present in human nature as in their goal. (*Sermo* XXII.32)

Presupposed is the preceding argument that the human being, because of its middle position in the hierarchy of creatures, is the only proper vehicle for the coincidence of Creator and creature. Such a creature would also be God "without confusion and without composition" (*DI* III.194).

Faith in the resurrection, Cusanus insists, requires the affirmation of the divinity and the humanity of Christ. In the thought of the perfect human being, Christ, time, and eternity are bent together. Death loses its sting.

> Christ is the center and the circumference of intellectual nature; and since the intellect encompasses all things, Christ is above all things. Nevertheless, as if in His own temple, He dwells in the holy rational souls and in the holy intellectual spirits, which are the heavens, declaring His glory. So, then, we understand that Christ—in that He "ascended above all the heavens, in order to fill all things"—

III. CHRIST'S BIRTH, DEATH, AND RESURRECTION

ascended above all space and time unto an incorruptible mansion, beyond everything which can be spoken of. Since He is God, He is all in all. Since He is Truth, He reigns in the intellectual heavens. And since as the life of all rational spirits He is their center, it is not the case that, with respect to location, He is seated on the circumference rather than at the center. And, therefore, He who is the "Fount of life" for souls, as well as their goal, affirms that the Kingdom of Heaven is also within men. (*DI* III.232)

With the statement "Christ is the center and the circumference of intellectual nature," Cusanus returns to the metaphor of the infinite sphere that figured so importantly in Books I and II. Applied to the Word it suggests that Christ is wherever there is intellect. Thus, to varying degrees, he is present in all human beings. Just as the human intellect enfolds all that is comprehensible, the Word enfolds all that is real. Since Christ is the union of both man and God, creation would not exist at all without man. And since Christ is present, if to varying degrees, in every human being, so is the Kingdom of Heaven. That Christ is said to have ascended to an incorruptible mansion "above all space and time" admonishes us not to try to picture in any way the mansion that awaits those who believe in Christ. Even talk of an afterlife is metaphorical and misleading.

IV. DEATH, DAMNATION, AND THE CHURCH

WE HAVE DISCUSSED Christmas, Good Friday, and Easter—that is, the birth, death, and resurrection of the incarnated Word. Those who believe in Christ are said by Cusanus to join him in that incorruptible mansion "above all space and time." But what sense can we make of such a dwelling above all space and time? How much content can Cusanus give to what awaits the faithful after death?

Let me interject here a question: why is the issue of immortality important for philosophy, especially for moral philosophy? How are morality and belief in an afterlife linked? The answer is perhaps obvious: If I am convinced that my death is my absolute end, why should I worry about what comes after me, what will happen to others, to the world? I, after all, shall be no longer. Nothing then will concern me. Nothing will have being for me. Does the finality of death not mean that I have only this one life to live and should do whatever is in my power to make this life as rewarding as possible? Will death not take away everything that could possibly happen to me? Why should I not think: After me the deluge! Belief in the finality of death and selfishness seem to go together. The moral life would seem to demand the conviction that what gives meaning to life transcends my death-bound life. That does not necessarily mean belief in an afterlife. Might a concern for those who will be when I am no longer not be sufficient?

It is of course possible to develop a self-centered morality. Remember Bentham's first principle: "Nature has placed mankind under the governance of two sovereign masters, pain and pleasure. It is for them alone to point out what we ought to do, as well as to determine what we shall do."[1] Not only Kant considers such a principle immoral.

1. Jeremy Bentham, *Principles of Morals and Legislation*, 1.

IV. DEATH, DAMNATION, AND THE CHURCH

Morality, I agree with Kant and, for that matter with Cusanus, is inseparable from an overcoming of such selfishness. It is inseparable from finding the courage to face death if necessary, as Socrates once faced it. But how will we find such courage unless we are convinced that our death does not have the last word? Recall Kant's claim that "the immortality of the soul is a postulate of pure practical reason."[2] This postulate presupposes a spiritual dimension of human being that reaches beyond death. This is what Plato hoped to show us in the *Phaedo*. How this spiritual dimension, this true home of the soul, is to be thought remains a question. But that the themes of morality and mortality are linked is impossible to deny.

Nothing that is said here, to be sure, does anything to establish the immortality of the soul. But those who are convinced of the immortality of the soul are also likely to think that life in what Cusanus calls the incorruptible mansion that awaits us after death will be a happy one for the just, where the meaning of such metaphors is shrouded in mystery. Cusanus attempts to shed some light on that mystery.

2. Kant, *Kritik der praktischen Vernunft*.

CHAPTER 9

Christ Is the Judge of the Living and the Dead

Who is a judge more just than He who is Justice itself? For Christ, the head and the source of every rational creature, is Maximal Reason, from which all reason derives. But reason judges discriminatively. Hence, Christ—who (while remaining God, who is the rewarder of all) assumed rational human nature with all rational creatures— is rightfully the judge of the living and the dead. (*DI* III.9:233)

Christ "is rightfully the judge of the living and the dead": *Vivorum et mortuorum iudex est.* Cusanus here follows the words of the Creed: *venturus est iudicare vivos et mortuos.* But the identification of Christ with Maximal Reason also invites us to read the words of the Creed met- aphorically: what judges us is Pure Practical Reason. Christ is said to embody that reason. Kant might well have agreed.

The discussion of light that follows may seem to lose sight of what we usually think of when we speak of Christ as Judge.

But through Himself and in Himself Christ judges—above all time— all things. For He embraces all creatures, since He is the maximum human being, in whom, because He is God, all things exist. As God He is Infinite Light in which there is no darkness. This Light illu- mines all things, so that in it all things are most manifest to it. For this infinite, intellectual Light enfolds, beyond all time, what is present

IV. DEATH, DAMNATION, AND THE CHURCH

> as well as what is past, what is living as well as what is dead—just as
> corporeal light is the basis (*hypostasis*) of all colors. (*DI* III.9:233)

The traditional understanding of every thing as *ens verum* comes to mind: the truth of things is their adequacy to the creative divine intellect. To it they owe their being. Their being can thus be said to be being illuminated by the infinite light that is the Logos. Light here has a function not altogether unlike that Hegel ascribes to spirit, not surprising, given that Christ is said to be maximal reason.

Cusanus would seem to come closer to what we associate with the last judgment with the transformation of metaphorical light into fire. Fire not only can illuminate; it can destroy and it can purify. Both figure in the Bible's use of the metaphor to describe God.

We should also keep in mind the Aristotelian and medieval hierarchy of the four elements, which places fire at the top. Cusanus was thinking of this when in Book II he likened God to fire:

> And, so to speak: earth is to fire as the world is to God. For fire, in its relation to earth, has many resemblances to God. [For example,] there is no limit to fire's power; and fire acts upon, penetrates, illumines, distinguishes, and forms all earthly things through the medium of air and of water, so that, as it were, in all the things which are begotten from earth there is nothing except fire's distinct activities. Hence, the forms of things are different as a result of a difference in fire's brightness. But fire is intermingled with things; it does not exist without them; and terrestrial things do not exist [without it]. God, however, is only absolute. Hence, God, who is light and in whom there is no darkness, is spoken of by the ancients as absolute consuming fire and as absolute brightness. All existing things endeavor, as best they can, to participate in His "brightness and blazing splendor," so to speak as we notice with regard to all the stars, in which participated brightness is found materially contracted. Indeed, this distinguishing and penetrating participated brightness is contracted "immaterially," so to speak, in the life of things which are alive with an intellective life. (*DI* II.13:177)

Although Cusanus refers to the way the ancients spoke of God as a consuming fire,[1] in Book II he is interested in the make-up of the earth, in the way the element fire is thought by him to be, to varying degrees, constitutive of all things. In analogous fashion those beings alive "with an intellective life" are said to participate in God's "blazing splendor." Judgment is not mentioned here.

---

1. Hb 12:29; Dt 4:24.

In his use of the metaphor Cusanus is indebted to Pseudo-Dionysius.[2]

> But Christ is as purest fire, which is inseparable from light and which exists not in itself but in light. And He is that spiritual fire of life and understanding which—as consuming all things and taking all things into itself—tests and judges all things, as does the judgment of material fire, which examines all things. (*DI* III.9:233)

Christ as judge is said to be an intellectual fire. In the First Letter to the Corinthians Paul makes use of this metaphor, likening himself to a master builder who has provided the Corinthians with the foundation that is Jesus Christ and admonishes them to take care with how they build on it:

> Now if anyone builds on that foundation with gold, silver, precious stone, wood, hay, stubble—each man's work will become manifest; for the Day will disclose it, because it will be revealed with fire, and the fire will test what sort of work each one has done. If the work any man has built on the foundation survives, he will receive a reward. If any man's work is burned up, he will suffer loss, though he himself will be saved, but only as through fire. (1 Cor 3:12–15)

Not all things are able to stand the test of fire; nor are all human beings.

> All rational spirits are judged in Christ, as what is heatable by fire [is judged] in fire. Of these [heatable things] the one, if it remains in the fire for a long time, is transformed into the likeness of fire (e.g., most excellent and most perfect gold is so gold and so intensely fire-hot that it appears to be no more gold than fire). (*DI* III.234)

The transformation of a human being by divine fire into a likeness of that fire, so that the difference between the individual and God disappears, recalls descriptions of mystical experience: Here is how Ruysbroeck describes such an experience:

> The spirit forever continues to burn in itself, for its love is eternal; and it feels itself ever more and more to be burnt up in love, for it is drawn and transformed into the Unity of God, where the spirit burns in love. If it observes itself, it finds a distinction and an otherness between itself and God; but where it is burnt up it is undifferentiated and without distinction, and therefore it feels nothing but unity; for the flame of the Love of God consumes and devours all that it can enfold in its Self.[3]

2. Dionysius Areopagita, *De cael. hier.* XV.2.
3. Ruysbroeck, *The Sparkling Stone,* chap. 3, cited in Clarence Edwin Rolt, *Dionysius*

IV. DEATH, DAMNATION, AND THE CHURCH

Even closer to the language of Cusanus is the description St. Bernard gives us of such an experience:

> As a little drop of water, blended with a large quantity of wine, seems utterly to pass away from itself and assumes the flavour and colour of wine, and as iron when glowing with fire loses its original or proper form and becomes just like the fire; and as the air, drenched in the light of the sun, is so changed into the same shining brightness that it seems to be not so much the recipient of the brightness as the actual brightness itself: so all human sensibility in the saints must then, in some ineffable manner, melt and pass out of itself, and be lent into the will of God.... The substance (i.e., personality) will remain but in another form.[4]

To experience such a passing out of oneself into the will of God is, according to St. Bernard "to be deified," a term familiar from the mystical theology of Pseudo-Dionysius. Are we to think of what awaits those firm in their faith at the end of time in the image of such a mystical experience?

Most believers, Cusanus knows, do not burn with such intensity that they deserve to be likened to gold. And so he continues:

> But some other thing does not participate in the intensity of the fire to such a degree (e.g., purified silver, bronze, or iron); nevertheless, they all seem to be transformed into fire, although each [is transformed] in its own degree. And this judgment belongs only to the fire, not to the things heated by fire, since each thing heated by fire apprehends in each other such thing only that very radiant fire and not the differences between each such thing. By comparison, if we were to see gold, silver, and copper fused in a maximum fire, we would not apprehend the differences of the metals after they had been transformed into the form of fire. However, if the fire were an intellectual [being], it would know the degrees of perfection of each [metal] and to what extent (according to these degrees) the fire's capability for intensity would be differently present in each thing. (*DI* III.234–35)

Cusanus both joins and opposes here the metaphors of light and fire.

> Hence, there are certain things—things heatable by fire, continuing incorruptibly in fire, and capable of receiving light and heat—which on account of their purity are transformable into the likeness of fire;

---

the Areopagite: On the Divine Names and the Mystical Theology (Grand Rapids, MI: Christian Classics Ethereal Library; London: SPCK, 1920), 21, http:www.//www.ccel.org/ccel/rolt/dionysius.html.

4. St. Bernard, *De diligendo Deo*, chapter x, cited in Rolt, *Dionysius the Areopagite*, 22.

and this occurs differently, according to greater and lesser degrees. But there are other things which, because of their impurity, are not transformable into light, even if they are heatable. In a similar manner, Christ, who is judge, according to one and the same most simple judgment, imparts most justly and without envy, at one instant and to all [rational spirits] (imparts not in the order of time but in the order of nature) the "warmth," so to speak, of created reason—in order to bestow, by the heat which is received, a divine, intellectual light from on high. Thus, God is all things in all things; and all things are in God through the Mediator; and [every rational spirit] is equal to God to the extent that this is possible in accordance with each's capability. (*DI* III.9:235)

What Cusanus has in mind here is not the Last Judgment but the constitution of all things. Christ is the Logos. Human beings participate in this Logos to varying degrees. Just as the light of the sun lets us see, the "intellectual light from on high" lets us understand.

But some things, because of the fact that they are more unified and pure, are able to receive not only heat but also light; other things are barely [able to receive] heat and are not [at all able to receive] light. Hence, since that Infinite Light is Eternity itself and Truth itself, it is necessary that a rational creature desiring to be illuminated by that Light turn to true and eternal things, which are above these mundane and corruptible things. (*DI* III.9:235)

The fundamental thought here is Platonic. And it is not surprising that immortality is then discussed in a way that recalls Plato's *Phaedo*.

However, when an intellectual spirit—whose operation is supratemporal and, as it were, on the horizon of eternity—turns toward eternal things, it cannot convert these things into itself, since they are eternal and incorruptible. But since it itself is incorruptible, it also is not converted into these things in such a way that it ceases to be an intellectual substance. Instead, it is converted into these [in such way] that it is absorbed into a likeness to the eternal things—[absorbed], however, according to degrees, so that the more fervently it is turned toward these things, the more fully it is perfected by them and the more deeply its being is hidden in the Eternal Being. But since Christ is immortal and still lives and is still life and truth, whoever turns to Him turns to life and truth. And the more ardently [he does] this, the more he is elevated from mundane and corruptible things unto eternal things, so that his life is hidden in Christ. For the virtues are eternal: justice remains forever, and so too does truth. (*DI* III.236)

Open to what is eternal, the intellect in us transcends our temporal being. It is capable of embracing eternal things, as it does when it is

IV. DEATH, DAMNATION, AND THE CHURCH

concerned with the truth. It offers the key to the desired homecoming to eternal being.

It is possible to read these chapters as asserting that only within the Christian church is salvation to be found. But it is also possible to offer a different reading. For if everyone who loves truth loves Christ, must not Plato, too, have been a lover of Christ, without being able to give the object of his love that name? Love of Christ here would name that power of self-transcendence that is a presupposition of the pursuit of truth. So understood, every truth-seeker could be said to love Christ, regardless of whether he or she ever heard of him. And the same could be said of every person who for the sake of others vanquishes his or her selfishness.

> Whoever turns to the virtues walks in Christ's ways, which are the ways of purity and immortality. Now, the virtues are divine illumina-tions. Therefore, if during this life someone turns by faith to Christ, who is virtue, then when he is freed from this temporal life, he will exist in purity of spirit, so that he can enter into the joy of eternal possession. But the turning of our spirit occurs when in accordance with all its intellectual powers our spirit turns by faith to the eternal and most pure truth (which it places before all else) and when it chooses and loves such truth as being alone worthy to be loved. For to turn by most assured faith to the truth which is Christ is to forsake this world and to tread on it in victory. (*DI* III.237)

The virtues Cusanus has in mind are faith in and love of the Truth, which is Christ. He opposes a life lived following Christ's ways to a worldly life. We may well want to question the way Cusanus valorizes the eternal and denigrates the temporal: are this earth and our earth-ly life not also divine gifts for which we should give thanks? Must our love of Christ not also be love of this earth? As Wenck charged, Christ as described here comes to resemble a timeless Platonic form, the res-urrection an ascent to a timeless realm that leaves time and the body and with it the individual behind. Must love of Christ not be love of the incarnated Word, and, that is to say, also love of the body and of all creation? Should the turn to the truth that is Christ be understood as a treading on the world in victory?

> Therefore, just as everyone who loves is within love, so all who love truth are in Christ. And just as everyone-who-loves loves through love, so all who love truth love it through Christ. Hence, no one knows the truth unless the spirit of Christ is in him. And just as it is impossible that there be a lover without love, so it is impossible that someone have God without [having] the spirit of Christ; only in

this spirit can we worship God. Accordingly, unbelievers—who are unconverted to Christ and who are incapable of receiving the light of transforming glory—have already been condemned to darkness and to the shadow of death, since they have turned from the life which is Christ. Through union [with Christ] all [who love Christ] are gloriously filled with His fullness alone. Later, when I shall speak about the church, I will add—on the same foundation and for the sake of our consolation—some more points regarding this union. (*DI* III.238)

Everyone who loves truth is said to be in Christ. Given an understanding of Christ as the Word, the Logos, a philosopher may well be prepared to grant this, but raise questions concerning the identification of Christ with the Logos. Cusanus, to be sure, as he has made clear, is speaking here not just as a philosopher, but "in sure faith." Hovering between philosophy and the traditional faith, these concluding chapters especially are profoundly ambiguous.

CHAPTER 10

The Judge's Sentence

In this chapter Cusanus turns more explicitly to the doctrine of damnation, even as he places it beyond our comprehension. Heavenly choirs praising God are dismissed as highly inadequate metaphors, as are hellfire and physical torment for what awaits the damned on Judgment Day.

> It is evident that no one among mortals comprehends the judgment and sentence of this judge. For since it is beyond all time and motion, it is not disclosed by comparative or inferential investigation or by vocal utterance or by such signs as indicate a delay or a protraction. But just as all things were created in the Word (for He spoke and they were created), so in the same Word, which is also called Reason, all things are judged. And there is no interval between the sentence and its execution, but what happens at an instant is the following: the resurrection and the securing of the respective end (viz., glorification with regard to the translation of the sons of God and damnation with regard to the exclusion of the unconverted) are not separated by a moment of time—[not] even by an indivisible [moment]. (*DI* III.10:239)

The following paragraph is once again quite within the Platonic tradition and in keeping with what had been said in the preceding chapters.

> The intellectual nature, which is beyond time and is not subject to temporal corruption, contains, in accordance with its nature, incorruptible forms—e.g., mathematical forms, which in their own way are abstract (but are also present in natural objects) and which are hidden away in the intellectual nature and are easily transformed. These [incorruptible forms] are, for us, guiding signs of the intellectual nature's incorruptibility; for [the intellect is] the incorruptible locus of incorruptible [forms]. Now, by its natural movement [the intellectual nature] is moved toward most abstract truth—as if toward the goal of its own desires and toward the ultimate and most delectable object. And since such an object as this is all things, because it is God, the intellect—insatiable until it attains thereunto—is immortal and incorruptible, for it is satisfied only by an eternal object. (*DI* III.10:240)

Possessing an intellect, we human beings transcend our time-bound existence. That transcendence manifests itself in our awareness of "incorruptible forms." Inseparable from this awareness is a desire that nothing temporal can fulfill. Like Plato, Cusanus, too, takes the life of us mortals to be ruled by a love of the eternal. Our insatiable search for truth springs from that desire. Mathematical forms are pointers that draw our intellect to God, who alone can truly satisfy us mortals created in his image. Love of God is the power that saves; to deny that love, to seek satisfaction in what is corruptible and fleeting is to engage in what we obscurely know is a vain pursuit.

> In that case, since (because of its turning away from truth at the hour of separation and because of its turning to what is corruptible) it falls toward corruptible objects of desire, toward uncertainty and confusion, and into the dark chaos of pure possibility (where there is no actual certainty): the intellect is rightly said to have descended unto intellectual death. Indeed, for the intellectual soul to understand is for it to be; and for it to understand the object of desire is for it to live. Hence, just as, for it, eternal life is finally to apprehend the unchanging, eternal object of its desire, so, for it, eternal death is to be separated from this unchanging object of desire and to be hurled into the chaos of confusion, where in its own manner it is eternally tormented by fire. [This manner is] graspable by us only analogously to the torment of someone who is deprived of vital nourishment and health—and [deprived] not only of these but also of the hope of ever obtaining them, so that he is ever dying an agonizing death, without extinction and termination. (*DI* III.10:241)

That the human intellect transcends time is a presupposition of Cusanus's understanding of damnation. The intellect cannot perish. But

IV. DEATH, DAMNATION, AND THE CHURCH

to really live, it must embrace the truth. If in the hour of death it has forsaken the truth, it descends into the chaos of possibility that according to the Platonic tradition precedes creation, and here is also understood as the end-state of the damned. No longer bound by truth, the intellect turns into a freedom that no longer knows where to turn, that is hurled, as Cusanus puts it, "into the chaos of confusion." Does damnation then mean freedom that, no longer bound by the body, fails to recognize anything to bind it, freedom without love?

Popular religion associates hell with physical pain, with devils torturing us poor humans. In Cusanus's account of the pains of the damned, the body does not figure. It is the intellectual soul that is eternally tormented. But if we are to do justice to the mystery of the resurrection, must we not be able to make some sense of the body's existence even after death? According to Cusanus, it is an existence only in the intellect—we may want to think of the way the body exists in our memories.

> Now, earlier I proved [all of the following]: The resurrection of men occurs above all motion and time and quantity and other [determinations] which are subject to time, so that the corruptible is resolved into the incorruptible and the animal is resolved into the spiritual. Accordingly, a whole [resurrected] man is his intellect, which is spirit; and a true body is engulfed by his spirit. Thus, the body does not exist in itself (i.e., in its corporeal, quantitative, and temporal relations) but exists as translated into the spirit (i.e., exists in a manner contrary to our present body). (*DI* III.10:242)

The body exists *aufgehoben*—that is, canceled and preserved in the intellect. There is a sense in which the body can be said to participate in the life of the intellect: think of the joy a lover feels in the presence of the beloved, of the pain he or she feels in his or her absence. In similar fashion Cusanus speaks of the "spiritual joys of the intellectual life" and the "infernal sorrows of spiritual death": they, too, are experienced by the body that is in the spirit. (*DI* III.242)

Cusanus is very much aware that all talk of heaven and hell can only be highly metaphorical:

> Therefore, with regard to all the musical and harmonic signs of joy, delight, and glory which, as signs for thinking what is known to us, are found to be indicators-of-eternal-life handed down by the Fathers: they are very remote perceptible signs—infinitely distant from the intellectual [realities], which are not perceivable by any imaging. Similarly, with regard to the punishments of Hell, which are likened to a fire of the element sulfur, to a fire from pitch, and to other

perceptible torments: these latter do not admit of any comparison with those fiery intellectual miseries from which Jesus Christ, our life and our salvation, deigns to save us. He is blessed forever. Amen. (*DI* III.243)

The ending of this chapter is surprising … *qui est in saecula benedictus* recalls the concluding words of Book One, *qui est super omnia in saecula benedictus* and of Book Two, *Qui sit in saecula benedictus*. Did Cusanus at one time think of this chapter as concluding the entire work? Hans Georg Senger raises this question.[1] The final *Amen* supports the conjecture. But Cusanus must have felt that the mysteries of faith required further discussion.

---

1. *PTW, DI* III:141n244.

CHAPTER 11

The Mysteries of Faith

The title raises the question of how the mysteries of faith to be discussed in this chapter are related to those mysteries already discussed, such as Incarnation, Crucifixion, Resurrection, and Last Judgment: is this chapter an inquiry into the essence of such mysteries rather than into particular mysteries?

The chapter begins by reasserting that faith is the beginning of understanding in a way that should pose few difficulties.

> All our forefathers unanimously maintain that faith is the beginning of understanding. For in every branch of study certain things are presupposed as first principles. They are grasped by faith alone, and from them is elicited an understanding of the matters to be treated. For everyone who wills to ascend to learning must believe those things without which he cannot ascend. For Isaiah says, "Unless you believe, you will not understand." Therefore, faith enfolds within itself everything that is understandable. But understanding is the unfolding of faith. Therefore, understanding is guided by faith, and faith is increased by understanding. Hence, where there is no sound faith, there is no true understanding. Thus, it is evident what kind of conclusion erroneous beginnings and a weakness of foundation imply. But there is no more perfect faith than Truth itself, which is Jesus. (*DI* III.11:244)

Cusanus makes the easy-to-grant point that all inquiry presupposes much that is taken for granted or taken on faith. He mentions Isaiah, but no doubt was also thinking of Aristotle, perhaps the most authoritative pagan among the mentioned forefathers, who called the conviction that "contradictory statements are not at the same time true"—the most indisputable of all beliefs."[1] While granting that this belief is presupposed by all rational inquiry, Cusanus, as we have seen, insists that such inquiry does not do justice to reality as it is in itself. Nor does it limit the reach of our intellect. With his assertion of the coincidence of opposites he calls what Aristotle calls the most indisputable of all beliefs into question. Aristotle's faith in the principle of non-contradiction is not yet the most perfect faith: Aristotelian reason cannot make sense of Cusanus's faith in Jesus, whom he identifies with the Truth itself.

Cusanus is of course right to point out that what is taken for granted and supposed to be not in need of supporting arguments may in fact be false. Faith may thus be more or less perfect. For Cusanus the measure of perfection is Truth itself, which he identifies with the divine Word. But faith in Jesus does not provide a measure that we can actually use to decide, for instance, which propositions in science are more or less adequate. That, as Cusanus is well aware, requires further inquiry into the matter at hand. Thus, while we can agree with Cusanus that "understanding is the unfolding of faith," we must distinguish cognitive from religious faith. Important would appear to be the distinction between faith that comes before persuasive considerations and is tested by them and faith that begins where persuasive considerations cease. The latter case raises the question: how are we to distinguish sound faith—that is, faith that is a gift from God—from false faith, faith that is a delusion? How are we to distinguish Kierkegaard's knight of faith, Abraham, ready to sacrifice Isaac in obedience to God's command, from a madman? Reason, it would seem, has no answer, but only sound faith.

> Since God is not knowable in this world (where by reason and by opinion or by doctrine we are led, with symbols, through the more known to the unknown), He is apprehended only where persuasive considerations cease and faith appears. Through faith we are caught up, in simplicity, so that being in a body incorporeally (because in spirit) and in the world not mundanely but celestially we may incomprehensibly contemplate Christ above all reason and intelligence, in the third heaven of most simple intellectuality. Thus, we see even the following: viz., that because of His excellence, God cannot be comprehended. And this is that learned ignorance through which

---

1. Aristotle, *Metaphysics* IV.6.1011b.13–14.

> most blessed Paul, in ascending, saw that when he was being elevated more highly to Christ, he did not know Christ, though at one time he had known only Christ. (*DI* III.11:245)

The passage is difficult to understand: how are we to understand "the third heaven of most simple intellectuality"? And what are we to make of that proximity to Christ that no longer knows Christ? The Apostle Paul spoke of this third heaven in his Second Letter to the Corinthians:

> I know a man in Christ who fourteen years ago was caught up to the third heaven—whether in the body or out of the body I do not know, God knows. And I know that this man was caught up into Paradise—whether in the body or out of the body I do not know, God knows—and he heard things that cannot be told, which man may not utter. (2 Cor 12: 2–4)

Paul here is telling of an ecstatic experience he once had that suspended his corporeal being, an experience of something that transcended what can be put into words. Cusanus speaks of the "third heaven of most simple intellectuality," where we should keep in mind that Cusanus tends to think of the intellect as the highest human faculty, which puts us in touch with the infinite, a faculty not bound by Aristotle's highest principle. The ascent to the "most simple intellectuality" thus must leave behind everything we can call knowledge. And thus it has to leave behind even the knowledge Paul in the First Letter to the Corinthians claims to have had of Christ: "For I decided to know nothing among you except Jesus Christ and him crucified" (1 Cor 2:2). That was sufficient for Cusanus to claim that Paul, "being elevated more highly to Christ,... did not know Christ, though at one time he had known only Christ." Absent such an ecstatic experience, we must wonder just how we are to understand this Christ above Christ. Meister Eckhart comes to mind:

> And if a fly could have the intelligence by which to search the eternal abyss of divine being out of which it came, we should say that God, together with all that God is, could not give satisfaction to that fly. Therefore, we beg God that we may be rid of God, and take the truth and enjoy it eternally, where the highest angels and the fly and the soul are equal, there where I stood and was what I wanted.[2]

---

2. "Beati pauperes spiritu, quia ipsorum est regnum coelorum," Quint 2: 492–94; trans. Meister Eckhart, *Meister Eckhart: A Modern Translation*, trans. Raymond B. Blakney (New York: Harper Torchbooks, 1969), 228–29. Translation changed.

Faith so understood requires that we transcend our bodily being and that mode of knowledge that is appropriate to the pursuit of worldly knowledge. Such knowledge may pursue the historical Jesus, but Christ is approached only by those whose faith has been formed by learned ignorance:

> Therefore, we who are believers in Christ are led in learned ignorance unto the Mountain that is Christ and that we are forbidden to touch with the nature of our animality. (*DI* III.11:246)

Jesus is said to be "the perfection of every creature," "the goal of all things" (*DI* III.11:247), "manifested to one who ascends to Christ by faith. But the divine efficacy of this faith is inexplicable," "as the deeds of the saints bear witness" (*DI* III.11:248).

Cusanus proceeds to apply his teaching of the coincidence of opposites to the required faith.

> In the preceding [sections] there can very frequently be found repeated [the doctrine] that the minimum coincides with the maximum. This doctrine applies to the faith which is unqualifiedly maximum in actuality and in power. This maximum [faith] cannot be in a pilgrim (*viator*), who is still not a full attainer (*comprehensor*) [of his goal], as was Jesus. However, the pilgrim actually must will to have for himself maximum faith in Christ—[to have it] to such an extent that his faith will be elevated to such a level of indubitable certainty that it will also be not at all faith but supreme certainty devoid of all doubt in any respect whatsoever. This is the mighty faith which is so maximal that it is also minimal, that it embraces all the things which are believable with regard to Him who is Truth. (*DI* III.11:248)

We are pilgrims in search of our true home, a home that we do not comprehend. Our faith could therefore always be greater. Perfect faith is said to be minimal because it coincides with comprehension. When we truly comprehend something faith vanishes. Jesus possessed such faith.

Cusanus here can appeal to Thomas Aquinas:

> A man is called a wayfarer from tending to beatitude, and a comprehensor from having already obtained beatitude, according to 1 Corinthians 9:24: "So run that you may comprehend [Douay: 'obtain']"; and Philippians 3:12: "I follow after, if by any means I may comprehend [Douay: 'obtain']." Now man's perfect beatitude consists in both soul and body, as stated in I-II:4:6. In the soul, as regards what is proper to it, inasmuch as the mind sees and enjoys God; in the body, inasmuch as the body "will rise spiritual in power and glory and incorruption," as is written 1 Corinthians 15:42. Now before His passion

IV. DEATH, DAMNATION, AND THE CHURCH

Christ's mind saw God fully, and thus He had beatitude as far as it regards what is proper to the soul; but beatitude was wanting with regard to all else, since His soul was passible, and His body both passible and mortal, as is clear from the above (Article 4; III:14:2). Hence He was at once comprehensor, inasmuch as He had the beatitude proper to the soul, and at the same time wayfarer, inasmuch as He was tending to beatitude, as regards what was wanting to His beatitude.[3]

Cusanus's understanding of us human beings as pilgrims, whose journey has its goal in beatitude, understood by him as the coincidence of faith and comprehension, invites the question of whether anyone is altogether without faith and therefore irredeemably damned. In Platonic fashion Cusanus understands the being of man as ruled by love, by the desire both to live and to comprehend, where only the latter allows the former to find satisfaction.

> For without love faith cannot be maximum. For if every living thing loves to live and if every understanding thing loves to understand, how can Jesus be believed to be immortal life and infinite truth if He is not loved supremely? For life per se is lovable; and if Jesus is most greatly believed to be eternal life, He cannot fail to be loved. For without love faith is not living but dead and is not faith at all. But love is the form of faith, giving to faith true being; indeed, love is the sign of most steadfast faith. Therefore, if for the sake of Christ all things are set aside, and if in relation to Christ the body and the soul are counted as nothing: this is a sign of maximum faith. (*DI* III.11:250)

Christ is the ideal we all bear within ourselves. One might accept this, but at the same time insist that the idea is self-contradictory and thus arrive at a position rather like Sartre's: what we most deeply desire is a contradiction. The doctrine of learned ignorance should make this reply more difficult by showing how much the infinite invades all our experience even as it transcends our comprehension.

In the very beginning of *On Learned Ignorance* Cusanus had asserted that no natural desire is vain. If this is accepted, it follows that Christ exists and that through him our desire can find satisfaction.

> Moreover, faith cannot be great apart from the holy hope of enjoying Jesus. For how would anyone have assured faith if he did not hope for what was promised him by Christ? If he does not believe that he will have the eternal life promised by Christ to believers, in what sense does he believe Christ? Or how is it that he believes that

---

3. *ST* III. q. 15., trans. Fathers of the English Dominican Province, online ed. copyright © 2017 by Kevin Knight.

Christ is truth if he does not have assured hope in His promises? How would he choose death for Christ's sake if he did not hope for immortality? (*DI* III.11:251)

The death of countless martyrs testifies to the power of faith,

this admirable gift of God which is such that we, who on this pilgrimage are constituted with frail flesh, can by the power of faith be elevated to this power over all the things which are not Christ through union? Be aware that as someone's flesh is progressively and gradually mortified by faith, he progressively ascends to oneness with Christ so that he is absorbed into Christ by a deep union—to the extent that this is possible on [this pilgrim's] pathway. Leaping beyond all things which are visible and mundane, he obtains the full perfection of his nature. (*DI* III.11:252)

The formulation "power over all the things which are not Christ through union [*quae Christus per unionem non sunt*]" invites the question, "What kind of power does Cusanus have in mind?" The formulation may bring to mind magicians who claim "that by faith and through certain practices a man ascends to a nature of influential spirits who are akin to himself—so that by the power of such spirits, with which the magicians themselves are united by faith, they perform many special wonders as regards fire or water or musical knowledge, visible transformations, the revealing of hidden matters, and the like" (*DI* III.11:253). We think of astrologers and alchemists. Cusanus does not deny that at times such magicians are successful in achieving their goals. But in all their achievements there is "deception as well as a departure from real life and from truth." Their faith is a false faith, the spirits in which they believe evil. Their power over nature is not the power Cusanus has in mind: The power that the gift of faith grants the Christian believer is the power to raise oneself above the sensible and mundane in such a way that it loses its power over us.

This chapter, too, concludes with a brief paragraph praising God:

Blessed is God, who by His own son has redeemed us from the darkness of ignorance in order that we may discern to be false and deceptive all the things which are sometimes done by a mediator other than Christ, who is truth, and by a faith other than [faith] in Jesus. For there is only one Lord—Jesus—who is powerful over all things, who fills us with every blessing, and who causes our every deprivation to be filled to overflowing. (*DI* III.253)

CHAPTER 12

The Church

The benediction that concludes chapter 11 once again suggests that it might have concluded the book, but Cusanus must have felt that his discussion of the concept of Jesus still remained incomplete, that something essential had not been given due consideration: the church, which is said by St. Paul to be the body of Christ. (Rom 12:5,1; Cor 12:12–27; Eph 3:6, 5:23; Col 1:18, 1:24). Just as human beings must be understood as essentially embodied, Christ must be understood as essentially embodied in the church. The simile suggests that just as the body is necessary to our human being, so human beings are necessary to Christ's being. God would not be God without the creation and human beings to recognize and praise him.

Cusanus had discussed the church in great detail in *De concordantia catholica*, written in the years 1432/1433 at the Council of Basel in support of the conciliarist cause. As mentioned, as the Council dragged on, he was to change sides, becoming a zealous defender of the authority of the pope. We might thus expect to find in this chapter some account of his changed understanding of the church. But the discussion here moves on a level of generality that leaves the pressing issues that so agitated the participants in the Council and that continued to threaten the unity of the church unaddressed.

Does the body metaphor help us think the unity of the church? When we think of a body, we think of a whole made up of members

428

gathered into an organic whole by the spirit dwelling in each such member. In analogous fashion, the metaphor suggests, the church is a whole made up of members, gathered into a whole by Christ dwelling in each such member. This makes understanding the church essential to understanding Christ.

Cusanus begins his discussion by repeating the obvious: no human being is just like another; and no person's faith is just like the faith of another; Christ is thus present in each person in a way that is uniquely his or her own.

> Since it is necessary that the faith in different men [*hominibus*] be of unequal degree and therefore admit of greater and lesser degree, no one can attain to maximum faith, than which there can be no greater power. (Similarly, no one [can attain] to maximum love either.) For if maximum faith, which could not be a greater power, were present in a pilgrim, he would also have to be an attainer [of his pilgrim's goal]. For just as the maximum in a genus is the supreme goal of the genus, so it is the beginning of a higher [genus]. Accordingly, unqualifiedly maximum faith cannot be present in anyone who is not also an attainer [of his pilgrim's goal]. Similarly, unqualifiedly maximum love cannot be present in a lover who is not also the beloved. Accordingly, neither unqualifiedly maximum faith nor unqualifiedly maximum love befits anyone other than Jesus. (*DI* III.12:254)

The passage restates what had already been said: we are all pilgrims longing for a beatitude that we desire or love and that our faith promises. In that sense every pilgrim is both a lover and a believer. But the beatitude we pilgrims long for we have not attained. Nor do we fully comprehend just what it is that we long for. Should love attain its goal, lover and beloved would be united and become one. But such unity is found only in Christ, our supreme goal. He is the maximum of the human genus. As such, in accord with what had been said in chapter 1 of Book Three, he is the beginning of a higher genus. But just as an infinite gap separates the maximum number from every finite number, so an infinite gap separates us mortals from Christ.

The fundamental thought is present already in Plato's *Symposium*: that plenitude or satisfaction that we mortals long for is denied to us by our temporal condition, but, according to Plato's Socrates, it calls us in the beautiful, awakening our love. The desire to attain what beauty promises is said to draw us ever higher until finally everything mundane and perishable has been left behind. This ascent culminates in a vision of absolute beauty: "What may we suppose to be the felicity of the man who sees absolute beauty in its essence, pure and unalloyed, who, instead of a beauty tainted by human flesh and colour and a mass of perishable rubbish."[1] For the Christian the place of Plato's absolute beauty is taken by Christ. The love of Christ, itself a gift of Christ's love for us human beings, gathers the faithful into the whole that is the church.

Jesus is said by Cusanus to be both *amor et caritas*, which Hopkins translates as "*is* love" (*DI* III.12:255). *Caritas* corresponds to the Greek *agape*, *amor* to *eros*. *Amor* is the more encompassing term, suggesting a desire to unite with the beloved, while *caritas* suggests a higher overflowing love, such as Mother Teresa's love for the poorest of the poor or Christ's love for us mortals. According to Thomas Aquinas, *caritas* is necessarily *amor*, but not the reverse.[2]

The church Cusanus understands as the body of Christ, gathered into a unity by love of Christ, which is a gift of Christ's love.

> Therefore, this union is a church, or congregation, of many in one—just as many members are in one body, each member existing with its own role. (In the body, one member is not the other member; but each member is in the one body, and by the mediation of the body it is united with each other member. No member of the body can have life and existence apart from the body, even though in the body one member is all the others only by the mediation of the body.) Therefore, as we journey here below, the truth of our faith can exist only in the spirit of Christ—the order of believers remaining, so that in one Jesus there is diversity in harmony. And once we are freed from this church militant: when we arise, we can arise only in Christ, so that in this way there will also be one church of those who are triumphant, each existing in his own order. And at that time the truth of our flesh will exist not in itself but in the truth of Christ's flesh; and the truth of our body will exist in the truth of Christ's body; and the truth of our spirit will exist in the truth of Christ Jesus's spirit—as branches exist in the vine. Thus, Christ's one humanity will be in all men, and Christ's one spirit will be in all spirits—so that each [believing individual] will be in Christ, so that from all [members] there will be one Christ. And then whoever in this life receives any one of those who are Christ's receives Christ; and what is done to one of the least of these is done to Christ. (By comparison, whoever injures Plato's hand injures Plato; and whoever harms the smallest toe harms the whole man.) And whoever rejoices in Heaven over the least one rejoices over Christ and sees in each one Jesus, through whom [he sees] Blessed God. Thus, through His son, our God will be all things

---

1. Plato, *Symposium* 94–95.
2. *ST* I-II, q. 26, a. 3c. See Senger, *PTW* I:152–53n254, 21f.

in all things; and in His son and through Him each [believer] will be with God and with all things, so that [each's] joy will be full, free of all envy and deprivation. (*DI* III.11:256)

In expected fashion Cusanus distinguishes the church militant from the church triumphant. The former is the community of the faithful, as it struggles here in the world against the countless temptations and challenges that would deflect it from its path, threatening to tear the church apart or even destroy it—threats that Cusanus, whose governing pathos had always been the desire to preserve the unity of the church, had to contend with again and again. The church triumphant is the community of the faithful as it will be when *tempus non erit amplius* (Rv 10:6), when there will be no more time and whoever believes will have arisen in Christ to eternal blessedness.

Cusanus discusses the state of blessedness as the coincidence of desire and satisfaction. Desire must be preserved, for it is constitutive of our human being. If all desire were to have been stilled, having given way to satisfaction, life would have given way to death. But what we most profoundly desire is from the point of view of our worldly reason a contradiction: eternal life, the coincidence of time and eternity. The fact that we must die weighs on us. *Tempus non erit amplius*: the time will come when time will be no longer for us. And what then? Nothing?

Now, our intellectual desire is [the desire] to live intellectually—i.e., to enter further and further into life and joy. And since that life is infinite: the blessed, still desirous, are brought further and further into it. And so, they are filled-being, so to speak, thirsty ones drinking from the Fount of life. And because this drinking does not pass away into a past (since it is within eternity), the blessed are ever drinking and ever filled; and yet, they have never drunk and have never been filled.[3] (*DI* III.12:258)

Cusanus's understanding of the state of blessedness is close to Kant's understanding of the highest good, the combination of supreme virtue and happiness, the attainability of which, Kant tells us, is a postulate of pure practical reason.

Cusanus had begun *De docta ignorantia* with, "We see that by the gift of God there is present in all things a natural desire to exist in the best manner in which the condition of each thing's nature permits this" (*DI* I.1:2). But if in all things we meet with this desire, a

---

3. Cf. Rv 21:6: "And he said unto me, It is done. I am Alpha and Omega, the beginning and the end. I will give unto him that is athirst of the fountain of the water of life freely."

satisfaction that would quench this desire would seem to be incompatible with such a thing's being. That would seem to be true especially of us human beings: if what we so profoundly desire were ever to be granted to us and our desire satisfied, would such satisfaction not mean death? Kant was right: the highest good or the state of blessedness cannot mean the end of desire. Cusanus therefore writes that the blessed remain ever desiring. In that sense the blessed are said to remain ever thirsty. And yet they are said by Cusanus to be ever filled, "drinking from the Fount of life." Lack and plenitude, time and eternity coincide here, another expression of the *coincidentia oppositorum*. That our reason cannot make sense of such a state of blessedness requires no comment. As Cusanus recognizes, the metaphor of drinking ever more deeply from the Fount of Life for the state of blessedness is profoundly inadequate. Aware of that inadequacy, he therefore adds, "And yet, they have never drunk and have never been filled."

That such metaphors must leave reason behind is evident. But Cusanus teaches that the reach of our intellect surpasses that of our reason.

> Blessed is God, who has given us an intellect which cannot be filled in the course of time. Since the intellect's desire does not come to an end, the intellect—on the basis of its temporally insatiable desire— apprehends itself as beyond corruptible time and as immortal. And the intellect recognizes that it cannot be satisfied by the intellectual-life-it-desires except during the enjoyment of the maximum, most excellent, and never-failing good. This enjoyment does not pass away into a past, because the appetite does not fade away during the enjoyment. (*DI* III.12:259)

Like Plato or Kant, Cusanus recognizes that we human beings possess a faculty that puts us in touch with the infinite and eternal. Our freedom and our ability to think, if not to comprehend, the maximum that is goal and ground of our existence are sufficient to demonstrate this. Our very desire for a blessedness that our temporal condition denies us is taken by Cusanus to testify to that power of self-transcendence that lets us long for the coincidence of time and eternity that awaits the faithful as members of the *ecclesia triumphans*.

In Platonic fashion Cusanus understands us human beings as in search of unity. As members of the *ecclesia triumphans* we are said to achieve the unity that is our goal and the goal of creation in a manner that preserves individuality. The nature of that union, however, is incomprehensible. Such incomprehensibility is confirmed by the way Cusanus relies in his attempts to shed some light on it on the *coincidentia oppositorum.*

Chapter and Book conclude by distinguishing between

1. The Absolute Union of God
2. The hypostatic union of humanity and divinity in Christ
3. The union of the blessed with Christ, which is at the same time the homecoming of creation to its origin.

And yet these three unions are said to be one.

Given the preceding, nothing that Cusanus has to say in these concluding paragraphs should seem surprising. Consider once more what Cusanus had said in chapter 8 of Book Three about the way that all human beings, damned and saved alike, will be forever.

> There is only one indivisible humanity and specific essence of all human beings. Through it all individual human beings are numerically distinct human beings, so that Christ and all human beings have the same humanity, though the numerical distinctness of the individuals remains unconfused. Hence, it is evident that the humanity of all the human beings who—whether temporally before or after Christ—either have existed or will exist has, in Christ, put on immortality. Therefore, it is evident that the following inference holds: the man Christ arose; hence, after [the cessation of] all motion of temporal corruptibility, all men will arise through Him, so that they will be eternally incorruptible. (*DI* III.8:227)

That all human beings, although numerically distinct, have the same humanity is easy to grant. That Christ's resurrection demonstrates that humanity does not entail mortality a believer will also have to grant. But that different human beings share their humanity does not mean that they therefore become in any meaningful sense one. But just this is what Cusanus asserts in his description of the church triumphant:

> This is the church of the triumphant, in which our God, who is blessed forever, is present. Here the true man Christ Jesus is united in supreme union, with the son of God—in so great a union that the humanity exists only in the divinity; it is present in the divinity by means of an ineffable hypostatic union—present in such a way that it cannot be more highly and more simply united if the truth [that is, the reality] of the nature of the humanity is to remain. Then every rational nature—provided that in this life it turn to Christ with supreme faith, hope, and love—is united with Christ the Lord (though the personal truth of each nature remains) to the following extent: (1) that all the angels and all the men (each [man] having the truth of his body absorbed and attracted through his spirit) exist only in

IV. DEATH, DAMNATION, AND THE CHURCH

> Christ, through whom they exist in God, so that each of the blessed,
> having the truth-of-his-own-being preserved, exists in Christ Jesus
> as Christ and—through Christ—in God as God; and (2) that God,
> while remaining the Absolute Maximum, exists in Christ Jesus as Je-
> sus and, through Jesus, in all things as all things. The church cannot
> in some other way be more one. For "church" bespeaks a oneness of
> many [members]—each of whom has his personal truth preserved
> without confusion of natures or of degrees; but the more one the
> church is, the greater it is; hence, this church—[viz. the church of
> the eternally triumphant]—is maximal, since no greater union of
> the church is possible. (*DI* III.12: 260–61)

The first part of the quote is in keeping with what the Council of
Chalcedon (451 A.D.) had declared concerning the hypostatic union:
that Jesus Christ is truly man and truly God, that there is no split between Christ's humanity and his divinity. This is orthodox doctrine.
What invites question is what follows: the way Cusanus would have us
think the union of those who truly believe in Christ in this life with
him when time shall be no more: they shall remain the individuals
they are and yet exist in Christ as Christ, and that means also, given
the orthodox understanding of the Trinity, in God as God, just as
God exists in Christ as Christ and in each individual as that individual, indeed in each thing as that thing. In the church triumphant the
greatest possible union is achieved between each believer and God.

That a Johannes Wenck should have objected to the claim "that
each blessed one is Christ and God" (*IL* 40) is to be expected. The
union of each believing individual with God is indeed ineffable.
Reason here suffers shipwreck. Cusanus insists that the individual is
fully preserved in this union, but reason cannot make sense of the
individual thus united with Christ and God. Cusanus would grant
that. But the coincidence of opposites, as he understands it, is like a
gate to that absolute union that is our goal, a goal that surpasses all
understanding.

> The Absolute Union is neither a greater nor a lesser [union] than
> the union of the natures in Jesus or [the union] of the blessed in
> Heaven. For it is the maximum Union which is (a) the Union of all
> unions and (b) that which is complete union. It does not admit of
> degrees of more or less, and it proceeds from Oneness and Equal-
> ity—as is indicated in Book One. And the union of the natures in
> Christ is neither a greater nor a lesser [union] than the oneness of
> the church of the triumphant; for since it is the maximum union
> of the natures, it therefore does not admit of degrees of more and
> less; hence, all the different things which are united receive their

oneness from the maximum union of the natures of Christ, through which union the union of the church is that which it is. But the union of the church is the maximum ecclesiastical union. Therefore, since it is maximal, it coincides on high with the hypostatic union of the natures in Christ. And since the union of the natures of Jesus is maximal, it coincides with the Absolute Union, which is God. And so, the union of the church, which is [a union] of individuals, [coincides] with the [Absolute Union]. (*DI* III.12:261–62)

As Cusanus himself points out, the claim that the three unions, the Absolute Union of God, the hypostatic union of humanity and divinity in Christ, and the union of the blessed with Christ are one union invites challenge: they seem very different, the first the strongest, the second somewhat weaker, the third weaker still. It is not difficult to understand Wenck's complaint: "By distinguishing, he confounds—as is typical of someone of learned ignorance. He shows that he does not know anything at all about the different unions of things" (*IL* 41). But, as Wenck would have gladly admitted, he, Wenck, does not belong with those who have become learned about their ignorance. Cusanus, however, can claim that the union of the three unions follows from the preceding:

And, assuredly, this [point] is seen quite clearly if attention is paid to what is repeatedly found earlier on. For the Absolute Union is the Holy Spirit. Now, the maximum hypostatic union coincides with the Absolute Union. Hence, necessarily, the union of the natures in Christ exists through and in the Absolute Union, which is the Holy Spirit. But the ecclesiastical union coincides with the hypostatic union, as was said. Hence, the union of the triumphant is in the spirit of Jesus, which spirit is in the Holy Spirit. Truth itself makes such a statement in John: "I have given them the glory which You have given me, in order that they may be one, as we also are one, I in them and You in me, so that they may be perfected in oneness" (Jn 17:22–23)—so that the church may be perfect in eternal rest that it could not be more perfect and may exist in so inexpressible a transformation of the light of glory that in all [the triumphant] only God appears. (*DI* III.12:262)

Hopkins calls Cusanus's claim "that the union of Christ's two natures, since it is maximal, coincides with the Absolute Union" (*DI* III.12:262:6–7) "theologically mistaken."[4] The Council of Chalcedon (451 A.D.) had declared Christ to be truly God and truly man, consubstantial with the Father according to his divinity and consubstantial

---

4. Hopkins, "Orienting Study, Part Two: Analysis of Specialized Topics," 89.

IV. DEATH, DAMNATION, AND THE CHURCH

with us humans according to his humanity, both natures, though distinct yet united in one person. As Hopkins points out, Cusanus was to correct himself in *De visione Dei*.[5] But the later revision— "the union of Jesus's human nature, qua human, to the divine nature is maximal, because it cannot be greater. But it is not maximal and infinite in an unqualified sense, as is the Divine Union."—invites the question: how are we to think the unity of Jesus's human and his divine nature? Reason cannot make sense either of the claim in *De docta ignorantia* that the union of Christ's two natures coincides with the Absolute Union nor of its revision in *De visione Dei*, granting that only the latter accords with orthodoxy. But in either case the doctrine of learned ignorance must come to the assistance of faith. The hypostatic union remains a mystery hidden beyond the coincidence of opposites. And so does the "union of the triumphant … in the spirit of Jesus," the way Jesus has robbed death of its sting.

Cusanus concludes the book with a prayer, affirming his faith in the Trinity.

> With very great affection we triumphantly aspire to this [glory]. And with humble heart we entreat God the Father that because of His immense graciousness He will to give—through His son, our Lord Jesus Christ, and in Him through the Holy Spirit—this [glory] to us in order that we may eternally enjoy Him who is blessed forever. (*DI* III:262)

What follows is only the letter to Cardinal Cesarini, which was discussed at some length earlier. In it Cusanus tells us that the central thought of the work, the thought that the incomprehensible Deity could be grasped only in learned ignorance, came to him as a divine inspiration when he returned from Constantinople late in 1437. On the moving ship, surrounded by water, he must have been struck by

---

5. Hopkins, "Orienting Study, Part Two: Analysis of Specialized Topics," 89. See Cusanus, *De Visione Dei* 20, 88: "You show me, O Light Unfailing, that the maximum union by which, in my Jesus, the human nature is united to Your divine nature is not in any way like an infinite union. For the Union by which You, God the Father, are united to God Your Son is God the Holy Spirit. And so, it is an infinite Union, for it attains unto an absolute and essential identity. But this is not the case when the human nature is united to the divine nature. For the human nature cannot pass over into essential union with the divine nature, even as the finite cannot be infinitely united to the Infinite. For the finite would pass over into an identity with the Infinite and thus would cease to be finite, since infinite would be predicated truly of it. Therefore, the union by which the human nature is united to the divine nature is only the attraction—in the highest degree—of the human nature to the divine nature, so that the human nature, qua human nature, cannot be attracted more highly. Therefore, the union of Jesus's human nature, qua human, to the divine nature is maximal, because it cannot be greater. But it is not maximal and infinite in an unqualified sense, as is the Divine Union."

the way our understanding is bound by whatever happens to be our perspective, which inescapably limits our access to reality. The truth of things eludes us. We must settle for conjectures. The other side of such reflections on the power of perspective is thoughts of the infinity of reality, be it that of the world, of some created thing such as a rose, of our human being, or of God. In a way we do not comprehend, the infinite in its different manifestations provides our conjectures with a measure. But only faith can provide the center that we need to live a meaningful life.

Concluding Personal Postscript

That I should have chosen to write what, given my health and age, is likely to be my swan song, as a commentary on *De docta ignorantia* by the fifteenth-century cardinal Nicolaus Cusanus, has made me wonder whether with this choice I was not escaping from the real world. Are there not countless more pressing matters that demand our time and engagement? What need is there for such a commentary? Does Cusanus have something important to teach us in these troubling times?

Such questions led me to consider what allowed me to be interested in Cusanus in the first place. What is it about his thought that has kept me returning to it? Through all these years, no thinker, except perhaps Martin Heidegger, has been such a constant companion. I see a connection between the way these two thinkers wrestled with what Heidegger called the question of Being, the way they both called the understanding of reality presiding over our modern world into question.

I have often wondered why Heidegger does not mention Cusanus in his many works. Heidegger knew medieval philosophy and theology very well, having once considered a career in that field. As a theology student at the University of Freiburg, he studied Logic and Metaphysics with Johannes Uebinger (1909–10), to whom we owe two early important studies of Cusanus, *Die Philosophie des Nicolaus Cusanus* (1880) and *Die Gotteslehre des Nikolaus Cusanus* (1888). Uebinger helped Ernst Cassirer recognize the significance of Cusanus.[1]

Heidegger's testimony suggests that Uebinger failed to excite him: "The lecture courses in philosophy that were prescribed at the time did not satisfy me much."[2] But Uebinger must have made Heidegger

---

1. Cassirer, *Das Erkenntnisproblem*, 1:24–25, 28, 48.
2. Thomas Sheehan, "Heidegger's Education, 1895–1915," corrected version, Academia. edu, 4.

aware of the works of Cusanus and, given Heidegger's high praise for Meister Eckhart, his failure to even mention, let alone confront Cusanus, who, as we have seen, owed so much to Eckhart, is surprising. Eckhart, whom Heidegger named the *Lese- und Lebemeister* and whom in a letter to Karl Jaspers (1948) he called the first of the three roots of his thinking,[3] had accompanied him ever since 1910. This makes his failure to even mention, let alone confront Cusanus, who, as we have seen, owed so much to Eckhart, surprising. I am convinced that such a confrontation would have led Heidegger to modify his thinking in significant ways, forcing him to reconsider his understanding of the history of metaphysics as a progressive forgetting of the meaning of Being.[4]

If Eckhart accompanied Heidegger ever since his student days, I can say the same of me and Nicolaus Cusanus. I don't recall when I first became interested in Cusanus. It must have been when I was an undergraduate at Yale University. I remember bringing Egil Wyller's *Platons Parmenides*,[5] which suggests a profound relationship between Cusanus's *De li non aliud* and Plato's dialogue, to a seminar I took with Robert S. Brumbaugh and discussing Wyller's work and that tetralogue, which I had read in Paul Wilpert's German translation, with him.[6] This was the gate through which I entered the vast edifice of Cusanus's thought. What then drew me to *De li non aliud* was the way it suggested the possibility of experiencing things in a way that transcends the reach of our language and logic. I saw a relationship between Cusanus's *non aliud* and what Meister Eckhart had to say about seeing the beauty of a flower,[7] Hugo von Hofmannsthal's "A pitcher, a harrow abandoned in a field, a dog in the sun, a neglected cemetery, a cripple, a peasant's hut—all these can become the vessel of my revelation,"[8] Martin Buber's "dialogical principle," his "Thou,"[9] and

---

3. The other two being the Greeks, especially Parmenides, and his own thought; letter to Jaspers of December 8, 1949, in Walter Biemel and Hans Saner, eds., *Martin Heidegger, Karl Jaspers: Briefwechsel 1920–1963* (Frankfurt, Munich, and Zürich: Klostermann, 1992), 181f. See also Eckard Wolz-Gottwald, "Martin Heidegger und die philosophische Mystik," pdf., 64, https://philosophisches-jahrbuch.de/wp-content/uploads/2019.

4. Cf. Peter J. Casarella, "Nicholas of Cusa and the Power of the Possible," *American Catholic Philosophical Quarterly* 64, no. 1 (Winter 1998): 9–12 and 30–34.

5. Egil A. Wyller, *Platons Parmenides in seinem Zusammenhang mit Symposion und Politeia: Interpretationen zur platonischen Henologie* (Oslo: I Kommisjon hos H. Aschehoug, 1960).

6. Nikolaus von Cues, *Vom Nichtanderen*, trans. Paul Wilpert (Hamburg: Meiner, 1952).

7. Meister Eckhart, *Meister Eckhart: A Modern Translation*, trans. Raymond B. Blakney (New York: Harper Torchbooks, 1957), 171.

8. Hugo von Hofmannsthal, "The Letter of Lord Chandos," in *Selected Prose*, trans. Mary Hottinger and Tania and James Stern (New York: Pantheon, 1952).

9. Martin Buber, *Die Schriften über das dialogische Prinzip* (Heidelberg: Schneider, 1954).

Wittgenstein's "There is indeed the inexpressible. This shows itself; it is the mystical."[10] They all spoke to me of the way I, too, at times experienced the magical presence of persons and things. Cusanus's "not-other" seemed to provide a pointer to what renders our lives meaningful. And I was looking for meaning.

As long as I can remember, nihilism has shadowed my life, at first a shapeless dark cloud, later a specter that I tried to address with my own thinking. That shadow haunts just about everything that I have written. I confronted it once more in my most recent books: *Wahrheit: Die Architektur der Welt* (2012), originally ten lectures I gave at the Leuphana University in Lüneburg, and its reworked English version, *The Antinomy of Being* (2019). This commentary, too, is a final attempt to drive away that specter.

I began to write about nihilism as an undergraduate. That time— I arrived at Yale as a freshman in 1954—now seems both very close and very distant. Less than three years had passed since my family left then still war-torn Germany. Memories of nightly air raids, images of the burning of Berlin, which we children could watch night after night from the attic of our house, of the bunker that was built in our garden, of strafing planes, of a prison camp on which my brother and I stumbled on the Grosse Gleichberg, horrified and frightened by the look of the prisoners; and then, after the war, of war-ravaged Munich, of hunger and living in the last, barely inhabitable story of an apartment building that had lost its roof—these and countless other memories were still fresh in my mind then and remain with me, especially when I watch the news. In that world there was no place for thoughts of an all-powerful, benign God.

But there were also positive memories of a land still beautiful, despite all that had ravaged it, of rococo churches that have lost nothing of their magic, of Munich's Maxgymnasium, which even though I attended it only for four short years, laid a firm foundation on which I could build. The beauty of the Bavarian landscape, along with that school and its teachers, made me not want to leave Germany when my parents chose to emigrate to the United States in 1951.

Although my grandfather Otto Grossmann was a Lutheran minister who in July 1933 bravely challenged Hitler from his Berlin pulpit only to be briefly arrested and then retired,[11] my parents were not

10. Ludwig Wittgenstein, *Tractatus Logico Philosphicus*, trans. C. K. Ogden (London: Routledge and Kegan Paul, 1922), 6:522.

11. See "Auszüge aus der Predigt von Pfarrer Großmann am 2. Juli 1933," *Archiv der Markusgemeinde*, https://www.markus-gemeinde.de.

religious. Regular church attendance was not part of my childhood. And this has not changed.

To be sure, in religion class I sang, without giving much thought to what I sang,

> Lobe den Herren, der alles so herrlich regieret,
> der dich auf Adelers Fittichen sicher geführet,
> der dich erhält, wie es dir selber gefällt;
> hast du nicht dieses verspüret?[12]

The hymn has remained with me. And has some higher power not kept me in a way that today I affirm? Despite so much I must condemn in the past that made me who I am, I do not wish for a different life. And must I not therefore affirm that past? But how can I reconcile such affirmation with events such as the Holocaust and the World War, not to mention more recent horrors? Do they not make talk of a God who rules all things so excellently seem absurd? Here is a Gordian knot that reason is unable to unravel.

As a boy I was interested in how things worked: watermills especially fascinated me; so did animals and trees. I dreamed of becoming a forester. As a young teenager I became interested in astronomy. Still in Germany, I got hold of a volume I still own that included an essay by Pascual Jordan on the expanding universe.[13] The questions about the origin and make-up of the universe it raised have stayed with me, as demonstrated by this commentary. Such questions led me to wonder even then about the limits of the objectifying reason that, presiding over our science and technology, has been shaping our life-world ever more decisively. That has remained a central concern. As an undergraduate at Yale University I thus drifted, after considering mathematics, classics, and history as possible majors, toward philosophy. But I ended up not majoring in any one subject. Yale's now unfortunately defunct Scholar of the House program freed me in my senior year from the normal course requirements. It required instead a dissertation-length essay. Mine had the title "Change and Permanence: A Study of Structure, Symbol, and Idea in Eight Major Prose

12. Praise the Lord who rules all things so excellently
    Who leads you securely on eagle's wings.
    Who supports you
    As you yourself wish;
    Have you not felt this?
13. Pascual Jordan, "Kosmogonische Anschauungen der modernen Physik," in *Naturwissenschaft—Religion—Weltanschauung: Clausthaler Gespräch 1948* (Clausthal-Zellerfeld, 1949), 25–33.

Works by Hermann Hesse." Quite a bit longer than my dissertation was going to be, that essay already attempted to address the nihilism that inescapably shadows the progress of reason. In all his writings, I argued, Hesse seeks to overcome the absurdity of life. That is especially true of his last major work, the utopian *Das Glasperlenspiel, The Glass Bead Game* (1943), set in the twenty-third century. Following Hesse, I described the game as "an attempt to find the divine in the world, to hear a harmony above the chaos. Pythagoras, Leibniz, Hegel, and especially Cusanus, but also the old Chinese, classical, and medieval philosophers are mentioned as its spiritual ancestors."[14] That is the first mention of Cusanus in any of my writings. The questions "To what extent can Cusanus be understood as such a glass bead player?" and "Are all philosophical attempts to find meaning in life perhaps a bit like Hesse's glass-bead game?" have remained with me.[15]

My dissertation, "Stranger in a Strange Land: An Exploration of Nihilism" (1961), confronted the loss of meaning directly. I had considered writing my dissertation on Cusanus but felt insufficiently prepared. Writing on nihilism seemed the more workable path. But that the two, Cusanus and nihilism, remained linked in my mind is shown by the way the dissertation's conclusion looks to Cusanus, especially to his understanding of the not-other, to find a way that might lead beyond nihilism:

> Unfortunately it is impossible to find for this last part of our journey a guide who speaks our own language. We have to go back to the late Middle Ages, back to Nicolaus Cusanus. Cusanus, more than Descartes, stood between two ages. He was the first one to see in all clarity that the Thomistic conception of the universe can no longer answer the questions that matter most, because of the modern turn to the subject. But the cardinal does not abandon the old value structure but attempts to lay new foundations for it.[16]

At that time I had spent a great deal of time on Wittgenstein's *Tractatus.* What Wittgenstein has to say there about language and its limits I still find challenging. To be sure, we must keep in mind that,

<hr>

14. Karsten Harries, "Change and Permanence: A Study of Structure, Symbol, and Idea in Eight Major Prose Works by Hermann Hesse," Scholars of the House Program, Yale University, 1958, 91.

15. I am not the only one to have found Hesse's association of Cusanus with the glass bead game suggestive. See Annarita Angelini, "Praecisio and Conjecture: Cusanus' Ball Game and the 'Learned Ignorance' of the World," *Nuncius* 28, no. 1 (January 2013): 5–18, https://doi.org/10.1163/18253911-028010.

16. Karsten Harries, "In a Strange Land: An Exploration of Nihilism" (Ph.D. diss., Yale University, 1961), 149.

as Wittgenstein himself came to acknowledge, what is called "language" here does not do justice to our language, either to ordinary language or to poetry. But his ideal language does do justice to the demand that language be clear and distinct, that meaningful propositions be either true or false, a demand that presides over our science as a regulative ideal. This demand, however, our language cannot meet. And it certainly cannot be reconciled with Cusanus's insight that all our propositions about reality are but sort of true, conjectures that inevitably fall short of the reality they claim to represent. As Wittgenstein knew, his logical space has no room for meaning or value. Nor does the world understood by him as the totality of facts and as such a subset of all possible facts, determined by logical space. Cusanus would have objected that the world so understood may not be confused with God's creation; it is our creation. Inseparable from this human construct is a loss of transcendence. So understood, the world does not know anything of what might make our lives meaningful. The young Wittgenstein would have agreed:

> 6.41 The sense of the world must lie outside the world. In the world everything is as it is and happens as it does happen. In it there is no value—and if there were, it would be of no value.
>
> If there is a value which is of value, it must lie outside all happening and being-so. For all happening and being-so is accidental.
>
> What makes it non-accidental cannot lie in the world, for otherwise this would again be accidental.
>
> It must lie outside the world.
>
> 6.42 Hence also there can be no ethical propositions. Propositions cannot express anything higher.[17]

In the world, as Wittgenstein understands it here, everything could be other than it happens to be. But if there were a value, it would have to present itself to us as not possibly other than it is. What the young Wittgenstein called the inexpressible, which is said "to show itself" (6.522), sheds some light on Cusanus's understanding of the not-other. As I put it in the dissertation:

> After having shown the inadequacy of all our attempts to seize the world, Cusanus proceeds to give a definition of God. Language, perception, and thought all operate by means of a logical space. This is the root of their inadequacy. But cannot language refer to its own inadequacy? We must find a name that forces us beyond the law of

17. Wittgenstein, *Tractatus Logico Philosphicus.*

contradiction, beyond logical space. This is what the poet tries to do. Cusanus gives a different and deceptively simple answer. If man cannot reach God because he operates within the mode of the *aliud* or the other, could not the *non aliud* be the name of God? The ideal name we imagined for the tree was the name that in no way fell short of the tree we are actually looking at. It is the object, not as it is in logical space, but as it is in itself. When I see the object in its ineffable particularity, I see it in the mode of the *non aliud*. The *non aliud* is what was called above the Thou; it is also God and the beautiful.[18]

These were rash, much too quickly made pronouncements. At that time, besides *De li non aliud*, of Cusanus's writings, I had only studied the *Idiota* dialogues, *De ludo globi, De beryllo,* and *De possest*. But what then prompted me to look to Cusanus still moves me: I remain convinced that a thoughtful return to the threshold that separates and joins the medieval and our modern world can help us proceed in a more promising direction. Key here is the difficulty we moderns have holding on to a robust awareness of transcendence. In contemporary philosophy, talk of transcendence is suspect. Like the neo-Kantians, most philosophers today are unable to make much sense of Kant's thing-in-itself. But as Kant recognized, the denial of the thing-in-itself leads to nihilism. The thing in itself, however, cannot be described or expressed in meaningful propositions. As the young Wittgenstein recognized, it must show itself. And it shows itself whenever we really engage and are open to another person.[19] It shows itself in the beauty of a flower or a work of art.[20]

At the time, my understanding of Cusanus's place on the threshold separating and joining the Middle Ages and our modern world owed much to Ernst Cassirer, who links the world-transforming originality of Cusanus to the way he emphasizes the problem of knowledge:

> The point of departure is here, too, the opposition between the being of the absolute and the empirically conditioned, the infinite and the finite. But this opposition is now no longer simply and dogmatically posited, but it is to be grasped in its ultimate depth, is to be comprehended in terms of the conditions of human knowledge. This stance towards the *problem of knowledge* characterizes Cusanus as the first modern thinker.[21]

18. Harries, "In a Strange Land," 153.

19. Cf. Kant, *Critique of Judgment*, 368. Freedom, by its effects, opens a window in nature to the supersensible.

20. Cf. Kant's discussion of "free beauty" in the *Critique of Judgment*.

21. Cassirer, *Individuum und Kosmos*, 10. See also Cassirer, *Erkenntnisproblem*, 1:32ff.

But, much as I admired Cassirer's scholarship and insight, his neo-Kantian reading of Cusanus left me dissatisfied. I felt that he failed to give sufficient weight to what I took to be Cusanus's insight that our life and thoughts become meaningful only when there is an awareness of a reality that transcends our reason, when we are touched by a reality radically other—for Cusanus, ultimately God. But God can be said to touch us whenever we are open to the unique presence of a person or thing. Every such experience is a revelation of the divine.

For Cassirer it is the translation of God into the human mind that justified his characterization of Cusanus as the first modern philosopher. "If the Middle Ages placed the goal of all knowledge in a transcendent being, so now the insight matures that it is only the immanent content of humanity that in the progress of the history of the spirit strives for clarity."[22] This at bottom Hegelian conception did not convince me. I gave voice to my dissatisfaction in my second published paper, "Cusanus and the Platonic Idea."[23] I concluded that essay with a discussion of the *non aliud*, which Cusanus took to be what Plato meant when he spoke of his ideas. Although much that I wrote then today leaves me dissatisfied, I still feel that I got hold of something important.

That *De li non aliud*, the work that introduced me to Cusanus, figures only marginally in Cassirer's Cusanus interpretation points to the different ways in which we approached his work. Cassirer mentions the *non aliud* just once in the *Erkenntnisproblem*, and in *Individuum und Kosmos* not at all. But that one mention is revealing:

> *Non aliud*: that means for one that the absolute is *not divorced* and separate from the empirical contents, but is precisely that which constitutes their inner immanent being; on the other hand, however, it is meant to express that the highest unity is not to be understood and defined as "this" or "that," not in the manner of a particular thing. "God is all in all and yet nothing of all"—Cusanus's metaphysics ends with this antinomy. But the opposition of these two theses can be resolved and understood if we—and once again Cusanus points the way—turn the proposition once more into the realm of consciousness. Every content of consciousness presupposes the original form and unity of consciousness and cannot arise or be thought without it; nevertheless, this form never presents itself fully and exhaustively in any content, and all pictures and concepts that

---

22. Cassirer, *Erkenntnisproblem*, 1:61.

23. Karsten Harries, "Cusanus and the Platonic Idea," *New Scholasticism* 7, no. 2 (1963): 188–203. My first published paper, "Heidegger and Hölderlin: The Limits of Language," *Personalist* 44, no. 1 (1963): 5–23, addressed what I took to be the same philosophical issue.

we take from the world of things and apply to it constitute a false and inappropriate application.[24]

The quotation suggests what Novalis had to say about the individual who succeeded in lifting the veil of Isis only to see himself. But such an idealistic replacement of God with the "original form and unity of consciousness" fails to do justice to what Cusanus had in mind when he spoke of the *non aliud*: when I see some rose as "nothing other" than just the rose it is, it is not myself that I see in the rose; I open myself to the rose's elusive transcendent being as I become aware of its mysterious *haecceitas* or "thisness."

Cassirer takes Cusanus to have anticipated the modern Platonism of Kepler and Galileo.[25] For Plato, Cusanus, and Cassirer, thought is a process by which the intellect, as it seeks to understand the given, seeks unity in what it confronts as its own true measure.[26] The form of that process is provided by mathematics. But, unlike Plato and like Cassirer, Cusanus, as we have seen, refuses to ground mathematical knowledge in a transcendent reality. Mathematicals have their foundation in an unfolding of the human mind. What is a priori is the mind's power to unify the manifold.[27] Similarly, Cusanus denies a realm of transcendent ideas, for Cassirer an anticipation of Kant's transcendental unity of the apperception. Cusanus takes Plato's ideas, too, to be human creations. But he recognizes an essential difference between mathematicals and ideas, as indeed Plato did when he distinguished the third and fourth levels of the divided line. Turning away from the materiality of the world, mathematics provided Cusanus with a model "of which all our knowledge [of reality] must necessarily fall short. but which it nevertheless strives to realize."[28] But if our knowledge of the world falls short of the truth we find in mathematics, because there we are concerned with our own creations, our creation of the ideas falls short of the truth of things that is God's creation.

Cusanus's insight into the creative power of the mind lets him, as we have seen, praise Protagoras and call the human being a second god. According to the Bible, God created us human beings in his image. As a second god the human being has his measure in God. The thought that the human being is *imago Dei* provides a key to Cusanus's

<hr>

24. Cassirer, *Erkenntnisproblem*, 56–57.
25. Cassirer, *Erkenntnisproblem*, 32.
26. See Plato, *Republic* VII.524E–25A.
27. Cassirer, *Erkenntnisproblem*, 33.
28. Harries, "Cusanus and the Platonic Idea," 192.

thought: whatever we understand about the world has its measure in God's creation; whatever we do similarly has its measure in the infinite God. But how can the infinite provide us finite human beings with a measure? Cassirer's answer: "Only in surrendering oneself (*Hingebung*) to the material of perception can true knowledge be gained and founded; but the more deeply we lose ourselves in this task, the more clearly the image of our own spirit and its thought creations emerges on the background of experience."[29]

But is the image of our own spirit, understood by Cassirer as the "original form and unity of consciousness," sufficient to provide our life and actions with the needed measure? The question points to what let Cassirer recognize in the later *Individuum und Kosmos* (1927) the importance of the third book of *De docta ignorantia*—that is, of Cusanus's understanding of the idea of Christ as a religious legitimation of the idea of humanity:

> Up to now the third book of the work *De docta ignorantia*, in which this turn is made, has been understood at times so little that one tried to excise it from the whole of Cusanus's philosophy, that one considered it an arbitrary "theological" appendix, which had its origin in a purely dogmatic interest. But such familiar separations cannot be introduced into the doctrine of Cusanus without thereby cutting into pieces its whole inner organization, without canceling its characteristic spiritual structure. In truth the introduction into and the speculative treatment of the Christ-idea in *De docta ignorantia* is not at all an external appendix, but rather what allows the moving force in Cusanus's thinking to fully unfold and express itself.[30]

While I very much agree that the third book of *De docta ignorantia* is an essential part of the whole, Cassirer's neo-Kantian framework transforms Christ into a regulative ideal that every human being bears within him- or herself. We are finite, embodied beings. As such we know of the infinite distance that separates us from the Absolute. But, Cassirer suggests,

> the consciousness of the difference includes the mediation of the difference. But this mediation cannot mean that the infinite, the absolute being, enters with the finite empirical self-consciousness into some sort of relation. Here a chasm gapes as before, which cannot be leapt over. A general self must take the place of the empirical self, the spiritual content of humanity must take the place of the human being as a particular existence. And it is this spiritual universal

29. Cassirer, *Erkenntnisproblem*, 32.
30. Cassirer, *Individuum und Kosmos*, 40.

content of humanity that Cusanus sees in Christ.... As Christ is the expression for *all* of humanity, as he means nothing other than its simple idea and essence, so, on the other hand, the human being, considered in its essence, includes the whole of all things within himself. In the human being as microcosm all things of the macrocosm converge.

But Christ, so understood, is not the cardinal's Christ, not the savior. If we look at Cusanus's works through Cassirer's neo-Kantian glasses, even if what we see can really be found there, much that is necessary to do justice to what mattered to the cardinal will escape us.

Cusanus's understanding of man as *imago Dei* is difficult to reconcile with the infinity of God. Cusanus recognizes this difficulty: If *infiniti ad finitum nulla est proportion*, how can the infinite God provide finite man with a measure? Cassirer's invocation of the universal content of humanity is indeed suggested by quite a number of passages in *De docta ignorantia*, passages that, as we saw, met with Johannes Wenck's vehement critique. But they should not be taken out of context. Cusanus is unwilling to rationalize the paradox of the incarnation.

Cusanus's understanding of the infinity of God provides the key or, perhaps we should say, the main obstacle to understanding *De docta ignorantia*. If *infiniti ad finitum nulla est proportio*, is not silence the only "discourse" adequate to God? "The plenitude and the contrary life of this world of appearances form the obstacle that denies us a genuine knowledge of God."[31] Are we then not left with an extreme version of negative theology? That this is not the case this commentary has shown. In *De docta ignorantia* Cusanus has a great deal to say about God. And this is even more true of the many works that were to follow. But what allowed him to do so? What justifies his reliance on a version of the doctrine of analogy?

In *Erkenntnisproblem* Cassirer does his best to remove this obstacle. Key here is the following passage from *De docta ignorantia*, discussed earlier:

Whatever is not truth cannot measure truth precisely. (By comparison, a non-circle [cannot measure] a circle, whose being is something indivisible.) Hence, the intellect, which is not truth, never comprehends truth so precisely that truth cannot be comprehended infinitely more precisely. For the intellect is to truth as [an inscribed] polygon is to [the inscribing] circle. The more angles the inscribed polygon has, the more similar it is to the circle. However, even if the

31. Cassirer, *Erkenntnisproblem*, 22–23.

> number of its angles is increased ad infinitum, the polygon never becomes equal [to the circle] unless it is resolved into an identity with the circle. Hence, regarding truth, it is evident that we do not know anything other than the following: viz., that we know truth not to be precisely comprehensible as it is. (*DI* I.3:10)

The passage suggests that while the infinite can never be known precisely, we can arrive at ever better approximations. We readily see that a regular polygon with 1,000 sides more closely approximates the circle than a polygon with 10 sides. This suggests that *infiniti ad finitum nulla est proportio* should not be understood to mean that there cannot be more or less fitting descriptions of the infinite. To be sure, just as the attempt to state the exact value of π can go on and on, so can our attempt to comprehend reality. "The interminability of this process now counts no longer as proof of an inner conceptual defect but as witnessing its power and specific nature: only in an infinite object, in a limitless progress, can reason become aware of its own capacity."[32] An awareness of the infinite is indeed part of our human nature. "Now infinity is no longer the limit, but the self-affirmation of reason."[33] Cassirer finds confirmation for his interpretation in this passage from *De visione Dei*:

> The reason You, O God, are unknown to all creatures is so that amid this most sacred ignorance creatures may be more content, as if [they were situated] amid a countless and inexhaustible treasure. For one who finds a treasure of such kind that he knows it to be altogether uncountable and infinite is filled with much greater joy than is one who finds a countable and finite treasure. Hence, this most sacred ignorance of Your greatness is a most delectable feast for my intellect—especially since I find such a treasure in my own field, so that it is a treasure which belongs to me. (*DVD* 71)

God is to be sought not without, beyond the sensible world, but within.

> The new age begins in both directions, the subjective as well as the objective, with a reversal of what previously had been thought. The object of its concern is immanent to the spirit; it is *consciousness* itself and its lawfulness that conditions and limits the object of knowledge. And yet the process, in which we seek to bring this new being to scientific determination, must be thought as in principle interminable. Finite empirical existence is never fully known, but lies as the task of research always ahead of us. The character of infinity has passed from the *object* of knowledge to the *function* of knowledge.[34]

---

32. Cusanus, *Erkenntnisproblem*, 26.
33. Cusanus, *Erkenntnisproblem*, 27.
34. Cusanus, *Erkenntnisproblem*, 28.

That the function of knowledge has the character of infinity we can grant Cassirer. It is indeed suggested by Cusanus's understanding of the human being as *imago Dei*. Just as our ability to count knows no limit, so does our attempt to understand nature. But unlike mathematics, science is not adequately understood as just an unfolding of the human mind. Whatever we understand about the cosmos is only a conjectural recreation of the divinely created cosmos. The awareness of what Cassirer calls the "original form and unity of consciousness" that we bear as a regulative idea, never to be fully realized, within may not be confused with the infinite that is the ground of our own being as it is the ground of the world of which we are but a part. When I experience the rose as not other than just this rose, what touches me is not the "original form and unity of consciousness," but something that I cannot comprehend: transcendence.

I taught a graduate seminar on Cusanus for the first time in 1964 at the University of Texas. A teaching award had enabled me to travel to Brixen to participate in the international congress *Nicoló Cusano agli inizi del mondo moderno* and to listen to a number of the then most active Cusanus scholars. That I should have found Egil A. Wyller's long contribution "Zum Begriff des 'non aliud' bei Cusanus"[35] especially thought provoking is not surprising, given my interest in that tetralogue.

When I returned to Yale in 1966, I continued to offer seminars on Cusanus. This commentary is indebted to the questions and comments of my students. They helped me to clarify my thoughts. A number of them—Clyde Lee Miller, Dermot Moran, Peter J. Casarella, Elizabeth Brient—went on to make significant contributions to the Cusanus literature.

Shortly after my return to Yale I discovered the writings of Hans Blumenberg. They helped guide my continuing explorations. I had little interest in Blumenberg's metaphorology, which excited some of my colleagues. What I found illuminating, but also finally unconvincing, was his account of the emergence of the modern world, developed at great length in the *Legitimität der Neuzeit*[36] and *Die Genesis der kopernikanischen Welt*,[37] as a response to nominalism: a world rendered

---

35. Egil A. Wyller, "Zum Begriff des 'non aliud' bei Cusanus," in *Nicolo' Cusano: Agli Inizi del Mondo Moderno*, 419–43.

36. Blumenberg, *Die Legitimität der Neuzeit: The Legitimacy of the Modern Age*, trans. Robert M. Wallace (Cambridge, MA: MIT Press, 1985).

37. Hans Blumenberg, *Die Genesis der kopernikanischen Welt* (1971; repr. Frankfurt am Main: Suhrkamp, 1981); in English Blumenberg, *The Genesis of the Copernican World*, trans. Robert M. Wallace (Cambridge, MA: MIT Press, 1987).

mute by the asserted absolute transcendence of God is said to have provoked a self-assertion that, finally dispensing with God, led to the worldliness of our modern world.[38]

Blumenberg's rejection of Cassirer's replacement of Descartes with Cusanus as the founding figure of modernity[39] resonated with my own reservations, but also challenged my conviction that Cusanus was a thinker who, precisely because he remained firmly rooted in his faith, even as many of his ideas anticipate what we have come to associate with modernity, remains relevant to this postmodern age, which, unable to break with its modernity, has yet come to question its legitimacy. The very title, *Die Legitimität der Neuzeit*, suggests that Blumenberg would have rejected such a suggestion. As the title *Die Genesis der kopernikanischen Welt* suggests, Blumenberg takes Copernicus to be the thinker who best marks the threshold to our modern world. To contest the claim that the pre-Copernican Cusanus deserves that "honor," Blumenberg contrasts him in the *Legitimität* with the post-Copernican Giordano Bruno, who owed so much to the cardinal. Bruno accepts the proposition *finiti ad infinitum nulla proportio*, which he cites in his interrogation by the Inquisition in Venice in his defense.[40] But as Blumenberg points out, while Cusanus responds to the abyss this proposition opens up by insisting on the Incarnation as the indispensable condition not just of our salvation, but of the intelligibility of the word, Bruno insists on its impossibility: the infinite God is infinitely distant from or infinitely close to everything. Bruno's God is not concerned with the fate of us human beings. That recognition is said to make Bruno a modern thinker, while Cusanus's attempt to preserve the old faith in the face of the challenge posed by his reflections on the infinite makes him a late medieval thinker. The transition from the final chapters of Book Two of *De docta ignorantia* to Book Three can be read as a reversal or a retreat from the unsettling vision of an infinite cosmos, which lets Cusanus liken the earth to a ship, adrift in boundless space, a return to the comfort provided by faith in Christ, which provides our lives and creation with a center, notwithstanding the decentering power of the infinite. I take this attempt by the cardinal to counter the decentering power of the infinite with a recentering granted by faith to present us with a continuing challenge: only some such recentering can render life meaningful. While there

38. On Blumenberg's understanding of Cusanus, see Elizabeth Brient, "Immanence of the Infinite."

39. Blumenberg, *Die Legitimität der Neuzeit*, 440.

40. Blumenberg, *Die Legitimität der Neuzeit*, 559.

is indeed a sense in which the post-Copernican Giordano Bruno can be said to be a modern thinker, while especially in Book Three of *De docta ignorantia* Cusanus presents himself to us as still thoroughly medieval, it is precisely his reversal that in my opinion makes him more relevant today than Bruno.

Given Blumenberg's understanding of Cusanus as a medieval thinker who cannot be said to have anticipated the scientist Copernicus in any very significant way, it is not surprising that in his monumental *Die Genesis der kopernikanischen Welt* Cusanus figures only on the margins of this thorough account. And yet the conclusion of the work made me think of Cusanus: If Cusanus saw a need to return from the decentering vision of the infinite cosmos to the centering power of grace, Blumenberg, too, in concluding his work, hints at the possibility of something like a secular grace. Especially suggestive is a comment, prompted by our failure to find any signs of extraterrestrials, that concludes *Die Genesis*: "Only as the experience of a reversal (*Rückwendung*) will it be accepted that for us human beings there is no alternative to the earth, just as there is no alternative to human reason."[41] I responded to this comment in concluding my lengthy review of the work:

> I find the first part of this statement clearer than the second. What renunciation does it invite? Would Blumenberg, forsaking the Cartesian dream of a science that seizes the truth without distortion, join those who would criticize the pursuit of objectivity in the name of care, the life-world, ordinary language, or myth? Where does Blumenberg locate reality, and where does he seek proper access to it? One wishes for a more systematic work that would furnish the answer. But I suspect that Blumenberg's diffidence and circumspection will never allow him to answer as unambiguously as one would like. Part of our Copernican inheritance is the uneasy coexistence of anthropocentric prejudice and the demand for liberation from all prejudice. The tensions between phenomenology and history, science and life-world, reason and sensibility, curiosity and care, cannot finally be resolved. Nor can reality be given a simple location.[42]

Much of my subsequent work can be understood as a response to Blumenberg's account of the genesis of the modern world and more especially to this closing remark. I dedicated *Infinity and Perspective*, which also tells the story of the emergence of the modern world, but

41. Blumenberg, *Die Genesis der kopernikanischen Welt*.

42. Karsten Harries, "Copernican Reflections," review of Hans Blumenberg, *Die Genesis der kopernikanischen Welt, Inquiry* 23 (1980): 253–69.

places Cusanus rather than Copernicus at the center of the narrative, to Blumenberg's memory.[43]

Key here is the decentering power of reflection on the way perspective distorts our understanding of reality, reflection that not only dethrones the earth from its central position, leaving us human beings adrift in infinite space, but also awakens a sense of freedom that recognizes no bounds and with it the need for a center to anchor our lives. If Cusanus met the decentering power of reflections on the infinite with the recentering power of faith, lacking such faith, Blumenberg met it with reflections that this fragile earth, now threatened by the power our science has given us, is yet the only home that we shall ever have, demanding our loving care.

In lectures, articles, and books I have attempted to unfold Blumenberg's claim that "for us human beings there is no alternative to the earth" by calling for a post-Copernican geocentrism.[44] Here the conclusion of *Infinity and Perspective*:

> Hans Blumenberg would have us remember that the earth, which once, because of its central position in a finite cosmos, was thought to provide human beings with a privileged place for the *theoria* of the cosmos, a place that allowed them to actually observe all that mattered, which then came to be understood as just another among countless stars, "as a result of the technology of space travel has unexpectedly 'shown' us a property that extends to us something rather like grace: that it is possible to come back home to the earth, if one has been sufficiently curious and self-assertive to leave it. Odysseus—once more and dressed in the space suit of a figure of humanity: To return to Ithaca—this much has not changed—requires and rewards the widest detour."[45]

Our ever farther-reaching explorations of space have only confirmed the uniqueness of our earth: "It is more than a triviality that the experience of returning to the earth could only have been made by leaving it. This cosmic oasis on which the human being lives, this miracle of an exception, this singular blue planet in the midst of the disappointing celestial dessert, is not just 'another star,' but the only one that seems to deserve that name."[46] Given the immensity and

---

43. Harries, *Infinity and Perspective*.

44. See, e.g., Karsten Harries, "Longing for Ithaca: On the Need for a Post-Copernican Geocentrism," in *From the Things Themselves: Architecture and Phenomenology*, ed. Benoit Jacquet and Vincent Giraud (Kyoto: Kyoto University Press; École francaise d'Extrême-Orient, 2012), 495–522.

45. Harries, *Infinity and Perspective*, 383.

46. Blumenberg, *Die Genesis der kopernikanischen Welt*, 793–94.

homogeneity of the cosmos, it would seem that there must be countless stars with intelligent life. Science cannot make sense of the supposedly unique. But our search for extraterrestrials has come up empty: as far as we know, we are alone. I accept Blumenberg's conclusion: "There is no alternative to the earth."

That also goes for Blumenberg's second claim: "There is no alternative to human reason." The claim may seem obvious: what would such an alternative look like? A medieval thinker such as St. Thomas might have pointed to the way God or perhaps angels know. Cusanus insisted that the abyss that separates our reason from reality will never be bridged; our science will never furnish us more than more or less well-founded conjectures. But inseparable from modernity is the dream that clear and distinct thought can build such a bridge. Consider once more the ideal language Wittgenstein proposed in his *Tractatus*; or Descartes's insistence that we take as false all that is not so patently true as to resist all our attempts to doubt it. In everything that we perceive clearly and distinctly, truth is said to present itself to us as not possibly other than it is. It leaves no room for doubt. Such perceptions can provide the edifice of thought with a firm foundation.

But the dream of a language totally adequate to reality cannot be realized, for it would have to elide the distinction between picture and pictured, between our logical constructs and reality. This does not mean that this ideal has not presided and should continue to preside over the progress of science. Descartes's promise of a science that would render us the masters and possessors of nature was no idle dream. The world we live in testifies to its power. But it is shadowed by the threat its very success poses to the long-term survival of humanity and to the meaning of life.

Koyré thinks it likely that Aquinas's discussion of angelic knowledge served as the source of Descartes's account of human knowledge.[47] Related is Thomas Nagel's construct of "The View from Nowhere," a totally objective "perspective," if we can call it that, uncontaminated by particular points of view,[48] as is the construct of an ideal observer. Objectivity presides over science as a regulative ideal. And as Plato already recognized, that ideal calls for the mathematization of nature. Cusanus,

47. Alexandre Koyré, *Essai sur l'idée de Dieu et les preuves de Son existence selon Descartes* (Paris: Leroux, 1922), 93. See also Étienne Gilson, *Études sur la rôle de la pensé médiévale dans la formation du système* cartésien (Paris: J. Vrin, 1967), 12.

48. Thomas Nagel, *The View from Nowhere*, rev. ed. (Oxford: Oxford University Press, 1989.

as we have seen, appropriates this Platonic insight. But he recognized that while mathematics provides us with a key to the construction of ever better conjectures, our propositions can claim absolute truth only in the realm of mathematics or, more generally, in the realm of concepts that are an unfolding of our own mind—for instance, "all roses are flowers." Here we are dealing with our own, not with God's creations. When studying nature or indeed anything real, we must content ourselves with conjectures.

To think that reality and our reason are commensurable is to substitute for reality a human construct. While it is impossible to deny the countless ways in which our science and technology have given us ever deeper insights into the mysteries of nature and improved our lives, it is equally impossible to deny that this very progress today endangers this fragile earth and the quality of our lives. The self-assertion that has built our modern world has also led to a selfishness that has too little concern for the stranger, for still unborn generations. Needed is a change of heart. But how do hearts change? We must temper the will to power that has built us our modern world with the recognition that what can give meaning to our lives must touch us from without, as another person can touch us. To give a different turn to Blumenberg's words: the caring encounter with others can "show" us a property that extends to us something rather like grace. Did not Christ say, "Whatever you did for one of the least of these brothers and sisters of mine, you did for me" (Mt 25:40)? In the other Cusanus would have us see God.

I wrote *Infinity and Perspective* to offer an alternative to Blumenberg's reflections on the emergence of the modern world. As the title suggests, my narrative had a sharper focus. Blumenberg might have objected that it does violence to the complexity of historical events.

Given that focus, it is not surprising that I should have made Cusanus the hero of my narrative. No thinker better illuminates the threshold that joins and separates the medieval and the modern world, where, as Blumenberg recognizes, a key is provided by the way the incomprehensibility of God provoked a human self-assertion that in the end was to lead to what Nietzsche called the death of God. Not that I see a sharp break between the medieval and the modern world. Wrestling with the infinity of God had to awaken thoughts that had to destroy the medieval world from within, awakening a new sense of freedom. In this connection Cusanus's relationship with Alberti, the way both defended the much-maligned Protagoras and his thesis that man is the measure of all things, became important to me.

Chapters 11 and 12 of Book Two of *De docta ignorantia* especially fit all too well into the picture of the emergence of the modern world I developed in that book. Long before starting work on *Infinity and Perspective* I had explored Cusanus's transference of the metaphor of the infinite sphere, which has its center everywhere and its circumference nowhere, from God to the cosmos in an article.[49] Shattering the fundamentally still Aristotelian medieval understanding of the cosmos, it casts a light on the theological roots of our modern scientific world picture. Presupposed by that transference is the freedom of the human intellect, to which we can also apply the metaphor of the infinite sphere: it has its center everywhere and its circumference nowhere. Our experience of reality is inescapably shaped by some perspective or other. We tend to think as central wherever we happen to be. But the infinity of the intellect calls into question every supposed center.

What prompted me to write this commentary was dissatisfaction with the way I had presented Cusanus in *Infinity and Perspective*. Not that I want to take back anything I wrote in that book. Although broadly reviewed, there has been no significant criticism of the narrative it presented. But its very focus prevented me from doing justice to the richness of Cusanus's thought, especially of *De docta ignorantia*. Instead of selecting passages that fit my narrative, I wanted to confront that work in all its complexity, allowing Cusanus's voice to be heard without distortion. I am all too aware that, as Cusanus teaches us, despite all my efforts, this commentary cannot claim to do full justice to the original. But I hope that it will make *De docta ignorantia* more accessible to a modern reader and exhibit its continued relevance.

In the introduction I wrote that this commentary attempts some steps toward answering the Kantian questions "What can I know? What should I do? What may I hope?" How Cusanus might have answered these questions should have been suggested by the preceding. But to briefly sum up:

Cusanus's answer to the first question is provided by the doctrine of learned ignorance. *Nulla proportio inter infinitum et finitum est.* There is no proportion between the infinite and the finite. God, the infinite ground of all that can be, cannot be known as he is. But all creatures, having their being from God, partake of his infinity. They too can therefore not be known as they are in themselves. The abyss that separates our knowledge from reality will never be bridged,

<hr>

49. Karsten Harries, "The Infinite Sphere: Comments on the History of a Metaphor," *Journal of the History of Philosophy* 13, no. 1 (1975): 5–15.

But just as the value of π can be determined ever more adequately, so our descriptions of things can be made ever more adequate. In the first case the measure of adequacy is provided by the thought of an inscribed polygon with infinite sides, which would be identical with the circle. Similarly, our descriptions of things have their measure in the thought of a totally adequate description, where description and thing would coincide. The truth, understood as *adaequatio intellectus ad rem*, as the adequacy of the intellect to the thing, has its measure in the truth understood as the identity of intellect and thing. As Hegel was to put it, "God alone is the true accordance of concept and reality; all finite things, however, possess an untruth: they have a concept and an existence, which, however, is inadequate to the concept."[50] We shall never know things as they are, but science can progress toward an ever more adequate, if inescapably one-sided, understanding of nature by subjecting what presents itself to our senses to our spirit's mathematical measures.

Cusanus's answer to the second question is less clear. *De docta ignorantia* does not develop an ethics. But Cusanus's understanding of the human being as *imago Dei* provides a significant pointer. Here Book Three is of special importance: Christ provides us human beings with a measure both of our thoughts and our actions. That measure is not just brought to us from without by the mystery of the Incarnation. Our sense of right and wrong does not depend on some external revelation. It is innate. If more or less imperfectly, every human being, having been created in the image of God, finds that measure within. The historical Jesus answers to an ideal that is inseparable from our human nature. That we have indeed been created in the image of God Cusanus takes to show itself in our freedom and our reason, which reach up to infinity. In a way that brings to mind Kant's pure practical reason, Cusanus seeks the origin of the laws that should rule our actions in our reason raised by the intellect above "the temporal and mundane" (*DI* III.6:215). These laws Cusanus takes to be universal, although, like the idea of God, inevitably refracted by differences of time and place.

The doctrine of learned ignorance does teach us that, except in the field of mathematics, where we are concerned not with God's creation but with an unfolding of our own mind, all our claims to be in possession of some unshakable truth must be rejected. That implies a demand for tolerance. To cite Cassirer:

---

50. Georg Wilhelm Friedrich Hegel, *Enzyklopädie*, §24, Zusatz 2. *Jubiläumsausgabe*, ed. Hermann Glockner (Stuttgart: Frommann), vol. 8.

The limiting thought of the infinite forms the uniform and essential core of all religions, no matter how they may determine and limit it in detail: *una est religio et cultus omnium vigentium, quare in omni diversitate rituum praesupponitur.*[51] The science of not knowing here has become the principle of religious tolerance and enlightenment. As much as Cusanus sought to hold on to the fundamental Christian dogmas and to approach the ideal of that single religion, the religion of the logos, so is nevertheless in this symbolic reinterpretation the dogma no longer the unconditioned measure, but the object that is being measured.[52]

That is indeed what reason, unaided by faith, must conclude. What allowed Cusanus to hold on to the fundamental Christian dogmas was his faith. That reason cannot make sense of what faith would have us believe Cusanus admits, but learned ignorance lets us recognize the limits of our reason. And must we not look for what gives meaning to our lives beyond these limits? Think of love! And can there be love without faith?

Cusanus's answer to the third question will not convince those who lack faith. Cusanus, too, cannot make sense of an afterlife, if we mean by this a transfigured spiritual life, rather like this life, that will be the reward for a good life here on earth. But he does believe that death does not mean the end of the individual, and that a good life will be rewarded and a bad life punished *sub specie aeternitatis.* In our essence we human beings transcend our temporal condition. Time is a mystery we cannot fathom. What awaits us when we die lies beyond the wall of paradise, which is the coincidence of opposites. Here our reason fails us. We would not have become learned about our ignorance were we to think we could somehow see what lies beyond that wall, be it paradise or nothing.

51. "Therefore for all those who are of sound understanding there is one religion and worship, which is presupposed in all the diversity of the rites"; *DPF* 16.

52. Cusanus, *Erkenntnisproblem*, 30.

BIBLIOGRAPHY

Cusanus

All citations from Cusanus's works use the translations by Jasper Hopkins, which
he has made generously available on his website: https://jasper-hopkins.info.

I compared these with the Latin original texts and the German translations published by Meiner Verlag Hamburg, many of which were republished
in four volumes by Felix Meiner Verlag/Wissenschaftliche Buchgesellschaft
as Nikolaus von Kues, *Philosophisch-theologische Werke*, Lateinisch-deutsch, intro.
Karl Bormnann, abbreviated *PTW*. A list of the works cited follows:

Apologia Doctae Ignorantiae: Nicolai de Cusa Opera Omnia. Vol. II. Edited by
Raymond Klibansky. Leipzig: F. Meiner, 1932. Translated by Jasper
Hopkins: *Nicholas of Cusa's Debate with John Wenck: A Translation and an
Appraisal of "De Ignota Litteratura" and "Apologia Doctae Ignorantiae."*
Minneapolis: Banning, 1981. See https://jasper-hopkins.info/:
Apologia Doctae Ignorantiae.
Compendium. Translated by Jasper Hopkins. In *Nicholas of Cusa on Wisdom
and Knowledge.* Minneapolis: Banning, 1996.
Coniectura de Ultimis Diebus: Nicolai de Cusa Opera Omnia. Vol. IV. *Opuscula* I.
Edited by Paul Wilpert. Hamburg: Meiner Verlag. 1959, 91–100.
Translation Jasper Hopkins, *A Surmise about the Last Days.* See
https://jasper-hopkins.info/: *Coniectura de Ultimis Diebus.*
Cribatio Alkorani. In Jasper Hopkins, *Nicholas of Cusa's and Cribatio Alkorani:
Translation and Analysis,* 2nd ed. Minneapolis: Banning Press, 1994.
See https://jasper-hopkins.info/: *Cribatio Alkorani.*
De Beryllo. Translated by Jasper Hopkins: *On [Intellectual] Eyeglasses.* In *Nicholas
of Cusa: Metaphysical Speculations.* Minneapolis: Banning, 1997. Page references in the text are to the Meiner edition, given also in the margin of the
translation. See https://jasper-hopkins.info/: *De Beryllo.* Abbreviated *DB.*
De coniecturis. Edited by Josef Koch, Karl Bormann, and Hans G. Senger.
Hamburg: Meiner Verlag, 1972. Translation *De coniecturis. On Surmises.*
by Nicholas of Cusa, In Nicholas of Cusa: *Metaphysical Speculations,* translated by Jasper Hopkins, 2:162–297. Minneapolis: Banning, 2000. See
https://jasper-hopkins.info/: *De coniecturis.* Page references to this and
the following texts are to the Latin text, found in the margins of Hopkins'
translation.

De dato patris luminum. 1445/1446. *Nicolai de Cusa Opera Omnia.* Vol. IV.
   Opuscula I, edited by Paul Wilpert. Hamburg: Meiner Verlag, 1959.
   Translation by Jasper Hopkins, "On the Gift of the Father of Lights,"
   in *Nicholas of Cusa's Metaphysic of Contraction,* 372–86. Minneapolis:
   Banning Press, 1983.
De docta ignorantia. Book I. Edited by Paul Wilpert. Hamburg: Meiner, 1964.
De docta ignorantia. Book II. Edited by Paul Wilpert. Hamburg: Meiner, 1963.
De docta ignorantia. Book III. Edited by Hans Gerhard Senger. Meiner:
   Hamburg, 1977.

The three books were republished as volume I of *PTW: De docta ignorantia.* English translation by Jasper Hopkins, *Nicholas of Cusa on Learned Ignorance: A Translation and Appraisal of De Docta Ignorantia.* Minneapolis: Banning Press, 1981. See
alsohttps://jasper-hopkins.info/: *De docta ignorantia.* References are to the books
and paragraphs of the Latin text, found in the margins of Hopkins's translation.

De li non aliud. Translated by Jasper Hopkins. In *On God as Not-Other: A Trans-
   lation and an Appraisal,* by Nicholas of Cusa. Minneapolis: Banning, 1987.
   See https://jasper-hopkins.info/: *De li non aliud.*
De Ludo Globi. Translated by Jasper Hopkins. In *The Bowling-Game* in *Nicholas
   of Cusa: Metaphysical Speculations.* Vol. 2. Minneapolis: Banning, 2000.
   See https://jasper-hopkins.info/: *De Ludo Globi.*
De Pace Fidei. Translated by Jasper Hopkins. *Nicholas of Cusa's De Pace Fidei and
   Cribatio Alkorani.* Translation and Analysis, 2nd ed. Minneapolis: Ban-
   ning, 1994, See https://jasper-hopkins.info/: *De Pace Fidei.*
De Theologicis Complementis. Translated by Jasper Hopkins. In *Complementary
   Theological Considerations,* in *Nicholas of Cusa: Metaphysical Speculations;
   Six Latin Texts,* translated by Jasper Hopkins. Banning: Minneapolis, 1998.
De Visione Dei. Translated by Jasper Hopkins. In *The Vision of God in Nicholas
   of Cusa's Dialectical Mysticism Text, Translation, and Interpretive Study of
   De Visione Dei.* 2nd ed. Minneapolis: Banning Press, 1988. See https://
   jasper-hopkins.info/: *De Visione Dei.*
Idiota de Mente. The Layman on Mind. Translated by Jasper Hopkins. In
   Nicholas of Cusa on Wisdom and Knowledge. Minneapolis: Banning, 1996.
   See https://jasper-hopkins.info/: *Idiota de Mente/.*
Idiota de Sapientia. The Layman on Wisdom. The translation of *Idiota de S
   apientia* was made from Codex Cusanus Latinus 218, folia 107r–014v.
   Abbreviated *IDS.* See https://jasper-hopkins.info/: *Idiota de Sapientia.*
   Page references are to the Latin text in *Nicolai de Cusa Opera Omnia,*
   reprinted in *PTW* 2.
Idiota de Staticis Experimentis. The Layman on Experiments Done with Weight-scales.
   Translated by Jasper Hopkins: *Nicholas of Cusa on Wisdom and Knowledge.*
   Minneapolis: Banning, 1996: 319–71. Translated. from Codex Cusanus
   Latinus 218, folia 132r–37v, as transcribed by Hopkins. See https://
   jasper-hopkins.info/: *Idiota de Staticis Experimentis.*
Nicholas of Cusa's Didactic Sermons: A Selection. Translated, with an introduc-
   tion by Jasper Hopkins. Loveland, Colo.: Arthur J. Banning, 2003.
   See https://jasper-hopkins.info/: *Cusa's Didactic Sermons.*
Nicholas of Cusa's Early Sermons. Translated and introduction by Jasper

Hopkins. Loveland, Colorado: Arthur J. Banning Press, 2003. See
https://jasper-hopkins.info/: *Cusa's Early Sermons.*
Trialogus de Possest. Translated by Jasper Hopkins. In *A Concise Introduction to
the Philosophy of Nicholas of Cusa*, vol. 3, *Actualized-Possibility.* Minneapolis:
Banning, 1980. See https://jasper-hopkins.info/: *De Possest\.*
Vom Nichtanderen. Translated by Paul Wilpert. Hamburg: Meiner, 1952.

Other Texts

Alanus ab Insulis. *Sermo de sphaera intelligibili: Textes inédits.* Edited by M. Th.
d'Alverny, 297–306. Études de Philosophie Médiévales 52. Paris: Vrin.
1965.
Alberti, Leon Battista. *On Painting.* Translated, with an introduction by
John R. Spencer, rev. ed. New Haven: Yale University Press, 1966.
Albertini, Tamara. "Mathematics and Astronomy." In Bellitto, Izbicki, and
Christianson, *Introducing Nicholas of Cusa.* 2004.
Albertson, David. "A Learned Thief? Nicholas of Cusa and the Anonymous
Fundamentum Naturae. Reassessing the Vorlage Theory." *Recherches de
Théologie et Philosophie médiévales* 77, no. 2 (2010): 351–90.
———. "Mystical Philosophy in the Fifteenth Century: New Directions in
Research on Nicholas of Cusa." *Religion Compass* 4, no. 8 (2010): 471–85.
———. "Gott als Mathematiker?" *Mitteilungen und Forschungsbeiträge der
Cusanus Gesellschaft* 33 (2012): 110–11.
———. *Mathematical Theologies: Nicholas of Cusa and the Legacy of Thierry of
Chartres.* Oxford: Oxford University Press, 2014.
———. "'Boethius noster': Thierry of Chartres's *Arithmetica* Commentary as
a Missing Source of Nicholas of Cusa's *De docta ignorantia*," *Recherches de
Théologie et Philosophie Médiévales* 83, no. 1 (2016): 143–99.
Angelini, Annarita. "Praecisio and Conjecture: Cusanus' Ball Game and the
'Learned Ignorance' of the World." *Nuncius* 28, no. 1 (January 2013):
5–18. https://doi.org/10.1163/18253911-028010.
Anselm of Canterbury. *De veritate.* Translated by J. Hopkins and H. Richardson.
New York: Mellen, 1976.
———. *Cur deus homo? Complete Philosophical and Theological Treatises of Anselm
of Canterbury.* Translated by Jasper Hopkins and Herbert Richardson.
Minneapolis: Arthur J. Banning, 2000.
Aquinas Thomas. *Summa Theologica.* In *The Basic Writings of St. Thomas Aquinas.*
2 vols. Edited by Anton C. Pegis. New York: Random House, 1945.
———. *Quaestiones disputatae de veritate Questiones Disputatae de Veritate.*
Questions, 1–9. Translated by Robert W. Mulligan, SJ. Chicago: Henry
Regnery, 1952.
Aristotle. *The Complete Works of Aristotle: The Revised Oxford Translation.* Edited
by Jonathan Barnes. 2 vols. Princeton: Princeton University Press, 1984.
Augustine. *The City of God.* Translated by Marcus Dods, D.D. (New York:
Random House, 1950).
———. *Confessions.* Translated by Edward B. Pusey. New York: Modern
Library, 1949.

Avicenna. *Metaphysica.* Opera Omnia. Venice, 1508. Reprint Louvain:
  Ed. de la bibliothèque S.J., 1961.
Baeumker, Clemens. "Das pseudo-hermetische 'Buch der 24 Meister'
  (Liber XXIV philosophorum): Ein Beitrag zur Geschichte des
  Neupythagoreismus und Neuplatonismus im Mittelalter." *Beiträge zur
  Geschichte der Philosophie und Theologie des Mittelalters* 25, 1928.
Baum, Wilhelm. *Nikolaus von Kues: Briefe und Dokumente zum Brixner Streit.*
  Vienna: Turia and Kant, 1998.
Baumgarten, Alexander Gottlieb. *Reflections on Poetry* (*Meditationes
  philosophicae de nonnullis ad poema pertinentibus*). Par. 66. Translated by
  Karl Aschenbrenner and William B. Holther. Berkeley and Los Angeles:
  University of California Press, 1954.
Bellitto, Christopher M., Thomas M. Izbicki, and Gerald Christianson,
  eds. *Introducing Nicholas of Cusa: A Guide to a Renaissance Man.* New York:
  Paulist Press, 2004.
Benedict XVI. "Regensburg Address." September 12, 2006.
———. General Audience, Wednesday, July 7, 2010. Vatican City: Libreria
  Editrice Vaticana, 2010. w2.vatican.va/content/benedict-xvi/en/
  audiences/.../hf_ben-xvi_aud_20100707.html.
Bentham, Jeremy. *The Principles of Morals and Legislation.* Amherst, NY:
  Prometheus, 1988.
Bertin, Francis. *Nicolas de Cues: Sermons Eckhartiens et Dionysiens, Introduction,
  traduction, notes et commentaires.* Paris: Les Éditions du Cerf, 1998.
Biechler, James E. "A New Face toward Islam: Nicholas of Cusa and John of
  Segovia." In Christianson and Izbicki, *Nicholas of Cusa: In Search of God
  and Wisdom,*185–202. Leiden: Brill, 1991.
———. "Interreligious Dialogue." In *Nicholas of Cusa: A Guide to a Renaissance
  Man,* edited by Christopher M. Bellitto, Thomas M. Izbicki, and Gerald
  Christianson, 270–96. New York: Paulist Press, 2004.
Biemel, Walter, and Hans Saner, eds. *Martin Heidegger, Karl Jaspers: Briefwechsel
  1920–1963.* Frankfurt, Munich, and Zürich: Klostermann, 1992.
Blumenberg, Hans, ed. *Nikolaus von Cues: Die Kunst der Vermutung; Auswahl
  aus den Schriften.* Bremen: Carl Schünemann Verlag, 1957.
———. *Legitimität der Neuzeit.* Frankfurt am Main: Suhrkamp, 1966. In En-
  glish: *The Legitimacy of the Modern Age.* Translated by Robert M. Wallace.
  Cambridge, MA: MIT Press, 1985.
———. *Schiffbruch mit Zuschauer: Paradigma einer Daseinsmetapher.* Frankfurt am
  Main: Suhrkamp, 1979.
———. *Die Genesis der kopernikanischen Welt.* Frankfurt am Main: Suhrkamp,
  1981. Originally published in 1971. In English: *The Genesis of the
  Copernican World.* Translated by Robert M. Wallace. Cambridge, MA:
  MIT Press, 1987.
Boethius. *De persona et duabus naturis Patrologia Latina.* Edited by J. Migne,
  64:1345. Paris: Migne, 1878–90.
———. *De institutione arithmetica.* Edited by G. Friedlein. Leipzig: Teubner,
  1867. Reprinted Frankfurt: Minerva, 1966.
———. *De trinitate.* Edited by C. Moreschini. Munich and Leipzig: Teubner,
  2005.

Bond, H. Lawrence. "Redefining *Via Negationis*." In *Introducing Nicholas of Cusa: A Guide to a Renaissance Man*, edited by Christopher M. Bellitto, Thomas M. Izbicki, and Gerald Christianson, 206–7. New York: Paulist Press, 2004.

Boockmann, Hartmut. "Johannes Lysura." *Neue Deutsche Biographie* 10 (1974): 560–61. Online version https://www.deutsche-biographie.de/pnd136317022.html#ndbcontent.

Boyle, Marjorie O'Rourke. "Cusanus at Sea: The Topicality of Illuminative Discourse." *Journal of Religion* 71, no. 2 (April 1991): 180–201.

Breazeale, Daniel. *Philosophy and Truth: Selections from Nietzsche's Notebooks of the Early 1870s*. Atlantic Highlands, NJ: Humanities Press, 1979.

Brient, Elizabeth. "The Immanence of the Infinite: A Response to Blumenberg's Reading of Modernity." Ph.D. diss., Yale University, 1995.

———. *The Immanence of the Infinite: Hans Blumenberg and the Threshold to Modernity*. Washington, DC: The Catholic University of America Press, 2002.

Broch, Hermann. "Einige Bemerkungen zum Problem des Kitsches." In *Essays*, vol. 1, *Dichten und Erkennen*, 295–309. Zurich: Rhein, 1955. English translation: "Notes on the Problem of Kitsch." In *Kitsch: The World of Bad Taste*, by Gillo Dorfles. New York: Universe, 1969.

Bruno, Giordano. *The Ash Wednesday Supper*. Edited and translated by Edward A. Gosselin and Lawrence S. Lerner. Hamden: Archon, 1977.

Buber, Martin. *Die Schriften über das dialogische Prinzip*. Heidelberg: Schneider, 1954.

Butterworth, Edward J. "Form and Significance of the Sphere in Nicholas of Cusa's *De Ludo Globi*." In Christianson and Izbicki, *Nicholas of Cusa: In Search of God and Wisdom*, 89–100. 1964.

Cajetan, Tommaso de Vio. *The Analogy of Names*. Translated by Edward Bushinski and Henry Koren. Eugene, OR: Wipf and Stock, 1953 and 2009.

Cantor, Moritz. *Vorlesungen über Geschichte der Mathematik*. New York: B. G. Teubner Verlagsgesellschaft, 1965.

Carman, Charles H. *Leon Battista Alberti and Nicholas Cusanus: Towards an Epistemology of Vision for Italian Renaissance Art and Culture*. Farnham Surrey: Ashgate, 2014.

Casarella, Peter J. "Nicholas of Cusa and the Power of the Possible." *American Catholic Philosophical Quarterly* 64, no. 1 (Winter 1998): 9–12 and 30–34.

———, ed. *Cusanus: The Legacy of Learned Ignorance*. Washington, DC: The Catholic University of America Press, 2006.

Cassirer, Ernst. *Das Erkenntnisproblem in der Philosophie und Wissenschaft der neueren Zeit*. Vol. 1. 2nd ed. Berlin: Verlag Bruno Cassirer, 1911. Reprinted Darmstadt: Wissenschaftliche Buchgesellschaft, 1994.

——— *Philosophie der symbolischen Formen*. Vol. I. Berlin: Cassirer, 1923.

———. *Individuum und Kosmos in der Philosophie der Renaissance*. Leipzig: Teubner, 1927.

———. *The Individual and the Cosmos in the Renaissance*. Translated, with an introduction by Mario Domandi. New York and Evanston, Ill.: Harper and Row, 1964.

Catà, Cesare. "Die paradoxale Frage der drei Weisen—Die Idee des *Unum infinitum* im Sermo CCXVI des Nikolaus von Kues." *Coincidentia: Zeitschrift für europäische Geistesgeschichte* 1–2 (2010): 13–22.

Christianson, Gerald, and Thomas M. Izbicki. *Nicholas of Cusa: In Search of God and Wisdom.* Leiden: Brill, 1991.

Clagett, Marshall. *The Science of Mechanics in the Middle Ages.* Madison: University of Wisconsin Press, 1959.

Colomer, Eusebio, SJ. *Nikolaus von Kues und Raimund Llull: Quellen und Studien zur Geschichte der Philosophie.* Vol 2. Berlin: De Gruyter. 1961.

Coreth, Emerich. "Nikolaus von Kues, ein Denker an der Zeitwende." In *Cusanus Gedächtnisschrift,* edited by Nikolaus Grass, 3–16. Innsbruck: Universitätsverlag Wagner, 1970.

Cranz, F. Edward. "The Transmutation of Platonism in the Development of Nicolaus Cusanus and Martin Luther." In *Nicolo' Cusano: Agli Inizi del Mondo Moderno.* 1964.

Creighton, Mandell. *The History of the Papacy During the Period of Reformation.* Vol. 2, *The Council of Basel—The Papal Restoration, 1418–1464.* London: Longmans, Green, 1882.

Daniels, Tobias. *Diplomatie, politische Rede und juristische Praxis- im 15. Jahrhundert: Der gelehrte Rat Johannes Hofmann von Lieser.* Göttingen: V. and R. Unipress GmbH, 2013.

Dantzig, Tobias. *Number: The Language of Science.* 1930. Repr. New York: Pi, 2005.

Denery, Dallas G. II. "Protagoras and the Fourteenth-Century Invention of Epistemological Relativism." *Visual Resources* 25, no. 1 (March 2009): 34–38.

Descartes, René. *The Philosophical Writings of Descartes.* Translated by John Cottingham, Robert Stoothoff, and Dugald Murdoch. 2 vols. Cambridge: Cambridge University Press, 1985.

Duclow, Donald P. "Nicholas of Cusa in the Margins of Meister Eckhart: Codex Cusanus 21." In Christianson and Izbicki, *Nicholas of Cusa: In Search of God and Wisdom:* 57–69. 1964.

———. "Mystical Theology and Intellect in Nicholas of Cusa." *American Catholic Philosophical Quarterly* 64, no. 1 (Winter 1990): 115–29.

Duhem, Pierre. "Thierry de Chartres et Nicolas de Cues. *Revues de Sciences Philos. et Théol.* 30 (1909): 325–31.

Dupré, Louis. "The Question of Pantheism from Eckhart to Cusanus." In Casarella, *Cusanus: The Legacy of Learned Ignorance,* 74–88. 2006.

Dupré, Wilhelm. "The Image of the Living God: Some Remarks on the Meaning of Perfection and World Formation." In Casarella, *Cusanus: The Legacy of Learned Ignorance,* 89–104. 2006.

Eckhart, Meister. *Meister Eckhart: A Modern Translation.* Translated by Raymond B. Blakney. New York: Harper Torchbooks, 1969.

———. *Predigten.* Edited and translated by Josef Quint. 3 vols. Stuttgart: Kohlhammer, 1936–1976.

———. *The Essential Sermons, Commentaries, Treatises, and Defense.* Translated and introduction by Edmund Colledge, OSA, and Bernard McGinn. Mahwah, N.J: Paulist Press, 1981.

Euler, Walter A. "Religionsfriede und Ringparabel: Die

religionstheologischen Ideen von Cusanus und Lessing." *Cusanus Jahrbuch,* 4 (2012): 3–24.

Fiamma, Andrea. "'Iudicium Staterae verius experimur': Augustinus von Hippo als Quelle der *De staticis experimentis* bei Nikolaus. von Kues." *Freiburger Zeitschrift für Philosophie und Theologie,* 63, no. 1 (2016): 175–95.

———. "Nicola Cusano ed Eimerico da Campo: Gli anni coloniensi." *Medioevo. Rivista di storia della filosofia* medievale XLI (2016): 217–57.

———. "La réception du Timéc par Nicolas de Cues (*De docta ignorantia* II, 9)." *Revue des sciences religieuses* 91, no 1 (2017): 39–55.

Filippi, Elena. *Umanesimo e misura viva: Durer tra Cusano e Alberti.* San Giovanni Lupatoto: Arsenale, 2011.

———. "The Heritage of Cusanus' New Anthropology and Its Impact on Visual Culture in Fifteenth-Century Germany and Flanders." *Newsletter: American Cusanus Society* 31 (2014): 34–43.

Firmicus Maternus. *Mathesis.* 2 vols. Edited by W. Kroll, F. Skutsch, and K. Ziegler. Leipzig: B. G. Teubner, 1913. Originally published in 1897.

Flasch, Kurt, "Cusano e gli intellettuali italiani del Quattrocento." In *Le filosofie del Rinascimento,* edited by Cesare Vasoli. Milan: Bruno Mondadori, 2002.

———. *Was Ist Gott? Das Buch der 24 Philosophen.* Lateinisch-Deutsch. Munich: Beck, 2011.

Floss, Pavel. *The Philosophy of Nicholas of Cusa: An Introduction into His Thinking.* Basel: Schwabe Verlag, 2020.

Führer, M. L. "The Theory of the Intellect in Albert the Great and Its Influence on Nicholas of Cusa." In Christianson and Izbicki, *Nicholas of Cusa: In Search of God and Wisdom,* 6–56. 1991.

Gadamer, Hans-Georg. "Nikolaus von Kues im modernen Denken." In *Nicolo' Cusano: Agli Inizi del Mondo Moderno,* 39–48.

Gandillac, Maurice de. *Nikolaus von Kues: Studien zu seiner Philosophie und philosophischen Weltanschauung.* Translated by Karl Fleischmann, vom Verfasser grundlegend überarbeitete Ausgabe. Düsseldorf: Schwan, 1953.

Gawlick, Günter. "Zur Nachwirkung cusanischer Ideen im siebzehnten und achtzehnten Jahrhundert." In *Nicolo' Cusano: Agli Inizi del Mondo Moderno,* 225–39. 1964.

Gerl-Falkovitz, Hanna-Barbara. "Nicolaus Cusanus, *De pace fidei.* 1454." In *Westliche Moderne, Christentum und Islam. Gewalt als Anfrage an monotheistische Religionen,* edited by Wolfgang Palaver, Roman A. Siebenrock, Dietmar Regensburger, 107–26. Edition Weltordnung. Innsbruck: Innsbruck University Press, 2008.

Gertsman, Elina. *Worlds Within: Opening the Medieval Shrine Madonna.* College Station: Pennsylvania State University Press, 2015.

———. "The Lives and Afterlives of Shrine Madonnas." *California Italian Studies* 6, no. 1 (2016): 4. https://escholarship.org/uc/item/6sboj1st.

Gilson, Étienne. *Études sur la rôle de la pensé médiévale dans la formation du système cartésien.* Paris: J. Vrin, 1967.

Hallauer, Hermann. "Die 'Schlacht' im Enneberg 1458: Neue Quellen zur Biographie des Nikolaus von Kues." In *Nicolo' Cusano: Agli Inizi del Mondo Moderno,* 447–69. 1964.

———. *Nikolaus von Kues als Bischof und Landesfürst in Brixen*, Trierer Cusanus Lecture. Vol. 6. Trier: Paulinus, 2000.

Harries, Karsten. "In a Strange Land: An Exploration of Nihilism." Ph.D. diss., Yale University, 1961.

———. "Cusanus and the Platonic Idea." *New Scholasticism* 7, no. 2 (1963): 188–203.

———. "Heidegger and Hölderlin: The Limits of Language." *Personalist* 44, no. l (1963): 5–23.

———. "The Infinite Sphere: Comments on the History of a Metaphor." *Journal of the History of Philosophy* 13, no. l (1975): 5–15.

———. "Decoration, Death, and Devil." In *Hermann Broch: Literature, Philosophy, Politics; The Yale Broch Symposium 1986*, 279–97. Columbia, SC: Camden House, 1988.

———. "The Philosopher at Sea." In *Nietzsche's New Seas: Explorations in Philosophy, Aesthetics, and Politics*, edited by Michael Allen Gillespie and Tracy B. Strong, 21–44. Chicago: University of Chicago Press, 1988.

———. *Infinity and Perspective*. Cambridge, MA: MIT Press, 2001.

———. "On the Power and Poverty of Perspective: Cusanus and Alberti." In Casarella, *Cusanus: The Legacy of Learned Ignorance*, 105–26. 2006.

———. "Longing for Ithaca: On the Need for a Post-Copernican Geocentrism." In *From the Things Themselves, Architecture and Phenomenology*, edited by Benoit Jacquet and Vincent Giraud, 495–522. Kyoto: Kyoto University Press; École francaise d'Extrème-Orient, 2012.

———. "The Antinomy of Being and the End of Philosophy." In *Division III of Being and Time: Heidegger's Unanswered Question of Being*, edited by Lee Braver, 133–48. Cambridge, MA: MIT Press, 2015.

———. *The Antinomy of Being*. Berlin: DeGruyter, 2019.

Haubst, Rudolf. *Das Bild des Einen und Dreieinen Gottes in der Welt nach Nikolaus von Kues*. Trier: Paulinus Verlag, 1952.

———. *Die Christologie des Nikolaus von Kues*. Freiburg: Herder, 1956.

———. "Der Evolutionsgedanke in der cusanischen Theologie." In *Nicolo' Cusano: Agli Inizi del Mondo Moderno*. 1964.

———. "Nikolaus von Kues und der Evoltionsgedanke." *Scholastik* 39 (1964): 481–94.

———. *Nikolaus von Kues: Pförtner der neuen Zeit*, Kleine Schriften der Cusanus-Gesellschaft, Heft 12. Trier: Paulinus, 1988.

———. *Streifzüge in die Cusanische Theologie*. Munich: Aschendorff, 1991.

Hauser, Arnold. *The Social History of Art*. 2 vols. Translated by Stanley Godman. New York: Vintage, 1951.

Hegel, Georg Wilhelm Friedrich. *Enzyklopädie*, §24, Zusatz 2. In *Jubiläumsausgabe*, edited by Hermann Glockner. Stuttgart: Frommann, 1965.

Heidegger, Martin. *Sein und Zeit*. 7th ed. Tübingen: Niemeyer, 1953. Translation: *Being and Time*. Translated by John Macquarrie and Edward Robinson. New York and Evanston, IL: Harper, 1962.

———. *Poetry, Language, Thought*. Translated and introduction by Albert Hofstadter. New York: Harper and Row, 1971.

———. "Vom Wesen der Wahrheit." In *Gesamtausgabe*, vol. 9. Frankfurt am Main: Klostermann, 1976.

————. *Einführung in die phänomenologische Forschung.* Wintersemester 1923/24. *Gesamtausgabe,* vol. 17. Frankfurt am Main: Klostermann, 1994.

————, *Vorträge und Aufsätze.* Gesamtausgabe. Vol. 7. Frankfurt am Main: Klostermann, 2000.

Heinz-Mohr, Gerd. "Bemerkungen zur Spiritualität der Brüder vom gemeinsamen Leben." In *Nicolo' Cusano: Agli Inizi del Mondo Moderno.* 1964.

Hermes Trismegistus. *Asclepius.* In *Corpus Hermeticum.* Vol. 2. Edited by A.D. Nock. 2nd ed. Paris: Société d'Edition "Les Belles Lettres," 1945.

Hilary of Poitiers. *De Trinitate* II-I. Translated by E. W. Watson and L. Pullan in *From Nicene and Post-Nicene Fathers,* Second Series, vol. 9. edited by Philip Schaff and Henry Wace. Buffalo, NY: Christian Literature Publishing, 1899. Revised and edited for New Advent by Kevin Knight, http://www.\\newadvent.org/fathers/3302.htm.

Hirschberger, Johannes. "Das Platon-Bild bei Nikolous von Kues." In *Nicolo' Cusano: Agli Inizi del Mondo Moderno.*

Hoenen, Maarten J. F. M. "'Ista prius inaudita': Eine neuentdeckte Vorlage der *De docta ignorantia* und ihre Bedeutung für die frühe Philosophie des Nikolaus von Kues." In *Medioevo: Rivista di Storia della filosofia medievale* 21 (1995): 435–36.

Hoff, Johannes. "Die sich selbst zurücknehmende Inszenierung von Reden und Schweigen: Zur mystagogischen Rhetorik des Nikolaus von Kues." In *Religion und Rhetorik. Entwicklungen und Paradoxien ihrer unvermeidlichen Allianz, Religionswissenschaft heute,* edited by Holt Meyer and Dirk Uffelmann. Stuttgart: Kohlhammer, 2007.

————. *The Analogical Turn: Rethinking Modernity with Nicholas of Cusa.* Grand Rapids, MI: Eerdmans, 2013.

Hofmann, Joseph Ehrenfried. "Einführung." In *Die Mathematischen Schriften,* by Nikolaus von Cues. Translated by Josepha Hofmann. Introduction and notes by Joseph E. Hofmann. Hamburg: Meiner, 1952.

————. *The History of Mathematics.* Translated by Frank Gaynor and Henrietta O. Midonick. New York: Philosophical Library, 1957.

————. "Sinn und Bedeutung der wichtigsten mathematicshen Schriften des Nikolaus von Kues." In *Nicolo' Cusano: Agli Inizi del Mondo Moderno.* 1964.

Hopkins, Jasper. "Preface." In *Nicholas of Cusa: On Learned Ignorance,* translated by Jasper Hopkins. Minneapolis: Arthur J. Banning, 1981.

————. *Nicholas of Cusa's Metaphysic of Contraction.* Minneapolis: Arthur J. Banning, 1983.

————. "Review of Special issue on Nicolaus Cusanus edited by Louis Dupré." *American Catholic Philosophical Quarterly* 64, no. 1, Winter 1990): 211–28.

————. *Nicholas of Cusa: Metaphysical Speculations.* 2 vols. Minneapolis: Arthur J. Banning, 2000.

————. "Nicholas of Cusa. 1401–1464: First Modern Philosopher?" *Midwest Studies in Philosophy* 26 (2002): 13–29.

————. "Nicholas of Cusa's Intellectual Relationship to Anselm of Canterbury." In Casarella, *Cusanus: The Legacy of Learned Ignorance,* 54–73. 2006.

Housley, Norman. *Crusading and the Ottoman Threat, 1453–1505.* Oxford: Oxford University Press, 2012.

Hundersmarck, Lawrence F." Preaching." In *Introducing Nicholas of Cusa: A Guide to a Renaissance Man*, edited by Christopher M. Bellitto, Thomas M. Izbicki, and Gerald Christianson, 232–69. New York: Paulist Press, 2004.

Hunter, A. Richard. "What Did Nicholas of Cusa Contribute to Science." In Christianson and Izbicki, *Nicholas of Cusa: In Search of God and Wisdom.* 1991.

Husserl, Edmund. *The Crisis of European Sciences and Transcendental Phenomenology: An Introduction to Phenomenological Philosophy.* Translated, with an introduction by David Carr. Evanston, IL: Northwestern University Press, 1970.

Hyman, Arthur, and James J. Walsh, eds. *Philosophy in the Middle Ages\.* Indianapolis: Hackett, 1973.

Jäger, Albert. *Der Streit des Cardinals Nicolaus von Cusa mit dem Herzoge Sigmund von Österreich als Grafen von Tirol.* 2 vols. Innsbruck: Wagner, 1861.

Jaspers, Karl, *Philosophie.* 3 vols. Berlin: Springer, 1932.

———. *Anselm and Nicholas of Cusa.* Edited by Hannah Arendt. Translated by Ralph Manheim. New York: Harcourt Brace Jovanovich, 1974.

Jordan, Pascual. "Kosmogonische Anschauungen der modernen Physik." In *Naturwissenschaft—Religion—Weltanschauung: Clausthaler Gespräch 1948,* 25–33. Clausthal-Zellerfeld, 1949.

Kant, Immanuel. *Kritik der praktischen Vernunft.* Translated by Thomas Kingsmill Abbott. In *Kant's Critique of Practical Reason and Other Works on the Theory of Ethics.* 4th rev. ed. London: Longman, Green, 1889.

———. *Kritik der reinen Vernunft.* Translated by Norman Kemp Smith as *Critique of Pure Reason.* New York: St. Martin's and Macmillan, 1929.

———. *Kritik der Urteilsraft.* Translated by Werner S. Pluhar as *Critique of Judgment.* Indianapolis: Hackett, 1987.

Kepler, Johannes. *De fundamentis astrologiae certioribus.* In *Opera Omnia,* vol. 1. Frankfurt am Main and Erlangen: Heyden and Zimmer, 1858.

Kirk, J. S., and Raven, J. E. *The Presocratic Philosophers.* Cambridge: Cambridge University Press, 1957.

Kny, Christian. "Einzelnes erkennt Einzelnes: Die Leistungsfähigkeit menschlicher Erkenntnis unter dem Gesichtspunkt der singularitas." In *Singularität und Universalität im Denken des Cusanus,* edited by C. Ströbele, 37–52. Regensburg: S. Roderer Verlag, 2015.

———. "Messen ohne Maß? Nicolaus Cusanus und das Kriterium menschlicher Erkenntnis." *Das Mittelalter* 23 (2018): 92–108.

Koch, Josef. *Die Ars coniecturalis des Nikolaus von Kues.* Cologne: Westdeutscher Verlag, 1956.

Koyré, Alexandre. *Essai sur l'idée de Dieu et les preuves de Son existence selon Descartes.* Paris: Leroux, 1922.

———. *From the Closed World to the Infinite Universe.* New York: Harper Torchbook, 1958.

Kozhamthadam Job, SJ. *The Discovery of Kepler's Laws.* Notre Dame, IN: Notre Dame Press, 1994.

Kraus, Franz Xaver. "Ulrich von Manderscheid." In *Allgemeine Deutsche Biographie,* 39: 234–35. Leipzig: M. Duncker and Humblet, 1895.

Krchnák, Alois. "Die kanonisschen Aufzeichnungen des Nikolaus von Kues in Cod. Cus. 220 als Mitschrift einer Vorlesung seines Lehrers Prosdocimus de Comitibus." In *Mitteilungen und Forschungsbeiträge der Cusanus-Gesellschaft*, 67–84. Mainz: Matthias-Grünewald-Verlag, 1962.

Lehmann, Paul. "Vom Mittelalter und der lateinischen Philologie des Mittelalters." *Quellen und Untersuchungen zur lateinischen Philologie des Mittelalters* V, no. 1 (1914).

Mahnke, Dietrich. *Unendliche Sphäre und Allmittelpunkt*. Halle: Nicmeyer, 1937.

Mandrella, Isabelle." Der wissenschaftstheoretische Primat im Denken des Cusanus: Mathematik oder Metaphysik?" In *Das Mathematikverständnis des Nikolaus von Kues: Mathematische, naturwissenschaftliche und philosophisch-theologische Dimensionen*. Mitteilungen und Forschungsbeiträge der Cusanus-Gesellschaft 29, edited by Friedrich Pukelsheim and Harald Schwaetzer, 183–200. Trier: Paulinus, 2005.

———. *Viva imago: Die praktische Philosophie des Nicolaus Cusanus*. Buchreihe der Cusanus-Gesellschaft. Münster: Aschendorff, 2011.

———. "Begriff und Funktion der Neuheit in der Philosophie des Nicolaus Cusanus." In *Die Modernitäten des Nikolaus von Kues: Debatten und Rezeptionen*, edited by Tom Müller and Matthias Vollet, 23–42. Bielefeld: Transcript, 2013.

———. "'Amor liber est': Liebe und Freiheit bei Nicolaus Cusanus." In *Trierer Cusanus Lecture*, Heft 20. Trier: Paulinus Verlag, 2016.

Mantese, Giovanni. "Ein notartielles Inventar von Büchern und Wertgegenständen aus dem Nachlass des Nikolaus von Kues." In *Mitteilungen und Forschungsbeiträge der Cusanus-Gesellschaft*, 2:85–116. Mainz: Matthias-Grünewald-Verlag, 1962.

McGinn, Bernard. "Seeing and Not Seeing: Nicholas of Cusa's *De visione Dei* in the History of Western Mysticism." In Casarella, *Cusanus: The Legacy of Learned Ignorance*, 44–47. 2006.

McTighe, Thomas P. "Nicholas of Cusa's Theory of Science and Its Metaphysical Background." In *Nicolo' Cusano: Agli Inizi del Mondo Moderno*. 318–19. 1964.

———. "*Contingentia* and *Alteritas* in Cusa's Metaphysics." *American Catholic Philosophical Quarterly* 64, no. 1 (Winter 1990): 55–71.

———. "Nicholas of Cusa's Unity Metaphysics and the Formula *Religio una in rituum varietate*. In *Nicholas of Cusa: In Seach of God and Wisdom*, edited by Gerald Christianson and Thomas M. Izbicki, 161–72. Leiden: Brill, 1991.

Markowski, Mieczyslaw. "Die kosmologischen Anschauungen des Prosdocimo de' Beldomandi." In *Studi sul XIV secolo in memoria di Anneliese Maier*, edited by Alfonso Maierù and Agostino Paravicini, 263–73. Rome: Ediz di Storia e Letteratura, 1981.

Maurer, Armand. "Nicholas of Cusa." In *Encyclopedia of Philosophy*, edited by Paul Edwards. Vol. 5. New York: Macmillan and Free Press, 1967.

Meier-Oeser, Stephan, *Die Präsenz des Vergessenen: Zur Rezeption des Nicolaus Cusanus vom 15. bis 18. Jahrhundert*, Buchreihe der Cusanus-Gesellschaft 10. Münster: Aschendorff, 1989.

Meuthen, Erich. *Die letzten Jahre des Nikolaus Cusanus.* Cologne and Opladen: Westdeutscher Verlag, 1958.

———. "Die Pfründen des Cusanus." In *Mitteilungen und Forschungsbeiträge der Cusanus-Gesellschaft,* vol. 2. Mainz: Matthias-Grünewald-Verlag, 1962.

———, ed. *Acta Cusana: Quellen zur Lebensgeschichte des Nikolaus von Kues.* Hamburg: Meiner, 1976.

———. *Nikolaus von Kues 1401–1464: Skizze einer Biographie.* 4th ed. Münster: Aschendorff, 1979.

———. *Nicholas of Cusa: A Sketch for a Biography.* Washington, DC: The Catholic University of America Press, 2010.

Miller, Clyde Lee. "Perception, Conjecture, and Dialectic in Nicholas of Cusa. "*American Catholic Philosophical Quarterly* 64, no. 1 (Winter 1990): 35–43.

———. "Nicholas of Cusa's *On Conjectures (De coniecturis).*" In Christianson and Izbicki, *Nicholas of Cusa: In Seach of God and Wisdom.* 1991.

———. *Reading Cusanus: Metaphor and Dialectic in a Conjectural Universe.* Washington, DC: The Catholic University of America Press, 2003.

Moran, Dermot. "Pantheism from John Scottus Eriugena to Nicholas of Cusa." *American Catholic Philosophical Quarterly* 64, no. 1 (Winter 1990): 131–53.

Nagel, Thomas. *The View from Nowhere.* Rev. ed. Oxford: Oxford University Press, 1989.

Nicholas of Autrecourt. *Exigit Ordo.* In J. R. O'Donnell, "Nicholas of Autrecourt," *Mediaeval Studies* 1 (1939): 179–280.

Nicolle, Jean-Marie. "Innovation in Mathematics and Proclusean Tradition in Cusanus' Thought." In *Nicholas of Cusa: A Medieval Thinker for the Modern Age,* edited by Kazuhiko Yamaki, 85–88. London and New York: Routledge 2011.

Nicolo' Cusano: Agli Inizi del Mondo Moderno, Atti del Congresso internazionale in occasione del V centenario della morte di Nicolò Cusano, Bressanone, 6–10 settembre 1964. Sansoni: Firenze, 1964.

Nietzsche, Friedrich. *"The Birth of Tragedy" and "The Case of Wagner."* Translated by Walter Kaufmann. New York: Vintage, 1967.

———. *Zarathustra.* Translated by Walter Kaufmann in *The Portable Nietzsche,* edited and translated by Walter Kaufmann. Harmondsworth: Penguin, 1976.

———. *Ecce Homo, Sämtliche Werke, Kritische Studienausgabe.* Vol. 6. Edited by Giorgio Colli and Mazzino Montinari. Munich, Berlin, and New York: Deutscher Taschenbuch Verlag and de Gruyter, 1980.

———. *On the Genealogy of Morals and Ecce Homo.* Translated by Walter Kaufmann and R. J. Hollingdale. New York: Vintage, 1989.

Nolan Michael. "What Aquinas Never Said about Women." November 1998. http://www.firstthings.com/article/1998/11/003-what-aquinas-never -said-about-women.

O'Collins, Gerald. "The Beauty of Christ." *The Way,* 44, no. 4 (October 2005): 7–20.

Ommeln, Miriam. "Die Aufnahme von Nietzsches Philosophie in die surre- alistischen Ideen oder: Die Verkörperung von Nietzsches Ästhetik ist der

Surrealismus." In *Die Auflösung des abendländischen Subjekts und das Schicksal Europas (Mit Nietzsche Denken)*, edited by Beatrix Vogel and Harald Seubert. Munich: Allitera Verlag, 2005.

Oresme, Nicole. *Le Livre du ciel et du monde*. Edited by Albert D. Menut and Alexander J. Denomy. Translated by Albert D. Menut. Madison: University of Wisconsin, 1968.

Patrologia Graeca. Edited by J. P. Migne, 161 vols. Paris: Fratres Garnier, 1857–66.

Patrologia Latina. Edited by J. P. Migne. 271 vols. Paris: Fratres Garnier: 1878–90.

Pavlac, Brian A. "Nicolaus Cusanus as Prince-Bishop of Brixen. 1450–64: Historians and a Conflict of Church and State." *Historical Reflections/ Reflexions Historiques* 21, no. 1 (1995): 131–53.

———. "Reform." In *Introducing Nicholas of Cusa: A Guide to a Renaissance Man*, edited by Christopher M. Bellitto, Thomas M. Izbicki, and Gerald Christianson, 71–83. New York: Paulist Press, 2004.

Peuckert, Will-Erich. *Die Große Wende: Das apokalyptische Saeculum und Martin Luther*. 2 vols. Darmstadt: Wissenschaftliche Buchgesellschaft, 1948.

Pick, Georg. *Nikolaus von Kues: Vom Moseljungen zum Kardinal und Philosophen*. 3rd ed. Frankfurt am Main: R. G. Fischer, 1996.

Plato. *The Collected Dialogues Including the Letters*. Edited by Edith Hamilton and Huntington Cairns. Bollingen Series. Princeton: Princeton University Press, 1962.

Plotinus, *Enneads*. Translated by Stephen MacKenna. London: Faber, 1956.

Popkin, Richard H. *The History of Scepticism from Erasmus to Descartes*. New York: Harper and Row, 1964.

Pseudo-Dionysius. *De mystica theologia* I.3. In PG 3:1000B. *Dionysiaca* I. 2 vols. Paris: Desclée de Brouwer, 1937.

———. *De divinis nominibus*: The Divine Names. *Dionysiaca* I.

———. *Epistula I ad Gaium*.V.8. PG 3:1065 A. Dionysiaca I.

———. *De coelesti hierarchia*. *Dionysiaca* II.

Radler, Gudrun. *Die Schreinmadonna/"Vierge Ouvrante."* Frankfurt: Kunstgeschichtliches Inst. der Johann-Wolfgang-Goethe-Universität, 1990.

Renz, Ursula. "Lebendiger Spiegel oder Spiegel des Lebendigen? Subjektivität und Performanz in Cusanus' Spiegelsymbolik." In *Präsenz ohne Substanz: Zur Symybolik des Spiegels*, edited by Paul Michel. Schriften zur Symbolforschung 14, 95–108. Zürich/Freiburg i. Br.: Pano, 2003.

Ripelin, Hugo. *Compendium Theologicae Veritatis*. Translated, with an introduction by Jasper Hopkins (August 2012). https://jasper-hopkins.info.

Rolt, Clarence Edwin. *Dionysius the Areopagite: On the Divine Names and the Mystical Theology*. Grand Rapids, MI: Christian Classics Ethereal Library; London: SPCK, 1920. http:www.//www.ccel.org/ccel/rolt/dionysius.html.

Rosenzweig, Franz. *Briefe*. Berlin: Schocken, 1935.

Ross, James Bruce, and Mary Martin McLaughlin, eds. *The Portable Renaissance Reader*. New York: Viking, 1953.

Russo, Eugen. "Philosophy of Paradox in the Fifteenth Century: Nicolaus

Cusanus' *De docta ignorantia* and Masaccio's *Trinity*." Master's thesis, Central European University, Budapest. September 2014.

Santinello, Giovanni. *Leon Battista Alberti: Una visione estetica del mondo e della vita*. Firenze: Sansoni, 1962.

Scharpff, Franz Anton. *Des Cardinals und Bischofs Nicolaus von Cusa wichtigste Schriften in deutscher Übersetzung*. Freiburg im Breisgau: Herder, 1862; reprint Frankfurt am Main: Minerva, 1966.

Schmid, Alexander, trans. *Cusanus, Nikolaus, Vom Wissen des Nichtwissens*. Hellerau: Jakob Hegner, 1919.

Schopenhauer, Arthur. *The World as Will and Representation*. 2 vols. Translated by E. F. J. Payne. New York: Dover, 1966.

Semler, Johann Salomo. *Des Kardinals von Cusa Dialogus von der Übereinstimmung oder Einheit des Glaubens*. Leipzig, 1787.

Sigmund, Paul E. *Nicholas of Cusa and Medieval Political Thought*. Cambridge, MA: Harvard University Press, 1963.

Sparber, Anselm. "Aus der Wirksamkeit des Kardinals Nikolaus von Kues als Fürstbischof von Brixen (1450–1464). In *Nicolo' Cusano: Agli Inizi del Mondo Moderno*, 523–35

Stammer, Dennis. "Nikolaus von Kues und die analogia entis? Eine zum Panentheismusbegriff leitende Streitfrage der systematischen Theologie in begriffshistorischem Kontext." Draft-Version zum privaten Gebrauch. https://www.academia.edu/43231365

Stieber, Joachim W. *Pope Eugenius IV, The Council of Basel and the Secular and Ecclesiastical Authorities in the Empire. The Conflict over Supreme Authority and Power in the Church*. Leiden: Brill, 1978.

———. "The 'Hercules of the Eugenians' at the Crossroads: Nicholas of Cusa's Decision for the Pope and Against the Council in 1436/37— Theological, Political, and Social Aspects." In Christianson and Izbicki, *Nicholas of Cusa: In Seach of God and Wisdom*. 1991.

Thierry of Chartres. *Lectiones in Boethii librum de Trinitate*, Edited by N. M. Haring. Archives de'Histoire Doctrinale et Littéraires de Moyen Age 33, 266–325. Paris: Librairie Philosophique J. Vrin, 1958.

———. *Commentum super Boethium de Trinitate. Librum hunc.* Edited by N. M. Haring. Archives de'Histoire Doctrinale et Littéraires de Moyen Age 35, 80–134. Paris: Librairie Philosophique J. Vrin, 1960.

———. *The Commentary on the "De arithmetica of Boethius."* Edited by Irene Caiazzo. Toronto: Toronto University Press, 2015.

Trinkaus, Charles. "Protagoras in the Renaissance: An Exploration." In *Philosophy and Humanism: Essays in Honor of Paul Oskar Kristeller*, edited by Edmund Mahoney. New York: Columbia University Press, 1976.

Vansteenberghe, Edmond. *Le Cardinal Nicolas de Cues: 1401–1464: L'Action– La Pensée*. Paris: Édouard Champion, 1920.

Volkmann-Schluck, Karl-Heinz. *Nicolaus Cusanus: Die Philosophie im Übergang vom Mittelalter zur Neuzeit*. Frankfurt am Main: Klostermann, 1957.

Vollet, Matthias. *Die Modernitäten des Nikolaus von Kues: Debatten und Rezeptionen*. Edited by Tom Müller and Matthias Vollet. Bielefeld: transcript Verlag, 2014.

von Bredow, Gerda. "Die Bedeutung des Minimim in der Coincidentia oppositorum." In *Nicolo' Cusano: Agli Inizi del Mondo Moderno*. 1964.

von Hofmannsthal, Hugo. "The Letter of Lord Chandos." In *Selected Prose of Hugo von Hofmannsthal*, translated by Mary Hottinger and Tania and James Stern. New York: Pantheon, 1952.

Wackerzapp, Herbert. "Der Einfluss Meister Eckharts auf die ersten philosophischen Schriften des Nikolaus von Kues," *Beiträge zur Geschichte der Philosophie in der Theologie des Mittelalters* 39, no. 3 (1962).

Watanabe, Morimichi. "The Origins of Modern Cusanus Research in Germany and the Establishment of the Heidelberg *Opera Omnia*." In Christianson and Izbicki, *Nicholas of Cusa: In Seach of God and Wisdom*. 1991.

———. "Political and. Legal Ideas." In *Introducing Nicholas of Cusa: A Guide to a Renaissance Man*, edited by Christopher M. Bellitto, Thomas M. Izbicki, and Gerald Christianson, 141–65. New York: Paulist Press, 2004.

———. *Nicholas of Cusa—A Companion to His Life and His Times*. London: Ashgate, 2013.

———. "'Cusanus, Islam, and Religious Tolerance." In *Nicholas of Cusa and Islam: Polemic and Dialogue in the Late Middle Ages*, edited by Ian Christopher Levy, Rita George-Tvrtković, and Donald Duclow. Studies in Medieval and Reformation Traditions 183. Leiden: Brill, 2014. https://doi.org/ 10.1163/9789004274761\.

Wenck, John. *De Ignota Litteratura*. In *Nicholas of Cusa's Debate with John Wenck: A Translation and an Appraisal of "De Ignota Litteratura" and "Apologia Doctae Ignorantiae,"* by Jasper Hopkins. Minneapolis: Banning, 1981.

Wittgenstein, Ludwig. *Tractatus Logico Philosphicus*. Translated by C. K. Ogden. London: Routledge and Kegan Paul, 1922.

Wolfsteiner, Andreas. "Die Natur löffelt nicht: Modellszenarien in den Laienschriften des Nicolaus Cusanus um 1450." In *Modell und Risiko: Historische Miniaturen zu dynamischen Epistemologien*, edited by Peter Löffelbein and Michael Lorber, 95–114. Wiesbaden: Harrassowitz, 2019.

Wyller, Egil A. *Platons Parmenides in seinem Zusammenhang mit Symposion und Politeia: Interpretationen zur platonischen Henologie*. Oslo: Aschehoug, 1960.

———. "Zum Begriff des 'non aliud' bei Cusanus." In *Nicolo' Cusano: Agli Inizi del Mondo Moderno*. 1964.

INDEX

Nicholas of Cusa's 'On Learned Ignorance': A Commentary on 'De docta ignorantia'
was designed in ITC New Baskerville and composed by Reflective Book Design
of Durham, North Carolina.